Solutions for Energy Security & Facility Management Challenges

Solutions for Energy Security & Facility Management Challenges

Proceedings of the
25th World Energy Engineering Congress
October 9-11, 2002
GeoExchange Conference & Expo
Energy Services Center
CHP Expo & Cogeneration Congress
Renewable Energy Technologies
Environmental Technology Expo
Facilities Security Expo
Plant & Facilities Expo

SOLUTIONS FOR ENERGY SECURITY & FACILITY MANAGEMENT CHALLENGES

Library of Congress Control Number: 2002112545

Printed in the United States of America
10 9 8 7 6 5 4 3 2 1

ISBN 0-88173-411-X

CONTENTS

SECTION 4: COMBINED HEAT & POWER/COGENERATION

SECTION 5: RENEWABLE ENERGY TECHNOLOGY

SECTION 6: ENVIRONMENTAL TECHNOLOGY

INTRODUCTION

This comprehensive reference is based on the papers presented at the 25th World Energy Engineering Congress (WEEC). The WEEC is the most comprehensive energy management and renewable energy conference in the world, continually reflecting the changes in technology and new forces shaping the energy industry. Since its inception in 1978 the WEEC has played a vital role in promoting technology transfer of energy information.

Today we are seeking solutions to ensure reliable energy supplies which are environmentally friendly. The oil embargo of 1973, the Iranian revolution of 1978-1979 and the Iraqi invasion of Kuwait in 1990 have demonstrated the direct link between U.S. economic vitality and energy supplies. The need for a Balanced National Energy Plan is critical for ensuring economic vitality and energy security. The technologies and theories presented in this reference cover the gamut of options available to reduce energy consumption and produce power through combined heat and power and renewable energy technology.

The Association of Energy Engineers (AEE), now in its 25th year, is the proud presenter of the WEEC and the companion Plant & Facilities Expo 2002, Facilities Security Exposition, Facilities E-Solutions Exposition, Geoexchange 2002, Combined Heat & Power 2002, Energy Services Center 2002, and the Renewable Energy Technology Expo 2002.

AEE will continue to play the leadership role in helping professionals reach their potential in energy management. We salute our member and the WEEC presenters for sharing information at this important conference. We congratulate our cosponsors and event sponsors, and thank them for supporting the WEEC and companion programs. These sponsors play a vital role in fostering information transfer.

- American Wind Energy Association
- American Bioenergy Association
- Defense Supply Center Philadelphia
- Energy Solutions Center
- Energy User News
- Georgia Tech Economic Development Institute
- National Association of State Energy Officials
- Solar Electric Power Association
- Solar Energy Industries Association
- TAC
- The Alliance to Save Energy
- The Geothermal Heat Pump Consortium

- The International Ground Source Heat Pump Association
- The National Association of Energy Service Companies
- The Power Marketing Association
- United Parcel Service
- U.S. Combined Heat & Power Association
- U.S. Department of Commerce
- USDOE Office of Power Technologies
- USDOE Federal Energy Management Programs (FEMP)
- USDOE Office of Energy Efficiency & Renewable Energy, Office of Outreach
- USEPA Energy Star

The sharing of information is critical for our industry to develop to its potential. We are proud to play a major role in presenting this important program.

Albert Thumann
Executive Director
Association of Energy Engineers

CONTRIBUTORS

Yousef Abouzelof, CEM
Harshweep Ahluwalia
Fatouh A. Al-Ragom, CEM
Paul Allen
Jolene Anderson-Sheil
John P. Archibald
W. Mark Arney, PE, CEM
Mahesh Bala
Kurt Bassett
Dagfinn Bell
Rob Bolin, PE
James M. Bolton, PE, CEM
Daryl R. Brown, CEM
Frits Bruggink
D. Victor Bush
Barney L. Capehart
Lynne C. Capehart
Walter H. Carter, CIAQP
Jason C. Chadee
Chao Chen
Hui Chen
Sool Yeon Cho
William D. Chvala, Jr., CEM
David E. Claridge
Kristyn L. Clayton, CEM
Bruce K. Colburn, PE, CEM
Gerry D. Crooks
Charles Culp
A.Z.D. Dalgleish
Song Deng
Patricia Dijak
James A. Dirks, CEM
Deepak M. Divan
Charles (Steve) S. Dixon, PE, CEM
Doug Dixon
Don Von Dollen
Dan Durham, PE
John M. Duff, CEM
Herbert Eckerlin
Mark Eggers
Robert Eidson
Stephen A. Fairfax
Larry J. Fisher
Ahmad R. Ganji, PE
P. Thomas Gard, PE
Thomas M. Giffin, PE
Geoffrey J. Gilg
Bruce Gilleland
Adrian Gillespie
Harry Goradia, PE
Trevor L. Grant
David Green
L. J. Grobler
Stanton W. Hadley
Randolph L. Haines, CEM, CLEP
Katherine H. Hamilton, CEM
K. Quinn Hart, PE
Greg Harrell, PE
Jon R. Haviland, PE, CEM
W.L.R. de Heijer
Derek Hengeveld
Raphael Herz
Rafael Herzberg, PE
Steve Hester
Andrew D. Holden, CEM
Bill Howe, PE
P.J. Hughes
W. David Hunt, CEM
Harry Indig
Richard Jendrucko, PE

Rene Jonker
Julia S. Kelley
L.D. Kicak
Keith L. Kline
Jason Kliwinski
Dragoljub Kosanovic
Chintamani V. Kulkarni
Tony Kushnir
Benson Kwong
Robert M. Lacy
Trina L. Larson, PE
James W. Leach
Mingsheng Liu
Jeff Mantel
Anthony C. Maurer
Diarmuid McSweeney
D. Paul Mehta
Aldo P. Melendez
Roy Michaelson
Lewis Milford
Dewayne R. Miller, CIAQP
Phil Mobley
Get W. Moy, PE
Martin A. Mozzo, Jr., PE, CEM, CLEP
John Nicol, PE
Terry Niehus, PE, CEM
Graham B. Parker
Klaus Pawlik
Terry Pease
James S. Peters
Ray Pugh
Ab Ream
James B. Redden, PE
Ray Reilly
Christopher Reohr
Bruce Ritchey
Stephen A. Roosa, CEM, CIAQP
John Salas
Marek Samotyj
Larry Seigel
Allen R. Shrum
Preston Schutt
Chandrabhan Sharma
Fred C. Shoeneborn, CEM
J.A. Shonder
Michael Simmons
Scott Sklar
Ronald B. Slosberg
Nick Stecky
William H. Steigelmann, PE
Alan F. Stewart, PE
Jeffrey G. Stringfield, PE
John M. Studebaker
Gregory P. Sullivan, PE, CEM
Robert B. Taylor, PE, CEM
Stephen Terry
W. Dan Turner
Wayne Turner
S. Kay Tuttle
Khaled A. Yousef, PE, CEM
Cisco L. Valentine, PE
John Van Gorp
Philip R. Walsh
James P. Waltz, PE, CEM
Mike Warwick
Guanghua Wei
Bill Westbrock
Tara Willey
Anthony L. Wright

ACKNOWLEDGEMENTS

Appreciation is expressed to all those who have contributed their expertise to this volume, to the conference chairs for their contributions to the 25th World Energy Engineering Congress, and to the officers of the Association of Energy Engineers for their help in bringing about this important conference.

The outstanding technical program of the 25th WEEC can be attributed to the efforts of the 2001 Advisory Board, a distinguished group of energy managers, engineers, consultants, producers and manufacturers:

Bob Billak
Department of Defense – Pentagon

Clint D. Christenson, C.E.M.
Johnson Controls, Inc.

Ted Collins
U.S. Department of Energy, FEMP

Michael D. Cuba, C.E.M., C.C.P.

John L. Fetters, C.E.M., C.L.E.P.
Effective Lighting Solutions, Inc.

Shirley J. Hansen, Ph.D., C.I.A.Q.P.
Hansen Associates, Inc.

Jon R. Haviland, P.E., C.E.M., C.L.E.P.
Marx Okubo Associates, Ltd.

Walter E. Johnston, P.E., C.E.M., C.C.P.
WEJ Energy Management Specialists

Marty A. Mozzo, Jr., P.E., C.E.M., C.L.E.P.
M & A Associates Inc.

Thomas D. Mull, P.E., C.E.M., C.L.E.P.
Carloina Consulting Group, Inc.

George R. Owens, P.E., C.E.M.
Energy & Engineering Solutions, Inc.

Graham Parker
Pacific Northwest National Lab

James J. Parker, P.E., C.E.M.
North Carolina State University – Industrial Extension Service

Steven A. Parker, P.E., C.E.M.
Pacific Northwest National Lab

W. Curtis Philips, C.E.M.
Southern Research Institute

Frank J. Richards, P.E., C.E.P.
The Richards' Energy Group

Patricia Rose

Stephen P. Sain, P.E., C.E.M., C.L.E.P., C.E.P.
Sain Engineering Associates, Inc.

Walter P. Smith, Jr., C.E.M.
ETSI Consulting, Inc.

T. Kenneth Spain, P.E., C.E.M., C.L.E.P.
University of Alabama in Huntsville

Jerry A. Taylor, P.E., C.E.M., C.I.A.Q.P., R.A.
Taylor Consulting Engineers

Albert Thumann, P.E., C.E.M., C.C.P.
Association of Energy Engineers

Wayne C. Turner, Ph.D., P.E., C.E.M.
Oklahoma State University

Eric A. Woodroof. Ph.D., C.E.M., C.E.P.
Johnson Congrols, Inc.

CORPORATE SUSTAINING MEMBERS

The following organizations have given outstanding support in promoting principles and practices to help achieve savings, greater productivity, and lower operating costs.

3M Energy Management
Alliance to Save Energy
Ameren CIPS
Ameresco,Inc.
American Hydrogen Association
Btech,Inc.
CEI Energy Group
CH2M Hill Inc
City of Corona
Company
Con Edison Solutions
Custom Energy
Defense Supply Center
Diesel & Gas Turbine Publicat
Dominion Virginia Power
Dynaire Corporation
E2MS, Inc.
Electrical & Mech Svcs Dept
Enbridge Consumers Gas
Energy Cybernetics
Energy Systems Group
Florida Power
FPL
Geothermal Heat Pump Consortium
Global Energy Solutions
H F Lenz Co
HQ USAMC/AMXIS M. Weaver
IBM Corp
Illinova Energy Partners
International District Energy Association
Johnson Controls, Inc.
Knoxville Utilities Board

M C Dean, Inc.
MagneTek Inc
MBNA America
NALMCO
Nicor
Obragas N V
Old Dominion Electric Coop
Options, Philip Morris USA
Otter Tail Power Co
PA Consulting Group
Powercell Corporation
PSEG
Rand Water
Raytheon
Refrigeration Service Eng Soc
REMA
Rocky Mountain Institute
Salas O'Brien Engineers Inc
Sempra Energy Services Company
Shanghai Soc of Engy Research
Siemens Building Technologies
Southern Company Energy Solutions
Starbucks Coffee Company
Stat Signal Systems, Inc.
Suncor Energy Inc.
Tampa Electric Company
The Boeing Company
United States Energy Assn
US Army Logistics Integration
US DOE-Chicago
USACERL
Virgin Islands Water & Power

Section 1
Energy Management

Chapter 1

HIGH FREQUENCY METAL HALIDE BALLAST

Diarmuid McSweeney, FIES, LC

ABSTRACT

Low Wattage HID and Fluorescent Electronic Ballasts have existed for some time. This paper discusses the introduction of a new High Wattage (400, 350, 320) Metal Halide High Frequency Ballast and its benefits.

Benefits include: Improved lamp lumen depreciation, Low watts loss, dimmability, low noise, power carry through, lamp mortality, power factor, ballast factor, FCC compliance, daylight harvesting.

ELECTRONIC 400 WATT METAL HALIDE BALLASTS

Companies and businesses are always looking for ways to reduce their operating costs. As energy conservation continues to be a focus, facility designers and managers are considering alternatives for their lighting systems. They want systems that are reliable and efficient over time. Yet, they want lighting that is unobtrusive and flexible enough to take advantage of energy saving opportunities such as daylight harvesting. New electronic ballasts for metal halide luminaires meet many of these requirements.

Actually, electronic ballasts are not new. The technology has long been used with fluorescent systems because of its dimming capabilities. In more recent years, electronic ballasts have been utilized in low power (175-watt or less) high intensity discharge (HID) luminaires. However, reliable electronic ballast technology is new to the higher wattage metal halide HID product class.

High wattage electronic ballast technologies are designed for use with 320-, 350- and 400-watt luminaires. The ballasts are used with both conventional and pulse start metal halide lamps to reduce energy costs, provide continuous dimming capabilities and improve lighting aesthetics. They also offer silent operation, improved color stability and flicker free illumination.

REDUCED ENERGY AND OPERATING COSTS

Rising energy costs and limited power availability in many regions of the country as well as a renewed focus on energy conservation have many firms searching for new ways to reduce energy consumption. Lighting systems are often viewed as the "low hanging fruit"—they provide an opportunity for quick payback with a reasonably low capital expenditure.

The advent of electronic ballasts for HID further improves energy consumption and can shorten payback. You can understand this better by comparing the operating characteristics of magnetically ballasted HID to electronically ballasted HID in regards to energy consumption.

During normal operation, all HID ballasts consume watts within the ballast that are not delivered to the lamp. For example, a metal halide fixture with a magnetic core and coil ballast can consume up to 460 watts to drive a 400-watt lamp. In comparison, an electronic ballast can consume 421 watts per lamp to deliver 400 watts to the lamp. The savings are 39 watts per lamp—a reduction that quickly adds up. This example of reduced watts loss represents a 9 percent savings in energy costs on a per luminaire basis.

Lamp lumen maintenance also affects the level of energy consumed by a lighting system. A lighting system with lower lamp lumen maintenance will require a higher quantity of fixtures in the lighting design. More fixtures increase the lighting system's energy consumption and boost installation and maintenance costs.

Electronic ballasts for HID systems hold great promise in the area of lamp lumen maintenance. A major lamp manufacturer tested its metal halide lamps with one of our company's new electronic ballast designs and reported a dramatic increase in the mean lumens. Mean lumen maintenance for a standard metal halide lamp increased from 65 percent to 75 percent, and from 75 percent to 85 percent for a pulse start lamp. Based on the test results, the lamp manufacturer is offering an improved light output warranty when its lamps are used with this particular ballast.

In Figure 1, note that a luminaire with a 400-watt standard metal halide lamp operating on a magnetic ballast will provide approximately 26,650 lumens burning at a mean life of 8,000 hours. A lamp with an electronic ballast will supply about 30,750 lumens at the same point in its operating life. At mean life (8,000 hours), the electronic ballast powered lamp supplies 4,100 more lumens (15 percent) than a magnetically ballasted lamp.

It is important to remember that the electronic ballast achieves this lamp output while consuming only 421 watts, compared to 460 watts consumed by the magnetic ballast/lamp system. This results in 73 mean lumens per watt for the electronically ballasted lamp compared to 58 mean lumens per watt for the magnetically ballasted lamp.

Electronic ballasts will outperform conventional ballasts when used with a pulse start 400-watt metal halide lamp (Figure 2). At mean lamp life (8,000 hours), the output from the unit with the conventional ballast is about 33,000 lumens. The luminaire with an electronic ballast will supply about 37,400 lumens.

At mean life (8,000 hours), the electronic ballast powered pulse start lamp supplies 4,400 more lumens (13

percent) than a magnetically ballasted pulse start lamp. Once again, it is important to note that the electronic ballast achieves this lamp output while consuming only 421 watts, compared to 460 watts consumed by the magnetic ballast/lamp system. This results in 89 mean lumens per watt for the electronically ballasted pulse start lamp compared to 72 mean lumens per watt for the magnetically ballasted pulse start lamp.

Improved lumen maintenance reduces the total number of luminaires required. Approximately 30 percent fewer units are needed for a project using electronic ballasts of this type compared to one using magnetically ballasted metal halide luminaires. The reduced luminaire count coupled with the lower watts loss in electronically ballasted luminaires results in annual energy savings of 36 percent!

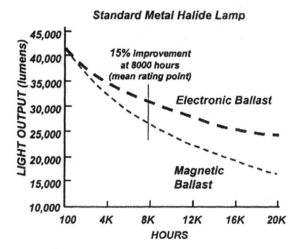

FIGURE 1.

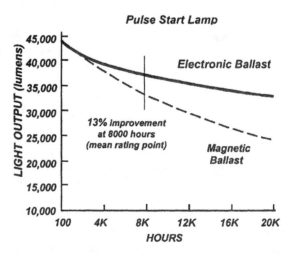

FIGURE 2.

4

DIMMING CAPABILITIES

Many facilities—particularly those on the coasts and in the south—take advantage of daylight harvesting by installing skylights to increase the amount of sunlight that comes into their buildings during the day. When light levels outdoors are sufficient to provide the required footcandle levels indoors through windows and skylights, the lighting system should respond with less light. Many HID systems currently provide dimming via a stepped or switchable system. These systems do not provide a smooth transition in light levels; the transitions are noticeable by people using the dimmed space.

The new ballasts allow facilities to accomplish smooth transitions in light levels and reduce energy consumption by continuously dimming metal halide luminaires—some down to as low as 25 percent of lumen output. Some electronic ballasts will reduce the power consumed from 100 to 50 percent of the rated wattage, resulting in a continuous dimming range from 100 to 25 percent of full lumen output.

This continuous dimming process allows the facility to take advantage of bright days and longer daylight hours—particularly during the summer. It important to note that lamp manufacturers typically have a lower limit to dimming power supplied to the lamp of 50%. Below this level, the lamp can become unstable and experience detrimental effects.

Some of the new electronic ballasts may be used with industry standard low-voltage control circuitry—including occupancy sensors or programmable controllers—to reduce light output when activity in the facility is reduced or terminated. This capability is particularly beneficial in warehouses and distribution facilities where areas may be occupied during a limited number of hours or in retail environments where light levels may be reduced for overnight merchandise restocking.

SILENT OPERATION

At some time, everyone has heard the annoying buzz produced by the vibration within magnetic core and coil HID ballasts. Magnetic ballasts produce noise—or unwanted sound—because of the changing magnetic field within the ballast. In a 60 Hertz system, the magnetic field changes 60 times per second, causing the metal laminations within the ballast to vibrate. As the vibration continues over time, the ballast pro-

duces more and more noise.

Luminaires with electronic ballasts have no laminations to vibrate. They operate at frequencies above the audible range, which results in silent operation. This benefit is essential in noise sensitive areas such as libraries, concert halls, assembly rooms and retail environments.

Some electronic devices generate "noise" in the form of electromagnetic or radio frequency interference. Electronic ballasts are no exception as a potential source of such interference. Electronic devices that operate above FCC limits for electromagnetic compatibility can wreak havoc on other sensitive electronic devices such as process controls in manufacturing facilities or point of sale systems in retail applications. When selecting a high power source such as a 400-watt HID electronic ballast, consider the FCC compliance relative to the ballast. This will reduce the likelihood of problems once the lighting system is installed.

IMPROVED COLOR STABILITY

Color stability is important in many applications, including commercial and retail establishments. A shift in lamp color will occur when the voltage to the fixture fluctuates, resulting in merchandise and displays that appear unattractive to the consumer. In manufacturing environments, lamp color shifts can change the appearance of color coded items.

Typically, a metal halide lamp operating on a magnetic ballast will experience a color shift when the voltage to the ballast changes. Electronic metal halide ballasts control power to the lamp so that the lamp power remains stable during power supply fluctuations. Electronic metal halide ballasts can have such high regulation that a plus or minus 10 percent voltage change can produce less than a plus or minus 1 percent change in lamp wattage, which means the lamp output remains consistent. By closely controlling the power to the lamp, color stability is better maintained.

The new electronic ballasts will continue to operate the lamps through multiple cycles of interrupted power. This capability is especially advantageous in areas that experience frequent power shifts and brownouts that may cause the lamps to extinguish. Electronic ballasts reduce nuisance outages of metal halide lamps by maintaining a supply of power to the lamp during brief power interruptions of several milliseconds duration.

FLICKER-FREE

Flicker illumination occurs with metal halide luminaires that have magnetic ballasts. Flicker can cause headaches, disrupt a person's concentration and lead to nausea. The resulting stroboscopic effect can lower productivity and create a serious safety hazard in environments with rotating equipment. Consumers shopping in stores where the luminaires are constantly flickering will tend to cut their visits short, reducing sales revenue. Electronic ballasts operate at a higher frequency than standard ballasts, which eliminates flicker.

FUTURE

The future looks very promising as far as higher wattage electronic metal halide ballast technology is concerned. Emerging metal halide lamp technologies coupled with developing electronic ballast technologies may enable HID mean lamp lumen maintenance to reach over 90 percent. Wider ranges of dimming for HID lamps may become possible with electronic ballasts.

These types of developments will require the cooperation of ballast designers and lamp companies. The integration of new controls for dimming such as the D.A.L.I. protocol or other individually addressable control protocols are certainly on the horizon for HID. Electronic ballast designs may provide opportunities to integrate other functionalities into HID luminaires, including those currently used with magnetically ballasted luminaires as well as functionalities not yet conceived.

THE AUTHOR

Diarmuid McSweeney is Vice President, Marketing and Product Development for Holophane Lighting located in Newark, Ohio. He oversees new product development and leads the company's marketing program. He is a Fellow of IESNA and recipient of the Distinguished Service Award and the President's Award. A past president of IESNA, he currently chairs the Industrial Lighting Committee.

Chapter 2

ENERGY EFFICIENCY OF ROTARY DRYERS IN MANUFACTURING PLANTS

Harshdeep Ahluwalia
James W. Leach
Stephen Terry

Mechanical and Aerospace Engineering
North Carolina State University
Raleigh, NC 27695-7910

ABSTRACT

This paper documents two preliminary studies conducted by the Industrial Assessment Center at North Carolina State University to estimate the potential for energy savings and the implementation costs associated with retrofit measures to improve the efficiency of rotary dryers operating in industrial settings. The first study deals with shell heat loss recovery from two large direct-fired rotary kilns at a paper mill. Previous works have shown that heat recovery in the form of pre-heated air for combustion can be realized if hoods are installed over hot sections of the kilns. Combustion air is preheated as it is drawn through the gap between the hood and the kiln. Economic analyses presented herein show that relatively large heat transfer areas can be justified. The heat recovery system must be designed such that the local kiln wall temperature does not exceed safe operating limits at the point where the hot air leaves the heat exchanger.

The second study addresses the minimization of stack losses in three low temperature rotary dryers at a mining facility. The parameters that limit energy savings made possible by adjusting the excess air in the burners are the allowable wall temperatures of the unlined dryers and the temperatures of the exhaust gases, which could damage downstream filters. It is difficult to estimate the wall temperatures accurately because the walls are in contact with combustion gases and wet solids. Also, different heat transfer correlations from the literature predict different exhaust gas temperatures. Significant energy savings can be realized by designing the burners and induced draft fans based on conservative calculations, but experiments will be needed to establish the true optimum flow of combustion air at this facility.

INTRODUCTION

Industrial dryers are used in chemical processing plants, paper mills, mining operations and a wide variety of other manufacturing facilities. Discussions of the advantages and disadvantages of the various types of dryers found in industrial settings are provided in Perry's Chemical Engineers Handbook [1] and from Williams-Gardner [2]. Analytical models for predicting dryer performance are described in more recent journal articles [3-8]. The Industrial Assessment Center at North Carolina State University has evaluated several large dryers over the past decade. A significant fraction of these dryers were inefficient and in need of repair or replacement. Very often the process or product at a plant will change, but the dryer remains the same. Sometimes a used dryer is purchased for economic reasons, even though it is not the right size or design. It is not uncommon to find dryers operating at 30% efficiency. By comparison, a typical industrial boiler would operate at 80% efficiency. Our experience indicates that there are significant opportunities for energy conservation in many industrial dryer operations. This paper documents two analytical studies of rotary dryers performed by the IAC this year. These are preliminary studies designed to establish the potential for energy savings and to estimate the implementation costs. They illustrate some typical cost-effective measures for conserving energy.

The first study evaluates a combustion air pre-heat system to reclaim energy being lost from the hot external walls of two direct-fired rotary kilns at a paper mill. Refractory lined kilns are used in place of ordinary bare walled rotary dryers for high temperature applications [1]. Kilns are equipped with internal refractory brick liners to prevent overheating of the carbon steel walls with resulting weakening. Although the exposed external surface temperature may approach 750 °F, additional insulation is

FIGURE 1. ROTARY KILN

usually impractical. External insulation would cause the metal temperature to exceed the tolerable limit, and additional internal refractory would interfere with the flow of gases through the kiln. However, heat could be radiated from the hot external surface to warm air needed for combustion. The combustion air would be drawn through an annulus formed by a cylindrical shroud placed around part of the kiln. Heat transfer calculations below show that the shroud can be designed such that it does not cause overheating of the kiln wall. A heat recovery system similar to this was installed on a lime kiln in Canada [9]. It preheated primary combustion air to 160°F, saved 5,210 MMBTU/yr, and had a payback period of 1.2 years. The two kilns at the paper mill are 210 ft. in length, and have diameters of 8 ft. and 10.5 ft. respectively. The shell heat loss from hot sections of the two kilns is estimated to be about 7.05 MMBTU/hr. Our calculations indicate that the heat recovery system would reduce the shell heat loss to about 1.06 MMBTU/hr, and would pay for itself in about 3 months. The heat exchangers evaluated in this work are larger than the one installed in Canada, and would preheat the combustion air well above 200°F.

Three dryers at a mining facility consume about 13 MMBTU/hr to remove moisture from mica particles that have been washed out of crushed rock. The dryers were purchased used, and modified by trial and error until they would dry the mica to the required moisture content. The plant engineers maintained records of materials throughput and energy consumption to establish the dryer efficiencies. They also asked the Industrial Assessment Center to make recommendations on ways to improve dryer performance. Measurements and analyses showed that the main cause of dryer inefficiency is high stack loss due to excess air in the combustion process. Also, analyses showed that the flow of combustion air could be reduced to improve energy efficiency without affecting the drying process and without overheat the carbon steel walls. Below, we describe the calculations involved in the optimization process. The analyses indicate that the flow of combustion air in two of the three dryers can be lowered to save about 2 MMBTU/hr.

COMBUSTION AIR PREHEAT SYSTEM
A section of one of the rotary kilns at the paper mill is shown in Figure 1. The kiln is 210 feet long and 8 feet in diameter. The temperature of the combustion gases at the entrance is about 2,400°F (1589K). The kiln has a refractory lining about 6 inches thick to reduce shell heat losses and to maintain the temperature of the metal wall at a tolerable level. The temperature of the bare exterior metal surface over the first 33 feet of the kiln is 720°F (655K). The temperature of the surface gradually decreases there onwards. The gas flow rate through the kiln is 64,000 lb/hr.

The heat recovery system would involve a cylindrical shroud that covers the first 33 feet of the kiln. Combustion air drawn through the annular space between the shroud and the kiln would be pre-heated using the energy that is now being lost to the atmosphere. Cool air drawn into the shroud by an induced draft fan would enter the annulus at both of the open ends, and would flow in the axial direction to an exhaust manifold located at the center of the 33 ft. section. Flow restrictions at the entrance to the exhaust manifold will insure that the flow is uniform around the perimeter of the kiln. The size of the heat exchanger must be determined by trial and error based on heat transfer calculations. The combustion air cannot be heated much above 300°F because the kiln wall temperature will exceed safe operating limits.

Below we summarize separate heat transfer analyses of the existing 33 ft. section of the kiln and analyses of the same section with the shroud in place. The first set of calculations is needed to establish the shell losses for the existing system, and to determine the unknown conductance of the refractory lining. The second set of calculations determines the effect of the shroud on the wall temperature, and predicts the energy savings.

Heat is now being transferred via conduction through the refractory and the metallic walls (shell) to the bare exterior surface. The surroundings pick up the heat from the hot kiln surface via natural convection and radiation as shown in Figure 2. The heat transfer from the walls can be estimated from the known surface temperature using well-established correlations [10] from the literature for the convective heat transfer coefficient and estimates of the surface emissivity. The internal resistance to heat transfer can then be determined from the calculated heat flux and the known internal gas temperature.

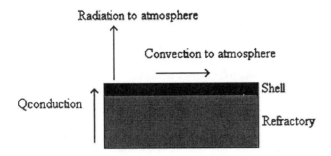

FIGURE 2. MECHANISM OF HEAT TRANSFER

The heat transfer coefficient for natural convection to the ambient air at 298 K is calculated as follows. The Grashoff Number is:

$$Gr = g \beta \Delta T\, d^3/v^2 = 8.41 \times 10^{10}$$

The Rayleigh Number is:

$$Ra = Gr \times Pr = 5.76 \times 10^{10}$$

The Nusselt Number for natural convection around the cylinder is given [10] by:

$$Nu = 0.125 \times Ra^{1/3} = 483$$

The heat transfer coefficient for natural convection is:

$$h_c = k \times Nu\, /d = 1.36\ \text{Btu/hr-ft}^2\text{-}^\circ\text{F}$$

The heat transfer from the exterior kiln surface via natural convection is:

$$Q_{convection} = h_c \times A_{kiln} \times \Delta T = 0.72\ \text{MMBTU/hr}$$

The heat transfer from the external surface to the surroundings by radiation is:

$$Q_{radiation} = \varepsilon \sigma A_{kiln} (T^4_{kiln} - T^4_{\infty}) = 1.82\ \text{MMBTU/hr}$$

The total heat being dissipated to the surroundings by the hot external surface is:

$$Q_{Total} = Q_{convection} + Q_{radiation} = 2.54\ \text{MMBTU/hr}.$$

Convection constitutes only 28% of heat loss and radiation constitutes the remaining 72%. This is because the kiln surface is at a fairly high temperature. The heat transferred to the surroundings must be equal to the heat conducted through the refractory and the metallic wall of the kiln. Expressed in terms of the internal resistance to heat transfer, the shell loss is:

$$Q_{Total} = (T_{interior} - T_{kiln})/R_w$$

Substituting for Q_{Total} from above, we obtain:

$$R_w = 6.6 \times 10^{-4}\ \text{hr-}^\circ\text{F/Btu}$$

The heat recovery system would employ a concentric metal cylinder surrounding the kiln at a separation distance of 3 inches. Heat is transferred via conduction through the walls of the kiln as shown in Figure 3. From the kiln surface, heat is transferred via radiation to the shroud and via forced convection to the air flowing in the annulus. The shroud absorbs radiation from the kiln surface and delivers heat to the combustion air via forced convection and to the external surroundings via both natural convection and radiation.

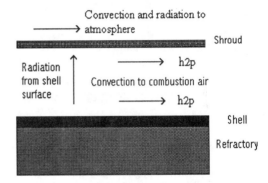

FIGURE 3. HEAT TRANSFER FROM THE SHROUD

The hydraulic diameter of the annulus is:

$$D_h = D_o - D_i = 6\ \text{inches}$$

The Reynolds number is given by:

$$Re_D = \frac{\rho u_m D_h}{\mu} = 51{,}498$$

The convective heat transfer coefficient, h_{2p}, for the turbulent flow is given [10] by:

$$h_{2p} = 0.023 \frac{k}{D_h} Re_D^{4/5} Pr^{0.4} = 5.186\ \text{Btu/hr-ft}^2\text{-}^\circ\text{F}$$

The heat transfer coefficient for the outer shroud surface is estimated to be $h_3 = 1.08\ \text{Btu/hr-ft}^2\text{-}^\circ\text{F}$, using correlations for natural convection as described above. A trial and error procedure is needed to solve the non-linear algebraic equations that govern the heat transfer. To begin, we will assume that the average combustion air temperature inside the annulus is 154°F. This assumption will be verified once the temperature of the shroud, the shell and the pre-heated combustion air exit temperature are determined.

Let Q_1 represent the heat radiated away from the shell. This is the difference between the conduction through the refractory and the convection from the shell surface.

$$Q_1 = (T_g - T_{kiln})/R_w - h_{2P} A (T_{kiln} - T_{air})$$

The net heat transfer by radiation from the shell to the shroud is also given [10] by:

$$Q_{1-2} = A_{kiln} \frac{\sigma(T^4_{kiln} - T^4_{shroud})}{\frac{1}{\varepsilon_1} + \frac{1}{\varepsilon_2} - 1}$$

Where,
$\sigma = 0.1714 \times 10^{-8}$ Btu/hr-ft^2-$^\circ$R^4
$\varepsilon_1 = 0.71$, Emissivity of kiln (carbon steel)
$\varepsilon_2 = 0.70$, Emissivity of shroud (stainless steel)

The heat transfer from the shroud to the combustion air and the external surroundings is given by:

$$Q_2 = A_{shroud} [h_{2P}(T_{shroud} - 154^\circ F) + h_3 (T_{shroud} - 77^\circ F) + \sigma \varepsilon_2 ((T_{shroud} + 460)^4 - (77^\circ F + 460)^4)]$$

All of the net radiation heat transfer to the shroud is dissipated by convection on the inside surface to preheat combustion air, by natural convection from the outside surface to the ambient air, and by radiation form the shroud to the ambient environment. Since Q_1, Q_{1-2} and Q_2 all represent the same flow of energy, they can be equated to determine T_{shroud} and T_{kiln}.

$$Q_1 = Q_{1-2} = Q_2$$

Solving these equations simultaneously, we obtain:

$$T_{kiln} = 604^\circ F \qquad T_{shroud} = 250^\circ F$$

The heat transfer to the combustion air is the sum of the convection heat transfer from the shell and from the inside of the shroud.

$$\begin{aligned} Q_{combustion\ air} = &\ h_{2p} \times A_{kiln} \times (604 - 154^\circ F) \\ &+ h_{2p} \times A_{shroud} \times (250 - 154^\circ F) \\ =&\ 2.379 \text{ MMBTU/hr.} \end{aligned}$$

The combustion air exit temperature can be determined from the following equation:

$$Q_{combustion\ air} = m\ C_p (T_{out} - T_{in})$$

Solving the above equation, we get $T_{out} = 232^\circ F$. The average temperature of the air in the annulus is 154°F, as assumed in the calculations above. The heat lost to the surroundings in the proposed system is calculated to be 0.345 MMBTU/hr. Since the shell heat loss for the

original system was 2.546 MMBTU/hr, the energy savings is about 2.20 MMBTU/hr. The cost of oil to fire the kilns is \$4.67/MMBTU, and the kilns operate 8,760 hrs/yr. Therefore, the annual savings for the 8 ft. diameter kiln is about \$90,000. The installed cost of a 3/16-inch thick stainless steel shroud is estimated to be about \$25,000, and the simple payback period is about 3 months.

The cost savings estimated above are for a representative shroud design. A larger shroud would recover more waste heat, and would provide greater savings. However, there is a limit imposed by the temperature of the pre-heated combustion air. The kiln surface temperature of 604°F calculated above is for an average combustion air temperature of 154°F. The local kiln surface temperature at the gas exit is expected to be about 50°F higher. Thus, to insure that the maximum kiln surface temperature does not exceed 750°F, the combustion air should probably not be preheated past about 300°F.

A second kiln at the paper mill has a diameter of 10.5 ft., and a gas flow of 102,000 lb$_m$/hr. Based on heat transfer calculations, it is estimated that a combustion air preheat system for this kiln would save about \$154,926 /yr. Results from the analyses of the two lime kilns are summarized in Table 1. The combined cost savings are \$244,926/yr with a total implementation cost of \$55,000 and a simple payback period of 3 months.

COMBUSTION AIR OPTIMIZATION STUDY

Plant engineers at a mica drying facility collected dryer production rate data and entering material moisture content data for three direct fired rotary dryers. The dryer efficiencies can be determined from this data, which is summarized in Table 2 below.

For example, the efficiency of dryer 1 is the ratio of the heat required to remove 0.8 tons/hr of moisture to the firing rate of 5.0 MMBTU/hr. The heat required to dry the moisture from the mica is:

$$Q_w = m_w \Delta h = 1,850,000 \text{ BTU/hr}$$

Thus, the efficiency of dryer 1 is:

$$\text{Efficiency} = 1,850,000 / 5,000,000 \text{ BTU/hr} = 37\%$$

To show the cause of this low efficiency, detailed estimates of the heat loads for dryer 1 are presented below. Heat loads for the other two dryers are calculated from similar analyses, and are summarized in Table 3. For the existing operating conditions, the heat absorbed by the mica in dryer 1 is:

$$Q_m = m_m C_p \Delta T = 98,784 \text{ BTU/hr}$$

10

TABLE 1. COMBUSTION AIR PREHEAT SYSTEM PREDICTED PERFORMANCE

	Kiln #1	Kiln #2
Existing Kiln External Surface Temperature	720 °F	820 °F
Kiln Diameter	8 ft.	10.5 ft.
Temperature of Combustion Gases	2,400 °F	2,400 °F
Gas Flow Rate	64,000 lbs/hr	102,000 lbs/hr
Existing Shell Heat Loss (32.8 ft. section)	2.546 MMBTU/hr	4.5 MMBTU/hr
Length of Proposed Shroud	32.8 ft.	32.8 ft.
Diameter of Shroud	8.5 ft.	11 ft.
Predicted Kiln Surface Temperature	604.5 °F	730 °F
Predicted Shroud Wall Temperature	250.6 °F	322 °F
Combustion Air Inlet Temperature	77 °F	77 °F
Predicted Combustion Air Exit Temperature	232 °F	242 °F
Heat Delivered to Combustion Air	2.38 MMBTU/hr	4.03 MMBTU/hr
Heat Lost to Surroundings	0.345 MMBTU/hr	0.72 MMBTU/hr
Shell Heat Loss Reduction	2.2 MMBTU/hr	3.79 MMBTU/hr
Annual Energy Savings (MMBTU)	19,282	33,175
Annual Fuel Cost Savings	$ 90,000 /yr	$154,926 /yr
Estimated Implementation Cost	$ 25,000	$30,000
Simple Payback Period	3 months	2 months

Since the firing rate in Table 2 is expressed in terms of the higher heating value, we must account for the heat required to evaporate water formed by the reaction of hydrogen in the fuel. For natural gas, about 90 lb_m of water is formed per MMBTU. Therefore:

$$Q_h = 90 \text{ lb/MMBTU} \times 5 \text{ MMBTU/hr} \times 1,000 \text{ BTU/lb}$$
$$= 450,000 \text{ BTU/hr}$$

The shell heat loss is estimated from temperature measurements made at various locations on the exterior surface. About two-thirds of the exterior surface of dryer 1 is insulated. Heat transfer coefficients accounting for natural convection and radiation were estimated at the measured temperatures using tabulated values from Mark's Mechanical Engineers Handbook [11]. The estimated shell heat loss is:

$$Q_{shell} = Q \text{ insulated surface} + Q \text{ uninsulated surface}$$
$$= 92,225 \text{ BTU/hr}$$

The flow rate of combustion air can now be estimated from the following equation, which accounts for all of the energy provided by the burner.

$$5,000,000 \text{ BTU/hr} = 1,850,000 + 98,784 + 450,000 + 92,225 + Q_{air}$$

The heat added to the combustion air is:

$$Q_{air} = 2,508,991 \text{ BTU/hr}$$

From this result, the flow rate of air is calculated to be :

$$m_{air} = 2,508,991 \text{ BTU/hr} / 0.244 \text{ BTU/lb-°F} (302 - 77°F)$$
$$= 45,700 \text{ lb/hr}$$

This is the second gas flow rate listed in Table 2. The first value was estimated by a dryer consultant based on his measurements of the oxygen content of the stack gases and the known firing rate. The discrepancy does not affect the

TABLE 2. DRYER DATA

	Dryer 1	Dryer 2	Dryer 3
Production Rate, tons/hr	1.12	1.5	2
Moisture removed, tons/hr	0.8	0.8	0.7
% Moisture	43	35	26
Gas exhaust temperature, °F	302	325	210
Mica leaving temperature, °F	270	260	168
% Excess air	980	690	1020
Gas flow rate from firing rate, lb/hr	40,000	29,337	23,229
Gas flow rate from energy balance, lb/hr	45,700	40,700	24,000
Firing rate, MMBTU/hr	5.0	5.0	2.8

TABLE 3. EXISTING OPERATING CONDITIONS FOR MICA DRYERS

Type of Loss	Dryer 1 Btu/hr	Dryer 2 Btu/hr	Dryer 3 Btu/hr
Heat absorbed by mica	98,784	100,000	92,000
Heat absorbed by moisture	1,850,000	1,850,000	1,550,000
Heat absorbed by air	2,508,991	2,400,000	798,000
Heat in combustion water	450,000	450,000	256,607
Drum loss	92,225	192,250	153,153
Total heat required	5,000,000	5,000,000	2,850,000
Efficiency	37%	37%	54%

conclusions or recommendations of this work. The percent excess air levels in Table 2 were determined from the estimated airflows and the stoichiometric flows. Calculations to establish the existing operating conditions for the other two dryers were done in the same way. Table 3 lists the results. The main cause of dryer inefficiency is high stack loss associated with the unusually high combustion airflows.

About half of the energy provided by the fuel leaves the dryers with the exhaust gases. Dryers of this size are capable of much higher heat transfer rates than are required in this application. It appears that the burners have been downsized to match the existing requirements, but that the airflows have not been adjusted for efficient operation. Heat transfer rates from the hot gases to the wet solids (dryer capacity) depend on the air velocity. However, analyses showed that the high airflows are unnecessary.

Table 4 below presents the results of the heat transfer analyses. The first row in the table gives the existing operating conditions. For lower airflows, the fuel flow has been adjusted until the flame temperature is high enough to dry the moisture from the mica. An empirical heat transfer correlation [1] was employed to estimate the heat transfer from the hot combustion gases to the wet mica.

$$Q \quad = \quad U \times V \times \Delta Tm$$
where,
U = volumetric heat transfer coefficient
V = dryer volume
ΔTm = mean temperature difference

Since most of this heat evaporates water, the mean temperature difference is given approximately by [1]:

$$\Delta Tm \quad = \quad \frac{T_1 - T_2}{\ln\left(\dfrac{T_1 - T_{wb}}{T_2 - T_{wb}}\right)}$$

where,
T_1 = entering gas temperature
T_2 = exit gas temperature
T_{wb} = entering gas wet-bulb temperature

Reference [1] discusses correlations from the literature for estimating the volumetric heat transfer coefficient. All of the published relationships can be reduced to the form:

$$U \times V \quad = \quad k \times L \times D \times G^N$$

where k and N are constants, L is the length of the dryer, D is the diameter, and G is the gas mass velocity, given by:

$$G \quad = \quad 4 \dot{m}_{gas} / \pi D^2$$

If the exponent, N, is specified, then k can be determined from the measured performance of the dryer at existing operating conditions. Reference [1] recommends N=0.67, whereas Reference [2] recommends N=0.16. Sample calculations showed that the value from Reference [1] is the most conservative. It predicts lower savings resulting from reductions in airflow through the dryer. Therefore the calculations in the tables below are based on N=0.67. From the existing production rates and temperatures for dryer 1, the corresponding values of the constant, k, is calculated to be k=0.217.

TABLE 4. DRYER 1 PREDICTED PERFORMANCE

m_{air} lb/hr	m_{fuel} lb/hr	U x V BTU/hr-°F	Flame Temp. °F	Exit Temp. °F	Efficiency %
45,700	210.0	7,864	481	302	36.8
35,700	199.9	6,669	568	336	39.1
25,700	188.5	5,357	718	389	42.3
15,700	175.2	3,860	1,042	485	47.1
10,700	168.0	2,974	1,418	577	50.8
5,700	162.5	1,976	2,431	776	56.3

TABLE 5. DRYER 2 PREDICTED PERFORMANCE

m_{air} lb/hr	m_{fuel} lb/hr	U x V BTU/hr-°F	T_1 °F	T_2 °F	Efficiency %
40,700	210.0	7,178	531	325	37.1
30,700	199.8	5,948	646	369	39.6
20,700	187.8	4,575	866	442	43.3
10,700	174.8	2,955	1,470	602	49.3
5,700	170.7	1,955	2,540	818	54.3

The results in Table 4 show that the fuel consumption drops from 210 lb/hr to 168 lb/hr when the combustion airflow is reduced from the existing value of 45,700 lb/hr, to 10,700 lb/hr. This represents a savings of 20%, or about 1 MMBTU/hr. The fuel cost savings is $18,723/yr.

At an airflow of 10,700 lb/hr the excess air is still 270%. However, the entering combustion gas temperature of 1,418 °F could be approaching a value that would overheat the carbon steel walls of the unlined dryer. The walls are also in contact with wet solids at 160°F. Experimentation will be needed to determine the minimum acceptable combustion airflow. Also, safe operating procedures will have to be established to insure that the burner does not operate for extended periods without wet solids in the dryer.

Another potential problem associated with lowering the airflow is high exhaust gas temperature. The exhaust gases must pass through a filter to remove dust. The heat transfer correlations from Reference [2] predict that T_2 will decrease when the airflow is reduced. For example, at m_{air} = 10,700 lb/hr, the correlation from Reference [2] predicts T_2=228°F which is significantly lower than the value of 577°F listed in Table 4. The actual values of T_2, and the minimum acceptable values of the airflow rate will have to be determined by experiment. However, we believe that the values in Table 4 are conservative in every respect.

The electric power required by the induced draft fans is expected to vary with the cube of the exhaust gas flow rate. Therefore the electrical energy consumption should be reduced by more than 90%. To be conservative, we will assume a 50% reduction. The predicted electrical energy savings are 59,899 kWh/yr and the electrical cost savings are $3,522/yr. The total energy cost savings for dryer 1 is estimated to be $22,245/yr.

Table 5 gives the predicted performance of dryer 2 for a range of combustion air flow rates. Assuming than an air flow of 10,700 lb/hr is acceptable, the fuel consumption can be reduced from 210 lb/hr to 174.8 lb/hr. The corresponding fuel cost savings are $25,803/yr. The electrical cost savings are $3,680/yr. The overall cost savings for dryer 2 are estimated to be $29,483/yr.

The results in Table 6 show that dryer 3 is relatively efficient in its present condition. Also, this particular dryer requires high airflows to transport the mica to the exit. The payback period for modifying dryer 3 is probably not acceptable.

The drives of the exhaust fans in dryer 1 and in dryer 2 will have to be modified. If the burners cannot be turned down to fire at less than full capacity, then some burner modification will also be required. The replacement cost of the drive pulleys of the belt driven fans is expected to be no more than a few hundred dollars. The cost of a new 4 MMBTU/hr burner is estimated to be about $5,000. Some experimentation will be required to optimize the system. Allowing for engineering and unforeseen costs, we estimate the total implementation cost to be about $50,000. The payback period is about 12 months.

CONCLUSIONS
The case studies illustrate some cost effective measures for reducing energy requirements of rotary dryers in industrial settings. Our analyses indicate that shell heat losses in high temperature rotary kilns can be economically recaptured to preheat combustion air. Relatively large heat exchangers can be justified. The heat transfer to the combustion air tends to lower the average kiln wall temperature. However, the local wall temperature may increase at the point where

TABLE 6. DRYER 3 PREDICTED PERFORMANCE

m_{air} lb/hr	m_{fuel} lb/hr	U x V BTU/hr-°F	T_1 °F	T_2 °F	Efficiency %
24,000	119.7	9,161	515	210	54.3
14,000	111.6	6,397	772	242	59.1
9,000	106.5	4,770	1,098	268	62.5
4,000	100.0	2,794	2,160	309	67.7

the hot air leaves the heat exchanger. This establishes the upper limit of the combustion air preheating and the energy savings. The second study shows that energy savings can be realized by reducing stack losses in low temperature rotary dryers operating with high excess air. The combustion temperature increases when the airflow is reduced, but the heat transfer coefficient between the combustion gases and the wet solids decreases. The parameters that limit the energy savings are the allowable wall temperature of unlined dryers and the allowable exhaust gas temperature. Established correlations from the literature predict significantly different exhaust gas temperatures. Also, it is difficult to estimate the temperature of the dryer wall, which is in contact with the combustion gases and the wet solids. Therefore, it appears that experimentation will be needed to establish the optimum combustion airflow at this facility.

REFERENCES

1) Perry, Robert H., and D. Green, Perry's Chemical Engineers Handbook, sixth ed., McGraw Hill Book Company, Section 20, p33, ISBN 0-07-049479-7, 1986.

2) Williams-Gardner, A., Industrial Drying, Chemical and Process Engineering Series, Leonard Hill Book Company, London, 1971.

3) C.T. Kiranoudis, Z.B. Maroulis and D. Marinos-Kouris, "Modeling and Optimization of Fluidized Bed and Rotary Dryers", Drying Technology, Vol. 15, No. 3-4, Mar-Apr, p 735-763.

4) C.T. Kiranoudis, Z.B. Maroulis and D. Marinos-Kouris, "Design and Operation of Convective Industrial Dryers", AIChE-Journal, Vol. 42, No. 11, Nov. 1996, p 3030-3040.

5) S.E. Papadakis, T.A.G. Langrish, I.C. Kemp and R.E. Bahu, "Scale-Up of Cascading Rotary Dryers", Drying Technology, Vol. 12, No. 1&2, 1994, p 259-277.

6) I.C. Kemp and D.E. Oakley, "Simulation and Scale-Up of Pneumatic Conveying and Cascading Rotary Dryers", Drying Technology, Vol. 15, No. 6-8, 1997, p 1699-1710.

7) F.Y. Wang, I.T. Cameron, J.D. Litster and P.L. Douglas, "A Distributed Parameter Approach to the Dynamics of Rotary Drying Process", Drying Technology, Vol. 11, No. 7, 1993, p 1641-1656.

8) J.R. Perez-Correa, F. Cubillos, E. Zavala, C. Shene and P.I. Alverez, "Dynamic Simulation and Control of Direct Rotary Dryers", Food Control, Vol. 9, No. 4, pp. 195-203, 1998.

9) Bruley, A. J., " Hood Installation to Pre-Heat Lime Kiln Primary Combustion Air", Energy Conservation Opportunities, 1981-1992, compiled by the Energy Committee Technical Section, Canadian Pulp and Paper Association, Vol. KP-56, ISBN 1-895288-34-7, 1986.

10) Incropera, F.P. and D.P. DeWitt, Fundamentals of Heat and Mass Transfer, John Wiley & Sons, New York, ISBN 0-471-30460-3, 1996.

11) Marks, B., Standard Handbook for Mechanical Engineers, 9th ed., McGraw Hill Book Company, p 4-90, ISBN 0-07-004127-x, 1987.

Chapter 3

Energy Information and How to turn it into KNOWLEDGE

Energy Stories... Let's start this with a few little stories, the names have been changed, but the story is still the same.... You are now the energy manager for a large corporation. Until this day you have worked as a line supervisor but this job paid more and the shift allowed you time to be with the family. First day on the job, the boss comes in your office and says we just got direction to cut costs 5%. Where do you start, how much money is that anyway?..... A utility rep has been questioned by a good customer that has two buildings they feel could be consolidated into one metering package to take advantage of the non-coincidental peaks of the "diversity" in the building. Rather than simply agreeing, you offer up services to monitor the building to compare the peaks. When the information is reviewed you find that there is a savings of $30 that month, but since it will cost an additional $50 for each meter, it's not worth it. You show the customer the information that since these buildings both peak with the air conditioning & heating loads, they would never save enough to pay for it. Now you have a customer that respects your opinion.... A new chiller system is being designed for your facility because they are not able to maintain conditions in the plant. The space was there, so you investigate the new installation. You call in a top-notch design firm that said for an extra few grand they will test the existing system to pinpoint the proper size of the chiller. You agree but with some reservations. Two weeks later they come up with a report that says the existing chillers are underutilized and one large flow control valve was oversized, causing the system to surge. Your project cost goes down 75% and you look like a hero.

Each of these stories is related to the fact that for us to do our jobs, an emphasis must be placed on the value of data and how we turn it into knowledge to make educated decisions. The energy manager has no idea what the overall energy consumption of a facility is until the information on each stream of energy is tabulated and compared to others. A utility rep can discuss the issues related to a customer's energy consumption based on a bill, but inorder to see the interaction of a facility, the data must be compiled on a interval basis to see the reaction to other variables. When a mechanical system has been in place and functioning, typically they have not been reviewed unless broken. Therefore, monitoring is the answer.

How to get started:.... Any project worth doing is worth planning. This planning can be as detailed as documenting what instrumentation you already have and logging on a website to review your usage, to developing specifications to install complex PLC monitoring. I like to tell people trying to get a handle on their energy consumption to start

at the billing and work backwards. Retrieving a copy of all the energy streams going into a facility for at least the last two years (two years will begin to show a trend) can be a difficult thing. Once the data has been retrieved, it should be placed in an easy-to-read format and summarized by meter, site & division. This will allow the user to review this in one document. Some utilities are offering the extraction of this information via a website or from their rep, or there are third party vendors that provide this service in conjunction with processing the invoices on a web-based interface.

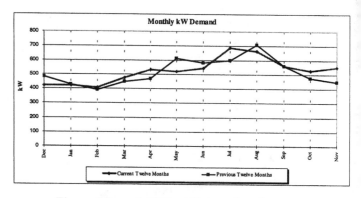

Figure 1 Billing History Table

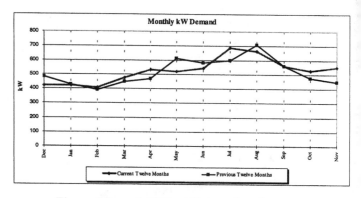

Figure 2 Sample Billing History Graph

Billing data does not tell the entire story, but it is a good place to start. By summarizing this information you can see anomalies and variations based on weather, production, and equipment that may not be functioning properly.

As we drill further into the operation of a building, the data becomes more "granular" or detailed. Again the planning will involve the investigation of what data is readily available. Some of the utility meters may already have the capability of recording load profiles within the memory of the meter or may be changed out for a low cost to one that does. Other times this data may be the by-product of a Building Management System (BMS) that has its own recording ability, or pulse modules that are part of the utility meter that provide a signal to a recorder onsite to display the consumption through the meter. Short term monitoring via single point metering can be done also to view what happens at a facility during a typical day, but this may not provide the complete picture of the events that happen at a location.

Table 1 Sample Profile for Selected Accounts on 05/26/2002

Time	Demo123 (kW)	RDU, NC (Fahren)	RDU, NC (RH)
00:15	1,000	72.00	57.00
00:30	1,068	72.00	57.00
00:45	1,088	72.00	57.00
01:00	908	72.00	57.00
01:15	928	70.00	59.00
01:30	912	70.00	59.00

The data can come in many different forms, and it is an art to turn that into useful information and knowledge that can be used to make decisions. Tables of information, like shown above, can be generated by BMS & utility systems, but unless you develop a plan for what you are searching for, you will be inundated with data and never turn it into true system knowledge. By reviewing specific pieces of data and turning them into specific information, such as the graphs below, you will increase your knowledge of the building system.

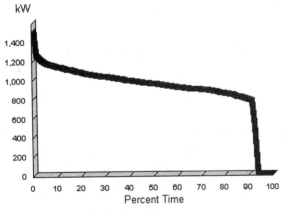

Figure 3 Typical Duration Curve

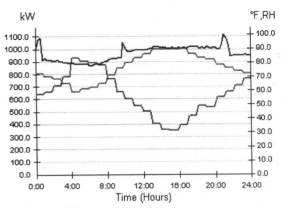

Figure 4 Typical Load Profile (red) with RH (purple) & Temp (green)

With this information available it becomes evident that three events raised the kW demand rapidly and then were not required. Reviewing the duration curve first gives an indication that only a few events caused the demand to elevate, and that the duration of these elevations was very short (i.e. a small percentage of time). Further investigation of the load profile would indicate that when overlaid with the outside temperature, it would not appear to be HVAC related, unless the equipment is not operating properly. Industrial batch process can drive demand so that can be investigated next, as well as operations that may be related to specific shifts.

You can take this a step further by finding the device that is causing the problems, and monitor it in detail. A water-cooled chiller can be monitored by collecting data (based on time) on the change in temperature through the chiller, the flow rate and the power consumption. With this data a

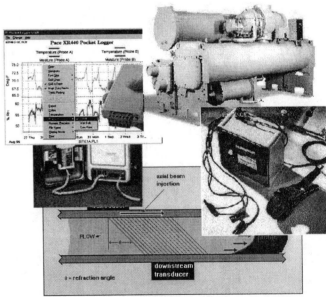

number of curves can be developed to indicate if a chiller or chiller plant is operating efficiently.

Figure 5 Chiller Monitoring Equipment

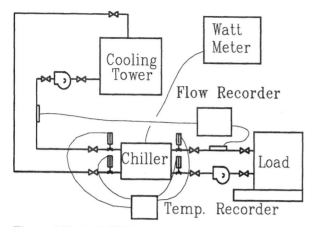

Figure 6 Typical Chiller Equipment Hookup

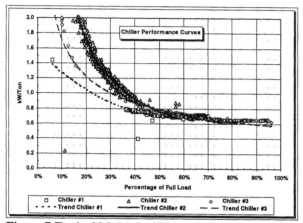

Figure 7 Typical Multiple Chiller Curve Output

When monitoring multiple chillers in a chilled water plant at the same time, it will become evident if the chillers are being loaded at the most efficient points. Also it can be extrapolated what the efficiency of the chiller is at certain load points and what the estimated power consumption of the chiller plant would be at certain load or outside conditions. Utilizing historic weather data, an estimated cost for the plant chilled water system can be given with a higher degree of accuracy. The pattern here is to "drill down" to the cause of the variations, then take that knowledge and create an action plan in order to reduce the demand variation and the operating cost of the facility.

What's next…..Now that we have used our information developed from the data to find the device that is causing our increased demand, what can we do to continuously improve the operation to help identify problems like this in the future? It is recommended to always review the detail of the utility billing, and track trends that may be developing. By creating a master database of your facility (s) it's easy to compare an operation with others in your company or typical facilities elsewhere in the world, where data is available. Identify specific areas or facilities that may be out of range. Then "roll up your sleeves" and dig deeper into the data that may be required to evaluate

the energy. Go as deep as you can to find the issues. Once the issues are identified, make a plan to come back and review the operation on a specific schedule to make sure the problem has been solved. Creating standard reports to review the facility on an ongoing basis can be very helpful.

In conclusion, remember that data is required to be turned into information before it can effectively create a knowledgeable person to solve a problem. If we theoretically look at the issues we have only partially reviewed the information. By taking measurements we can make more definite decisions that are based on more than just theory and may be easier to explain to others as an added value.

Chapter 4

RESULTS FROM THE INDUSTRIAL ASSESSMENT CENTER (IAC) STEAM TOOL BENCHMARKING SUPPORT PROJECT

Dr. Anthony L. Wright
BestPractices Steam
Oak Ridge Natl. Lab.

Dr. Kurt Bassett
South Dakota
State Univ.

Dr. Herbert Eckerlin
North Carolina
State Univ.

Dr. Ahmad Ganji
San Francisco
State Univ.

Derek Hengeveld
South Dakota
State Univ.

Dr. Richard Jendrucko
Univ. of Tennessee,
Knoxville

Dr. Dragoljub Kosanovic
Univ. of Massachusetts,
Amherst

Dr. Wayne Turner
Oklahoma State
Univ.

ABSTRACT

The U. S. Department of Energy's (DOE) Office of Industrial Technology (OIT) BestPractices effort is developing a number of software tools to assist industrial energy users to improve the efficiency of their operations. One of the software tools developed is the "Steam System Scoping Tool." In the summer of 2001, six of the DOE Industrial Assessment Centers (IACs) completed a project to provide data on the usefulness of the Steam System Scoping Tool. These six IACs performed eighteen plant steam system assessments; as part of these assessments the Steam System Scoping Tool was used and evaluated. This paper presents the results from these steam system assessments, and the results of the evaluations of the Steam System Scoping Tool.

INTRODUCTION

The U. S. Department of Energy's (DOE) Office of Industrial Technology (OIT) BestPractices effort is developing a number of software tools to assist industrial energy users to improve the efficiency of their operations. One of the software tools that have been developed is the "Steam System Scoping Tool." The Steam Scoping Tool is an Excel spreadsheet that can be applied by industrial steam users to: a) evaluate their steam system operations against identified best practices; and b) develop a greater awareness of opportunities to improve their steam systems.

The Steam Scoping Tool was developed by BestPractices Steam (the Best Practices and Technical subcommittee of BestPractices Steam); the tool was initially released in August 2000.

In June 2000, the IAC Steam Tool Benchmarking Support project was started. DOE Industrial Assessment Centers provide energy, waste, and productivity assessments at no charge to small to mid-sized manufacturers. These assessments help manufacturers maximize energy efficiency, reduce waste, and improve productivity. The assessments are performed by teams of engineering faculty and students from participating universities/IACs across the United States.

The IAC Steam Tool Benchmarking Support project had three main tasks:

Task 1: Compile steam system benchmarking data from past IAC steam assessments;

Task 2: Perform one-day focused steam system assessments to test new steam assessment tools and to develop new steam benchmarking data; and

Task 3: Document the results of the Task 2 efforts.

Six IACs participated in this project:

University of Massachusetts, Amherst;
North Carolina State University;
Oklahoma State University;
San Francisco State University;
South Dakota State University; and
University of Tennessee, Knoxville.

This paper summarizes the results for the key efforts of the project – the results from the eighteen steam system assessments, and the results of the evaluations of the Steam System Scoping Tool.

RESULTS FROM THE EIGHTEEN IAC STEAM SYSTEM ASSESSMENTS

Each of the six IACs performed three one-day steam system assessments in industrial plants. As part of the effort to perform these assessments, two BestPractices Steam assessment tools were utilized:

a. The Steam System Scoping Tool; and
b. The Steam System Survey Guide. This guide (a published BestPractices Steam document) was written by Dr. Greg Harrell from the University of Tennessee, Knoxville. It is a reference document that provides a technical basis for identifying and assessing many potential steam system improvement opportunities. Although the Survey Guide was provided to the IACs to use as a resource, the main focus of this project was to evaluate the usefulness of the Steam Scoping Tool.

Table 1 lists the industrial plant types for the one-day steam assessments. The IACs obtained annual data on the fuel cost to produce steam for fifteen of the assessed plants. These annual fuel bills ranged from about $79,000 to $14,800,000 per year; the average for the fifteen plants was about $1,600,000 per year.

The key activities associated with each of the eighteen steam assessments were the following:

a. Working with the plant people to obtain answers to questions in the Steam Scoping Tool;
b. Performing the individual steam assessments;
c. Documenting the results of each of the individual steam assessments in summary reports; and
d. Documenting the results of each of the completed Steam Scoping Tool evaluations.

Individual summary reports were prepared for each of the eighteen steam assessments. In addition, completed Steam Scoping Tool spreadsheets for each of the plant assessments were prepared.

Steam improvement opportunities, cost savings, implementation costs, and anticipated paybacks were identified for each of the eighteen steam assessments. Eighty-nine improvement opportunities were identified. Sixty-eight of the identified improvements had yearly savings less than $20,000 per year; twenty-one of the identified improvements had yearly savings greater than $20,000 per year.

The total identified annual energy savings from these assessments was $2,800,000; the average yearly savings for each of the identified eighty-nine improvements was about $31,500 per year. The total identified implementation costs for the eighty-nine was about $1,600,000; the average overall payback for the eighty-nine improvements was about 7 months.

Table 2 shows data for annual fuel costs to produce steam and annual identified savings, as a percent of annual fuel costs, for the eighteen steam assessments. For eight of the assessments, annual identified savings were greater than 9% of the annual fuel costs. The average identified energy savings for the eighteen steam assessments was 12.5% of the individual plant energy bills.

Table 3 shows data for individual steam system improvement opportunities identified that had projected annual savings greater than $20,000/yr.

The Steam System Scoping Tool [1] includes seven worksheets associated with identifying steam system improvement opportunities:

a. Introduction;
b. Steam System Basic Data;
c. Steam System Profiling;
d. Steam System Operating Practices – Total Steam System;
e. Steam System Operating Practices – Boiler Plant;
f. Steam System Operating Practices – Distribution, End Use, and Recovery; and
g. Summary Results.

A steam user has to answer 26 questions to complete the Steam Scoping Tool; the maximum score that can be achieved in completing the Steam Tool (100%) is 340 points. Figure 1 illustrates the individual plant scores achieved for the IAC steam assessments. The individual plant scores ranged from a low of 37.1% to a high of 85.9%.

Table 4 shows average question responses and standard deviations of question responses for the IAC steam assessments. The results shown in Table 3 illustrate the following:

a. For three of the general areas – Steam System Profiling, Boiler Plant Operating Practices, and Steam Distribution, End

Use, and Recovery Operating Practices –
the average overall score was about 50%.
For example, out of 90 points available
for Steam System Profiling, the average
score for the eighteen IAC steam
assessments was 44 points;

b. The highest scores were achieved in the
area of Steam System Operating
Practices - out of 140 available points the
average score was 102 points (about
73%);

c. The scores varied the most (highest
relative standard deviation) for the Steam
System Profiling area – for this area, the
standard deviation of responses was 28
points out of the available 90 points.
This suggests that the plants differed the
most in their responses to the Steam
Profiling questions.

STEAM SCOPING TOOL EVALUATION RESULTS

The IACs prepared an individual summary report for
each of the eighteen steam system assessments. In
addition, each participating IAC prepared a separate
report summarizing the overall results of each of their
efforts.

A key part of the Steam Scoping Tool evaluation
reports was to identify the following types of
information:

a. How useful was the Steam Scoping Tool
to the plant personnel?
b. How can the Steam Scoping Tool be
improved?
c. How can the usefulness of the Steam
Scoping Tool to plant personnel be
improved?

All of the individual evaluation comments on the
Steam Scoping Tool have been reviewed, and many of
the suggested improvements will be included in the
next release of the Steam Scoping Tool. Some of the
key comments made by the IACs are summarized
below:

a. A number of the IACs indicated that the
question on Options for Reducing Steam
Pressure (PR1) needs to be improved.
Many facilities will not have the option
of reducing pressure using backpressure
turbines, and the Steam Tool should
reflect this.

b. Many of the plant personnel who
completed the Steam Scoping Tool felt
that it helped them to understand areas
where they could improve their steam
systems.

c. A number of the plant personnel
indicated that they would not have
completed the Steam Scoping Tool if
they had not been selected to have a free
steam system assessment. The responses
from the IACs suggest a number of ways
to enhance the usefulness of the software
tool; for example: 1) provide information
on cost savings associated with different
improvement opportunities; 2) provide
feedback to steam users, after they
complete the Tool, providing more
details on how improvements can be
made; and 3) provide plants with
corresponding summary results from
other plants to illustrate how their scores
compare with other similar plants.

d. A number of the IACs suggested that
some measure of comparison be
provided on the relative merits of
different scoring ranges, e.g., 300-340
excellent, 250-299 very good, etc.

e. Finally, a number of the IACs suggested
that improving the overall formatting of
the software tool would improve its
usefulness.

SUMMARY AND CONCLUSIONS

In summary, this was a successful project. When the
project was started, the Steam System Scoping Tool
was about to be released, and there was no measure of
how useful the software tool would be for assessing
steam systems or where the software tool could be
improved. As a result of the project, a number of
areas for improving the Tool and the usefulness of the
software tool to steam users have been identified.

Based largely on the improvements suggested from
this project, an updated version (1.0d) of the Steam
System Scoping Tool has now been published. Efforts
are underway to convert the Microsoft Excel version
of the Scoping Tool to a Visual Basic format (a
recommendation from this project).

The results from the eighteen steam system
assessments will also prove valuable to the overall
BestPractices Steam effort.

The Steam Scoping Tool and other BestPractices Steam resources are available from this web site: **www.oit.doe.gov/bestpractices/steam**.

REFERENCES

1. *The Steam System Scoping Tool: Benchmarking Your Steam System Through Best Practices*, Anthony Wright (Oak Ridge National Laboratory) and Glenn Hahn (Spirax Sarco Inc.), 23rd National Industrial Energy Technology Conference, Houston, TX May 2001.

ACKNOWLEDGEMENTS

The authors acknowledge the U.S. Department of Energy Office of Industrial Technologies for providing financial support for this project.

TABLE 1. PLANT TYPES FOR THE 18 IAC STEAM ASSESSMENTS

Cheese and Whey Products
Chemicals
Corrugated Containers (2)
Fabric Dying Facility
Frozen Food Producer
Hardwood Mouldings
Industrial Cleaning Compounds and Sanitizers
Inorganic Chemical Intermediates
Pulp and Paper Plants (3)
Redwood Lumber
Rubber Tires
Shopping Cart Manufacturer
Styrofoam Cups
Textiles
Vinyl Flooring

TABLE 2. ANNUAL FUEL COST TO MAKE STEAM AND IDENTIFIED ANNUAL ENERGY SAVINGS AS PERCENT OF ANNUAL STEAM FUEL COST, FOR THE 18 IAC STEAM ASSESSMENTS.

Annual Fuel Cost to Produce Steam ($)	Annual Energy Savings as Percent of Annual Steam Fuel Cost
$532,940	1.8%
$1,579,231	2.6%
$157,862	3.4%
$261,558	4.3%
$661,391	4.6%
$173,222	5.6%
$14,790,000	6.0%
$244,124	6.2%
$3,131,040	6.7%
$1,224,997	7.0%
$1,000,000	9.4%
$78,934	10.3%
$136,791	13.9%
$415,337	15.4%
$1,744,680	20.2%
$183,889	25.3%
$619,016	33.5%
$1,456,000	49.2%

TABLE 3. ANNUAL COST SAVINGS, PAYBACKS FOR IAC STEAM ASSESSMENT IMPROVEMENTS HAVING PROJECTED ANNUAL SAVINGS GREATER THAN $20,000/YR.

Description of Improvement	Annual Cost Savings ($)	Payback Period
Retune Boiler And Purchase Combustion Analyzer	$20,736	0.3 years
Use Water From Fresh Water Tank As Boiler Makeup Water	$24,500	3 months
Install Economizer On Boiler, Reduce Stack Temperature By 100+ F	$28,000	3.5 years
Use Water Spray In Lieu Of Live Steam To Moisten Board Before Adhesive Bonding	$28,190	0.4 years
Install Automatic Boiler Air/Fuel Ratio Controls	$33,580	0.7 years
Install Economizer On 600 HP Boiler	$34,291	0.6 years
Insulate Hot Exterior Surfaces Of Presses	$35,467	0.3 years
Install An Economizer To Reduce Exit Flue Gas Temperature And Improve Efficiency	$44,160	1.5 years
Repair Steam Leaks	$46,670	<0.1 years
Shut Steam Valves Feeding Unused Presses	$54,060	0.3 years
Use Cogeneration For Electricity Production	$54,400	5.3 years
Refurbish And Tune Up Burner On Each Boiler To Reduce Excess Air At The Lower Load Ranges	$66,300	0.3 years
Control Steam Bleeding At Platens	$75,509	0.3 years
Use Economizer To Preheat Boiler Feedwater	$84,500	1 month
Install Automatic Boiler Air/Fuel Ratio Controls	$150,030	0.1 years
Reduce Excess Air In Boiler	$174,785	0.6 years
Reduce Excess Air In Boiler	$174,785	0.6 years
Reduce Excess Air In Boiler	$226,925	0.4 years
Recover Heat From Wastewater	$241,800	1 year
Reduce Excess Air In Boiler	$315,564	0.3 years
Convert To Single Boiler Operation, Reduce Wear And Tear On Boilers	$600,000	Minimal

TABLE 4. SUMMARY OF STEAM SCOPING TOOL RESULTS FOR THE IAC STEAM ASSESSMENTS

Scoping Tool Areas and Questions	Possible Score	Average, IAC Responses	Std. Deviation, IAC Responses
1. STEAM SYSTEM PROFILING			
STEAM COSTS			
SC1: Measure Fuel Cost to Generate Steam	10	7	5
SC2: Trend Fuel Cost to Generate Steam	10	6	5
STEAM/PRODUCT BENCHMARKS			
BM1: Measure Steam/Product Benchmarks	10	4	5
BM2: Trend Steam/Product Benchmarks	10	4	5
STEAM SYSTEM MEASUREMENTS			
MS1: Measure/Record Steam System Critical Energy Parameters	30	18	9
MS2: Intensity of Measuring Steam Flows	20	5	7
STEAM SYSTEM PROFILING SCORE	**90**	**44**	**28**
2. STEAM SYSTEM OPERATING PRACTICES			
STEAM TRAP MAINTENANCE			
ST1: Steam Trap Maintenance Practices	40	24	7
WATER TREATMENT PROGRAM			
WT1: Water Treatment – Ensuring Function	10	8	3
WT2: Cleaning Boiler Fireside/Waterside Deposits	10	9	3
WT3: Measure Boiler TDS, Top/Bottom Blowdown Rates	10	8	4
SYSTEM INSULATION			
IN1: Insulation – Boiler Plant	10	9	3
IN2: Insulation – Distribution/End Use/Recovery	20	14	8
STEAM LEAKS			
LK1: Steam Leaks – How Often	10	6	5
WATER HAMMER			
WH1: Water Hammer – How Often	10	8	3
MAINTAINING EFFECTIVE STEAM SYSTEM OPS.			
MN1: Inspecting Important Steam Plant Equipment	20	16	6
STEAM SYSTEM OPERATING PRACTICES SCORE	**140**	**102**	**18**
3. BOILER PLANT OPERATING PRACTICES			
BOILER EFFICIENCY			
BE1: Measuring Boiler Efficiency – How Often	10	6	4
BE2: Flue Gas Temperature, O2, CO Measurement	15	9	6
BE3: Controlling Boiler Excess Air	10	6	4
HEAT RECOVERY EQUIPMENT			
HR1: Boiler Heat Recovery Equipment	15	6	6
GENERATING DRY STEAM			
DS1: Checking Boiler Steam Quality	10	3	4
BOILER OPERATION			
GB1: Automatic Boiler Blowdown Control	5	3	3
GB2: Frequency of Boiler High/Low Level Alarms	10	9	2
GB3: Frequency of Boiler Steam Pressure Fluctuations	5	4	2
BOILER PLANT OPERATING PRACTICES SCORE	**80**	**45**	**13**
4. STEAM DISTRIBUTION, END USE, RECOVERY OPERATING PRACTICES			
MINIMIZE STEAM FLOW THROUGH PRVs			
PR1: Options for Reducing Steam Pressure	10	5	3
RECOVER AND UTILIZE AVAILABLE CONDENSATE			
CR1: Recovering and Utilizing Available Condensate	10	8	3
USE HIGH-PRESSURE STEAM TO MAKE LOW-PRESSURE CONDENSATE			
FS1: Recovering and Utilizing Available Flash Steam	10	1	3
DISTRIBUTION, END USE, RECOVERY PRACTICES SCORE	**30**	**14**	**6**
TOTAL STEAM SCOPING TOOL SCORE	**340**	**205**	**47**
TOTAL STEAM SCOPING TOOL SCORE (%)		**60%**	**14%**

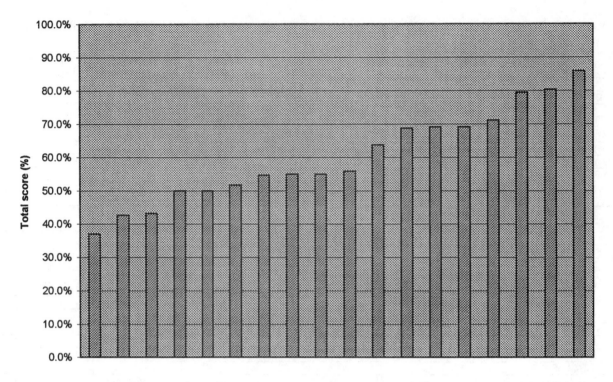

FIGURE 1. STEAM SYSTEM SCOPING TOOL TOTAL SCORES FROM IAC STEAM ASSESSMENTS

Chapter 5

25th World Energy Engineering Congress
Association of Energy Engineers
October 9-11, 2002
Atlanta, Georgia

Proceedings Submittal

Fred C. Schoeneborn, CEM
FCS Consulting Services, Inc.
July 2002

The Industrial Partnership of ENERGY STAR®

ENERGY STAR, a voluntary government program, offers businesses and consumers clear information on the best in energy efficiency helping them to save money while protecting the environment for future generations. Participating organizations join and partner with ENERGY STAR by making a commitment to:

- Measure, track, and benchmark their organization's energy performance by using tools such as those offered by ENERGY STAR;
- Develop and implement a plan to improve energy performance in facilities and operations by adopting the successful energy management strategy promoted by ENERGY STAR; and,
- Educate staff and the public about their partnership with ENERGY STAR, and highlight achievements with the ENERGY STAR label, where available.

The Industrial Partnership of ENERGY STAR promotes and encourages superior corporate energy management, providing tools and resources specific to the needs of manufacturers. The Partnership currently enjoys the participation of over 470 companies of varying sizes.

The Industrial Partnership's unique resources for manufacturers include opportunities to participate in sector-focused activities, networking with other industrial energy managers in the broad partnership, the Industrial Web site, and assistance in developing or improving a corporate energy performance program. Each year, the Industrial Partnership identifies certain manufacturing sectors to engage in focus activities. These activities include an in-depth study and assessment of energy efficiency opportunities within the sector, development of an energy performance indicator for plants within the sector, and sector-specific working groups, including focus meetings, aimed at improving corporate energy performance. In 2002, the Industrial Partnership of ENERGY STAR is conducting focus activities with two manufacturing sectors – the Motor Vehicle Assembly and Brewery industries.

In addition to taking advantage of industrial-specific resources, partners are also encouraged to take advantage of other program-wide tools and resources, including the benchmarking tool for office buildings and corporate headquarters, a financial value calculator and other technical resources.

Annually, ENERGY STAR recognizes partner organizations that have demonstrated a commitment to superior energy performance. In 2002, ENERGY STAR honored General Motors Corporation with an award for Excellence in Energy Management. General Motors, a world leader in vehicle manufacturing, has a comprehensive corporate energy management program that tracks energy performance for its business operations worldwide.

General Motors established its global Energy and Environment Strategy Board to integrate energy and environmental issues with core business decisions. As a result, the world-class corporate energy program includes aggressive continuing energy performance improvement goals, a clear procurement policy covering energy purchasing and the acquisition of manufacturing process and building operation equipment, benchmarking of plant energy performance internally as well as with key competitors, and the Energy $avings Project Implementation Process to promote energy projects on an equal ground with other core business operations. General Motors uses its partnership with ENERGY STAR to promote energy performance throughout the corporation.

General Motors' corporate energy commitment has saved over $400 million in the past six years and expects a reduction of 4.8 trillion Btu from its 2000 levels in 2001. The cost savings for the reduction in 2001 translates to an equivalent profit margin for vehicle sales of $800 million.

Another outstanding example of achievement by an ENERGY STAR partner is Eastman Kodak Company's development of a world-class communication effort designed to promote its strong energy management program. Kodak has carefully developed highly effective communications directed to various stakeholders. For example, the Kodak Neighborhood *Update* is a newsletter designed to keep the community around its plants informed about the company's continuous improvement in energy efficiency and its positive impact on the environment. Other examples include posters and stickers to increase employee awareness, an environmental annual report demonstrating Kodak's environmental commitment to the investor community and an Energy Scorecard, used to show management both progress toward goals and the financial benefits the program is generating.

A sample of companies participating in the Industrial Partnership of ENERGY STAR include:

3M
The Adolph Coors Company
Anheuser-Busch, Inc.
Apple Computer
Dow Chemical Company
Eastman Kodak Company
Ford Motor Company
General Motors
Honeywell, Inc.
IBM Corporation
Kellogg Company
Johnson & Johnson
Lockheed Martin Company
Raytheon

To learn more about ENERGY STAR tools and resources designed to help your organization improve energy performance, visit the ENERGY STAR Web site www.energystar.gov or call 1-888-STAR-YES.

Chapter 6

IS COMMISSIONING ONCE ENOUGH?

David E. Claridge, Associate Director and Professor
W.D. Turner, Director and Professor
Energy Systems Laboratory, Texas A&M University
Mingsheng Liu, Associate Professor
Architectural Engineering, University of Nebraska
Song Deng, Assistant Director
Guanghua Wei, Assistant Director
Charles Culp, Associate Director
Hui Chen, Research Associate
SoolYeon Cho, Research Associate
Energy Systems Laboratory, Texas A&M University

ABSTRACT

The Energy Systems Laboratory has developed a commissioning process called Continuous Commissioning[SM] over the last decade. This process is used to resolve operating problems, improve comfort, optimize energy use, and sometimes to recommend retrofits. The process has produced average energy savings of about 20% without significant capital investment in well over 100 large buildings in which it has been implemented. Payback has virtually always been under 3 years with most at two years or less.

This paper describes the process and presents recent evidence of the need for follow-up commissioning when indicated by consumption increases. A case study is presented that specifically shows the value of this follow-up.

INTRODUCTION TO CONTINUOUS COMMISSIONING[SM]

Continuous Commissioning (CC[SM]) started at the Energy Systems Laboratory (ESL) of Texas A&M University as an attempt to achieve energy and cost savings with operations and maintenance (O&M) procedures (Liu et al. 1994). It evolved into a commissioning process that is a way of problem solving in buildings, which helps problems stay fixed longer than conventional trouble-shooting procedures and simultaneously helps reduce energy costs (Liu et al. 1999). It requires knowledge of the fundamentals of humidity, airflow, water flow, and heat flow. This knowledge must be combined with a practical and fundamental knowledge of building systems and building operation to diagnose the cause(s) of problems (Liu et al. 1996). These elements are then combined to solve the problems. Use of this approach typically not only makes problems stay fixed longer; it makes a building operate more efficiently and hence at lower cost. This process attempts to optimize building operation for current requirements. It has primarily been applied to existing buildings, and in that respect resembles what has come to be called retro commissioning. However, it has also been applied to new buildings where it differs from conventional new building commissioning with its emphasis on performance optimization. On-going monitoring of energy consumption with commissioning follow-up as needed has been recommended as an integral part of the process since the mid-1990s.

To date CC has been applied to well over one hundred large buildings with a total floor area of well over 10 million square feet and has reduced energy costs by an average of 20% without appreciable capital investment. Gregerson (1997) investigated existing building commissioning in 1997 and reported average savings of 11.8% for 13 buildings which had undergone conventional commissioning. The average savings noted for the 21 buildings that had undergone CC was 23.8%.

Buildings that have had retrofits and buildings that have not had recent upgrades to the HVAC equipment comprise two significantly different categories to which the CC process has been applied. The average savings due to the process in buildings that had already been retrofit were about 20% beyond the retrofit savings (Claridge et al. 1996). A more recent paper (Claridge et al. 2000) reported that application of the CC process to buildings that had not generally been retrofit produced savings averaging 28% for cooling, 54% for heating, and savings of 2 to 20% for other electrical uses.

THE CONTINUOUS COMMISSIONING PROCESS

The Continuous Commissioning Process is shown schematically in Figure 1 as outlined in Claridge et al (2000).

The first step in the CC process is to perform an initial survey of the building and discover the comfort and operational problems that are present. During this survey,

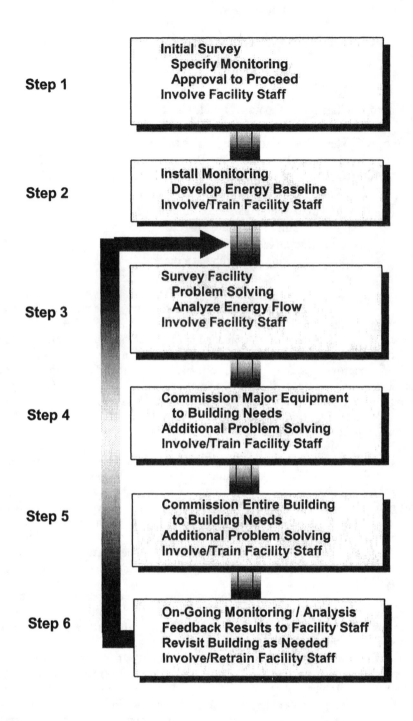

FIGURE 1. THE CONTINUOUS COMMISSIONING PROCESS

an initial estimate of the potential CC savings and an estimate of the monitoring requirements are made. One of the fundamental requirements for CC to be effective is to involve the facility staff in each of the steps so that they will understand and support the planned enhancements to the operations and the facility. Training in Step 1 is usually informal and generally involves discussions as the CC engineer surveys the facility.

A method for measuring and modeling the baseline performance of the facility must be established to determine the impact of the CC process. Equipment is normally installed to separately monitor at least heating, cooling, and other electric consumption on at least an hourly basis and a baseline started in Step 2. This equipment may be installed and owned by the utility or may be owned by the facility. If the metering will be maintained by the building staff, they need to be involved in the installation and should be given installation responsibility if possible. This creates ownership and will allow a much faster repair of sensors when needed. The training in Step 2 is informal and should involve hands-on participation in the installation process.

The CC engineer next performs a detailed facility survey in Step 3. This survey utilizes data from the energy monitoring equipment, the control system, and numerous one-time measurements of temperatures, pressures, and flows made throughout the building. Any broken components or any causes of discomfort are identified and fixed. Also, a team must be formed between the CC engineers and the facility staff. Getting the building back up to proper function is very important as this provides an immediate benefit to the occupants. Having the facility person involved with this step helps to minimize actions by operators to "undo" changes implemented as part of the repair process if complaints occur. Before proceeding, the facility environment should be comfortable and the equipment should be operating acceptably. For example, if the airflow through air handler 5 is increased to improve the temperature in the Dean's Office, discomfort may be created in the EE Department Head's office, two doors down. The CC team identifies these problems, develops a plan for solving them and then solves them. The CC engineers work with the facility staff until solutions are identified and in place. The CC engineer must have an excellent fundamental understanding of the systems in the building combined with substantial practical experience with these systems.

Commissioning the equipment to the facility needs and then commissioning the entire facility to the facility needs are completed in Steps 4 and 5. Commissioning to facility needs involves problem analysis and solution. When equipment is oversized, a typical finding, the operation is usually non-optimal. The CC engineer must understand the operation of the equipment in the equipment room and also how energy is transported in the facility.

Monitoring, in Step 6, is key to measuring the changes and being able to report the savings obtained. Monitoring also serves as an early warning if changes were made in the facility which degrade the operation or savings. A CC engineer needs to visit to facility to review the operation whenever the building consumption increases significantly. Often facility staff change and retraining is important. Also, facility use often changes and these visits will be useful for identifying additional needs at the site. The CC process optimizes the building as it was being operated.

For example, if one-half of a floor of offices was converted to labs, it is very likely the energy use of the space will have changed and will need to be optimized. Additional information on the CC process is provided in Liu et al. (1994, 1999) and in Claridge et al. (2000)

CASES WHERE CONTINUOUS COMMISSIONING MAY BE USED

The CC process has been applied almost exclusively to buildings with a floor area of at least 5,000 m^2. About 90% of the buildings to which the process has been applied are in cooling dominated climates where typical cooling consumption in large buildings is at least two times the heating consumption. However, it has also been successfully applied to buildings in the coldest parts of the continental United States. It is a relatively labor intense process at this time, making it generally more applicable to buildings with large air handlers and large total energy use. Automated control systems tend to simplify implementation of CC and it has been particularly effective in buildings that exhibit significant simultaneous heating and cooling. If the CC process were to be implemented in all in the commercial buildings larger than 50,000 ft^2 in the United States, and achieve comparable savings, it would have the potential to reduce consumption in the commercial buildings sector by 8%. Of course, if it were successfully implemented on that scale, it can be anticipated that a variety of automated techniques would make it applicable to smaller buildings and expand the potential impact.

CASE STUDY - KLEBERG BUILDING

The Kleberg Building is a teaching/research facility on the Texas A&M campus consisting of classrooms, offices and laboratories, with a total floor area of approximately 165,030 ft^2. Ninety percent of the building is heated and cooled by two (2) single duct variable air volume (VAV) air handling units (AHU) each having a pre-heat coil, a cooling coil, one supply air fan (100 hp), and a return air fan (25 hp). Two smaller constant volume units handle the teaching/lecture rooms in the building. The campus plant provides chilled water and hot water to the building. The two (2) parallel chilled water pumps (2×20 hp) have variable frequency drive control. There are 120 fan-powered VAV boxes with terminal reheat in 12 laboratory zones and 100 fan-powered VAV boxes with terminal reheat in the offices. There are six (6) exhaust fans (10-20 hp, total 90 hp) for fume hoods and laboratory general exhaust. The air handling units, chilled water pumps and 12 laboratory zones are controlled by a direct digital control (DDC) system. DDC controllers modulate dampers to control exhaust airflow from fume hoods and laboratory general exhaust.

A CC investigation was initiated in the summer of 1996 due to the extremely high level of simultaneous heating and cooling observed in the building (Abbas, 1996). Figures 2 and 3 show daily heating and cooling consumption (expressed in average kBtu/hr) as functions of daily average temperature. The Pre-CC data heating given in Figure 2 shows very little temperature dependence as indicted by the regression line derived from the data.

Data values were typically between 5 and 6 MMBtu/hr with occasional lower values. The cooling data (Figure 3) shows more temperature dependence and the regression line indicates that average consumption on a design day would exceed 10 MMBtu/hr. This corresponds to only 198 sq.ft./ ton based on average load.

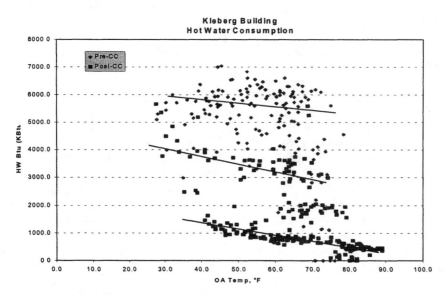

FIGURE 2. PRE-CC AND POST-CC HEATING WATER CONSUMPTION AT THE KLEBERG BUILDING VS DAILY AVERAGE OUTDOOR TEMPERATURE.

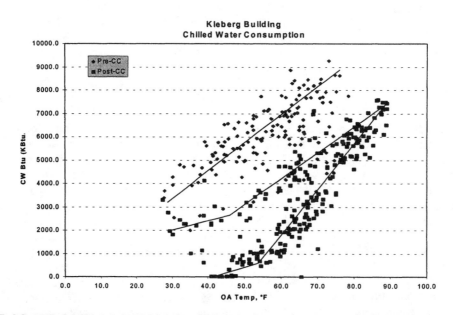

FIGURE 3. PRE-CC AND POST-CC CHILLED WATER CONSUMPTION AT THE KLEBERG BUILDING VS. DAILY AVERAGE OUTDOOR TEMPERATURE.

It was soon found that the preheat was operating continuously, heating the mixed air entering the cooling coil to approximately 105 F, instituted in response to a humidity problem in the building. The preheat was turned off and heating and cooling consumption both dropped by about 2 MMBtu/hour as shown by the middle clouds of data in Figures 2 and 3. Subsequently, the building was thoroughly examined and a comprehensive list of commissioning measures was developed and implemented. The principal measures implemented that led to reduced heating and cooling consumption were:

- Preheat to 105 F was changed to preheat to 40 F

- Cold deck schedule changed from 55 F fixed to vary from 62 F to 57 F as ambient varies from 40 F to 60 F

- Economizer – set to maintain mixed air at 57 F whenever outside air below 60 F

- Static pressure control – reduced from 1.5 inH2O to 1.0 inH2O and implemented night-time set back to 0.5 inH2O

- Replaced or repaired a number of broken VFD boxes

- Chilled water pump VFDs were turned on.

Additional measures implemented included changes in CHW pump control – changed so one pump modulates to full speed before second pump comes on instead of operating both pumps in parallel at all times, building static pressure was reduced from 0.05 inH2O to 0.02 inH2O, and control changes were made to eliminate hunting in several valves. It was also observed that there was a vibration at a particular frequency in the pump VFDs that influenced the

operators to place these VFDs in the manual mode, so it was recommended that the mountings be modified to solve this problem.

These changes further reduced chilled water and heating hot water use as shown in Figures 2 and 3 for a total annualized reduction of 63% in chilled water use and 84% in hot water use. Additional follow-up conducted from June 1998 through April 1999 focused on air balance in the 12 laboratory zones, general exhaust system rescheduling, VAV terminal box calibration, adjusting the actuators and dampers, and calibrating fume hoods and return bypass devices to remote DDC control (Lewis, et al. 1999). These changes reduced electricity consumption by about 7% or 30,000 kWh/mo.

In 2001 it was observed that chilled water savings for 2000 had declined to 38% and hot water savings to 62% as shown in Table 1. Chilled water data for 2001 and the first three months of 2002 are shown in Figure 4. The two lines shown are the regression fits to the chilled water data before CC implementation and after implementation of CC measures in 1996 as shown in Figure 3. It is evident that consumption during 2001 is generally appreciably higher than immediately following implementation of CC measures. The CC group performed field tests and analyses that soon focused on two SDVAV AHU systems, two chilled water pumps, and the Energy Management Control System (EMCS) control algorithms as described in Chen et al. (2002). Several problems were observed as noted below.

TABLE 1. CHILLED WATER AND HEATING WATER USAGE AND SAVING IN THE KLEBERG BUILDING FOR THREE DIFFERENT YEARS NORMALIZED TO 1995 WEATHER.

Type	Pre-CC Baseline (MMBtu/yr)	Post-CC Use/Savings		2000 Use/Savings	
		Use (MMBtu/yr)	Savings (%)	Use (MMBtu/yr)	Savings (%)
CHW	72935	26537	63.6%	45431	37.7%
HW	43296	6841	84.2%	16351	62.2%

Problems Identified

- The majority of the VFDs were running at a constant speed near 100% speed.

- VFD control on two chilled water pumps was again by passed to run at full speed.

- Two chilled water control valves were leaking badly. Combined with a failed electronic to pneumatic switch and the high water pressure noted above, this resulted in discharge air temperatures of 50F and lower and activated preheat continuously.

- A failed pressure sensor and two failed CO2 sensors put all outside air dampers to the full open position.

- The damper actuators were leaking and unable to maintain pressure in some of the VAV boxes. This caused cold air to flow through the boxes even when they were in the heating mode, resulting in simultaneous heating and cooling. Furthermore some of the reheat valves were malfunctioning. This caused the reheat to remain on continuously in some cases.

- Additional problems identified from the field survey included the following: 1) high air resistance from the filters and coils, 2) errors in a temperature

33

sensor and static pressure sensor, 3) high static pressure set points in AHU1&AHU2.

A combination of equipment failure compounded by control changes that returned several pumps and fans to constant speed operation had the consequence of increasing chilled water use by 18,894 MMBtu and hot water use by 9,510 MMBtu. This amounted to an increase of 71% in chilled water use and more than doubled hot water use from two years earlier

These problems have now been largely corrected and building performance has returned to previously low levels as illustrated by the data for April-June 2002 in Figure 4. This data is all below the lower of the two regression lines and is comparable to the level achieved after additional CC measures were implemented in 1998-99.

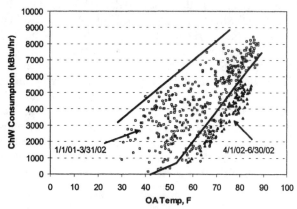

FIGURE 4. CHW DATA FOR THE KLEBERG BUILDING SINCE JANUARY 2001.

WHEN IS FOLLOW-UP COMMISSIONING NEEDED?

For the Kleberg Building, it is clear that a combination of control changes and component problems led to a need for follow-up commissioning measures. In principle, these measures could be viewed as routine maintenance, but since they had not led to comfort problems, it is unlikely that they would have been addressed unless they ultimately resulted in a comfort problem. Even then without the evidence of the $66,500/year increase in consumption, it is unlikely that a comprehensive follow-up effort would have occurred. But how often do such problems occur?

The ESL has conducted a study of 10 buildings on the A&M campus that had CC measures implemented in 1996-97. Table 2 shows the baseline cost of combined heating, cooling and electricity use of each building and the commissioning savings for 1998 and 2000. The baseline consumption and savings for each year were normalized to remove any differences due to weather (see Turner, et al. 2001 for details).

Looking at the totals for the group of 10 buildings, savings decreased by over $207,258 (17%) from 1998 to 2000, but were still very substantial. However, it may also be observed that almost ¼ of this decrease occurred in two buildings, the Kleberg Building, and G. Rollie White Coliseum. The increased consumption of the Kleberg Building was due to a combination of component failures and control problems as already discussed. The increased consumption in G. Rollie White Coliseum was due

TABLE 2. COMMISSIONING SAVINGS IN 1998 AND 2000 FOR 10 BUILDINGS ON THE TEXAS A&M CAMPUS.

Building	Baseline Use ($/yr)	1998 Savings ($/yr)	2000 Savings($/yr)
Kleberg Building	$ 484,899	$ 313,958	$ 247,415
G.R. White Coliseum	$ 229,881	$ 154,973	$ 71,809
Blocker Building	$ 283,407	$ 76,003	$ 56,738
Eller O&M Building	$ 315,404	$ 120,339	$ 89,934
Harrington Tower	$ 145,420	$ 64,498	$ 48,816
Koldus Building	$ 192,019	$ 57,076	$ 61,540
Richardson Petroleum Building	$ 273,687	$ 120,745	$120,666
Veterinary Medical Center Addition	$ 324,624	$ 87,059	$ 92,942
Wehner Business Building	$ 224,481	$ 47,834	$ 68,145
Zachry Engineering Center	$ 436,265	$ 150,400	$127,620
Totals	$ 2,910,087	$ 1,192,884	$ 985,626

to different specific failures and changes, but was qualitatively similar to Kleberg since it resulted from a combination of component failures and control changes. The five buildings that showed consumption increases above 5% from 1998 to 2000 were all found to have different control settings that appear to account for the

changed consumption (including the decrease in the Wehner Business Building).

This data does not explicitly answer the question "When is follow-up commissioning needed?", but the authors believe it suggests that tracking consumption and investigating the reasons for significant increases is likely to provide real benefits.

ACKNOWLEDGEMENTS:

The authors are pleased to acknowledge cooperation and assistance of Homer Bruner and numerous others in the Physical Plant Department at Texas A&M University and to acknowledge the financial support of the Physical Plant Department for implementing CC work on the Texas A&M campus. The support of the California Energy Commission in funding the study of commissioning savings persistence through Lawrence Berkeley National Laboratory under the Public Interest Research Program is also gratefully acknowledged.

REFERENCES

Abbas, M., 1996. "CC at the Kleberg Building," Internal ESL Memo, August.

Chen, Hui, Song Deng, Homer Bruner, David Claridge and W.D. Turner, 2002. "Continuous Commissioning[SM] Results Verification And Follow-Up For An Institutional Building - A Case Study," *Proc. 13th Symposium on Improving Building Systems in Hot and Humid Climates*, Houston, TX, May.

Claridge, D.E., Liu, M., Zhu, Y., Abbas, M., Athar, A., and Haberl, J., 1996. "Implementation of Continuous Commissioning in the Texas LoanSTAR Program: 'Can You Achieve 150% of Estimated Retrofit Savings' Revisited," *Proceedings 4, Commercial Buildings: Technologies, Design, and Performance Analysis. ACEEE 1996 Summer Study on Energy Efficiency In Buildings*, American Council for an Energy Efficient Economy, Washington, D.C., pp. 4.59-4.67.

Claridge, D.E., Culp, C.H., Liu, M., Deng, S., Turner, W.D., and Haberl, J.S., 2000. "Campus-Wide Continuous Commissioning[SM] of University Buildings," *Proc. of ACEEE 2000 Summer Study on Energy Efficiency in Buildings*, Pacific Grove, CA, Aug. 20-25, pp. 3.101-3.112.

Gregerson, Joan, 1997. "Cost Effectiveness of Commissioning 44 Existing Buildings," Fifth National Conference on Building Commissioning, Huntington Beach, CA April 28-30.

Lewis, T., H. Chen, and M. Abbas, 1999. "CC summary for the Kleberg Building," Intrenal ESL Report, July.

Liu, M., Houcek, J., Athar, A., Reddy, A. and Claridge, D., 1994. "Identifying and Implementing Improved Operation and Maintenance Measures in Texas LoanSTAR Buildings," *ACEEE 1994 Summer Study on Energy Efficiency In Buildings Proceedings: Commissioning, Operation and Maintenance*, Vol. 5, American Council for an Energy Efficient Economy, Washington, D.C., pp. 153-165.

Liu, M., Zhu, Y., Abbas, M., de La Cruz, R., Perez, J., and Claridge, D.E., 1996. "An O&M Story of an Old Building," *Proceedings of the 2nd National Commissioning Conference*, Portland, OR, May 3-4, 13 pp.

Liu, Mingsheng, Claridge, David E. and Turner, W.D., 1999. "Improving Building Energy System Performance by Continuous Commissioning," *Energy Engineering*, Vol. 96, No. 5, pp. 46-57.

Turner, W.D., Claridge, D.E., Deng, S., Cho, S., Liu, M., Hagge, T., Darnell, C., Jr., and Bruner, H., Jr., "Persistence of Savings Obtained from Continuous Commissioning[SM]," *Proc. of 9th National Conference on Building Commissioning*, Cherry Hill, NJ, May 9-11, 2001, pp. 20-1.1 - 20-1.

Chen, Hui, Song Deng, Homer Bruner, David Claridge and W.D. Turner, 2002. "Continuous Commissioning[SM] Results Verification And Follow-Up For An Institutional Building - A Case Study," *Proc. 13th Symposium on Improving Building Systems in Hot and Humid Climates*, Houston, TX, May.

Chapter 7

CENTRAL PLANT RETROFIT CONSIDERATIONS

Jon R. Haviland, P.E., CEM
Marx/Okubo Associates, LTD

ABSTRACT

Refrigerant changes, along with normal aging, are driving the need to retrofit or replace chillers within a central plant at a much greater pace than ever before. This is an opportunity to improve the efficiency of the chiller as well as the overall performance of the plant. The key to taking advantage of this opportunity is to "re-engineer, not replace." In addition to issues relating to type and size of chillers, chilled water piping, control systems, cooling tower selection and condenser water piping should be addressed to ensure maximum benefit from the cost of the retrofit.

INTRODUCTION

The central cooling plant is a critical component of any building or facility. As with all mechanical equipment, there is a finite useful life for the equipment. While an aggressive and extensive maintenance program can extend this useful life, there comes a time when replacement of the equipment is necessary. In addition, retrofit projects can be undertaken as part of a refrigerant management strategy, a desire to improve efficiency or as a result of changes in the use or needs of the facility. The major component is the chiller, however the cooling tower also deserves specific consideration. Because this system is generally deemed to be critical to the operation and because it is a major energy consumer within the facility, special consideration should be given to the retrofit process. Since a significant cost is anticipated and budgeted, changes that will improve efficiency and reliability may be easier to justify based on the incremental cost and savings. In addition, life cycle cost analysis is more likely to be used since these projects are generally undertaken directly by the owner.

RE-ENGINEERING

The first consideration in undertaking a central plant retrofit project is that the scope of the project should not be limited to simple replacement of the components. Because this project is usually taking place at least 20 years after the facility was originally constructed, the system should be re-engineered based on the current and presently anticipated loads and usage of the facility. This will help to promote the goals of increasing efficiency and reliability and position the facility for the long term. While it may not be possible to create an ideal new central plant, the re-engineering process should strive to create as efficient and effective a plant as possible.

There are a number of reasons for this re-engineering. The first involves the original equipment selection. In general, engineers are conservative in their load calculations and equipment selection. While this is generally good, as the intent is to ensure adequate cooling even if the system is slightly overloaded or not operating at full capability, too much of a good thing can lead to inefficient operation. A second reason for re-engineering is due to changes in the peak load and/or load profile for the facility. This can be either an increase, such as added equipment, or a decrease, such as the results of lighting retrofits or other efficiency improvements in the facility. Another example is changes due to a change in occupancy or use of the space. This can lead to a change in the design load of the facility as well as to changes in the operating profile which affects equipment selection. Changes in the operating profile are very common because of the proliferation of 24/7 operations and the increased need for continuous cooling for specific areas within a facility.

Technology changes are another big reason for re-engineering the central plant. One major advance is in the area of control systems. Today's control systems have much greater capacity than the systems that were available when the plant was first constructed, and the limitations in control strategies sometimes played a significant role in the design of the central plant. An offshoot of this is the inclusion of digital control panels on the equipment. This greatly improves the operation of the equipment as well as providing availability of better information on the operation of the equipment. Strategies like variable flow in chillers were difficult to achieve with analog control panels. Another big change is the availability of variable speed drives and the efficiency improvements that can be gained from their proper application. Potential uses are for secondary pumping systems, chilled water and condenser water pumps for variable flow chillers, chillers and cooling tower fans.

ALTERNATIVES TO CONSIDER

As is always the case with engineering, there are multiple solutions to any problem and different ways to design a system that will produce the desired result, cooling for people and/or equipment. Each option will have good features and bad features that must be weighed to determine what system should be chosen for a particular application. There is no one best solution for every application. This section will present some of the alternatives that should be considered and some of the good and bad features of each, as well as some of the criteria that should be considered. The final evaluation is generally site-specific and requires a detailed engineering analysis to properly evaluate the various factors to choose the best system for the particular operation. Among the factors that must be considered are electric costs and rate structure, natural gas rates, maintenance requirements and costs, electric deregulation impact and potential changes in operation.

Hybrid Plants

The first alternative comes under the general heading of hybrid cooling plants. There are a number of different technologies that will provide cooling and a hybrid plant incorporates more than one of these technologies. These technologies include electric chillers, absorption chillers, engine-drive and/or dual-drive chillers, thermal storage systems and use of a water-side economizer cycle. Most of these choices seek to provide some or all of the cooling without using electricity during the high cost, peak period. Thus the electric rate structure is one of the primary determinants of the choice of cooling medium. Hybrid plants are generally a better option because the cost of cooling with electricity during some periods is less than the cost of cooling with natural gas.

Absorption chillers, especially double-effect, offer a good option for utility rate structures with high peak period demand or usage charges or rate schedules with ratchet clauses for the demand charges. There is a significant first cost premium for this equipment. Maintenance costs are generally comparable with electric chillers, although the absorption chiller requires better day-to-day maintenance.

Engine-driven chillers provide an alternative to absorption chillers when a natural gas cooling is desired. Engine-driven chillers utilize the same type of equipment as electric chillers for cooling, but replace the electric motor with a natural gas fueled engine. One problem with this equipment is that the maintenance and operation people are unfamiliar with the requirements of the engine. Especially for truck-derivative engines, maintenance costs are significant and must be accounted for in the operating cost analysis. Noise and vibration are significant concerns that must be addressed. A major benefit of engine-driven chillers is the opportunity to capture waste heat from the engine as a mechanical cogeneration system. An offshoot of these units is the limited availability of dual-drive chillers with both an electric motor and a natural gas engine available to drive the chiller.

Thermal storage systems are useful to shift cooling load from the high cost times to low cost times. While there were equipment and application problems when these systems were first being installed, most of these have been corrected. There are several good design and equipment guides for these systems. The major design concern is allowing for sufficient storage and re-charging capacity to allow for some load and temperature increase for over-night periods. There is significant danger of poor operation and inability to fully transfer load if some reasonable spare capacity is not provided in the design of these systems.

Water-side economizers are of use in areas with low wet bulb temperatures, especially when the use of an air-side economizer cycle is not feasible. One problem that must be considered in the design is the change-over from economizer operation to chiller operation since the low condenser water temperature may affect the operation of the chiller. The use of a water-side economizer also affects the cooling tower selection as there is additional benefit to providing a larger than necessary cooling tower.

Primary-Secondary Chilled Water Distribution

Primary-secondary chilled water distribution systems were developed to allow constant flow through chillers, required by the chiller manufacturers, with variable flow for the load side of the system to improve efficiency. The primary applications were for multi-building systems or systems with larger variations in load. The advent of variable speed drives and DDC control systems made the operation of these systems much more effective. Newer chillers with digital control panels are able to operate effectively and safely with variable flow, and they can be used in a simplified system to achieve the savings of variable flow in the load-side loop. Another significant advantage of the primary-secondary system is the system flexibility that it offers. This type of system makes it easier to incorporate hybrid systems, as well as thermal storage systems and water-side economizers. Depending on the piping and valving arrangement, the system can load chillers evenly, load chillers sequentially or allow for preferential loading of particular chillers as is required for a hybrid system to gain the maximum benefit. The complexity of these systems also requires a well developed sequence of operations to ensure that the control system will provide the proper operation.

Chiller Sizing

Over the years, engineers have gotten into the habit of specifying equal size chillers for multiple chiller installations. The primary argument for this is to reduce the complexity of the system and make it easier to maintain the equipment. In addition, control systems did not have the intelligence to deal with different size chiller effectively. With the advent of DDC control systems and the trend away from stocking of spare parts, these reasons no longer apply. For most applications, such as office buildings and retail, there appears to be a definite benefit to providing two different sized chillers. For many applications, sizing at 60% and 40% of design load seems to provide better operation, although this should be confirmed in the analysis phase. The benefits are twofold. First, one chiller can supply all the requirements for the building for more hours, thus reducing the total hours of chiller operation. Second, fewer of the hours of operation of the chillers are at less than 50% of capacity where the machines are less efficient.

Condenser Water System

Typically, condenser water systems for electric chillers are designed with a 10° F temperature differential. Absorption chiller systems have been designed with higher temperature differentials due to the greater amount of heat rejected from these units. There may be benefits for electric chiller systems in using a larger temperature differential for the condenser water system. The primary benefit is the reduction in the quantity of water to be pumped for the condenser water system to reject the same amount of heat. This allows the use of smaller piping and pumps. This is especially useful if the system capacity is being increased and the condenser water pipe size is a limiting factor. The higher temperature will improve the efficiency of the cooling tower, but will reduce the efficiency of the chiller. There is a reduction in first costs due to the smaller pumps and piping, with no change in the cooling tower or the chiller. Note that there may be a minor change in the cooling tower, but having an oversize cooling tower is generally beneficial so no change is recommended. Oversizing the cooling tower provides additional capacity and allowance for equipment problems

for the least additional cost. For operating costs, there is a reduction in pumping energy, possibly a reduction in cooling tower energy, offset by an increase in chiller energy. The net impact depends on the size of the system, amount of pumping, climate and hours of operation, but generally results in a net reduction in energy consumption.

RETROFIT PROCESS

While the basic process of a retrofit project is similar to a new construction project, there are some special considerations in a retrofit project. Most of these stem from the difference between working with the existing system and design versus the ability to start with a clean sheet of paper for a new system. It is very beneficial to the process if the engineer and contractor have some experience working with retrofit projects.

Engineer Selection

As noted above, having an engineer experienced with retrofit projects is an important criteria in the selection of an engineer. Typically the best option is an engineer with some background in facilities management or engineering. As one who has a facilities management background, not a design background, I can attest to the potential problems caused by engineers who do not have the experience of living with a system over a period of time. Generally, these are sins of omission, not commission, in that they have not had this type of experience to guide their thinking about systems and equipment. Locating these engineers may not be easy, and the best source is people who have recently completed a similar project. Another consideration in the selection of an engineer is having someone who is willing to work with and listen to a peer reviewer and to the operating personnel. Because of the complex nature of most retrofit projects, the inclusion of a peer review activity, primarily as part of the commissioning process, is important. This person provides another set of opinions and brings a different range of experiences to the project. Both parties have to keep in mind that there is always more than one option that will provide the desired results and they must help the owner evaluate these options. Both parties should have the best interests of the owner in mind, but also must remember that the ultimate responsibility belongs to the engineer of record.

Information Sources

The first step in the information gathering process is a site visit. This is an opportunity to review the original design documents of the plant as it currently exists and to determine the history of changes that have occurred. This also provides the engineer an opportunity to review the current method of operation of the plant. The site visit is also an opportunity to interview the operators about the plant.

The operator interview should elicit information about the general operation of the plant, operational history of the existing equipment, plant history and a discussion of any idiosyncrasies that may exist with the plant or facility. While it is important that the engineer be willing to talk with and listen to the operators, this does not mean that everything they say is to be taken as gospel and that all problems they refer to need to be addressed. Given the opportunity, they will be sure to gild the lily to make their job easier without necessarily providing real benefit to the owner.

The site visit is also an opportunity to review the operating logs for the equipment. The engineer needs to review these to evaluate the reliability of the information they contain. Assuming they contain reliable information, this can provide information to support, or to refute, the information provided by the operators. Unfortunately, sometimes the information is not collected properly and inaccuracies are not questioned. In these cases, the logs have limited value to the process.

The final information source that may or may not be used is monitoring of the plant operation. The use of monitoring data is most prevalent when retrofit projects are part of a larger energy services agreement. In these cases, the financial backers of the project are interested in a better baseline than can be provided by other methods. Monitoring can utilize an existing building management system, although additional inputs and memory capability may be required, or may be done with temporary data logging equipment. If the project is part of an energy services project, then utilizing the existing BMS is a good option since the same information will be required for post implementation monitoring to confirm the savings.

Evaluation of the Alternatives
Because there will be several options that will provide the desired results, the evaluation of these alternatives is important. In addition, this is somewhat more involved than it is for new construction because in most cases the facility will continue to operate during the retrofit project. This means that the constructability of the proposed design is an important factor. Ideally, having a contractor involved as part of the team throughout the process may help address this issue. This is a case where the contractor should be reimbursed for his time if he has no guarantee of getting the job. If the owner has one contractor he is comfortable working with, then this contractor should be brought into the process early and can work on a negotiated contract basis. The second important consideration is the opinion of probable costs. It is necessary to have a good idea of the first costs of each option to provide a good base for the analysis. Again, the involvement of a contractor will help improve this part of the process.

The major factor in the evaluation will be the estimates of operating costs. Note that since there will be a significant investment in the retrofit project, it may be easier to justify efficiency improvements based on incremental costs and savings instead of having to justify the entire cost of a project solely by the anticipated efficiency gains. There are several levels of estimates of operating costs that can be utilized, and the extent of the analysis will depend on the extent of the project. In addition, the simpler methods may be used as a screening tool to reduce the amount of simulation work that may be required. The simplest methods are generally spreadsheet approaches that frequently rely on bin weather data. A second step that may or may not have application is to use simple programs that evaluate specific equipment or proposed changes. The ultimate analysis tool is a full energy simulation, using DOE 2 or one of the proprietary programs that are available. As a reality check, the results of the analysis should be compared to current utility bills.

Design Phase
After one of the alternatives has been selected, the next step is the design phase. Again, the commissioning agent should be involved throughout and provide the peer review function as well. The plant operators should have the opportunity to review and comment on the design as it progresses. Again, this is additional input that should be considered, but the final responsibility lies with the engineer of record. Contractor input continues to be valuable, especially in developing the sequence of construction. This also needs to be reviewed with management in terms of the number and length of any shut-downs that may be required. A very important part of the design includes the development of the sequence of operations. This is necessary to guide the controls contractor in developing his programming to ensure the operation follows that developed through the analysis phase.

Construction Phase
These considerations carry over to the construction phase. Proper coordination between the contractor and the operating personnel is critical to the success of the project. Contractor selection should, to the extent possible, be limited to those who have had experience with similar projects. Especially critical is the attitude of the on-site superintendent and project manager, who should be interviewed as part of the selection process.

Commissioning
The final step to ensure the success of the retrofit project is commissioning of the system. Development of the commissioning plan must proceed with the design and construction phases, especially since it is likely that completion of the project will occur in stages over time. The commissioning information provides a baseline to check proper operation of the plant over time, especially if

there are operations people who get involved in changing the operation in perhaps mis-guided efforts to improve the operation. After the project is completed, there should be some on-going monitoring of the operation. This is to ensure that the systems continue to operate as intended, as well as to provide the information for possible refinement of the sequence of operations.

SUMMARY

In summary, a retrofit project needs to be approached in some ways as if it were a new installation and the opportunity should be taken to examine all feasible options that will improve the efficiency of the system. The process should focus on the system efficiency, not just on the individual components. The process is complicated by the limitations imposed by the existing plant, available space and need to keep the system operating during the construction phase. For these reasons, the choice of engineers and contractors is critical to the success of the project.

This paper was originally presented at the 22nd World Energy Engineering Congress, sponsored by the Association of Engineers, October 1999.

Chapter 8

EXHAUST AIR: CONTROL IT AND SAVE MONEY

Chao Chen, PE
Snohomish PUD

ABSTRACT

Exhausting contaminated air to outside is an effective way to provide safe and comfortable working environment for industrial workers. Many exhaust systems are designed for peak demand and operate 24/7 with little or no controls. Normally one fan controls several exhaust inlets. There are no dampers to close the inlets that are not in use. The fans are usually single speed and are not controlled by the building control system. They are manually turned on and run 24/7 in most cases. Most of exhaust fans are small fans in the range of ¼ hp to 15 hp. Since exhaust fans do not directly consume a lot of energy comparing to other HVAC equipment in the building, many plant operators do not pay attention to their efficient operation. In manufacturing buildings, exhaust air needs to be made up by fresh outside air. Due to high air exhaust, some manufacturing buildings use almost 100% outside air during winter heating season. For electronic manufacturers, reducing exhaust air means lower heating and humidifying. With the help of the local utility, an aerospace electronic manufacturer implemented a control project to reduce exhaust air by up to 30% for the first shift and 60% for the rest of the time and achieved great savings with one year simple payback. The project is basically to close the exhaust inlets by dampers and control the exhaust fan speeds with variable frequency drives (VFD). Exhaust fans are now monitored and controlled by the building direct digital controls (DDC) system to ensure proper operation and save energy. The presentation explains how to evaluate energy savings of exhaust air reduction, and lessons learned in the project.

INTRODUCTION

A basic industrial ventilation system consists of a supply system and an exhaust system. The supply system is to create a comfortable environment in the plant and replace the air exhausted out by the exhaust system. Exhaust system is to remove the contaminated air and reduce the heat concentration locally. Exhaust system can be divided into general exhaust and local exhaust. Local exhaust is more effective due to the fact it is close to the source of contamination. Local exhaust can be a very costly process if they are not designed and operated properly. In electronic manufacturing plants, temperature and humidity are controlled to ensure worker comfort and product quality. When excessive exhaust occurs, the supply system would need to supply more outside air than the minimum required for proper ventilation, resulting in more heating and cooling energy.

THE FACILITY

The industrial facility involved in the project is Eldec Corporation, an aerospace electronic manufacturer. The facility has three buildings with sizes ranging from 70,000 to 80,000 square feet (SF). Exhaust system retrofit has been done in two buildings while the third building is in the process of retrofit. The HVAC systems are variable air volume (VAV) systems. Minimum 30% relative humidity is controlled in the production buildings. All the three buildings have a similar operating schedule. We will focus on one of the buildings that is already retrofitted. This building is a two-story building with 70,000 SF. Two packaged units serve the majority of the building. Both units combined have maximum supply air of 72,000 CFM and a minimum supply air of 44,000 CFM. Total exhaust CFM before retrofit was 34,650 CFM constant.

EXHAUST AIR CONTROLS

Figure 1 shows some typical types of the exhaust inlets and exhaust hoods in the building after the retrofit. Before the retrofit, the exhaust system was manually controlled, by turning off fans. There were no dampers to close the inlets and no flow controls for the fans. Since those are local exhausts, heat recovery is not possible. Most inlets or hoods shared fans, so it was not possible to switch off a fan if any inlet was in use. Although some fans could be turned off but that was not the case. As it is indicated above, the exhaust air volume was about the same as the minimum supply air. The floors were open spaces so the air was moving around the floor and transferred from one floor to the other by pressure differences. Although there was a minimum outside air setting in the packaged units, outside air had to make up the exhaust by supply air from the packaged units and infiltration. The work schedule was flexible. Even though the building operated on one-shift schedule, workers could be in the building working any time of the day. Some equipment were operating unmanned 24/7. The exhaust system ran 24/7 constantly. Due to exhaust, the HVAC systems had to operate the same way all the time.

The building had been operated this way by design for many years. During 2000 to 2001, the power rate increased dramatically due to the energy crisis in the West Coast. It became a high priority for the facilities engineers to find ways to reduce the power usage for cost control. One area they identified was the exhaust system. A survey of all of the exhaust fans revealed a big surprise. The exhaust air was very high and unnecessary especially during unoccupied hours. Two things needed to be done: close the inlets and slow done or turn off the fans. As explained before, there were no dampers in most of the exhaust inlets and no automatic controls on the fans. Since this project had no benefits other than energy savings, the project had to meet the company's investment criteria to receive company funding. With this in mind, a low cost approach was taken, that is, using manually operating dampers. Dampers were custom made in house. When a few test dampers were installed. It closed the inlets ok but noise generated from the seal was annoying. It turned out that the seal was too thin. Replacing that with a thicker seal solved the problem. This trial and error method worked well in this project considering that the success or failure of the project heavily depended on the cooperation of the workers on the floor. If they kept the dampers open, the amount of exhaust reduction would be difficult to achieve. Some modifications were made through the process, resulting in easier operating dampers, such as using magnetic to hold the dampers open and

relocating the dampers in the right places so they would not obstruct the normal operation.

To control the fans, two methods were implemented. One was to install or relocate the switches in a location the workers could easily operate. To ensure the exhaust fans would be on when any of the inlets was in use, visible warning lights were installed to indicate if the associated exhaust fans were on or off. This applied to the fans that were only used for short time in a day. Another way was to control the fans by variable frequency drives (VFD). Since the building had a direct digital control (DDC) system, the VFDs were linked into the DDC system to schedule and monitor the operation.

Through education and training, workers were able to close dampers and turn off fans when they were not needed. The DDC system would monitor the VFD operation to see if they were operating normally. When the building was in unoccupied mode, the VFDs were set to run at minimum. After the project was implemented, the building achieved 30% reduction during occupied hours and 60% during unoccupied hours.

ENERGY SAVING ESTIMATES

Accurately estimating the energy savings from the project was critical in two ways: one was that the utility conservation incentive was calculated based on savings, and the project needed to have a quick payback to get funded. Some of the standard practices were to use computer building simulation program such as DOE-2 program or use bin data analysis. To be able to simulate the savings by DOE-2 program, internal load had to be accurately estimated. Using DOE-2 program would require more time. On the other hand, a bin data analysis was a more straight forwarded process and less time consuming. A bin data analysis was used for the saving estimate. One idea was to demonstrate a method that can be used and understood by engineers who have not used any energy simulation program.

To be able to get good results on the saving estimates, the first thing was to measure the amount of the existing exhaust air. Using manufacturer's data on the exhaust fans combining with field measurements of static pressures, the flow rates of all the exhaust fans could be determined accurately. The next thing was to estimate how much exhaust air could be reduced and what would be the best control of them. Through observation and interview of the workers on the production floor, the facilities engineers were able to make estimates on how much exhaust air could be reduced. Also environmental safety standards were used to check if the exhaust amounts were enough. As it is common in manufacturing building, constant changes in production configuration may not result in reconfiguration of the exhaust system. Most likely there is more exhaust than that is required. Through design, the facilities engineers figured 30% could be reduced during occupied hours and 60% during unoccupied hours.

With the bin data, a spreadsheet was created to estimate the savings. In this project, the total exhaust air was much higher than the minimum outside air required for proper ventilation. Any exhaust air reduction would result in energy usage reduction. Table 1 shows the energy usage per CFM per year in Seattle, Washington area. When OSA temperature was in the range of 57°F to 67 °F, the economizer cooling was in effect so there was little or no extra energy usage by excessive OSA. The method in constructing Table 1 can be utilized in other buildings and other climates. One caution is that only the exhaust air that excesses the minimum OSA should be used to estimate savings. For example, if the minimum OSA is 5,000 CFM and the exhaust air is to be reduced from 10,000 CFM to 6,000 CFM, Table 1 can be applied directly to the 4,000 CFM reduction. If in the same situation, the exhaust air is to be reduced from 10,000 CFM to 3,000 CFM, only 5,000 CFM reduction will result in savings. To estimate the total savings, we need to figure out the amount of exhaust reduction and the associated hours. For a building with no humidifier, the table can be modified by just using temperature differences to calculate heating energy. The cooling energy calculation should be the same.

The following shows the savings estimates for this project:

Max supply air: 72,000 CFM
Min supply air: 44,000 CFM
Existing exhaust: 34,650 CFM
Exhaust reduction: 30% during occupied hours,
          60% during unoccupied hours
Occupied hours: 3070 hours/year, about 35%
Unoccupied hours: 5690 hours, about 65%

Cooling savings:
34,650 CFM x (30%x35%+60%x65%) x 1.3351 kWh/CFM/year = 22,899 kWh/year

Heating savings:
34,650 CFM x (30%x35%+60%x65%) x 35.4338 kWh/CFM/year = 607,751 kWh/year

Total savings:
630,650 kWh/year or $40,992 at 6.5 cents/kWh

The building used about 4,900,000 kWh before the retrofit, so about 13 % was saved by exhaust reduction. The building also implemented a temperature setback during unoccupied hours at the same time the retrofit took place. The temperature was setback from 70°F heating to 65°F during unoccupied hours. 65°F was to be maintained to accommodate workers who might come to work at any time. In the seven months since the retrofit and temperature setback, the power usage has dropped about 730,000 kWh. Figure 2 shows the data for these seven months.

Power sub-metering were done before and after the retrofit for the heater in one unit and half of the humidifier in the same unit. Although the weather conditions were not exactly the same, the intention was to get some understanding on the power consumption on the heater and humidifier in the similar weather conditions. Pre-metering was done in late February while the post-metering was done in late November. Figure 3 shows the power consumption comparison of the heater in one of the two packaged units before and after for a week. Figure 4 shows the data for one quarter of the humidifier in the building. The data clearly indicate that the power consumption dropped significantly.

The total cost for retrofitting the two buildings was about $300,000. The project saved close to 1,400,000 kWh/year or $80,000 in power cost. The local utility contributed about 70% of the total cost toward project as an incentive, so the net cost to Eldec on the project was $90,000. The project resulted in about one year simple payback.

SUMMARY
Exhaust air could be excessive in industrial buildings especially those built in the past when energy cost was very low. Excessive exhaust can be costly as demonstrated in this paper. A simple and effective way to reduce exhaust air is

to close inlets when they are not in use and turn off fans or slow them down. To estimate energy savings from exhaust air reduction, we need to know how much the existing exhaust is and how much can be reduced. We can do that by using fan data and actual measurements. A bin data analysis can be easily done to get a good estimate on the energy savings.

ACKNOWLEDGEMENT
Dale Cheatham, Senior Facilities Engineer of Eldec Corporation provided some information used in the paper. The author sincerely thanks Mr. Cheatham for his assistance in preparing this paper.

BIBLIOGRAPHY
1. American Conference of Governmental Industrial Hygienists, Industrial Ventilation, A Manual of Recommended Practice, 24th Ed. 2001.

2. American Society of Heating, Refrigerating and Air-Conditioning Engineers, Inc, 1993 ASHRAE Handbook, Fundamentals.

3. Seattle Bin Data

4. Los Alamos National Laboratory, DOE-2 Reference Manual (Version 2.1A), Part 1, 1981.

Figure 1: Exhaust Inlets

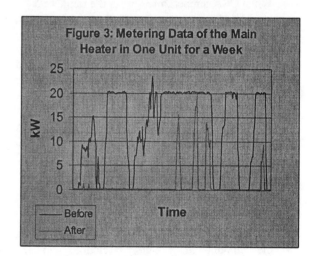

Figure 3: Metering Data of the Main Heater in One Unit for a Week

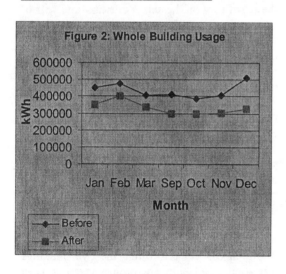

Figure 2: Whole Building Usage

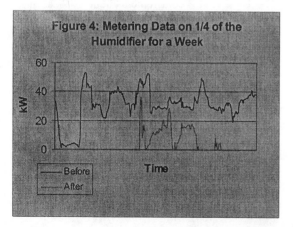

Figure 4: Metering Data on 1/4 of the Humidifier for a Week

Table 1: Energy Usage Per CFM OSA

Seattle Bin Data				Indoor Conditions		Energy Usage			
Annual HR	Mean Dry Bulb	MCWB	OSA enthalpy BTU/lb dry air	Cooling 74°F (30% RH min)	Heating 70°F (30% RH min)	Btu/hr/ per CFM OSA (Cooling, COP=3)	Btu/hr/ per CFM OSA (Heating, electric resistance)	Annual kWh/CFM (cooling)	Annual kWh/CFM (heating)
1	97	71	34.6	23.8		16.20		0.0047	
5	92	70	33.8	23.8		15.00		0.0220	
27	87	68	32.3	23.8		12.75		0.1009	
84	82	66	30.7	23.8		10.35		0.2547	
166	77	64	29.2	23.8		8.10		0.3940	
326	72	62	27.7	23.8		5.85		0.5588	
566	67	59	25.7	23.8	21.8	0.00	0.00	0.0000	0.0000
1000	62	57	24.2	23.8	21.8	0.00	0.00	0.0000	0.0000
1332	57	53	21.9	23.8	21.8	0.00	0.00	0.0000	0.0000
1415	52	49	19.6		21.8		9.90		4.1045
1573	47	45	17.7		21.8		18.45		8.5033
1258	42	40	15.4		21.8		28.80		10.6154
687	37	36	13.4		21.8		37.80		7.6087
214	32	31	11.7		21.8		45.45		2.8498
57	27	25	9.7		21.8		54.45		0.9094
25	22	20	7.8		21.8		63.00		0.4615
15	17	16	6.0		21.8		71.10		0.3125
3	12	12	4.4		21.8		78.30		0.0688
0	8	8	3.2		21.8		83.70		0.0000
Total								1.3351	35.4338

Chapter 9

MAKING BUILDINGS WORK...
A Case Study of an Innovative Cold Air Retrofit

James P. Waltz, P.E., C.E.M., A.C.F.E.

The first cost focus of new construction can often result in buildings that don't work—particularly the HVAC systems. This article presents an innovative cold air retrofit that corrected designed-in HVAC inadequacies in an office building. By utilizing cold air, the retrofit overcame insufficient airflow and insufficient cooling capacity at the air handling units, thereby avoiding a massive, and very disruptive retrofit of a fully occupied office building. The resulting retrofit cost less than half of the conventional alternatives and was easily implemented during a weekend hours. It resulted in a building that actually worked for the first time since its original construction some 15 years prior The author's more than two decades of experience in restoration and remediation of existing buildings provides some valuable insight into how to creatively and cost-effectively fix nagging comfort problems in existing buildings. The author additionally provides some reflection on the energy-efficiency impact of the project and energy-related implications for new building designers.

James P. Waltz, P.E., C.E.M., A.C.F.E.
President, Energy Resource Associates, Inc.

INTRODUCTION

In reading this article, it is important to realize that the world of retrofit is a poorly understood and completely unique niche of the building construction industry, We find that most building owners and most design professionals don't understand this. By and large, traditional design professionals, who grew up in the world of new construction, are ill equipped to face the constraints of fixing problems in existing buildings—short of wholesale replacement of systems (which gets us right back to "clean sheet" or new construction design, right?), In the world of retrofit, all those little problems that were resolved in the field by the original builders, and all those remodels and modifications all need to be identified and dealt with by the retrofit engineer. Frequently whole-building testing is necessary to identify the cause of the complaints. In addition, retrofit frequently requires that the building be modified while the building is fully occupied, meaning that working conditions are difficult, and major disruption to the occupants cannot be allowed. We frequently liken it to performing a heart transplant on a marathon runner—during a marathon. The project described herein is just such a project.

THE SITUATION

We were called into the project by the service contractor for the building, who was trying to figure out how to help the owner keep their tenants happy. They weren't very happy as the building was uncomfortably warm nearly all year long in its Northern California climate. Only during the coldest months of the year was the building comfortable. Just as in our expert testimony work, we set about to ferret out the source of the problem. What we learned was that the original designer made some fundamental conceptual errors in determining the operating parameters of the air handling equipment—which effectively resulted in under-sizing of both the airflow and the cooling coils. This was in spite of the fact that he had done a good job of estimating the cooling needs of the building. The problem wasn't in the capacity or the chiller, or in the apparent capacity of the air handling units. There was a problem, though, in the performance of the air handling units.

There are a couple of aspects of load calculations that, as the cartoon character Dilbert is wont to say about nuclear energy, "can be used for good or evil." Those aspects have to do with space loads versus system loads. Astute HVAC system designers are very careful when considering these loads, realizing that any cooling load that can be kept out of the occupied space allows the designer to reduce the supply air quantity needed to cool the space, and in turn allows the use of a smaller air handling unit. Seems pretty obvious, right?

Well, in this case the designer assumed that 100% of the heat from the lights would go into the return air instead of the space. After all, he was assuming that return-air-troffer lighting fixtures would be used, and therefore all the heat from the lights would go into the return air passing through the fixtures. On the surface this seems plausible. However, certain fixture manufacturers actually document the percent of the total heat from a fluorescent fixture that is transferred into the air stream. The highest value we've seen so far is about 30%, and we think even that is a bit optimistic. When you consider that the lighting system heat gain can contribute as much as 40 to 60% of the total heat gain in an occupied space, this had a dramatic effect on the calculated supply air cfm. Add to this the fact that the HVAC system was designed for a "shell" building and the eventual tenant build-out did not employ return air troffer lighting fixtures, you can start to get an idea of how much trouble this building was in. But there's more…

The "more" is the other effect of the designer's assumption about the space loads—it's effect on the load the system experiences. You see, if you assume that 100% of the heat from the lights goes into the return air, instead of a return air temperature of, say, 76 degrees, you will calculate a return air temperature of more like 86 degrees. This means that, when combined with a fairly high ambient design temperature, the mixed air temperature will calculate out to about 88 degrees—instead of a more correct value like 78 degrees. This only becomes a problem when selecting a cooling coil for your (already undersized!) air handling unit. Since there will be more heat transferred from 88-degree air to 45-degree chilled water than

from 78-degree air (total temperature difference is now thought to be 88-45 or 43 degrees rather than 78-45 or 33 degrees) it will appear that you can get all the cooling done that you need with a pretty small coil (i.e., fewer rows and/or fewer fins per inch). Indeed, such an under-sized coil was selected by the system designer.

The net-net of all the above is that by making one "fatally" wrong assumption, the system designer put into the building an air side system that could never cool the building—and indeed it didn't.

SOLVING THE "PUZZLE"

Once we understood the root source of the problem, then we had to face the question of what to do about it.

The immediately obvious solution was to yank out the air handling units and replace them—what we would call the "traditional" approach. After all, this would correct the fundamental error that was made in the first place. The problem with this approach were, not surprisingly, many fold, and included:

- the air handling units were located in interior mechanical rooms in the "core" area of each floor and replacing them would require knocking out walls and seriously disrupting the occupants and operations of the building

- increasing the horsepower of the air handling units would require significant cost for electrical work as all the air handling units were fed electrical power from the basement and the entire conduit and conductor riser would need to be replaced as it had no excess capacity

- the mechanical rooms were very cramped and there really was no room at all in them for larger air handling units, and would require re-configuring the floor plan layout of the "core", another very expensive proposition (and likely not really feasible)

Recognizing that a more traditional approach really didn't constitute a suitable solution for this problem (and was likely the reason the problem had gone unresolved for 15 years) ERA set about to "re-engineer" the HVAC system from the inside out, assuming that the air handling units themselves could not be replaced, nor could their fan horsepower be increased (due to the limitations of the building's power distribution system). Grinding away with a computerized coil selection program and rethinking other parts of the HVAC system, we determined that the air handling units *could* be made to perform by:

- replacing the existing 4-row chilled water coils with 8-row coils of equal air pressure drop (examination of factory certified dimension drawings confirmed that they would fit in the air handling units)

- increasing the chilled water flow through the coils (feasible with a much higher horsepower pump, and within the allowable flow rate for the chiller—and requiring more than twice the original horsepower to achieve a 30% increase in flow)

- reducing the chilled water supply temperature (from 45 to 40 degrees, also with the allowable operating parameters for the chiller)

- installing new air handling unit temperature controls (to reset the planned very-low supply air temperature upwards during cool weather, else "cold" complaints would replace the prior "hot" complaints)

Without negatively impacting the air handling systems' air supply rate, the new system would be capable of supplying 46-degree air, and thereby produce the actual cooling needed to satisfy the occupied space. As shown in the table below, some pretty interesting results can be achieved by optimizing the coil selection in particular!

MAKING THE FIX

Upon completion of the study, *ERA* was engaged to prepare final installation documents. This work was performed in collaboration with the owner's selected contractor so as to achieve maximum integration of design concepts and the contractor's working knowledge of the building (the contractor had the service contract for the building). Final selection of equip-

ment was made, simplified installation drawings were prepared and the project installed and put into operation over a 90 day period, including start-up. No tenant disruption was caused during the installation (which would have been the case had the conventional approach of replacing the air handling units been followed). Upon completion of the project, the building's HVAC systems provided comfort for the first time in the 15-year life of the building! The utterly prosaic business of HVAC engineering doesn't get any more exciting than this.

SOME INTERESTING CONCLUSIONS

One of the lessons that can be learned from this project is that the age-old tradition of linking engineering fees to construction cost—our traditional way of paying design professionals—would not have allowed this project to take place. After all, it took a lot of engineering to avoid spending money. So engineering fees went up, and construction costs went down, making the engineer's fees look "large" as a percent of construction costs. Many building owners would insist that less money be spent on engineering—with the result that the engineer is forced to get his eraser out to create a "clean sheet of paper" and do a very simple design—that doubles or triples construction costs. Voilà! The engineer's fees, look "small" as a percent of construction. Building owners, take heed.

Another, perhaps more technical, lesson to be learned, is that by understanding the essential nature of the engineering problem being faced, it is often possible to re-engineer a system from the inside out and make it work, even when it seems impossible. Design engineers, take heed.

A final lesson for new building HVAC designers, is that if you want to build a little "safety" into your HVAC system, selecting a cooling coil with more rows (and perhaps a few less fins per inch) is really, really cheap "insurance."

Readers may have noticed that this retrofit would likely have the effect of increasing the energy use of

DESCRIPTION	ROWS/FPI	EDB/EWB	LDB/LWB	EWT/LWT	GPM	APD	MBH
EXISTING	4/12	74/60	53.5/51.8	45/58.5	30	.69	203
RETROFIT	8/9	74/57	45.8/44.6	40/54.4	39	.70	281

this building. Our charter from the building owner on this project was to make the building work. They were not at all interested in energy conservation—much to the contrary. The truth is, even in today's energy-sensitive environment, making buildings work, i.e., having them provide the function they were intended to provide (a comfortable and productive work environment) is equally if not more important than saving a few dollars on the utility bill (and this coming from an award-winning energy engineer).

For energy engineers, the lesson is that cold air works—and offers some interesting energy-saving opportunities. If you were designing this building from scratch, using a conventional design would have required a larger (and probably more powerful air handling unit), so cold air would have saved a lot of air circulation energy. Since the fans run whenever the building is occupied (or even longer), these savings would be dramatic. While we ran the chiller at a colder evaporator temperature, in a new building design the cooling tower could have been oversized (at relatively minimal cost) to compensate and keep the total chiller "lift" (which is what you pay for in terms of chiller power) the same as a conventional design, or even better. In this retrofit we had to increase pump power—rather dramatically. In a new design, a nominal (and relatively cheap) oversizing of the piping could have been done, and the system configured for variable flow (see our Contracting Business article on our web site for this) and the pumping power kept to a minimum as well. Finally, an energy engineer "worth his salt" would include variable speed drives on the fans and a digital control system to precisely reset supply air temperature (to minimize reheating) and manage the operation of the chilled water system and optimize run hours of the entire HVAC system.

ABOUT THE AUTHOR

James P. Waltz, President of Energy Resource Associates, Inc., is an acknowledged pioneer in the field of energy management. Prior to the Arab Oil Embargo of 1973, Mr. Waltz made a personal commitment to energy management as the focal point of his engineering career Since that time, he has served as energy management program manager for the Air Force Logistics Command and the University of California's Lawrence Livermore National Laboratory. In addition he has worked as an energy manage-

ment engineer for consulting and contracting firms. In 1981 he founded Energy Resource Associates for the purpose of helping to shape the then-emerging energy services industry—and did so through a multi-year assignment to create a (still) successful energy services business unit for a Fortune 500 temperature controls manufacturer.

Specializing in the renewal of mechanical, electrical and control infrastructure systems of existing buildings, Mr. Waltz's firm has accomplished a wide variety of facilities projects, recently including a corporate-wide energy management program review for a major hospital chain, design of a replacement chilled water plant for a northern California hospital, on-site recommissioning of the entire building automation system for another large northern California hospital and audit and expert testimony relating to a failed energy services contract for a large southern California hospital.

Mr. Waltz's firm was the State of California's sole performance contracting consultant for the development of the State's ESPC program and provides performance contracting owner's representative services for such clients as the Veterans Administration (in 18 western states).

Mr. Waltz's credentials include a Bachelors Degree in Mechanical Engineering, a Masters Degree in Business Administration, Professional Engineering Registration in three states, charter member of and Certified Energy Manager of the Association of Energy Engineers (AEE), member of the Association of Energy Services Professionals (AESP), Demand Side Management Society (DSMS) and the American Society of Heating Refrigeration and Air Conditioning Engineers (ASHRAE).

Mr. Waltz served as a member of the DOE's measurement and verification protocol technical committee, which is responsible for the International Performance Measurement and Verification Protocol (IPMVP), originally known as the North American Energy Measurement & Verification Protocol (NEMVP).

Mr. Waltz was named International Energy Engineer of the Year in 1993 by the Association of Energy Engineers (AEE) and teaches a nationwide performance contracting seminar through the AEE. He maybe reached at www.eraenergycom.

Chapter 10

TECHNOLOGY DEMONSTRATION: MAGNETICALLY-COUPLED
ADJUSTABLE SPEED DRIVE SYSTEMS

William D. Chvala, Jr., CEM
David W. Winiarski
Pacific Northwest National Laboratory[1]
U.S. Department of Energy, Federal Energy Management Program

ABSTRACT

Adjustable speed drive (ASD) technologies have the ability to precisely control motor system output and produce a number of benefits including energy and demand savings. This paper examines the performance and cost effectiveness of a specific class of ASDs called magnetically-coupled adjustable speed drives (MC-ASD), which use the strength of a magnetic field to control the amount of torque transferred between motor and drive shaft. The MagnaDrive™ Adjustable Speed Coupling System (referred to hereafter as the MagnaDrive Coupling) uses fixed rare-earth magnets and varies the distance between rotating plates in the assembly. The PAYBACK® Variable Speed Drive (referred to hereafter as the PAYBACK Drive) from Coyote Electronics uses an electromagnet to control the speed of the drive.

Laboratory testing was conducted at the Motor Systems Resource Facility at Oregon State University, to evaluate performance for the MagnaDrive, PAYBACK, and a common variable frequency drive (VFD) when connected to a 50-hp motor driving three different load profiles: fan, low head pump, and high head pump. The testing consistently showed that in the upper speed range (80 to 100% of full speed) the MC-ASD efficiency was typically between 2 to 4% less than a comparable VFD. However, in the lower speed range (less than 50%), the VFD was substantially more efficient, often using less than one half of the energy of the MC-ASDs.

Based on the test data, a life-cycle cost analysis was performed using a 50-hp fan retrofit as an example. The VFD performed the best, saving 61,120 kWh/yr over the baseline conditions. Assuming $0.06 per kilowatt-hour with no demand charges produced a simple payback of 2.4 years. The PAYBACK Drive had the best simple payback at 1.9 years because of its low purchase and installation costs. The MagnaDrive, which has the highest initial cost (purchase and installation), produced a simple payback of 4.6 years. Long-term operations and maintenance costs were not considered, which skews the comparison because technologies like MC-ASD are designed with reduced maintenance costs in mind.

Based on the results of this study, the MC-ASD technology shows good potential for new construction and retrofit application in Federal facilities. The MagnaDrive appears best suited for direct-drive loads, especially on very large motors. The design of the PAYBACK Drive makes it ideal for belt-driven loads.

INTRODUCTION

Most large electric motors run at a nearly constant speed, although the devices they drive – particularly pumps, fans, or blowers – represent loads that vary over time. Commonly, flow is regulated by partially closing a valve or damper in the system (throttling) or allowing some of the flow to go through a bypass loop. These methods are effective, yet inefficient in terms of energy consumption of the system. ASD technologies provide a better method

---

[1] Pacific Northwest National Laboratory is operated by Battelle Memorial Institute for the U.S. Department of Energy under contract DE-AC06-76RLO 1830.

of control by either causing the motor to rotate at varying speeds, as is the case with a VFD, or by providing a clutch between the motor and load to introduce some "slip" in the system, causing the output drive speed to be variable. A number of different products fall into the latter category, where the motor speed remains relatively constant and the speed of the output shaft is adjustable. These include variable diameter pulleys, mechanical clutches, and a unique category called magnetically-coupled adjustable speed drives (MC-ASD). The MC-ASD uses changing magnetic field strength within a coupling attached to the motor shaft to adjust the amount of torque transferred to, and thus the speed of, the drive shaft. This demonstration focuses on two unique applications of the MC-ASD technology – a fixed magnet coupling and a uniquely packaged electromagnetic coupling.

ASDs can save substantial energy when applied to variable-torque loads, such as fans, blowers, and most centrifugal and axial pumps. All fluid flow is governed by the Affinity Laws, whose equations describe pressure differences and fluid flow in closed systems. The Affinity Laws state that, for a fixed system, the torque of the motor varies in proportion to the square of the speed of the fluid flow. In addition, the horsepower (work input) varies in proportion to the cube of speed. This cubic relationship between speed and input power is where energy savings are realized. For example, if fan speed is reduced by only 20%, motor horsepower (and therefore energy consumption) is reduced by nearly 50%. The ability to control output speed is important because even small reductions in speed will produce significant savings because of the cubic relationship. Although the energy savings mechanism for all ASDs is the same, in reality inefficiencies in the design of different speed control technologies introduce losses, resulting in different levels of motor power savings.

The purpose of this demonstration is to quantify the performance of two MC-ASDs in a controlled laboratory environment and address the benefits and limitations of each. The U.S. Department of Energy and Pacific Northwest National Laboratory do not specifically endorse or sponsor the devices or manufacturers described in this study, other than to present the specific data collected during this study.

ABOUT THE TECHNOLOGY

The MC-ASD technology can be divided into two types: fixed magnet and electromagnet. This demonstration focused on two unique applications of the MC-ASD technology: The MagnaDrive Coupling, marketed by MagnaDrive, Inc, and the PAYBACK Drive, marketed by Coyote Electronics.

The MagnaDrive Coupling is a fixed magnet MC-ASD that uses permanent rare-earth magnets fixed to a rotating disk to generate eddy currents in a copper conductor assembly fixed to the load shaft (see Figure 1). By mechanically varying the physical distance between the conductor assembly that rotates at motor speed (shown in crosshatch pattern) and the magnet rotor assembly that rotates at the load speed (shown in gray shading), the amount of torque produced on the load shaft can be varied. A photo of an actual installation is shown in Figure 2, with the protective shroud removed for illustration purposes. The MagnaDrive Coupling is controlled by a mechanical actuator that uses a pneumatic or electronic process control signal to modulate the speed or torque output of the coupling.

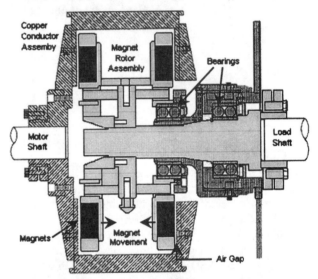

FIGURE 1. MAGNADRIVE SCHEMATIC

FIGURE 2. PHOTO OF MAGNADRIVE COUPLING WITH PROTECTIVE SHROUD REMOVED

The MagnaDrive Coupling is available in horizontal and vertical mounted designs. Drives are named by their size and will handle peak torque ranging from 1,200 to 19,320 lb-in. depending on the model chosen. This represents applications ranging from 25-hp, 900-rpm motors all the way up to 500-hp, 3600-rpm motors.

The PAYBACK Drive uses an electromagnet to transfer torque across a fixed-width air gap (see Figure 3). Changing the current supplied to the permanent electromagnet in the assembly varies the magnetic field and the amount of torque transferred. The PAYBACK Drive clamps to the motor shaft. Its internals rotate at motor speed (shown as light gray) and the external casing is mounted on a bearing, allowing it to rotate independently at load speed (shown as dark gray). This design makes the PAYBACK Drive, with its integrated belt grooves, ideally suited for belt-driven loads. It can also be used in a direct-drive system by purchasing an assembly that connects the belts to a shaft assembly, which in turn can be directly connected to any direct-driven load. A photo of a motor-drive assembly is shown in Figure 4 with a protective shroud in place surrounding the entire drive assembly.

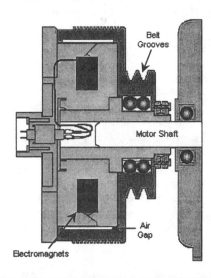

FIGURE 3. SCHEMATIC OF PAYBACK DRIVE

FIGURE 4. PAYBACK DRIVE AND MOTOR PACKAGE

The PAYBACK Drive is currently available in nine models, which fit 3- to 200-hp motors. The speed controller for the PAYBACK Drive operates on 115 volts AC (no more than 3 amps are needed for the controller) and provides adjustable voltage output to the drive's electromagnets. The controller accepts current, voltage, or pressure transducer signal inputs, and can interface with most energy management systems. The controller is also equipped with a potentiometer to manually vary output speed.

Installation
Both types of MC-ASD technologies are well-suited to retrofit applications and new installations. These devices can be used in either a solid shaft connection or a belt-driven connection between motor and load.

For direct-drive systems, where the motor shaft is connected directly to the load, the shaft is disconnected or cut to insert the MC-ASD coupling. When using the MagnaDrive Coupling, the motor is generally moved 12 to 18 in. further from the load shaft to provide space to insert the coupling between the motor and driven load. The conductor assembly is bolted to the motor drive, and the magnet rotor assembly is bolted to the load shaft. The two shafts should be in good alignment, although the MagnaDrive Coupling will tolerate a significantly greater degree of misalignment than would be suitable for a solid shaft connection between load and motor. Finally the control signal is connected.

The PAYBACK Drive can also be used in a direct-drive process, but requires installation of the direct-drive assembly at additional cost. The direct-drive assembly requires approximately the same amount of floor space, because the motor is mounted above a new drive shaft. Installation requires good alignment of the new drive shaft with the driven load and some alignment of the belts between the PAYBACK Drive and the new drive shaft. Finally the control signal is connected.

For belt-driven systems, such as most fans and blowers, the PAYBACK Drive is often a simple replacement of the pulley assembly attached to the motor. Disconnect the existing pulley, bolt on the coupling, install and align the belts, connect the control signal, and it's operational. Generally there is no need to move the motor itself. The MagnaDrive Coupling can also be used in belt-driven applications by either converting the belt-driven system to a direct-driven system if that can be done, or adding a pulley to the output shaft of the drive. In either event, it is likely that the position of the motor would have to be changed.

Benefits
When compared to a motor system with no speed control, the MC-ASD systems (and most VFD systems) offer many benefits in addition to energy savings. Systems where flow is controlled by throttling with a valve or damper often have vibration problems from turbulent flow, cavitation, and water hammer. These affects are eliminated with the addition of an ASD system. ASD

systems provide a method of slowly starting a motor to reduce initial in-rush current and prevent a lowering of distribution system supply voltage. Smaller size motors are possible because motors no longer have to be oversized for large starting loads or shock absorption of instantaneous peak loads. MC-ASDs (and some VFDs) can be easily implemented in retrofits as well as new construction.

In addition to these benefits, the MC-ASD systems provide the following additional benefits, which are not found in electronically controlled ASDs (e.g., VFDs). The motor shaft and drive shaft in the MagnaDrive Coupling are physically separated by an air gap, making it tolerant of some degree of misalignment. MC-ASDs introduce an insignificant amount of harmonic distortion to the power grid and will not shut down during voltage sags like some VFDs. When a VFD slows down a motor, it also reduces cooling from internal motor fans, which could potentially damage the motor's internal windings. MC-ASDs control speed while operating the motor at full speed. MC-ASDs do not require inverter-duty motors, which can cost 30% more than standard, high-efficiency motors and are recommended for VFD systems. Finally, MC-ASDs are primarily mechanical devices and are more easily serviced, repaired, or replaced by on-site staff. Their simple design is intended for long-life and serviceability.

APPLICATIONS

The MC-ASD is suitable for use anywhere an ASD could be applied, commonly pumps, fans, and blowers. In general, all large loads with throttled output (partially closed dampers or valves) or bypass loops to control flow velocity or pressure should be evaluated for ASD retrofit. For ASDs to be cost effective, the motor/load system should have significant operating time at part load.

When deciding which MC-ASD technology to use, there are two primary factors to consider: drive type (direct- or belt-driven) and drive size. The PAYBACK Drive is generally more suited to belt-driven systems and is an easy retrofit, with drives sized for 3- to 200-hp motors. The MagnaDrive Coupling can also be used for belt-driven applications by installing an additional pulley and shaft support.

In small to medium size direct-drive systems it is possible to use either MC-ASD technology. The MagnaDrive Coupling is the easiest to connect to direct-drive loads. The PAYBACK Drive can also be connected to a jackshaft (available from the manufacturer), which itself is directly connected to the load shaft. In very large direct-drive systems, the MagnaDrive Coupling is the only option. It can operate on motors between motors of all speeds with sizes up to 1500 hp and with voltage greater than 2840 volts.

Constant torque systems should be avoided because the large amount of slip generates a significant amount of heat in the coupling. Situations where the MC-ASD provides a great amount of speed control for a large percentage of its operating hours should be avoided. Providing a large amount of slip decreases drive efficiency because energy is lost in dissipated heat. For example, an MC-ASD should not be used in a direct connection to attempt to drive a fan at 750 rpm when connected to an 1800-rpm motor. If by motor downsizing, changing pulley ratio, or staging a series of motor/pumps the motor will operate a greater portion of the time at higher speeds, this will improve the suitability for the MC-ASD devices. These actions should be considered anytime an MC-ASD is applied to get the smallest motor and MC-ASD coupling possible.

Maintenance

Both MC-ASD technologies require little additional maintenance. The MagnaDrive Coupling has two bearings and four pivot assemblies that require periodic greasing. After about 40,000 hours of operation, the drive should be checked and, if needed, the bearings replaced. The PAYBACK Drive uses sealed for life bearings that require no maintenance. Power is supplied to the drive through a brushless rotary connector that should be replaced every 3 years. Both MC-ASDs can be repaired using off-the-shelf parts by local mechanical staff.

Costs

Costs for the MC-ASD drives as of January 2002 are shown in Table 1. As more units are produced and more orders received, the cost of the MC-ASD drives continues to decrease. The drive manufacturer will help determine

TABLE 1. MC-ASD STANDARD COST SHEETS FOR 2002

MagnaDrive Coupling					PAYBACK Drive		
Model Size	Approx. Motor, hp	Retail Price	GSA Pricing		Model	Approx. Motor, hp	Retail Price
8.5	≤ 25	6,440	6,096		EASY-1	3-5	1,600
10.5	25-50	9,090	8,581		EASY-2	7.5-10	1,800
12.5	50-75	10,582	9,974		EASY-3	15-25	2,500
14.5	75-125	11,830	11,147		EASY-4	25-30	3,300
16.5	125-150	15,160	14,244		EASY-5	40-50	4,900
18.5	150-200	18,410	17,269		EASY-6	60-75	7,200
20.5	200-250	21,385	20,047		EASY-7	100-125	9,400
22.5	250-350	24,800	23,320		EASY-8	150	14,000
24.5	350-500	29,600	27,740		EASY-9	200	16,800
26.5	500+	34,400	32,160				

which drive is needed through an engineering evaluation of the motor/load system.

Installation costs can vary significantly for each facility and each motor. On average, it should take two mechanics between 2 and 4 hours to retrofit an MC-ASD to an existing motor system. It is important to note that these devices do not require an inverter duty motor or additional electronics cabinetry or cabling. Contact your local utility because many offer technical support and financial incentives for motor speed control technologies.

LABORATORY TESTING

To accurately compare the two MC-ASD technologies under identical conditions, these devices were tested at the Motor Systems Resource Facility (MSRF) located on the campus of Oregon State University. The goal was to test the system efficiency of three different ASD systems connected to the same 50-hp motor. Each ASD system was used to drive three different load profiles: 1) a variable-flow fan, 2) a variable-flow pump with high static head, and 3) a variable-flow pump with low static head. Each load profile was represented using a dynamometer to ensure repeatability.

System efficiency was measured for each load profile in four separate configurations: 1) a VFD, 2) a MagnaDrive Coupling directly coupled to the load shaft, 3) PAYBACK Drive installed in a belt-drive system using the integral belt grooves and a 1:1 pulley ratio, and 4) MagnaDrive Coupling with an attached pulley in a belt-driven system using a 1:1 pulley ratio. A schematic of the four tests is shown in Figure 5.

Complete results of the laboratory testing will be available from the Federal Energy Management Program (FEMP) in a New Technology Demonstration Program document in summer 2002. A summary of the laboratory testing that highlights important issues is provided as follows.

Test Results: Fan Load Profile

Each of the four test configurations was used to drive the fan curve test profile, as shown in Figure 6. The VFD operated more efficiently than the MC-ASDs over the full range of speed control; although near full speed, the efficiencies of the three drives were similar. For example, at 1705 rpm (96% of full motor speed), the VFD used approximately 34 kW, the PAYBACK Drive used 36.3 kW, the

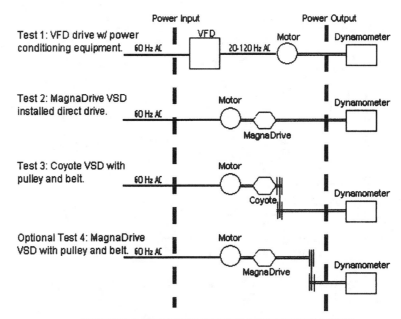

FIGURE 5. TESTING EQUIPMENT SCHEMATIC

MagnaDrive-Direct used 37.6 kW, and the MagnaDrive-Belt used 38.4 kW. The MC-ASDs use approximately 2.3 to 3.6 kW (6.8 to 13%) more power than the VFD at this speed. As fan speed is reduced, the MC-ASDs become much less efficient. However, because the overall power consumption is reduced at lower speeds, the MC-ASDs consume slightly more power. At 50% speed (~890 rpm), the VFD fan consumed 5.55 kW, while the PAYBACK, MagnaDrive-Direct, and MagnaDrive-Belt consume 5.74 (3%), 7.05 (27%), and 8.0 kW (44%) more power, respectively.

Dividing the output motor shaft power by the input electrical power at each point calculates the efficiency of each combined motor/drive system. Figure 7 shows the drive efficiency as a function of fan shaft power (in kW). Notice that the VFD operated between 88% and 92% efficiency from the maximum power tested down to approximately 35% of maximum power consumption, with a sharp decline in efficiency below 35% output power. Both the MagnaDrive and PAYBACK showed a rapid degradation in efficiency as speed was reduced over the entire range of speeds tested.

The testing protocol called for meeting target torque values (rather than output speed values) across the range of operations to characterize each drive. This created a problem because the upper torque target represented the fan torque at 1800 rpm, which was above the nominal motor speed and unattainable for MC-ASDs. By over-driving the system, the drives were able to meet the target torque value, but at a lower speed. This point deviates from the fan curve being tested and gives a false value for the top speed of the MC-ASD devices. Likewise, the VFD system was able to meet the target torque at a full 1800 rpm, but accomplished this by supplying power at greater than 60 Hz. This also provides a false value for

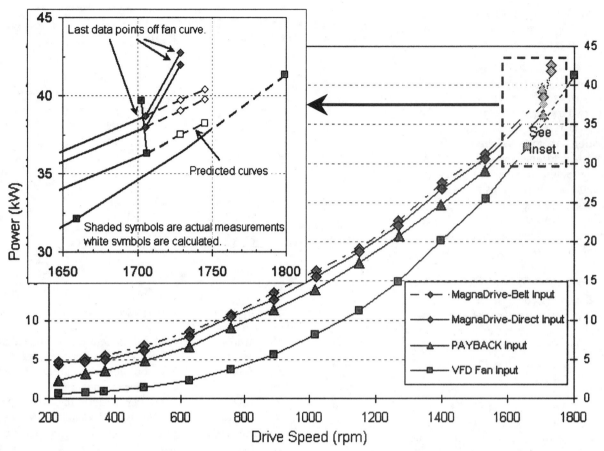

FIGURE 6. POWER CONSUMPTION OVER RANGE OF SPEED FOR FAN LOAD

the top speed because, in practice, full motor speed is a nominal value less than synchronous speed. Extrapolating each of the MC-ASD curves to a drive speed of 1750 rpm suggests maximum system efficiencies from 85.2% to 89.6% for the MC-ASDs and 90.6% for the VFD. Additional testing is being considered to explore what the curves should look like in this upper range and to determine what the true maximum speed is for each ASD.

The MagnaDrive-Direct appears to consume 1.5 to 2.3 kW more power than the PAYBACK for the fan speeds tested and is not influenced by changes in drive efficiency. This difference is most likely the result of the bearing losses and aerodynamic drag from the rotating magnet assembly. Discussion with the manufacturer revealed that these values were higher than expected and could be attributed to selecting a larger coupling than was needed. As the size and torque transmission

capabilities of the models increases, the aerodynamic losses would be expected to become a much smaller fraction of the total power transmitted through the unit.

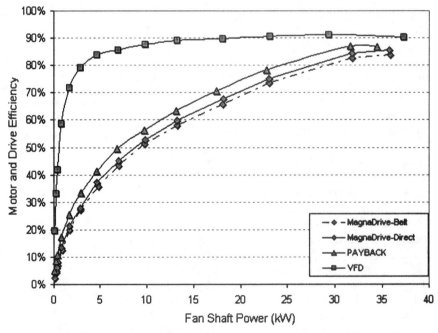

FIGURE 7. SYSTEM EFFICIENCY VERSUS SHAFT POWER

58

These "windage" losses and the problems determining the full speed point on the fan curve prevented the testing from proving if the MagnaDrive energy use would dip below the VFD curve near full load speed as the manufacturer claims it should. These tests were unable to substantiate this claim.

Tests also showed that the energy required to energize the electromagnetic in the PAYBACK Drive was almost negligible to the performance of the drive. Below 1600 rpm, the drive used between 13 to 24 watts to control slip within the drive. Above 1600 rpm, power consumption climbed steeply, but still used no more than 90 watts.

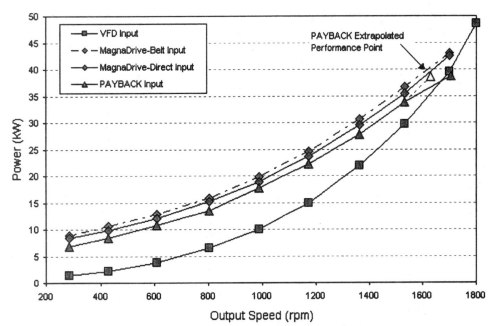

FIGURE 8. LOW HEAD PUMP POWER CONSUMPTION OVER OUTPUT SPEED

Test Results: Low Head Pump Application

Figure 8 shows power consumption over a range of output speed for each of the three technologies in a low head pump application.

In comparing the three systems, the VFD clearly showed the lowest power consumption. The MagnaDrive-Direct again consumed a roughly constant 1.5 kW more than the PAYBACK Drive, except at the very highest rpm point tested. At 1705 rpm, the PAYBACK Drive was not able to maintain the desired torque required for the pump curve. The torque requirements for this low head pump curve were approximately 16% higher than that of the fan test near 1700 rpm. This appeared to have been more torque than this size PAYBACK Drive could provide at that speed and is shown as a dip in the PAYBACK curve at top speed.

Test Results: High Head Pump Application

Figure 9 shows the power consumption in a high head pump application. In this application, the head pressure encountered by the pump was not purely a function of flow but was instead the sum of static and dynamic (flow) head. The principle impact of this was that the torque on the high head pump shaft is not a linear function of shaft rotational speed, making the power consumption of the pump a more complicated function of flow.

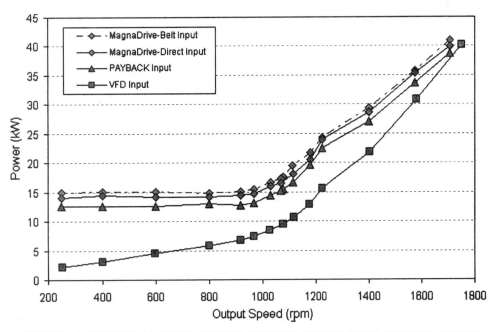

FIGURE 9. HIGH HEAD PUMP POWER CONSUMPTION OVER OUTPUT SPEED

High head pump applications appear to be an ideal application for MC-ASDs because they will operate a greater portion of the time at higher speeds, and being direct driven loads, are well-suited for the MagnaDrive Coupling. Unfortunately, problems determining the upper test points during laboratory testing do not reveal if the MC-ASD curves cross the VFD curve at high speeds.

Power Factor
Power factor for the VFD was lower than that of the MC-ASDs; however, total power was also lower. In a building application, it is the total kilovolt-amp reactive power (kVAR) produced by the motor drive system that is important. Total kVAR produced by each drive system (including the Payback electromagnetic controller) is shown in Figure 10. The kVAR produced by the VFD is higher at full load than that of the MC-ASDs, but drops below that of the MC-ASDs at about 1200-rpm drive speed. The reactive power curve produced by all MC-ASDs is nearly identical and appears to follows the typical reactive power curve for the motor in moving from an unloaded to a fully loaded condition.

It is important to also consider the ability to "control" the building power factor. The reactive power produced by the MC-ASD systems is the result of induction devices and is readily corrected through the addition of capacitance at the building electrical distribution level. The power factor generated by the VFD is the result of harmonics generated by the VFD electronics and is not easily corrected at either the building or drive level.

Test Conclusions
For all tests, the VFD was more efficient than the MC-ASDs at all speeds; however, the differences were relatively small at the highest speeds (above 1700 rpm). The PAYBACK Drive performed more efficiently than the MagnaDrive, typically saving the equivalent of 3 to 4% of the full-load power over the entire operating range. The MagnaDrive-Belt configurations also invariably used the equivalent of 1 to 2% of full-load power more than the MagnaDrive-Direct configuration, presumably as a result of belt losses.

The choice between using the MagnaDrive in a direct- or belt-driven configuration is expected to be driven by the use of either a fan or pump in most cases. Most pumps are designed to operate at near the full-load motor speed (corresponding to synchronous speeds of 900, 1800, or 3600 rpm) in a direct-drive application and would be sized accordingly to meet peak loads. Most large fans, however, are typically designed to be operated as a belt-and-pulley-driven load, with the choice of pulleys used to fine-tune a particular fan size to the peak air flow needed. Because the full-load fan speed required for the system being retrofit is less likely to be near the nominal full-load motor speed, using a MagnaDrive-Direct configuration is likely to result in unacceptable levels of slip losses, and a MagnaDrive-Belt configuration (or PAYBACK) represents a more reasonable choice despite the pulley losses.

These results highlight the importance of carefully considering the load profile when selecting the drive type (VFD or MC-ASD), as well as sizing the drive correctly for the application. If a large portion of the time is spent below about 80% of full speed, the VFD would outperform the magnetically coupled drives in terms of efficiency and expected energy savings. However, if the system operates primarily in the 80 to 100% of full flow range, the additional efficiency obtained from the VFD may be a relatively small fraction of total energy requirements. This test suggested that for high head pump applications using MC-ASDs, there may be a fixed speed below which there is little if any energy advantage obtained with speed reduction using a MC-ASD. Wide variations in flow requirements for these pumps suggest either the use of a single variable speed pump, or the use of multiple pump/motor combinations, some of which may use magnetically coupled drives.

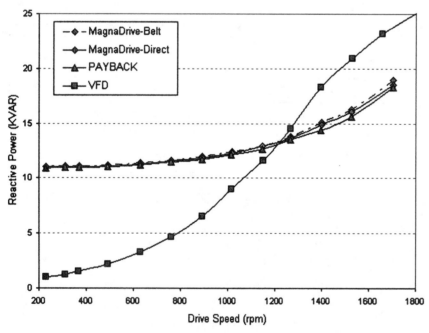

FIGURE 10. REACTIVE POWER GENERATED DURING FAN CURVE TEST

60

SAVINGS POTENTIAL

The life-cycle cost (LCC) of a potential retrofit is the present value of all the costs associated with the investment over the life of the equipment. The Building Life Cycle Cost (BLCC) program, developed by the National Institute of Standards and Technology, allows users to compare the life-cycle cost of several alternatives. LCC analysis is required of Federal agencies by 10 CFR Part 436.

Energy data from the 50-hp motor tested in the laboratory was used to construct a LCC analysis for a sample fan system typically found in Federal facilities. The three ASDs tested were compared to the "do nothing" conditions (often called the *baseline*). The following inputs were identified and included in the analysis:

- **Installed Cost.** The installed cost includes the cost of equipment (as of January 2002) and the labor required to install the ASD on a typical 50-hp motor retrofit. Note that the cost of the VFD does *not* include the replacement with an inverter-duty motor, which is recommended but not required.

- **Energy Cost.** Because the testing was performed without a specific city or region in mind, the energy cost was assumed to be $0.06 / kWh with no demand charges. Demand reduction was ignored because determining a good estimate for demand costs is problematic.

- **Energy Use.** The energy consumption for each drive systems was generated using the performance testing data from OSU and typical load profiles from QuikFan. QuikFan is an EnergyStar® software product designed to estimate the cost efficacy of retrofits on fan systems. QuikFan uses the performance curves of fan systems, typical or user supplied binned load profiles, and total hours of operation to estimate the total annual energy consumption for the same fan system with different drive systems or control applications. Default duty cycles representing typical fan systems were used to estimate annual energy consumption for the 50-hp motor used in testing.

- **Maintenance Costs.** Estimating long-term maintenance costs – including lubrication, routine parts replacement, and failures – proved difficult. Although MC-ASDs are expected to have reduced long-term costs, because they are a relatively new technology no hard data exists. Obtaining data for VFDs proved even more difficult, despite checking a number of sources. Conversations with in-field personnel seem to indicate that a VFD would be unlikely to reach a 20-year service life without any additional service and/or replacement. Unfortunately this information is largely anecdotal, with no solid data to substantiate these claims. It was decided that long-term maintenance costs would be omitted from the economic analysis because of the lack of solid data. This definitely skews the comparison because technologies like MC-ASD are designed with reduced maintenance costs in mind.

Life-Cycle Results for Fan Application

The sample system for the BLCC analysis is a typical 50-hp fan system, where speed control will be retrofit where none existed before. The fan system chosen operates on a 12-hour, workday-only schedule (3,476 hour per year) over a study period of 20 years (see Table 2).

The baseline option required no initial investment, but was expected to use 109,133 kWh/year, which is nearly double any of the alternatives. Compared to no speed control, any of the ASDs would be a smart retrofit, with simple payback ranging from 1.9 to 4.6 years.

The VFD used the least energy (41,013 kWh/year) and had the best life-cycle cost among the alternatives ($44,995). The Savings-to-Investment (SIR) of the VFD alternative was 6.74, with a simple payback of 2.4 years. Even if $5,000 for the purchase of an inverter duty motor

TABLE 2. BLCC PROGRAM INPUTS

Equipment Type	Purchase Price	Install Cost	Energy Use[1] (kWh/yr)	Life-Cycle Cost	SIR[2]	AIRR[3]	Simple Payback
Base case	$ 0	$ 0	109,133	$ 94,229	N/A	N/A	N/A
VFD	$ 8,582	$ 1,000	41,013	$ 44,995	6.74	13.64%	2.4 years
MagnaDrive	$ 11,147	$ 750	66,205	$ 69,061	3.26	9.58%	4.6 years
PAYBACK	$ 4,900	$ 500	59,160	$ 56,481	8.70	15.10%	1.9 years

[1] Energy consumption (kWh) per year based on test results over 20 year study period.

[2] Savings-to-Investment (SIR) ratio compares the investment for an alternative versus baseline. Higher numbers are better.

[3] Adjusted Internal Rate of Return (AIRR).

were added to the analysis, the life-cycle cost is still best at $50,395, with a simple payback of 3.9 years.

The MagnaDrive Coupling and the PAYBACK Drive were also excellent options compared to the base case, with life-cycle costs of $69,061 and $56,481, respectively. Although the VFD still performed more efficiently overall, these devices were competitive and may be more attractive given some of the additional benefits.

At 59,160 kWh/year, the PAYBACK Drive uses 45% less energy than the base case. With the lowest purchase and installation cost, it provides a simple payback of 1.9 years. The PAYBACK Drive had the best SIR of 8.70, indicating that it provided good savings (although not the most savings) with the least initial investment. For retrofits that fit its inherent design, it appears to be the ideal choice.

Of the three alternatives, the MagnaDrive Coupling used the most energy, 66,205 kWh/year, or 39% less than the base case. At $11,400, it was also the most expensive to install among the alternatives. A 50-hp motor is at the low end of the range of applications for MagnaDrive Couplings. In larger sizes, economies-of-scale make the purchase price more competitive. Even so, with a simple payback of 4.6 years, it can be an attractive option for certain retrofit applications on direct-driven loads, where operations and maintenance considerations (which were not considered in this analysis) are important.

Although a life-cycle cost analysis for a pump application is a natural next step, constructing a baseline scenario proved difficult without making a number of assumptions and was not specified in the laboratory testing. Both MC-ASDs are most efficient near full-load speeds and a pump application (especially with a high static head) would tend to operate at or near full speed a greater percentage of time.

CONCLUSIONS

Implementing speed control in motor systems represents an opportunity to gain additional control over system operations while yielding substantial energy savings. More traditional types of speed control (e.g., variable frequency drives) will continue to be a good option. This study has shown that the MC-ASDs will provide similar energy savings under certain conditions. The MC-ASDs are flexible for a variety of applications and are an easy retrofit. The simplicity of these devices remains a strong selling point because installation, maintenance, and repair can all be performed by in-house mechanical staff. The facilities that are using MC-ASDs have been happy with their performance and, in most cases, have purchased additional units after their initial

experience. Although the MC-ASD technologies are fairly new (less than 10 years old), both products have been through several design iterations and have a well-established product.

ACKNOWLEDGEMENTS
This work was supported by the Department of Energy - Office of Federal Energy Management Programs (FEMP) under the New Technology Demonstration Program, whose mission is to reduce the cost of Government by advancing energy efficiency, water conservation, and the use of solar and other renewable technologies. A more detailed report on this project is available from the New Technology Demonstration Program. The authors wish to thank Mr. Ted Collins (FEMP) for supporting the work, the Motor Systems Resource Facility at Oregon State University for performing the testing, and MagnaDrive Corporation and Coyote, Inc. for their support and equipment loans.

ABOUT THE AUTHORS
Bill Chvála, Jr. (pronounced Koala, like the bear) is a senior research engineer in the Technology Systems Analysis group at Pacific Northwest National Laboratory (PNNL). Bill holds Bachelor of Science degrees in physics and applied mathematics from Nebraska Wesleyan University and a Master of Environmental Science degree, Energy emphasis from Miami University, Oxford, Ohio. Bill has been involved in field technology demonstrations, demand-side management, and load-shedding projects for FEMP. He manages the FEMP Design Assistance and Distributed Energy Resources technical assistance tasks at PNNL.

David Winiarski received a Bachelor of Arts and Science Degree in Physics from Oregon State University and a Master of Science degree in Mechanical Engineering from Texas A&M University with an emphasis on energy systems. During his academic career, David worked in the Energy Analysis and Diagnostic Centers at both Oregon State University and Texas A&M University. David also served 2 years as a Peace Corp Volunteer in Belize Central America where he taught high school physics and mathematics. David is currently a senior research engineer with Pacific Northwest National Laboratory's Energy and Engineering Technical Resources group.

REFERENCES
Chvála, W.D., Jr., Winiarski, D.W., and Mulkerin M.C. *Technology Demonstration of Magnetically-Coupled Adjustable Speed Drive Systems.* PNNL-13879 Pacific Northwest Laboratory, Richland, Washington, anticipated publication April 2002.

Chapter 11

ADD CHP—Accelerated Development and Deployment of Combined Cooling, Heat and Power at Federal Facilities

Keith L. Kline, Stanton W. Hadley, and Julia S. Kelley,
Oak Ridge National Laboratory (ORNL)

ABSTRACT

Fuel-efficient distributed energy generation systems such as combined cooling, heat and power (CHP or cogeneration) are attracting increasing attention among project developers and policy makers because they can make significant contributions to mitigating key power sector constraints. These systems can meet increased energy needs, reduce transmission congestion, cut emissions, increase power quality and reliability, and increase the overall energy security for a site. The U.S. Department of Energy's (DOE's) Federal Energy Management Program (FEMP) recently completed a national market assessment to estimate the potential impacts of CHP in the federal sector [Ref. 1]. That study suggests that CHP could be successfully applied in 9% of large federal facilities, annually conserve 50 trillion Btus of primary energy, reduce CO_2 emissions by 2.7 million metric tons, and cut utility bills by $170 million. Although many CHP technologies are proven and the potential savings and benefits are significant, project development lags behind potential in the federal sector.

This paper describes FEMP Programs to "ADD CHP" (Accelerate Development and Deployment of Combined Cooling, Heat and Power) at federal facilities and other CHP outreach efforts including FEMP's New Technology Demonstration Program (NTDP). ADD CHP works to identify and reduce barriers to installation of CHP technologies in federal buildings. FEMP's role, CHP market potential in the federal sector, issues affecting CHP deployment, the strategy to expedite CHP projects, and progress to date are all discussed herein.

What is CHP?

CHP goes by many names—cogeneration; building cooling, heating, and power; and combined heat and power—all referring to a system that efficiently generates electricity (or shaft power) and uses the heat from that process to produce steam, hot water, and/or hot air for other purposes. The most common building applications use a prime mover (gas turbine or engine) coupled with a generator to produce electricity and capture the waste heat for process steam and space heating. Or boiler steam passes through a turbine to generate electricity in addition to serving other thermal applications. One of the simplest systems employed recently at a federal site replaced steam pressure-relief valves with a low-cost backpressure steam turbine and electric generator.

A CHP system recovers the heat from electricity generation for productive uses. Normally, conventional power plants waste this heat. And because a CHP system generates electricity near the point of use, CHP also avoids transmission losses from distant central stations. For these reasons, properly designed CHP systems can be much more efficient than the average U.S. fossil fuel power plant and boiler combination.

CHP Efficiency: Site versus Source Energy Savings

A CHP system alone is generally not more efficient at producing electricity than the central grid, and properly maintained boilers alone can be more efficient at producing thermal energy than a CHP system. But the combined generation of electricity and thermal energy on-site by a well-designed CHP system is more efficient overall than the combined efficiencies of these two alternatives. One key to ensuring an efficient CHP system is to maximize the use of thermal energy (waste heat) from the generation process. Emissions or other site-specific factors may override electrical efficiency or operating and maintenance (O&M) costs when determining which CHP system is best for a facility.

Because CHP uses energy to generate electricity on site, and because it is slightly less efficient for thermal purposes than a regular boiler, the energy use at the site will increase with a CHP system. However, because losses associated with generating and distributing the electricity (from the alternate central source) will be avoided, CHP results in a net savings of primary or *source* energy.

A Proven Technology

CHP systems play an essential role in our nation's present energy supply and future plans. The United States has more than 50 gigawatts (GW) of installed CHP capacity producing about 7% of the nation's electricity. The National Energy Policy Report highlights the importance of CHP to help effectively meet critical goals related to emissions reduction, reliability, and new energy production cost. Federal agencies have a mandate to lead by example in meeting national energy and environmental goals, and an Executive Order specifies that agencies "shall use combined cooling, heat and power systems when life-cycle cost-effective."

FEMP's Role and Rationale for CHP

FEMP's mission is to reduce the cost of the federal government by advancing energy efficiency and water conservation, promoting the use of renewable and distributed energy, and improving utility management decisions at federal sites. FEMP's criteria for emphasizing a technology are that it must be commercially available, be proven but underutilized, have a strong constituency, offer large energy savings, and carry sufficient federal market potential. CHP meets these criteria. And Executive Order 13123 directs all federal facilities to use CHP when life-cycle cost analysis indicates energy-reduction goals will be met. FEMP can help facilities conduct this analysis. FEMP programs respond to federal partners who wish to reduce energy costs and emissions. More and more federal partners are requesting information on CHP.

CHP systems can help federal agencies meet goals related to energy security, cost reduction and environmental quality. Recognizing the benefits of CHP, DOE, the Environmental Protection Agency, and the private sector have embarked on a joint effort to double the amount of CHP capacity in the U.S. by 2010 (Fig. 1). FEMP efforts to expand CHP in federal sites are an integral part of the strategy developed with other agencies and sectors, including the Environmental Protection Agency and the U.S. Combined Heat and Power Association (USCHPA).

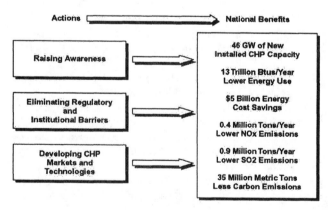

FIG. 1. NATIONAL CHP ROADMAP, OBJECTIVES FOR 2000–2010.

CHP may present some challenges, but more than 50 federal sites have benefited from CHP systems in the past, and as of February 2002, another 50 sites were actively developing opportunities to install 100 MW of additional CHP capacity.

Potential for CHP in the Federal Sector

To give FEMP a better understanding of the federal sector's CHP potential, ORNL created a simple model that calculates the energy use and costs in different types of federal buildings across the country. This model was used to estimate when and where CHP would be most likely to offer a cost-effective alternative to traditional (grid and boiler) systems. The model allows the user to select various parameters regarding CHP technology, energy prices, and energy use. It then calculates the financial payback of CHP to determine the amount that could be implemented within prescribed parameters. The market assessment [Ref. 1] base case included only those buildings with simple payback periods of less than ten years. In a typical federal installation like those modeled for this market assessment, CHP is assumed to provide thermal energy for heating and cooling a building while at the same time generating a portion of its electricity needs. While other applications (process steam for industry, laboratories, laundry, hot water, dehumidification) and more complicated systems are possible and often result as site-specific conditions are analyzed, it was impractical to make assumptions about these alternatives in the present assessment. Site-specific information is critical to verify CHP potential.

Potential CHP Capacity

The total amount of CHP potential capacity for federal facilities nationwide is estimated to be between 1500 and 1600 MW [Ref. 2]. Under base-case assumptions, the CHP systems would produce 7.7 terawatt hours (TWh) of electricity representing about 13% of the 57 TWh total electricity the federal government purchased in FY 2000 (FEMP 2002). This CHP capacity would provide electricity and thermal energy for about 580 million ft^2 of building space in 9% of all federal sites. The potential will be greatest in large sites with central plants or mechanical rooms and high electricity rates. Key assumptions behind these numbers are summarized here:

- reciprocating gas engines are used at their current estimated cost and efficiencies;
- energy prices are at 2000 industrial rates for each state;
- CHP supplies 75% or 50% of estimated electric demand with load factors at 85% or 35%, depending on building type and size;
- only the percentage of CHP-compatible federal facilities was considered;
- all recoverable waste heat is assumed utilized by the site; and
- only systems with a simple payback less than ten years were counted in the totals.

Changing these parameters can produce great variation in amounts of CHP potential and energy savings.

Under the base case, federal hospitals are the building category with the highest potential for CHP. They also show the most promising target of opportunity, since more than two-thirds of large hospitals are expected to have CHP potential. Industrial buildings are next in potential capacity at 340 MW and are second in percentage of sites at 42%. This result is partly influenced by the fact that these two categories were modeled using a 24/7 load-following CHP

TABLE 1: NATIONAL CHP POTENTIAL BY BUILDING CATEGORY AT FEDERAL FACILITIES USING MARKET ASSESSMENT [REF. 1] BASE CASE ASSUMPTIONS

	Hospital	Industrial	Office	Prison	R&D	School	Service	Total
Total Mft^2, all buildings[a]	141	115	514	41	144	136	463	2757[b]
Mft^2 buildings with CHP payback <10 years	113	80	146	16	100	42	82	579
Total number of sites[a]	331	181	2302	99	421	917	1033	8182[b]
Number of sites with CHP payback <10 years	235	75	167	38	70	42	74	700
% of sites with CHP potential	71	42	7	38	17	5	7	9
Potential TWh of electricity from CHP	2.9	2.3	0.8	0.2	0.8	0.1	0.7	7.7[c]
Potential CHP Capacity, MW	440	340	250	40	270	20	210	1570[c]

[a] Includes buildings in General Services Administration database >25,000 ft^2, even those without CHP potential.
[b] Total includes other building types not shown.
[c] Row total differs due to rounding.

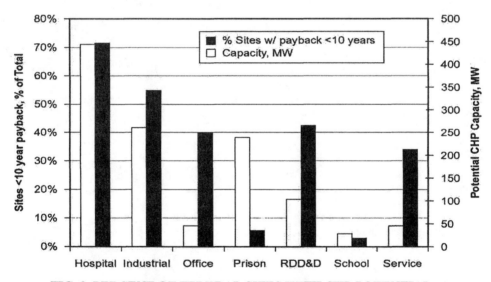

FIG. 2. PERCENT OF FEDERAL SITES WITH CHP POTENTIAL BY BUILDING CATEGORY AND CORRESPONDING CAPACITY (MW).

profile. And since this scenario assumes a relatively high capacity factor (75%), they also represent more than two-thirds of the total electricity and potential savings estimated by the model.

R&D facilities, office buildings, and service buildings provide similar amounts of capacity (270, 250, and 210 MW, respectively) under the base case. These three categories were modeled in the base case as using the weekday occupation load profile (CHP provides 50% of electricity at a 35% capacity factor) rather than the 24/7 load-following CHP profile. Some R&D and service facilities may be more appropriately modeled using the higher loads assumed for hospitals and industrial sites. Under that alternative load

profile, R&D CHP capacity increases 45%, from 270 to 390 MW. Figure 2 shows the percentage of buildings with CHP potential (payback less than 10 years) in a given category and compares that percentage to corresponding MW of capacity. Hospitals, prisons, and industrial sites offer the greatest likelihood of having CHP potential.

CHP Costs and Savings
Table 2 shows the average costs, payback, and annual savings expected if all the CHP identified in the base case were implemented at federal sites. Costs include one-time installation, annual operating, and annual gas purchase expenses. Estimated installed costs range from $600–

TABLE 2: CHP COSTS, SAVINGS, AND PAYBACK BY BUILDING CATEGORY, UNDER BASE CASE ASSUMPTIONS

	Hospital	Industrial	Office	Prison	R&D	School	Service	Total
Capacity, MW	446	342	248	36	265	18	211	1567
Installation cost, M$	319	222	174	28	163	14	135	1055
Operating cost, M$	23	17	6	2	6	0	5	59
Gas costs, M$	55	42	15	4	16	1	12	145
Electricity savings, M$	138	100	44	11	44	3	35	375
Net annual savings, M$	60	41	23	5	22	2	18	171
Average payback, years	5.3	5.5	7.5	5.8	7.4	7.5	7.4	6.2

$1300/kW, and O&M from $5.5–$12/MWh, depending on system size and technology (considering gas turbines or internal combustion gas engines). The thermal benefits of CHP are incorporated in the gas cost because the amount of gas needed is the amount to make the electricity minus the amount displaced by CHP waste heat utilization. Dollar savings come from reduced electricity purchases, and the net annual savings ($171 million/year) are these savings less annual costs. "Simple payback" is the installation cost divided by the annual net savings, to show the number of years until the installation cost is recovered. The payback numbers reflect national averages for each building category for states where that category showed payback less than ten years. Hospitals, industrial, and prison facilities show the shortest payback periods. Besides the amount of floor space and energy intensity in any state, a key factor is the relative price of natural gas and electricity. States with low gas prices and high electricity prices are the best candidates for CHP. Contrarily, high gas prices and low electricity prices make CHP less attractive.

Figure 3 illustrates the national amount of potential CHP capacity, and Fig. 4 shows the states with the highest difference between electricity and gas prices (spark spread). Note that there is a strong correlation between the two figures. Exceptions exist primarily because states with higher numbers of large federal buildings are more likely to have higher CHP potential.

CHP Potential by Federal Agency

Table 3 estimates the potential CHP capacity for each agency by building type. Many agencies showed little potential as calculated using the base case parameters. (The sum does not exactly match the earlier analysis, because agency-by-agency averages by state have slightly different paybacks compared to the building category averages that go above or below the threshold ten years for simple payback.)

Nearly all CHP potential is found among nine agencies: the three military services, Veterans Affairs (VA) hospitals, DOE, the National Aeronautics and Space Administration (NASA), the General Services Administration (GSA), the U.S. Postal Service, and the Department of Justice (Fig. 5). And the military, VA, and DOE represent 83% of the total CHP potential identified in the base case. The military services (more than 50% of total) have significant potential

CHP capacity in most types of buildings, while the VA's capacity is in hospitals. Energy and NASA capacity is concentrated in R&D and industrial buildings, while GSA and the Postal Service have capacity in the office category.

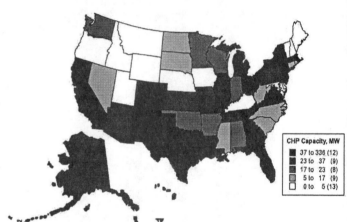

FIG. 3: FEDERAL CHP POTENTIAL CAPACITY UNDER BASE CASE, MW.

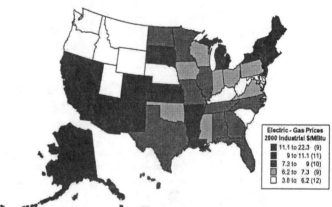

FIG. 4: "SPARK SPREAD" DIFFERENCE IN ELECTRIC AND GAS PRICES IN $/MBTU.

TABLE 3: POTENTIAL CHP CAPACITY BY FEDERAL AGENCY AND BUILDING CATEGORY, MW.

Agency	Hospital	Industry	Office	Prison	R&D	School	Service	Total
Air Force	43	57	31	0	85	7	116	339
Veterans Affairs (VA)	311	0	1	0	1	0	0	314
Army	55	101	52	2	24	3	33	270
Navy	27	36	39	0	43	2	58	205
Department of Energy	0	113	15	0	64	0	2	195
National Aeronautics and Space Administration (NASA)	0	17	10	0	43	0	3	73
General Services Administration (GSA)	0	1	68	0	0	0	0	69
United States Postal Service	0	0	48	0	0	0	0	48
Justice	0	3	0	34	0	0	0	37
Health and Human Services	6	0	0	0	2	0	0	9
Treasury	0	8	0	0	0	0	0	8
Transportation	0	0	2	0	4	0	0	7
Interior	0	2	2	0	0	3	0	7
Agriculture	0	0	0	0	3	0	0	3
Other	0	0	0	0	2	0	0	7
Grand total	443	338	269	36	274	16	212	1588

Note: "Other" refers to Commerce, Corps of Engineers, National Science Foundation, Environmental Protection Agency and Education. Other federal agencies considered showed no potential under the assessment parameters.

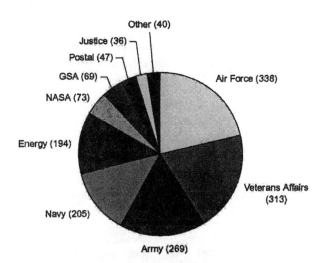

FIG. 5. POTENTIAL CHP CAPACITY FOR MAJOR FEDERAL AGENCIES (MW, TOTAL = 1590).

Conclusions: Market for CHP in the Federal Sector
There is significant potential—1000 to 2000 MW of capacity—for CHP to serve federal facilities. Regions with the greatest CHP potential are the southwest, northeastern metropolitan areas, and the southeast. The actual potential could be higher or lower depending on the specific conditions of any given site. Where the federal government can obtain low-cost electricity, CHP will have difficulty competing. But if on-site energy is required for security, CHP can make the system more efficient and cost-effective.

As energy prices increase and CHP system costs decrease, the amount of cost-effective CHP potential will rise.

The 1.5 GW identified under the base-case scenario would be sufficient to power more than a million homes and save the federal government $170M per year in energy costs. To install the 1.5 GW of electrical CHP generating capacity (all cases where the simple payback period is under ten years) would require an estimated $1.5–$2 billion in capital investments. Since the average simple payback period for these projects was about 7 years, many could be financed through existing credit mechanisms supported by FEMP and agency partners [energy saving performance contracts (ESPCs), utility energy service contracts, enhanced use lease agreements, etc.]. The source (primary) energy savings from this level of CHP investment are estimated to be 50 trillion Btus per year, and projected carbon dioxide emissions would be reduced by 2.7 million metric tons per year compared to gas-fired central electric power and thermal alternatives.

Hurdles for CHP in Federal Sector
Although CHP technologies are proven and the potential savings and benefits are significant, project development over the past decade has been modest in the federal sector. Given the potential for CHP, why haven't more federal facilities installed this technology? Preliminary discussions with facility managers reveal several reasons including:
- low historical tariffs for electricity;
- high initial cost of CHP systems;
- limited budgets (agencies rarely have sufficient appropriations for even much smaller energy conservation investments);

67

- complexity of CHP systems partly because of the need for custom engineering and design of different components for each site;
- a lack of time and capability for facility managers to evaluate potential applications and benefits to their site;
- obstacles related to local regulations and policies for interconnection, backup/standby fees, siting and emissions [Ref.1];
- high maintenance costs of many old thermal distribution (steam) systems;
- lack of adequate fuel (gas) supply at the site; and
- a lack of trusted sources of information about the costs, operation, and performance of CHP systems.

FEMP's Strategy to Expedite Projects: ADD CHP
DOE and FEMP are working to address many of the obstacles discussed here through technical assistance, project financing, applied R&D, education, and outreach. All these activities depend upon teaming with private and public partners for success.

The ADD CHP initiative is an integral part of FEMP's technical assistance program aimed at addressing the obstacles to CHP at federal sites. The strategy is to facilitate sound investments in CHP systems by providing qualified technical support and information focused on federal sites with good potential and champions motivated to develop a CHP project. ADD CHP offers federal agency partners support in areas such as:
- conducting CHP quick technical screening for interested federal sites;
- performing site survey and feasibility verification;
- fostering partnerships among federal, state, and private-sector project developers that bring financing if needed;
- collecting baseline data;
- fostering partnerships between federal sites and industry developers of "packaged" CHP;
- providing design and technical assistance to projects selected under FEMP calls for projects;
- providing support in addressing policy and regulatory constraints—siting and permitting, grid interconnection requirements, exit fees, standby/backup charges;
- providing conceptual design, component matching, and sizing verification (thermal/power profiles); and
- evaluating technical/price proposals.

CHP systems are costly to design and build. Federal agencies almost never have appropriated funds for this type of investment. Therefore, private partners who can provide financing and support design and construction are critical for success. While many private partners are already working with federal sites on traditional energy conservation measures, only a few have ventured into CHP projects. Private partners typically use their own at-risk funds to design projects and must get site approval of the design before moving forward. They naturally tend to first propose investments that can be designed at a low cost and are very likely to be approved. Uncertainties about future fuel and energy costs, changing rules and regulations related to permitting and interconnection, reluctance to "get into the power business," and the complexity of the initial design are all strong deterrents to CHP. If the site is not already

convinced that CHP will be a cost-effective, mission-enhancing investment, private partners are unlikely to put their time and money at risk.

Federal facility managers do not typically have time and resources to investigate whether CHP will work for their site. Therefore, FEMP offers free screening for CHP potential at federal sites. The screening provides an initial estimate of site-specific economics for a CHP project and helps determine if further investigation of CHP opportunities is worth the effort. Basic criteria that influence CHP project economics are described to the site along with the assumptions behind the analysis and the simple payback period for a proposed CHP system under reported fuel prices. A graphic presentation of the project illustrates the sensitivity of the project economics to energy prices and waste heat utilization. If the screening shows that the CHP system offers a simple payback in less than ten years, a set of recommendations for next steps is offered.

ADD CHP—Results to Date
As of June, more than 80 sites had requested CHP screening from FEMP. Requests have come in from 15 different states as well as Puerto Rico and the Virgin Islands, and from a broad range of federal agencies: VA; DOE; the National Guard; the Air Force, Army, and Navy; NASA; the Department of Justice (Bureau of Federal Prisons), GSA, and the U.S. Postal Service. The screening form guides agency managers to focus on large buildings and campus-style sites with more than 1 MW of minimum electricity demand and clearly defined thermal needs. About 50% of the sites merited further study of their CHP potential. FEMP and the private sector partner with sites to facilitate next steps. Examples of the teaming efforts on a few sites are described below.

Fort Bragg, North Carolina. A memorandum of understanding formalized an ongoing relationship among FEMP, the U.S. Army's Ft. Bragg, and the Honeywell Corporation involving the evaluation of a CHP project at Fort Bragg, North Carolina. The primary private partner, Honeywell, is developing an ESPC task order to install 5–12 MW of CHP capacity to reduce energy consumption at a central heating and cooling plant at the base. Fort Bragg, FEMP, and Honeywell have agreed to collaborate to enable FEMP to develop performance models and conduct an independent evaluation of this advanced turbine CHP project.

National Park Service, New York. State, federal, and private partners are collaborating to fund the design and construction of a CHP microturbine demonstration project in the Gateway National Recreation Area in Brooklyn, New York. Microturbines will generate about 175 kW and supply heating and cooling to a Park Service building at Floyd Bennett Field. The installation will form part of the Park Service's living demonstration of more sustainable urban development. The project is supported by the New York State Energy Research and Development Administration (NYSERDA) with cost sharing by the National Parks Service, FEMP, DOE's Office of Power Technologies (OPT), and Keyspan Energy (a gas distribution company). Landsberg Engineering received the competitive award from

NYSERDA to implement the project and Capstone (turbines) and Broad USA (chiller) manufacturers are supporting the design.

Twenty-nine Palms Marine Corps Base, California. Another example of recent teaming to implement CHP involves a CHP plant now being installed for the Marine Corps. The U.S. Naval Facilities Engineering Service Center requested FEMP support to review the proposal from an Energy Services Company (ESCO) for a 7-MW cogeneration project to be installed under an ESPC at a large U.S. military facility. The Core Team provided a detailed examination of (a) the proposed design, to ensure that the system would function according to specifications; (b) the ESCO's engineering analysis, to ensure that the methodology used to model the system supported the guaranteed energy savings; and (c) the measurement and verification plan for the project, to ensure that the savings achieved from the project could be quantified to the Navy's satisfaction. Again, the project is possible due to the partnering with the private sector. In this case, the local gas company supported the original design and feasibility study, the ESCO prepared the project proposal and financing package, and FEMP supported the site with design review and technical guidance.

About 50 federal sites (Fig. 6) are in different stages of investigating and implementing their CHP potential, including several that have already awarded contracts for design and construction.

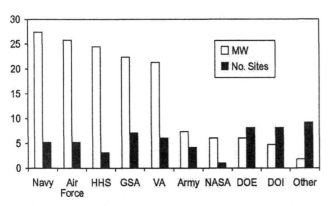

FIG. 6. FEDERAL SITES PLANNING AND DEVELOPING CHP (JAN. 2002).

The New Technology Demonstration Program and CHP Outreach
Many federal sites are still unaware of CHP potential and FEMP services. FEMP's New Technology Demonstration Program (NTDP) plays a key role in outreach to federal agencies. Two recent CHP-related NTDP publications help draw attention to CHP and FEMP. The first, *Energy Efficiency Improvements Through the Use of Combined Heat and Power (CHP) in Buildings*, [Ref. 3], examines the increasing options available to Federal energy managers to provide electric power and thermal energy (heating, cooling and humidity control) to buildings and processes and integrating proven technologies (e.g., engines, gas turbines, boilers, absorption chillers, desiccant dehumidifiers, electric air conditioners) to maximize the use of recoverable thermal energy. It also provides a glimpse into the arena of emerging technologies (e.g., microturbines, fuel cells).

The second publication focuses on integrated systems [Ref. 4]. These systems bring together gas-fired and electrically driven equipment to provide heating, cooling, dehumidification, and electrical service to commercial and public buildings. The principle configurations of integrated systems include CHP systems that include on-site electrical power generation with heating and cooling space conditioning and potable hot water production. Developments in the integration of on-site power generation, heating, cooling, and dehumidification are moving rapidly as a result of the changing economics of commercial building electric rates.

Other CHP Outreach Efforts
Other CHP outreach efforts include participating in a wide variety of workshops and conferences to help get the word out. During 2002, FEMP is sponsoring a series of four Distributed Energy Resource Workshops that focus on teaming with the private sector to get projects rolling and implemented. FEMP also produces additional high quality publications and maintains a distributed energy resources (DER) website (including CHP) to facilitate information dissemination.

REFERENCES
1. ORNL 2002. *Analysis of CHP Potential at Federal Sites*, ORNL/TM-2001/280, Kline et al. Available from the ORNL FEMP website:
www.ornl.gov/femp/pdfs/chp_market_assess.pdf

2. FEMP 2002. *Annual Report to Congress on Federal Government Energy Management and Conservation Programs Fiscal Year 2000. (Draft)* USDOE, EERE. Washington, D.C.

3. *Technology Focus: Energy Efficiency Improvements Through the Use of Combined Heat and Power (CHP) in Buildings*, DOE/EE-0239, October 2000.
www.eren.doe.gov/femp/prodtech/pdfs/chp_tf.pdf.

4. *Federal Technology Alert: Integrated Systems*, DOE/EE-0234, September 2000.
www.eren.doe.gov/femp/prodtech/pdfs/FTA_IntSys.pdf

Other References
FEMP 1999. Executive Order 13123, "Greening the Government Through Efficient Energy Management." www.eren.doe.gov/femp/aboutfemp/exec13123.html.

NEPDG 2001. National Energy Policy Development Group 2001, *National Energy Policy Report, Reliable, Affordable, and Environmentally Sound Energy for America's Future*, Office of the President of the United States, May. www.whitehouse.gov/energy/

USCHPA 2001. United States Combined Heat and Power Association, in cooperation with DOE and EPA, *National CHP Roadmap, Doubling Combined Heat and Power in the United States by 2010*, October. www.nemw.org/uschpa or www.eren.doe.gov/der/chp.

Chapter 12

INVESTMENT GRADE AUDITS...
Fact, or Fiction

James P. Waltz, P.E., C.E.M., A.C.F.E.
President, Energy Resource Associates, Inc.
Member, 1997 International Performance Measurement and
Verification Protocol Technical Committee

ABSTRACT

Performance contracting is all the rage for facility managers in the late 1990's and early 2000's. Everybody talks about "energy audits " and "investment grade audits," but what's the difference, and what is an audit, really? This article provides a down-to-earth discussion of the need for and benefits to be derived from doing investment grade audits. It also provides a detailed description of what an investment grade audit should be—as based on the author's more-than-two-decades of experience in the performance contracting field and from his nationwide seminar on performance contracting and forthcoming book by The Fairmont Press.

INTRODUCTION

Depending upon who you talk to in the performance contracting industry the concept of the "investment grade audit" is either waived aside as a foolishly expensive techno-babble academic exercise—or a critical element in developing a successful project, While it ran in fact be either one (mostly depending upon who's doing the audit), what you will read in the following is a rather strong statement of the case in favor of the investment grade audit, in one "flavor" or another. In fact it is not just a statement in favor of investment grade audits, but a statement in favor of doing performance contracting in such a way that the door is opened to investment grade audits and makes them an integral part of the process, rather than an almost "accidental" part of the process.

A PROBLEM EXISTS

One of the problems with the performance contracting industry (or "energy services" as it was known in the early 1980's when we helped to formulate the industry), is that it has always been sort of a "rogue" business—not failing into any existing category of business, sort of hard to understand, and therefore inclined towards freelancing and not following any particular standards, nor really even having it's own "standard of care" as such things are referred to in legal circles. Some have claimed that as the industry has matured the "hit and run" ESCo's "are no longer with us," Unfortunately nothing could be farther from the truth.

The dichotomy that exists in this industry is that on one hand the business proposition is compellingly simple, but on the other hand the actual implementation is devilishly tricky.

First of all we have to deal with the technical and organizational problems associated with determining actual existing field conditions. Then we have to conceive, design and build a complex retrofit project (like doing a heart transplant on a marathon runner... during a marathon), Finally we have to keep it working when the end users may actually be in resistance (to lighting controls, building automation, etc.). After scaling these hurdles, we then have to deal with the fact (as mentioned in the Spring 1998 *Energy & Environmental Management* article "Measurement & Verification Options") that **savings cannot actually be measured**. That is to say, cost avoidance can be accounted for, but the actual stream of savings is a use of energy that no longer exists and it is therefore physically impossible to slap a clamp-on ammeter around it to measure it. Combine this with the owner's greed occasionally getting in the way (ala Alameda County v. Western Energy Management, et al) and the Owner actually encouraging unethical Energy Service Company (ESCo) behavior, and you have significant potential for calamity—especially when the unwary owner and the unscrupulous ESCo collide, but also when other well-intended parties (on both sides) pursue performance contracting in relative ignorance. Given the rush of Energy Service Providers (ESP's—as opposed to ESCo's) to add energy service offerings to their commodity portfolio, calamities are inevitable (and already occurring).

THE "SALESMAN'S" POINT OF VIEW

I do not present this point of view spuriously. It is real, in many cases fairly held, and it continues to recur as turnover in sales staff takes place every few years. It is, however, largely wrong.

This point of view (perhaps unfairly named) holds that the whole business of performance contracting is simply one of marketing—specifically product packaging and sales. The salesman's point of view is that there is a need in the marketplace and that the smart company (and salesman) simply provides what it is that the customer thinks they need. Within this mindset:

- the project is just a somewhat unique assembly of widgets (lighting, digital controls, some chillers, perhaps a few rooftop units, etc.)

- engineering is a commodity at best (in fact it really is only needed to identify the parts needed, not to really do any analysis or design)

- energy audits and studies use things like impossible-to-understand-or-prove computer simulations

- it is really the owner's ultimate responsibility to make everything work

- the "guarantee" is only there because the competition offers it as well

Combine this with levels of sales performance bonuses that are generally unequaled elsewhere in the

HVAC: industry, and you have very little motivation for taking the performance contracting process seriously.

And the truth is, given buildings of low complexity, a large inventory of facilities over which to spread risk, a little bias on the salesman's part towards ethical behavior, a company possessing some actual, practical energy retrofit acumen, and you can actually produce workable projects.

But "accidents" don't equal good policy & good procedure—as, for example, a few ESCo's learned in the recent past.

The first of these was competing for the large project described in the Summer 1998 *Energy & Environmental Management* article "What Do Customers Want Besides Lower Energy Costs?" During the interviews at the ESCo's office, this one ESCo responded to an inquiry regarding their engineering resources by rattling off five consulting firms' names in a single breath. What this told us (and the owner) was that this ESCo viewed engineering as a pure commodity (the firms they named ranged in capability from not-good-enough-to-build-a-dog-house to the best in the business—frightening indeed!), and that they had so many names meant that they did not have a solid working relationship with any of these firms. This, among other reasons, got them "cut from the squad." Curiously, we later learned that the performance contracting manager (and interview leader) for this ESCo had "learned" the business working for a competitor best known for their marketing skills rather than their execution skills.

The second of these was another Fortune-500 that had signed an audit agreement with a medium sized school district (21 sites, 900,000+ square feet). This one page agreement provided for the ESCo to prepare a "detailed energy audit" (yes, those three words were the entire specification for the audit) for a fee of $75,000. Upon completion of their work, they presented the owner with a 36 page audit report. This was very disconcerting to the owner, who requested that more detailed information be provided. After a few more submissions by the ESCo (a total of four, one original and three supplements), we were finally brought in to assist the owner. Amazingly, after four submissions, there was still not a single energy savings calculation in the audit report(s)! When privately questioned on this later, the ESCo replied, "Well, we don't give our customers detailed information, because they trust us." Based upon our recommendations, the owner insisted that the ESCo fill in the details (in spite of the fact that they trusted their ESCo) and eventually closed the deal with this Fortune 500 on a $3,000,000 performance contract. The ESCo in this case has still not figured out the folly of their strategy or that it cost them almost a year's delay in the project (this lack of "corporate memory" is one of the bad side effects of rapid turnover in this relatively volatile industry). Curiously, the sales manager for this Fortune 500 later joined Enron as a performance contracting manager!

The third of these was a Fortune 500 that was completing the first of (they hoped) a series of performance contracts for a large school district in the Southwest. As the first phase project was completing, the owners project manager got nervous and called in a consultant to audit the project. What the consultant discovered was that the work promised by the performance contractor was, to a large extent, incomplete. The ESCo had promised in writing to restore existing HVAC equipment to a like-new condition, but actually never really intended to do this—a bit of sales chicanery if you would—claiming instead that only work needed to produce the guaranteed energy savings was ever intended. The consultant interpreted the contract language literally and reported his findings accordingly. The ensuing dispute resulted in future large projects being canceled and the Fortune 500 incurring large legal fees attempting to restore their integrity in the eyes of the bystanders.

A BETTER POINT OF VIEW

* truly better point of view is one which serves the (long term) best interests of all the parties involved. As developed over nearly two decades of experience in the field, presented in our nationwide seminar on performance contracting and as embodied in the performance contracting program we developed for the State of California (and for our clients like the San Francisco Unified School District) is an open-book, process-oriented, qualification-based, pay-as-you-go approach to performance contracting. This approach is as follows, and due to its very nature opens the door for the use of investment grade audits:

- The owner prepares a preliminary assessment of conservation potential to gauge the opportunity and likelihood of success of a performance contract.

- ESCo's are considered and selected on the <u>basis of their qualifications</u>—in return for which they agree to an open book process and pre-agreed margins and definitions of project costs.

- The ESCo is <u>paid</u> for doing the investment grade audit and must meet a fairly stringent criteria for the audit, including full disclosure of all the audit information, including cost estimates and sub/vendor quotes—and making a commitment to a (reasonable) minimum level of savings, else they do not get paid (see further comment on this below).

- The Owner participates in developing the audit and selecting the final package of retrofit measures to be implemented under the program.

- The parties enter into an Energy Services Agreement (ESA) which is a third-party document that both parties examine at the very beginning of the process, and is finalized following completion of the audit.

- The project is designed, documented, installed and commissioned according to fairly stringent criteria in the ESA.

- Ongoing measurement and verification is conducted for only a fairly short "guarantee demonstration period" (nominally 14 months) following completion of the installation so as to <u>keep M&V costs to a minimum</u> and to <u>focus the concentration of both parties on making sure everything works</u>—rather than waiting for a year or more to even check the results (which is <u>very</u> often the case).

This approach solves virtually all the ills we have discovered in the process of creating a performance contracting business unit for a Fortune-500 company and doing lots of expert testimony and remediation work in this field. Moreover, it solves the problem of the investment grade audit—<u>that it all too often isn't done</u>.

WHY INVESTMENT GRADE AUDITS ARE IMPORTANT

The foundation of every performance contract or energy services project is the technical problems in a facility which cause it to perform poorly and waste energy. It is identifying the problems, or <u>opportuni-</u>

ties, developing technically and organizationally workable fixes, and putting those fixes in place that makes the whole process work. Treating the audit like a commodity, then, is like getting your quadruple bypass diagnosis from your physician's receptionist. No matter how good he is, the receptionist's opinion is of little value. No indeed, when considering major surgery, nothing short of a Mayo Clinic physical is what most of us would insist upon. Then why do anything less for your building when considering major surgery for it?

Besides laying the foundation for the entire project, the investment grade audit does some other good things for the project as well. These benefits, by the way, **benefit the ESCo** as well as the building owner, and include:

- it dramatically increases the retrofit team's familiarity and knowledge of the facility—which will help the savings analysis, cost estimating, design and installation

- it increases the documentation shared by the parties, which will help to resolve change orders and other potential disputes later in the process

- it puts the numbers "on the table" so that the owner sees exactly what the costs are and serves to co-opt the owner into the process—which helps to avoid buyer's remorse down the road (but also prevent the unscrupulous ESCo from employing "value pricing," i.e., exorbitant mark-ups—this is good for all you "straight-up" ESCo's!!)

- it provides a set of construction documents that allows the more effective management of subs, commissioning, construction coordination, commissioning, etc.

- it provides a solid base of data for establishing the baseline which will be used during measurement & verification

In our experience, we have never found a single ethical ESCo who wouldn't "kill" for the chance to open his books in return for being part of a qualifications-based-selection and negotiated contract process. Only those who have admitted to us that their policy is "rape, pillage and burn" have found this approach unworkable. But, hey, too bad for them.

THE INVESTMENT GRADE AUDIT DEFINED

So what is this thing we're referring to as an "investment grade audit"? Well, it's a lot of things, but mostly it is a process of investigation and creation and documentation. Our criteria runs quite a few pages in the contract documents we prepare for our clients, but basically it includes the following:

- Energy Accounting. Before anyone even steps into the buildings, the very first step should be the gathering of all the energy data for the facilities and analyzing it to develop energy use and cost indices. This data can be used to triage multiple facilities (such as school districts) into three groups of facilities (big/bad energy "hogs," big-and-moderately-bad/small-but-seriously-bad, and the "don't waste your time") so that effort on the audit and on the retrofit program can be directed accordingly. We saw one Fortune-500 some years ago spend as much money retrofitting 40,000 Btu/sf/yr elementary schools as they did on 100,000 Btu/sf/yr schools for lack of understanding this step (the whole project team were later given the opportunity to find new jobs, by the way).

- Field surveys. We identify two basic types, The first of these is the "observation" survey during which the auditors look at what is going on in the building—and why. This survey is intended to identify problems (but not yet quantify them). The second type is the "data gathering" survey, in which name plate data, instantaneous measurement or time-series data is gathered for quantification of the energy used and the potential for savings. Following the field survey, the ESCo is required to issue a preliminary report and make a go/no-go recommendation. If the ESCo's commitment to a minimum level of savings that can be financed in a self-funded project cannot be met, this is the time for them to pull out and cut their losses (far superior to having a bunch of ESCo's doing "B.S." audits on speculation and "ginning up" savings figures out of the "ether' during a request-for-proposal process).

- Energy balance/computer modeling. As we have explored in numerous papers (and in our Fairmont Press book published in 2000), computerized simulation does not have to be costly, especially if modest approaches (such as spreadsheet models) are used. Some avoid building simulation due to their perception of its high cost. However, whether it is used or not, at some point an accounting of all the sources and use of energy (sound familiar to you MBA's out there?) must be done. The purpose of the energy balance is to prevent double counting of savings and to keep all the estimates of savings bounded by the energy attributed to the end use processes being retrofitted. Don't laugh. One Fortune-500 we know of guaranteed $150,000 per year in gas savings on a building that only used $50,000 worth of gas to begin with!

- Energy Conservation Measure (ECM) development. Each ECM under consideration should have developed for it an outline scope of work, preliminary sizing calculations, preliminary equipment selection, sketches (for complicated ECM's), detailed cost estimates, and both a statement of the principles of how the ECM will save energy and how that energy savings will be estimated (e.g., "air handlers run at night when it is cool and the space served needs cooling—we will add outside air economizers for "free" cooling and simulate on DOE-2 by adding economizers to the retrofitted air handling systems").

- Detailed savings calculations. Someone at some point has to sit down and say what they think the savings from a given retrofit is going to be. This needs to be documented, by type of energy saved, by piece of equipment being modified, as a percent of the equipment/end use being modified (numbers greater than 100 not allowed!) and the M&V approach planned for the retrofit (yes, M&V starts at the beginning, not the end of the project).

- Audit report. All the data gathered above and all of the analysis needs to be bundled up in the final report. This report should be presented to the owner in draft form, the ECM "package" discussed and negotiated, and the report then finalized.

Our standards for doing this work also include criteria for the engineer performing the audit as well. Generally we are primarily looking for engineers other than traditional consultants who do new construction, as it is rare that new-construction consultants have practical retrofit expertise. Similarly, we avoid what we call the 'study kings," i.e., those firms

that have traditionally specialized in audit work for "low buck" government agencies and have little expertise in designing and commissioning actual projects, We generally look for design-build experience, control system experience and building simulation experience in selecting consultants for our clients. Building owners are cautioned here as many of the folks out there in the performance contracting business are unable to discriminate between competent energy engineers and the rest—which actually (and unfortunately) reinforces the "salesman's" point of view discussed above when a less-than-competent auditor is employed.

Now, the above describes a pretty rigorous process, and if you're doing a 1,000,000 square foot high rise in the center of town, this is definitely the way to go. However, and as we have previously alluded to above, if you're working with an elementary school district, a much "lighter" approach would make sense. We would still call this an investment grade audit, thought the level of site investigation and the rigor of the energy balance/building simulation would be significantly relaxed. The documentation would be commensurately lighter as well, though we would still expect it to be fully comprehensive in nature.

As a rule of thumb, we expect to spend 10 to 300 per square foot, or 5 to 10% of the annual energy bill in doing investment grade audits. Generally this represents a value in a range of 5 to 10% of the overall value of the project. This is another area where intimate involvement between the owner's and the ESCo's organization is important as the allocation of the engineering resources to the various facilities should really be a collaborative endeavor.

FINAL

To some, this rigorous form of energy audit is new. Well, some energy engineers, your author included, have been doing instrumented surveys and investment grade audits since the late 1970's. At that time we could not imagine asking our employers to "roll the dice" on anything but a rigorously-performed audit.

In fact we found it both curious (and frustrating) that only government agencies and other quasi-government institutions felt that "ordinary' audits lacking in rigor, were acceptable. We could only conclude that accountability apparently had a lot to do with the judgment of what was acceptable, Perhaps this also explains why the vernacular 20 years ago used by real energy engineers when referring to rigorous audits was "engineering feasibility studies"—to avoid the stigma of the term "audit'.

To close, we believe that it is important to observe that not a single project that has followed our process has ever come to naught. While some have bemoaned the "high cost" of investment grade audits, we can think of no better (or cheaper) "insurance" for success than doing the homework, and doing it right.

ABOUT THE AUTHOR

James P. Waltz, President of Energy Resource Associates, Inc., is an acknowledged pioneer in the field of energy management. Prior to the Arab Oil Embargo of 1973, Mr. Waltz made a personal commitment to energy management as a key focus of his engineering career. Since that time, he has served as energy management program manager for the Air Force Logistics Command and the University of California Lawrence Livermore National Laboratory. In addition he hay worked as an energy management engineer for consulting and contracting firms. In 1981 he founded Energy Resource Associates for the purpose of helping to shape the then-emerging energy services industry—and did so through a multi-year assignment to create a still successful energy services business unit for a Fortune 500 temperature controls manufacturer.

Specializing in the mechanical, electrical and control systems of existing buildings, Mr. Waltz's firm hay accomplished a wide variety of facilities projects, recently including a corporate-wide energy management program review fir a major hospital chain, design of a replacement chilled water plant for a northern California hospital, on-site recommissioning of the entire building automation system for another large northern California hospital and audit and expert testimony relating to a failed energy services contract for a large southern California hospital.

Mr. Waltz's firm was the State of California's sole performance contracting consultant during their performance contracting program development and provides performance contracting owners representative services for such clients as the Veterans Administration in 18 western states.

Mr. Waltz's credentials include a Bachelors Degree in Mechanical Engineering, a Masters Degree in Business Administration, Professional Engineering Registration in three states, charter member of and Certified Energy Manager of the Association of Energy Engineers (AEE), board certified Forensic Engineer, member of the Association of Energy Services Professionals (AESP), Demand Side Management Society (DSMS) and the American Society of Heating Refrigeration and Air Conditioning Engineers (ASHRAE).

Mr. Waltz's serves as a member of the DOE's measurement and verification protocol technical committee, responsible for the 1997 International Performance Measurement and Verification Protocol (IPMVP), formerly known as the North American Energy Measurement & Verification Protocol (NEMVP).

Mr. Waltz was named International Energy Engineer of the Year in 1993 by the Association of Energy Engineers(AEE) and taught a nationwide performance contracting seminar through the AEE. He may be reached at www.eraenergy.com.

Chapter 13

ADVANCED TOOLS FOR ENERGY AUDITING

W. Mark Arney, P.E., CEM   Senior Engineer
Facility Dynamics Engineering

ABSTRACT

Energy audits are typically performed in two phases. The first is a preliminary [or walkthrough] audit. The second is more comprehensive and is often called an investment grade audit. This paper will present two advanced techniques that are useful for conducting a comprehensive energy audit. These techniques are short term diagnostic testing and functional performance testing.

Even though a building remains comfortable to occupants, operation and maintenance problems may still exist. Short-term diagnostic testing, which is the application of specialized software and hardware tools to gather and analyze data for the evaluation of the performance of building energy systems, can be used as tool to uncover "hidden" operational problems that are difficult, if not impossible, to identify in any other way. These problems can cause excess energy consumption and/or equipment damage. Short-term diagnostic testing can also verify the presence, magnitude, and nature of other problems that were suspected by the operations staff or discovered through on-site audits. The monitored data can be used to estimate the savings from the tune-up work.

Functional performance testing is a process used in building commissioning and is used to verify the performance of HVAC system components and controls. Typically a system [for example an air hander or chiller] is forced through all possible modes of operation to test the control sequences. This is done after a thorough inspection of individual devices such as valves and dampers.

The concept of continuous commissioning, where periodic checks of operational parameters are made on a regular basis, is another advanced technique that can be applied to the energy auditing process.

The paper will describe these three techniques and will show some examples of their application.

INTRODUCTION

Short-term diagnostic testing is the application of specialized software and hardware tools to gather and analyze data for the evaluation of the performance of building energy systems. In addition to O&M assessments and commissioning, short-term diagnostic testing results are useful for calibration of building simulation models, impact evaluation of utility demand-side management programs, and baselining for energy service companies.

THE APPLICATION OF SHORT TERM DIAGNOSTIC TESTING TO ENERGY AUDITING

Previously published papers (1, 2) have presented in-depth information on the application of short-term diagnostic testing to the building commissioning process. A summary of this process, as it applies to energy auditing, is as follows:

- survey buildings
- develop monitoring plan.
- install data loggers and sensors
- retrieve and analyze data
- develop list of fixes
- perform fixes

Optional steps:
- re-install monitoring equipment on affected systems

- retrieve and analyze post-fix data to verify that problems were fixed
- calculate savings from fixes using monitored data and other references.

The selection of monitoring points is tailored to the type of systems found within a building and is prioritized by equipment size, energy savings potential, and ease of monitoring. If there is a large number of similar equipment, such as packaged rooftop units, a representative sample is chosen. Monitoring equipment is typically installed at three levels: 1) plant level, this may include boilers, chillers and associated pumps, 2) system level, including air side and fan measurements, 3) zone level, including measurements made at the terminal boxes and the conditioned space. The zone level monitoring is generally limited to areas of known problems or complaints, since the tune-up of terminal equipment has minimal energy impacts. Any other special equipment with major loads or suspected problems can be included.

A wide range of operational items with energy saving potential can be discovered with short-term diagnostic testing. Some general types of problems are as follows:

- scheduling: equipment found on at night, weekends and during other times when it was assumed to be off
- system operation above or below setpoint
- excessive cycling of equipment
- malfunctioning controls (economizers, reset)
- simultaneous heating and cooling
- EMS loops not working optimally
- controls permanently overridden by building operators

OTHER METHODS FOR ENERGY AUDITING
More traditional methods for O&M assessment include on-site auditing/spot testing, utility bill analysis, and EMS trend logs. Usually a combination of these methods will be used. An on-site meeting and walkthrough is always necessary to interview operators, assess documentation, and to obtain an understanding for how O&M is approached in the building. This method can easily detect problems that are apparent from a visual inspection such as dirty filters, loose belts, failing insulation, leaky valves, etc.

Spot checking equipment with hand held instruments may turn up additional problems. However, these tests only observe the operation of the equipment at one instant in time. Functional testing using the EMS to simulate various conditions can provide additional information. However, it is costly and time-consuming to check everything by hand. Utility bill analysis can only assess the gross level operations information such as a high EUI or off season operation of major equipment. Utility bill trending can indicate that a problem exists, but generally cannot identify the source of the problem.

The primary advantages of short-term diagnostic testing as compared to these methods are that dynamic interactions of components comprising the system can be observed. Monitoring systems over a period of days or weeks can uncover problems that could not be found with simple one-time tests.

EMS point trending has many similarities to short-term diagnostic testing, but also has some limitations as a diagnostic tool. Some of the most important limitations of this approach are as follows:

- sampling rates are too slow to discover many problems
- memory is limited, so large data sets cannot be saved in one file
- only a small set of points can be trended at one time
- the data can't be trusted unless sensors have been calibrated
- building operator may not know how to set up trends
- consistent time-series data are difficult to gather
- points critical to short-term diagnostic testing are not available
- output format is often difficult to import into analysis tools such as spreadsheets

APPLICATIONS OF DIAGNOSTIC TESTING
Five buildings from different climate zones are presented. In general these buildings have an on-site operator, an age of two to ten years, size over 50,000 ft^2, and are part of the retail or office sector. Table 1 presents a brief summary of the buildings.

TABLE 1. SUMMARY OF MONITORED BUILDINGS

Building	Type	Location	Size (ft²)
1	Office	Oregon	278,000
2	Office	Tennessee	250,000
3	Office	Arizona	80,000
4	Retail	Colorado	122,000
5	Retail	Massachusetts	107,000

The following section presents one of the most informative diagnostic plots from each building. Thirty to forty plots similar to these are typically plotted and analyzed for each audited building.

Building 1

The Oregon building, a 15 story Class A office structure in downtown Portland, is heated with in-line electric resistance duct heaters located in each zone which are controlled by a zone thermostat. A few years prior to the audit an EMS was added to the building. As part of the EMS retrofit, relays were installed on each floor to help control the duct heaters and reduce heating costs. A control strategy that locked out the heaters whenever the average zone temperature on each floor was above 72.5°F **and** the ambient air temperature was between 60°F-70°F (depending on the compass face of the building) was implemented. This strategy was deemed successful and quickly paid for the entire cost of the EMS.

While developing the monitoring plan for this building, the engineer decided to monitor a sample of duct heaters to assess the control of the heaters and analyze the potential for energy savings. Sixteen circuits on three floors were monitored, representing 8% of the total connected load. Figure 1 shows the data from three monitored circuits on one of the floors. The plot indicates that all three circuits operated extensively during the monitoring period (July 21 through August 4), even at temperatures above 80°F, indicating a control strategy problem. The different grouping of data points represent the times when all circuits were off; or one, two, or three, circuits were energized.

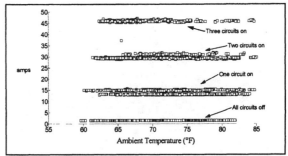

FIGURE 1. PORTLAND DUCT HEATERS

A new control strategy was proposed to lower the ambient lockout temperatures and change the conditional statement from **and** to **or**, so that meeting only one of the conditions would shut off the heaters.

Post fix monitoring was performed on the same circuits as in the pre-fix phase. In general, the edited control routine appeared to be working, with one major exception. The controls contractor was called in and found a burned out relay that was preventing the heaters from being locked out in one area.

A linear regression model was developed from the duct heater kWh and ambient temperature data. A comparison of the pre and post fix data indicates an annual savings of $3,330 from the fix. The potential savings could be much greater than this if the lockout temperatures are further reduced. Many office buildings in the Portland area do not use any heating in the summer months, so it seems reasonable to assume that this building could be operated in a similar fashion. Additional strategies to reduce summer heating will include adjustment of VAV box minimum air settings and implementation of a supply air reset strategy.

Building 4

The mechanical systems of the Denver building, a two story department store anchoring a shopping mall, were comprised of a single multizone air handler, and a central plant consisting of two chillers and two boilers. During the cooling season, a precooling routine in the EMS was set to start the systems at 5 a.m. and bring in 100% outdoor air whenever the ambient enthalpy was below the interior enthalpy. Figure 2 shows the upper floor space temperature over a two week period in August.

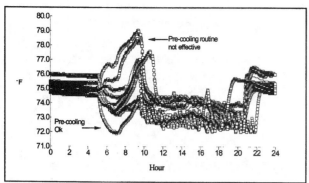

FIGURE 2. DENVER SPACE TEMPERATURE

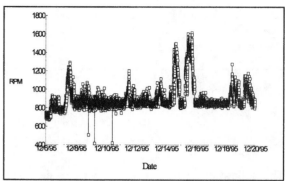

FIGURE 3. NASHVILLE CHILLED WATER PUMP

As one can see from the plot, there were times when the precooling routine resulted in preheating instead, actually increasing the startup load on the chillers. The problem is that the EMS sequence runs this routine at too small of a difference between indoor and ambient enthalpies, and the fans and motor both add heat to the supply air stream. The fix for this problem was to increase the difference in enthalpy that controlled the precooling loop. By the time the fix was completed the building was well out of cooling season, so no data are available to verify if the new setpoints were successful.

Building 2
This large institutional office building in Tennessee is connected to both district chilled water and district steam loops. A single 40 horsepower chilled water pump supplies water to air handlers located on each floor of this high-rise. The pump must run 24 hours per day year-round in order to serve a few mainframe computer rooms. Prior to the assessment, the variable frequency drive (VFD) controlling the motor was frequency tripped, thus defaulting the pump operation to full speed (1800 rpm). Even with the VFD operating, the pump ran at full speed due to faulty EMS control loop logic, a larger than necessary pressure setpoint and a number of heretofore unknown chilled water bypasses and leaks. With such low off-season and night time flow requirements, getting the VFD to modulate the pump speed was identified as a key fix for this building.

Figure 3 is a time-series plot of chilled water pump RPM for the post-fix monitoring period. Prior to this, the control logic was improved, bypasses reduced and the pressure setpoint lowered. Another round of adjustments in setpoints and control logic has resulted in reducing the minimum flow rate to 25% of full speed.

Periods with higher RPM were warm days when the air handlers were calling for cooling. Otherwise the pump was running close to minimum speed for most of the two week monitoring period. Shaft RPM, or trending the control signal, are the preferred ways to measure performance of VSDs because of power quality problems that confound accurate current and power measurements, and the non-linearity of current relative to motor speed.

DOE2 was used to calculate an annual savings of $7,311 for this measure, based on a minimum operating speed of 30%. The long-term goal is to run the pump at a lower minimum flow rate by installing a new differential pressure sensor to improve the overall system control.

Building 3
This four story office building in Phoenix contained a water loop heat pump system. As one would expect, the system rarely operates in the heating mode. When the assessment team began work, the building had recently changed management, and the new staff was anxious to remedy some of the past ignorance of proper O&M procedures and capture some energy savings. In particular, the system scheduling controls had been bypassed so the building was being operated as though it was occupied 24 hours a day. From the initial building walkthrough, it was obvious that the main loop circulating pump, cooling tower fans and spray pumps were all energized at all times. The night time behavior of the zone heat pumps could not be determined from a day time walkthrough.

Forty-five of the building's 95 heat pumps were monitored at the circuit breaker level. Each circuit powers three to five individual heat pumps. Three circuits (480 volt, three phase) were grouped together on four different current transformers to reduce monitoring costs. Figure 4 shows a three day time-series plot from one of the current transformers. This profile is typical for all days of the monitoring period (November 10 to November 24). As one can see, there is significant night time operation of the heat pumps. Note that November 18th was a Saturday, which is an unoccupied day.

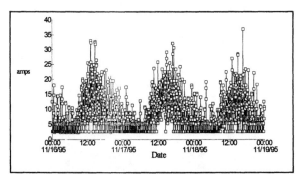

FIGURE 4. PHOENIX HEAT PUMPS

In Phoenix, November is considered part of the swing season. One would expect much more cooling energy to be used in the summer months. In addition, the occupants have control of the zone thermostats. This could also tend to increase cooling requirements if the thermostat was lowered on hot afternoons and left there until the next morning.

Typical weekend and weekday profiles similar to the one shown above were analyzed to calculate the average number of kWh per day for weekends and weekdays as well as the occupied/ unoccupied energy use for the weekdays. The estimated savings from proper scheduling of the heat pumps is 177,000 kWh per year resulting in an annual operating cost savings of $8,850.

Building 5
This single story "big box" type building in eastern Massachusetts has a large refrigeration load. There are two large compressor racks, one serving low temperature (frozen) cases and the other serving medium temperature cases. There are eleven separate electric defrost circuits in these cases. Figure 5 presents a two day profile showing all the defrost circuits. One leg of the three phase, 480 volt circuits was monitored.

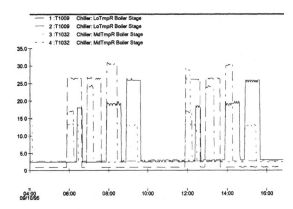

FIGURE 5. MASSACHUSETTS DEFROST HEATERS

Each stage is set to operate four times per day. During each cycle, there are times when up to four defrost circuits are coincident. The coincident demand of these circuits is about 68 kW. During the tune-up work, the defrost schedules were reprogrammed. Post tune-up data revealed the coincident demand had been reduced 18 kW per month for a resulting annual savings of $3900.

FUNCTIONAL PERFORMANCE TESTING
Functional Performance Testing (FPT) is a key component of the building commissioning process that also has direct applications to energy auditing. When commissioning is applied to existing buildings the term retrocommissioning is often used. Many steps in the retrocommissioning process are very similar to task done in a comprehensive energy audit, especially in the initial part of the projects.

Functional performance testing verifies the intended operation of individual components and system interactions under various conditions and modes of operation. The systems are run through all of the sequences of operation and the response of components is verified. Testing proceeds from components to subsystems to systems, and finally to interlocks and connections between systems. For example: on a typical built up air handler the dampers s and valves are fully inspected and stroked before testing control sequences. Prior to on site testing a test plan is developed for a particular piece of equipment based on the configuration of the equipment and sequence of operation.

One key advantage of FPT over short term diagnostic testing is the ability to test all modes of operation. In short term test only a portion of the full functionality of a system is tested.

81

CONTINUOUS COMMISSIONING

Another term coined in the commissioning industry is continuous commissioning. This is where systems, components, and controls are checked on a regular periodic basis, as opposed to just a single time in the traditional commissioning process. This helps to guarantee that the persistence of savings is maintained. Automated tools are available to assist in continuous commissioning. They are usually backed by a database application such as Microsoft Access that can handle large amount of data. For this process data from the EMS as opposed to data loggers is ideal.

CONCLUSIONS

The power of information technology can greatly enhance the energy auditing process. Many "hidden" O&M problems can be found with short-term diagnostic testing. Other known problems can be verified and quantified. Functional performance testing and continuous commissioning are other techniques that can be applied to the energy auditing process.

BIBLIOGRAPHY

(1) Arney, W.M. and D.F. Frey. 1994. "Short Term Diagnostic Testing to Streamline Commissioning," *Proceedings from the Third National Conference on Building Commissioning.* Portland Energy Conservation, Inc.

(2) Waterbury, S.S., D.J. Frey, K. F. Johnson. 1994. "Commercial Building Performance Evaluation System for HVAC Diagnostics and Commissioning," *Proceedings from The ACEEE 1994 Summer Study for Energy Efficiency in Buildings*, Volume 5. American Council for an Energy Efficient Economy, Washington, D.C.

AUTHOR'S BIO

W. Mark Arney, a Senior Engineer at Facility Dynamics Engineering, is responsible for project management, energy analysis, commissioning, measurement and verification (M&V), and system diagnostics for projects in the building industry. Mr. Arney has been involved in building energy analysis and facilities management since 1981. He is a registered Professional Engineer in the State of Colorado and is a Certified Energy Manager.

Chapter 14

AIR FORCE PERFORMANCE CONTRACTING IN THE US AND OVERSEAS

Jeffrey G. Stringfield, P.E.
Solutions Development Team Lead
Honeywell International Inc.
&
K. Quinn Hart, P.E.
Air Force Facilities Energy Program Manager
HQ Air Force Civil Engineer Support Agency

INTRODUCTION

Performance contracting for the Federal market has been growing rapidly the last several years. The contracting vehicles from various Federal agencies are different and present different challenges to the energy savings performance contractors (ESCOs) performing the work. This paper will highlight performance contracting solutions development for the Air Force Bases in the US and the Air Bases overseas. The process reviewed in this paper is geared for that mandated by the Air Force Region 5 Contract. It is not necessary for this process to be followed by other contract vehicles.

The total Air Force performance contracting is divided into Six regions in the US. Honeywell is the ESCO for the work in Region 5, which includes Air Force installations located in Washington, Oregon, Arizona, Utah, California, Hawaii, Alaska, Idaho, Nevada, and South Korea (Osan and Kunsan only). The contract maximum is $250,000,000. The dollar amount is calculated as "sum total of scheduled Government payments over the life of the contract, inclusive of the total contractor investment (direct labor (including subcontractor markups), materials, and equipment), operations and maintenance costs, finance charges in the form of interest, profit, and overhead"[1]. Although interest is an allowable cost, Honeywell is not allowed to add any markup to the financing cost. This cost

is a direct pass through cost from the financing institution. The Region 5 Contract term is 25 years from the date of award (10 Sep 1998).

The task orders for each base are performed in three phases. This paper will cover a process used for the Air Force for the three phases and concentrate on the most intensive process - Phase II, which is the Solutions Development and Detailed Proposal phase. Phase II includes the Investment Grade Survey, measurements and testing, baseline development, calculations, proposal development and negotiations prior to the Project Implementation Phase III.

The paper will cover what is required in developing the Phase I, Preliminary Report and transitioning to the Phase II, Investment Grade Survey and Detailed Proposal. The Phase I Report is a preliminary report recommending the Energy Conservation Projects (ECP) and estimates the project implementation costs and savings (energy and maintenance). The Phase II Proposal includes the Investment Grade Survey (IGS) and surveys, evaluates and recommends the ECPs to be implemented in the Phase III, Construction.

SUMMARY OF PAPER

The areas that will be discussed will be as follows:
- Three Phases of Air Force Contract
  - Phase I Report
  - Phase II IGS and Proposal
  - Phase III Construction
- Typical ECPs
- IGS Process
  - Systems Surveyed
  - Base Information Gathering
  - Base Access
  - Utility Analysis

- Baseline Measurement and Testing
- Measurements and Verification Plan
- ECP Level of Design
- Energy Projects
- Pricing and Subcontractors
- Modeling Techniques
  - Lighting Retrofits
  - Daylighting Retrofits
  - HVAC Retrofits
- Commissioning Recommendations
- Warranties and Guarantees
- Maintenance Recommendations
- US and Overseas Differences
- Challenges for Air Force.

THREE PHASES OF AIR FORCE CONTRACT

The Air Force contracting vehicle is divided into three Phases of work as follows:

- Phase I - Preliminary Site Survey and Report
- Phase II - Facility Energy Audit and Economic Analysis and Proposal
- Phase III - Project Implementation and Operation/Maintenance.

This paper will discuss the first two Phases because they are considered the solutions and development phases. The three Phases are defined as follows:

Phase I Report

The initial Phase I Report includes the preliminary survey and calculations to develop a feasibility report. The report highlights the recommended Energy Conservation Projects (ECP) and estimated implementation costs, savings and paybacks. Prior to starting the survey the Air Force Base Contracting Officer submits a release letter prioritizing the facilities and giving the ESCO the approval to develop the Phase I Report. Phase II also requires a Contracting Officer release letter.

The scope of the report will include the energy conservation opportunities evaluated in the prioritized facility listings identified in the Phase I Release Letter. Preliminary site survey and feasibility study including the following activities.

- Preliminary survey of facilities included in the scope
- Utility analysis of electric, gas, fuel oil, water, and other utilities
- Listing of Recommendation, deferred and rejected ECPs
- Financial analysis including:
  - Implementation cost
  - Energy savings
  - O&M savings
  - Payback
  - Financial term of lease (do you mean "Loan")
  - Financial analysis
  - Construction schedule
  - Maintenance & M&V recommendations.

The scope definition allows the ESCO to survey and provide a report giving the energy savings potential of the facility and possible recommended ECPs to be proposed. The Phase I study gives the base the potential of energy savings and infrastructure improvements and gives them the ability to select the projects that will provide the most cost-effective energy savings and upgrades.

Executive Order 13123 requires Federal Buildings to reduce their energy consumption by 30% by the year 2005 and 35% by the year 2010. The energy savings resulting from the various task orders will help the base and the Air Force meet these aggressive energy goals.

Table 1 summarizes the Region 5 Air Force bases implemented and proposed task orders.

TABLE 1 – REGION 5 AIR FORCE BASES TASK ORDERS PHASE I, II AND III

Air Force Base	No. of Task Orders/Pending Projects	Projected Savings
Luke Air Force Base, Phoenix, Arizona Davis-Monthan Air Force Base, Tucson, Arizona Fairchild Air Force Base, Spokane, Washington Travis Air Force Base, Sacramento, California Los Angeles Air Force Base, Los Angeles, California Hickam Air Force Base, Honolulu, Hawaii Hill Air Force Base, Salt Lake City, Utah Mountain Home Air Force Base, Boise, Idaho Kunsan Air Base, Gunsan, South Korea Osan Air Base, Songtan, South Korea	13/ 6	$197,589,768*

* These costs are for 13 awarded contracts and 6 Phase I reports or Phase II Proposals submitted to the Air Force. The costs are the total dollars expended or the total dollars saved for the term of the contract.

Phase II Proposal
The Phase II includes the Investment Grade Survey (IGS) and the detailed proposal for the recommended ECPs. The Proposal is divided into the following Exhibits.

- Exhibit A - Synopsis of Proposed ECM
- Exhibit B - Calculation of Savings & M&V Plan
- Exhibit C - ESCO Compensation Format
- Exhibit D - Buildings
- Exhibit E - Baseline Data
- Exhibit F - ESCO Post-Implementation Responsibilities
- Exhibit G - Government Post-Implementation Responsibilities
- Exhibit H - Standards of Service
- Exhibit I - Final Performance Tests
- Exhibit J - Equipment Availability and ECM Implementation Schedule
- Exhibit K - Termination or Buyout Costs
- Exhibit L - Pre-Existing Equipment Inventory
- Exhibit M - Subcontracting Plan
- Exhibit N - ECPs Evaluated - Not Recommended for Implementation

Phase III Construction
The Phase III is the construction and implementation of the task order and includes the construction, testing, commissioning and on-going activities of the project. This paper will not detail this phase because it is not considered part of the solutions development. This is not to say that Phase III is not important. Implementation and follow-up can be the most important part of a successful energy savings project. This subject will be saved for another paper because of the extensive nature.

TYPICAL ECPs FOR AIR FORCE
Table 2 summarizes the types of Energy Conservation Projects (ECP) implemented for Region 5. Not all of the Air Force bases have implemented all the facilities and ECPs possible. There are a variety of reasons not all the facilities and ECPs are implemented.

- Most -Reimbursable facilities do not participate in the program
- Reimbursable facilities may need to have separate Task Orders from base facilities because of avoiding mixing funds
- Reimbursable customers may not wish to participate in program
- Military facilities may be very secure and not accessible for surveys and construction
- A portion of facilities are scheduled for demolition in the future
- Some buildings do not have HVAC or lighting systems

- Hazardous and low-use buildings do not have good energy paybacks.

IGS PROCESS
The Investment Grade Survey (IGS) is the most important step in the Phase II process. The Air Force believes the baseline, and measurements and verification development sets the accuracy and possibility for success of the energy savings. The energy savings and maintenance dollar savings pay for the project retrofits. If there is inaccuracy in the baseline energy usage and if the measurements and verification is not correctly applied, the customer will not realize the full energy savings dollars.

The IGS includes the survey, testing, preliminary design, and pricing for the development of the detailed proposal. When a base-wide survey is planned, it is important to make sure the IGS is organized and planned to provide an accurate and complete assessment of the possible ECPs for the entire base. The baseline development is the first thing to organize and the remaining IGS steps dovetail into the baseline structure.

Systems Surveyed in IGS
The following seven energy-consuming systems should be broken out for all the facilities studied in order to perform the IGS accurately.
1. Lighting systems
2. Control systems
3. Fan systems
4. Pump systems
5. Cooling systems
6. Heating systems
7. Industrial and Miscellaneous systems (compressed air, plating, irrigation, etc.)

These seven systems can make up the majority of the energy consumed on a military base. All of these systems contain energy generating savings that can help cash flow the entire task order. The energy generating ECPs can be developed and bundled with lower energy saving projects (projects not cash-flowing separately).

Typical Cash-generating ECPs are as follows:
- Lighting Retrofits
- Energy Management Control Systems
- Daylighting
- Occupancy Sensors and lighting controls
- Water and Sewer Conservation
- Conversion of Central Steam or HTHW to Distributed Boilers
- Central Steam or Chilled Water Retrofits

TABLE 2 – AIR FORCE BASES AND TYPES OF ECPs

Air Force Base	Types of Projects Proposed and Implemented
Luke Air Force Base, Phoenix, Arizona Davis-Monthan Air Force Base, Tucson, Arizona Fairchild Air Force Base, Spokane, Washington Travis Air Force Base, Sacramento, California Los Angeles Air Force Base, Los Angeles, California Hickam Air Force Base, Honolulu, Hawaii Hill Air Force Base, Salt Lake City, Utah Mountain Home Air Force Base, Boise, Idaho Kunsan Air Base, Gunsan, South Korea Osan Air Base, Songtan, South Korea	• Lighting Retrofits • Bi-level Lighting Controls • Lighting Occupancy Sensors • Workstation Occupancy Sensors • Energy Management Control Systems • HVAC Retrofits • Natural Daylighting and Controls • Water and Sewer Conservation • Building Total Systems Upgrades for 45,000 SF Facility • Central Steam Plant Conversion to Distributed Heating • Plate-and-Frame Free-Cooling Installation for Central Chilled Water Plant • Infrared Heating for Hangers & Warehouses • Steam Trap Retrofits • Solar Hot Water Heating • Solar Attic Ventilators • Chiller Replacements • Boiler Replacements • Variable Speed Pumping for Gas-Engine Driven Central Chilled Water Plant • Variable Volume HVAC System Installation • Water-Source Heat Pump Installation

There are other ECPs that can generate excess cash flow, but a lot depends on the utility rates, utility rebates, and maintenance savings. ECPs such as HVAC retrofits and installation intensive ECPs do not generate cash and normally need some of the above cash-generating ECPs to cash flow the project.

The most cost-effective base-wide IGS is to concentrate on the cash-generating ECPs and include only the number of cash-hog ECPs that will stay within the payback criteria of the entire task order. Studying more ECPs that don't fit within the cash flow of the entire bundle wastes IGS dollars and extends the timeline of the IGS. The Air Force contract allows a maximum simple payback of 10 years. "A ten-year simple payback is defined as the contractor's capital investment cost divided by the annual guaranteed savings"[1].

Base Information Gathering

The timeline of the IGS is very critical. The first task before starting the IGS is to gather the necessary information and documents, so as not to perform unnecessary tasks. It is best to develop a document that details the information necessary to streamline the IGS.

The following is a highlight of the information necessary to start the IGS.

• At least three years of utility usage and costs for base
• Utility rate structures
• Electronic listing of all facilities on base with square feet, user, and other pertinent information
• Listing of all buildings scheduled for demolition and year planned
• Listing of all reimbursable customers and buildings occupied
• Document listing all buildings planned for capital improvements and maintenance improvements
• Listing and telephone numbers of all building managers
• Listing of all facilities and HVAC equipment. Prefer list include sizes, type, model numbers, year installed, etc.

A standardized survey form should be developed to be used by each type of surveyor so complete information is gathered during the survey, and it is not necessary to back-track when it is discovered more information is needed.

Base Access

Base access is important to not delay the IGS. The following items and tasks should be completed before starting the IGS.

- Obtain mechanical room key
- Base should inform all base managers and commands of impending IGS
- All surveyors should get base access badges
- Obtain listing of all buildings needing special access requirements
- Surveyors should wear visible badges indicating surveyor is a contractor
- Surveyors should carry proof that they are allowed to perform survey.

Utility Analysis

After obtaining three or more years of utility usage and costs (including rate structure contracts) a utility analysis is required to determine the energy savings potential of each ECP evaluated. Example: If the electric rates include a ratchet clause or power factor penalty this will affect the type of ECP evaluated and the resulting savings.

Baseline Measurements and Testing

A Baseline Measurement and Testing Document should be developed and reviewed with the customer to get approval of the methodology used during the IGS. This is the most important part of the IGS and set the starting point and can make or break the ECPs. This is also a prerequisite to developing the Measurements and Verification program to be used for the task order.

Measurements and Verification Plan

A Measurements and Verification Plan (M&V) is required to set the parameters to be measured for the life of the task order. Meetings should be set up prior to submitting the detailed proposal to get agreement on the M&V. The associated costs for the M&V activities will be included as on-going costs for the project and these costs take away from the positive cash flow of the project. Unnecessary M&V should be avoided to not waste dollars and necessary M&V should be included to make sure the ESCO verifies that the energy savings are realized.

ECP Level of Design

Performance contracting is a form of design-build. Since solutions development includes the preliminary design for various ECPs, unnecessary expenditures of design dollars can be wasteful and take away from the cash flow of the task order. The following ECPs do not need a high level of traditional design in order to obtain good and accurate implementation costs or energy savings.

- Lighting retrofits, occupancy sensors and lighting controls
- Daylighting
- Water and Sewer conservation
- Energy Management and Control Systems (EMCS)
- Pumping and fan variable frequency drives.

The following ECPs can require more design effort.

- HVAC retrofits
- Central plant retrofits
- Other installation-intensive ECPs.

The level of preliminary design depends upon the amount of information to calculate accurate energy and maintenance savings and price accurate costs for the ECPs. The amount of design also needs to be sufficient to allow the Air Force to review and know what they are getting. Design dollars spent over that necessary for accurate dollars could be wasted if the ECP drops out of the task order bundle. This is why it is important to capture all the cash-generating ECPs and have the base prioritize the ECP projects. The ESCO is at risk for project development dollars spent in the IGS, even if the base decides to not implement the ECP.

Energy Projects

An energy project is an ECP that has energy savings associated with the retrofit. Projects such as landscaping, interior renovations, and structural improvements may not provide utility savings and may not be allowed to be included in the task order. Interior renovations and structural improvements may be included when it becomes necessary to perform interior retrofits or structural changes to meet the requirements of an ECP. The Air Force looks at the nature of the retrofit and if the work is associated with an energy project. The ESCO will loose the IGS development dollars and jeopardize the entire task order.

Pricing and Subcontractors

The development work with the subcontractors runs in parallel with the design and calculations part of the IGS. Scopes of Work (SOW) and Instructions to Bidders (ITB) need to be developed for competitive bidding of the various ECPs included in the detailed proposal. Copies of the successful bidders bids will be included in the proposal for review by the Air Force. The Air Force will require the ESCO to provide information that verifies that the different ECPs are competitively bid and the best bid was selected for the task order. If an ECP is not competitively bid, the ESCO will be subjected to additional pricing review to prove the pricing is reasonable. Other pricing and financial processes will not be covered in the paper.

Other Cost Considerations

When developing the SOWs and ITBs, the following pointers are recommended when obtaining bids from subcontractors.

- Include in the ITB package a detailed SOW, copy of the ESCO Subcontractor Agreement and applicable drawings. This will allow the subcontractor to provide a complete bid for the ECPs.
- Be very specific on the requirements for meeting IES lighting standards and detail exactly the buildings and areas, and the reason for not meeting IES.
- Detail exactly the requirements for disposal of lamps, ballasts and other hazardous waste disposal
- Asbestos will be encountered on the most complex projects. Highlight if the subcontractor or the Government will be responsible for asbestos removal and disposal.
- Include a detail schedule showing the milestone dates needed for the ECPs.

MODELING TECHNIQUES

The IGS calculations are performed using various models that determine the baseline energy usage and resulting energy savings. Normally simpler ECPs such as lighting and water conservation do not need complex calculation models. However, when dealing with numerous facilities and complex rate structures, careful development of savings formulas are necessary. It is best to use subcontractors performing the calculation models to perform the calculations to provide all the necessary outputs and information needed in the detailed proposal. The following listing of information and outputs are needed for the ECPs listed.

Lighting Retrofits

1. Building-by-building listing of energy, demand and burn-hours.
2. Space-by-space listing showing the existing lights and recommended retrofit.
3. Space-by-space listing showing the base energy usage, and demand savings.
4. Calculation of HVAC heating and cooling adjustment of savings.
5. Detail of lighting lamps and ballasts to dispose and the resulting disposal costs.
6. Material maintenance baseline and post-case costs and savings for proposed retrofits.
7. Number of each type of lamp, ballast, and fixture for existing and proposed.

Daylighting Retrofits

1. Building-by-building listing of energy, demand and burn-hours with number of fixtures controlled by daylight control module.

2. Building-by-building listing showing the base energy usage, and demand savings.
3. Size of each daylighting module unit and layout of each unit showing no interference with existing structure or fire protection pipes.

HVAC Retrofits

The more complex calculations are usually the ones dealing with heating, ventilating and air conditioning (HVAC) systems. Because there are so many variables affecting the energy usage complex models are needed. These include retrofits such as HVAC and central plant ECPs using varying types of baseline and energy savings models. When the facilities or recommended retrofits are very complex models such as DOE2 or Trace 700 can be used. If the use of these two canned-models are not cost effective the ESCO can development their own model for calculating the baseline and energy savings. At a minimum the following parameters should be taken into consideration when calculating the baseline and energy savings.

- Weather data including hourly or bin-temperature data
- HVAC per and post-operating schedules
- Number of building occupants
- Actual lighting kW and kWh (include lighting retrofit if applicable)
- Internal equipment heat gain affecting HVAC usage
- Temperature set-points for spaces affecting usage
- Space set-back criteria and other HVAC control modifications affecting usage.

There are much additional input necessary for an accurate model of baseline and energy savings. The baseline usage needs to be compared to the information gathered and tested during the IGS. This will calibrate the model, and the changes in the model input for the retrofit will provide accurate energy savings estimates.

ACCEPTANCE RECOMMENDATIONS

After installation is complete the ESCO needs to follow an accepted Acceptance Plan. This Acceptance Plan includes the method of startup, testing and measuring the installed equipment to verify the baseline usage and develop the necessary data for use in the on-going measurements and testing. It is important for the Acceptance Plan to include all the necessary equipment data to measure during the startup of the system and develop the data in an acceptable format. The Acceptance Plan will be given to the customer to approve so the ECPs can be accepted. Until all the task order ECPs are accepted the energy savings do not start accruing and payments cannot be made to the financing company for the subject project. "The Government will begin making payments to the ESCO beginning the month following the first full calendar month after acceptance of the energy conservation measure by the Government."[1]

WARRANTIES AND GUARANTEES

The detailed proposal will contain all the manufacturer's warranties. The Air Force Contract requires the ESCO to be responsible for maintaining and repairing the installed systems as well as achieving the energy savings for the entire term of the task order. This includes ensuring that the maintenance is being performed in accordance with the recommended maintenance procedures included in the detailed proposal. If the base is performing the maintenance tasks, this does not relieve the ESCO of responsibility for assuring the required tasks are performed.

The Region 5 Contract requires installed equipment to have a 1-year warranty. However, some materials and equipment having longer warranties are passed through to the Government. Some equipment manufacturers offer extended warranties that will cover labor and materials. This may be a benefit to the base and the ESCO to keep the maintenance costs down and generate more savings to cash-flow the project.

MAINTENANCE RECOMMENDATIONS

Maintenance requirements are different between ECPs and bases. Some equipment and systems will require maintenance to be provided from the ESCO and other will remain being maintained by the base staff. No matter who performs the maintenance the ESCO will be responsible to maintain the integrity of the system, so the savings are realized through the term of the contract. Through the measurements and testing activities the ESCO will need to determine if the maintenance is being performed and, if not, corrective action should be taken to get the system maintained.

US AND OVERSEAS DIFFERENCES

There are varying differences between implementing performance contracts in the US and overseas. The Region 5 Contract includes Air Force bases in the Western United States and Air Bases in South Korea, specifically Osan and Kunsan. Performing the required tasks for an IGS, subcontracting plan, measurements and verification and maintenance can be a challenge in South Korea or other overseas installations.

The complexity of doing overseas performance contracts is much more difficult than US-based contracts. The following areas need careful attention when doing projects overseas.

- Develop longstanding relationships with manufacturers and subcontractors.
- Military bases require project work to conform to US standards, so working with foreign manufactures and subcontractors should be avoided in certain cases.

- The major ECPs should be installed by the ESCO or the ESCO should contract with US-based contractors. Let the subcontractors deal with the foreign contractors.
- Davis Bacon Wage Rates do not apply to oversea work, but the country will probably have Labor Wage Laws that do apply.
- Consider contracting the on-going measurements and verification activities with a US contractor or the ESCO should perform the M&V.
- Develop only base-wide task orders and bundle large task orders in order to keep IGS costs down.
- Consider performing more Phase III services for the military base to help provide consistency long-term. Most military personnel rotate out of their jobs on a yearly basis.
- Include sufficient schedule time in the Phase I and Phase II activities to allow for working with foreign contractors, working with frequent military personnel in South Korea changes and dealing with the higher security.

Buy American Act
This Region 5 Air Force contract states the following regarding the Buy American Act.

First, products from the following countries, in addition to Canada and Mexico [NAFTA] are exempt from the Buy American Act [in our contract]:

(a) As a result of memoranda of understanding and other international agreements, the DoD has determined it inconsistent with the public interest to apply restrictions of the Buy American Act/Balance of Payments Program to the acquisition of defense equipment which is mined, produced, or manufactured in any of the following countries (referred to in this part as "qualifying countries")

- Australia, Belgium, Canada, Denmark, Egypt, Federal Republic of Germany, France, Greece, Israel, Italy, Luxembourg, Netherlands, Norway, Portugal, Spain, Switzerland, Turkey, United Kingdom of Great Britain and Northern Ireland.

Second, the 50% rule applies to the "End Product". Here is how the DFARS defines "End Product" for Buy American Act purposes:

"End product" means those articles, materials, and supplies to be acquired for public use under the contract. For this contract, the end products are the line items to be delivered to the Government (including supplies to be acquired by the Government for public use in connection with service contracts, but excluding installation and other services to be performed after delivery).

In other words, on an HVAC retrofit, 50% of the total equipment and materials shall be manufactured in the US or any of the countries listed above.

Status of Forces Agreement
Air Force work overseas may require special military access requirements above that required in the US. In South Korea, US contractors performing work long term will require obtaining Status of Forces Agreement (SOFA) passes. SOFA status will be required of construction managers, US-based subcontractors and other ESCO employees spending a long time in South Korea. Along with SOFA status ration are necessary to be able to purchase gas for automobiles driven on base. These passes can allow workers to operate and have the same privileges as the military workers.

CHALLENGES FOR AIR FORCE
There is a tremendous potential for energy savings in the Federal market. The Air Force has a contracting vehicle for performing much of the ESCO work. The US market uses six regional contracts to perform this ESCO work. Only one of the contracts added foreign bases to the scope of work (Region 5). Most of the remaining locations outside the US have used their own contracting vehicles for implementing their energy services needs or have Memorandum of Agreements/Understandings in place with other services. These foreign contracts have not been as successful as the US region contracts.

Successfully performing the Solutions Development required in the Phases I and II can help to fully develop the energy savings potential in the US and abroad.

It is estimated that at the current rate the Region 5 ESCO will implement 50% of the total potential energy savings. Each Regional Contract has an upper limit to the dollars the ESCO can utilize. In the future these contracts will be re-bid with higher maximum contract dollar amounts. The foreign Air Bases (except for South Korea) do not fall under any of the Region Contracts. If, in the future, the Air Force decides to include remaining foreign bases into new contracts, the US-based ESCOs can implement a great amount of energy savings work.

BIO FOR JEFF STRINGFIELD
Mr. Stringfield works for Honeywell International and is the Solutions Development Team Lead for Federal projects

in the Western States. Jeff works in Honeywell's Federal Energy Services Business Unit and is responsible for solutions development of several Federal customers, including many of the Region 5 Air Force projects (including South Korea).

Jeff is a mechanical engineer (Kansas State University), is registered in 20 states, and has an MBA from Arizona State University.

Contact Information
Jeffrey G. Stringfield, P.E.
2626 West Beryl Avenue
Phoenix, Arizona 85021

(602) 684-9753
(602) 861-4553 Fax

jeffrey.stringfield@honeywell.com

BIO FOR K. QUINN HART
Mr. Hart manages the Air Force's Facility Energy Program. In this capacity, he is responsible for directing the implementation of energy conservation programs for Air Force facilities worldwide. He manages the Facilities Energy Team that administers the Energy Conservation Investment Program (ECIP), Energy Savings Performance Contracts (ESPC), Defense Utility Energy Reporting System (DUERS), energy program training, and various energy awareness/awards programs. The Air Force has six regional ESPCs that have awarded over $259 Million in investments to date.

Mr. Hart is a registered Professional Engineer with a Masters of Science in Engineering and Management Systems from the University of Nebraska.

Contact Information
K. Quinn Hart, P.E.
Air Force Facilities Energy Program Manager
HQ Air Force Civil Engineer Support Agency
Tyndall, AFB, FL 32403

(850) 283-6361
(850) 283-6219 Fax

Quinn.Hart@tyndall.af.mil

REFERENCES
1. AFCESA (Sept 10, 1998). Region 5 Contract, FO4626-98-DO103.

Chapter 15

OPERATIONS AND MAINTENANCE FOR FEDERAL BUILDINGS: CAPTURING THE POTENTIAL

Ab Ream (Department of Energy, Federal Energy Management Program)
W. David Hunt, CEM (Pacific Northwest National Laboratory[1])
Gregory P. Sullivan (Pacific Northwest National Laboratory[1])

ABSTRACT

The verdict is in: Improved operations and maintenance (O&M) offers significant energy and cost savings opportunities. It is conservatively estimated that O&M improvements in Federal facilities could result in a 10% reduction in energy use. But simply identifying this opportunity is not enough. If these opportunities are to be captured, Federal agency O&M needs must be strategically addressed. This paper summarizes the past and planned efforts of the Federal Energy Management Program (FEMP) to work with Federal agencies in developing an O&M Program that will realize both energy savings and facilities operations improvements.

INTRODUCTION

Over the last two decades, energy-efficiency programs in the Federal sector have largely concentrated on retrofitting old energy consuming equipment with newer, more energy-efficient equipment as a way of meeting legislated and mandated energy reduction goals. Total Federal expenditures for energy-efficiency retrofits and capital equipment for the period covering fiscal years 1985 through 1999 has been reported at $2.4 billion. During this period, the corresponding energy reduction was 20.7 percent on a Btu per square foot basis [1]. Further, a recent analysis estimated a remaining cost effective retrofit potential in the Federal building goal inventory of $5.2 billion. It was also estimated that this additional investment would result in a corresponding reduction in energy use of 19% [2].

Of late, other opportunities for energy efficiency in the Federal sector have been addressed. The U.S. Department of Energy's FEMP Procurement Challenge Program helps agencies select energy-efficient products for their buildings and facilities. Also, many Federal agencies are now looking at reducing energy use in new buildings, primarily through developing and implementing sustainable building designs and policies. Energy efficiency is a significant part of sustainable building designs, even though this concept addresses much more than energy efficiency.

With all these past and on-going activities aimed at reducing energy use in Federal buildings through improved efficiency, why should Federal agencies be interested in improved operations and maintenance (O&M)? In short, Federal agencies should be very interested in improving O&M capabilities and performance because of the following well documented benefits:

- 10 to 30% savings are typical
- extended equipment life
- less capital intensive than equipment replacement
- improved occupant satisfaction and comfort.

WHAT IS O&M?

The term "O&M" is used in many ways. It is difficult to define a term that captures two distinctly different components – operations and maintenance. The definition of O&M developed for the FEMP O&M business case and strategy is as follows:

> Decisions and actions regarding the control and upkeep of property and equipment inclusive but not limited to the following: actions focused on scheduling, procedures, and work/systems control and optimization; and performance of routine, preventive, predictive, scheduled and unscheduled actions aimed at preventing equipment failure or decline with the goal of increasing energy efficiency, reliability, and safety.

[1]Operated for the U.S. Department of Energy by Battelle Memorial Institute under contract DE-AC06-76RLO1830.

The need for effective O&M is demonstrated in Figure 1, which shows how, over time, the performance of a building (and its components) will eventually degrade and that the service life of the building is prolonged through effective O&M. Not shown in this figure is the additional benefit of reduced building (energy) operating costs resulting from effectively maintaining mechanical and electrical equipment (e.g., lighting; heating, ventilation and air conditioning (HVAC); controls; and on-site generation).

In terms of energy-efficiency programs, it is not always easy to differentiate between O&M activities and retrofit/capital replacement activities. Figure 2 helps demonstrate the relationship between O&M activities and those that are typically considered for project retrofit.

OPPORTUNITIES FOR IMPROVEMENTS
A significant part of establishing a business case for a FEMP O&M program focused on identifying the potential energy savings attainable through improved practices. An extensive literature search was conducted to satisfy this requirement. The results are compelling; many studies of

commercial buildings show an estimated energy saving potential from improved O&M between 5% and 30%. Consider this potential in relation to the fiscal year 1999 Federal building energy use of 0.34 quads at a cost of $3.4 billion [1]. Not only would this resulting energy reduction significantly contribute to Federal agencies meeting or eclipsing the 2005 and 2010 energy reduction goals of 30% and 35%, respectively, the corresponding annual energy cost savings would be in the range of $170 million to $1.0 billion.

The results of the literature search are backed up to some degree by the results of the Assessment of Load and Energy Reduction Techniques (ALERT) Program. The ALERT Program was developed in response to the 2001 energy crisis as a way to identify low- and no-cost energy-efficiency measures and assist Federal sites in reducing and managing peak electric loads, and energy use and costs. In fiscal year 2001, 25 Federal sites in California were assessed by the ALERT team. Some examples of the O&M improvement opportunities identified by the ALERT teams include:

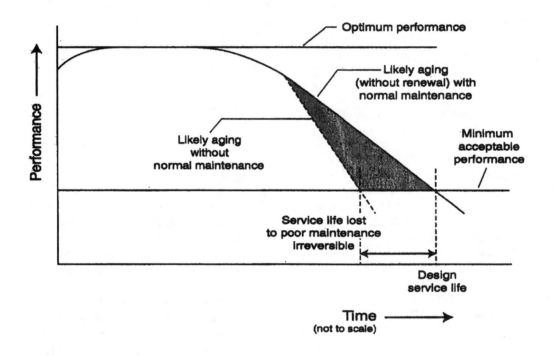

FIGURE 1 – EFFECT OF ADEQUATE AND TIMELY MAINTENANCE AND REPAIRS ON THE SERVICE LIFE OF A BUILDING [3] Reprinted with permission from "The Fourth Dimension in Building: Strategies for Minimizing Obsolescence". Copyright 1993 by the National Academy of Sciences. Courtesy of the National Academy Press, Washington, D.C.

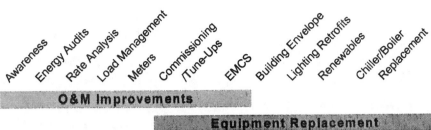

FIGURE 2 – THE ENERGY MANAGEMENT CONTINUUM[2]

- Revise operation schedules for central cooling systems and fans
- Reset chilled water setpoint
- Repair/replace motors, dampers, sensors, and gauges
- Clean heat exchanger coils
- Cycle air handler units
- Balance air systems.

The average estimated potential savings for these 25 sites are a 9.1% reduction in demand (kW), 11% reduction in energy consumption (kWh), and a 9.9% reduction in electric costs. It must be noted that the ALERT visits were focused on reducing summer peak loads, so opportunities for heating season improvements were not examined. However, the results of the ALERT assessments are in agreement with the findings of the literature search on the potential energy and cost savings available through improved O&M.

AGENCY O&M NEEDS
The second major component of the FEMP O&M business case was identifying the O&M program needs of the Federal agencies. By identifying these needs, the FEMP O&M program was able to identify specific strategies and tools that the agencies want and will be likely to use.

The primary method of identifying agency needs was interviews of agency O&M staff at the programmatic (headquarters) and site (field) levels. Input was also obtained by administering an informal survey at the end of the FEMP Operations and Maintenance Management workshops held in 2001 and 2002.

---

[2]Figure from Energy 2002 presentation "How Well Do You Know Your Building" by Ab Ream, Sara Farrar-Nagy (National Renewable Energy Laboratory), and John Hail (Pacific Northwest National Laboratory).

Below is a brief summary of the most significant needs identified in these interviews:

- Technical skills of in-house O&M contract administration staff must be enhanced and/or augmented to effectively manage outsourced O&M.

- Performance incentives language for inclusion in O&M contracts to encourage contractors to operate energy intensive equipment in an energy-efficient manner.

- Contract language that articulates proper and necessary O&M requirements.

- Increased funding to address training, staffing, and equipment needs.

- More technical guidance on issues such as building and equipment commissioning and recommissioning; design, operation and maintenance of direct digital control systems; and primers on technologies and strategies (e.g., metering and reliability centered maintenance).

- More O&M training offerings including training specifically targeting systems such as boilers, chillers, and building controls.

The fact that the needs identified in the first three bullets above address O&M contracting at first seems a bit out of place. However, based on the information provided by the agency O&M managers, it is estimated that O&M is outsourced for well over 50% of the Federal floor space. Further, the outsourced square footage is expected to grow in the coming years, especially in Department of Defense facilities, as a result of renewed interest in the

Federal "Commercial Activities" or A-76[3] process. Thus, the needs associated with improving the O&M outsourcing contract and its administration appear to be the greatest area of concern, as well as the greatest area of opportunity for the FEMP O&M Program.

FEMP'S O&M PLAN OF ACTION

In fiscal year 2002, the FEMP O&M Program activities centered around developing a business case for a broader, more active O&M Program, along with a strategy for implementing this program. A key product in fiscal year 2002 was completion of "Operations and Maintenance Best Practices: A Guide to Achieving Operational Efficiency." This guide provides a variety of information on O&M including general definitions, guidance on managing an O&M program, a summary of maintenance program approaches, information on predictive maintenance technologies, O&M ideas for major equipment types (boilers, steam traps, chillers, cooling towers, energy management/building automation systems, pumps, fans, motors, air compressors, and lighting), and an introduction to new O&M technologies. Visit the FEMP home page for information on obtaining a copy of this guide.

Over the past few years, FEMP has sponsored Texas A&M's Energy Systems Laboratory to develop a Continuous Commissioning Guidebook, based on real-life experiences with over 130 buildings. Continuous commissioning is an ongoing process to resolve operating problems, improve comfort, optimize energy use, and identify retrofits for existing commercial and institutional buildings and central plant facilities. Continuous commissioning focuses on optimizing HVAC system operation and control for existing building conditions. The final draft of this guide is under review and we hope to have it published in the very near future. This guide will be available through the FEMP home page.

In fiscal year 2003, the FEMP O&M Program will aggressively address the O&M needs identified by agencies. Activities planned for fiscal year 2003 include:

- Work with a Federal agency to develop and pilot model contract language for new contracts and performance incentives for amendment to existing contracts.

- Develop guidance for obtaining commissioning services including generic statements of work as the need for improved and increased use of commissioning across the Federal building sector is widely recognized.

- Develop guidance for facility metering/sub-metering to assist sites in better managing their energy use and in response to provisions on Federal energy efficiency in the pending (as of July 2002) comprehensive energy legislation.

- Demonstrate automated diagnostics at Federal facilities. FEMP will look to install the Whole Building Diagnostician[4] at a number of Federal sites to evaluate not only the resulting energy-efficiency improvements, but to also document the benefits of automated diagnostics realized by the site O&M staff.

- Make available more FEMP O&M training course offerings.

CONCLUSIONS

Clearly there is a tremendous opportunity for Federal facilities to reduce energy use and save money through improved O&M practices. Many of these savings can be realized through low- and no-cost actions. In addition to being well documented, this improvement potential is already recognized by the Federal O&M staff contacted by FEMP in support of the FEMP O&M business case. That said, the real issue becomes developing tools and strategies that Federal agencies want and will use.

The fact that most O&M of Federal building floor space is outsourced is important to recognize. Providing guidance on improved O&M practices to Federal staff is not enough because contractors (not Federal staff) are completing most of this work. FEMP can best assist agencies by working with them to develop model contract and performance incentives language that will require (in new contracts) and encourage (in existing contracts) the contractors to do a better job operating and maintaining energy intensive equipment.

Finally, there appears to be a great need government-wide to accept and apply advances in O&M technologies, approaches, and strategies. Examples include building and equipment commissioning, metering and sub-metering, and predictive and reliability centered maintenance-based programs. Lack of acceptance may in large part be caused by a lack of awareness and training to help people be aware of these advances. However, FEMP can be instrumental in assisting agencies in the area by providing the technical resources to evaluate and demonstrate these advances and promote them through targeted awareness programs.

---

[3]Circular A-76 established the Federal policy for the performance of Commercial Activities in procedures (including O&M activities) for studying and eventual private transfer.

[4]Visit http://www.pnl.gov:2080/wbd/features.htm for more information on the Whole Building Diagnostician.

FOR MORE INFORMATION

For more information on the FEMP O&M Program, contact Mr. Ab Ream at ab.ream@hq.doe.gov.

To obtain information on the FEMP Operations and Maintenance Best Practices Guide and the Continuous Commissioning Guidebook, visit the FEMP Home Page at http://www.eren.doe.gov/femp/

Federal agencies are encouraged to contact their regional DOE offices for assistance. To determine the DOE regional contact for your site visit http://www.eren.doe.gov/femp/aboutfemp/doe_regional_office.html

REFERENCES

1. FEMP. 2001. *Annual Report to Congress on Federal Government Energy Management and Conservation Programs, Fiscal Year 1999.* DOE/EE-0252, U.S. Department of Energy – Federal Energy Management Program, Washington, DC.

2. Brown, D.R., J.A. Dirks, and D.M. Hunt. 2000. *Economic Energy Savings Potential in Federal Buildings.* PNNL-13332. Pacific Northwest National Laboratory, Richland, Washington.

3. NRC (National Research Council). 1993. The Fourth Dimension in Building: Strategies for Minimizing Obsolescence. Building Research Board, National Research Council. Washington, DC. National Academy Press, Washington, D.C.

Chapter 16

FEMP'S O&M BEST PRACTICES GUIDE
A Guide to Achieving *Operational Efficiency*

Gregory P. Sullivan, PE, CEM (Pacific Northwest National Laboratory[1])
Aldo P. Melendez (Pacific Northwest National Laboratory[1])
Ray Pugh (Pacific Northwest National Laboratory[1])

ABSTRACT

FEMP's Operations and Maintenance Best Practices Guide (O&M BPG) highlights O&M programs targeting energy efficiency, which are estimated to save 5% to 20% on energy bills without a significant capital investment. Depending on the Federal site, these savings can represent thousands to hundreds-of-thousands of dollars each year, and many can be achieved with minimal cash outlays. In addition to energy/resource savings, a well-run O&M program will:

- Increase the safety of all staff because properly maintained equipment is safer equipment.
- Ensure the comfort, health and safety of building occupants through properly functioning equipment, providing a healthy indoor environment.
- Confirm the design life expectancy of equipment is achieved.
- Facilitate compliance with Federal legislation such as the *Clean Air Act* and the *Clean Water Act*.

The focus of this guide is to provide the Federal O&M/energy manager and practitioner with information and actions aimed at achieving these savings and benefits. The O&M BPG was developed under the direction of the Department of Energy's Federal Energy Management Program (FEMP).

GUIDE DESIGN AND LAYOUT

This guide is intended to be a "living document," that is, one that is amended as things change. For this reason, a three-ring binder format was selected. In addition, the three-ring binder will provide storage room for newsletters, seminar announcements, and other supplementary information you may wish to include. Eventually, a Web-based version is anticipated.

The guide currently consists of nine chapters. Chapter 1 provides an introduction and an overview. Chapter 2 provides the rationale for "Why O&M?" Chapter 3 discusses O&M management issues and their importance. Chapter 4 examines computerized maintenance management systems (CMMS) and their role in an effective O&M program. Chapter 5 looks at the different types of maintenance programs and definitions. Chapter 6 focuses on maintenance technologies, particularly the most accepted predictive technologies. Chapter 7 explores O&M procedures for the predominant equipment found at most Federal facilities. Chapter 8 describes some of the promising O&M technologies and tools on the horizon to increase O&M efficiency, and Chapter 9 provides 10 steps to initiating an *operational efficiency* program.

The O&M environment is in a constant state of evolution and the technologies and vocabularies are ever expanding. Therefore, the guide contains a glossary of terms is presented in Appendix A. Appendix B provides a list of Federal contacts for training and assistance. Appendix C includes a list of organizations and trade groups that have interest or are related to O&M. And finally, Appendix D is a form that can be used to submit suggestions or revisions to the guide.

The goal of this paper is to provide an overview of the O&M BPG, how and why it was developed, and present in highlight form some of its sections. Each highlighted section will be referenced in parentheses in this paper's section title.

INTRODUCTION (O&M BPG Chapter 1)

Effective O&M is one of the most cost-effective methods for ensuring reliability, safety, and energy efficiency. Inadequate maintenance of energy-using systems is a major cause of energy waste in both the Federal government and the private sector. Energy losses from

[1]Operated for the U.S. Department of Energy by Battelle Memorial Institute under contract DE-AC06-76RL01830.

steam, water and air leaks, uninsulated lines, maladjusted or inoperable controls, and other losses from poor maintenance are often considerable. Good maintenance practices can generate substantial energy savings and should be considered a resource. Moreover, improvements to facility maintenance programs can often be accomplished immediately and at a relatively low cost.

The purpose of the O&M Best Practices Guide (O&M BPG) is to provide the operation and maintenance/energy manager and practitioner, with useful information about O&M management, technologies, and cost-reduction approaches. To make this guide useful and to reflect the facility manager's needs and concerns, the authors met with O&M and energy managers via Federal Energy Management Program (FEMP) workshops. In addition, the authors conducted extensive literature searches and contacted numerous vendors and industry experts. The information and case studies that appear in this guide resulted from these activities.

It needs to be stated at the outset that the guide is designed to provide information on effective O&M as it applies to systems and equipment typically found at Federal facilities. The guide *is not* designed to provide the reader with step-by-step procedures for performing O&M on any specific piece of equipment. Rather, the guide first directs the user to the manufacturer's specifications and recommendations. In no way should the recommendations in the guide be used in place of manufacturer's recommendations. The recommendations in the guide are designed to supplement those of the manufacturer, or, as is all too often the case, provide guidance for systems and equipment for which all technical documentation has been lost.

DEFINITIONS (Chapter 2)

Operations and Maintenance: Decisions and actions regarding the control and upkeep of property and equipment inclusive but not limited to the following: actions focused on scheduling, procedures, and work/systems control and optimization; and performance of routine, preventive, predictive, scheduled and unscheduled actions aimed at preventing equipment failure or decline with the goal of increasing efficiency, reliability, and safety.

Operational Efficiency represents the life-cycle cost-effective mix of preventive, predictive, and reliability-centered maintenance technologies, coupled with equipment calibration, tracking, and computerized maintenance management capabilities, all targeting reliability, safety, occupant comfort, and system efficiency.

O&M POTENTIAL, ENERGY SAVINGS, AND BEYOND (Chapter 2)

It has been estimated that O&M programs targeting energy efficiency can save between 5% and 20% on energy bills without a significant capital investment [1]. From small to large sites, these savings can represent thousands to hundreds-of-thousands of dollars each year, and many can be achieved with minimal cash outlays. Beyond the potential for significant cost and energy/resource savings, an O&M program operating at its peak "operational efficiency" has other important implications:

- A well-functioning O&M program is a safe O&M program. Equipment is maintained properly, mitigating any potential hazard arising from deferred maintenance.

- In most Federal buildings, the O&M staff are responsible for not only the comfort, but also the health and safety of the occupants. Indoor air quality (IAQ) issues within these buildings are of increasing productivity (and legal) concern. Proper O&M reduces the risks associated with development of dangerous and costly IAQ situations.

- Properly performed O&M helps to ensure that the design life expectancy of equipment can be achieved, and in some cases exceeded. Conversely, the costs associated with early equipment failure are usually not budgeted for, and often come at the expense of other planned activities.

- An effective O&M program aids in a facilities compliance with Federal legislation, such as the *Clean Air Act* and the *Clean Water Act*.

- A well functioning O&M program is not always reactive (answering complaints); rather, it is proactive in its response, and corrects situations before they become problems. This model minimizes callbacks and keeps occupants satisfied while allowing more time for scheduled maintenance.

O&M MANAGEMENT (Chapter 3)

O&M management is a critical component of the overall program. The management function should bind the distinct parts of the program into a cohesive entity. From our experience, the overall program should contain five very distinct functions making up the organization [2]: **Operations, Maintenance, Engineering, Training,** and **Administration—OMETA.**

Beyond establishing and facilitating the OMETA links, O&M managers have the responsibility of interfacing with other department managers and making their case against ever-shrinking budgets. Their roles also include project implementation functions, as well as the need to maintain persistence of the program and its goals.

Developing the Structure (Chapter 3)

Five well-defined elements of an effective O&M program include those presented above in the OMETA concept [2]. While these elements (Operations, Maintenance, Engineering, Training, and Administration) form the basis for a solid O&M organization, the key lies in the well-defined functions each brings and the linkages between organizations. A subset of the roles and responsibilities for each of the elements is presented in the guide; further information is found in Meador [2].

Obtain Management Support (Chapter 3)

Federal O&M managers need to obtain full support from their management structure to carry out an effective maintenance program. A good way to start is by establishing a written maintenance plan and obtaining upper management approval. Such a management-supported program is very important because it allows necessary activities to be scheduled with the same priority as other management actions. Approaching O&M by equating it with increased productivity, energy efficiency, safety, and customer satisfaction are ways to gain management attention and support.

Measuring the Quality of Your O&M Program (Chapter 3)

Traditional thinking in the O&M field focused on a single metric, reliability, for program evaluation. Every O&M manager wants a reliable facility; however, this metric alone is not enough to evaluate or build a successful O&M program.

Beyond reliability, O&M managers need to be responsible for controlling costs, evaluating and implementing new technologies, tracking and reporting on health and safety issues, and expanding their program. To support these activities, the O&M manager must be aware of various indicators that can be used to measure the quality or effectiveness of the O&M program. Not only are these metrics useful in assessing effectiveness, but they are also useful in the justification of cost for equipment purchases, program modifications, and staff hiring.

Below are a number of metrics that can be used to evaluate an O&M program. Not all of these metrics can be used in all situations; however, a program should use as many metrics as possible to better define deficiencies and, most importantly, publicize successes. The O&M BPG describes each of these metrics in detail.

- capacity factor
- work orders generated/closed

- backlog of corrective maintenance
- safety record
- energy Use
- inventory
- overtime worked
- environmental record
- absentee rate
- staff turnover.

Selling O&M to Management (Chapter 3)

To successfully interest management in O&M activities, O&M managers need to be fluent in the language spoken by management. Projects and proposals brought forth to management need to stand on their own merits and be competitive with other funding requests. While evaluation criteria may differ, generally some level of economic criteria will be used. O&M managers need to have a working knowledge of economic metrics such as:

- *Simple payback* – The ratio of total installed cost to first-year savings.

- *Return on investment* – The ratio of the income or savings generated to the overall investment.

- *Net present value* – The present worth of future cash flows minus the initial cost of the project.

- *Life-cycle cost* – The present worth of all costs associated with a project.

Program Implementation (Chapter 3)

Developing or enhancing an O&M program requires patience and persistence. Guidelines for initiating a new O&M program will vary by agency and management situation; however, some steps to consider are presented below:

- *Start small* – Choose a project that is manageable and can be completed in a short period of time, 6 months to 1 year.

- *Select troubled equipment* – Choose a project that has visibility because of a problematic history.

- *Minimize risk* – Choose a project that will provide immediate and positive results. This project needs to be successful, and therefore, the risk of failure should be minimal.

- *Keep accurate records* – This project needs to stand on its own merits. Accurate, if not conservative, records are critical to compare before and after results.

- *Tout the success* – When you are successful, this needs to be shared with those involved and with management. Consider developing a "wall of accomplishment" and locate it in a place where management will take notice.

- *Build off this success* – Generate the success, acknowledge those involved, publicize it, and then request more money/time/resources for the next project.

O&M Contracting (Chapter 3)

Approximately 40% of all non-residential buildings contract maintenance service for heating, ventilation, and air conditioning (HVAC) equipment [3]. Discussions with Federal building managers and organizations indicate this value is significantly higher in the Federal sector, and the trend is toward increased reliance on contracted services. The O&M BPG explores this trend further and offers guidance on O&M contracting.

COMPUTERIZED MAINTENANCE MANAGEMENT SYSTEMS (Chapter 4)

A computerized maintenance management system (CMMS) is a type of management software that performs functions in support of management and tracking of O&M activities. CMMS systems automate most of the logistical functions performed by maintenance staff and management. CMMS systems come with many options and have many advantages over manual maintenance tracking systems. The O&M BPG presents the major capabilities, benefits, and potential pitfalls of CMMS.

TYPES OF MAINTENANCE PROGRAMS (Chapter 5)

What is maintenance and why is it performed? Past and current maintenance practices in both the private and Government sectors would imply that maintenance is the actions associated with equipment repair after it is broken. The dictionary defines maintenance as follows: "the work of keeping something in proper condition; upkeep." This would imply that maintenance should be actions taken to prevent a device or component from failing or to repair normal equipment degradation experienced with the operation of the device to keep it in proper working order. Unfortunately, data obtained in many studies over the past decade indicates that most private and Government facilities do not expend the necessary resources to maintain equipment in proper working order. Rather, they wait for equipment failure to occur and then take whatever actions are necessary to repair or replace the equipment. Nothing lasts forever, and all equipment has some predefined life expectancy or operational life. For example, equipment may be designed to operate at full design load for 5,000 hours and may be designed to go through 15,000 start and stop cycles.

The design life of most equipment requires periodic maintenance. Belts need adjustment, alignment needs to be maintained, proper lubrication on rotating equipment is required, and so on. In some cases, certain components need replacement (e.g., a wheel bearing on a motor vehicle) to ensure the main piece of equipment (in this case a car) lasts for its design life. Anytime maintenance activities intended by the equipment's designer are not performed, we shorten the operating life of the equipment. But what options do we have? Over the last 30 years, different approaches to how maintenance can be performed to ensure equipment reaches or exceeds its design life have been developed in the United States. In addition to waiting for a piece of equipment to fail (reactive maintenance), we can utilize preventive maintenance, predictive maintenance, or reliability centered maintenance.

The O&M BPG provides a detailed description of each major maintenance program type (reactive, preventive, predictive, and reliability centered), including each program's advantages and disadvantages.

PREDICITIVE MAINTENACE TECHNOLOGIES (Chapter 6)

Predictive maintenance attempts to detect the onset of a degradation mechanism with the goal of correcting that degradation prior to significant deterioration in the component or equipment.

The diagnostic capabilities of predictive maintenance technologies have increased in recent years with advances in sensor technologies. These advances, breakthroughs in component sensitivities, size reductions, and most importantly, cost have opened up an entirely new area of diagnostics to the O&M practitioner.

As with the introduction of any new technology, proper application and *TRAINING* is of critical importance. This is particularly true in the field of predictive maintenance technology, which has become increasingly sophisticated and technology driven. Most industry experts would agree (as well as most reputable equipment vendors) that this equipment should not be purchased for in-house use if there is not a serious commitment to proper implementation, operator training, and equipment upkeep. If such a commitment cannot be made, a site is well advised to seek other methods of program implementation—a preferable option may be to contract for these services with an outside vendor and rely on their equipment and expertise.

Chapter 6 presents a detailed description and applications for predictive technologies including: thermography, oil analysis, ultrasonic analysis, vibration analysis, motor analysis, and performance trending.

O&M IDEAS FOR MAJOR EQUIPMENT TYPES (Chapter 7)

At the heart of all O&M lies the equipment. Across the Federal sector, this equipment varies greatly in age, size, type, model, fuel used, condition, etc. While it is well beyond the scope of this guide to study all equipment types, we tried to focus our efforts on the more common types prevalent in the Federal sector. The objectives of this chapter in the guide are:

- Present general equipment descriptions and operating principles for the major equipment types.

- Discuss the key maintenance components of that equipment.

- Highlight important safety issues.

- Point out cost and efficiency issues.

- Provide recommended general O&M activities in the form of checklists.

- Where possible, provide case studies.

The major equipment types covered in Chapter 7 include: boilers, steam traps, chillers, cooling towers, energy management/building automation systems, pumps, fans, motors, air compressors, and lighting. At the end of each section in Chapter 7, a checklist of suggested O&M activities is provided. These checklists are not presented to replace activities specifically recommended by equipment vendors or manufacturers. In most cases, these checklists represent industry standard best practices for the given equipment. They are presented here to supplement existing O&M procedures, or to merely serve as reminders of activities that should be taking place.

O&M FRONTIERS (Chapter 8)

As old a topic as O&M is, there are a number of new technologies and tools targeting the increased efficiency of O&M. As with most new technology introduction, these tools are in various stages of commercialization; for up-to-date information on each tool, contact information is provided. This chapter serves to highlight some of the more promising technologies targeting improved O&M and efficiency.

TEN STEPS TO *OPERATIONAL EFFICIENCY* (Chapter 9)

As defined, operational efficiency is: the life-cycle cost-effective mix of preventive, predictive, and reliability-centered maintenance technologies, coupled with equipment calibration, tracking, and computerized

maintenance management capabilities, all targeting reliability, safety, occupant comfort, and system efficiency. Chapter 9 presents 10 simple steps to begin the path toward improved O&M and ultimately *operational efficiency*.

APPENDICIES

Four appendices are provided in the O&M BPG. These include: Appendix A, a glossary of common terms; Appendix B, the FEMP staff contact list; Appendix C, a variety of O&M resources including relevant trade organizations and web sites; and Appendix D, a form to submit offering suggestions for the next version of the O&M BPG.

CONCLUSIONS

As FEMP starts up its O&M program, the O&M BPG will provide valuable guidance to Federal building managers, O&M program managers, and building operations staffs. This guidance provides not only a starting point in terms of establishing clear objectives and understanding benefits, but also can be used to establish an effective, long-range plan that involves all O&M related staff functions, measure program performance, upgrading existing practices, and planning for the future. This Guide will ultimately assist Federal building managers realize significant cost-effective energy savings and improve occupant satisfaction.

FOR MORE INFORMATION

For more information on the FEMP O&M Program, contact Mr. Ab Ream at ab.ream@hq.doe.gov.

To obtain information on the FEMP Operations and Maintenance Best Practices Guide and the Continuous Commissioning Guidebook, visit the FEMP Home Page at http://www.eren.doe.gov/femp/

Federal agencies are encouraged to contact their regional DOE offices for assistance. To determine the DOE regional contact for your site visit http://www.eren.doe.gov/femp/aboutfemp/doe_regional_office.html

REFERENCES

1. PECI. 1999. *Operations and Maintenance Assessments*. Prepared by Portland Energy Conservation, Inc. for the U.S. Environmental Protection Agency and U.S. Department of Energy, Washington, D.C.

2. Meador, RJ. 1995. *"Maintaining the Solution to Operations and Maintenance Efficiency Improvement."* World Energy Engineering Congress, Atlanta, Georgia.

3. PECI. 1997. *Energy Management Systems: A Practical Guide.* Portland Energy Conservation, Inc., Portland, Oregon.

Chapter 17

BUILDING CONTINUOUS COMMISSIONING^{SM} GUIDEBOOK

W. Dan Turner, Director and Professor
David E. Claridge, Professor
Energy Systems Laboratory
Texas A&M University

and

Mingsheng Liu, Associate Professor
Architectural Engineering Program
University of Nebraska-Omaha

ABSTRACT

The concept of building and plant Continuous Commissioning^{SM} (CC) originated within the Energy Systems Laboratory around 1993 when our engineers started looking at low-cost, no-cost operating practices which could be implemented in buildings to reduce operating costs. These "O&M" operating practices mostly involved shutting down systems during nights and weekends or turning off unnecessary components, such as two boilers operating when one would satisfy the loads. ESL engineers then started taking a more in-depth look at the HVAC system operation, and the Continuous Commissioning process was begun around 1995. The energy-savings results from CC have been extremely good, typically ranging from 15-25% of the facility energy bill. As a result of these successes in over 100 buildings, the U. S. Department of Energy provided a grant to the Energy Systems Laboratory to produce a Continuous Commissioning Guidebook which can be used by building energy managers and facility operators to reduce energy consumption. This paper will introduce the Guidebook and provide a case study from the book, the Continuous Commissioning of a DOD hospital, the Brooke Army Medical Center (BAMC) in San Antonio, TX.

INTRODUCTION

The Continuous Commissioning (CC) process, as originated by the Energy Systems Laboratory within the Texas A&M University System, focuses on improving overall system control and operations for the building as it is currently being utilized. CC is more than just an O&M program. It is a team effort between the commissioning engineer, energy manager, owner, operator, and maintenance staff to optimize the energy consumption of the building or plant and <u>continue</u> to operate the facility at its optimum energy consumption. The CC engineer, after the facility is commissioned, will continue to work with the staff through a continuing contract, to ensure proper

operation. It is important to point out that the Continuous Commissioning process purpose is not to restore the building operation to the original design intent. Rather it is to optimize operation as the facility is currently utilized. In the process of CC, occupant comfort is improved, which should improve overall worker productivity and reduce absenteeism. In a few buildings, particularly those with poor indoor air quality, the CC process could actually increase energy consumption, by bringing in more outside air, for example.

A formal definition for the Continuous Commissioning process is:

"An ongoing process to resolve operating problems, improve comfort, optimize energy use, and to identify retrofits for existing commercial and institutional buildings and central plant facilities."

The CC process has been applied to relatively new buildings, i.e., Capitol Extension Building in Austin, TX, Brooke Army Medical Center (BAMC) in San Antonio, TX and to the Matheson Courthouse in Salt Lake City, UT, among others. It has been applied to retrofitted buildings in the Texas LoanSTAR program, and to older buildings which have not received any retrofits. The results are generally the same, i.e., a 15-25% annual energy reduction. [Refs. 1, 2, 3, 4, 5] For example, the entire Texas A&M International University campus (six buildings plus a central plant) at Laredo, TX, a relatively new campus, was commissioned and achieved a 20% reduction in energy consumption. Two new buildings on that campus are currently undergoing the CC process.

Because of the thoroughness of the CC process in each building and central plant, CC engineers often identify capital retrofit opportunities, which, if implemented, will improve operations and provide additional energy savings. It should be emphasized at this point that the 15-25% savings achieved through the CC process normally does not involve major hardware additions or retrofits. These savings are achieved largely through operational optimization.

MEASUREMENT AND VERIFICATION
Measurement and verification (M&V) are key elements to the CC process as developed by the ESL. We feel it is key to project success for several reasons:
1) first and foremost, is the assurance that is provided to the customer that savings are being achieved as projected.
2) the initial energy baseline provides a "yardstick" on which savings are measured and allows energy analysts to track the persistence of savings over time
3) hourly or 15-minute data provide a much finer description of how the building is using energy and helps to identify additional CC opportunities.

For example, the massive commissioning effort on the 15 million square feet Texas A&M University campus in College Station, TX, was approved by the university administration in the spring of 1995. However, the actual CC did not start until April 1996. The reason for the time delay was the installation of building electrical and thermal meters on the 80 largest buildings, the central plant, and the satellite thermal plants. The ESL wanted to obtain 6-9 months of metered data to:
1) establish a pre-CC baseline
2) identify the buildings which were the biggest energy users as the starting places for the CC effort.

In most of the buildings commissioned by the ESL, we use existing interval meters, i.e., those installed by the Texas LoanSTAR program, or we install a stand-alone energy information system (EIS), i.e., Texas A&M University campus. In some facilities EMCS data are used, provided sufficient trending capability exists. These trend logs are also used to identify potential CC opportunities. We also will utilize interval electrical data from the utility when it is available.

Finally, monthly utility bills (both gas and electric) will be utilized for both the baseline and savings analysis. This approach is the least preferred because it does not provide much useful information on how the building uses energy.

The approaches used to calculate savings are consistent with the International Performance Measurement and Verification Protocols (IPMVP). Option C, the whole building or whole campus approach, is most often used. Some of the analysis methodologies developed by the Energy Systems Laboratory are, in fact, included in the IPMVP.

CONTINUOUS COMMISSIONING GUIDEBOOK
The guidebook will contain chapters on how to commission all major HVAC and controls systems. These include: chillers, boilers, air handlers, cooling towers, economizers, thermal storage systems, controls, pumping, central plants, and water distribution systems. Case studies are provided which illustrate the CC process for each measure.

Detailed case studies are also provided which detail the CC process. One of the detailed case studies is the DOD Army Hospital in San Antonio, TX, the Brooke Army Medical Center (BAMC). Portions of that case study are excerpted from the Guidebook and presented below.

CASE STUDY – CONTINUOUS COMMISSIONING AT BROOKE ARMY MEDICAL CENTER (BAMC)

INTRODUCTION
At the time of our commissioning, the facility was operated for the Army by a third-party company, and it was operated in accordance with the original design intent. As has been discussed throughout this guidebook, the CC process looks at the facility as it is being operated and attempts to optimize the energy-using systems. This case study illustrates a wide range of CC opportunities. [Refs. 6, 7, 8, 9]

We would like to acknowledge the assistance and cooperation of Chuck Cameron, Lead Operator, and Ben Keeble, Project Manager, of Johnson Controls, Inc., and Roy Hirchak, Chief, BAMC Facility Management, for their contributions to the BAMC Continuous Commissioning.

BUILDING AND HVAC SYSTEMS
The Brooke Army Medical Complex is a large, multi-functional medical facility. It consists of the medical center (main hospital), a research building (R) and a central energy plant (CEP). The medical center consists of the C building (4 stories), M building (6 stories), A building (6 stories) and B building (8 stories) with a total floor of 1,349,707 ft^2. The research building is a 3-story building with a floor area of 118,886 ft^2. Figure 1 is the typical floor layout of the complex.

The complex primarily consists of outpatient clinic rooms, nuclear medicine, pharmacy areas, ICUs, CCUs, surgical areas, inpatient beds, emergency rooms, diagnostic areas, research labs, offices, animal holding areas, a cafeteria, computer rooms, training classrooms and an auditorium.

The complex is equipped with a central energy plant, which has four 1,200 ton water-cooled electric chillers. Four primary pumps (75 hp each) are used to pump water through the chillers. Two secondary pumps (200 hp each), equipped with VFDs, supply chilled water from the plant to the building entrance. Fourteen chilled water risers equipped with 28 pumps totaling 557 hp are used to pump chilled water to all of the AHUs and small FCUs. All of the chilled water riser pumps are equipped with VFDs.

There are four natural gas fired steam boilers in this plant. The maximum output for each boiler is 20 MMBtu/hr. Steam is supplied to each building where heating water is generated. The steam pressure set point for the boilers, prior to CC, was 125 psig.

There are 90 major AHUS serving the whole complex with a total of 2,570 hp. VFDs are installed in 65 AHUs while the others are constant volume systems.

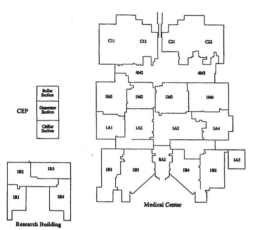

FIGURE 1. TYPICAL LAYOUT OF BAMC COMPLEX

In the complex there are 2,700 terminal boxes of which 27% are dual duct variable volume (DDVAV) boxes, 71% are dual duct constant volume (DDCV) boxes, and 2% are single duct variable volume (SDVAV) boxes. There are no terminal boxes for the warehouse and auditorium.

The HVAC systems (chillers, boilers, AHUs, pumps, terminal boxes and room conditions) are controlled by a York DDC control system. Individual controller-field panels are used for the AHUs and water loops located in the mechanical rooms, which are also accessed by the central control system through an interface-ProComm plus and Facility Manager. The program and parameters can be changed either by the central computers or at the panels.

METERING INSTALLATION
Once the contract was signed for the commissioning, metering was installed on the whole facility and the central plant to monitor whole facility energy consumption. Because the metering was not installed in time to get the pre-CC baseline, monthly utility bills were used for the pre-energy consumption baseline. The hourly data were

used to determine the post-CC consumption. Some short-term loggers were also installed.

CONTINUOUS COMMISSIONING PROCESS
The first steps in the CC process were to determine the details of current system operation, which included a survey of every room to determine the current function, operating hours, etc. It was also determined that the facility was being well maintained by the facility operator in accordance with the original design intent. The EMCS was used extensively during this process. The following controls were being utilized by the EMCS.
1. hot deck reset control for AHUs
2. cold deck reset during unoccupied periods only for some units
3. static pressure reset between high and low limit for VAV units
4. hot water supply temperature control with reset schedule
5. chilled water pumps VFD control with P set point (no reset schedule)
6. box level control and monitoring

This building was considered energy efficient for a large hospital complex. Nevertheless, significant energy savings were identified through the commissioning audit process.

COMMISSIONING ACTIVITIES
Because the case study hospital is such a multi-functional complex, the commissioning activities were performed at the terminal box level, AHU level, loop level and central plant level. Several different types of improved operation measures and energy solutions were implemented in different HVAC systems due to the actual function and usage of the areas and rooms. Each measure will be discussed, starting with the air handling units.

1.   AHU LEVEL
OPTIMIZE THE OPERATION OF VAV AHUS
There are a total of 54 VAV AHUs serving the clinic areas, diagnostic areas, pharmacy, research laboratory, food services areas, offices, lobby areas, maintenance areas and storage rooms. The cold deck (CD) temperature set points were operated with a constant set point, ranging from 55 to 57 F and were occasionally adjusted by the operator during occupied periods. The hot deck (HD) temperature set points were modulated between a low limit and a high limit according to the box requirement. If there is no call for heat from the box, the hot deck will be maintained at the low limit. If there is a call for heat from a box, the hot deck will be increased up to the high limit until there is no longer a call for heating.

The actual measured results from the site measurements and short-term data loggers showed that HD temperatures ranged from 75 F to 93 F during the hot summer. The static pressure set points were modulated between the low and high limits according to the box conditions. The supply fan ranged from 55 Hz to 60 Hz for different AHUs during the site visit period.

Table 1 shows the control schedules before commissioning.

TABLE 1: TYPICAL SET POINTS FOR THE HD AND STATIC PRESSURE BEFORE COMMISSIONING

Limit	HD Set Point	Static Pressure Set Point
High limit	110 F if Toa<30 F, 90 F if Toa>70	1.8" H20 (fixed value)
Low limit	90 F if Toa<30 F, 70 F if Toa>70 F	1.4" H20 (fixed value)

The outside air intakes were constant for both day and night. The relief and return air dampers were 100% open for all units.

Through our investigation, it was found that the high hot deck temperature caused excessive heating and cooling consumption and caused hot calls during the summer. The cold deck set points with a reset schedule can better satisfy the building load under different weather conditions and reduce simultaneous cooling and heating consumption during winter conditions. Measurements of the static pressures indicated the static pressures could be much lower than the designed value. The higher static pressure consumed more fan power and provided excess cold and hot air to the building. Based on measurements and calculations, the commissioning control schedules are presented in Tables 2, 3, and 4.

TABLE 2. POST-CC HD TEMPERATURE RESET SCHEDULES FOR DDVAV AHUS

Limit	HD Set Point
High limit	94~98 F if Toa<30 F, 75 F if Toa>78 F
Low limit	74~76 F if Toa<30 F, 70 F if Toa>78 F

TABLE 3. POST-CC HD TEMPERATURE RESET SCHEDULES FOR DDVAV AHUS

Time	CD Set Point
Occupied period	60 F if Toa<45 F, 56 F if Toa>80 F
Unoccupied period	Keep existing reset schedule 80 F if Tret<55 F, 55 F if Tret>80 F

TABLE 4. POST-CC STATIC PRESSURE SET POINT LIMITS FOR DDVAV AHUS

Limit	C building Inch H20	M building Inch H20	A building Inch H20	B building Inch H20	R building Inch H20
High limit	0.9~1.3	1.0~1.8	1.0~1.8	1.0~1.8	1.5~1.8
Low limit	0.5	0.5~0.7	0.5~0.7	0.5	0.5

Note: The static pressure set point limits are determined based on the duct condition, box condition, damper condition, and special resistance factors such as HEPA filters.

Prior to CC, the preheat set points were 2-5 degrees below the cold deck set points, which caused some simultaneous heating and cooling if the temperature sensors had some error. The new preheat set points after CC are 40 F for all the AHUs.

Before commissioning, 12 AHUs in the C building had 2 hours of shut down at night and the control philosophy allowed the indoor temperature to swing from 65 F to 85 F. In order to reduce the swing for the indoor air conditions, the AHUs are now run 24 hours a day after the commissioning.

As one of the commissioning measures during unoccupied periods, in order to reduce the outside air intake after hours, the relief air dampers were closed for all the units. To maintain the building pressure, some of the exhaust fans were shut down as well.

The optimized operation schedules were tested and implemented in all 54 VAV AHUs. The commissioning team also performed troubleshooting and fine-tuning on the AHUs and associated terminal boxes. The indoor conditions were improved and the fan power consumption, as well as thermal energy consumption, was reduced significantly.

OPTIMIZE THE OPERATION OF DUAL DUCT CONSTANT VOLUME AHUS

There are a total of 9 constant volume AHUs serving the diagnostic areas, pharmacy, offices, classroom areas and health promotion center. Seven constant volume AHUs serve inpatient areas, which have special requirements such as indoor temperatures for burn patients.

The cold deck temperature set point was operated with a constant set point, ranging from 55 F to 57 F, and was occasionally adjusted by the operator during occupied periods. The hot deck (HD) temperature set points were modulated between the low limit and the high limit according to the terminal box requirements. The limits were almost the same for the AHUs and can be seen in Table 5.

TABLE 5: TYPICAL SET POINTS FOR HD BEFORE COMMISSIONING

Limit	HD Set Point
High limit	110 F if Toa<30 F, 90 F if Toa>70 F
Low limit	90 F if Toa<30 F, 70 F if Toa>70 F

The outside air intakes were constant day and night. All dampers stayed in the same position day and night. The relief and return air dampers were 100% open for all units.

The post-commissioning control schedules are presented in Tables 6 and 7.

TABLE 6. POST-CC HD TEMPERATURE RESET SCHEDULES FOR DDCV AHUS

Limit	HD Set Point
High limit	94~98 F if Toa<30 F, 75 F if Toa>78 F
Low limit	74 F if Toa<30 F, 70 F if Toa>78 F

TABLE 7. POST-CC CD TEMPERATURE RESET SCHEDULES FOR DDCV AHUS

Time	CD Set Point
Occupied period	60 F if Toa<50 F, 56 F if Toa>80 F
Unoccupied period	Keep existing unoccupied schedule 80 F if Tret<55 F, 55 F if Tret>80 F

The new preheat set points after commissioning are 40 F for all the AHUs and the relief air dampers will be closed for all the units. To maintain positive building pressure, some of the exhaust fans were shut down.

Due to special inpatient requirements, there was no modification for 7 AHUs. After implementation of the measures, the hot calls were reduced and thermal energy usage was reduced.

2.   TERMINAL BOX LEVEL

There are a total of 2700 terminal boxes supplying the conditioned air to the rooms. Twenty-seven per cent are DDVAV boxes, 71% are DDCV boxes, and 2% are SDVAV boxes.

DDVAV BOX CONTROL LOGIC

The original control logic of the DDVAV boxes was the same as the constant volume terminal box operation except there were different CFM settings at minimum and maximum conditions. The minimum air flow CFM setting for the VAV boxes were the same both day and night and ranged from 30% to 90% with an average of 60% of maximum air flow for the box. Current operation consumes excess heating and cooling air under normal room load condition. Also, the heating capacity was limited for some boxes due to the existing box design setting. In some cases, the boxes supplied a limited amount of hot air even in the full heating mode even though the hot duct of the boxes could allow more flow.

To meet the minimum air flow requirements, the boxes used more cold air than was necessary.

A new control logic was developed, which made the box run on a VAV operation schedule. As a result, simultaneous cooling and heating were reduced significantly during normal load conditions for the box. The hot air capacity was increased by 30% on average, in the full heating mode. The minimum supply air flow was also satisfied.

UNOCCUPIED PERIOD SETBACK FOR VAV BOXES
The setback control is as follows:
1. The room temperature set points will be kept the same as occupied periods (BAMC request).
2. Reduce total flow minimum value to 0. The box can provide enough air when the load increases.

UNOCCUPIED PERIOD SETBACK FOR THE CV TERMINAL BOXES
The setback control is as follows:
1. The room temperature set points will be kept the same as occupied periods (based on existing set points--BAMC request).
2. Reduce total flow to a certain percentage of the design flow. The percentage is determined based on the building pressure analysis. Generally, the percentage is from 30% to 70% for different AHUs.

TROUBLESHOOTING
During the commissioning period, it was found that some terminal boxes could not provide the required air flow before and after the control program modification. The major reason is due to higher flow resistance from the flexible and kinked ducts to the terminal boxes. The authors performed detail checks for every box on the computer first, then conducted field measurements for all the trouble boxes. The specific problems were identified for about two hundred boxes. The operation and maintenance personnel fixed the problems following our recommendations.

3.   LOOP LEVEL
There are 14 chilled water risers equipped with 28 pumps which provide chilled water to the entire complex. One pump per riser is needed. The second pump is standby.

During the commissioning audit phase, the following were observed:
1. All the riser pumps were equipped with VFDs and they were running from $41H_3$ to 60 Hz.
2. All the manual balancing valves on the risers were balanced 30% to 60% open.
3. The ΔP sensor for each riser was located 10 to 20 feet from the far-end coil of the AHU on the top floor.
4. Differential pressure set points for each riser ranged from 13 psi to 26 psi.
5. There is no control valve on the return loop.
6. Although most of the cold deck temperatures were holding well, there were 13 AHUs whose cooling coils were 100% open but could not maintain cold deck temperature set points.

COMMISSIONING MEASURES
Since the risers are equipped with VFDs, traditional manual balancing techniques are not appropriate. All the risers were rebalanced initially opening all of the manual balancing valves. The actual pressure requirements were measured for each riser, and it was determined that the P for each riser could be reduced significantly. Table 8 summarizes the riser conditions before and after the commissioning and the hp savings for each riser pump.

TABLE 8. SUMMARY OF CHILLED WATER SYSTEM CONDITION BEFORE AND AFTER RESET AND NEW SET POINTS

Riser	Before Reset				After DP Reset				% of rated HP	Rated HP
Name	DP set point	Time	DP meas.	Pump Hz	DP set point	Time	DP meas.	Pump Hz	Savings	
C11/C12	13	14:00	13.1	41.3	6	10:20	6.2	27.7	23%	15
C21/C22	16	14:20	16.1	49.1	7	15:50	7	33.8	37%	15
M1	15.2	11:00	15	45	7	13:40	7	29.1	31%	15
M2	25	11:10	25	60	8	13:45	8	37	77%	20
M3	25	15:00	24.5	60	8	16:00	7.8	35.4	79%	20
M4	26	15:10	24	59.8	8	16:06	8	40	69%	20
A1	20	9:00	20.5	50.5	8	10:50	8	33	43%	20
A2	16	13:15	16.2	40.3	13	16:19	13.1	36.7	7%	40
A3	15.2	11:20	15	43.8	8	15:00	8	32	24%	20
A4	16.2	13:50	16.3	53	12	13:16	12	45.3	26%	15
B1	14	14:00	13.6	50.7	8	14:30	8	42.7	24%	15
B2	17	14:00	17	55.7	9	13:42	8.7	42.2	45%	15
R1/R2	14	11:40	14	54.7	8	15:50	8	44.1	36%	15
R3/R4	16	11:45	15	50.4	8	15:54	7.1	36	38%	25
Ave/Tot									40%	270
Total Saving										108hp (80kw)

4. CENTRAL PLANT AND LOOPS

BOILER STEAM PRESSURE AND BOILER OPERATION

The original steam pressure was set to 125 psig. However, the actual required pressure for BAMC was less than 125 psig. The recommendation was made to reduce the boiler pressure to 100 psig, thus reducing losses and gas consumption. The operations staff was not comfortable with 100 psig, but agreed to drop the pressure to 110 psig. The boiler efficiency increased after the implementation of the new steam pressure set point. Also, the practice at BAMC was to run two boilers year round, and as part of commissioning one boiler was shut down during the summer and swing seasons.

CHILLED WATER LOOP

Before the commissioning, the blending valve separating the primary and secondary loops at the plant was 100% open. The primary and secondary pumps were both running. The manual valves were partially open for the secondary loop although the secondary loop pumps are equipped with VFDs. The following was implemented.
1. Open the manual valves for the secondary loop
2. Close the blending stations
3. Shut down the secondary loop pumps, except in extreme summer conditions

As a result, the primary loop pumps provide required chilled water flow and pressure to the building entrance for most of the year, and the secondary pumps stay offline for most of the time. The operator drops the online chiller numbers according to the load conditions and minimum chilled water flow can be maintained to the chillers. At the same time, the chiller efficiency is also increased.

RESULTS

Major commissioning activities were completed in April 1999, and the Energy Systems Laboratory continued to monitor BAMC through June 2000. We worked with the operations staff to assist with troubleshooting and to continue to fine-tune the operation. The commissioning started in October 1998, and the 1997-98 utility bills were used to establish the energy baseline. Since the commissioning process extended over a seven-month period, savings were calculated to be approximately $105,000 during the implementation phase. For the fourteen-month period (May 1999-June 2000) savings were measured to be nearly $410,000, or approximately $30,000/month, based on 1997-98 energy prices. Total savings from the commissioning process (October '98 to June 2000) was about $515,000. The ESL cost to meter, monitor, commission, and provide a year's follow-up services, was less than $350,000. This cost does not include any time for the facilities operations staff who repaired kinked flex ducts, replaced failed sensors, implemented some of the controls and subroutines, and participated in the CC process.

REFERENCES

1. Y. Zhu, M. Liu, D. E. Claridge, D. Feary, T. Smith, 1997, A Continuous Commissioning Case Study of a State-of-the-Art Building, *Proceedings of 5th National Conference on Building Commissioning*, Huntington Beach, California, Session 13.

2. M. Liu, Y. Zhu, D. E. Claridge, 1997, Use of EMCS Recorded Data to Identify Potential Savings Due to Improved HVAC Operation & Maintenance (O&M), *ASHRAE Transaction-Research, Vol. 103, part 2, pp. 122-129.*

3. D. E. Claridge, M. Liu, Y. Zhu, et al., 1996, Implementation of Continuous Commissioning in the Texas LoanSTAR Program: "Can You Achieve 150% of Estimated Retrofit Savings" Revisited, *Proceedings of ACEEE, Vol. 4*, pp. 4.59-4.67.

4. Y. Zhu, W D. Turner, D. E. Claridge. *1999*, Report of Energy Efficiency Study and Metering/Utilities Profile for Electricity Deregulation at Texas A&M International University, Laredo, Texas, ESL-TR/99-12/03.

5. Y. Zhu, M. Liu, D. E. Claridge, W. D. Turner, et al., 1998, A Novel Procedure to Determine Optimal Air Static Pressure Set-points and Reset Schedules in VAV Air Handling Units, *Proceedings of 10th Symposium on Improving Building Systems in Hot and Humid Climates*, Fort Worth, pp. 294-301.

6. Y. Zhu, M. Liu, T. Batten, J. Zhou, et al., 2000, Continuous Commissioning Report for Brooke Army Medical Center, ESL report.

7. M. Liu, Y. Zhu, D. E. Claridge, et al., 1999, Airflow Reduction to Improve Building Comfort and Reduce Building Energy Consumption-A Case Study, *ASHRAE Transaction-Research, Vol. 105, Part I.*

8. Y. Zhu, M. Liu, J. Zhou, T. Batten, et al., 2000, Optimization Control Strategies for HVAC Terminal Boxes, *Proceedings of 12th Symposium on Improving Building Systems in Hot and Humid Climates*, San Antonio, Texas.

9. Y. Zhu, M. Liu, T. Batten, et al., 2000, A Simple and Quick Chilled Water Loop Balancing for Variable Flow Systems, *Proceedings of 12th Symposium on Improving Building Systems in Hot and Humid Climates*, San Antonio, Texas.

Chapter 18

SOFTWARE MAINTENANCE
A MUST FOR ENERGY MANAGEMENT PROGRAMS

Yousef Abouzelof, M.S., C.E.M.
Zions Securities Corporation
10 East South Temple, Suite 1500
Salt Lake City, Utah 84133
(801) 321-7562
abouzelofy@zsc.com

ABSTRACT

There are many reasons for implementing a preventive maintenance (PM) program; to lower power consumption, extend the life of equipment, and to maintain or improve tenants thermal comfort. However, all the efforts to service and improve the performance of the HVAC system may be promoted or hindered by the building automation system (BAS). While the PM program may provide a certain level of assurance that the HVAC system is working at optimal performance, the BAS is the one dictating the load level as well as the duration of operation, thus impacting the entire cost of operation of the facility. For that reason, I suggest including software maintenance as an integrated part of the PM program. This article will discuss the various aspects of software maintenance and its impact on the power consumption of the facilities and its operating cost. Also, I will present a list of critical BAS items to be included in the software maintenance program.

DEFFINATIONS

The PM program is usually associated with the maintenance of the physical aspects of facilities: air handlers, chillers, boilers, cooling towers, air compressors, pumps, valves, dampers, etc. The tasks include brushing of tubes, changing of air filters, greasing of pumps, and calibration of dampers. A software maintenance program, on the other hand, deals primarily with the auditing and upkeep of the BAS software programs. Since the BAS is the one controlling the equipment schedule, water and air temperature set-points, and has the ultimate power over the tenants individual cooling or heating variable air volume (VAV) boxes, it is of utmost importance to maintain the system at optimal efficiency.

MAIN REASON FOR SOFTWARE MAINTENANCE

The main reason for implementing a software maintenance program is to reduce the operating costs of the facility. It is good to remember that not long ago the BAS used to be called Energy Management System. The push for integration, speed, and colorful graphics, all but obscured the fundamental reason for building controls, which is to operate the building efficiently and reduce the power consumption of the facility while maintaining a good thermal comfort for the tenants. The BAS is being integrated into building access systems, life and safety equipment, etc. However, the integrity and accuracy of BAS programs will ultimately be the one impacting the operation of the HVAC system, the power consumption and cost of operation for the facility.

START WITH A GOOD PM PROGRAM

Software maintenance is a supplement to the facilities' BAS PM program and should not be considered as a substitute. A comprehensive and effective PM program is needed in order to get the most performance and response out of the BAS. The basic requirements are as follows:

- **Complete inventory of the equipment to be serviced.** This inventory should include all the facilities' main systems as well as their components. Chillers, boilers, cooling towers, air handlers, fans, pumps, dampers, air compressors, roof top units, VAV boxes, fan coils, exhaust fans, water treatment equipments, etc. should be included in this inventory.
- **Provide O&M manuals for all equipment.** The manuals will provide the level of maintenance and frequency as required by the equipment manufacturer.
- **Supply all necessary tools.** The maintenance staff should be provided with the necessary and required tools to perform the various aspects of the PM program.

- **Purchase energy efficient equipment.** Using first cost as the only qualification to purchase a piece of equipment is not the most economical way to operate a facility. Life cycle cost; measuring the cost of purchase and the cost of operation of the equipment over its expected life, is much more effective measure than first cost.
- **Proper training of the maintenance staff.** The in-house maintenance staff should be trained and qualified to operate and maintain the equipment they are trying to service. Training cannot be overemphasized. Handing an untrained maintenance staff member a grease gun will not guarantee that the person will use the correct type of grease. Staff members are the only ones able to maintain or extend the life of equipment, or cut that life by half.
- **Outsource maintenance.** Many facilities are outsourcing part or the entire PM program. There are many advantages and disadvantages to outsourcing based on the size of the facility, staff expertise and operating budget. Some facilities utilize partial outsourcing in which the maintenance staff performs lower level maintenance while highly technical or specialized pieces of equipment are handled by outside vendors. It is worth remembering that outsourcing may solve your training issues, however, you get what you pay for. The lowest bid may not provide the level of maintenance that you would like to have in your facility.

LEVEL OF BAS INTENSITIES

The level of automation and investment in BAS varies between facilities. Some facilities incorporate Direct Digital Controls (DDC) to the latest integration methods to upgrade and optimize their BAS system. On the other hand many facilities are still trying to enter the DDC world very carefully. Here is a list of the different level of automation being experienced by various facilities:
- **Single BAS system for the entire facility.** The facility's BAS utilizes one control company or is being integrated into one master system. Most, if not all of the facilities' equipment are connected to the BAS. This includes chillers, boilers, central air handlers, and VAV boxes. All programs' set points and alarms report back to a central control room PC computer with a graphics user interface monitor. Acknowledgement of alarms, changing of set points and updating of time schedules can be accomplished with ease at the graphics monitor. This is the most comprehensive and automated BAS that a facility can install.
- **Multiple BAS systems.** Economic realities make it very difficult to upgrade the BAS in all of the facilities at the same time. Older but operable systems are maintained as long as possible. The conversion to new BAS is usually based on capital budget requirement, high operating costs and tenants thermal comfort. System integration between old multiple BAS systems, is not widely practiced.
- **In-between BAS upgrades.** A new BAS is being installed in the facility. The upgrade may impact one system; chiller plant, VAV boxes, or may impact an entire building. There are many energy saving opportunities during this upgrade.

- **Partial BAS and manual operation.** Economic and investment reasons may dictate such a system. New BAS is being installed on a particular system, i.e. chiller plant, while the rest of the building will maintain time clocks and stand alone systems.

SOFTWARE MAINTENANCE BASIC TOOLS

The basic tools needed to initiate a software maintenance program are as follows:
- **Master point list.** Every facility should have a master point list, hard copy or on a CD disk. The list will include all the original set points that the BAS engineers has programmed to the system. Some of these points may have been changes to correct for any operating difficulties. However, these points will serve as a reference for the software maintenance program.
- **Sequence of operation.** Each facility should have a clearly defined sequence of operation. This sequence will describe the mechanical engineer's design specification for the equipment.
The sequence of operating will state the operating set points of the mechanical system as well as the operating parameters of the chillers, boilers and air handlers.
- **As-built drawing for VAV boxes locations.** As built drawing showing the correct locations and addresses of VAV boxes is very important document to keep and update if needed.
VAV boxes' temperature set points influence the temperature and the load of the central air handler, and indirectly the chiller and boiler plant loads, thus impacting the power consumption of the entire facility.
- **Training.** Since the introduction of the PC computers during the mid 1980s, more and more BAS vendors are selling the concept that BAS are so intelligent that operator intervention is rarely required. The color graphics are very easy to under stand that minimal training is all it takes to operate the BAS, hence the HVAC system. Nothing could be further from real life day-to-day operation of the HVAC system.
Understanding the basic concepts of the HVAC operation and basic understanding of the BAS terminology is very critical in the operation of the BAS system as well as controlling the energy consumption and cost of the facility. It is important to remember that the operating staff will raise or reduce the capabilities of any BAS to their level of understanding. If the facility lacks the trained personnel to conduct the software maintenance, paying an outside vendor is highly recommended.
- **Accessibility and security of the BAS system.** There are four aspects of accessibility and security of the BAS. **First**, outside hackers, especially if the BAS is a web based system. Internet firewall and security passwords should be utilized to prevent any access to the system. **Second**, maintenance staff members with limited BAS experienced. This group should have limited access to the programming portion of the BAS, however, access to the graphics interface points should be granted. This group will have the most impact on the operation of the facility because of their ability to modify the set points.
Changing the set points on the central air handler, chiller or boiler plant will directly impact the load on the equipment, hence, the power consumption of the facility. **Third**, trained

BAS technicians should have total access and the tools needed to connect remotely to the system. **Fourth**, the BAS system provider may have access to the system using a modem to remotely connect to the BAS and trouble shoot any problem. It is of utmost importance that the facilities manager approves such an arrangement. For security reasons, this arrangement should be evaluated on regular basis.

MAIN ELEMENTS OF THE SOFTWARE MAINTENANCE PROPGRAM

An energy management based software maintenance program should include all the programs and set-points that would impact the energy consumption of the facility, as well as the wear and tear on equipment, and finally the tenants thermal comfort. The following are points to include in your software maintenance program:

- **Time schedule.** This is one of the easiest programs to modify and at the same time the most expansive if abused. Facilities may utilize this program to control the HVAC system as well as lighting schedule. HVAC time schedule controls the operation of central air handlers, chillers, boilers, VAV boxes and so on. The cost penalty of using the wrong time schedule can be obtain by multiplying the KW consumption of all equipment that are running, but not needed, by the extra hours, days or weeks to obtain the total KWH. This total KWH should be multiplied by the facilities' cost per KWH to obtain the total cost of the wasted energy. The time schedule should be evaluated and reviewed on a regular time, but no less than twice a year, especially at the beginning of the cooling and heating seasons.

- **Set points.** The set points of the central air handlers discharge and mix air temperature, and the air duct static pressure should be evaluated and reviewed. Also, VAV boxes' set points for occupied and unoccupied temperatures as well as the CFM settings should be checked regularly.

- **Reset schedule.** Most BAS utilize a reset schedule for air handler discharge air temperature as well as chilled and hot water temperatures. The reset schedule will change the parameters of the hot, chilled water or the discharge air temperature of the central air handler supply fan whenever full cooling or heating is not needed. For example, if the outside air temperature is 30° F or lower, the hot water supply from the boilers can be set at 180° F, however, if the outside air temperature is 50° F or above, then the hot water supply will be reset down to 140° F. The reset schedule should be evaluated and reviewed at least twice a year at the beginning of the heating and cooling seasons. The cost associated with the wrong reset schedule is that the air handler, chiller and coiler plants will end up producing cooler or hotter water temperature than required by the space which translate into higher energy consumption and cost to the facility.

- **Alarms.** All BAS provide the ability to assign a numeric priority to each alarm event for which notification is desired. This includes change of status, change of value, command failure and out of range alarms. Excessive or nuisance alarms are a clear indication of low tolerance between assigned values.

All efforts should be made to adjust or correct the assigned values and all nuisance alarms should be eliminated. There are two costs associated with nuisance and false alarms. First, the labor time required to check these false alarms and second, the more alarms received at the control room, the less likely a true and serious alarm will be caught in time. Regular evaluation and review of the alarms' points and their priority levels should be conducted at least twice a year at the beginning of the heating and cooling seasons.

- **Notification Classes.** The ability of the BAS system to direct alarms to different destinations based on the type of alarm, the day of week, and time of day. Most facilities will distribute alarms by specifying the recipient of each type of alarms. Some alarms may be specified to go to BAS PC computer, audible or visual signal, an emergency printers, or to go to certain technicians' phones or pagers. This program should be evaluated and all phone numbers and pagers should be evaluated for accuracy. The notification program should be checked against changes in maintenance staff assignments and/or their responsibilities.

- **Message updates.** Many facilities utilize the messaging file as an instruction media source for the operating staff. These messages may instruct the staff to check on a piece of equipment, call a vendor for service, or call a technician for help. Review the message file and be sure that all the information is correct, that the vendor is still responsible to respond to call, or the technicians listed are still employed by the facility.

- **After-hours accounting.** Most commercial facilities provide after-hours service such as HVAC and lighting at a predetermined cost. After-hours are defined as any time after the normal business hours, usually between 6:00PM and 7:00AM, Saturday, Sunday and holidays. This service is provided at the tenant's request, and is accomplished by pushing on a button or turning a switch connected to a VAV box in the tenants' own space. The length or duration of the after hours service is usually two or three hours of service. The hourly cost of this service is based on the facilities' operating costs plus any markup and administrative fees. This program could be considered as an added revenue source to an owner or a cost reduction program for a facility. Review the duration time and the cost per hour once a year.

- **Trending.** Trending is the accumulation of time and value pairs at a specified rates for a specified duration. A trending program can be used to track a zone temperature, a chilled water supply temperature, frequency of chiller startups, or any other point in the system. Trending is a valuable tool, however, it is allocated a certain memory size in the BAS PC computer. Most technicians will initiate the program and watch it for a week, then leave it running for months. When trending information reaches its allocated memory size it starts replacing the oldest information with the most recent. Twice a year, check and disable all unnecessary programs from the computer.

- **Lead-lag program.** This program will allow multiple equipment to be assigned the role of lead or lag based on size, capacity or efficiency. For example, if the facility has two boilers, one of the boilers will be assigned the role of lead while the other boiler will lag. If the lead boiler is unable to satisfy the needs of the facility the lag boiler will come on. The lead -lag program can also serve as a backup function. If lead boiler failed to start, the lag boiler will start instead. This is especially import during winter months when freeze protection is of utmost important. This feature also allow multiple equipment to alternate at a predetermined value, i.e. the first of the month or every 300 hours, thus equating the run time and wear and tear on equipment.

EXAMPLES OF SOFTWARE MAINTENANCE

My interest in software maintenance came as a byproduct of retro or re-commissioning of building systems. I re-commissioned two office towers totaling 650,000 sq/ft. One building was in the process of upgrading the BAS, thus both BAS systems were active. The second building had one BAS. The following are examples of what was discovered:

• **Changing of duct static pressure settings.** The building engineer changed the set points on the main air duct of the air handler from 1.5 to 3.0 inches. The change in the static pressure caused the VFD to operate close to 60 Hertz, thus converting a VAV fan system to constant speed. The set-point change was done on 13 of 22 air handlers. All static pressure set points were adjusted back to 1.5 inches and the VFDs backed off to the mid 40s Hertz.

• **Changes in the CFM set points of the VAV boxes.** The building engineer, who had very limited experience with VAV boxes, handled all tenants' thermal comfort complains by changing the CFM setting of the VAV boxes. Thus a max 1,200 CFM VAV box was changed to 2,000 CFM, even though the box was fully open at 1,200 CFM with no possible increase in the amount of airflow. So many VAV boxes were changed up and down that the entire floor had to be reset back to its original balancing report set points.

• **Time schedule changes.** Even though one office tower has 22 air handlers (one per floor), the time schedule for the air handlers was different. The normal business hours of the office tower was 7:00 AM to 6:00 PM, however, some of the fans started as early as 1:00 AM while others did not start until 6:30 AM. Some were running seven days a week while others ran Monday through Friday. Once again, there is no logical reason for this difference in the time schedule. After reviewing the time schedule with the building management and the tenants, the time schedule was corrected.

CONCLUSION

The main purpose of any energy management program is to reduce energy consumption and cost while maintaining the highest level of tenants' thermal comfort. Checking and maintaining the BAS software programs at an optimal level will result in lower power consumption, less wear and tear on equipment, and improve tenants' thermal comfort. Combining a PM program with a software maintenance program will greatly improve the life cycle cost of all controlled equipment.

Chapter 19

IF BUILDINGS WERE BUILT LIKE CARS -
THE POTENTIAL FOR INFORMATION AND CONTROL SYSTEMS
TECHNOLOGY IN NEW BUILDINGS

Barney L. Capehart, University of Florida
Harry Indig, KDS Energy
Lynne C. Capehart, Consultant

ABSTRACT

The purpose of this paper is to compare the technology used in new cars with the technology used in new buildings, and to identify the potential for applying additional technology in new buildings. The authors draw on their knowledge of both new cars and new buildings to present a list of sensors, computers, controls and displays used in new cars that can provide similar and significant opportunities for our new buildings. Some thoughts on how this new technology could be integrated into new buildings are also discussed. The authors hope that calling attention to using new car technology as a model for new building technology will stimulate recognition of the potential for new buildings, and ultimately lead to the implementation of similar technological improvements in new buildings.

INTRODUCTION

A great deal of new technology is available for buildings. Smart Buildings and Intelligent Buildings are labels that have been around for years. But this paper will show that although this wealth of new technology for buildings exists in pieces and as products from many different companies, virtually no newly constructed building utilizes a significant amount of this new technology. Most buildings constructed today are almost identical to the buildings of the 1970's. Even though new materials, design and construction methods, and new ASHRAE building codes have made major improvements in new buildings, these buildings still look and operate much like they did twenty years ago. While it is true that most new buildings have new technology in the form of new equipment and insulation, there is little new technology for the building occupants to see and use.

In contrast, every new automobile – regardless of its price – is filled with new technology compared to the automobile of the 1970's. A new car typically comes with eleven separate computers, has around thirty seven sensors, and provides about twenty electronic display and control functions. It does this for as little as $20,000, and the new car information and control system commonly requires little or no maintenance or repair for a period of three to five years. This technology is often visible, it can be used by the driver and passengers, it is generally STANDARD on new cars, and it is inexpensive and reliable. There is much fancier technology available if you want to pay for it, but the main point is that the majority of the new automotive technology is found on every new car.

Even with all this new technology, today's cars are much more reliable and have significantly reduced maintenance requirements. In the 1970s, an automobile needed a tune up every 10,000 miles. Today, a typical new car does not need a tune up for 100,000 miles. Older cars needed new brakes about every 20,000 miles. Now it's every 50,000 miles. One of the authors bought a new mini van in 1998, and did not need to take it back to the dealer for any service for 40,000 miles! The vehicle did get several oil changes in that period, but no mechanical or electrical work had to be performed.

In comparison, our buildings need maintenance people from the moment we start using them. We're not talking about janitorial work, but about real maintenance of lights, air conditioners, switches, controls, doors and windows. This is like the old days with our cars, when we started making a list of things to be fixed as soon as we drove the car off the dealer's lot. Why can't a new building operate for six months, a year, or even several years without needing any maintenance? Our cars do.

What is the potential for using reliable, comprehensive, integrated, and inexpensive components in our new buildings to create a transparent and efficient information and control system? And what should we do in terms of buying new buildings? It is clear that progress in adapting and implementing technology for new buildings has a long way to go. Nonetheless, we should demand more technology – a lot more. Technological improvements should be standard features that come with every new building without question rather than options that add significant cost to the building. The only question should be where do we draw the line between standard features and additional new, super high tech technology that we will pay extra for?

FEATURES OF AUTOMOBILES THAT WE COULD USE IN BUILDINGS

Individual Control Systems: One of the most noticeable features of new automobile technology is how it provides the driver and often the passengers with individual control systems. Compared to a building, a new car has far more sensors, controls and displays for a much smaller space. There are individually controllable air supplies for the driver and the front passenger. Large vehicles often have air controls for the rear seat passengers too. Temperature ranges for heating or air conditioning are individually controllable, often for the front passenger as well as the driver. The air velocity is controllable with a multispeed fan. The outlet vents are movable and can direct the airflow onto or away from the person. The amount of ventilation air can be controlled by selecting fresh air or recirculation. Some lights such as headlights and interior dome lights are automatic with their sensors. Other lights are individually controllable. The driver or the passenger can turn on selected interior lights, can often dim these lights, and can direct the light to the area where it is needed. The moon roof can be opened or closed by the driver or front passenger. Both front seats are individually adjustable for horizontal position, height, tilt, and back support; and many are heated, too. In addition, in some cars, these individually settings or preferences for

functions like HVAC and seat positions are provided through a memory setting tied to an electronic key.

Compare this technology to the control systems currently available in a common new building. A typical room in a new building may have a thermostat with a control setpoint and a temperature display at that location. It also usually has an unseen VAV control function, and in a few instances a humidistat with a setpoint control and a display of the relative humidity at that location. Lighting is controlled with a single light switch or possibly a single occupancy sensor for lighting. Otherwise, the occupants most likely have no other sensors, controls or displays in that room.

In addition to these personal comfort controls, the new car also a large number of automatic control systems to optimize and control its own operation. Engine control systems insure fuel efficiency and reduce air pollutants from the combustion process. Sensors for inlet air temperature and relative humidity allow optimum fuel flow control and optimum combustion. System computer modules also control the ABS, transmission, cruise control, and body controller.

Display Systems: In terms of maintenance and repair needs, new cars tell the owner much of what needs to be done, and certainly notify us whenever one of our major systems is in need of attention. The new car has sensors that report tire pressure, unclosed doors, lights or other controls left on, unfastened seatbelts, brake fluid status, and many other operational features related to the safety of the car and the occupants. Even a cursory comparison shows that our new buildings lag very far behind the existing use of technology in new cars.

Much of the information on car maintenance and safety is aimed at the driver. What comparable information does a building operator get about maintenance needs of the building or the various rooms in a building? Things that would be helpful to know include whether the air handling system filters were dirty, whether the refrigerant was at the proper level, whether sensors were working properly, whether lights were burned out, or whether the doors were left open.

The present system in buildings is essentially a manual system. Filters are checked manually on a time schedule. Maintenance workers often depend on "human" sensors to notify them of burned-out lights, improperly functioning photosensors, or temperature problems in individual rooms.

Options: New cars have options, and new buildings have options—but these mean very different things. An option available for a new car means that the item or function can be installed on the car at extra cost—but it does not need any additional design engineering, integration or testing. For a building, an option is an item or function that an owner wants to add at extra cost, but most often requires expensive additional design, engineering integration and testing work before it can be installed and operated.

Table 1 below summarizes many of the sensor control and display functions of new cars, and provides a model for desired technology in new buildings.

HOW DID THE AUTOMOTIVE INDUSTRY DO THIS?

To see how to utilize similar innovations in the building industry, we must understand what allows new automobiles to have so much new technology at such a low cost, and why they are so reliable?

Engineering Analysis and Design – A significant amount of engineering analysis and design goes into both the structural and operational features of a new car. In addition, significant engineering analysis and design also goes into the manufacturing and production processes for assembling the new cars. One of the main benefits of this approach is that not only are each of the car's components engineered, the entire system and subsystems are carefully engineered. For example, the electrical power consumption of the components and systems in a new car are carefully analyzed, built and selected to make sure that the total power demand is not greater than the capacity of the electrical power supply system, i.e., the 12-volt battery. Thus, with cars, there is a built in need for energy efficient electrical systems right from the start.

When a building is designed, the electrical load is specified first, and then a power supply system is specified that is big enough to handle the load of the building. Little or no thought is given to minimizing the electrical load itself because there are generally no constraints on the amount of power the utility will supply to the building. Furthermore, utility bills are not part of the first cost of a building, so they are not of concern to the designer.

Overall Quality Control Programs – The reliability of the new car is the result of the significant amount of engineering that goes into the car design, as well as the manufacturing process. Quality and quality control start with the engineering design, and are strongly emphasized during the manufacturing and assembly of the car. Individual components are designed and made with quality and reliability as major goals. Next, subsystems are similarly produced, and finally, systems –including the

entire car – are similarly produced. Ordinary and accelerated life testing are conducted on the car's components, subsystems and systems. Effects of temperature, moisture, mechanical and thermal stress, and other factors are included in these extensive tests. The result is that most of the car's components and systems will last at least three years or 36,000 miles. Warranties on new cars are now available for seven years or 70,000 miles.

Quality control and warranties in building design and construction are very different. Unlike automobiles where the auto manufacturer provides the warranty for the entire vehicle (with the possible exception of the tires), the systems in new buildings are likely to be under several different warranties. The HVAC manufacturer covers the HVAC system; the flooring manufacturer guarantees the carpet/flooring; the plumbing manufacturer guarantees the plumbing fixtures; etc. There is usually no centralized quality control or warranties for a new building in the sense of what we have with cars.

Widespread Use of Microprocessors and Computers – Much of the technology and operational features of our new cars comes from the use of microprocessors and microcomputers. A new car may have as many as 50 separate microprocessors and 11 major computer-based systems. Some new luxury cars have up to 90 microprocessors. A frequently heard statement is that a new car has more computer power in it than our first manned space capsule. The computer-based systems are found in the System Modules for new cars, and account for much of the engine performance, the reduced emissions, the sophisticated diagnostics, and many of our comfort and convenience features. The ECU or Engine Control Unit is the most powerful computer in the car, and it has the demanding job of controlling the fuel economy, the emissions from the engine and the catalytic converter, and determining the optimum ignition timing and fuel injection parameters. These computers, microprocessors and system modules greatly simplify the diagnostic job of finding problems with the car, and providing information on what kind of repair or replacement work is needed.

While a large new buildings with a sophisticated BAS or Building Automation System may well have 50 or more microprocessors attached to it, it doesn't match the new car in terms of having any kind of equal computing power per room or per group of rooms with 2 to 4 occupants. The rooms and offices in our buildings don't have monitoring and self-diagnostic features. They could, because the technology, equipment and systems exist, but they are not supplied as a standard item, and they are not available in the sense that options are available on new cars.

TABLE 1: SENSOR, CONTROL AND DISPLAY COMPARISON FOR CARS AND BUILDINGS

S=Sensor   C=Control   DI=Display
D=Driver   FP=Front Passenger   RP=Rear Passengers
CBO=Controllable by Occupant   NCBO=Not CBO

Function	Cars			Buildings	
	All	Mid-cost	Luxury	All	Some
I. Comfort and convenience					
A. Climate Control (HVAC)				Yes	
1. Zone of Control					
Single Zone	D	D	D	Few	
Dual Zone		D, FP	D, FP	Very Few	
Multi-Zone			D, FP, RP	Most	Individual Zone, CBO
2. Temperature				Yes	
Lever setting (C, DI)	D	D, FP	D, FP	Some	
Thermostat (S, C, DI)	–	D, FP	D, FP	1 per zone	Individual Zone, CBO
3. Air Supply					
Directional Vents (C, DI)	D, FP	D, FP, RP	D, FP, RP	Partial	
Multi-Speed Fan (C, DI)	D	D, FP	D, FP, RP	No	
Ventilation (S, C, DI)	D	D, FP	D, FP	Yes, NCBO	
Recirculation (C, DI)	D	D	D	Yes, NCBO	
4. Humidity (S, C)	–	–	Yes	Some, NCBO	Yes, CBO
5. Air Quality (S, C) (CO, NO$_2$)	–	–	Yes	Yes, NCBO	Yes, On/Off
6. Advanced Features					
Reheat Operation			Some	Most, NCBO	Yes, CBO
Window Fog Control			Some	No	
Air Filters			Some	Yes	
Sun Sensors			Some	No	
B. Seating BT=Back Tilt					
1. Basic – Mech or Elec (C)	D, FP	D, FP	D, FP, RP (BT)	Yes	–
2. Horiz Position + Back Tilt (BT)					
3. Six-Way (C)	–	D, FP	D, FP		Yes
4. Back Support (C)	–	D, FP	D, FP		Yes
5. Heated (C)	–	D	D, FP		No
6. Memory Function (C)		D	D, FP	No	No
C. Visual (Inside Lighting)					
1. Dome Light (C)	Yes	Yes	Yes	Yes	
With Occupancy Sensor (S,C)	Yes	Yes	Yes	No	Yes
Delayed Dimming (S, C)	No	Yes	Yes	No	No
2. Overhead/Task (C)	No	Yes	Yes	Some	Yes
Directional (C)				Few	Yes
3. General					
Door, Glove Box (S, C)	Yes	Yes	Yes	No	?
Visor, Map (C)	No	Yes	Yes	No	?
D. Windows					
Power Windows	No	Yes	Yes	No	
Power Sunroof	No	Yes	Yes	No	Yes
II. Normal Operation					
A. Speedometer (S, D)	Yes	Yes	Yes	No	*
Cruise Control (S, C, DI)	No	Yes	Yes	No	*
B. Odometer (S, C, DI)	Yes	Yes	Yes	No	*

C. Tachometer (S, DI)	No	Yes	Yes	No	*
D. Fuel (S, DI)	Yes	Yes	Yes	No	*
III.Safety and Maintenance					
A. Engine					
1. Engine Control Module (S, C) Temperature, Oil Pressure, Check Engine	Yes	Yes	Yes		
Status Light (S, DI)	Yes	Yes	Yes		
Gauges (S, DI)	No	Yes	Yes		
B. Auxiliary Systems					
1. Electrical					
Generator (Charge)					
Status Light (S, DI)	Yes	Yes	Yes		
Voltage Gauge (S, DI)	No	Yes	Yes		
Lights					
Headlights (C)	Yes	Yes	Yes		
Backup Lights	Yes	Yes	Yes		
2. Brakes					
ABS (S,C)	No	Yes	Yes		
Status Light (S, DI)	Yes	Yes	Yes		
Brake Light Out (S, DI)	No	No	Yes		
3. Others					
Seat Belt (S, DI)	Yes	Yes	Yes		
Turn Signals On (S, DI)	No	Yes	Yes		
Headlights On (S, DI)	No	Yes	Yes		
Low WW Fluid (S, DI)	No	Yes	Yes		
Door Not Closed (S, DI)	No	Yes	Yes		
Exterior Temp (S, DI)	No	Yes	Yes		
IV. Pleasure & Entertainment					
A. Audio System					
Radio	Yes	Yes	Yes		
Satellite Radio			YES		
CD Player	No	Yes	Yes		
B. Video System					
TV	No	No	Yes		
VCR, DVD	No	No	Yes		
C. Computer	No	No	Some		
Internet	No	No	Option		
D. Communications					
Cell phone	No	Yes	Yes		
Internet	No	No	Option		
V. Advanced Systems					
A. Navigation Systems	No	No	Yes		
B. Collision Avoidance Systems	No	No	Option		
C. Rain Sensing Wipers	No	No	Option		
D. DewPoint & Glass Temp Sensors	No	No	Option		
E. Voice Commands	No	No	Option		

System Modules – As discussed above, the System Modules are where the computer-based systems reside in new cars. These System Modules are highly complex, and highly important systems in new cars. Many of our highly desirable performance and comfort features are provided by these System Modules. Typical System Modules in a new car are: the Engine Control Unit, the Instrument Panel Module, the Climate Control Module, the Transmission Control Module, the Power Distribution Box Module, the Airbag Module, the Driver's Door Module, the ABS Module, the Body Controller Module, and the Cruise Control Module. These are just the System Modules that we expect to see on every basic car. They do not include the additional System Modules that we find as options for lower priced cars, or as standard features of higher priced cars. These include Navigation Control Modules, Entertainment System Modules, Advanced Comfort Control Modules and Communication Control Modules for our computers, cell phones and internet access.

Communication Buses -The use of standardized communications buses along with these System Modules makes both designing and building new cars much easier than it was in the old days. Two major services must be accessible to every area of a new car – electric power, and the communications bus. All of the System Modules on a car must be able to communicate with each other, and must be able to receive signals from most of the sensors in the car, and must be able to send signals to the control components, systems and actuators. Without the communications bus, the job of wiring up a car during the assembly operation would simply be too labor and time consuming to have a reasonable cost product. Using a communications bus greatly simplifies the wiring, reduces the number of data sensors, and implements additional features at very little additional cost. Also, the speed of communications is so important now that only a digital bus has the speed and capacity to handle the data collection and data transfer load for a new car.

The communication bus and the System Modules work together to make the design and building of the car much easier. Information is sent over the communication bus in a standard communications protocol – usually the SAE J1850 standard, or the Controller-Area Network (CAN) standard. Recent emphasis has been on using FlexRay, which is a faster and more sophisticated communication bus Data is sent in packets with a standard structure – a label and some data, such as Speed for the label and 52.5 for the speed in MPH. This information packet is picked up by the Instrument Control Module and it can refresh the indication on the speedometer with this new data. With this standard communications bus, the design of the various System Modules becomes much more straightforward. In addition, the sensors in the car now need only to send packets of data out to the communications bus, and it is not

necessary for the car maker to deal with the problem of a particular sensor putting out a strange voltage or current signal that must be converted somewhere into a true physical parameter of the car's operation. For example, it might otherwise have been necessary to have told the Instrument Panel Module maker that the signal for speed was going to be a 4 – 20 mA current loop value, and that 10 mA was equivalent to 40 MPH.

The use of the standardized communication bus also greatly increases the ability to use outside suppliers and sources for many of the components and systems in a new car. The carmaker does not have to worry about how a specific sensor or module works internally; they only need to know that the data will be transmitted in a known, standardized manner, and that it will have a known, standardized structure. Much of the success with using modern technology in cars, and much of the reliability of that technology comes from using this simplified approach with a standardized communications bus.

We basically know how to do this in our new buildings. We have BACnet, LONWorks, and TCP/IP as our most common standard communication protocols. TCP/IP may be the ultimate answer, but we will also need another level of standardization to insure that the data that comes across TCP/IP means the same thing to each different piece of equipment in our facility. Most of our buildings are being wired for a Local Area Network (LAN) with either co-axial cable or fiber optic cable. We have the hardware, we have the software, but we don't have the organizational structure in place to require and enforce the standardized interconnection of all of our building components, subsystems and systems like carmakers do. Without this standardized communication bus running through our entire facility – together with accessible electric power – we will never have the kind of technology that cars have, and we will never have the cost benefit or the reliability that this kind of technology can bring to our buildings.

Smart Sensors – Most of the basic sensors that cars have used in the past to read continuous physical parameters such as temperatures, pressures, flows and levels operated on the principle of producing a voltage or current output proportional to the real value of the parameter. The output of these sensors was almost always nonlinear, and also varied with the temperature or other physical parameters. This resulted in poor measurements, or required the use of more equipment and processing power to correct the sensor reading for the nonlinearity and to provided temperature compensation curves to get accurate readings. Today, smart sensors are used to provide these functions initially with the sensor, and output data to a microprocessor or System Module. The sensor output is read as an input to the microprocessor, and the sensor reading is digitized, corrected, temperature compensated and sent out over the standardized communications bus.

These smart sensors interface directly to the communications bus, and provide fast and accurate measurements. Since the sensor package contains a microprocessor, much of the load is taken off of the System Module that the smart sensor is supporting. Designed and built as an integrated package, the smart sensor fulfills its mission reliably with a low initial cost.

In our buildings, the sensors are expensive, and many of them are not very reliable. They are certainly not reliable in comparison to those in cars. In particular, the relative humidity sensors and CO_2 sensors are notoriously unreliable, and require frequent cleaning, calibration and general maintenance. That level of performance would be unacceptable for the sensors in a car. Why shouldn't the sensors in buildings work reliably for a period of three to five years before they need any significant attention?

Wiring Harnesses and Standard Connectors – The use of pre-assembled wiring harnesses and standard connectors has made the task of wiring up a new car much easier. It is important to use stranded, not solid, wire cable. Each length of stranded wire consists of a twisted bundle of very thin thread-like wires. Solid wire, on the other hand, is a single thick wire segment. The advantage of stranded wire is that it is much more flexible than solid wire, and also less susceptible to breakage. One thread of a stranded wire can break without affecting the performance of the connection, but if a solid wire breaks the connection is lost. Also, if there is one weak link in the reliable performance of any electrical or electronic system, it is the connectors. With this in mind, the importance of carefully and correctly built standardized connectors cannot be overemphasized.

Use of Skilled Assembly Workers – The auto industry has succeeded in recent years by having a large supply of skilled workers at its design, engineering and assembly operations. These skilled workers receive training in their specific jobs as well as training in quality control and process improvement techniques. Many of the manufacturing and design improvements in new cars have come from the production workers themselves. In addition, the skilled workers have made a great improvement in the overall reliability and quality of the new cars. Autoworkers are usually highly paid compared to those working in other industries or services.

The problems we have with the construction of new buildings often come from the use of workers with minimal or insufficient skills for the job. Finding skilled workers may be difficult, and is certainly expensive. The transient nature of much building construction also impedes the retention of skilled workers. As a result there may not be a large pool of highly qualified building construction workers available when a particular building is being built.

One of the most common problems in building structures is the roof, which is the subject of the greatest number of lawsuits in building construction. Most roofs leak, and leak from the day the building is occupied. Roof leaks are the result of poor installation and construction rather than problems with roofing technology and materials. When a roof leaks, water leaks into the walls and is not noticed until mildew and rot are visible; by then the building may be significantly damaged. Mold, mildew and IAQ problems in the building will require more time and money to fix. Using sensors in new buildings to identify roof and wall leaks when they occur is a critical application of automotive type technology in our new buildings. New cars use infrared reflectance sensors to identify rainfall on windshields, and automatically start up the windshield wipers. These sensors, or other types of moisture sensors, if installed throughout our new buildings, would quickly identify leaks and moisture buildup and alert building operational people to this serious problem.

Poor workmanship can cause many other problems in buildings. Even the HVAC system can be affected since random testing has shown that many air conditioning systems are installed with an improper charge of refrigerant. In economic terms, the problem of workers with insufficient skills and quality concerns results in the need to commission buildings to check and see if the building components and systems work as they should. (See discussion on Commissioning below.) This expense is clearly attributable to lack of adequate engineering, lack of quality control measures, and especially lack of highly trained workers.

WHY DOESN'T NEW BUILDING CONSTRUCTION INCLUDE MORE NEW TECHNOLOGY AS STANDARD EQUIPMENT AND SYSTEMS?

Automobiles are built according to a standard plan; building architects on the other hand reinvent the wheel each time they design another building. This lack of standardization in buildings impedes the introduction of new technology in new building construction. Other factors also influence this difference in approach.

Unlike new cars, most new buildings are site built, and are built to "cookie cutter" specifications that emphasize lowest first cost of construction. Even "custom built" buildings are held hostage to the lowest first cost syndrome. Thousands of different construction companies build residential and commercial buildings.

Hundreds of different companies build fairly large commercial buildings. These companies range in size from small businesses to major architectural and engineering firms and major construction firms. It is extremely difficult to implement standards of technology when this many individual companies are involved. It is not impossible by any means – it is just not easy!

The fact that most buildings are site built impedes the assembly line and systems approach to installing new technology that is used in the auto business. One area of building construction that is immediately amenable to the assembly line approach of the carmakers is in the construction of prefabricated or modular buildings. This manufacturing sector is in a perfect position to use the knowledge from the automotive assembly sector to produce buildings with the same level of technology and reliability that we see in new cars. The engineering and the quality control functions are much more cost effective in this sector. The use of more computers, more microprocessors, more System Modules, more Smart Sensors, and definitely a standardized communications bus, would be relatively easy for this sector to provide.

Cars are constructed in a factory assembly line and moved to their ultimate market and user. The factory environment makes it easier to train workers in installing the equipment in new cars as well as training them in quality control procedures. Buildings are constructed at the point of use. Construction workers may work for a long time on a single building doing all types of work. Their training is not likely to be technology specific. Auto assembly workers typically specialize in some part of the assembly process, and therefore can be trained on this more limited work task. In addition, they become quite knowledgable on this part of the assembly operation, and soon become able to add value to the company by suggesting improved methods of designing and constructing components and systems that they assemble. Quality control is more easily stressed in this environment, and many of the workers actually see the final result of their work drive off the assembly line, which serves to positively reinforce the need for a high skill level and the need to perform high quality work. In fact, these workers often own and drive cars produced by the company they work for. Few of these workers will willingly accept poor quality parts, components, systems and assembly procedures as a result of their skill and training level.

More new cars are sold each year than new buildings, so there is a larger market for the technology and the price can be reduced due to bulk purchase of the equipment. This is certainly true at face value, but when the scale of use of technology for buildings is considered, the numerical superiority of the cars goes away. If we consider that the unit of interest in buildings is rooms, and

that we are interested in having the same technology level in each room that we have in a car, we now have a very different prospective. There may very well be more rooms than cars built each year. Thus, the comparison of a room to the car, rather than a building to a car, will lead to a much greater economy of scale for new building construction, and should provide a strong economic incentive to move in this direction for buildings.

Cars have a shorter lifetime than buildings, so new technology can be introduced faster, and the customers can develop a faster appreciation for what it does. Cars certainly do have a shorter lifetime than buildings, but on the other hand, most buildings end up being refurbished, or equipment and systems retrofitted, so there is still a lot of opportunity to use new technology in older buildings. Sensors, controls, System Modules and many of the other features of new car technology can be added to our older buildings when they are needed. In general, the most cost effective way to build an energy-efficient and functionally superior building is to do it right the first time, rather than retrofit it later. However, there is new equipment, and especially new information technology that can be added to rooms and to the entire building. It is not always easy to install co-axial or fiber optic cable in an older building, but most of us have experienced just that. It would have been easier and cheaper to put it in when the building was built, but we still have managed to find a way to get the LAN cable and connections into our rooms and offices so we could network our PCs.

Purchasers of new cars are influenced by features they have seen on other cars. Therefore, consumer demand is important in increasing the marketability of new technology options. This is one of the reasons we need to start getting some of this new technology in our buildings. Once building owners, managers and occupants start seeing what can be done in our buildings, and how much more enjoyable and productive it is to work in buildings with this advanced technology, they will start to demand more technology as a result. It is somewhat amazing that the people who drive cars with all this new technology will go happily to work in buildings that do not come close to providing similar comfort and operational features of technology!

WHAT DOES THE BUILDING CONSTRUCTION INDUSTRY NEED TO DO?
Establish an integrated design and build engineering and management structure. The amount of engineering work that goes into a new building needs to increase significantly. The building structure needs to be designed with high technology use in mind, and needs to utilize new technology to deliver the performance and comfort features that we want in our new buildings. In addition, quality

control and reliability need to be designed and engineered into the building from the start of the project. Then, quality management techniques need to be employed so that the building is actually constructed to provide the quality and reliability features that we expect.

Build more modular buildings. The solutions to providing greater use of technology in new buildings and providing quality and reliable buildings are much easier when the buildings are a modular type with significant pre-site construction performed in a factory or controlled environment. High-tech components and equipment can be installed more easily in prefabricated and modular buildings within a controlled environment and with highly skilled and quality control trained workers.

Impose standards on equipment and system suppliers. Most major construction companies are already in a position to do this. They have the financial leverage to specify components and equipment that meet their exact requirements. The residential manufactured housing sector in particular could do this quite easily. The Federal Sector, States and large companies also have excellent opportunities to set these standards. One of the most important standards is to require a standardized communications bus in a building with all sensors and controls interfacing directly with that standardized communications bus.

Use equipment and system modules. This approach has facilitated the use of so much new technology in new cars at a reasonable cost, and with extremely good reliability. However, as stated above, the standardized communications bus has mode the most dramatic difference. With the standardized communication bus and the system modules, car technology could be transferred to buildings relatively easily. Individual HVAC modules for occupants, individual lighting modules, other comfort modules such as for seating, and building operation and maintenance modules can all be used to greatly increase the performance and reliability of our buildings and yet allow us to build them at reasonable costs. Again, certain sectors such as the residential manufactured housing sector, the hotel/motel sector, and many office buildings could easily adopt this approach.

Are Codes, Standards or Legislation Required To Increase the Use of New Technology in Buildings? There is no question that building codes and standards have been responsible for much of the improvements in standard buildings. With minimum equipment efficiencies, minimum thermal transfer levels, and minimum structural standards in place, companies that construct buildings must meet these minimum standards – regardless of whether it increases the first cost of the building. Without minimum standards such as the ASHRAE 90.1 standard, many of our

buildings would still have inferior equipment and poor insulation, because it was cheaper to put in initially. The standards for utilizing new technology could be set voluntarily by large companies and big purchasers of buildings like the Federal Sector, the States, schools, and the hotel/ motel sector. Certainly the auto industry has incorporated many of the new technological features without needing government intervention.

Integrate new building technology with the desktop computers and BAS (Building automation systems) that are already being installed in new buildings. In truth, the types of smart sensors, system modules and standardized communication buses that the authors have been recommending for use in new buildings should be considered an integral part of our overall Building Automation System. All of these components, systems and equipment must work together seamlessly to provide the expected level of performance and comfort and all the desktop computers should be tied in to these systems through a Local Area Network.

The desktop computer can be the equivalent of the car dashboard or instrument panel, and it should be our personal interface to an expanded BAS. It could tell us what the space temperature is and how much ventilation is being provided. It should allow us to set our personal preferences for lighting levels, seat positions, window or skylight openings, etc. It should also let us enter our new desired values of these space parameters.

BENEFITS OF STANDARDIZED COMMISSIONING OF BUILDINGS

Commissioning a building is defined in ASHRAE Guideline 1 – 1996 as: The processes of ensuring that building systems are designed, installed, functionally tested over a full range, and capable of being operated and maintained to perform in conformity with the design intent (meaning the design requirements of the building). Commissioning starts with planning, and includes design, construction, start-up, acceptance and training, and can be applied throughout the life of the building.

Commissioning a building involves inspection, testing, measurement, and verification of all building functions and operations. It is an expensive and time consuming activity, but it is necessary to insure that all building systems and functions operate according to the original design intent of the building. Commissioning studies on new buildings routinely find problems such as: control switches wired backwards, valves installed backwards, control setpoints incorrectly entered, time schedules entered incorrectly, bypass valves permanently open, ventilation fans wired permanently on, simultaneous heating and cooling occurring, building pressurization actually negative, incorrect lighting ballasts installed, pumps running backwards, variable speed drives bypassed, hot and cold water lines connected backwards, and control dampers permanently fully open. And this is just a short list!

The process of commissioning a building constructed in the manner of a new car, and using the new car-like technology would be far quicker and simpler, as well as being much less expensive. The use of standardized components, subsystems and systems could actually eliminate the need to check and test these items each time they are used in a new building. A factory or laboratory, standardized commissioning test could well determine their acceptability with a one-time procedure. The use of a standardized communication bus would dramatically shorten the time and effort of on-site testing of the building components, subsystems and systems. Data from all sensors and controls would be accessible on the communications bus, and would allow a significant amount of automated testing of basic functions and complex control actions and responses in the building. A Commissioning Module could also be added to the building systems, and would even further automate and speed up the Commissioning process. This Commissioning Module would remain as a permanent building system, and would not only aid in the initial Commissioning process, but also the Re-Commissioning process, and the Continuous Commissioning process.

Presently, the cost of Commissioning a new building is around 2 to 5 percent of the original cost of construction. The use of Standardized Commissioning tests, and the use of a Commissioning Module, would greatly reduce this cost. Although Commissioning has been shown to be a cost effective process – usually having a payback time of one to two years – many building owners do not want to spend the additional money upfront for the Commissioning effort. A prevailing attitude is "I have already paid to have the job done correctly. Why should I have to be the one to pay to check to see that it has actually been done correctly?" This is a difficult attitude to overcome, and it is often a hard sell to convince new building owners that they will actually come out ahead by paying this cost to verify that their building does work as it was designed to work.

One final note on Commissioning is that from one of the author's energy audit experience, many problems found in conducting audits of existing buildings are clearly ones where the problem has been there since the building was constructed. For example, in the audit of a newspaper publishing company it was found that the cost of air conditioning was excessive. Further checking showed that the heating coil and the cooling coil of the major air handling unit were both active during the hottest part of the summer. Even further checking showed that the control specifications specifically called for that simultaneous

heating and then cooling! Once that original problem was corrected, not only did the air conditioning bill go down dramatically, but the reports from the building occupants stated how much better they thought the air conditioning system was working since they were much more comfortable.

DO NEW BUILDINGS NEED "DASHBOARDS?"

The dashboard and instrument panel is the heart of the driver – car interface. Status information on the car's operation is presented in easily understood form here. Why wouldn't it make sense to have a similar feature in a new building? Not the complex HMI or GUI from a BAS, but a simplified display for average building occupants, and maybe even one for the building engineer or maintenance supervisor. Why not a "dashboard" type of display for each floor of a building? This could be located in a visible place, and occupants could see the status of energy use in terms of peak cost or off-peak cost, daily use of kWh and therms of gas, could see temperature and RH conditions at a glance, and could get red light/green light indicators for energy use and maintenance actions. These "dashboards" could be provided on each floor of the building, and several could be provided to the operation and maintenance staff. These simplified "dashboard" type of displays could also be available on the PCs of the occupants and operating personnel. Cars provide a powerful model for us to use in many building technology applications.

ADDITIONAL CONSIDERATIONS

The increasing sophistication of information technology coupled with its rapidly falling costs are making possible ever "smarter" buildings with increased capabilities for customizing the workplace to the needs of the workers and their employers. Smarter buildings cannot happen without extensive use of the basic building blocks of sensors, actuators and controllers. Many more are needed in new buildings. The economics of replacing existing structures with wholly new ones is daunting, and so new technologies are especially desirable if they can be retrofitted into existing spaces, replacing existing infrastructures to support change.

Research opportunities exist at the interface of how people work, where people work, and how they can be made more effective in buildings as they have become in their cars. Much of the research agenda needs to develop a more quantitative evaluation of productivity gains brought about by innovations in information and control technologies in new buildings. We not only need to focus on general purpose commercial buildings, but consider special purpose buildings, such as schools or hospitals. They are significantly affected by the new information technologies; including cable TV and computers. These research needs in commercial buildings are certainly worthy of further investigation and continued development and application of new sensors, actuators and controllers.

CONCLUSION

New buildings have not kept up with technological advances, especially when compared to automobiles. All we need to do is to make one trip in a new car, and then make one visit to a new building to see this for ourselves. Comfort level, safety levels, reliability levels, quality control levels and automation levels are all much higher in new cars than in buildings. The imagination and creativity that goes into new car technology and manufacture should be harnessed for our new buildings as well. We really do need to start building our new buildings like we build our new cars.

BIOGRAPHICAL SKETCHES OF AUTHORS

Barney L. Capehart, PhD, CEM is a Professor Emeritus of Industrial and Systems Engineering at the University of Florida in Gainesville, FL. He has broad experience in the commercial/industrial sector having served as the Founding Director of the University of Florida Energy Analysis and Diagnostic Center /Industrial Assessment Center from 1990 to 1999. He personally conducted over one hundred audits of industrial and manufacturing facilities, and has helped students conduct audits of hundreds of office buildings, small businesses, government facilities, and apartment complexes. He regularly taught a University of Florida course on Energy Management, and currently teaches Energy Management Seminars around the country for the Association of Energy Engineers (AEE). He is a Fellow of IEEE, IIE and AAAS, and a member of the Hall of Fame of AEE. He is the co-author of *Guide to Energy Management*, author of the chapter on Energy Management for the *Handbook of Industrial Engineering*, and wrote the chapter on Energy Auditing for the *Energy Management Handbook*.
Capehart@ise.ufl.edu

Harry Indig, BSME, MSME, has worked in the automotive industry for over twenty-five years. During this time he became involved in energy and alternate fuels. He specializes in testing, systems development, and project management, and has completed numerous challenging positions in product development at Ford Motor Company in testing as a technician, technologist and product engineer. General Motors Corporation sponsored Harry's Master Thesis in the fabrication of an inwardly opposed engine and Harry worked in the engineering laboratories and in Design and Release for GM Trucks. Harry worked on projects designed for development several years in the future. As Energy Engineering became intertwined with the automotive industry, Harry became more interested in the applications and needs for energy alternatives in the United States. He has joined the Association of Energy Engineers and has started a company, KDS Energy Alternatives, LLC which is working on anaerobic digestion energy process. Harry is an active member in the American Society of Mechanical Engineers, and a member of the Society of Automotive Engineers. He is the author of several SAE papers.
HIndig@Comcast.net

Lynne C. Capehart, BS, JD is a consultant in energy policy and energy efficiency, and resides in Gainesville, FL. She received a B. S. with High Honors in Mathematics from the University of Oklahoma, and a JD with Honors from the University of Florida College of Law. She is co-author of *Florida's Electric Future: Building Plentiful Supplies on Conservation;* the co-author of numerous papers on PURPA and Cogeneration Policies; and the co-author of numerous papers on commercial and industrial energy efficiency. She was Project Coordinator for the University of Florida Industrial Assessment Center from 1992 to 1999. She is a member of Phi Beta Kappa, Alpha Pi Mu, and Sigma Pi Sigma.
Lynneinfla@aol.com

BIBLIOGRAPHY

Argonne National Laboratory program on sensor development, www.transportation.anl.gov/ttrdc/sensors/gassensors.html

Automated Buildings website, www.automatedbuildings.com

Automotive Electrics and Electronics, Third Edition, 1999, Robert Bosch, GmbH, Stuttgart, Germany, in association with the Society of Automotive Engineers, Warrendale, PA.

Court Manager's Information Display System, www.ncsc.dni.us/bulletin/V09n01.htm

Delphi Automotive Electronics Website, www.delphi.com/automotive/electronics

How Car Computers Work, www.howstuffworks.com/car-computer.htm

New car features, www.autoweb.com.au

Smart Energy Distribution and Consumption in Buildings, CITRIS – Center for Information Technology Research in the Interest of Society, www.citris.berkeley.edu/SmartEnergy/SmartEnergy.html

Chapter 20

MAXIMIZING REVENUE POTENTIAL THROUGH REMOTE AUTOMATION SYSTEMS

Frits Bruggink at Echelon Corporation

Today's buildings incorporate a wide array of new technologies that enable owners and property managers to achieve cost-effective operations, reduced capital equipment and operational expenses, remote management capabilities, enhanced comfort and security features, and energy savings.

Intelligent device networks facilitate the exchange of real-time information between remote devices and mission-critical applications and building systems. These "smart" devices have the ability to communicate with each other over virtually any wireless or wireline communications pathway, including existing power lines. A non-proprietary control system is essential, because it provides an open network to which many systems can be integrated. As new portions of a building are upgraded, users are free to select products and services based on performance, features, and costs from any vendor they choose—and are assured of interoperability.

A single, non-proprietary Building Automation System (BAS) using LonWorks™ networks can benefit building owners and managers in many ways. Accessible through the Internet from anywhere, an intelligent device network gives owners and facility managers a real-time, detailed view of every system throughout the building or campus—from HVAC and lighting to security and landscaping irrigation—24 hours a day. Alarms indicating fluctuations in equipment performance enable managers to often anticipate problems before the system fails. Scheduled repairs replace costly breakdowns, and systems are maintained with minimal disruption to tenants. System problems can be corrected on-line, such as adjustments to air handlers, lighting, and heating or cooling. Improved preventive maintenance leads to longer equipment life, again reducing costs.

This ability to remotely access real-time information through intelligent device networks allows building operations to be far more efficient. The operator can be at the building site or at a remote location and access the devices via the Internet using a PC. This remote control is enabled by an Internet Protocol (IP) backbone to route the building's sub-systems data to the remote operator. It allows for the management of critical functions like energy management, security, lighting, and inventory control over the Internet—from corporate headquarters, or even using a laptop with mobile Internet access.

The ability to share more information makes possible many long sought-after applications, including integrated energy control systems. For example, in response to access control reader data and daylight illumination sensors, the HVAC and lighting systems can automatically adjust the comfort and illumination levels in different work areas based on individual preferences to reduce energy costs. Lighting can be adjusted on an office-by-office basis to adjust for peak daylight and weather changes—either automatically or through commands entered from a user's PC via the corporate LAN. Heating and air conditioning can be similarly tailored.

Additionally, as more and more disparate systems are tied together, corporations can gain other benefits of efficiency and integration. Besides enabling devices to communicate with one another, information can be captured and used to better analyze energy costs and requirements for product development, fostering greater understanding of requirements and procedures to reduce costs. Fuji Electric recently announced their commitment to help corporations achieve these efficiencies by creating a business that uses a leading control network platform to tie automation systems with enterprise applications like MRP, ERP, CRM, etc.

The applications are numerous for companies in diverse industries to use open, intelligent device networks to increase productivity and cut costs.

Italian giant Enel is a case in point on using control networks for automation and energy conservation. Enel has committed to installing the LonWorks technology in twenty-seven million homes, eliminating the need for meter readers and expensive data collection, while empowering customers with information on personal electricity use and conservation. Cost savings are expected to be a half a billion dollars a year, drawing the attention of other utility companies interested in achieving similar savings.

St. Charles Parish Waterworks tracks filter runs, monitors breakdowns and determines more efficient backwashing procedures for more than 40,000 people that it provides water to from plants on both sides of the Mississippi River. Plants, such as St. Charles Parish, can save 30 percent on installation and 50 percent on cabling using LonWorks systems.

MST Measurement systems uses intelligent device networks to help semiconductor companies better manage power, monitor and control hazardous gas leaks, and collect more detailed information, such as status of the alarm, sensor cells, general system status and concentration levels. With control systems, MST can save these companies 40 percent in installation costs.

France Telecom is tying together the existing and new LonWorks networks in over 40 of its buildings for centralized monitoring and control of HVAC, security and lighting systems. The centralized building management system helps to cut back on increasing building management, maintenance and surveillance costs, and the open nature of the platform is conducive to further expansion down the line as new devices, systems and buildings are added.

In the commercial and entertainment sectors, Trump Tower, The San Diego International Airport and the Knickerbocker Hotel in Chicago are using LonWorks technology for automating and adjusting temperature control.

Others using LonWorks networks to save money and automate business processes include: Nestle, General Motors, W.R. Grace, Texaco, Shell, Trump Tower and the Knickerbocker Hotel in Chicago and Proctor & Gamble.

Open networking standards and turnkey, end-to-end control systems are revolutionizing the way building owners and managers monitor critical operations by enabling this information to be easily and readily accessed through a Web browser in real-time. Better ways of managing heating and refrigeration, lighting and air conditioning, and the ability to monitor and adjust this information across the board can provide a corporation with a competitive edge. Costs of these systems often pay for themselves many times over with savings that are achieved through automation and conservation. In the future, intelligent device networks will become an essential component of building control systems to reduce energy costs, improve efficiency and operating margins and facilitate overall decision-making processes.

Frederic "Frits" Bruggink is the senior vice president and general manager of the service provider group at Echelon Corporation. The service provider group works with electric utilities and other service providers such as telecommunications companies, cable operators, and Internet Service Providers (ISPs) on the development of open standards.

Echelon Corporation is the creator of the LonWorks™ platform, a widely used standard for connecting everyday devices such as appliances, thermostats, air conditioners, electric meters, and lighting systems to each other and to the Internet. Echelon's hardware and software products enable manufacturers and integrators to create smart devices and systems that lower cost, increase convenience, improve service, and enhance productivity, quality, and safety. Thousands of companies have developed and installed more than 18 million LonWorks-based devices into homes, buildings, factories, trains, and other systems worldwide.

Chapter 21

STRATEGY FOR DEVELOPING 10-YEAR ENERGY MANAGEMENT PLANS AT U.S. ARMY FORCES COMMAND INSTALLATIONS

Graham B. Parker, Program Manager
Pacific Northwest National Laboratory

Adrian Gillespie, Energy Engineer
U.S. Army Forces Command

Doug Dixon, Program Manager
Daryl Brown, Staff Engineer
Ray Reilly, Senior Program Manager
Mike Warwick Staff Scientist
Pacific Northwest National Laboratory

ABSTRACT

In order to reach the energy reduction and sustainability goals of the Executive Order 13123, and to minimize overall energy and water costs, the U.S Army Forces Command (FORSCOM) has embarked on a program to develop comprehensive 10-year *Energy Management Plans* for each of the 11 major FORSCOM installations. These plans will identify activities and projects critical to the installations reaching the Executive Order (E.O.) goals as well as help ensure a reliable and secure energy supply. Each FORSCOM installation will be responsible for developing a plan that is closely linked with the installation Master Plan. The *Energy Management Plan* will cover both demand side (efficiency) elements and supply side (commodity procurement), as well as energy/water security assessments and funding/financing resource requirements.

At FORSCOM's request, the Pacific Northwest National Laboratory (PNNL) will be assisting the installations with plan development.[1] On the demand side, PNNL is working with each installation to 1) establish the baseline from which to measure progress (energy, water and greenhouse ga s baselines), 2) identify specific activities/projects to reduce energy/water use and emissions (e.g., energy efficiency retrofit projects, replacing equipment on failure, new construction), and 3) identify sources of funding for implementing these activities (e.g., government funds, Energy Savings Performance Contracting, Utility Energy Services Contracting, other third party financing). On the supply side, PNNL is working with the suppliers of energy commodities and the installations to ascertain future options for engaging in the deregulated energy markets, the potential for on-site/distributed generation (including green power/renewables), wholesale electrical customer status and energy security. The installation plans will be rolled up to form a total *FORSCOM Energy Management Plan*. The goal is to have the installation and FORSCOM Plans in place by mid-FY2003.

To date, the plan development activity has been initiated at Forts Lewis (WA), Riley (KS), Hood (TX), Campbell (KY), and Bragg (NC). The Plan for Fort Lewis is currently being drafted based on the analysis completed in the third quarter of FY2002.

This paper highlights the results of the Fort Lewis analysis, which serves as an example of the type of analysis and plan development being undertaken for the remaining 10 installations.

INTRODUCTION

FORSCOM requested that each installation

---

[1] Operated for the U.S. Department of Energy by Battelle Memorial Institute under contract DE-AC06-76RL01830

develop a 10-year *Energy Management Plan* for submission by August 2002. [1] Subsequent changes by the Department of the Army in the organization of the management of Army (and FORSCOM[2]) installations have delayed the development of the plans by several months; however, they still need to be developed. These plans are intended to achieve two major objectives: First, to lay the groundwork to ensure that the goals of Executive Order 13123 will be met. Second, to budget (as instructed by the E.O.) for the resources necessary to meet those goals. [2] The installation-level plans will be integrated into a detailed *FORSCOM Energy Management Plan* that will be used to project future budgets for supporting energy projects and activities at installations. FORSCOM has requested that PNNL assist installations in development of the plans, primarily with analytical and budgeting activities.

Each installation will develop a plan that meets its own energy management needs. Installations may want to expand the plan to cover all infrastructure, or include additional energy management elements. However, in order to support development of the overall FORSCOM Plan and budget projections, the following elements are to be included, at a minimum, in each installation's plan.

Demand Side Requirements
For the demand side, each plan is expected to:

1. Project annual installation energy-use intensity (EUI) on a million Btu/ft^2 basis from FY2002 through FY2010, covering all installation facilities. The plan should document the FY1985 baseline, the current (FY2001) level, and the energy consumption reduction goals levied by the E.O.

2. Document numerically how the goals will be reached through contributions from new construction, rehabilitation, demolition, efficiency retrofit, improved O&M, and energy awareness activities. If the installation believes that it cannot achieve

compliance with the E.O. goals, the plan should include a detailed explanation.

3. Describe how the installation will manage compliance with the water conservation, petroleum use reduction, Energy Star® procurement, and greenhouse gas emission requirements of the E.O.

4. Describe how the installation will manage compliance with the E.O. requirement that the entire installation be audited every 5 years.

5. Identify, on an annual basis, the financial resources that will be required to achieve E.O. objectives. These resources might include utility modernization funding for non-privatized utilities and central heating/cooling systems, installation-level funding including environmental program funding, design assistance to improve the energy performance of construction and rehabilitation projects, Energy Conservation Investment Program (ECIP) funding, Energy Savings Performance Contract (ESPC) funding, Utility Energy Services Contracting (UESC) funding, Resource Efficiency Manager (REM) positions, energy/water efficiency awareness materials, and/or other available mechanisms. The plan should document funding requirements such that required resources can be identified and submitted to the Department of the Army as unfunded requirements.

Supply Side Requirements
The following are the expected requirements for characterizing the supply side:

1. Describe how the installation plans to work with franchise (energy) suppliers, or within competitive markets, to procure energy commodities and minimize commodity costs.

2. Describe how the installation will meet green power/renewables, and reduced power plant air emission requirements of the E.O.

3. Describe any plans for onsite generation—including small-scale distributed generation—of electricity.

Energy Security Requirements and Activities
Energy security is of critical importance to today's installations and thus will be

---

[2] FORSCOM HQ will become the HQ of the Department of the Army Southeast Regional Office (SERO) on 10/02 with responsibility for 19 Army installations located in the Southeast Region (IV). Nevertheless, the *Energy Management Plan* is to be developed for all FORSCOM installations, even those that fall outside of the SERO.

incorporated into the 10-year Plan. Thus, the plan will:

1. Describe any plans for working with commodity suppliers to enhance the reliability/security of delivered energy and water commodities.

2. Describe any plans to assess and improve the security and protection of energy and water systems on the installation.

PLAN EXAMPLE ANALYSIS

A generic example of the summary "compliance pathway" for achieving the E.O. energy use intensity goals is shown in Figure 1. PNNL works with each installation energy manager to develop the analysis for compiling the data shown in this figure. The analysis is based on information provided by the energy manger as well as information collected during on-site meetings and data collection activities.

Table 1 shows an example of an associated "resource requirements" table. This table is a summary of the resources (funding) required to meet the energy use goals and thus forms the basis for budgeting for appropriated federal funding (e.g., ECIP), private sector funding (e.g., UESC, ESPC) technical assistance (e.g., design assistance or sustainability compliance) necessary to achieve the forecasted savings and thus achieve the EUI goal.

FORT LEWIS EXAMPLE ANALYSIS

Below is a discussion of the analysis undertaken by PNNL to support the Fort Lewis energy manager in the development of the *Energy Management Plan* for Fort Lewis. PNNL initiated the 10-year plan development for FORSCOM with a site visit to Fort Lewis in early FY2002. During the site visit, a series of meetings were held with site staff to describe the Plan development process and to gather data that are critical to the analysis and development of the plan.

Analytical Approach

The analytical approach was to develop a model of the buildings and other energy-related infrastructure at Fort Lewis, calibrate that model to actual FY2001 energy use, and then utilize the model to predict the energy consumption impact of each of the bulleted items above.

Building inventory data for Fort Lewis were obtained from the Headquarters Executive Information System (HQEIS) databases. Approximately 30 generic building proxies were developed to represent buildings across FORSCOM. Each of the buildings at Fort Lewis was assigned to one of the generic proxies. The median building size (square footage) and vintage (age) were then calculated for each proxy based on the building inventory specific to Fort Lewis. Building characteristics were developed from a combination of inferencing relationships within the Facility Energy Decision System (FEDS) model (driven by building type, size, climate, and vintage) and walk-through audits of selected buildings at Fort Lewis during a site visit [3].

Development of the Fort Lewis energy model included characterization of non-building energy-related infrastructure as well. Natural gas consumption and steam production data at Fort Lewis central energy plants were used to estimate boiler energy conversion efficiencies and thermal distribution losses. Rules-of-thumb based on more detailed assessments conducted at other FORSCOM installations were used to estimate energy consumption for non-building lighting, water pumping, and electricity distribution.

Building energy use was simulated with FEDS and combined with the non-building energy infrastructure characterization to predict the total site energy consumption for FY2001. Uncertain elements of the modeling assumptions were adjusted until the model's energy consumption prediction matched "reasonably well" with actual energy consumption for FY2001 as reported by Fort Lewis in its annual energy and water reporting to the Department of the Army.

RESULTS

Energy impacts are measured by the reduction in site energy intensity (MMBtu/ksf—million Btu/ 1000 ft^2) resulting from the prospective event being evaluated. All events affect energy use; some affect both energy use and building square footage. The results are the combined effect of both energy consumption and building square footage changes on overall site energy intensity. Fort Lewis energy intensity is reported as 91.98 MMBtu/ksf in FY2001 in the Army reporting database, dropping from 118.11 MMBtu/ksf in the FY1985 baseline (reference) year [4]. Thus, Fort Lewis will have to drop its energy intensity to 76.77 MMBtu/ksf to meet the FY2010 energy goal as determined by the E.O.

Weather is assumed to have a significant impact on site energy consumption. For example, variation in weather from a typical meteorological year can increase or decrease energy use by as much as 10%. Thus at Fort Lewis, a reduction of about 3 MMBtu/ksf in site energy intensity was predicted for FY2001 if a typical meteorological year had occurred rather than the actual weather. While a return to typical weather cannot be predicted for any specific year, estimating future energy consumption based on typical weather is the best assumption possible. Note that site infrastructure characteristics and the model calibration process were based on the actual weather for FY2001. The impacts of prospective changes to the infrastructure were based on weather for a typical meteorological year.

Impact of Specific Site Activities on EUI

Figure 2 shows the impact on site energy use intensity of replacement of equipment upon failure. Included here are HVAC and service hot water (SHW) equipment in buildings. This equipment is assumed replaced, on average, at the end of its expected service life. Technological advances and more rigorous building codes have generally resulted in improved efficiency of current equipment compared to existing stock. The cumulative effect of this activity was an estimated reduction in site energy intensity of about 2 MMBtu/ksf, occurring uniformly from FY 2002 through 2010.

Figure 3 shows the impact on site energy use intensity of building demolition on energy intensity, calculated to result in a cumulative reduction in site energy intensity of about 2 MMBtu/ksf through FY2010. The impact of building demolition was calculated by removing buildings on the Facility Reduction Program list and temporary buildings constructed from 1941-1945 within A, B, C, D, E, and F block codes in the real property inventory. Total demolition was 1946 ksf and was assumed to occur uniformly over the assessment period. The average energy consumption avoided for demolished buildings was 114 MMBtu/ksf.[3]

---

[3] This figure, and similar figures quoted for new building construction, includes the impact of electricity distribution losses at Fort Lewis in addition to energy consumed within the buildings.

Figure 4 shows the impact on site energy use intensity of new barracks construction. About 2300 ksf of new barracks are planned for construction at Fort Lewis through FY2010. Future barracks were assumed to have energy-related features similar to building #12630. Energy simulations predicted a contribution of 40 MMBtu/ksf for the new barracks. The cumulative impact on the site's energy intensity was a reduction of nearly 5 MMBtu/ksf, with the year-by-year impact proportional to the planned construction schedule. Note that the impact of demolishing old barracks was included in the building demolition impact described above.

The impact on site energy intensity of family housing construction is shown in Figure 5. The cumulative impact on site energy intensity through FY2010 is a reduction of 1.3 MMBtu/ksf. Approximately 700 ksf of family housing are planned for construction as part of the Residential Communities Initiative (RCI). Per advice received from Fort Lewis RCI representatives, the new housing was presumed to be gas heated, but constructed to Washington State energy codes for electrically-heated housing and use Energy Star appliances. Energy simulations predicted a contribution of 48 MMBtu/ksf for the new housing. Planned housing construction was assumed to occur uniformly from FY2003 through FY2010.

The impact on site energy use intensity of new construction other than barracks or family housing is shown in Figure 6. Although about 500 ksf of "other" new buildings are planned for construction through FY2010, the cumulative reduction in site energy intensity was only 0.5 MMBtu/ksf. Although newer buildings are generally less energy intensive than existing stock, housing is significantly less energy intensive than non-housing, so has a greater impact on reducing energy intensity per sf constructed. Specifically, the mix of "other" new buildings was predicted by energy simulations to consume 67 MMBtu/ksf.

In recent years, Fort Lewis has shut down two central boiler plants and installed building-level heating systems. Although not currently planned, this strategy could be employed for the remaining central boiler plants, namely Division Area, Madigan Hospital, and Building 9785. Thermal distribution losses are still a significant part of energy consumption at Fort Lewis. Total thermal distribution losses were estimated to be about 120,000 MMBtu/year. Incorporating the corresponding boiler conversion losses (based on 75% boiler plant efficiency) increases the effective distribution loss to about 160,000 MMBtu/year, or about 7 MMBtu/ksf per year.

Thermal distribution losses are nearly constant whenever the distribution system is energized. During the summer, when end-use loads are often limited to SHW, much of the steam production leaving the boiler plant is merely keeping the piping warm. The monthly thermal distribution loss was estimated to be two-thirds of the monthly load for August in the Division Area and one-third of the monthly load for August at Madigan. A lower loss fraction was assumed for Madigan because of the significantly higher SHW loads experienced by a hospital compared with other buildings. Steam production data were not available for the smaller 9785 boiler plant, so its distribution system was assumed to be 80% efficient on an annual basis.

The total estimated reduction in energy intensity for utility modernization and decentralization of boilers is shown in Figure 7 for the three boiler plants at Fort Lewis. This reduction was estimated to be about 8 MMBtu/ksf, which includes elimination of the thermal distribution losses described above and an additional reduction of energy (natural gas) consumed to provide the energy used (steam or hot water) by the buildings served. The additional savings of 1 MMBtu/ksf stems from an assumed improvement to 80% conversion efficiency for new distributed boilers compared with 75% for the existing boilers.

The potential impact of cost-effective, energy-specific retrofits via performance contracting is shown in Figure 8. The total potential reduction in site energy intensity was estimated to be about 8 MMBtu/ksf based on a retrofit analysis conducted with FEDS.[4] The August 17, 2001, proposal by the installation energy savings performance contractor (ESCO) estimated annual energy savings of 86,199 MMBtu for its proposed projects or about 4 MMBtu/ksf if spread over the entire site. The ESCO proposal did not cover the entire site, however; rather, the proposal was limited to 73 buildings, mostly in the Division Area, and specifically excluded existing housing and the hospital.

Therefore, a site-wide estimate of 8 MMBtu/ksf appears reasonable and possibly conservative. The availability of lower cost government financing was estimated to result in a potential reduction in site energy intensity of about 11 MMBtu/ksf. Of course, government funding for energy-specific retrofits is less likely to be available.

Cumulative Impacts and Findings
The combined annual and cumulative site energy intensity impacts of all prospective infrastructure changes evaluated for Fort Lewis are shown in Figures 9 and 10, respectively.[5] These figures include the impact of a typical meteorological year compared with actual FY2001 weather, which is included as part of the reduction shown for FY2002.

The estimated cumulative potential reduction in energy intensity (30 MMBtu/ksf) would appear to be twice the reduction needed (15 MMBtu/ksf) to meet the FY2010 energy savings goal. ***Thus, the analysis indicates that installation can likely achieve the E.O. energy reduction goals through these actions.*** However, three caveats are noted.

1. The results presented in Figures 2-10 were calculated without considering the interactive effects of the individual events. For example, the benefits derived from replacement of equipment upon failure and energy-specific retrofits will not be seen in buildings being demolished. In addition, declining marginal impacts result in the combined effect of constructing new barracks, housing, and other buildings being less than the sum of the individual effects. Accounting for these interactive effects results in a net cumulative potential reduction in energy intensity of ~28 MMBtu/ksf, or an ~7% reduction in savings.

2. Consideration should also be taken regarding the likelihood of each event occurring. A return to typical weather, on average, is practically a certainty.

---

[4] FEDS summary results are presented in detail in Table 2.

[5] Note that in Figure 10, the cumulative reduction is not adjusted for any interactive effects.

Replacement of equipment upon failure requires no special planning or budget request. Funding for near-term construction and demolition projects is likely, but long-term (FY2006-2010) projects are more uncertain.

3. There are no current plans to eliminate the remaining thermal distribution systems, and the total energy savings potential via ESPC financing will have to be proved through additional work by the site ESCO.

4. Finally, uncertainty exists in the various assumptions incorporated in the Fort Lewis energy model developed for this evaluation. However, calibration results suggest the model accuracy is acceptable for the intended use of the results.

OTHER APPLICATIONS OF ANALYSIS APPROACH

This analytical approach has also been broadly applied to all 11 FORSCOM installations to estimate the potential impact on FORSCOM's combined energy intensity in 2010 from key planned or prospective changes to the installation energy-related infrastructure [5]. This includes changes from the natural turnover of certain energy-related equipment, ongoing or currently planned programs, and retrofit with cost-effective energy efficiency measures.

The study results indicated that the combination of currently planned infrastructure changes coupled with cost-effective energy efficiency measures would allow FORSCOM—as a whole— to meet its E.O. energy goals.

REFERENCES

[1] Memorandum from Col. Gene A. DeWulf, FORSCOM Engineer, to FORSCOM DCS and Installation Management Personnel, 19 September 2001.

[2] Executive Order 13123 *Greening the Government Through Efficient Energy Management*, June 3, 1999. See http://www.eren.doe.gov/femp/aboutfemp/exec1 3123.html

[3] Facility Energy Decision System (FEDS), Release 5.0, Pacific Northwest National Laboratory, April 2002. See www.pnl.gov/FEDS.

[4] Redesigned Army Defense Utility Energy Reporting System Data System (RADDS). See www.hq.usace.army.mil/isd/YellowPages/info/ra duersd.html.

[5] Brown, D.R., and J.A. Dirks. *Prospective FORSCOM Energy Intensities*. Proceedings of the 2002 World Energy Engineering Congress, October 9-11, 2002. Atlanta, GA.

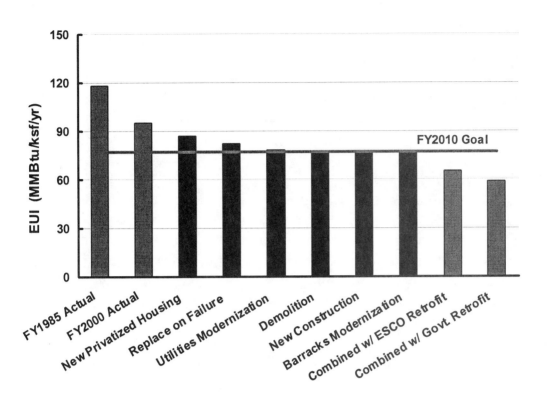

FIGURE 1. EXAMPLE OF COMPLIANCE PATHWAY TO MEET E.O. GOALS

TABLE 1. EXAMPLE OF PROJECTED SUPPLEMENTARY SOURCE REQUIREMENTS
TO FUND PROJECTS TO MEET E.O. GOALS

Supplementary Resource Requirements for Energy Projects										
	FY2001	FY2002	FY2003	FY2004	FY2005	FY2006	FY2007	FY2008	FY2009	FY2010
	$1,000	$1,000	$1,000	$1,000	$1,000	$1,000	$1,000	$1,000	$1,000	$1,000
Expanded Utility Modernization Funding [EUMP]		$95	$2,200	$2,400	$1,200					
Other Federal Implementation Funds (ECIP, etc. for projects infeasible through ESPC)			$300			$400			$375	
Energy Design Assistance			$40	$40	$40	$10				
Other Technical Assistance Support (Improved O&M, energy awareness, resource energy						$20	$30	$30		
TOTAL Auxiliary Federal Funds Required	$0	$95	$2,540	$2,440	$1,240	$430	$30	$30	$375	$0
Anticipated ESPC Contractor Investments	$1,500	$2,500	$6,000	$2,500	$15,000	$2,500	$2,500	$2,500		

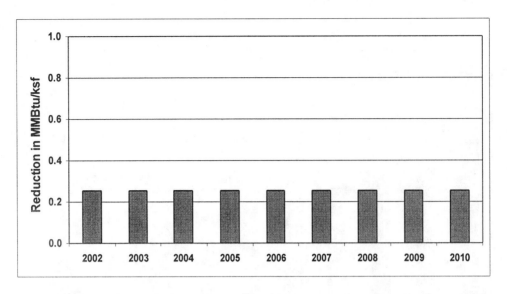

FIGURE 2. IMPACT ON SITE ENERGY INTENSITY OF REPLACING EQUIPMENT UPON FAILURE

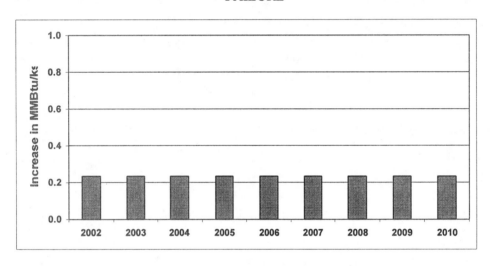

FIGURE 3. IMPACT ON SITE ENERGY INTENSITY OF BUILDING DEMOLITION

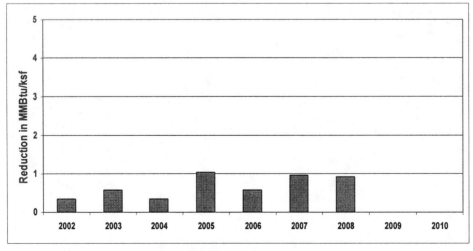

FIGURE 4. IMPACT ON SITE ENERGY INTENSITY OF BARRACKS CONSTRUCTION

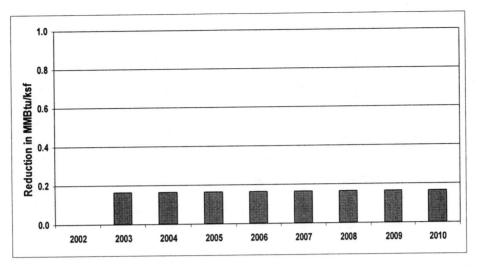

FIGURE 5. IMPACT ON SITE ENERGY INTENSITY OF HOUSING CONSTRUCTION

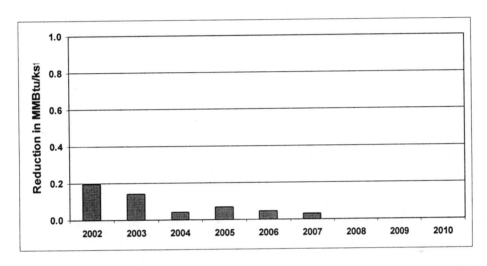

FIGURE 6. IMPACT ON SITE ENERGY INTENSITY OF OTHER BUILDING CONSTRUCTION

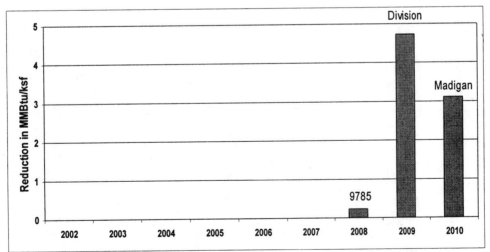

FIGURE 7. IMPACT ON SITE ENERGY INTENSITY OF UTILITY MODERNIZATION (DECENTRALIZATION OF BOILERS)

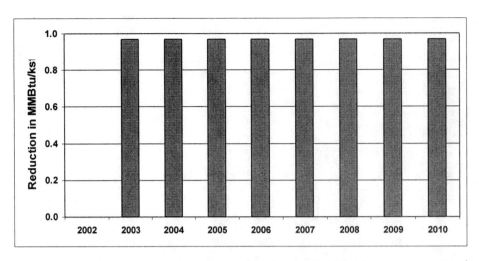

FIGURE 8. IMPACT ON SITE ENERGY INTENSITY OF ENERGY-SPECIFIC RETROFITS VIA PERFORMANCE CONTRACTING

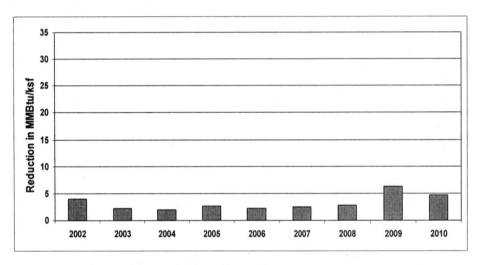

FIGURE 9. COMBINED IMPACTS ON SITE ENERGY INTENSITY – ANNUAL TOTAL REDUCTION

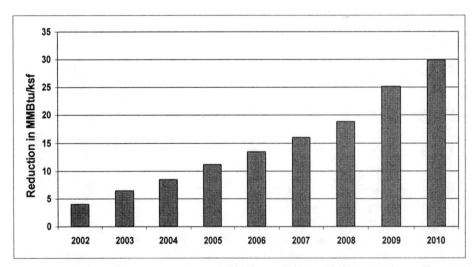

FIGURE 10. CUMULATIVE REDUCTIONM ON SITE ENERGY INTENSITY: FY2002-2010

TABLE 2. FEDS ANALYSIS RESULTS SHOWING PERFORMANCE CONTRACTING COSTS AND SAVINGS

Building Retrofit	Installed Capital Cost, $	Annual Energy Savings, MMBtu	Net Present Value, $
Automatic Electric Dampers	31,830	12,486	449,498
Natural Gas Furnaces	364,655	5,998	70,855
Service Hot Water Retrofits[6]	301,519	89,641	2,988,212
CFLs	1,108,912	12,984	6,443,324
Exit Panels	1,025,754	10,027	6,398,177
T-8 Fluorescents	5,252,053	20,150	1,674,004
Attic/Ceiling Insulation	277,062	10,010	47,849
Totals	8,361,785	161,566	18,071,919

---

[6] Includes low-flow showerheads, faucet aerators, lowering tank water temperature, and insulating tanks.

Chapter 22

Real-Time Risk Management In the Energy Market - Goals and Challenges

Risk Management has evolved in the last 10 years from an activity that was performed perfunctorily by traders on their trading desks, into an activity that is now viewed by most large companies as a critical enterprise-wide requirement for many reasons, including recognition and mitigation of risk at the executive level, satisfaction of regulatory requirements, gaining increased market valuation, better use of assets, and higher returns on risk capital.

Hardware, software and mathematical modeling technologies have also flourished. Today, the combination of powerful hardware, sophisticated software, highly refined mathematical processes, and the web, have enabled risk managers to manage risk on extremely large numbers of transactions from simple spot natural gas purchases to highly complex exotic derivatives.

Additionally, electronic sensors in wells, pipelines and grids communicating back to the corporate office allow operators and risk managers to receive relevant operational information reliably when needed.

However, despite the growth of various technologies, energy industry risk managers continue to face significant challenges, such as
1) the inability to calculate enterprise market risk and credit risk exposures in real-time, and;
2) the related inability to recognize, in real-time, threats to the enterprise caused by constantly changing complex combinations of conditions (such as gas pipeline congestion, generation plant outages, gas price changes, electricity price changes, grid congestion, customer demand changes) and;
3) the resulting inability to take immediate appropriate action based on that recognition and;
4) the difficult task of integrating the metrics (such as cash-flow-at-risk) of physical operating assets with the traditional metrics for trading desks (Market VaR and Credit VaR).

Early Beginnings

As software vendors began bringing enterprise market risk, credit risk and operational risk applications to market in the 1980s and 1990s, the statistical methods employed to calculate risk exposures were crude by today's standards.

For market risk, Value at Risk (VaR) is probably the most well-know measure of risk. The first widely accepted version was Parametric VaR, introduced by JP Morgan in the 1980s. It made the assumption that all transactions involved linear instruments (such as cash and forward trades). Since the valuation formulas of linear instruments involve very simple closed-form algebraic solutions, the calculations using them were extremely fast. Thus, Parametric VaR could be calculated quickly on books containing large numbers of transactions. However, the assumption of linearity that allowed calculation speed was also an Achilles heel. Since most trading books contain non-linear instruments (such as options), the accuracy of the Parametric VaR method suffered for these trading books.

To mitigate this optionality problem, Historical Monte Carlo VaR was introduced. While not quite as fast as Parametric VaR, it was more accurate for options since it used each instrument's specific valuation formula thus making no assumption about linearity. However, there were two serious drawbacks to this method. First, the use of historical data to calculate forward-looking risk implicitly assumed that future price movements would behave like past price movements, a rather heroic assumption. For example, in California thoughts of recent electricity price history repeating itself have put pressure on the state government and it is using its considerable influence and power to prevent such an event. The second drawback is that different choices of historical period would give materially different results. This brings to mind the story of the insurance company president asking the actuary "What do the numbers tell us?" and the actuary replying, "Sir, what do you want them to tell us?"

The latest entry in the risk sweepstakes is the Full Monte Carlo Simulation VaR, for both market risk and credit risk. It is the method of choice offered by the most sophisticated enterprise risk software vendors. It is however slow in comparison to the earlier methods since it uses thousands, sometime tens of thousands, of simulated future market parameter paths and each transaction in the trading book must be evaluated along each time point on each path. Additionally, it makes some assumptions about distributions of future price movements as relates to distributions of past price movements, but these assumptions are less intrusive than those in the Historical Monte Carlo VaR method. While still a weakness, when choosing between Historical Monte Carlo VaR and Full Monte Carlo VaR, speed considerations aside, risk managers usually choose Full Monte Carlo VaR as the more accurate and lesser of two evils. Also, Full Monte Carlo VaR can be used to calculate both enterprise market risk and portfolio credit risk with a degree of accuracy most risk managers find acceptable.

Risk Management Challenges Today

The job of risk managers in the energy industry is more difficult than in other markets due to complexities unique to energy. For example, in the power industry, purchasing and delivering fuel to the generating plants, optimizing the use of those plants, and selling and scheduling the power that is produced all depend on complex combinations of conditions. The number of inputs required to make purchasing, generating, trading and scheduling decisions is significantly larger than other markets. Efficiently gathering, digesting, and making decisions based upon such a vast amount of constantly changing data is more than the human brain can do in real time.

The issues bedeviling risk managers are best summarized by the following questions recently posed by a power risk manager: "Between constantly changing conditions and the immense amount of real-time data, how can I recognize threats to the company when they occur? How can I discriminate between different threats and their importance to the company? How can I then take the appropriate action in real-time if more than one of these threats occurs?"

To answer these question, there is a movement in the industry to coordinate the trading desks with the operating assets to enhance the returns on the latter. This involves integrating metrics to measure the risks of operating assets (such as cash-flow-at-risk) with the metrics to measure trading risks (market risk, credit risk, settlement risk, etc.). To add another wrinkle, full

integration of these metrics can only occur when trade capture systems are operated in real-time. This means that traders enter their trades as soon as they are executed and their front, mid, and back office systems must be integrated to enable straight-through processing. This is a daunting task for many energy companies.

An equally important goal is to enable the integrated risk measurements to be triggered in real time when pre-defined complex events occur.

Advances in Risk Management Technology

New "sense and respond" technology allows energy industry risk managers to define threats or opportunities ("events") in advance, so that when these events occur, pre-specified action can be taken in real time to mitigate risk. These events can be quite complex, involving multi-dimensional combinations of conditions.

- For example, a risk manager might be concerned about the ability of his company to procure natural gas for its Phoenix plant should a spike in electricity demand in the southwest occur. This will directly affect his company's ability to produce and deliver power for which it had previously contracted and this in turn could raise the risk of financial penalties.
  For short-term contracts, the risk manager must be able to detect these complex events in real time and also take corrective action immediately.
- For a second example, a risk manager might be concerned that one of the trading desks is approaching its Gamma and Vega limits. He wants to be alerted as soon as usage of any of these limits reaches 80% of the limit so that he can warn the trading desk immediately. Additionally, he must be alerted immediately should a breach of the actual limit occur.
- For a third example, a company with trading desks in North America, Europe and Asia may be at risk for settlement limits breaches. This can occur when all three desks "load up" on settlement risk with the same favorite highly-rated counterpart. Since the three desks operate in different time zones, they may do this unbeknownst to each other and the risk manager might not detect this until it is too late.

Using real time "sense and respond" technology, risk managers, traders, power plant operators, planners and engineers can all be apprised of changes in the extended environment as they occur and take appropriate action immediately. Not only will this greatly enhance company performance, but will also lead to higher market valuations which means greater value for the shareholders.

Conclusion

While risk managers in all industries are wrestling with the problems of performing real-time risk measurement and mitigation, energy industry risk managers face additional complexities due to the nature of the business. Optimizing generation plant usage, electricity selling prices and delivery schedules, natural gas prices and deliveries, oil pipeline usage, and cash flows all in real-time, is a formidable task.

However, recent innovations in hardware and software technology, as well as improvements in mathematical modeling techniques, allow risk managers to approach the Nirvana of real-time risk management. Risk managers who can sense and respond to specified changes in the energy industry environment and take appropriate action in real-time, are able to dramatically increase the financial and operational performance of today's power companies. They will also enjoy a significant competitive advantage.

Author bio: Jeff Mantel, Product Marketing, iSpheres

Jeff Mantel is Director, Risk Management Solutions and Product Marketing for iSpheres Corporation. He has 22 years of experience in trading, risk management, financial software, and insurance having held senior positions at Westpac Bank, Phibro Salomon, Deutsche Bank, Iron Speed, Mysis, and SunGard.

Chapter 23

ARMY'S SUSTAINABLE DESIGN AND DEVELOPMENT PROGRAM FOR MILITARY FACILITIES

Harry Goradia, P.E., Mechanical Engineer
U.S. Army Corps of Engineers

ABSTRACT:

The U.S. Army Corps of Engineers (USACE), in conjunction with the Office of Assistant Chief of Staff for Installation Management (OACSIM), developed the Sustainable Project Rating Tool (SPiRiT), an easy-to-use system which allows building delivery teams to score various design features defining how sustainable a facility will be over its life cycle.

ARMY'S SUSTAINABLE DESIGN AND DEVELOPMENT PROGRAM FOR MILITARY FACILITIES:

SDD can be described as a holistic way to approach planning design, construction and demolition. An integrated design undertaking, it emphasizes a whole system plan, multidisciplinary teams, and improving environmental goals and procurement practices.

SDD is not a new concept. It goes back to the Greece of Aristotle and Colonial America of Thomas Jefferson. More recently, in 1996, the President's Council on Sustainable Development published a report that identified three overarching areas (efficiency, environmental health and social well-being and equity) in which to strive for balance as part of promoting the principles of SDD. To achieve sustainable goals, the Council's report stated that these considerations are interdependent and should be followed simultaneously, in a balanced manner.

Recent Executive Orders and the strong support of our Army leaders have rejuvenated interest in the SDD concept. This renewed emphasis has enabled OACSIM and USACE to develop the Army's SDD program so that the Army can build healthier and more livable communities for our personnel.

To improve mission capabilities and quality of life at its Army bases, OACSIM has developed a policy to create Sustainable Army Communities. This Sustainable Army Communities Policy calls for incorporating the principles of SDD into all actions and decisions that affect Army installations.

While today's SDD has many definitions, USACE has adopted one that practicing engineers and architects (A/Es) can associate with easily. This definition appears in the USACE Technical Letter (ETL) 1110-3-491:

"SDD is the design, construction, operation and reuse/removal of the built environment in an environmentally and energy efficient manner. It meets the needs of today without compromising the ability of future generations to meet their needs"

By now, all of Army personnel dealing with any aspect of facilities should have heard about the USACE/DA SDD program. This systematic engineering process provides guidance on how-to-do-it, checklists, tools and scoring systems that integrate environmental concerns into the design and development process.

Architect/Engineer (A/E) communities feel that many of the things they do inherently have some, if not all, sustainable features built in. Much of the USACE technical guidance has incorporated SDD. However, we still need measuring tools to track our progress as we design greener and greener facilities.

The U.S. Green Building Council (USGBC), which is made up of volunteers, developed a rating tool called Leadership in Energy and Environmental Design (LEED). This tool is used extensively by practicing A/

Es. Many local and state authorities have developed their own tools.

The Army has enhanced LEED by adding some military specific criteria and is calling it the Sustainable Project Rating Tool (SPiRiT). SPiRiT allows us to score our designs for sustainability with four levels of achievement, Bronze, Silver, Gold and Platinum.

Recently issued DA and USACE policies require all Army projects to be scored against SPiRiT and to achieve the Bronze level. To help educate our practicing designers, USACE has conducted SDD workshops at every District designing military facilities.

The OACSIM and USACE have identified some projects in FY 02 and beyond as SDD showcase facilities. The intent is to achieve a higher level of sustainability in these projects and validate the life cycle cost effectiveness of some of these measures.

SUSTAINABLE PROJECT RATING TOOL (SPiRiT):

USACE, in conjunction with OACSIM has developed SPiRiT, an easy-to-use rating tool which allows building delivery teams to score various design features defining how sustainable a facility will be over its life cycle. SPiRiT v.1.4 is a Microsoft Word formatted document with point summary sheets in Microsoft Excel, making it both easier for users to print and use while allowing for automated tallying of point scoring results. SPiRiT v.1.4 can be downloaded from the web at http://www.cecer.army.mil/sustdesign/SPiRiT.cfm.

In the development of SPiRiT, USACE reviewed a broad representation of rating schema available at the time to score facility design sustainability, including the USGBC LEED" Green Building Rating System Version 2.0. USACE and DA staff decided to use LEED"†2.0, supplemented with criteria more germane to military installation planning, design, and construction, to achieve Army sustainable design and development goals. SPiRiT supplements LEED" 2.0, providing guidance to ensure that sustainable design and development are considered in Army installation projects to the fullest extent possible, balanced with funding constraints and customer requirements.

The ultimate goal is to partner with the USGBC in development of a standard commercial rating tool equally applicable to military infrastructure. USACE

has recently become a member of the USGBC Steering Committee and is actively participating in the development of a suite of LEED" products. SPiRiT will be used in the interim until LEED" 3.0 is released.

USACE SDD WEB PAGE:

A new SDD web site is now available to the public at http://www.cecer.army.mil/SustDesign. The web site is intended to help the Army and USACE Districts plan, design, build, and operate facilities in a sustainable manner. This web page contains reference information to help people comply with current sustainability criteria. It contains links to case studies, policy, training resources, important conferences and events, and the best available sources of information. The SDD website will be kept up-to-date to provide timely guidance.

Major topics include:
- What Is Sustainable Design and Development (SDD)?
- How Do You Do SDD?
- What Is the Corps Doing? (SPiRiT)
- What Are Other Federal Agencies Doing?
- Current Events
- Frequently Asked Questions
- SDD Resources

AUTHOR'S BIO:

Mr. Harry Goradia, P.E. is a mechanical engineer with HQ U. S. Army Corps of Engineers, 441 G. Street, NW, Washington, DC 20314. Phone: (202) 761-7170, Email: harry.goradia@USACE.ARMY.MIL.

At present he is the main Point of Contact for sustainable design and development program for military facility design. He has degrees in mechanical and electrical engineering and is a registered Professional Engineer in the state of Nebraska. He has over 30 years of experience in design, engineering management and overseeing large Army-wide programs. Prior to this position he was Chief of Mechanical and Energy Division at U.S. Army Center of Public works where his Division provided assistance to Army installations in Operation and Maintenance arena. Mr. Goradia has spoken at many conferences on energy conservation, sustainable design and design of mechanical systems. As an ambassador for the Army Energy Program he oversaw awareness activities throughout the Army, represented Army at DoD and DoE. As the focal point for sustainable design he oversaw and conducted training at every Corps District performing military facility design.

Chapter 24

SUCCESSFUL DEVELOPMENT AND PRIVATIZATION
OF ENERGY PLANTS THROUGH ENHANCED LEASING

Michael Simmons and Tony Kushnir, Patton Boggs, LLP
Robert Eidson, Energy Systems Group, LLC

SUCCESSES AT THE
DEPARTMENT OF VETERAN AFFAIRS

In June 2001, Deputy Secretary, Dr. Leo Mackay formally dedicated the "Mountain Home Energy Center," Department of Veterans Affair's (VA) first privately financed and operated energy development and operation. The energy center was also a "first" in the federal government in that it was developed and financed with minimal, short-term federal commitments in lieu of the traditional long-term leaseback or energy purchase arrangements. This state-of-the-art cogeneration facility, designed in harmony with the historic Beaux Arts campus architecture at the James H. Quillen VA Medical Center (Mountain Home) in Johnson City, TN will not only serve the energy needs of the VA Medical Center, it will also produce and sell energy products to the neighboring East Tennessee State University's James H. Quillen College of Medicine, as well as to others in the local community for many years to come.

This arrangement produced immediate and substantial program and financial benefits to the Department, veterans, and to the local community. From a Departmental perspective, it enabled VA to realize more than $16 million in discounted recurring cost savings and more than $26 million in life-cycle (20 years) cost savings from the higher energy efficiencies put into place from the new plant. Further, the local VA Medical Center will also receive a percent of the revenues from energy sales to non-VA customers. Projected revenues from this plant are expected to be in excess of $5 million. Veterans benefited from the arrangement in that the local VA Medical Center plans to use the savings and revenues from this project to fund improvements to its primary care and community-based outpatient clinics. Finally, although the underlying land was still federal property, the energy facility was subject to local taxes and resulted in an increased tax-base for the local community. From a legal and real estate management perspective, the results were equally impressive. VA leveraged over $26 million of financial benefits from a parcel of vacant VA property that was appraised at $300,000. More importantly, other than leasing the site, the Department made no long-term commitments or obligations regarding the purchase of energy products or services. There were no long-term VA purchase guarantees or termination liabilities.

On May 21, 2002, VA used this authority again to close a transaction that provides for the development of a privately financed and operated energy center on the campus of the VA Medical Center in North Chicago, Illinois. This center includes 5MW of electric generating capacity and 150,000 lb/hr of steam generating capacity, which will serve not only the VA Medical Center but also some Navy activities at the Great Lakes Naval Training Center and a neighboring Medical School as well. Other third party users will be added as the market allows. This project will yield immediate cost avoidance and savings of $13.6 million in development costs as well as substantial operational savings (estimated in the area of $800,000 yearly after year two of the operation) and revenues to VA. More importantly, it guarantees that the users will obtain needed energy at the most cost effective rate and on terms that provide future flexibility. The terms for this transaction did not vary significantly from those in the Mountain Home transaction. The new energy center will begin operations in April 2004.

A third energy transaction is now underway using this same approach and is scheduled for closing in August 2002. This project is located on a VA Medical Center that is situated in the Illinois Medical District in Chicago, Illinois. Like its other siblings, this project, when executed, will provide for a privately financed, developed and operated cogeneration plant that will provide electricity, steam and chilled to the VA Medical Center, a VA office building and other potential users in the Medical District. VA will be able to obtain energy upgrades and its energy requirements from a state-of-the-art facility without obligating scarce construction funding while at the same time lowering its operating budget. Projected date to begin operations is June 2004.

The Department was able to achieve these benefits through the use of an asset management tool called the "Enhanced-Use leasing authority" and a unique legal and financing structure specifically developed to implement this legal authority. Using this two-step approach, VA is able to develop and then incorporate a capital asset management program into its strategic mission objectives. This capital asset management program relies upon a central principle that each VA-controlled property must be managed in a manner that promotes or enhances a VA program or mission. Such management may be either by direct VA-use or by its redevelopment by non-VA (public or private) users.

BACKGROUND

VA, the second largest agency in the federal government in number of employees, has as its unique mission the delivery of comprehensive assistance and benefits to the nation's veterans and their families. VA, through its Veterans Health Administration, is one of the largest direct providers of health care in the world. The Department is also a major land holding agency, with an extensive and diverse portfolio of properties including over 23,000 acres of land and over 4,600 buildings at approximately 270 locations, in addition to over 550 leased spaces nationwide.

To manage its property, VA uses all of the traditional authorities available to federal agencies. However, in many instances these authorities do not adequately

address the needs of specific mission or developmental issues. Because of these limitations, exacerbated by on-going budgetary constraints, privatization and income-generation programs have become increasingly important to the Department. In an effort to obtain significant operating cost reductions and pursue alternative funding sources for veterans programs, VA is constantly developing and implementing new programs, such as Enhanced-Use leasing.

Traditionally, VA properties have been viewed as cost centers. In contrast, the Enhanced-Use leasing concept was designed to:

- Encourage VA program and facility managers to view VA property holdings as program resources and potential revenue centers;

- Attract other public or private sector investment in VA facilities through broad-based market-based opportunities rather than upon reliance upon current or future federal programs;

- Redirect VA's capital budget program toward facilities that are involved in the delivery of veteran services by encouraging private sector development and operation of non-core functions and uses (e.g., energy production, parking, administrative office space, etc.);

- Enable VA to acquire otherwise unaffordable services or facilities; and

- Allow VA to realign its property holdings to reflect current and projected program requirements.

WHAT IS ENHANCED-USE LEASING AND WHAT MAKES IT WORK?

Enhanced leasing, otherwise known as Enhanced-Use Leasing within VA and other federal agencies, is a cooperative arrangement for the development of public property, under which that property is made available to a public or private entity through a long-term lease. At VA the leased property may be developed for non-VA and/or VA uses, and in return for the lease, the Department obtains fair consideration in the form of revenue, facilities, space, services, money or other consideration.

VA has specific authority to enter into these types of

arrangements. Originally enacted in August 1991, the Enhanced-Use leasing authority is now codified at Section 8161 through Section 8169 of Title 38, United States Code. The technical elements of this authority are:

- The term of an Enhanced-Use lease may be up to 75 years;

- The site to be leased must be controlled by the Secretary;

- All uses must be consistent with and not adversely affect the Department's mission;

- VA may use "minor" construction funds (up to $4 million) as a capital contribution in connection with an Enhanced-Use lease;

- VA may purchase services, space or facilities in connection with the lease;

- VA must hold a public hearing at the location of any proposed Enhanced-Use lease to obtain veteran and local community input;

- VA must provide two notices to its congressional oversight committees prior to entering into an Enhanced-Use lease.

One of the major elements of VA's Enhanced-Use leasing authority is that unlike traditional federal leasing authorities in which generated proceeds must deposited into a general treasury account, the Enhanced-Use leasing authority provides that all proceeds (less any costs that can be reimbursed) are returned to medical care appropriations. The ability to keep proceeds creates an economic incentive for VA and its property managers to fully utilize their existing capital assets and to begin to view these assets as potential resources to fund needed programs or facility requirements. To underscore Congress' intent to provide VA with sufficient latitude to undertake and practice asset management, the statute addresses several key legal issues that are critical to successful public/private transactions by:

- Providing the Department with the ability to enter into long-term agreements so as to enable amortization of private sector capital investments;

- Clarifying the ability of the Department to un-

dertake this authority from the myriad of other substantive and procedural laws relating to government procurement, management and disposal of property or services;

- Enabling the Department to enter into these agreements in a timely fashion to address market demands;

- Providing the Department with the flexibility to address a broad spectrum of market and financial conditions to address specific project requirements so long as the activity was within established statutory requirements and Department mission.

In addition, close coordination with and reliance upon the local government and community as full partners in the development process is a key element of project success.

While the Enhanced-Use leasing authority provides that any development on VA property can be based on VA building and development standards in lieu of local requirements, the Department has used this authority very cautiously. There are two reasons for this caution.

First, in order to maximize project efficiencies and minimize development costs, the Department relies, to the greatest extent possible, upon local building codes, safety requirements, construction standards and local government inspection services as they pertain to any non-VA development. If the project involves direct VA control over the management and operation of a facility or if VA occupies a significant portion of the Enhanced-Use development, the project is considered in the context of applicable VA standards. In such instances, VA requirements are reviewed in the context of how such standards integrate with applicable local codes and standards.

The second, and perhaps the more important reason why Enhanced-Use leasing stresses local government and local community involvement is to assure that the development is integrated in the local planning process. Close integration enables VA to spot any potential community concerns (scope and intensity of the development, traffic impacts, business impacts, etc.) and to address those issues early on in the process.

For energy projects, this means that, notwithstanding that federal property is involved, the project will likely be subject to the same or similar state and local environmental and development requirements that would be otherwise applicable if the project occurred on non-federal lands. However, the flexibility to use federal or local development standards does provide opportunity to negotiate project development issues including site development, building and safety code compliance, and building codes. As such, the agency must assume a leadership role in coordinating and negotiating with applicable state and local authorities. The energy developer/provider serves a critical supporting role by furnishing the necessary project development information and taking an active role in establishing relationships with the applicable local authorities. Environmental issues such as obtaining state and federal permits as well as dealing with hazardous materials are strictly complied with and incorporated into the project planning process.

The last "piece of the puzzle" for a successful project is developing a "project structure" that enables the project to secure private financing yet comply with the strict federal budgetary and fiscal rules governing capital leasing and long-term federal commitments. Federal fiscal policy directs that if a VA project is solely or substantially based on the public funding to accomplish predominately public sector capital objectives, the venture should be treated as a "public venture" and that project be accomplished through federally appropriated funds rather than by private financing. This result, of course, frustrates the very reason for public/private ventures such as the Enhanced-Use leasing program. Further, since the project by definition involves federal property, VA cannot subordinate the fee title to the property. While there is no single "magic bullet" that addresses the federal fiscal policy mandates, the legal and financial structure developed for the VA energy projects have not only complied with these strict federal fiscal policy requirements they have also successfully secured low-cost, private financing. These elements include securing the participation of an investment grade energy developer/provider, avoiding long-term federal commitments, and crafting contractual protections to the financing source that are comparable to those in the private sector. Great care must be exercised in structuring these types of transactions. Recent experiences by other federal agencies indicate that federal fiscal rules will be strictly interpreted for compliance. This year, $300 million were scored against the budget authority of the Tennessee Valley Authority by the Office of Management and Budget on the basis that lease payments that TVA is making,

under a complex leasing transaction involving a natural gas plant in western Tennessee, are obligations that should be treated as a capital debt under the above-mentioned fiscal rules. It should be noted that the energy projects developed for VA have secured OMB's review and approval as being in compliance with federal fiscal policy.

WHAT TYPES OF PROJECTS HAVE WORKED AT VA?

Obviously, sound development economics are the foundation of Enhanced-Use projects. But some factors within VA's control can contribute to the likelihood of success. Enhanced-Use leasing works best when government requirements can be defined in private sector terms. Energy plants are excellent examples. VA's objective in this transaction is simply to secure a reliable source of energy for its requirements. This allows the private sector to design, construct and operate the facility in its customary manner. VA then benefits from the efficiencies of organization and delivery processes that have been honed over time by the developer/lessee. VA can also improve the value of its projects by working to reduce project uncertainties, private sector risk and the cost of borrowing capital. This can be achieved through a variety of means such as use of local building codes, VA participation in entitlement discussions with local authorities, or addressing the concerns of potential financing sources early in the development process.

In addition to the energy plants, VA has, to date, successfully completed a number of other projects, including office buildings, research facilities, medical space, senior living residential facilities, medical facilities, child development centers and elder day care centers, single room occupancy housing (homeless shelters) and management and operation of VA golf courses.

WHO MAY BENEFIT FROM ENHANCED-LEASING?

While VA has been at the forefront of successfully developing and implementing its Enhanced-Use Leasing authority, it is not by any means the only entity with the ability to take advantage of the benefits of enhanced-leasing. Several other federal departments are seeking similar authority and others have been granted such authority recently. The enhanced leasing concept provides public agencies (federal, state, municipal, and local), not-for-profit entities, universities and colleges (domestic and foreign), and others the ability to utilize the value in their existing capital assets to secure consideration in the form of cash or construction and management benefits without the need to totally divest themselves of the asset - and to successfully secure the necessary financing.

LESSONS LEARNED

In implementing its Enhanced-Use leasing authority, VA has discovered several key points to developing a successful public/private development program. The single most important is the enabling statute itself. This authority must provide sufficient flexibility to allow the agency to be innovative in its approach to secure private investment into its facilities. While preserving the integrity of governmental processes, that public agency's implementation procedures must be tempered so as to be responsive to the broad span of market, environmental, political, and legal issues that arise in the development of federal property. The agency officials involved in the process must be committed to the effort's success and, while attempting to be responsive to the legitimate demands of the private sector, they must remain committed to structuring each transaction in a manner that will not obligate future appropriations and federal programs. To accomplish this objective, the agency must participate fully as equal partners with the developer/lessee in project's development, financing and local community review. Finally, securing a qualified and experienced team of professionals in structuring and developing the project is necessary to address the multitude of legal, fiscal, and program issues that arise from such development. Successful implementation is dependent not only on a strong agency commitment but also on securing a strong development team that not only has the management and financial resources to execute the project but also has the necessary experience in and understanding of the fundamental issues, disciplines and responsibilities involved in project development on federal property.

Chapter 25

ASSESSMENT OF NON-ELECTRIC COOLING ALTERNATIVES TO REDUCE THE ELECTRIC DEMAND ON NEW YORK'S POWER GRID

Khaled A. Yousef, PE, CEM, CDSM, Senior Engineer
Science Applications International Corporation

Ronald B. Slosberg, Program Manager
Science Applications International Corporation

Mark Eggers, RA, Program Manager
New York State Energy Research and Development Authority

Christopher Reohr, Project Manager
New York State Energy Research and Development Authority

ABSTRACT

Electric cooling technologies impose significant demand on the utility grid. For instance the cooling system for a 200,000 square foot building could add over 300 kW of electric load onto the grid during peak summer periods. A typical 600,000 square foot building has an electric chiller plant that peaks at nearly 1MW. Natural gas and steam chillers, on the other hand, impose only a fraction of these loads on the electric grid.

This paper highlights the potential of state government subsidies and incentive programs in promoting non-electric cooling technologies to help reduce the peak demand load on the New York power grid. The results obtained also provide valuable equipment installed costs and energy/demand parameters for both electric and non-electric chillers.

The technical and economic viability of five non-electric cooling technologies are compared to standard practice electric chillers. The five non-electric cooling technologies are:
1. Gas Engine-Driven Chiller
2. Two-Stage Gas-Fired Absorption Chiller
3. Two-Stage Steam-Fired Absorption Chiller
4. Single-Stage Steam-Fired Absorption Chiller
5. Steam-Turbine Driven Centrifugal Chiller

The energy consumption and peak summer demand were calculated for the chillers in each of three different size ranges. Installed cost estimates were developed for each chiller technology in two regions of New York State.

The results presented here will help design consultants, estimators, utilities, and government energy officials assess preliminary estimates for installed costs, energy savings, and incremental maintenance costs. Normalized costing indices such as $/ton, $/hp, $/sqft. and $/lin.ft and operating

characteristics such as full load hours and kW/ton rules-of-thumb for the chiller and plant components are also presented.

The study reports typical office building savings and economic paybacks. Chiller operation of 800 equivalent full load hours (EFLH) for Upstate New York sites and 850 EFLH for Downstate/NYC sites were used.

PROJECT DESCRIPTION AND SUMMARY OF FINDINGS

Non-electric cooling technologies offer the potential to dramatically reduce electric energy consumption and peak electric demand load.

Various non-electric cooling technologies were evaluated and compared to standard practice electric chillers. The impacts of financial incentives on the comparative economics were also investigated.

The baseline electric chillers were assumed to meet NYSERDA's New Construction Program (NCP) Standard Practice Guidelines (based on ASHRAE Standard 90.1-1999 Minimum Efficiency Requirements). The study used the following electric chiller efficiencies:

- Full load and IPLV COP of 6.10 (0.576 kW/ton) for chiller capacities greater than 300 tons. Centrifugal chillers were used as baseline electric equipment for this size category.
- Full load COP of 4.90 (0.718 kW/ton) and IPLV COP of 4.95 (0.710 kW/ton) for chiller capacities that are less than 300 tons and greater than 150 tons. Positive displacement (rotary screw and scroll) chillers were used as baseline equipment type for this size category.

For the large size category, the ASHRAE Standard full load COP value was equal to the IPLV COP value based on the ARI 550 test procedure and certification program. For the small size category, the ASHRAE Standard IPLV COP value was slightly better then the full load COP value. For both size categories, full load efficiencies were used for electric demand savings calculations and IPLVs were used for the electric energy savings calculations.

The energy consumption (kWh) and peak summer demand (kW) were calculated for chillers in 3 size ranges. Energy and demand savings were calculated as the difference between the electric baseline and each of the non-electric cooling technologies. The evaluation was completed for typical office-type building applications. The chiller size ranges were:

- Large – chiller capacities greater than 1,000 tons (a 1,200 ton centrifugal example was used)
- Medium – capacities greater then 300 tons and less than 1,000 tons (a 600 ton centrifugal example was used)
- Small – capacities less then 300 tons and greater than 150 tons (a 200 ton positive displacement example was used)

Data from chiller manufacturers, vendors, design consultants, and contractors were used to support the development of cost estimates for a complete chiller system installation. In situations where vendors were reluctant or unable to provide specific information, RS Means estimating guides and other published sources were used.

More than 90% of the costing was developed through interviews with industry professionals.

Installed cost estimates were developed for each chiller technology in two regions:
- Upstate New York Region
- Downstate / New York City Region

Under NYSERDA's NCP, cost-effective measures are eligible for incentives of up to 70% of the incremental cost over standard practice. Using NYSERDA's New Construction Screening Tool, we evaluated the electric benefit/cost ratio[1] and potential incentive for each technology compared to the standard practice electric chiller.

A number of Tables were provided to summarize and illustrate the results of this study:

Table 1A presents a summary of potential incentive levels calculated in this study by region calculated at 70% of the incremental system first cost.

Table 1B presents a summary of the electric benefit to cost ratios by region.

Table 2A presents a summary of the simple economic payback (SPB) ratio *before* applying the incentive.

Table 2B presents a summary of the simple economic payback (SPB) ratio *after* applying the incentive.

TALBE 1A   Incentive Level Summary

	Single-Stage Absorber	Gas Engine, Two-Stage Gas Absorber, Two-Stage Steam Absorber, Steam Turbine	All Five Cooling Technologies
Upstate New York Region	$177	$428	$378
Downstate New York and New York City Region	$205	$466	$414
Average for both Regions	$191	$447	$396

TABLE 1B   Electric Benefit to Cost Ratio Summary

	Single-Stage Absorber	Gas Engine, Two-Stage Gas Absorber, Two-Stage Steam Absorber, Steam Turbine	All Five Cooling Technologies
Upstate New York Region	4.3	1.8	2.3
Downstate New York and New York City Region	3.7	1.7	2.1
Average for both Regions	4.0	1.6	2.2

[1] The electric benefit to cost ratio is defined as the value of avoided electricity and demand over the measure life (20 years) divided by the incremental first cost.

TABLE 2A Simple Payback Economic Summary (before the incentive)

Region	Single-Stage Absorber	Gas Engine, Two-Stage Gas Absorber, Two-Stage Steam Absorber, Steam Turbine
Upstate New York Region	NA as savings < $0	28.0
Downstate New York and New York City Region	Very long payback (~60 years) for Med/Large absorbers and about ~9 years for the small absorbers	8.5
Average for both Regions	**NA due to Upstate results**	18.3

TABLE 2B Simple Payback Economic Summary (after the Incentive)

Region	Single-Stage Absorber	Gas Engine, Two-Stage Gas Absorber, Two-Stage Steam Absorber, Steam Turbine
Upstate New York Region	NA as savings < $0	8.4
Downstate New York and New York City Region	Relatively long payback (~18 years) for Med/Large, but short payback (2.6 years) for small absorbers	2.5
Average for both Regions	**NA due to Upstate results**	5.5

Tables 3A and 3B present a summary of the study results. For each technology/region/option or scenario, chiller capacity, baseline equipment installed cost, non-electric equipment installed cost, net incremental equipment installed cost, B/C ratio, potential incentive level based on 70% of the incremental cost, simple payback (SPB) *before* the incentive, SPB *after* the incentive and the incentive per ton are all presented. All measures had a 20-year measure life as assumed in the NYSERDA Screening Tool.

Table 4 presents some of the inputs, assumptions, and the energy rates used in the analysis.

Tables 5A and 5B present normalized equipment costing as well as analysis details for only one of the chiller size/region groups. For illustrative purposes only one group, representing a large 1,200-ton chiller in a large in large commercial office building in Downstate/NYC, is presented (*before* applying the incentive).

Assessment Results

The effect and the importance of financial incentives were very clear with the gas engines, two-stage gas absorbers, two-stage steam absorbers, and steam turbine chillers. The economic payback in the Upstate region improved from 28.0 years to 8.4 years, which is a very significant. Also, the economics payback in the Downstate Region improved from 8.5 years to a very attractive 2.5 years. This illustrates the importance and value of incentives to help promote the installation of non-electric cooling alternatives, which will in turn reduce summer peak electric demand loads.

Despite the relatively long SPBs for the single-stage absorbers, a similar trend was observed. The payback in the Downstate region for medium and large chillers was reduced from 60 years to 18 years after the incentive. For the small chiller size range, paybacks were reduced from 9 years to 2.6 years after the incentive for Downstate sites. A payback calculation was not possible for the Upstate sites with single-stage absorbers because the additional fuel and O&M costs exceeded the savings from selecting steam chillers in place of electric units.

Overall economic paybacks were reduced from an average of 18.3 years for all 30 scenarios to 5.5 years when the recommended incentives were included. The incentive calculations and equipment installed costs in this study were primarily for new construction, however, we expect similar results to apply in retrofit situations.

As shown in Tables 3A (Upstate) and 3B (Downstate), it was found that potential non-electric chiller incentives for both regions (when calculated at 70% of the incremental first cost) range between $328 to $600/ton for all technologies except for the single-stage steam absorption chillers. The potential incentive for the single-stage steam absorption chillers analyzed ranged from $150 to $257 per ton. It should be noted that energy and demand savings resulted in electric benefit to cost ratios that were greater than one for all scenarios.

155

The average calculated incentive for all scenarios was $396 per ton. The average incentive for single-stage absorption chillers was $191 per ton, which is about ½ the average calculated for all scenarios. For all technologies except for the single-stage absorption chiller, the average incentive was $447 per ton.

The average electric benefit to cost ratio for all scenarios was 2.2. The average benefit to cost ratio for single-stage absorption chillers was 4.0[2]. For all technologies except for the single-stage absorption chiller, the average electric benefit to cost ratio was 1.8.

Chillers Smaller than 150 Tons

Chiller capacities less than 150 tons are not common non-electric cooling applications for three of the technologies studied. As such, they were excluded from this study. For capacities less then 150 tons, the non-electric chiller market is limited to the single-stage steam or gas absorbers and gas-engine units.

Notes and Observations Regarding Single-Stage Absorption Chiller Economic Results

Single-stage absorption chillers are fuel inefficient when compared to two-stage chillers. However, single-stage chillers are often installed because they are the least expensive non-electric option to install and also because they do not require a stationary engineer (in NYC).

Single-stage absorbers can be ideal for generating cooling when waste heat is available or in combination with cogeneration applications as they utilize low-grade steam (~ 15 psig).

In the smaller Downstate/NYC absorber applications, it should be noted that the economic payback for the small size chillers (2.6 year) was much better than that for the med/large capacity (~ 18 years) primarily because of the ASHRAE Standard electric baseline used. In the small chiller scenario, a 0.718 kW/ton (COP of 4.90) positive displacement (rotary screw or scroll) chiller was assumed to be the baseline standard practice.

Notes and Observations Regarding Gas Engine, Two-Stage Gas Absorber, Two-Stage Steam Absorber, and Steam Turbine Chillers Economic Results

Average Downstate/NYC paybacks without the incentive (8.5 years) are much better than Upstate's (28 years). This is because of the energy rates used in the analysis (See Table 4 for energy cost details). In Downstate/NYC, electricity is much more expensive than Upstate (almost double), whereas the Downstate fuel costs are about 45% higher than Upstate's.

The service market in the Downstate market has more experience with non-electric chiller technologies. Therefore, additional O&M costs for the non-electric cooling technologies in the Upstate market were assumed to be higher than in the Downstate market.

---

[2] It is important to note that the electric benefit to cost ratio does not account for fuel/steam and additional maintenance costs associated with non-electric chillers. Therefore, even though a single-stage absorber operates at a low COP, its lower initial cost compared to the two-stage absorber results in higher (artificially look favorable) electric benefit to cost ratios. However, economic SPB and recommended incentive levels accounted for fossil fuel/steam and maintenance costs to provide a real life economic payback.

TABLE 3A: Summary and Findings (Upstate New York)

Group # and Option #	Estimated Installed Cost ($)	Incremental Cost ($)	Electric Benefit / Cost Ratio	NCP Incentive based on 70% Incremental Cost	SPB without Incentive (years)	SPB with Incentive (years)	Normalized Incentive ($ / ton)
Group 1 of 6 - 1,200 ton Chiller - Office Building in Upstate New York							
Electric Baseline (0.576 kW/ton)	$837,000						
1: Gas Engine Driven Chiller	$1,555,450	$718,450	1.8	$502,915	16.5	5.0	$419
2: Two-Stage Gas Fired Absorption Chiller	$1,501,300	$664,300	1.8	$465,010	38.5	11.6	$388
3: Two-Stage Steam-Fired Absorption Chiller	$1,417,900	$580,900	2.1	$406,630	33.8	10.1	$339
4: Single-Stage Steam-Fired Absorption Chiller	$1,112,500	$275,500	4.3	$192,850	(10.4)	(3.1)	$161
5: Steam-Turbine Driven Centrifugal Chiller	$1,696,450	$859,450	1.5	$601,615	39.2	11.8	$501
Group 2 of 6 - 600 ton Chiller - Office Building in Upstate New York							
Electric Baseline (0.576 kW/ton)	$433,500						
1: Gas Engine Driven Chiller	$783,600	$350,100	1.8	$245,070	16.1	4.8	$408
2: Two-Stage Gas Fired Absorption Chiller	$757,650	$324,150	1.9	$226,905	37.6	11.3	$378
3: Two-Stage Steam-Fired Absorption Chiller	$714,450	$280,950	2.1	$196,665	32.7	9.8	$328
4: Single-Stage Steam-Fired Absorption Chiller	$561,750	$128,250	4.6	$89,775	(9.7)	(2.9)	$150
5: Steam-Turbine Driven Centrifugal Chiller	$852,600	$419,100	1.5	$293,370	38.2	11.5	$489
Group 3 of 6 - 200 ton Chiller - Office Building in Upstate New York							
Electric Baseline (0.718 kW/ton)	$142,000						
1: Gas Engine Driven Chiller	$279,200	$137,200	1.9	$96,040	12.9	3.9	$480
2: Two-Stage Gas Fired Absorption Chiller	$271,200	$129,200	2.0	$90,440	20.5	6.2	$452
3: Two-Stage Steam-Fired Absorption Chiller	$256,100	$114,100	2.2	$79,870	18.2	5.4	$399
4: Single-Stage Steam-Fired Absorption Chiller	$204,700	$62,700	4.0	$43,890	(64.4)	(19.3)	$219
5: Steam-Turbine Driven Centrifugal Chiller	$300,400	$158,400	1.6	$110,880	32.3	9.7	$554

Table 3B: Summary and Findings (Downstate New York and New York City)

Group # and Option #	Estimated Installed Cost ($)	Incremental Cost ($)	Electric Benefit / Cost Ratio	NCP Incentive based on 70% Incremental Cost	SPB without Incentive (years)	SPB with Incentive (years)	Normalized Incentive ($ / ton)
Group 4 of 6 - 1,200 ton Chiller - Office Building in Downstate/NYC							
Electric Baseline (0.576 kW/ton)	$958,050						
1: Gas Engine Driven Chiller	$1,739,130	$781,080	1.6	$546,756	6.7	2.0	$456
2: Two-Stage Gas Fired Absorption Chiller	$1,682,910	$724,860	1.7	$507,402	9.8	3.0	$423
3: Two-Stage Steam-Fired Absorption Chiller	$1,574,280	$616,230	2.0	$431,361	8.5	2.5	$359
4: Single-Stage Steam-Fired Absorption Chiller	$1,270,785	$312,735	3.8	$218,915	61.0	18.3	$182
5: Steam-Turbine Driven Centrifugal Chiller	$1,873,110	$915,060	1.4	$640,542	11.5	3.5	$534
Group 5 of 6 - 600 ton Chiller - Office Building in Downstate/NYC							
Electric Baseline (0.576 kW/ton)	$494,025						
1: Gas Engine Driven Chiller	$879,180	$385,155	1.7	$269,609	6.6	2.0	$449
2: Two-Stage Gas Fired Absorption Chiller	$852,495	$358,470	1.7	$250,929	9.7	2.9	$418
3: Two-Stage Steam-Fired Absorption Chiller	$795,660	$301,635	2.0	$211,145	8.3	2.5	$352
4: Single-Stage Steam-Fired Absorption Chiller	$643,913	$149,888	4.0	$104,921	58.5	17.5	$175
5: Steam-Turbine Driven Centrifugal Chiller	$943,650	$449,625	1.4	$314,738	11.3	3.4	$525
Group 6 of 6 - 200 ton Chiller - Office Building in Downstate/NYC							
Electric Baseline (0.718 kW/ton)	$164,113						
1: Gas Engine Driven Chiller	$316,735	$152,623	1.8	$106,836	5.7	1.7	$534
2: Two-Stage Gas Fired Absorption Chiller	$308,585	$144,473	1.8	$101,131	7.3	2.2	$506
3: Two-Stage Steam-Fired Absorption Chiller	$288,580	$124,468	2.0	$87,127	6.4	1.9	$436
4: Single-Stage Steam-Fired Absorption Chiller	$237,448	$73,335	3.4	$51,335	8.8	2.6	$257
5: Steam-Turbine Driven Centrifugal Chiller	$335,610	$171,498	1.5	$120,048	10.0	3.0	$600

TABLE 4: Energy Rates and Other Analysis Inputs

	Upstate	Downstate
Electric Energy ($/kWh) =	$0.095	$0.160
Electric Demand ($/kW) =	$12.00	$30.00
Number of Demand Months =	5.0	5.0
Fuel $/Therm (Gas and/or Steam) =	$0.52	$0.75
Additional Operational and Maintenance		
for Non-Elec Chillers $/Ton-Hr =	$0.010	$0.012
Additional Space & Structure Cost		
w/ gas/steam chillers ($/sqft of plant area) =	80	120
Annual Operating Hours =	1400	1600
Equivalent Full Load Hours (EFLH) =	800	850
Chiller Design Load Factor (DLF) =	0.90	0.90

Important notes and assumptions:

1 Cooling Tower Fan (kW/ton) and Condenser Pump (kW/ton) are shown normalized based on chiller tonnage, not on cooling tower size.

2 Condenser water pump annual operating hours were assumed to be equal to the annual operating hours for the chiller.

3 Annual operating hours of non-electric chiller ancillary equipment were assumed to be equal to those for the chiller.

4 Cooling Tower Fan EFLH was estimated to be the average of the chiller annual operating hours and chiller EFLH.

5 Fuel $/Therm (Gas and/or Steam) is an average price that accounts for gas service or steam service.

DETAILED WORK APPROACH

The analysis of operating costs used equipment operating hours and equivalent full load hours (EFLH) to calculate the energy usage for each of the chiller alternative. The chiller usage characteristics were based on past project experience, analysis of chillers logs (from prior projects), simulation work, and interviews with building personnel, etc.

Installed costs for the chiller equipment were obtained from interviews with design professionals, equipment vendors and contractors. The purpose for utilizing these resources was to obtain pricing based on actual past projects within each region for the various chiller technologies. To facilitate the presentation of all costs and to provide an easy comparison of all scenarios, prices were normalized on per ton, per horsepower, per linear foot, and per square foot basis for the different components in each of the scenarios.

The normalized costs and analysis summary are shown in Tables 5A and 5B for one of the chiller size/region groups. The example shown represents a large 1,200-ton chiller in a large commercial office building in Downstate/NYC (Manhattan, NY). This size installation is likely to be one of the most prevalent non-electric chiller applications.

Tables 5A and 5B also present common items for all chiller options (electric and non-electric):
- Chiller - Material in $/ton
- Chiller - Installation/Rigging in $/ton
- Condenser Water Pump/Motor Main - Material in $/hp
- Condenser Water Pump/Motor StdBy - Material in $/hp
- Condenser Water Pump (Main & StdBy) - Installation in $/hp
- Condenser Water Piping/Fitting - Material & Installation in $/lft
- Cooling Tower - Material in $/ton
- Cooling Tower - Labor in $/ton
- Design Fees, Construction Management, Contingency, Insurance - all combined in $/ton
  Note: Cooling tower material and labor $/ton are based on "chiller" tonnage, not on "cooling tower" tonnage.

The items listed below are additional to steam/gas cooling technologies only:
- Surface Condenser - Material & Installation in $/ton. Only applicable to steam turbine driven centrifugal chillers
- Additional Gas or Steam Service in $/ton. Applies to all non-electric chiller options
- Additional Space and Structure in $/sqft. Applies to all non-electric chiller options.

The comparison of the chiller analyses resulted in electric energy (kWh) and peak summer demand (kW) savings. It also resulted in the economic simple payback for each of the options.

These kWh and kW values, along with the incremental costs for each chiller option were used in NYSERDA's NCP Screening Tool. The screening tool determined the electric benefit to cost (B/C) ratio for each scenario. The additional costs for gas or steam and maintenance associated with non-electric chillers were not included in the B/C Screening Tool. For all scenarios, the B/C ratio was greater than 1.0.

Pricing Assumptions and Limitations
Listed below are some of the assumptions and limitations used in the pricing process.

Prices include design fees, standard commissioning, small contingency, and a moderate construction management budget. These "soft cost" components totaled somewhere between 10% to 12% of the installed cost for each of the alternatives.

Limited chiller controls (built-in microprocessor control) are included within the labor and material categories of the cost estimates. This does not include any "control transfer" functions, which interface the new chiller with the building energy management system.

Costs for obtaining buildings permits, excessive staff training, and equipment balancing that are above and beyond a typical installation are not included.

Contractor overhead and profit is already included under each of the plant component cost estimates.

Equipment prices and labor did not include taxes.

It was assumed that on-site boilers would provide the majority of the steam in the Upstate Region, whereas in the Downstate/NYC Region steam is either purchased (as is available in part of Manhattan) or can be provided by in-house boilers. The installed cost of steam boilers is not included in this assessment. One average fuel rate was assumed for all Downstate/NYC sites. This average rate represents a mix between purchased steam (Manhattan) and site-generated steam (the non-Manhattan Boroughs and Westchester).

Chilled water pumping and piping were not included in the comparison because they were assumed to be the same between the electric baseline and the non-electric cooling technologies.

Simulation Assumptions

Chiller EFLH: Buildings in the Downstate/NYC area will typically have higher equivalent full load hours (EFLH) and operating hours than those in the Upstate New York region. This is primarily due to three major reasons: (1) many of the Manhattan buildings may have limited economizer (air-side and/or water side) abilities compared to Upstate sites, (2) Downstate is generally hotter and more humid compared to Upstate, and (3) buildings in Manhattan typically have slightly longer operating hours than those Upstate.

Chiller Peak Design Load Factor (DLF): The analysis utilized a 0.90 design load factor for the chillers in both the Downstate and Upstate regions and for all chiller sizes.

Cooling Tower Fans: To estimate the EFLH for the tower fans, we assumed a mix between towers that (1) have VFD controls, (2) have multiple speed fans or multiple cells, and (3) have no controls. Therefore, it was assumed that the EFLH for the tower fans to be higher than the chiller EFLH, but lower than the annual operating hours of the chiller. This was done in an effort to simulate a case that represents the average for a typical installation. The value used was simply the mathematical average between chiller EFLH and chiller operating hours.

Condenser Water Pumps: The analysis assumed constant flow condenser water pumps. Therefore, the annual hours of operation of the condenser water pumps (during the mechanical cooling mode, not free cooling) was assumed to be the same as the annual hours of operation for the chiller. That is, whenever the chiller is operated, condenser water pumps are energized to pump a constant amount of flow across the condenser at all times.

Non-Electric Chiller Parasitic: The analysis assumed that the annual hours of operation of the parasitic components is equal to the annual hours of operation for the chiller itself. That is, whenever the chiller is operated, its parasitic components are energized regardless of chiller load.

Baseline Electric Chiller Efficiency: ASHRAE Standard 90.1-1999 was used to determine baseline chiller efficiency, or standard practice baseline. Full load efficiencies were used for electric demand savings calculations and IPLVs were used for the electric energy savings calculations.

Non-Electric Cooling Chiller Efficiency: We relied on manufacturer information to estimate chiller COPs. We selected what appeared to be new equipment with typical to higher efficiencies based on interviews with equipment vendors and chiller manufacturers. The efficiencies of the non-electric chillers used in this study were slightly better than the ASHRAE Standard 90.1-1999.

Surface Condenser

The surface condenser is a necessary component whose specific function is to condense the steam leaving the condensing steam turbine that is providing the shaft power to the centrifugal compressor in the steam turbine driven chiller. The analysis assumed 125 psig dry and saturated entering steam, and leaving at an exhaust vacuum of 3" to 4" of mercury absolute (HgA) with moisture content of about 10%. This information was obtained from both chiller and turbine manufacturers.

No Heat Recovery Benefit was Assumed with the Gas-Engine Driven Chiller Analysis:
This was assumed to ensure equal comparison between the different technologies and because heat is not always recovered from engine driven chillers. If heat recovery was taken into consideration, the customer's simple payback period for the gas engine chiller would have been improved.

Sources of Data

- More than 90% of the material and labor costing information has been obtained through interviews with equipment vendors, contractors, and design consultants.
- Where possible, market information was compared to reference information. Adjustments to pricing were made when necessary.
- Simplified values for non-electric chiller incremental maintenance costs were used, as detailed values were not available.

TABLE 5A Normalized Equipment Costing and Analytical Details for only one of the groups (a large 1,200 ton chiller in a large commercial office building in Downstate/NYC) *before* applying the incentive

1,200 ton Chiller - Office Building in Downstate/NYC

Electric Baseline (0.576 kW/ton)

Estimated Installed Cost	Capacity	Units	x	$/Unit	=	Cost	%of tot
Chiller - Material	1,200	tons	x	300 $/ton	=	$360,000	38%
Chiller - Installation/Rigging	1,200	tons	x	196 $/ton	=	$235,200	25%
Cond Pump/Motor Main - Mat	100	hp	x	75 $/hp	=	$7,500	1%
Cond Pump/Motor StdBy - Mat	100	hp	x	75 $/hp	=	$7,500	1%
Cond Pump (Main & StdBy) - Install	200	hp	x	210 $/hp	=	$42,000	4%
Condenser Water Piping/Fitting Material &	300	ft	x	188 $/lft	=	$56,250	6%
Cooling Tower - Material	1,500	tons	x	60 $/ton	=	$90,000	9%
Cooling Tower - Labor	1,500	tons	x	42 $/ton	=	$63,000	7%
Design Fees, CM/Contgcy, Insur	1,200	tons	x	81 $/ton	=	$96,600	10%
Total =				798 $/ton		$958,050	100%

Energy Related Inputs:				
Annual Operating Hours =	1,600	Equivalent Full Load Hours (EFLH) =	850
Chiller Design Load Factor =	0.90	Sizing Tower/Chiller Factor =	1.25
Chiller Rated Efficiency	0.5764	Chiller IPLV Efficiency =	0.5764
Clg Tower Fan (kW/ton) =	0.035	Condenser Pump (kW/ton) =	0.055

Annual Electric Energy Usage										kWh/year	%of tot
Chiller	1,200	tons	x	850	EFLH	x	0.576	kW/ton	=	587,928	79%
Clg Twr Fan	1,200	tons	x	1,225	EFLH	x	0.035	kW/ton	=	51,450	7%
Cond Wat Pmp	1,200	tons	x	1,600	HR	x	0.055	kW/ton	=	105,600	14%
Annual Electricity Energy Usage Calc (kWh/year) =										744,978	100%

Annual Ton-Hour Load = 1,020,000 tons

Monthly Electric Demand:										kW	%of tot
Chiller	1,200	tons	x	0.90	LF	x	0.576	kW/ton	=	623	85%
Clg Twr Fan	1,200	tons	x	1.00	LF	x	0.035	kW/ton	=	42	6%
Cond Wat Pmp	1,200	tons	x	1.00	LF	x	0.055	kW/ton	=	66	9%
Peak Monthly Electric Demand Calculation (kW/moth) =										731	100%

Option 1 of 5: Gas Engine Driven Chiller

Estimated Installed Cost	Capacity	Units	x	$/Unit	=	Cost	%of tot
Chiller - Material	1,200	tons	x	577 $/ton	=	$692,550	40%
Chiller - Installation/Rigging	1,200	tons	x	401 $/ton	=	$481,650	28%
Cond Pump/Motor Main - Mat	125	hp	x	75 $/hp	=	$9,375	1%
Cond Pump/Motor StdBy - Mat	125	hp	x	75 $/hp	=	$9,375	1%
Cond Pump (Main & StdBy) - Install	250	hp	x	210 $/hp	=	$52,500	3%
Condenser Water Piping/Fitting Material &	300	ft	x	200 $/lft	=	$60,000	3%
Cooling Tower - Material	1,680	tons	x	60 $/ton	=	$100,800	6%
Cooling Tower - Labor	1,680	tons	x	42 $/ton	=	$70,560	4%
Design Fees, CM/Contgcy, Insur	1,200	tons	x	165 $/ton	=	$198,000	11%
The Items Listed Below are Additional to Steam/Gas Cooling Only:							
Surface Condenser - Mat & Install	-	tons	x	- $/ton	=	$0	0%
Additional Gas or Steam Service	1,200	tons	x	34 $/ton	=	$40,320	2%
Additional Space and Structure	200	sqft	x	120 $/sqft	=	$24,000	1%
Total =				1,449 $/ton		$1,739,130	100%

Energy Related Inputs				
Annual Operating Hours =	1,600	Equivalent Full Load Hours (EFLH) =	850
Chiller Design Load Factor =	0.90	Sizing Tower/Chiller Factor =	1.40
Ancillary kW/ton =	0.010	Chiller IPLV COP =	1.80
Clg Tower Fan (kW/ton) =	0.038	Condenser Pump (kW/ton) =	0.058
Surface Condenser/Chiller Factor =	.		

Annual Electric Energy Usage										kWh/year	%of tot
Chiller Ancillary	1,200	tons	x	1,600	HR	x	0.010	kW/ton	=	19,200	10%
Clg Twr Fan	1,200	tons	x	1,225	EFLH	x	0.038	kW/ton	=	55,860	30%
Cond Wat Pmp	1,200	tons	x	1,600	HR	x	0.058	kW/ton	=	111,360	60%
Annual Electricity Energy Usage Calc (kWh/year) =										186,420	100%

Gas consumption, cost, and added maintenance costs are not parts of screening tool - Included FYI:

Assumed Gas $/Therm =	$0.75	Additional Maint Gas $/Ton-Hr =	$0.012			
Therm / year =	1,200	tons	x	850 EFLH /	1.80 COP	
			x	12,000 Btu/tor /	100,000 Btu/Thrm =	68,000

Monthly Electric Demand:										kW	%of tot
Chiller Ancillary	1,200	tons	x	0.90	LF	x	0.010	kW/ton	=	11	9%
Clg Twr Fan	1,200	tons	x	1.00	LF	x	0.038	kW/ton	=	46	36%
Cond Wat Pmp	1,200	tons	x	1.00	LF	x	0.058	kW/ton	=	70	55%
Peak Monthly Electric Demand Calculation (kW/moth) =										126	100%

Outputs of the above analysis become inputs to the NYSERDA Screening Tool:				
Annual Energy Savings (kWh) =	558,558	Summer Peak demand Reduction (kW) =	605	
Incremental Cost ($) =	$781,080	Winter Peak demand Reduction (kW) =	-	**SPB**
Savings Aggregate $/kWh =	$0.322	Winter Peak demand Reduction (kW) =	NA	6.7

Option 2 of 5: Two-Stage Gas Fired Absorption Chiller

Estimated Installed Cost	Capacity	Units	x	$/Unit	=	Cost	%of tot
Chiller - Material	1,200	tons	x	534 $/ton	=	$641,250	38%
Chiller - Installation/Rigging	1,200	tons	x	371 $/ton	=	$444,600	26%
Cond Pump/Motor Main - Mat	150	hp	x	75 $/hp	=	$11,250	1%
Cond Pump/Motor StdBy - Mat	150	hp	x	75 $/hp	=	$11,250	1%
Cond Pump (Main & StdBy) - Install	300	hp	x	210 $/hp	=	$63,000	4%
Condenser Water Piping/Fitting Material &	300	ft	x	200 $/lft	=	$60,000	4%
Cooling Tower - Material	1,920	tons	x	60 $/ton	=	$115,200	7%
Cooling Tower - Labor	1,920	tons	x	42 $/ton	=	$80,640	5%
Design Fees, CM/Contgcy, Insur	1,200	tons	x	160 $/ton	=	$191,400	11%
The Items Listed Below are Additional to Steam/Gas Cooling Only:							0%
Surface Condenser - Mat & Install	-	tons	x	- $/ton	=	$0	0%
Additional Gas or Steam Service	1,200	tons	x	34 $/ton	=	$40,320	2%
Additional Space and Structure	200	sqft	x	120 $/sqft	=	$24,000	1%
Total =				1,402 $/ton		$1,682,910	100%

Energy Related Inputs				
Annual Operating Hours =	1,600	Equivalent Full Load Hours (EFLH) =	850
Chiller Design Load Factor =	0.90	Sizing Tower/Chiller Factor =	1.60
Ancillary kW/ton =	0.025	Chiller IPLV COP =	1.10
Clg Tower Fan (kW/ton) =	0.042	Condenser Pump (kW/ton) =	0.062
Surface Condenser/Chiller Factor =	.		

Annual Electric Energy Usage										kWh/year	%of tot
Chiller Ancillary	1,200	tons	x	1,600	HR	x	0.025	kW/ton	=	48,000	26%
Clg Twr Fan	1,200	tons	x	1,225	EFLH	x	0.042	kW/ton	=	61,740	33%
Cond Wat Pmp	1,200	tons	x	1,600	HR	x	0.062	kW/ton	=	119,040	64%
Annual Electricity Energy Usage Calc (kWh/year) =										228,780	123%

Gas consumption, cost, and added maintenance costs are not parts of screening tool - Included FYI:

Assumed Gas $/Therm =	$0.75	Additional Maint Gas $/Ton-Hr =	$0.012			
Therm / year =	1,200	tons	x	850 EFLH /	1.10 COP	
			x	12,000 Btu/tor /	100,000 Btu/Thrm =	111,273

Monthly Electric Demand:										kW	%of tot
Chiller Ancillary	1,200	tons	x	0.90	LF	x	0.025	kW/ton	=	27	21%
Clg Twr Fan	1,200	tons	x	1.00	LF	x	0.042	kW/ton	=	50	40%
Cond Wat Pmp	1,200	tons	x	1.00	LF	x	0.062	kW/ton	=	74	59%
Peak Monthly Electric Demand Calculation (kW/moth) =										152	120%

Outputs of the above analysis become inputs to the NYSERDA Screening Tool:				
Annual Energy Savings (kWh) =	516,198	Summer Peak demand Reduction (kW) =	579	
Incremental Cost ($) =	$724,860	Winter Peak demand Reduction (kW) =	-	**SPB**
Savings Aggregate $/kWh =	$0.328	Winter Peak demand Reduction (kW) =	NA	9.8

TABLE 5B Normalized Equipment Costing and Analytical Details for only one of the groups (a large 1,200 ton chiller in a large commercial office building in Downstate/NYC) *before* applying the incentive

Option 3 of 5: Two-Stage Steam-Fired Absorption Chiller

Estimated Installed Cost	Capacity	Units	x	$/Unit	=	Cost	%of tot
Chiller - Material	1,200	tons	x	513 $/ton	=	$615,600	39%
Chiller - Installation/Rigging	1,200	tons	x	309 $/ton	=	$370,500	24%
Cond Pump/Motor Main - Mat	150	hp	x	75 $/hp	=	$11,250	1%
Cond Pump/Motor StdBy - Mat	150	hp	x	75 $/hp	=	$11,250	1%
Cond Pump (Main & StdBy) - Install	300	hp	x	210 $/hp	=	$63,000	4%
Condenser Water Piping/Fitting Material &	300	ft	x	200 $/ft	=	$60,000	4%
Cooling Tower - Material	2,160	tons	x	60 $/ton	=	$129,600	8%
Cooling Tower - Labor	2,160	tons	x	42 $/ton	=	$90,720	6%
Design Fees, CM/Contgcy, Insur	1,200	tons	x	149 $/ton	=	$178,200	11%
The items Listed Below are Additional to Steam/Gas Cooling Only:							0%
Surface Condenser - Mat & Install	-	tons	x	- $/ton	=	$0	0%
Additional Gas or Steam Service	1,200	tons	x	17 $/ton	=	$20,160	1%
Additional Space and Structure	200	sqft	x	120 $/sqft	=	$24,000	2%
Total =				1,312 $/ton		$1,574,280	100%

Energy Related Inputs			
Annual Operating Hours =	1,600	Equivalent Full Load Hours (EFLH) =	850
Chiller Design Load Factor =	0.90	Sizing Tower/Chiller Factor =	1.80
Ancillary kW/ton =	0.025	Chiller IPLV COP =	1.25
Clg Tower Fan (kW/ton) =	0.045	Condenser Pump (kW/ton) =	0.065
Surface Condenser/Chiller Factor =	-	Boiler Eff (needed to generate steam) =	0.90

Annual Electric Energy Usage										kWh/year	%of tot
Chiller Ancillary	1,200	tons	x	1,600	HR	x	0.025	kW/ton	=	48,000	26%
Clg Twr Fan	1,200	tons	x	1,225	EFLH	x	0.045	kW/ton	=	66,150	35%
Cond Wat Pmp	1,200	tons	x	1,600	HR	x	0.065	kW/ton	=	124,800	67%
						Annual Electricity Energy Usage Calc (kWh/year) =				238,950	128%

Gas consumption, cost, and added maintenance costs are not parts of screening tool - Included FYI:

Assumed Gas $/Therm =			$0.75	Additional Maint Gas $/Ton-Hr =			$0.012	
Therm / year =	1,200	tons	x	850 EFLH	/	1.25 COP		
	/	0.90	BlrEff	x	12,000	Btu/tor /	100,000 Btu/Thrm =	108,800

Monthly Electric Demand:											%of tot
Chiller Ancillary	1,200	tons	x	0.90	LF	x	0.025	kW/ton	=	27	21%
Clg Twr Fan	1,200	tons	x	1.00	LF	x	0.045	kW/ton	=	54	43%
Cond Wat Pmp	1,200	tons	x	1.00	LF	x	0.065	kW/ton	=	78	62%
						Peak Monthly Electric Demand Calculation (kW/moth) =				159	126%

Outputs of the above analysis become inputs to the NYSERDA Screening Tool:

Annual Energy Savings (kWh) =	506,028	Summer Peak demand Reduction (kW) =	572
Incremental Cost ($) =	$616,230	Winter Peak demand Reduction (kW) =	-
Savings Aggrigate $/kWh =	$0.329	Winter Peak demand Reduction (kW) =	NA

SPB **8.5**

Option 4 of 5: Single-Stage Steam-Fired Absorption Chiller

Estimated Installed Cost	Capacity	Units	x	$/Unit	=	Cost	%of tot
Chiller - Material	1,200	tons	x	338 $/ton	=	$406,125	32%
Chiller - Installation/Rigging	1,200	tons	x	238 $/ton	=	$285,000	22%
Cond Pump/Motor Main - Mat	150	hp	x	75 $/hp	=	$11,250	1%
Cond Pump/Motor StdBy - Mat	150	hp	x	75 $/hp	=	$11,250	1%
Cond Pump (Main & StdBy) - Install	300	hp	x	210 $/hp	=	$63,000	5%
Condenser Water Piping/Fitting Material &	300	ft	x	200 $/ft	=	$60,000	5%
Cooling Tower - Material	2,400	tons	x	60 $/ton	=	$144,000	11%
Cooling Tower - Labor	2,400	tons	x	42 $/ton	=	$100,800	8%
Design Fees, CM/Contgcy, Insur	1,200	tons	x	121 $/ton	=	$145,200	11%
The items Listed Below are Additional to Steam/Gas Cooling Only:							0%
Surface Condenser - Mat & Install	-	tons	x	- $/ton	=	$0	0%
Additional Gas or Steam Service	1,200	tons	x	17 $/ton	=	$20,160	2%
Additional Space and Structure	200	sqft	x	120 $/sqft	=	$24,000	2%
Total =				1,059 $/ton		$1,270,785	100%

Energy Related Inputs			
Annual Operating Hours =	1,600	Equivalent Full Load Hours (EFLH) =	850
Chiller Design Load Factor =	0.90	Sizing Tower/Chiller Factor =	2.00
Ancillary kW/ton =	0.025	Chiller IPLV COP =	0.70
Clg Tower Fan (kW/ton) =	0.049	Condenser Pump (kW/ton) =	0.069
Surface Condenser/Chiller Factor =	-	Boiler Eff (needed to generate steam) =	0.90

Annual Electric Energy Usage										kWh/year	%of tot
Chiller Ancillary	1,200	tons	x	1,600	HR	x	0.025	kW/ton	=	48,000	19%
Clg Twr Fan	1,200	tons	x	1,225	EFLH	x	0.049	kW/ton	=	72,030	29%
Cond Wat Pmp	1,200	tons	x	1,600	HR	x	0.069	kW/ton	=	132,480	52%
						Annual Electricity Energy Usage Calc (kWh/year) =				252,510	100%

Gas consumption, cost, and added maintenance costs are not parts of screening tool - Included FYI:

Assumed Gas $/Therm =			$0.75	Additional Maint Gas $/Ton-Hr =			$0.012	
Therm / year =	1,200	tons	x	850 EFLH	/	0.70 COP		
	/	0.90	BlrEff	x	12,000	Btu/tor /	100,000 Btu/Thrm =	194,286

Monthly Electric Demand:											%of tot
Chiller Ancillary	1,200	tons	x	0.90	LF	x	0.025	kW/ton	=	27	16%
Clg Twr Fan	1,200	tons	x	1.00	LF	x	0.049	kW/ton	=	59	35%
Cond Wat Pmp	1,200	tons	x	1.00	LF	x	0.069	kW/ton	=	83	49%
						Peak Monthly Electric Demand Calculation (kW/moth) =				169	100%

Outputs of the above analysis become inputs to the NYSERDA Screening Tool:

Annual Energy Savings (kWh) =	492,468	Summer Peak demand Reduction (kW) =	562
Incremental Cost ($) =	$312,735	Winter Peak demand Reduction (kW) =	-
Savings Aggrigate $/kWh =	$0.331	Winter Peak demand Reduction (kW) =	NA

SPB **61.0**

Option 5 of 5: Steam-Turbine Driven Centrifugal Chiller

Estimated Installed Cost	Capacity	Units	x	$/Unit	=	Cost	%of tot
Chiller - Material	1,200	tons	x	556 $/ton	=	$666,900	36%
Chiller - Installation/Rigging	1,200	tons	x	371 $/ton	=	$444,600	24%
Cond Pump/Motor Main - Mat	125	hp	x	75 $/hp	=	$9,375	1%
Cond Pump/Motor StdBy - Mat	125	hp	x	75 $/hp	=	$9,375	1%
Cond Pump (Main & StdBy) - Install	250	hp	x	210 $/hp	=	$52,500	3%
Condenser Water Piping/Fitting Material &	300	ft	x	200 $/ft	=	$60,000	3%
Cooling Tower - Material	2,400	tons	x	60 $/ton	=	$144,000	8%
Cooling Tower - Labor	2,400	tons	x	42 $/ton	=	$100,800	5%
Design Fees, CM/Contgcy, Insur	1,200	tons	x	176 $/ton	=	$211,200	11%
The items Listed Below are Additional to Steam/Gas Cooling Only:							0%
Surface Condenser - Mat & Install	840	tons	x	155 $/ton	=	$130,200	7%
Additional Gas or Steam Service	1,200	tons	x	17 $/ton	=	$20,160	1%
Additional Space and Structure	200	sqft	x	120 $/sqft	=	$24,000	1%
Total =				1,561 $/ton		$1,873,110	100%

Energy Related Inputs			
Annual Operating Hours =	1,600	Equivalent Full Load Hours (EFLH) =	850
Chiller Design Load Factor =	0.90	Sizing Tower/Chiller Factor =	2.00
Ancillary kW/ton =	0.005	Chiller IPLV COP =	1.09
Clg Tower Fan (kW/ton) =	0.049	Condenser Pump (kW/ton) =	0.062
Surface Condenser/Chiller Factor =	0.70		

Annual Electric Energy Usage										kWh/year	%of tot
Chiller Ancillary	1,200	tons	x	1,600	HR	x	0.005	kW/ton	=	9,600	5%
Clg Twr Fan	1,200	tons	x	1,225	EFLH	x	0.049	kW/ton	=	72,030	36%
Cond Wat Pmp	1,200	tons	x	1,600	HR	x	0.062	kW/ton	=	119,040	59%
						Annual Electricity Energy Usage Calc (kWh/year) =				200,670	100%

Gas consumption, cost, and added maintenance costs are not parts of screening tool - Included FYI:

Assumed Gas $/Therm =			$0.75	Additional Maint Gas $/Ton-Hr =			$0.012	
Therm / year =	1,200	tons	x	850 EFLH		1.09 COP		
			x	12,000	Btu/tor /	100,000 Btu/Thrm =		112,300

Monthly Electric Demand:											%of tot
Chiller Ancillary	1,200	tons	x	0.90	LF	x	0.005	kW/ton	=	5	4%
Clg Twr Fan	1,200	tons	x	1.00	LF	x	0.049	kW/ton	=	59	42%
Cond Wat Pmp	1,200	tons	x	1.00	LF	x	0.062	kW/ton	=	74	54%
						Peak Monthly Electric Demand Calculation (kW/moth) =				139	100%

Outputs of the above analysis become inputs to the NYSERDA Screening Tool:

Annual Energy Savings (kWh) =	544,308	Summer Peak demand Reduction (kW) =	592
Incremental Cost ($) =	$915,060	Winter Peak demand Reduction (kW) =	-
Savings Aggrigate $/kWh =	$0.323	Winter Peak demand Reduction (kW) =	NA

SPB **11.5**

SUMMARY AND CONCLUSIONS

This study illustrates the potential of financial incentives in promoting non-electric cooling technologies in office buildings. Without the incentive, the selection of non-electric chillers are difficult to justify in many cases. Whereas with incentives, paybacks were reduced significantly making non-electric chillers a potentially attractive technology choice for many customers.

The effect and the importance of incentives were very clear with the gas engine, two-stage gas absorber, two-stage steam absorber, and steam turbine chillers. The economic payback in the Upstate region improved from 28.0 years to 8.4 years, which is very significant. Also, the economic payback for the Downstate Region improved from 8.5 years to a very attractive 2.5 years. The above clearly illustrates the importance and value of the incentive.

It was found that potential non-electric incentives (calculated at 70% of the incremental system first cost) ranged between $328 to $600/ton for all technologies except for the single-stage steam absorption chillers. The potential incentive for the single-stage steam absorption chillers analyzed ranged from $150 to $257 per ton. It should be noted that energy and demand savings resulted in electric benefit to cost ratios that were all greater than one for all scenarios.

The average incentive for all scenarios was $396 per ton. The average incentive for single-stage absorption chillers was $191 per ton, which is about ½ the average value for all scenarios. For all technologies except for the single-stage absorption chiller, the average incentive was $447 per ton.

The average electric benefit to cost ratio for all scenarios was 2.2. The average electric benefit to cost ratio for single-stage absorption chillers was 4.0. For all technologies except for the single-stage absorption chiller, the average electric benefit to cost ratio was 1.8.

When selecting non-electric chillers, efficiency levels should meet or exceed ASHRAE Standard 90.1-1999 as not to introduce significant gas or steam penalties.

Single-stage absorption chillers are not good fuel conversion applications from a cooling/thermal efficiency viewpoint. They are often used because they are the least expensive non-electric chiller option to install and they do not require a stationary engineer (in NYC). However, single-stage absorbers can be ideal for generating cooling when inexpensive waste heat is available from a process or during cogeneration applications. They can utilize low-grade steam (~ 15 psig) and can be very beneficial if inexpensive heat is available from another source. Though they do not seem to be good office building applications, they can be ideal elsewhere, which is not part of the scope of this study as it focused on commercial office buildings only.

Simple payback periods in NYC are better than those Upstate because NYC's electricity costs are close to double those Upstate, whereas NYC's fuel costs are only 45% more than those Upstate.

Alternative steam system configurations such as the use of backpressure steam turbines (instead of condensing turbines) should be investigated as that may enhance the overall efficiency. Backpressure steam turbines can be used for onsite power generation or to drive a centrifugal chiller in a piggybacked assembly with single-stage absorption chillers.

To improve overall system efficiency, chiller sizing/combinations should be selected in a way that best meet the varying building load profiles.

The study focused on typical office building applications. The economics for non-electric chillers can be improved by carefully selecting the system application. For instance, facilities with longer cooling seasons, low cost steam, waste heat recovery opportunities, etc. will have shorter payback periods than the office application studied here.

This analysis did not address heat recovery. The economics of non-electric cooling can be optimized in industrial situations where gas-engine waste heat can be utilized as a heat source for an industrial process where a heat sink exists during the cooling season.

ACKNOWLEDGMENTS
The New York State Energy Research and Development Authority (NYSERDA) sponsored the majority of this study. Valuable information was provided during the data collection process and during the sizing and pricing of the different alternatives from a number of vendors, contractors, and design professionals. A total of 13 professionals were consulted during the generation of this paper as well as our in-house expertise with the subject of the report.

REFERENCES
1. ASHRAE Standard 90.1-1999 – Energy Standards for Buildings Except Low-Rise Residential Buildings
2. RS Means Mechanical 2002 Cost Data 25th Annual Edition (HVAC and Controls)

3. Much of the information used in the development of system costs was obtained through interviews with equipment vendors, contractors, and design consultants.

AUTHOR'S BIOs

Khaled A. Yousef, P.E., CEM, CDSM is a Senior Engineer with the Energy Solutions Division of Science Applications International Corporation (SAIC). He has over twelve years of comprehensive energy analysis and modeling experience. Provided technical building energy/analysis services to over 120 customers domestically and internationally. Examined the technical and economic feasibility of many energy efficiency technologies. Participated in over 300 energy audits and energy efficiency studies and was the technical lead in many of them.

His energy expertise includes the intensive use of building simulation software, such as DOE-2 and ASEAM (both developed by the US Department of Energy) and other bin and custom methods. Participated in the evaluation and verification of the DOE-2.1E Beta releases during the early 1990s. His simulations, coupled with engineering expertise, are used to evaluate the energy and economic impacts of a wide range of energy efficiency measures (EEMs) for: technical feasibility/assistance studies, utility demand side management (DSM) programs, energy savings performance contracts (ESPCs), design assistance, commissioning energy management and control systems (EMCS), and radon mitigation/indoor air quality (IAQ) measures. Computed the savings and incentive levels in many of the state government incentive programs, participated in the development of many of them and served as QC/QA lead on reported results. Developed and implemented measurement and verification (M&V) programs for impact assessment.

Science Applications International Corporation (SAIC)/Energy Solutions Division, 421 New Karner Road, Albany, New York 12205
Phone: 518 452-8800 Ext. 214, Fax: 518 452-8111,
e-mail: Khaled.A.Yousef@saic.com, http://www.saic.com

Ronald Slosberg is a Program Manager with Science Applications International Corporation. For the past seventeen years, Ron has focused on providing energy conservation and cost reduction solutions to customers, helping improve their business operations and profitability. He has provided energy consulting to many commercial, industrial, institutional, and municipal facilities, completing energy audits and energy use evaluations, recommendations, and implementation support. Ron has also completed many DSM and market transformation program design and evaluation projects, working for clients such as NYSERDA, New England Electric, Consolidated Edison, and Northeast Utilities. Ron was involved with program design for the standard performance contract program and the new construction program. He is also currently providing implementation assistance to these programs. SAIC/Energy Solutions Division, 421 New Karner Road, Albany, New York 12205, Phone: 518 452-8800 Ext. 216, Fax: 518 452-8111, e-mail: Ronald.B.Slosber@saic.com, http://www.saic.com

Mark Eggers, RA is a Registered Architect who has over two decades of experience with building energy efficiency and energy codes. Mark also holds a Masters degree in Business Administration. He is a Program Manager of the New Construction/Green Buildings/Energy Codes Unit at the New York State Energy Research and Development Authority (NYSERDA), where he currently directs the $45 million New Construction Program for commercial buildings, which provides technical assistance to design teams and financial incentives to building owners. He also directs NYSERDA's technical support activities for the New York State Energy Conservation Construction Code and has authored three successive DOE grant awards totaling $1.2 million for energy code activities in New York.

Mark has managed several innovative residential, commercial and industrial energy programs for New York State during his career, including the NYSTAR builders program, the Energy Advisory Service to Industry, and the Energy Efficient Procurement Collaborative.

NYSERDA is the New York State Energy Research & Development Authority located on 286 Washington Avenue Extension, Albany, New York 12203
Phone 518 862-1090 Ext 3308, Fax 518 862-1090,
e-mail: MSE@nyserda.org, http://www.nyserda.org/

Chris Reohr is a Project Manager with NYSERDA. He helped create and currently manages the New Construction Program (NCP) for the New York State Energy Research and Development Authority (NYSERDA). In addition to developing and refining this program, he oversees the management of over 250 individual projects and manages 25 Outreach Project Consultants that promote and manage NYSERDA's activities across New York State. Chris also holds an MBA in Finance.
Phone 518 862-1090 Ext 3363, Fax 518 862-1090,
e-mail: CJR@nyserda.org, http://www.nyserda.org/

Chapter 26

HYBRID PLANT EXPANSION: A CASE STUDY AT SJSU

John Salas
Principal
Salas O'Brien Engineers, Inc.

Abstract:

The sophisticated Physical Plant at San Jose State University has become a state of the art, high efficiency hybrid plant. Strategic campus planning has allowed San Jose State University to remain energy resourceful, despite the recent energy crises. Innovative, well planned projects have permitted this high tech showcase to support future growth demands with sustainable system approaches.

plant consists of a 5 MW gas fired generator, which converts waste heat to steam for re-injection in the turbine (Cheng cycle) and for steam driven absorbers (two at 1300 ton). The plant also contains two 750 ton electric chillers. The hydraulic system consists of primary pumps for each chiller, multiple secondary pumps with variable speed drives serving the campus loop, with tertiary pumps being added to the buildings in phases. The entire plant is controlled and

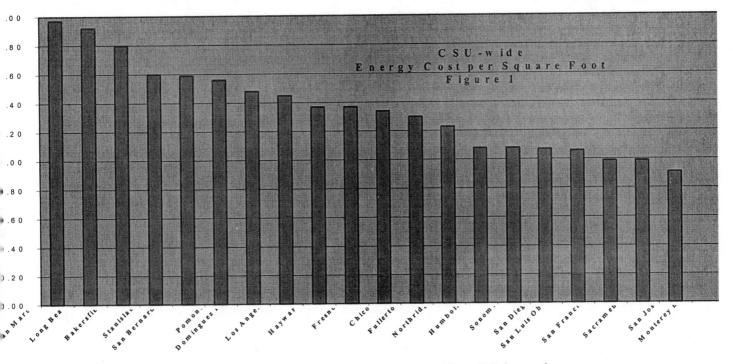

CSU-wide
Energy Cost per Square Foot
Figure 1

The existing San Jose State University Physical Plant has evolved over the years as expansion has occurred. It has become the most efficient and diversified heating, cooling and generating power plant in the CSU system (See Figure 1). The

monitored by a digital control system.

Expansion of the campus plan included a new 500,000 sq.ft. Library, which was to be the first joint city and university library in the U.S. Also planned was an expansion in student housing

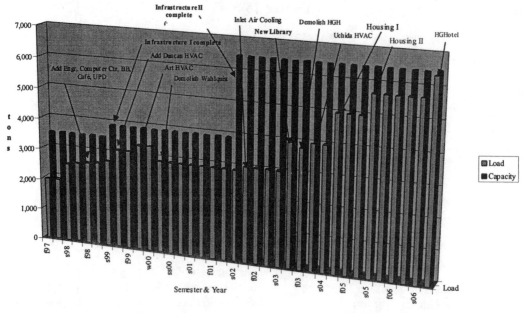

FIGURE 2

complex (700,000 SF) to accommodate the expected growth in enrollment on campus. Smaller expansions include Building renovations and some building replacements. All this planning was taking place during an energy crisis. This focused the attention on energy efficiency based solutions. The plant capacity would have to expand by almost double in the 5 year plan for the campus. See Figure 2.

The Physical Plant had some challenges relative to space. The cooling tower expansion area was taken by the cogeneration system installed in 1986. As such, expansion capability of the tower was limited to an increase in the fan motor horsepower. This, in addition to the benefits associated with limiting demand increases led to the proposal for an ice storage system. The ice system would allow the physical plant to meet the future capacity with little to no increase in electric demand. It would also not require any cooling

tower capacity increase as the ice would be made at night when the tower loads would be significantly less.

In order to provide the future demands, the campus load profiles were analyzed using the Building automation system. The DDC system has flow meters and temperature instrumentation on all the chillers, so exact loads could be trended continuously (See Figure 3). The proposed expansion loads were added to this profile. This information led to the design of an approximately 16,800 ton-hr ice system, consisting of a 2000 ton chiller, and a plate and frame heat exchanger. The ice tanks could not be manufactured tanks, as there was not enough space available. A 644,000 gallon tank was to be constructed with 3/4 of the depth of the tank to be underground. In conjunction with this addition, an inlet air cooler was proposed to increase the power output of the cogeneration system.

OPTION #1 SUMMARY LOAD PROFILE
Figure 3

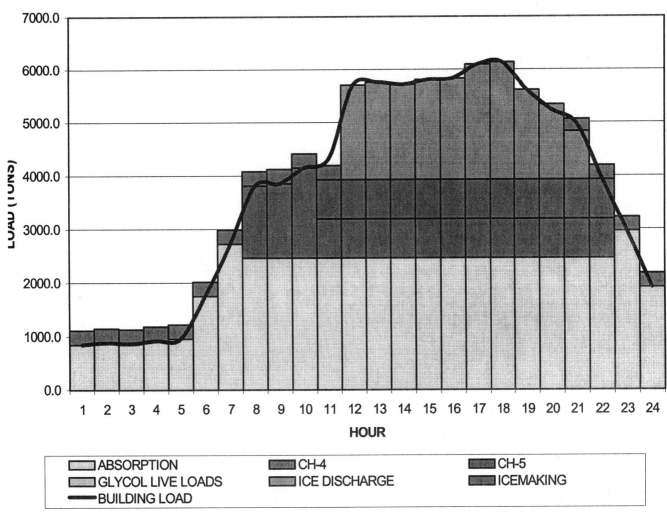

The infrastructure project included underground services, chilled water, steam, and power. The entire project construction cost was approximately $8 million. The ice storage system was able to displace approximately 2600 Tons, estimated to be 1300 KW of demand reduction. The addition of the inlet air cooler on the Cogen system displaced another 300 KW for a total reduced demand of 1600 KW.

Chapter 27

Variable Air Volume and Ventilation (VAV^2)

Alan F. Stewart, P.E.
Stewart Engineering Services Corp.

Abstract

The paper considers alternative engineering approaches to energy efficient cooling and heating systems. Traditional HVAC design considers systems to be continuous flow. With the robust control technologies available, we may need to think batch flow concepts to meet required part load operation efficiency and ventilation requirements. The need for greater cooling capacity is a significant problem for the office facilities designed in the 1960's. And having high internal computer system heat loads.

Overview

The challenge for building owners with energy efficient mechanical systems has evolved into how to properly care for the building occupants, ensuring proper ventilation to meet the statutory requirements. ASHRAE Standard 62-2001 requires 15-20 CFM per person depending on the facility type. Ventilation requirements may be higher yet if the actual mixing of out side air with facility return air is not uniform. The following plan details how to use technology to solve a problem with required airflow and energy efficiency imperatives. To begin, we must scope the problem.

Typical VAV installations operate on the premise that the local thermostat will have available the necessary thermal solution for the space. The role of the thermostat is to regulate the amount (volume) of, typically, cooling for any given space. (There are many variants of VAV boxes, with fan powered heating units. These will not be the subject of this work, but are a logical extension of the thought process). In twinned in the available cooling is the proportion of ventilation air for the entire area served by the air handler. During the normal daily cycle, when occupants are present, lights are on and the heat load to be extracted as drags along some ventilation air. At the end of the day the lights are turned off, and the space heat load

may go to almost zero. Our early designs for VAV would let the VAV box shut off the flow of air to the space. Now we know that some limited airflow must continue into these spaces with no cooling load. The approach is to set the minimum flow for the VAV box to say 10-30 percent and provide reheat to prevent the space from over cooling. Given the typical pneumatic controls implementation for VAV, the reheat option solved the problem of overcooling. In the retrofit of existing buildings with VAV we are posed with a serious challenge. How do we distribute reheat systems throughout existing facilities, when the facility will remain in service during the renovation work.

Traditional VAV systems

Before we solve the need for reheat problem we must have some common definition for how the VAV systems operate in the traditional manner. To do this, let us work back from the liberation of the heat by the cooling tower to the occupied space and define all of the control parameters from the cooling tower (or air cooled condenser) to the space. A diagram of the full sequence is shown below.

Working backward in the heat rejection process, from the tower to the space we have the following:

The cooling tower functions by passing water over the fill material, designed to create the greatest water and air contact, and into the tower basin. The tower fan will be operated to control water temperature in the basin to some desired level by forcing air to flow up through the tower. Even without the fan the hot water from the chiller will cause some level of convection airflow, due to the temperature differences. Not shown in the example drawing is the condenser water bypass valve that can divert water into the tower basin in cold weather and low load. Freeze protection is provided by tower basin heaters.

CONDENSER LOOP   CHILLED WATER LOOP   AIR SIDE

STATIC PRESSURE CONTROL@ 3PSI

FAN

COOLING TOWER

CHILLER

AIR HANDLER

VAV

SPACE

RETURN AIR

The condenser water pump operates the condenser water loop. The pump is selected to move the design quantity of water, gallon per minute, (GPM) through the condenser water barrel in the chiller. With safety factors the pump can be over sized.

The chiller compressor is sized to transfer the heat from the evaporator to the condenser. This compressor operational working range is usually defined over a narrow set of operating curves, specifying entering water and leaving water temperatures. Very cold condenser water generally limited to 10 degrees F above chilled water (verify requirements from the chiller manufacturer) can cause internal refrigerant flow problems for the compressor.

The evaporator water pump or pumps are designed to get the chilled water to the air handler. There are many possible configurations for the chilled water design. (See the chilled water design example.)

The air handler is designed to convey the airside heat to the chilled water, and to supply the cooled air to the space. There are many design variations here also. In this example we consider variable air volume (VAV) as the airside control. The air handler may use a variable frequency drive, inlet air dampers or outlet air dampers to vary the airflow. Typically the air handler controlled to provide a fixed pressure output to the ductwork. The operating pressure was established in the design analysis.

The airflow is conveyed to the VAV box, which based on the local sensor will cool as necessary to meet the temperature set point.

Each of the above system components function as an autonomous elements, controlled by individual set points.

Let's go back through my simple example and determine how many control loops exist:

Cooling tower-
    Divert water through the tower or to the basin (1)
    Operate the fan speed (1)
    Operate the basin heaters, if freezing weather (1)

Condenser water
    Pump with pressure verification generally on/off (1)

Chiller
    Condenser water flow, for chiller shut down
    Compressor inlet vane control to maintain chilled water temperature (1)
    Chilled water flow, for chiller shut down

Chilled water pump(s)
    Pump with pressure verification, generally on/off (1)

Air handler
    Chilled water flow through the cooling coil (1)
    Fan start/stop (1)
    Fan pressure control set point (1)
    Minimum outside air for ventilation (1)

VAV box
    Flow control based on space set point (1)
    May have minimum flow set point with reheat (1)
    Space humidity (1)

Recognizing this to be a simple system we have about 15 control loops total. For those of pure heart we will only consider the loops marked with a (1) as controlling energy. Even in this simple example we have 13 loops that all have an impact on the energy consumption for the entire system.

Further I submit that if the information available to the 13 individual control loops were available to all 13-control loops the decision-making would further reduce facility energy consumption.

Software Solutions to Hardware Problems
Let's look at some examples.

1. The airflow from the air handler is maintained a preset static pressure. The pressure should be controlled by the flow needs of the VAV box with the greatest load. I have used this technique effectively in many facilities (subject to minimum throw for the terminal diffusers). To avoid conflicting control loop activity between the fan speed and VAV box, I assign the worst-case space temperature plus one degree as the set point for the fan speed control. That way the worst-case VAV box is fully open and I drive the system air volume from that space. The other spaces operate the VAV normally. A second benefit of this approach is the reduced effect of noise created by throttling the central fan airflow through the VAV box.

2. The system can be examined during low load periods to minimize reheat by floating the fan supply air temperature to prevent overcooling.

3. The chiller supply water temperature can be reset based on knowing the actual sensible and latent load requirements of the space.

4. Condenser and chilled water loops can be flow/delta temperature controlled, within limits, to reduce chiller operating cost.

5. Actual performance can be measured and compared to manufacturer specification for chillers, pumps, air handlers, cooling towers and other components. For example, if some of the cooling tower nozzles were fouled the performance degradation would show up over time, as the tower would not continue to meet part load performance. Using the method of today, the tower will degrade until even running the fans on high will not meet condenser water set point.

6. Even overloaded air handlers can be aided by developing lower chilled water supply temperatures. The reason for the overload should be determined. This approach can solve seasonal air handler overload due to ventilation cooling loads, at least until permanent solutions are developed.

7. One project I worked had significant production swings in the electrical demand. By allowing the thermal mass of the chilled

water system to absorb short periods, 5–15 minutes, of reduced chiller demand, we were able to reduce facility site demand by over 100 KW per month, a saving of over $15K per year. This was accomplished by reducing chiller load during peak periods of demand. And recovering the cooling thermal mass during the reduced production demand. This cycle operated several times during a day in the hot weather without comfort interruption. Key here was available cooling capacity beyond breakpoint such that the chilled water system could recover quickly.

8. Return airflows may be monitored for carbon dioxide. Given reasonable testing and familiarity with these devices over ventilation may be reduced, or as part of a fault tolerance solution available cooling can be better utilized when equipment failures prevent all the required cooling from operating. The key here is the knowledge of actual operating parameters allows informed decision-making.

9. Dual duct installations can also profit from the current state of automation and controls. A recent job had seen the typical explosion of plug devices throughout the facility, computers, printers and copiers to name a few. The air handler and ductwork were taxed out to supply cooling for the loads. With automation we can determine the entire area cooled by the dual duct to be in cooling mode. At that time we have interconnecting ductwork to the hot deck, which we now use as a parallel cold deck. This approach allows use of the hot deck to reduce fan horsepower. The normal cold deck is still primary with cold flow on the hot deck dictated by worst-case zone loads.

Two inter-related principles have been discussed above. The existing approach of multiple, single loop control subsystems, where the loops are not working together has tremendous energy savings opportunity. Secondly, shortcomings in the existing subsystems may be overcome by operating the system as a single loop reset with data from each subsystem. In practice other sub-systems can cover some or all, of the shortfall from parts of the larger system

Renovation Projects
Above we set the stage for consideration of the complete HVAC system for a facility as a single loop. Additionally, we have the dilemma of installing reheat throughout facilities in operation. What if we depart from traditional thinking, particularly since we have control and

automation systems with tremendous untapped power. Let us restate the operating parameters:

1. Normal operation, say, during day load when people are present, the lights are on and office equipment is in use. During this condition we have sufficient heat load to require cooling and byproduct ventilation.

2. Low load periods, say, during late evening or night. Perhaps there is limited staff working, motion sensors have the lighting on low level, and our green computers have spun down to minimum energy consumption.

During normal periods the outside air will be reasonably distributed. Local test instruments, measuring carbon dioxide variation throughout the facility, can verify this. Areas that are candidates for consideration, small area with no heat loads, can be instrumented with a carbon dioxide sensor. How do we get the ventilation to these spaces?

There are several potential ways to accomplish this task:

1. On a regular schedule, perhaps once an hour raise discharge air temperature by 5-10 degrees. And automatically command VAV boxes with low flow to some new minimum. Due to the variety of configurations of airflows and space requirements "rule of thumb" procedures are difficult to propose. However, you may consider 1 air change per hour as a good starting place.

2. Should the space in low load areas over cool, consider closing the chilled water valve, reduce to minimum out side air/no outside air, command low flow areas to high flow. This procedure is for use during light occupant loads with the return air carbon dioxide well toward outside air PPM. Typical carbon dioxide values are 330-350 for outside air but may go as high as 700 PPM in some industrial areas. ASHRAE std. 62-2001 allows carbon dioxide levels 700 PPM above ambient as allowable. For our use I would expect return air with a target carbon dioxide PPM of 200-300 PPM over ambient to provide good dilution for lightly occupied spaces.

3. Pretreatment of outside air may be necessary. This can be accomplished by using multiple technologies to conserve energy. Sensible or sensible and latent heat wheels recover energy of the exhausted air. Conditioning of the outside air at one location will be far less costly than implementing multiple reheat installations throughout a facility. (We will not cover methods to obtain dehumidified outside air here, only presume it to be possible). Once conditioned air is available, it can be routed through the ductwork in a timed fashion to solve particularly thorny ventilation issues. Or just solving day-to-day problems, you know at 8:00 PM someone makes popcorn, with one or two outcomes. The popcorn smell permeates the whole building, worse yet if the popcorn is burned. With the concepts presented here we can spin down all VAV zones to say 10 percent, and 100 percent to the area with the popcorn machine. Then operate the maximum available outside air with full exhaust.

4. Consider that large common areas served by VAV zones can use one carbon dioxide sensor as the partial pressure of the carbon dioxide will assure a degree of uniformity higher than the temperature from zone to zone in a common area.

5. The primary goal here is to think of the ductwork system as having a new axis of freedom. We already vary the temperature, flow rate and outside air percentage. Now we add the ability during non-peak periods to time phase different air flow conditions customized for specific spaces.

Summary

The discussion above opens a new opportunity to solve facility airside problems with VAV and Dual Duct installations. When we decouple the ductwork from continuous temperature flow and begin to think in terms of the High Occupancy Vehicle (HOV) lanes on the highways. Now we can use the ductwork by time phasing the temperature and quality of the air and routing that air to the area with special needs.

About the Author

Owner, Stewart Engineering Services Corp, develops Solutions Engineering projects for a broad range of customers desiring to reduce facility ownership costs through technology and technical services. A ten-year veteran of Honeywell Inc, he developed a wide variety of facility and process solutions for fortune 100 companies. He is a Honeywell President's Club member and recipient of the Johnson and Johnson Quality award. He served twenty-one years in the U.S. Air Force in a variety of engineering and technical roles both in flight simulation systems and facility operation and design. Alan has published several technical articles from Energy Auditing, Facility Simulation to Fiber Optic local area network design. He is active in AEE, ASHRAE and NSPE. Alan is a licensed engineer in four states. His bachelor of electrical engineering degree is from Rutgers University and his graduate studies in mechanical engineering were through the Air Force Institute of Technology.

Chapter 28

THE CHANGING ROLE OF THE ENERGY MANAGER

D. Victor Bush, Practice & Technology Leader
URS Corporation

ABSTRACT
The traditional energy manager has been primarily focused on the demand side management or energy conservation aspects of energy management. As a result the energy manager's responsibilities were limited to finding energy conservation opportunities (ECOs), performing economic justifications and submitting proposals to management for funding. In many cases, the ECOs had to compete with operational projects for capital funding or the energy manager had to be able to sell and manage a performance contract, a formidable task in itself.

In addition to the above requirements, today's energy manager must take on a much broader scope of responsibilities and authority to accomplish the objectives of an energy program. The past few years have made CEOs and CFOs aware of the importance of corporate energy management and its effect on the company's financial bottom line and stock valuation.

Today's energy manager must understand financial and physical energy risk management and be able to value corporate energy risk with regard to reliability and energy costs. Once the energy manager defines corporate risk, a plan must be developed to mitigate that risk through alternate energy sources, financial derivatives and/or load management plans. These plans must take into account lost production costs and the possibility of future energy risks in the cost-benefit analysis.

From an implementation standpoint today's energy manager must have the authority to make the end users of energy responsible for their energy consumption. The energy manager must also have direct input into the day-to-day decision making if the corporate energy program objectives are to be achieved.

ENERGY SAVINGS –VS- STOCK VALUE
A comprehensive energy management program will almost always result in a return on investment and improve cost competitiveness. This holds especially true for the energy intensive industries where a significant portion of their overhead costs are attributable to energy costs. Energy cost savings go directly to the bottom line of the corporation and can equate to several multiples of sales revenue. For example if a health care company's net profit is 7.8% and it was to implement an energy conservation measure that saves $50,000, that same company would have to generate over $640,000 in sales to achieve the same "bottom line" results. In fact the stock price of a corporation has been shown to go up with just the announcement of corporate energy conservations projects.[1]

These facts and correlation would seem would seem to make the decision to implement an energy management program or project and easy sell. Unfortunately, energy conservation projects tend to directly compete with other capital improvement projects from the maintenance and operations groups. The challenge for the new energy manager is to present energy conservation investment opportunities in CFO language, demonstrating the return on investment using whatever financial criteria is dictated by finance. This will require the energy manager to develop the trust and confidence of the corporate financial team. This is also very much to the benefit of the company in demonstrating wise investment of corporate funds and socially responsible leadership.

A NEW ERA OF ENERGY ENGINEERING
For most, energy issues in the past have involved the basics of energy management actions that have included lighting modifications, ventilation control, facility

173

management system controls, motor controls, etc. Now, especially with the growing interest/disdain regarding deregulation and its impact on utility costs, energy is again taking a center stage in many offices and boardrooms.

Physical and Financial Risk Management

The new energy manager must now be able to assess and identify the source of risks inherent in the business and be able to measure the impact of those risks on the financial statements of the company. This objective will now require the energy manager to be intimately aware of maintenance and operational concerns, production schedules, etc. to effectively understand the costs associated with loss of power (physical risk) and/or increasing power costs (financial risks).

Based on identified, measured and valued risks, the new energy manager must develop risk management strategies that will meet the company's goals and objectives. Once the value of the risk has been identified, the energy manager can now use this information to execute the appropriate strategy. It is easy to say, but much more difficult to value these risk.

Physical risk evaluation will value the cost of not having power or downtime. This value can then be used to justify physical risk management through back-up generation, co-generation, fuel switching, natural gas storage, burying the electrical distribution lines, etc..

Financial risk evaluation will value the cost/benefit of using derivatives to hedge energy costs for firm delivery at fixed prices. In the past this was not a concern of the energy manager because there was no option for purchasing power. Even today's energy manager can transfer risk to the energy marketer but it will come at a cost. The more risk the energy manager can take from the provider and manage, the better the price for power the energy manager will be able to negotiate. In addition to using derivatives, today's energy manager will also coordinate the demand side management activities to minimize consumption during periods of supply shortage and high prices. This will be discussed in more detail later in this paper.

Management's Aversion to Derivatives

For that portion of the power that must be firm at a fixed price, derivatives can be a useful tool. But again the energy manager must be able to sell this concept to a potentially reluctant upper level management team, especially since the financial debacles of Enron. Another potential impediment is the accounting rules applying to derivatives such as FAS 133 (Statement of Financial Accounting Standards No. 133). FAS 133 require

companies to recognize all derivative instruments as either assets or liabilities on their balance sheet, and to measure those instruments at fair market value. This rule has forced virtually every public company to revisit its derivatives accounting

The new energy manager will be challenged to demonstrate the value of energy derivatives to the financial managers of the company. "A successful hedging program coupled with the right derivatives accounting strategy transforms and uncontrollable risk into a strategic advantage. It allows companies to leverage those advantages over their competition, to handle compliance issues more efficiently, and spend more time running core operations and increasing profitability"[2].

REAL TIME (SPOT MARKET) PRICING

In most cases, the best price for electrical power will be on the real time market with the exception of short duration, highly volatile prices due to shortages or constraints. Therefore, it stands to reason that the more load that can be purchased on the real time (spot) market, the lower the overall price will be. But for those short duration highly volatile price spikes, the energy manager will have to shed previously identified and isolated non-critical loads. The energy manager will now be required to coordinate the demand side program with the supply side program to minimize costs and maximize efficiency.

The strategies for managing cost are limited only by the energy manager's imagination. A few of the many strategies include load shedding, load scheduling, load shifting, fuel switching and co-generation. The challenge for the energy manager is to maintain close coordination with operations and maintenance to ensure there are no adverse ramifications for production or productivity. It will require a close working relationship with the management of maintenance and production and a strong buy in from top-level management including the CEO and CFO.

TOTAL ENERGY ASSET MANAGEMENT (TEAM)[SM]

The URS Corporation has utilized the term TEAM[sm] (Figure 1) to represent the new era of energy management. The TEAM[sm] approach captures the variety of approaches that should be considered in the development of a comprehensive energy management program. The primary purpose for using this approach is to insure that great opportunities are not missed, or worse yet, compromised by actions taken in another area. The following are the key links in the value chain that represents the TEAM[sm] concept.

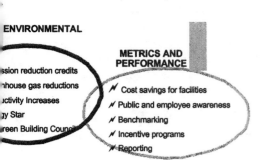

ENVIRONMENTAL

...ssion reduction credits

...nhouse gas reductions

...uctivity Increases

...gy Star

...reen Building Council

METRICS AND PERFORMANCE

- Cost savings for facilities
- Public and employee awareness
- Benchmarking
- Incentive programs
- Reporting

Integrated Resource Planning (Often the Link between Supply Side and Demand Side Management Programs and Other Asset Management Functions)

Integrated Resource Planning (IRP) is This has been one of the foremost management practice leadership concepts in bringing together various cost saving opportunities in one program. With the increased ability to consider supply-side management options, the link to demand–side management practices has become more important. This has also many times required the financial divisions of an organization to coordinate projects with the facility's services divisions. The projects and services in this area include:

Figure 1. Total Energy Asset Management Value Chain.

- Strategic Energy Management
- Integrated Resource Planning
- Demand Side Management
- Environmental
- Metrics and Performance

Strategic Energy Management (Supply Side Management)

This is probably one of the newest areas (certainly the most expanded area) to be added as a standard part of a comprehensive energy management program. The roots of this section go back to the rate and tariff analyses that were performed prior to deregulation. However, now, even rate and tariff analysis has taken on an increased responsibility to insure the best end result for energy management programs.

In a deregulated environment, this area concentrates on finding ways to reduce the cost of energy. Potential savings can range from a nominal amount to twenty percent or more. This all depends on specifics of the location including load factor, usage, vendor, risk management features, etc. This area includes the following processes, projects and services:

- Supplier selection and negotiation
- Financial and physical risk management
- Tariff analysis and optimization
- Aggregation analysis
- Real time pricing

- Bill Consolidation
- Load Management Studies
- Strategic Planning
- Deregulation Awareness
- Usage Auditing

Demand Side Management (Traditional Energy Management Practices)

This practice area includes many of the traditional services performed for energy management programs. The scope of work typically involves controlling equipment and/or replacing equipment and/or systems with more energy efficient options. Projects may include:

- Chilled water equipment, systems, and distribution
- Boiler equipment, systems, and hot water and/or steam distribution
- Building envelope
- Control/facility management systems
- Electrical distribution
- Lighting
- Ventilation/air handling systems
- Production equipment

Environmental (The Extended Impact of Energy on the Environment)

This topic includes the impact on energy programs as a result of environmental programs or vice versa. Many environmental projects can be enhanced through the development of energy management programs. Of great interest is where facility equipment and systems improvement options can have a significant impact on reducing pollution and energy costs. The projects to be considered include:

- Emission reduction programs
- Greenhouse gas reductions
- Productivity increases
- US EPA programs including Green Lights and Energy Star
- US Green Building Council

Metrics and Performance

This topic represents many of the management functions that deal with the measurements, public relations, planning, reporting, and goal setting activities related to the development of energy management programs. Without this section, the ability to adequately measure results and plan for future projects is minimized. Most importantly, the ability to develop a long-term program is compromised or at worst, doomed to failure. These projects include:

- Cost saving measurements
- Public and employee awareness programs
- Benchmarking
- Incentive programs
- Reporting systems

FINANCIAL ALTERNATIVES

There are generally three ways to finance energy conservation measures. Those being, internal capital funds, lease/purchase, and shared savings or performance contracting. In general a capital investment in the energy conservation measure will result in the highest return on investment but the funds may not be available. If corporate funding is not an option, then the second best return on investment would be through lease/purchase financing through third party financing. If neither the capital purchase or lease/purchase options are available to the energy manager, then performance contracting would still be better than forgoing the upgrades. If performance contracting is the financing of choice, the energy manager must understand and work through numerous administrative issues to make the program work.

The new energy manager will have to understand the corporate investment criteria and financial alternatives if he or she is to effectively implement energy cost saving measures.

CONCLUSION

The new corporate energy manager will have a new level of corporate responsibility that will have a significant affect on the company's bottom line and indirectly on the company's stock value. He or she will have to understand the financial alternatives available to him and be able to communicate the value of life-cycle costing to corporate financial personnel.

Due to the expanded scope of the new energy manager's responsibilities he or she will have to be able to leverage their resources through team development internally and externally. The energy manager will need to constantly sell the energy program throughout the company and communicate the latest news to the team participants. In short, the corporate energy manager will be required to wear several hats such as project finance, risk management, communications and program selling. To accomplish this job, the energy manager must have support from the highest levels within the organization.

REFERENCES

1. Wingender, J. and Woodroof E. (1997) "When Firms Publicize Energy Management Projects Their Stock Prices Go Up", Strategic Planning for Energy and the Environment 17(1), p. 38-51.

2. Emanuelsson, J. (2002) "Derivatives Accounting Compliance", Demystifying Derivatives Accounting, KIODEX Report, July 2002.

THE AUTHOR

Victor Bush is currently the Practice and Technology Leader, Energy Management Services, Global Accounts for URS Corporation. He has more than 28 years of professional experience in energy engineering. He holds a B.S. degree in Engineering from the Colorado School of Mines and is an AEE Certified Energy Manager, Certified Energy Procurement Professional and a Certified Demand Side Management Professional.

Chapter 29

Heat Recovery Strategies for Low Temperature Heat Sources.

D. Paul Mehta, Ph.D.
Professor & Chairman of Mechanical Engineering Department
Director, Industrial Assessment Center
Bradley University, Peoria, IL. 61625

And

Chintamani V. Kulkarni
Graduate Research Assistant
Industrial Assessment Center
Bradley University, Peoria, IL. 61625

ABSTRACT

In small and medium sized manufacturing facilities, several situations exist where sources of waste heat and sinks needing heat coexist. However, generally sources of waste heat like drained hot water streams from water-cooled manufacturing equipment are low temperature waste heat sources while heat sinks like drying and preheaters for fluids operate at higher temperatures. Commercially available heat recovery devices such as heat pumps and heat pipes become unfeasible for heat recovery from low temperature sources because of their low efficiency and high first cost. This results in meeting the heating requirements by burning fossil fuels or even by using electric heaters while available waste heat is dumped to the surrounding environment. This practice results in: a) energy waste, b) global warming, and c) economic inefficiency.

The objective of the work reported in this paper was to develop strategies for enhancing the efficiency and to reduce the first cost of low temperature heat recovery devices with the purpose of making the application of these devices more feasible to replace combustion of fossil fuels with recovered heat in order to save energy, prevent pollution, and to enhance the competitiveness of the manufacturers.

The heat exchangers used in the heat pumps and heat pipes were modeled. Available literature on the techniques for enhancing heat transfer in the heat exchangers was reviewed. Significant design parameters were identified and analyzed to quantify their impact on improving heat transfer in these heat exchangers. Specific recommendations were developed to optimize the design of four commercially available heat exchangers for heat pumps and heat pipes.

Introduction

The advantages of heat pumps and heat pipes for low temperature heat recovery have long been recognized. However, the application of these devices for low temperature heat recovery is rendered unfeasible due their low efficiencies. Research into improving their performance has been an on going concern for industrial and academic organizations. Heat transfer enhancement through surface modifications and thereby increasing the capacity or reducing the size and cost has become a common method of increasing the efficiency of the heat exchangers of these devices. (Ravigururajan and Bergles, 1995). Enhancement of heat transfer has been of interest to the researchers and practitioners since the earliest documented studies of heat transfer (Bergles, 1988). During the past decade numerous studies on flow in enhanced tubes and over fins have resulted in various enhancement techniques. For instance several correlations have been developed that can be used to calculate heat transfer coefficient and friction factor for rib roughness.(Ravigururajan and Bergles, 1985, 1986; Webb, Narayanamurthy and Thors, 2000), Similarly, Chamra, Webb and Randlett, (1996); and Schlager, Pate and Bergles, (1989, 1990) reported work on micro fin tubes for refrigerant evaporation and condensation. Nakayama, W and Xu, L. P, (1983) and Ayub, Z. H and Bergles, (1985) published research work for fins for air-cooled heat exchangers and pool boiling respectively.

The objective of the work reported in this paper was to apply the heat transfer enhancement techniques developed and reported by the various researchers for improving the efficiency of heat pumps and heat pipes. The purpose of improving the heat transfer in the components of these devices was to improve their performance, reduce their size, and cut their first cost so that they become feasible for recovery of waste heat in low temperature heat sources. It is expected that it will result in reduced use of fossil fuels for meeting heating requirement leading to save energy, prevent pollution, and enhance the competitiveness of the manufactures.

To accomplish the stated objectives, the heat exchangers used in heat pumps and heat pipes were modeled. Focus of modeling in the case of heat pumps was on liquid to refrigerant heat exchangers. The impact of enhancement techniques on commercially available models of heat pumps and heat pipes for improving the performance was quantified.

Heat Sources and Heat Recovery

The technical and economic performance of heat pumps and heat pipes is closely related to the characteristics of the heat source. An ideal heat source for heat pumps and heat pipes in buildings should have a high and stable temperature during the heating season, and should be abundantly available. It should not be corrosive or polluted and should have favorable thermo physical properties. Its utilization should require low investment and operational costs. In most cases, the availability of heat source is the key factor determining its use. Industrial processes are an important source of waste heat. Hot water from various cooling processes, exhaust air from ovens and furnaces, and water for cooling towers are probably the most common waste heat sources. Heat pumps can be operated for sources, having temperature up to 150 °F while heat pipes can be operated for source temperatures up to 450 °F. Table 1 shows the available heat sources and source temperature for heat recovery.

Table 1. Different Heat Sources and Their Range

Heat Source	Temperature Range
Ambient Air	-13 to 50
Exhaust Air	59 to 77
Ground Water	0 to 50
Lake Water	0 to 20
Waste Heat (Warm Water, exhaust Air Cooling Tower	> 50

There are many examples in a manufacturing facility where the heat in effluent streams is allowed to dissipate to the atmosphere. Heat recovery systems aim to transfer this heat to fluids, which require heating. This "free" heat replaces heat, which would otherwise be derived from the combustion of fuels. Heat recovery can reduce fuel cost, help conserve natural resources and reduce environmental pollution. Wide ranges of well-developed technologies are available. The main concern in implementing these techniques is their feasibility.

Heat Transfer Enhancement

Heat exchangers in heat pumps and heat pipe systems use plain or smooth heat transfer surfaces. The performance of these systems can be increased or improved if the UA^* (overall heat conductance) value is increased per unit length. This can be achieved by changing the heat transfer surface and its structure.

An enhanced heat transfer surface has a special surface geometry that provides higher overall heat transfer coefficient. The enhancement ratio (E) is the ratio of the hA value of an enhanced surface to that of a plain surface. Thus,

$$E_h = \frac{hA}{(hA)_p}$$

(1)

The heat transfer rate for a two fluid heat exchanger is given by the equation:

$$q = UA\Delta T_m$$

(2)

The performance of the heat exchanger will be enhanced if the value of UA is increased. The increase in the overall heat conductance per unit tube length can be used for one of the two objectives (Webb, 1993):

1. Size reduction: if the heat transfer rate q is held constant, the heat exchanger length may be reduced. This will provide a smaller heat exchanger.
2. Increased UA: This can be used in two ways:
    a) Reduced ΔT_m: if q and the total tube length L are held constant, ΔT_m may be reduced. This provides increased thermodynamic process efficiency and yields a saving of operating costs.
    b) Increased heat exchange: Keeping the length of the heat exchanger L constant, the increased UA/L will result in increased heat transfer rate for fixed fluid inlet temperatures.

An enhanced surface can be used to provide any of the above-discussed objectives. The improvement accomplished will depend on the designer's objective.

---

* See nomenclature at the end.

Enhancement Techniques

Bergles, (1988) has identified several enhancement techniques. These techniques can be divided into two groups as passive and active techniques. Passive techniques are employed for surface geometries for enhancement and require no direct application of power. The active techniques require external power such as electric or acoustic fields and surface vibration.

Passive Techniques

Rough Surfaces: These are integral to the base surface or may be made by placing a roughness adjacent to the surface. Integral roughness is formed by machining or restructuring the surface of a plain tube. The configuration is generally chosen to promote turbulence rather than to increase the heat transfer surface area. The application of rough surfaces is primarily in the area of single-phase flow. Various rough surfaces such as helical- ribs and corrugated tubes are shown in Figure 1.

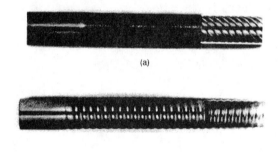

(a)

(b)

Figure 1. Illustration of Commercially used Enhanced Tubes. a) Helical-Rib Turbo- Chil Tube. b) Corrugated Korodense Tube. (Webb, 1993)

Extended Surfaces: The thermal resistance may be reduced by increasing the heat transfer coefficient h or the surface area A or both h and A. Special shape extended surfaces may also increase h. Extended surfaces such as fins provide area increase. The types of extended surfaces for liquids are internally finned tubes, externally finned tubes (integral fins) and fins for gases over the tubes. For instance, internally finned tubes such as micro fin tubes for evaporation and condensation are shown in Figure 3, externally finned tubes such as integral fins tubes for shell side evaporation and condensation, in Figure 6 and enhanced fins for gases over the tubes are shown in Figure 7. Extended surfaces use smaller fins heights for liquids than those used for gases.

Coated surfaces: They involve metallic and non-metallic coatings on the surface. Examples include a nonwetting coating such as Teflon to promote drop wise condensation. A fine scale porous coating may be used to enhance nucleate boiling.

Insert devices: Insert devices are the devices inserted into the flow channel to improve energy transport at heated surfaces. They can be used within single and two phase flow.

Active Techniques: Various surface vibration techniques are surface vibration, fluid vibration and application of electrostatic fields.

Rough Surfaces for In-Tube Side Single Phase Flows

Various types of surface roughness have been tested for single-phase liquid flow for inside tubes. Figure 2 shows various types of two dimensional rib roughness tubes. These tubes provide waterside heat transfer enhancement in the range of 70-250 percent. Webb, Narayanamurthy and Thors, (2000), studied the performance of helical rib roughness as shown in Figure 2a. They studied the effect of rib height (e), rib axial pitch (p_a), and the helix angel (α) and the number of starts (n_s) on the tube performance. The correlations presented by (Webb, Narayanamurthy and Thors, 2000), equations 3 and 4 can be used to calculate the heat transfer coefficient and friction factor for these tubes. Enhancement ratio of 2.37 can be obtained for heat transfer coefficient by using these tubes.

The heat transfer correlation is given in terms of j factor by:

$$j = St\,\mathrm{Pr}^{2/3} = 0.00933\,\mathrm{Re}^{-0.181}\,n_s^{0.285}\,(e/d_i)^{0.323}\,\alpha^{0.505} \tag{3}$$

The friction factor is given by:

$$f = 0.108\,\mathrm{Re}^{-0.283}\,n_s^{0.221}\,(e/d_i)^{0.785}\,\alpha^{0.78} \tag{4}$$

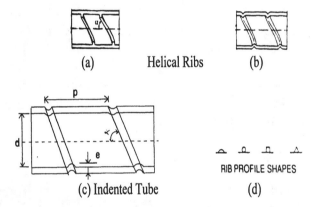

Figure 2. Illustrations of Different Methods of Making Two-Dimensional Roughness in Tubes. a) Integral Helical Rib. b) Helically Corrugated Rib. c) Spirally Indented Rib. d) Different Possible Profile Shapes of Roughness. (Ravigururajan and Bergles, 1985, 1986)

Ravigururajan and Bergles, (1985, 1986, 1995), carried out work on internally ribbed tubes as shown in Figure 2c. Ravigururajan and Bergles, (1995), determined the Prandtl number influence on the performance of spirally indented tubes. They studied the effect of rib height on the performance of the tube. The rib height to diameter ratio of 0.02 provides the best overall performance. The experiments were carried out for water with Prandtl Numbers varying from $5.8 \leq \mathrm{Pr} \leq 10.2$. The correlations for heat transfer and friction factor are given be equations 5 and 7.

The heat transfer for the enhanced tube flow is given by:

$$Nu_a / Nu_s = \{1 + [2.64\,\mathrm{Re}^{0.036}\,(e/d)^{0.212}\,(p/d)^{-0.21}\,(\alpha/90)^{0.29}\,(\mathrm{Pr}^{-0.024}]^7\}^{1/7} \tag{5}$$

where

$$Nu_s = (f/2)\text{Re}\Pr/\{1+12.7(f/2)^{0.5}(\Pr^{2/3}-1)\}$$ (6)

The friction factor is given by:

$$f_a/f_s = [1+\{29.1\text{Re}^{Y1}(e/d)^{Y2}(p/d)^{Y3}(\alpha/90)^{Y4}(1+2.95/n)\sin\beta\}^{15/16}]^{16/15}$$ (7)

where

$Y1 = 0.67 - 0.06(p/d) - 0.49(\alpha/90)$
$Y2 = 1.37 - 0.157(p/d)$
$Y3 = -1.66\,\text{Re}/10^{-6} - 0.33(\alpha/90)$
$Y4 = 4.59 + 4.11\,\text{Re}/10^{-6} - 0.15(p/d)$
$f_s = (1.58\ln\text{Re}(-3.28))^{-2}$ (8)

Extended Surfaces for In-Tubes and Over Tubes for liquids and Gases

Internally Finned Tubes for Refrigerant Evaporation and Condensation

The recent studies that are representative of the work in this area include: Khanpara, Bergles and Pate, (1986), Schlager, Pate and Bergles, (1989, 1990), and Chamra, Webb and Randlett, (1996). Most of this work measured the effects of the fin geometry, fin dimensions, and fluid properties on the condensation and evaporation characteristics, and developed empirical equations for heat transfer and pressure drop. The micro-fin tubes provided enhancement of heat transfer from 100% or more for both evaporation and condensation when compared to smooth equivalent tubes. Figure 3b shows the micro fin tubes geometry.

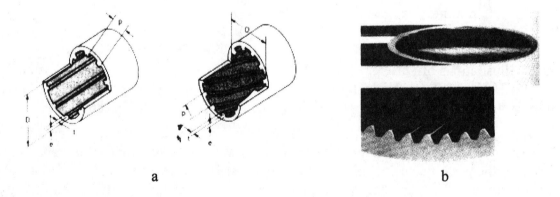

a   b

Figure 3. a) Axial and Helical Internal Fins. b) Micro-Fin Tube. (Webb, 1993.)

Chamra, Webb and Randlett, (1996), developed new internal geometries of micro-fin tubes (single helix and cross-grooved tubes) having higher evaporation and condensation coefficients than the existing single-groove micro-fin designs. The cross-grooved geometries were formed by applying a second set of grooves at the same helix angle, but opposite angular direction as the first set.

The single helix and cross-grooved tubes tested by Chamra and Webb in 1996 showed higher heat transfer coefficient compared to the existing single helix tubes. The heat transfer and pressure drop increases as the helix angle increases.

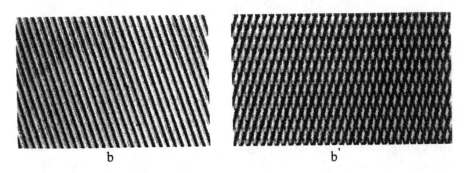

Figure 4. Advanced Micro Fin Tubes (Plain View), a) Single Helix, b) Cross Grooved. (Chamra, Webb and Randlett, 1996)

Externally Finned Tubes for Liquids

Various enhanced surfaces have been developed for boiling and condensation of refrigerants and water on the horizontal tubes.

Ayub and Bergles, (1985), performed pool boiling heat transfer test on Gewa-K and Gewa-T tubes. Figure 5 shows the Gewa surface profiles. The gap width for the Gewa-T tubes ranged from 0.15-mm to 0.55-mm. The tests were performed with R-113 and water. The enhanced surfaces tested by them showed higher performance than the smooth tubes.

Figure 5. Gewa-K and Gewa-T Tubes for Enhanced Boiling. (Webb, 1993)

For Gewa-T surfaces, the best enhancement for water was obtained with a gap width of 0.35 mm and the best enhancement for R-113 was obtained with a gap width of 0.25 mm.

Figure 6 shows the integral fin tube for refrigerant condensation over the horizontal tube. Webb et al., (1985) performed condensation tests on horizontal integral tube for refrigerants. They showed that the heat transfer coefficient increases with increasing fins per unit length.

183

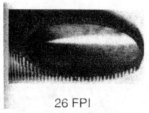

26 FPI

Figure 6. Horizontal Integral Tube. (Webb, 1993)

Externally Finned Tubes for Gases

Fin tube heat exchangers have been used for heat exchange between gases and liquids. Use of enhanced fin geometries will provide higher heat transfer coefficients than the plain surfaces. Figure 7 shows the various types of enhanced fin geometries for tubes. The offset strip fin is shown in Figure 7b has been applied to finned-tube heat exchangers with plain fins. Nakayama and Xu, (1983), studied offset strip fins and compared the heat transfer coefficients with the plain fins. The offset strip fin provides a heat transfer coefficient, which is 150% higher than that of the plain fin at the same flow rate. Generalized correlations for heat transfer have not been developed for the offset strip fin around tubes. However Nakayama and Xu, proposed in 1983 empirical correlations to define the enhancement level.

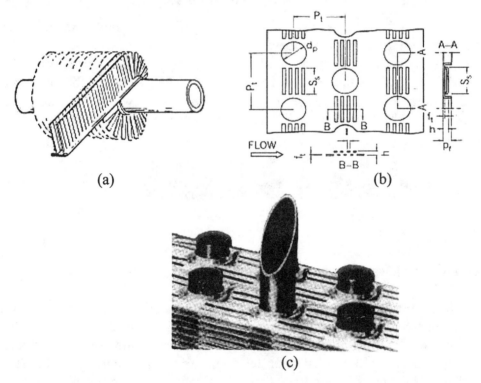

(a)

(b)

(c)

Figure 7. Enhanced Fin Geometries, a) Spine Fin. b) Offset Strip Fin. c) Convex Louver Fin. (Webb, 1993.)

Optimization of Heat Exchangers

For quantifying the effect of energy efficient strategies on the performance of heat exchangers of heat pumps and heat pipes, specific heat transfer enhancement techniques discussed in this paper were applied to the commercially available models of heat pumps and heat pipes.

Heat Pump Heat Exchangers

Two models of heat pump heat exchangers were considered. Model 1 is a coaxial water to refrigerant evaporator where water flows through inside tube and refrigerant evaporates on the outside tube. Model 2 is a coaxial water to refrigerant condenser where water flows through the inside tube while refrigerant condenses on the outside tube. The inside tubes for both the models are made of copper. Internally helically-rib roughness, which gives an enhancement factor of 2.37, was applied to Model 1 and spirally indented tube roughness, which gives an enhancement factor of 1.47, was applied to Model 2 in order to enhance heat transfer coefficients. Figure 8 shows an application of heat pump heat exchanger for heat recovery.

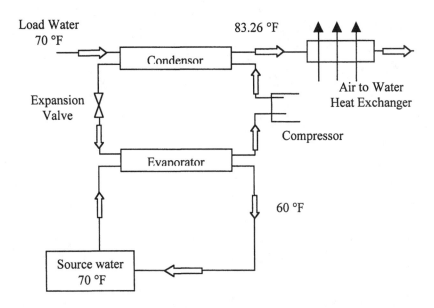

Figure 8. Application of Heat Pump Heat Exchanger For Heat Recovery.

Heat Pipe Heat Exchangers

Two models of air-to-air heat pipe heat exchangers were considered. Model 1 is used in heating mode while Model 2 is used in cooling mode. Offset strip fins are used for the airside (over the tube) heat transfer coefficient enhancement. The offset fin tube will give an enhancement factor of 1.50.

Results and Conclusions

Table 2 shows the increase in capacity and cost savings after application of enhanced surfaces for the considered models of heat exchangers. As seen in this table, heat recovery in heat pump heat exchangers with enhanced heat transfer techniques can improve the capacity by 41 % for the evaporator and by 30 % for the condenser. This will result in annual fuel cost saving of $ 1,554 for the model analyzed. Similar quantifications for the heat pipe heat exchangers result in an annual savings of $ 1,093. The implementation cost for replacing plain tubes with the rough surface tubes in the heat exchangers is going to be not more than $200.

Thus these modifications result in very short pay back periods and energy savings over the entire life of these devices.

Acknowledgements

The financial support from the U.S. Department of Energy (DOE) to carry out this work is gratefully acknowledged.

Table 2. Summary of Results

Heat Exchangers	Capacity Without Enhancement (Btu/h)	Heat Recovery Without Enhancement (MMBtu/yr)	Cost Savings Without Enhancement ($/yr)	Capacity After Enhancement (Btu/h)	Heat Recovery After Enhancement (MMBtu/yr)	Cost Savings After Enhancement ($/yr)	% Increase In Capacity
Heat Pumps							
Model 1, evaporator	25,100.00	137.00	471	35,411	193.34	665	41.00
Model 2, condenser	36,300.00	198.20	682	47,332.65	258.40	889	30.40
Heat Pipes							
Model 1	13,136.58	75.03	277	19,697.16	112.50	415	49.94
Model 2	5,667.49	17.13	452	8,499.54	25.70	678	49.96

187

Nomenclature

A   Heat transfer surface area, m^2 or ft^2

d Envelop (maximum inside) diameter, m or ft

d_i Internal tube diameter, m or ft

e Rib height (average value), m or ft

E_h Enhancement ratio

f Fanning friction factor, dimensionless

h Heat transfer coefficient, W/m^2-°C or Btu/h-ft^2-°F

j Colburn j factor ($= St\,Pr^{2/3}$), dimensionless

L   Length of flow path in heat exchanger, m or ft

m   mass flow rate, kg/s or lbm/s

n_s Number of starts, dimensionless

Nu   Nusselt number, dimensionless

p Pitch of the roughness

Pr   Prandtl number, dimensionless

q Heat transfer rate, Watts or Btu/h

Re   Tube-side Reynolds number, dimensionless

St   Stanton number, dimensionless

Δt_m Log mean temperature difference, °C or °F

U Overall heat transfer coefficient, W/m^2-°C or Btu/h-ft^2-°F

Greek Letters

α Helix angle, degree

β Included angle between sides of ribs

Subscripts

a   Augmented Tube

e   Enhanced surface

p   Plain surface

References

Ayub, Z. H., and Bergles, A. E., 1985, "Pool Boiling from GEWA Surfaces in Water and R-113," Augmentation of Heat Transfer in Energy Systems, HTD-Vol. 52, pp. 57-66.

Bergles, A. E., 1988, "Some Perspective on Enhanced Heat Transfer-Second Generation Heat Transfer Technology," Journal of Heat Transfer, Vol. 110, pp. 1082-1096.

Chamra, L. M., Webb, R. L and Randlett, M. R., 1996, "Advanced Micro-Fin Tubes for Condensation," International Journal of Heat and Mass Transfer, Vol.39, pp. 1839-46.

Chamra, L. M., Webb, R. L and Randlett, M. R., 1996, "Advance Micro-Fin Tubes for Evaporation," International Journal of Heat and Mass Transfer, Vol.39, pp.1827-38.

Khanpara, J. C., Bergles, A. E., and Pate, M. B., 1986, "Augmentation of R-113 in Tube Evaporation with Micro-Fin Tubes," ASHRAE Transactions, Vol.92, Part2B, pp. 506-524.

Nakayama W., and Xu, L. P., "Enhanced Fins for Air Cooled Heat-Exchangers –Heat Transfer and Friction Correlations," Proceedings of the 1983 ASME-JSME Thermal Engineering Conference, Vol. 1, pp. 495-502.

Schlager, L. M., Pate, M. B and Bergles, A. E., 1989, " Heat Transfer and Pressure Drop During Evaporation and Condensation of R-22 in Horizontal Micro-Fin Tubes," International Journal of Refrigeration, Vol. 12, pp. 6-14.

Schlager, L. M., Pate, M. B and Bergles, A. E., 1990, " Evaporation and Condensation Heat Transfer and Pressure Drop in Horizontal, 12.7 Tom Micro-Fin Tubes with Refrigerant 22," Journal of Heat Transfer, Vol. 122, pp.1041.

Ravigururajan, T. S., and Bergles, A. E., 1985, "General Correlations for Pressure Drop and Heat Transfer for Single Phase Turbulent Flow in Internally Ribbed Tubes," Augmentation of Heat Transfer in Energy Systems, ASME HTD, Vol. 52, pp. 9-20.

Ravigururajan, T. S., and Bergles, A. E., 1986, "An Experimental Verification of General Correlations for Single-Phase Turbulent Flow in Ribbed Tubes," Advances in Heat Exchanger Design, ASME HTD-Vol. 66, and pp. 1-11.

Ravigururajan, T. S., and Bergles, A. E., 1995, "Prandtl Number Influence on Heat Transfer Enhancement in Turbulent Flow of Water at Low Temperature," Journal of Heat Transfer, Vol. 117, pp. 276-282.

Webb, R. L., Rudy, T. M., and Kedzierski, M. A., 1985, "Prediction of Condensation Coefficient on Horizontal Integral-Fin Tubes," Journal of Heat Transfer, Vol. 107, pp. 369-376.

Webb, R. L., 1993, Principles of Enhanced Heat Transfer," John Wiley & Sons, Inc.

Webb, R. L., Narayanamurthy, R., and Thors, P., 2000, "Heat Transfer and Friction Characteristics of Internal Helical-Rib Roughness," Journal of Heat Transfer, Vo.122, No1 pp.134-42

Chapter 30

DELIVERING ENERGY EFFICIENCY SERVICES TO WISCONSIN'S INDUSTRIES: ACTIONS, EXPERIENCES AND RESULTS FROM THE FOCUS ON ENERGY PROGRAM

Thomas M. Giffin, P.E., Industrial Sector Manager
Science Applications International Corporation

Jolene Anderson-Sheil, Contract Manager Business Programs
Wisconsin Department of Administration

Preston Schutt, Program Manager
Wisconsin Department of Administration

Terry Pease, Program Manager
Wisconsin Department of Administration

John Nicol, P.E., Program Manager
Science Applications International Corporation

ABSTRACT

Under its electric utility restructuring, Wisconsin established a series of energy efficiency programs with major components devoted to serving Wisconsin's industries. This paper presents experiences and lessons from working with Wisconsin industry and their suppliers in an action-oriented approach to implement energy-efficient projects and practices.

In 1999, Wisconsin began a pilot program called Focus on Energy for the development, testing, and delivery of energy efficiency market transformation programs. In 2001, a statewide Focus on Energy program was initiated to enhance and expand the scope, territory and variety of programs offered and markets served. While the pilot work focused on testing energy efficiency services with industry, in contrast, the statewide industrial programs have been action-oriented, focusing on getting energy-efficient projects and practices in-place with industry and their suppliers.

These industrial programs experienced many diverging and interesting results from early successes, to missed opportunities, to surprise interests. The lessons of these experiences have been now incorporated into the many program services and offerings including in-plant technical support, targeted financial incentives, specialized marketing, and advanced technology support to better service Wisconsin's industries.

Over 400 industrial companies and municipal water/wastewater facilities have taken advantage of these energy efficiency services, saving over $9,000,000 in energy costs.

These partners and allies have used the program to support such actions as project development, in-plant assessments, facility energy management planning, staff training, specialty process enhancements and advanced technology assessment and demonstration, all to act upon energy efficiency opportunities to improve plant operation costs.

The challenges and experiences in the Wisconsin industrial programs serve as a valuable guide to the design, development and implementation of energy efficiency in industrial organizations, facilities and processes. Case examples from planning through delivery of projects, from starting and continuing activities, are presented to illustrate how energy efficiency implementation can be advanced and achieved.

INTRODUCTION

Under its electric utility restructuring, Wisconsin established a series of energy efficiency programs with major components devoted to serving Wisconsin's industries. This paper presents experiences and lessons from working with Wisconsin industry and their suppliers in an action-oriented approach to implement energy-efficient projects and practices.

Background

In 1999, Wisconsin began a pilot program called Focus on Energy for the development, testing, and delivery of energy efficiency market transformation programs. In 2001, a statewide Focus on Energy program was initiated to enhance and expand the scope, territory and variety of programs offered and markets served. While the pilot work focused on testing energy efficiency services with industry, in contrast, the statewide industrial Business Programs have been action-oriented, focusing on getting energy-efficient projects and practices in-place with industry and their suppliers

The industrial sector of the Wisconsin Business Program is budged to deliver over $18 million of energy-efficient services, support and incentives over a 3-year period. Three industrial programs are offered: 1) General Industrial services, 2) Water and Wastewater facilities, and 3) Industries of the Future. The primary missions of the programs are to deliver near-term resource acquisition, while encouraging market transformation for energy efficiency. In particular, the program services include on-site opportunity identification, actions planning, project facilitation, support to program allies, and financial mechanisms to provide for early identification and implementation of energy efficiency improvements, which is one if the primary goals in Wisconsin's programs.

In the first year, the industrial sector programs mobilized over 50 people across 6 organizations to deliver over $7 million of services and support back to Wisconsin ratepayers. The General Industrial and Water and Wastewater programs were focused on developing near-term resource acquisition, while Industries of the Future program focused on addressing long-term advancements with the intent of bringing market transformation to key industries. The programs delivered energy efficiency to the market through a host of methods including on-site technical assistance, financial incentives, specialized training including Building Operator Certification, Best Practices and Compressed Air Challenge, special strategic partnerships with providers of energy-efficient products and services, and coordination with affiliated programs that also serve the market

Key Program Missions
The Business Programs of Focus on Energy in the industrial sector aim to help participants adopt the energy management process whereby the industrial end-user adopts an Action Plan leading to the implementation of energy efficiency improvements. Based on overcoming market barriers, the Wisconsin Focus on Energy approach expands upon this through developing relationships between the industrial Partners, Trade Allies, and other support programs. The programs are designed to provide participants with technical assistance for improving those internal processes that will enable them to implement energy efficiency projects as an ongoing activity. The programs were also designed to foster relationships between Trade Allies and participants to build a market infrastructure that is able to carry energy efficiency projects forward and result in the marketing of new projects. Further enhancements also include marketing, and education and training support. It is noted that the participation in the program is voluntary; the program design is based on the theme that energy efficiency is a profitable business practice.

DESCRIPTION OF INDUSTRIAL PROGRAMS AND STRATEGIES
Three programs are offered to the industrial market.

1. The General Industrial Program serves all types and sizes of industries across Wisconsin with technical, financial and educational assistance to advance energy efficiency practices and projects.
2. The Water and Wastewater Program serves water utilities and municipal and industrial wastewater treatment facilities. This program delivers similar services as the General Industrial Program, but with a focus on this specific market sector.
3. The Industries of The Future Program serves 8 specific industrial sectors with services and financial support to advance innovative technologies and practices. The Program has a long-term perspective to affect change in industrial practices and the related market.

Each of these programs employs strategies that are targeted to overcoming market barriers; specific program activities, offerings and components are designed to influence specific market barriers. The following provides a more detailed description of each of the Focus on Energy Business Programs for the industrial sector.

GENERAL INDUSTRIAL PROGRAM
Program Description
The key goal of the general industrial program is to promote the adoption of energy efficiency measures and practices by end-users, by changing energy using behaviors both short-term and long-term. In the short-term, the program seeks to achieve specific energy savings, environmental improvement, and economic development goals as a direct result of the energy savings projects implemented. Over the long-term, the program hopes to cultivate an energy saving ethic in industrial end-users, leading them to institute energy saving practices and procedures in their facilities. The program also seeks to transform the equipment stocking and sales practices of equipment suppliers and distributors, leading them to actively promote energy-efficient measures to their customers. This program has a broad orientation and is offered to all industries throughout Wisconsin.

To further educate and transform end-users, the General Industrial program offers a wide array of tools and services.

The program offers a wide array of educational courses, industrial sector "Best (energy use) Practices" technical information, and end-user services (including energy audits and analyses) in order to address end-users' extensive and varied technical information needs. Importantly, to meet their financial requirements and improve the economics of proposed energy efficiency projects, the program provides many different types of financial assistance. For larger industries, the program also works with senior managers of corporations in Year 2, educating them on how their current energy management practices compare with those of their peers in the industry and providing them with specific strategies they can implement to improve.

The program also works with organizations on the supply-side, seeking to change their attitudes towards stocking and selling energy-efficient equipment. In large part, this is accomplished by increasing demand for energy efficiency measures (through interventions offered on the demand-side). However, the program also works directly with trade allies to develop specific action plans geared toward their organizations that will shift their focus toward promotion of energy-efficient measures.

The program delivers services and support to the industrial sector by the following:

Provide Planning Assistance: Develop Action Plans for end-users and Strategic Business Action Plans for trade ally partners to increase their adoption of energy-efficiency practices and sale and promotion of energy-efficient products or services, respectively.

- Foster partnerships and collaborations
- Establish partnerships with trade ally partners and key allied program organizations that can assist with program delivery.
- Provide technical assistance
- Provide technical support to industrial partners, including energy efficiency opportunity identification, technical and financial analysis of recommended measures, and development of energy management Action Plans to facilitate with implementation of recommended measures.
- Provide education and training to partners, trade allies, and key organizations.
- Educate end-users and trade allies regarding energy-efficiency Best Practices.

Provide Financial Support: Provide various types of financial incentives to assist with reduction of project costs and reduction of project paybacks to levels competitive with other investment opportunities available to partners. Provide a source of project financing for those partners that need it.

Achieve Savings Goals: Implement energy efficiency improvements that achieve the specified energy savings and market effects goals.

Key Barriers and Strategies for Overcoming Them
The General Industrial program has strategies that are targeted to specific markets and their barriers as follows:

Small Industrial: One of the key barriers in this sector is a lack of infrastructure to reach and impact the efficiency of this market; providers of products and services are not highly proactive in promoting energy efficiency. The strategy is to increase the ability of the program allies to deliver information and products to this market. Part of this strategy includes increasing the demand for efficiency by providing a self assessment tool to the end-users. Prescribed incentives for appropriate technologies can make it easy for the end-user and the allies to understand the grants available. Allied organizations such as the technical colleges, libraries also play a key role to reach this market for the program.

Medium Industrial: The key barriers for this market segment where the program can have the greatest impact are: the lack of knowledge about opportunities and, the lack of performance knowledge about their level of efficiency. The strategy to overcome both the knowledge of opportunities and to show a basic level of efficiency performance uses the Best Practices CD. This technical resource provides a framework to guide the user on implementing Best Practices for as series of common energy systems (compressed air, refrigeration, etc.) found in industries. For each system there are up to 10 standard steps to insure the system is as efficient as economically possible or the "Best Practices".

Large Industrial: The key barrier for this segment is the commitment of the upper management to more effectively manage their energy use. One of the key factors preventing "buy-in" to this practice is the lack of knowledge on the relative performance of their facilities. The first need to develop the commitment from upper management is to get their attention; there are many different approaches including using high level executives in the utilities, marketing group or branches of government. The program delivers a management approach that keys in on organizational interaction, accountability and continuous improvement to will fit with many of their quality improvement and cost reduction strategies. Using leaders in the industrial community, demonstration of the cost effectiveness of investing in energy management strategies can be promoted.

Program Allies: One of the greatest barriers for program allies to promote energy efficiency is the use of first cost as the primary determinant in a customer's purchase decision.

The program provides support through fact sheets and training to assist the allies to overcome this resistance and provide a niche of selling long-term, life-cycle costs. Part of the effort is to connect with program allies to gain knowledge on what new projects are being considered by companies to help them influence on-going facility expansions or improvements.

Allied Organizations and Utilities: A big barrier for connecting and using allied organizations is their competing priorities. They are usually very limited in time to give to any issue beyond their direct mission. The program coordinates with them to add enough value for their constituents.

WATER AND WASTEWATER PROGRAM
Program Description
The Water and Wastewater program is designed to promote adoption of energy efficiency measure and practices by Wisconsin's water and wastewater facilities. This program offers many of the same types of interventions as the General Industrial program; however, they are tailored specifically to meet the unique needs of water/wastewater industrial and municipal facilities. This sector is unique in other ways, many of which should enhance the success of this program.

Municipal water/wastewater districts are semi-autonomous from other parts of government operations, which facilitates the energy efficiency decision-making process in general.

The sector itself is highly networked making it relatively easy to "spread the word" about successful, cost-effective, energy efficiency measures.

Many recommended energy savings measures are highly replicable across the entire sector, which streamlines the measure identification and analysis process for the sector as a whole.

The program promotes energy efficiency for several sub-markets within the water and wastewater sector (see Figure 1).

To further educate and transform end-users, the Water/Wastewater program offers a wide array of tools and services. The program provides in-plant and formal training opportunities, sector-specific "Best (energy use) Practices" technical information, and end-user services (including energy audits and analyses) in order to address end-users' extensive and varied technical information needs. Importantly, the program provides many different types of financial assistance to meet their financial requirements and improve the economics of proposed energy efficiency projects.

> The Water/Wastewater Program Serves:
>
> - Municipal water treatment facilities,
> - Surface water facilities,
> - Well water facilities,
> - Municipal wastewater treatment facilities,
> - Industrial wastewater treatment operations, and
> - Water and wastewater design contractors, product suppliers, and service companies.

FIGURE 1. WATER/WASTEWATER SUBMARKETS

Key Barriers and Strategies for Overcoming Them
The Water and Wastewater program addresses the following barriers and strategies to program implementation and market transformation.

For the Water and Wastewater Facilities:
Barrier: Lack of initial labor resources to identify and prioritize energy efficiency opportunities. **Strategy:** Establish a "partnership" with key management and operators. Provide on-site assistance identifying energy efficiency opportunities and addressing barriers to their implementation. Provide facilitation to advance energy efficiency projects towards implementation in consort with the partner through the Action Plan process.

Barrier: Energy costs are not a priority, and/or they are the responsibility of others. Energy efficiency is seen as a one-time action where prior audits, retrofits, or actions are perceived as completing projects rather than as an on-going practice. **Strategy:** Encourage adoption of energy efficiency practices as part of the regular business in the organization. Gain top management buy-in to energy efficiency practices by establishing a partnership agreement and Action Plan. Advance knowledge of energy efficiency technical options and energy management practices via in-plant and formal training.

Barrier: Lack of, or competition for, capital. **Strategy:** Encourage energy efficiency project advancement and implementation through financial assistance. Offer custom and expanded financial incentives, such as project implementation grants, feasibility assessment grants, leasing options, etc.

Barrier: *Small-to-Medium facilities:* Market is difficult to reach cost-effectively for other energy efficiency market actors. **Strategy:** Use existing industry associations to deliver energy efficiency knowledge through their existing support services. Establish a systematic and standardized approach to get information and tools to this dispersed market.

Barrier: *Small-to-Medium facilities:* Limited knowledge of energy efficiency options and energy efficiency Best Practices. **Strategy:** Use simple self-help tools, education, and training to enable the small facilities to independently assess their energy opportunities and to advance energy efficiency project implementation and practices.

Barrier: Emergency repair responses dominate many equipment purchase decisions. **Strategy:** Encourage water/wastewater facility end-users to request suppliers to offer and stock typical energy-efficient equipment.

For Trade Allies:

Barrier: Lack of sales processes to educate the water/wastewater market regarding the benefits of energy efficiency. **Strategy:** Provide energy efficiency sales support specifically for program allies with key technologies for the water/wastewater markets, e.g., fine-bubble aeration, biogas, adjustable speed drives, etc. Provide allies with a Strategic Business Action Plan to increase long-term sales and identify ways to provide program services

Barrier: Competition with other investments (low first-cost bid mentality). **Strategy:** Provide program ally with training, tools, and support to explain the benefits of lifecycle analysis to overcome first cost barriers.

Barrier: Lack of program ally promotion of technologies specifically beneficial to water/wastewater facilities. **Strategy:** Provide key technology financial incentives to encourage allies to promote energy efficiency technologies. Identify opportunities for program ally technology applications via partnership agreement and Strategic Business Action Plan.

For Related Organizations and Allied Programs:

Barrier: Lack of knowledge regarding how energy efficiency affects non-partners (i.e., those with no specific connection to the Focus on Energy program). **Strategy:** Develop and implement an energy efficiency training curriculum for the Water/Wastewater Operators training certification program. Develop design guidelines and implement an energy efficiency review service for water/wastewater facilities in cooperation with the DNR. Implement energy efficiency training activities in conjunction with established allied program events.

INDUSTRIES OF THE FUTURE PROGRAM
Program Description

The Industries of the Future (IOF) program seeks to further the goal of energy efficiency adoption in the most energy-intensive industry categories through a strategy that involves commercialization of new industry-specific technologies that solve energy-related needs and other challenges facing these industries in the future. The IOF

program uses a multi-faceted strategy to identify and develop these new technologies as described in Figure 2.

> The Industries of the Future Program targets the following industries:
>
> - Forest Products
> - Metal Casting
> - Food Processing
> - Biotechnology
> - Printing
> - Chemicals
> - Glass.
> - Water and Wastewater

FIGURE 2. INDUSTRIES OF THE FUTURE TECHNOLOGIES

The IOF Program takes a long-term perspective in facilitating the adoption of new technologies and practices in Wisconsin industry. In this respect, its goals and approaches are primarily oriented on market transformation effects. Figure 3 illustrates the development sequence. Here, a technology or concept is to be developed over the longer-term period ranging from 1 to 10 years. The IOF Program's role is to then advance promising technologies toward industry acceptances through demonstration by supporting first applications. Over time, the new technology is adopted as a Best Practices; this is similar to the service that The General Industrial Program is intended to delivers. Then after widespread adoption, the technology becomes standard practice affecting change in the market.

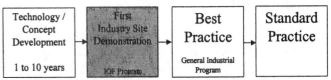

FIGURE 3. SEQUENCE OF NEW TECHNOLOGY ADOPTION TO INDUSTRIAL MARKET

The IOF program has several activities. First, a series of Industry roundtables are held with key stakeholders in each industry. Stakeholders include end-users, equipment suppliers, and technology developers. The purposes of these roundtables are to:

- Identify and discuss key issues and challenges facing the industry during the next several years;
- Identify and describe industry needs in detail with respect to the following areas: manufacturing process; materials technology; environmental, regulatory and technical; energy reliability; and products and market needs. As part of this process, identify new technologies that can be developed to address these needs;

- Specify a set of actions that can be taken to address these needs;
- Form action teams to address priority needs;
- Develop an industry roadmap from the above. This roadmap is a written report that documents the roundtable discussions and thus contains detailed information on industry-specific issues, needs, new technologies, and action teams/plans. The roadmap also includes a resource directory containing information on funding sources, possible sponsor organizations for new technology RD&D;
- Generate leads for new technology demonstration (pilot) projects with information gleaned from the roundtable/ road mapping process. The pilot projects are designed to directly address the needs identified within the industry roadmaps. These projects involve demonstration of new energy-efficient technologies that are highly replicable to the sector as a whole. The program seeks to develop a small number of pilot projects each year.

Expanding upon the Roundtable consensus buildings, the Program also uses process experts for industrial site visits to identify needs and convey information on new technologies; if promising projects are identified; they are referred to the action teams for subsequent follow-up. In addition, the IOF Program provides progress grants to support demonstrations to overcome the risk of an industry adopting a new technology.

Key Barriers and Strategies for Overcoming Them
The Industries of the Future program addresses the following barriers with strategies for program implementation and market transformation. The primary focus is on achieving long-term improvement in key industries in Wisconsin.

Barrier: Inadequate communication between industry and technology developers regarding industry needs and potential technology solutions. **Strategy:** Increase the quantity and quality of communication regarding new technologies between industry and technology developers through events, project action teams, and information products.

Barrier: Real and perceived risks of adopting new technologies that could fail to work as anticipated. **Strategy:** Identify and overcome specific concerns raised by industry through technology evaluation services. Ease the technology adoption process for industry through facilitation by third-party enablers.

Barrier: Competition with other capital investments. **Strategy:** Assist management decision-making by supporting economic evaluation studies that quantify all benefits of adopting new technologies and the risks of not adopting new technologies.

Barrier: Numerous and complex issues to address when adopting a new technology. **Strategy:** Ease the technology adoption process for industry through facilitation by third-party enablers.

Barrier: Inadequate support and funding throughout the technology development process. **Strategy:** Target support to new technologies with high market potential using an industry-needs driven selection process.

Barrier: Difficulty of obtaining production trials to refine new technologies for industrial use. **Strategy:** Overcome industry resistance to production trials by providing third-party facilitation, technology evaluation, and funding to support production trials.

Barrier: No single technology transfer enabler provides all of the competencies required for successful technology commercialization (soliciting funding, patents, licensing, marketing, sales, business creation and administration, joint ventures, etc.). **Strategy:** Provide key competencies for commercialization through facilitation by third-party enablers.

Barrier: Limited resources (staff time and money) to support new technology development. **Strategy:** Focus resources on new technologies with high potential using an industry-needs-driven process for prioritizing and selecting opportunities to pursue.

Barrier: Difficulty of assessing the technical and market viability of proposed new technologies. **Strategy:** Assist technology transfer enablers assess new technologies by providing technical and financial support for technology evaluation.

LESSONS AND EXPERIENCES
Experiences and lessons from working with Wisconsin industry and their suppliers in an action-oriented approach to implement energy-efficient projects and practices provide insight to the decision-making and approaches that affect energy efficiency adoption.

Serving the Needs of Trade/Program Allies.
Providers of products and services are part of the program market transformation and resource acquisition delivery mechanisms in the Wisconsin Focus on Energy programs. One of the original program strategies was to involve Trade Allies in promoting the program. A cross program function was established to gather and organize information of providers of energy-related products and services for the whole of the Business Programs. This function registered and made available listing of firms who were Program Allies with the intent that this could be used as a resource for end-users to find providers.

However, in the early stages of the industrial programs it became apparent that there were a few major providers who were key industrial market players for whom the basic program ally program services were not of interest. One of the over-arching impediments to the development of an active Trade Ally involvement was whether the Trade Allies could use the Program to support their development and sales needs, or whether the Program would bring Partners to them as potential customers. It was found that while many Trade Allies could see the benefits of the Focus on Energy Program to support their products and services, they were far too busy to undertake any special sales or development to promote the Program. Also, at the early stages of the Focus on Energy Program, Trade Allies were a bit hesitant to fully subscribe without knowing if there would be any return through increase business opportunities with participating industries.

Working with the program representatives and the Program Allies, the industrial programs developed enhanced approaches to this part of the market. The Action Plan approach that was successfully being used with the end-use customers was adapted to the Program Allies; a Strategic Business Action Plan is now used to develop specific strategies for the Program Ally's participation and coordination in the industrial programs. Here, essentially a series of specific activities are agreed upon where the Program and the Trade ally can work together. The Business Action Plan specifies tasks, steps, responsibilities and schedules so that the Trade Ally is provided a specific set of progressive actions. Oftentimes, the Business Action Plan is oriented to tasks that support the ultimate sale and delivery of an energy-efficient product for service by the Program Ally. This approach has proved to be highly successful in creating specific opportunities for the program and its allies to deliver energy efficiency products and related services to the end-market customer.

As and example of how this approach has been used, the Focus on Energy program began assisting with a major industrial compressed air supply and service company. As part of the Strategic Business Action Plan, detailed tasks were defined and implemented to approach selected industrial customers about energy-efficient approaches with the Focus program representative working in consort with the Program Ally. The value that the Focus on Energy brought to the transaction was to provide an independent assessment of the validity of the energy savings opportunities. At the same time, Focus on Energy was undertaking training for compressed air system fundamentals; however, the initial sign-up activity was slow to develop. To increase the sign-up for attendance, discounted fees were put in place, and offered to industrial customers through the Program Ally's relationships. This situation created opportunity for both Focus and the Program Ally where by more indusial staff attended the training, and at the same time the Program Ally received recognition for bringing the training opportunity to the industrial company.

Action-Oriented Education and Training
The Industrial Program coordinated several technical and informational training programs including:

- Making Sense of Energy and Environmental Programs
- Compressed Air Fundamentals
- Advanced Compressed Air
- Steam Challenge

Free tuition to many training sessions was offered as an incentive to join the Program for new Partners and as a reward for existing Partners.

At the mid-point of the first year, however, feedback on the early education and training events while positive, did not appear to be causing any noticeable change in the participants' energy efficiency practices. Furthermore, resource acquisition missions in the programs were becoming amplified in response to the client and market requests. To response to these customer considerations, the indusial programs under took a re-evaluation and a re-direction in the approach and techniques for educational and training programs in early 2002.

The education and training programs were modified to include more of an action-oriented approach. Elements were added to the instructional approach to include the development of in-class actions plans for each participant. The programs, implemented through the Energy Center of Wisconsin, have added adult learning techniques, "hands-on" training with take-home, action-oriented tools. For example, a building operator attending compressed air training would take-home an Action Plan of things to do in his facility to improve compressed air systems. As a result the trainees get to apply what they learned.

Additionally, more technical sessions (as opposed to general information programs) are planned for future education programs to respond to the desire of participants to expand specific energy-related skills. Also, as noted above, these can be integrated with the coordination activities for Program Allies who have products and service related to the technical training.

This approach has changed how the programs are reaching some of the industrial market. Often now, new participants are coming to the programs for further support as an outcome of the education and training programs. Also, these participants appear to be more advanced or at least interested in energy efficiency from the beginning of their program involvement.

Coordination Across Industrial Programs

Because the industrial programs had the possibility of reaching some of the same customers, efforts were required to be coordinated across the programs. For example, the General Industry program could approach industries that were part of the Industries of the Future key industrial sectors, or wastewater facilities could be in industrial plants requiring interface coordination with the Water and Wastewater Programs.

Therefore, coordination between the three industrial programs was needed so that the services and approaches of the programs were an integrated approach to the market. In simple terms, the customer should "see" the Focus on Energy programs as a single entity, and gain access to all available programs through a single contract.

The services and approaches for the programs were designed to inter-related and coordinated, but additional enhancements were made to streamline these processes. Also, Program representatives were cross-trained to provide access to the services of both programs. The improved program process gave the customer a single point of program contact to both programs and established a consistent message.

Responding to Extensive Demand for Program Services

After the initial start-up months, the Water and Wastewater program began to have a tremendous amount of requests for services, however, the program resources were at the same time beginning to become committed. To respond to this potentially overwhelming program demand, a "Fast Track" project application and approval process was designed and put in place. This allowed customers to, in effect, self-initiate their program participation with only limited assistance, typically over the phone, from the program representatives. After a simple automatic FAX announcement (see Figure 4) of this program option, over 50 customers inquires were received through the Fast Track process.

This Fast Track approach also captured energy efficiency projects that would otherwise not have been supported by Focus on Energy. For example, a small rural water utility called Focus on Energy on a Friday afternoon, after receiving the Fast Track announcement the previous day. They had just had a well pump motor burn out and were about to rewind the motor to repair it. They wondered if the Focus on Energy program would be able to help support the purchase of a new premium efficiency motor, rather than repairing the old motor. They needed to make a decision by Monday morning because the town water supply was operating without this pump being available. Working with the town's motor supplier, Focus performed a quick assessment of savings and was able to offer a partial incentive for the premium efficiency motor. Armed with the energy savings and the partial financial incentive, on Monday morning the water plant operators were able to convince the town manager to commit the extra monies needed for the premium efficiency motor.

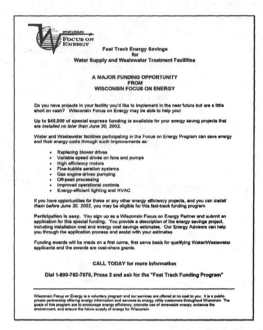

FIGURE 4. FAX ANNOUNCEMENT

Throughout its operation, also, recruiting for the Water and Wastewater Program has only been through word of mouth; no significant recruiting or marketing campaigns have been needed to exceed participating goals. One good example how the work is spreading in this close-knit community is that Program has served every wastewater plant in Door County, Wisconsin. This occurred because the first participant proceeded to tell others in his county about the program, and his success with it, and advised them to also become partners in the program.

Unexpected Opportunities

In some cases there were unexpected results. For example, under the General Industrial Program, a large paper manufacturer was approached for participation in the program. However, the company was in the process of being sold, and as such, the management, while fully understanding the benefits, was unwilling to participate in the Focus on energy program. After several meetings with the plant manager and engineering manager, no progress was made.

After many months of inactivity and little communication, the General Industrial Program received a phone call requesting that the Program Representative come to the site to work with an assessment team. It turned out that the new owner had initiated a "top-to-bottom" review of the plant processes, and when asked how energy would be considered in this review, the plant and engineering managers noted that they would use the Focus on Energy program support.

As a result, the Focus representative became part of the engineering team in the plant review. While working with the company team, the representative put in place methods for assessment of energy, and he provided energy assessment training to others on the team. The end result was to embed energy efficiency considerations into the detailed assessments that were being done by the company under its new ownership.

SUMMARY AND CONCLUSION

Over 400 industrial companies and municipal water/wastewater facilities have participated in these energy efficiency services, putting in place implemented projects with over $9,000,000 in energy costs savings. These partners and allies have used the program to support such project development, in-plant assessments, facility energy management planning, staff training, specialty process enhancements and advanced technology assessment and demonstration, all to act upon energy efficiency opportunities to improve plant operation costs.

Furthermore these over 400 industrial and municipal partners are building a foundation of future energy efficiency savings, with over $2 million in financial incentives leveraged to commit over 150 energy projects, with savings commitments of over 70 Million kWh's, 10 MW's and 3 million therms of savings.

These industrial programs experienced many diverging and interesting results from early successes, to missed opportunities, to surprise interests. The lessons of these experiences have been now incorporated into the many program services and offerings including in-plant technical support, targeted financial incentives, specialized marketing, and advanced technology support to better service Wisconsin's industries.

The challenges and experiences in the Wisconsin Focus on Energy industrial programs serve as a valuable guide to the design, development and implementation of energy efficiency in industrial organizations, facilities and processes.

AUTHOR'S BIO

Thomas M. Giffin, P.E.
Senior Program Manager
Science Applications International Corporation
6314 Fly Road
East Syracuse, NY 13057
Phone: (315) 437-1869
Fax: (315) 437-1866
E-mail: *giffint@saic.com*

Chapter 31

ENERGY 101
TEN WAYS TO REDUCE FACILITY ENERGY COSTS
OR
WHAT TO LOOK AT FIRST

Terry Niehus, P.E., CEM
President
Lakeshore Consulting

ABSTRACT

In my experience as an energy management instructor and energy auditor, I have found that certain items always seem to be included in the list of energy saving recommendations. These items are included because they typically have a reasonable payback for the effort. I have put together a list of what I have found to be the "top ten" of these energy saving measures. These measures tend to be more applicable to commercial buildings, but some of them, particularly the motor recommendations and utility concerns, may be appropriate for industrial facilities.

This list can be used as a general guide as to what to examine first when looking at ways to save energy and reduce operating costs. The paybacks shown are of a "first cut" accuracy, and do not reflect maintenance or capital expenditure savings that can be included in a life cycle analysis. Further and more detailed analysis is recommended prior to the implementation of any of these measures. These paybacks shown are based on a range of average electrical and gas costs, and assume a capital cost for the energy conservation measure.

The top ten items discussed include: converting standard fluorescent lighting systems to T8s systems with electronic ballasts; utilizing compact fluorescent lamps to replace incandescents; replacing exit signs containing incandescent or fluorescent lamps with LED exit signs; installing occupancy sensors for lighting control; using programmable thermostats for setback/setup control; replacing standard motors with energy efficient models; purchasing new energy efficient motors in lieu of rewinding, and converting water heating from electric to gas. Also addressed are understanding utility rates, tracking utilities, and the benefits of forming a working relationship with the utility representative.

TEN WAYS TO REDUCE FACILITY ENERGY COSTS OR WHAT TO LOOK AT FIRST

In my twenty-five years of experience as an energy auditor and instructor, I have found that specific items always seem to be included in the list of energy saving recommendations; they tend to have a reasonable simple payback for the effort. I have put together a list of what I have found to be the "top ten" of these energy saving measures. These measures are applicable to commercial buildings, but some, particularly the energy efficient motor recommendations and utility concerns, can also be appropriate for industrial facilities.

This "top ten" list can be used as a general guide as to what to examine first when looking at ways to save energy and reduce operating costs. The simple paybacks shown are based on a range of average electrical costs, and assume a capital cost for the energy conservation measure. Labor is assumed to be performed in-house. When evaluating these measures, ensure that the utility rates accurately reflect the charges for your specific facility, and obtain pricing data and technical specifications from reputable vendors. Operating hours also impact the calculations, so make sure that your estimates are reasonable.

Important note- The following recommendations are based on a "first cut " analysis, and should be used only as a guideline for more detailed project analysis. Also, I have not taken into account capital savings, maintenance savings, or the cost of money over the life of the project. These additional considerations may make the energy conservation measures more attractive in the long run.

The ten ways to reduce your facility energy cost are described as follows. The corresponding figures are included at the end of the article.

THE TEN WAYS

1) Replace fluorescent 40W – T12 lamps with 32W – T8 lamps and electronic ballasts.

Explanation: The T8 lamps with electronic ballasts are more efficient than the standard T12 lamps with standard ballasts. In addition, the quality of lighting may be improved due to the higher CRIs (Color Rendition Index) of the T8s as compared to the standard T12s. Figure 1 illustrates the simple paybacks that would occur for various average electric costs if a 4 lamp-4 foot fluorescent fixture with standard ballasts and 40 W – T12 bulbs (192 W per fixture) was replaced with a 4 lamp-4 foot fixture using 32 W- T8s with electronic ballasts (111 W per fixture). At an average electric cost of 8 cents/kWh and a fixture cost of $75, the payback is 5.8 years for 2,000 hours of annual operation, 2.9 years for 4,000 hours, and 1.9 years for 6,000 hours. Obviously, more operating hours and/or higher electric costs will result in lower paybacks. *Fixture wattage – EPA Lighting Upgrade Manual*

2) Replace incandescent bulbs with energy efficient compact fluorescent lamps.

Explanation: Compact fluorescent lamps (CFLs) are very efficient when compared to the standard incandescent bulb. The CFLs use approximately 1/3 to 1/4 the wattage of the incandescent bulb to produce an equivalent amount of light. In addition, CFLs can have a rated life as high as 10,000 hours life, as opposed to 750-1,000 hours for most incandescents.

Figure 2 illustrates the simple paybacks realized by changing out a 100 W incandescent lamp with a 28 W CFL. For this example, the price of the CFL was estimated at $12. As the price of CFLs continues to drop, the paybacks will get lower. For an electric cost of 8 cents/kWh, and with more than 2,000 hours of operation, the payback can be about one year; for more than 4,000 hours about six months and for more than 6,000 hours less than 4.2 months. *Fixture wattage – EPA Lighting Upgrade Manual*

3) Replace incandescent or fluorescent exit signs lights with LEDs

Explanation: Exits signs should operate continuously by law, or approximately 8,760 hours per year. If these signs are illuminated by incandescent bulbs, the total wattage can be as high as 40 W. The fluorescent signs (compact fluorescent lights or *CFLs*) typically have lower wattages, in the 10 to 15 W range. The LED (*Light Emitting Diode*) signs operate on about 2 W, and therefore consume significantly less energy than the other types mentioned.

Figure 3 shows the simple paybacks for different electric costs if a 2-20 W incandescent lamp exit sign is retrofitted with LEDs. Paybacks are also shown for retrofitting a 10 W CFL exit sign with LEDs. Note that the LEDs have a life of over 25 years, meaning that the maintenance and associated costs are much less than the other types of exit signs examined. For an electric cost of 8 cents/kWh, the payback can be about 8 months for incandescent replacement and approximately 3.2 years for fluorescent lamp replacement. *Fixture wattage – EPA Lighting Upgrade Manual*

4) Use occupancy sensors in areas where lighting is left on when no one is there.

Explanation: In most facilities there are places where lights are typically left on when the areas are unoccupied. Occupancy sensors, when properly installed, can ensure that the lights are turned off when the area is vacant, and on when occupied. The energy savings from occupancy sensors depends on the total hours that the lights are normally on, and the percentage of hours that they can be turned off. Savings for an office building operating 4,000 hours annually can be in the range of 10% to 50%, depending on area traffic. The actual percentage of hours that the lights can be turned off can be tracked with an inexpensive lighting data logger.

Figure 4 shows the paybacks that could be realized for various electricity costs by installing occupancy sensors in a room with six fluorescent fixtures consisting of four-34 W T12 lamps with standard ballasts (164 W per fixture). For a electrical cost of 8 cents/kWh, the payback for a 10% reduction in lighting hours is about 3.2 years. For a 25% reduction the payback drops to around 1.3 years, and for a 50% reduction in lighting hours, the payback is under 8 months. *Fixture wattage – EPA Lighting Upgrade Manual*

5) Install programmable thermostats

Explanation: Programmable thermostats can be used to setup or setback temperatures during facility non-occupied hours, therefore reducing energy costs. These increases in temperature during the cooling season and decreases in temperature during the heating season can result in significant savings in energy usage. The savings realized from installing programmable thermostats are not easy to quantify, as they depend on numerous variables which include: efficiencies of the heating and cooling equipment, weather, facility integrity, hours of operation and setback/setup duration. Manufacturers typically overstate the percent energy savings with estimates going as high as 50%. A more reasonable and generally used estimate is 1% savings for each degree of an eight-hour setback. A building simulation program can be used to more accurately estimate the annual savings. My experience has been, using a building energy simulation program, that the paybacks for installing programmable thermostats in office buildings range from 8 months to 1.5 years. The costs of programmable thermostats range from $50 to over $200, depending on the functions.

6) Replace motors that have burned out with energy efficient ones.

Explanation: Energy efficient motors use less energy to operate than standard motors due to their higher efficiency. A few percent increase in efficiency can save a significant amount of money in the course of a year, especially if the motor has high operating hours.

Figure 5 illustrates the paybacks for various electric rates for changing out a burned-out 70% loaded 10 HP- 86.5% efficient motor with a 10 HP- 91.7% efficient motor. The cost of the standard motor was $294 and the high efficiency one was $390. For an average electric cost of 8 cents/kWh, and with 4,000 hours of operation, the payback is less than 11 months. For 6,000 hours, the payback drops to approximately 7 months.

7) Replace motors with energy efficient ones rather than rewind.

Explanation: Rewinding motors can lower their efficiency and consequently increase operating costs. It is generally better, for motors less than 25 HP, to replace the motor with a high efficiency equivalent rather than rewind. Also, rewound motors may not last as long as new ones, so the long term economics will generally favor the new motor alternative.

Figure 6 illustrates the paybacks realized by purchasing a new energy efficient motor rather than rewinding the existing one. A 2% loss in efficiency of the rewound motor was assumed based on experience. The cost of the rewind was estimated at 50% the cost of a new motor. The motor parameters used were the same as in the previous example. At 8 cents/kWh, motors operated 4,000 hours annually had paybacks of approximately 1.3 years. For 6,000 hours, the payback drops to about 11 months.

8) Replace electric water heaters with gas water heaters.

Explanation: Heating water with electricity can be more expensive than heating it with gas, even though the electric water heaters are more efficient than the gas ones. This is because the cost per Btu of gas has typically been less than electricity. Note: If this pricing hierarchy

changes, due to gas shortages or other economic conditions, then the electric to gas conversion may not be as favorable. Figure 7 shows the paybacks realized for changing out an electric water heater with a gas equivalent at various gas and electric rates. The payback calculations assume an annual hot water usage of 30,000 gallons per year, a sixty degree temperature rise, and a $600 installation cost for changing out a 40 gallon electric water heater for a gas one. The electric and gas water heater energy factor used were 90% and 70% respectively. At an average electric cost of 8 cents/kWh, the paybacks range from 1.8 years with gas at $3/MCF to 3 years with gas at $9/MCF.

9) Understand the utility rate structures and track billing histories

In my years as an energy auditor and instructor, I have been amazed at how little some facility managers know about their utility rates. They know the building operation and equipment inside and out, yet they don't take the time to understand *how* they are being billed; many of them have never seen the utility bills. In order to control utility costs, it is necessary to fully understand the utility rate that the building is billed on. Know how the demand and energy charges are calculated, and how they impact facility operating costs. Also, in order to save energy, it helps to understand how your building has performed in the past. Track your utility usage for at least the previous twelve months and graph this information. Commercial software programs designed to do this tracking/graphing are readily available, or you can develop your own with spreadsheets. At a minimum, track monthly demand, energy usage and dollar amounts. This will enable you to quantify savings due to energy management improvements, and can even help you spot billing errors.

10) Work with your utility representatives

The utility representative can be a valuable asset in controlling energy costs. Deregulation has placed pressure on utilities to pay more attention to their current customers, especially the larger facilities. This means that most utilities want to do all that they can for their customers in order to keep them from even thinking about switching to other suppliers or generation alternatives. Here are some questions to ask your representative:

- How does my rate work?- Can you get me a copy of the tariff?
- Am I on the best possible rate? If not, how can I get on it? What are my rate options?
- Does my rate include a ratchet charge?
- What is the demand period?
- Do you offer any incentives for equipment replacement? Financing?
- Can you help me reduce my utility costs?

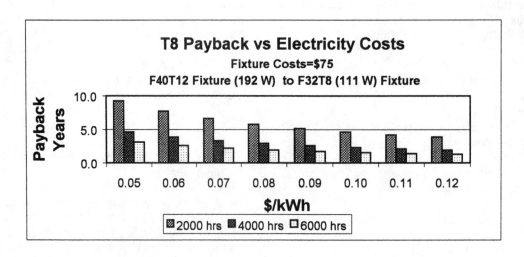

FIGURE 1 – T8 PAYBACK VS ELECTRICITY COSTS

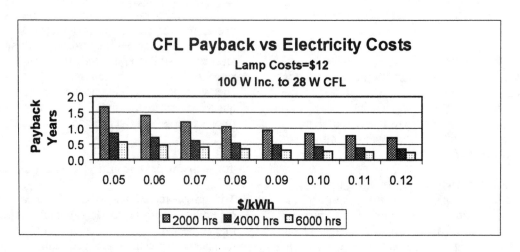

FIGURE 2 – CFL PAYBACK VS ELECTRICITY COSTS

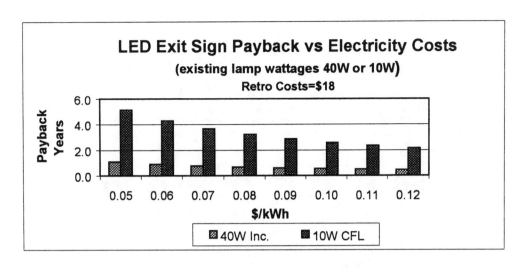

FIGURE 3 – LED EXIT SIGN PAYBACK VS ELECTRICITY COSTS

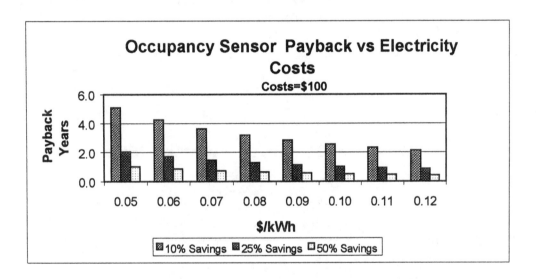

FIGURE 4 – OCCUPANCY SENSOR PAYBACK VS ELECTRICITY COSTS

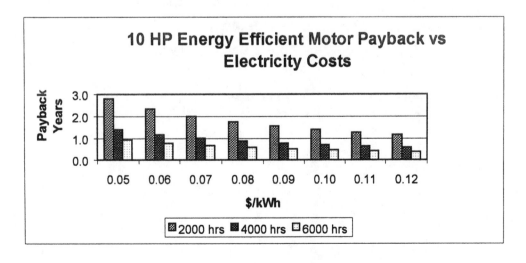

FIGURE 5 - 10 HP ENERGY EFFICIENT MOTOR PAYBACK VS ELECTRICITY COSTS

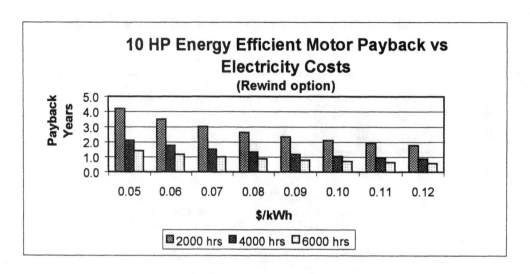

FIGURE 6 - 10 HP ENERGY EFFICIENT MOTOR PAYBACK VS ELECTRICITY COSTS
(REWIND OPTION)

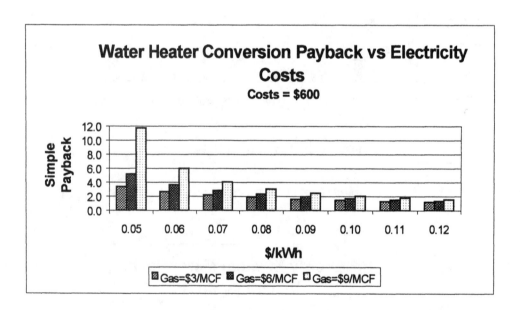

FIGURE 7 - WATER HEATER CONVERSION PAYBACK VS ELECTRICITY COSTS

Conclusions

The energy conservation opportunities addressed in this paper, if properly implemented, will help reduce your energy costs. The next step in this process would be to have an energy audit performed to identify which of the energy conservation opportunities discussed would be applicable to your building *and* to identify any other energy saving opportunities. The audit could be performed in-house, using this paper as a preliminary guideline, or as a checklist for an outside auditor. If an outside auditor is used, make sure that at the *very least* they look at the energy conservation opportunities discussed in this article. If they do not, then you may want to consider consulting with a more experienced auditor.

BIOGRAPHY

Terry Niehus is the founder of Lakeshore Consulting, a firm based in Atlanta specializing in energy auditing and technical training. His lists of clients include numerous electric and gas utilities, the Army National Guard, the Corps of Engineers, and hundreds of commercial and industrial businesses. Terry's unique qualifications include practical, hands-on experience as an energy consultant.

Mr. Niehus is an accomplished trainer and has taught courses in commercial building energy systems, motors and drives, residential systems, commercial cooking equipment, HVAC, compressed air, domestic water heating, gas facts, cogeneration and thermal energy storage.

These courses focus on understanding the technical aspects of the subject matter, and how they apply to commercial, industrial and governmental facilities. In addition to teaching these classes, he has written numerous training manuals including the technical resource manual for motors/drives, commercial building energy systems, commercial HVAC, compressed air, commercial cooking systems, domestic water heating and thermal energy storage.

Terry's unique qualifications include extensive experience as an energy auditor. He has performed over 1,000 energy analyses for governmental, commercial and industrial facilities. He is well versed in life cycle costing analyses and building simulation programs. This comprehensive auditing experience ensures that the training and energy analyses performed by Mr. Niehus are practical, results oriented and technically sound.

Mr. Niehus is a registered Professional Engineer and a Certified Energy Manager. He holds a B.S. in Electrical Engineering and an M.S. in Industrial Engineering. He is a member of the Association of Energy Engineers and ASHRAE. He can be contacted at tniehus@aol.com, or 770-447-1675

Chapter 32

Leveraging Power:
How To Use Energy Management Systems to Track
Power and Negotiate Better Prices
by Robert M. Lacy and Anthony C. Maurer

Energy costs are a significant portion of the operating expenses for many commercial and industrial enterprises. Within the new energy environment, energy suppliers, service companies and large consumers are well positioned to take advantage of opportunities to challenge and manage these prices; however, most do not have the tools to support informed decisions that will help them control energy and improve operational efficiencies. New enterprise energy management tools offer a solution to ensuring operational efficiency and controlling overall costs.

What Attendees Will Learn:

- Today's Energy Management Challenges—How to manage and control energy costs. Find out how businesses on both the supply and demand side of energy can:
    - Combat rising prices
    - Locate inefficient energy use
    - Eliminate waste

- What Are EEM Systems? —Learn how an EEM system acts as a layer of information technology accompanying an enterprise's set of energy assets. By collecting, storing and analyzing mountains of real-time data for historical trend reports, the system enables management, accounting, engineering and maintenance personnel to make optimal decisions regarding enterprise-wide energy control.

Technology Demonstrations
This interactive session will navigate the latest technology designed for enterprise energy management. Discover how engineers, operators, managers and executives can utilize the EEM interface as a decision support tool.

Practical How-To Advice on Using EEM
The session will reveal how using EEM systems can help enterprises integrate data with existing systems for increasing operational efficiency and cost-effective decision-making. In addition, learn how large energy consumers can monitor energy use by creating load profile reports and implementing alarm notifications on the system

Real-World Case Study
A case study will illustrate how some large energy users-- such as universities, manufacturing plants and large commercial buildings-- are leveraging EEM systems to save money by gaining control of enterprise energy use.

Power costs can be modeled using classic supply and demand theory. Electricity is a commodity that must be used simultaneously as it is produced – it cannot be economically stored for future use. For this reason, energy demand must be forecasted very accurately. Any significant excess of supply will significantly reduce the price on the spot market and any circumstances where an electricity provider is required to provide more power than it is able to supply will cause it to purchase power on the spot market. Power available on the spot market is priced at a significant premium, many times the cost of producing the power, and many times the average retail price received from the end user.

This potential for extreme market volatility is causing all providers and users of energy to focus on managing demand to avoid the pitfalls of doing business on the spot market. Energy providers are partnering with their largest users to assist with peak-period usage management and to identify methods of reducing/controlling peak demand in order to avoid the potentially catastrophic financial impact of buying power on the spot market. The largest commercial customers of the energy provider have incentives to manage peak usage and not exceed certain thresholds, as prices for peak hour energy usage beyond those thresholds ratchet up in a volatile fashion, resembling the volatility of the spot market.

The commercial customer bears a significant economic risk if they exceed critical thresholds. In order to reduce these risks, the customer must have a plan to limit utilization instead of incurring spot market pricing. By having a plan to shut down non-essential assets, or switch to alternate energy sources such as generators, the end user can avoid spot market risks. Enterprise Energy Management (EEM) systems can provide all of the information necessary to prepare such a plan and can monitor real-time usage, alarming when plan execution is necessary.

WHAT IS AN ENTERPRISE ENERGY MANAGEMENT SYSTEM?
The foundation of an EEM system is an integrated set of control systems, meters, monitoring devices and data points. The database and software portion of an EEM system should include the following capability:
- o   Store mountains of information and retrieve that information very quickly for analysis purposes
- o   Maintain a real-time load profile
- o   Provide sophisticated usage information for activity-based costing down to the lowest metered level
- o   Incorporate reference data from external sources (a reference module) such as utility bills, schematics, contract utility rates, process information, weather information and live information feeds from the internet
- o   Generating billing for individual users and departments

The Foundation
In order to begin to understand the demands for energy throughout a business and manage the usage effectively, it is necessary to capture the utilization information at the sub-meter level. In many cases, individual machines require a dedicated meter in order to measure and report usage at the lowest level of material energy usage.

In addition to monitoring energy usage at the lowest level of material usage, large operations environments should have control systems in place to allow for automatically or remotely switching to alternate sources of energy during peak demand periods. In addition, the control system could remotely shutdown equipment when it is left on during non-business hours and for remote power-interruption in the event of a peak-demand emergency. Of course, power interruption would only occur during execution of a well thought out peak energy conservation plan.

The EEM system foundation also includes data points that can help analyze usage, measure the rationality of usage and compare current usage to other similar periods (with respect to weather, production rates, etc.). It is essential to have as many relevant data points as possible in order to monitor usage on a real-time basis and make objective observations and management decisions in a dynamic fashion.

The Database and Software
The database of an EEM system should be a real-time database capable of capturing, and analyzing many data points and storing the data accurately in a very efficient manner. The database should be able to manage the stored data in a distributed fashion to allow endless historical archiving. In addition, data retrieval rates should be very fast to facilitate real-time analysis.

The EEM system software must be capable of maintaining a load profile and comparing that load profile to process data or other relevant reference data. This capability allows management to analyze usage relative to the activities that drive energy usage and identify illogical trends in usage relative to these activities. The load profile is compiled from historical data within the EEM database; it is used as a base line to adjust current energy needs and can be used to predict future requirements. This load profiling must have the capability to create an up-to-the-minute picture of a facility's energy usage by month, week or day. The load profile should be down to the lowest sub-meter level. A load profile is also used to identify inefficient processes and identify non-critical loads that can be shed or shifted to avoid peak demand charges. Last, but not least, the load profile is critical to the energy contract negotiation process and it can be used to verify compliance with utility contracts. Exhibit A is an example of a profile trend.

Sophisticated usage reporting capability is a requirement of any EEM software. The application must be able to produce energy costs down to the lowest metered level for cost accounting purposes throughout the manufacturing environment and for allocating costs to administrative departments. The reporting capability should apply to real-time information and historical information. This gives management the information they need to identify consumption patterns, set benchmarks and compare current consumption to prior periods. Usage inefficiencies can be identified real-time with this reporting capability.

In addition to reporting on activity captured from all monitoring devices, the EEM software should include a reference module with the capability of incorporating other data relevant to management and analysis. The reference module can include data from many disparate sources. Utility bill information, fed electronically from the provider, can facilitate automatic reconciliation of billed usage. Billing inaccuracies will be identified very easily using this process. Exhibit B is an example of invoicing and analysis that can be prepared using an EEM system. Facility schematics (from the CAD drawings of the facility) are valuable for correlating meter data with physical locations, enabling operations and security personnel to pinpoint illogical usage; for example, usage at points in a building that are not occupied. Storing utility contract rates is necessary in order to accurately determine costs for allocation purposes and for reconciling the energy invoices from the provider. Historical weather data and a live feed from the Internet can be correlated with energy usage to improve the accuracy of load profiling and to enhance real-time analysis. Real-time spot-market energy prices can be monitored via an Internet feed in the resource module, making this critical information available to managers facing a peak demand crisis.

Profile Trend

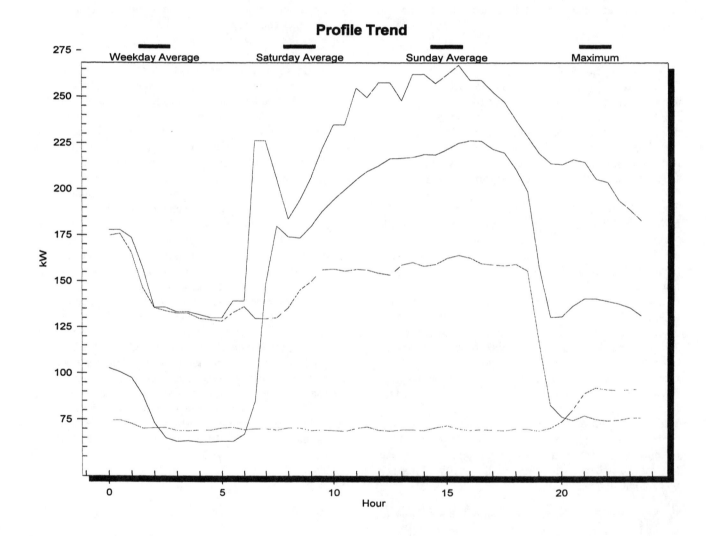

Weekday Average   Saturday Average   Sunday Average   Maximum

Exhibit A

Description	Usage	Units	Price	Sub Total
Meter: HAMILTON.CALC.750_ELEC at 100%				
Energy Charge - Peak	11,733.48	kWh	0.05	589.26
Energy Charge - Off Peak	5,710.95	kWh	0.02	121.24
Energy Charge Peak	4,889.29	kWh	0.02	103.80
Demand Charge (Summer1)	239.33	kW	16.41	3,927.47
Demand Charge (Summer2)	0.00	kW	6.51	.00
Demand Charge (Winter 1)	0.00	kW	16.41	.00
Demand Charge (Winter 2)	0.00	kW	5.03	.00
Non-Meter Charges				
Monthly Customer Charge			246.39	246.39
Total				**$4,988.16**

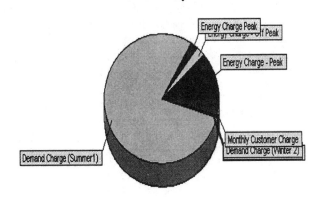

Invoice Analysis

Site Name	Max Demand	Load Factor	Consumption
750 Lake Cook Rd	249	0.54	22,743
Total			**22,743**

Exhibit B

213

The following case study illustrates the EEM benefits experienced by a large university in the Midwestern U.S.

Case Study: Collection and Invoicing of Electric Meter Data at a Midwest University   by InStep Software, LLC

Background:
A large university in the Midwestern U.S. leases a large amount of square footage and has difficulty providing accurate bills to tenants and verifying usage with the local utility company.

Need:
The university receives a monthly bill for all electricity used throughout the campus, which includes leased space within the buildings. Verifying that the rates reflected in the monthly bill are consistent with the contract rates is a manual process. The facilities staff allocates the electricity costs to the leased tenants using a square footage and estimated hourly usage formula. Tenants are not confident in the accuracy of invoices and the university staff is unable to substantiate tenant usage with this method of allocation.

Solution:
InStep Software developed the Enterprise Energy Management (EEM) suite of tools that is wrapped around the core eDNA product. The university uses InStep's EEM solution to create invoices for their commercial and retail tenants and to provide an audit trail for their utility bills. They compare their internally generated invoices to the utility bill to validate the accuracy. Reading these meters in near real-time, the facilities staff can monitor consumption and compare this usage against the budget. In addition, they can now do "what if" scenarios with the rates and tariffs being proposed by the local utility company.

Benefits:
Tenant invoices are automatically generated. The facility staff can provide detailed tenant invoices if needed; including the time of day that usage occurred. The tenants feel they are dealing with a knowledgeable group and the invoice is very similar to the invoice the utility company issues. In addition to being intuitive and easy to use, the flexibility and scalability of the program make it capable of expanding in the future to include natural gas, water and steam. University officials rely upon InStep's EEM solution to help them verify the monthly utility bill and substantiate billing inaccuracies. The usage information is retrieved instantly from the eDNA database in varying report formats and graphs to meet any communication or discussion needs. The eDNA trending tools show any time-span of usage graphically. The Trending tools can help assist the Facility Group in spotting any equipment malfunctions or inefficiencies of equipment.

SMALL COMPANY EEM BENEFITS

The benefits of an EEM system are not just focused on large companies with astronomical energy usage. Small companies are benefiting from installing EEM systems as well. The knowledge provided by an EEM system can help a small company understand exactly what drives the company's energy usage and unnecessary energy usage can be isolated. Information included in the company's load profile can improve its negotiating position when making energy purchasing commitments. On average, if the company can save 5% of it's energy costs by using an EEM system, the payback on such a system is less than 12 months.

CONCLUSION

The energy market-pricing model rewards companies that plan and manage their energy utilization. Conversely, a company that fails to manage its' utilization will bear the astronomical cost of purchasing excess energy at spot market prices. Energy utilization planning, management and control can yield significant savings for large and small companies alike. Regardless of size, energy costs are a significant percentage of many companies' operating costs. Implementing an EEM system is the most efficient and effective way for a company to monitor and control these costs, thereby minimizing them.

A complete EEM system will provide all of the necessary usage and cost information required to make intelligent management decisions and minimize energy costs. Such a system will enable management to identify usage reduction opportunities, negotiate optimal prices for energy, and plan for alternate energy source utilization in order to avoid spot market costs. Integrated with a sophisticated control system, EEM systems can actually shed or shift excess energy usage in order to avoid peak usage spot market rates. All businesses with significant energy costs should deploy an EEM system. In many cases, the payback period will be less than one year.

REFERENCES

Barrie Murray, "Electricity Markets Electricity Markets", 1998 John Wiley & Sons Ltd

Chapter 33
ENERGY MANAGEMENT CHALLENGES IN THE WATER/WASTEWATER INDUSTRY

Mr. Robert B. Taylor, PE, CEM, Energy Manager
Washington Suburban Sanitary Commission (WSSC)

ABSTRACT
The municipal water and wastewater industry is facing
enormous changes never before encountered in its long
and stable history. Facing a huge backlog of aging
infrastructure improvements, new, more stringent
environmental requirements, increasing competitiveness
from privatization, and recent security concerns, utilities
are increasingly exposed to the risks inherent in a
deregulated electricity market. This paper addresses the
unique ways utilities are coping with the challenge, and
management of the second largest direct cost of their
organization. Specifically, it outlines the energy
management approach of the Washington Suburban
Sanitary Commission (WSSC), the nation's seventh
largest water/wastewater utility, and WSSC's specific
objectives.

OVERVIEW OF THE WATER/WASTEWATER INDUSTRY

Municipal Water/Wastewater utilities in the United States
spend an estimated $6.5 billion annually representing
about 3% of the nation's total electricity use. Electricity is
used to power pumps, fans and blowers, mixers,
centrifuges, ozone generators, and ultraviolet disinfecting
equipment, and represents 25-50% of the average yearly
operating budget, second only to wages and salaries.
Nearly 80% of this electric energy is used for pumping
water.[1] Water and wastewater treatment plants typically
operate well under capacity to insure permit compliance
and equipment reliability and redundancy.
In addition, water and sewer infrastructure improvements
have been drastically under-funded due to municipalities
funding restraints. The Congressional Budget Office
estimates that a minimum of $500 billion is needed over
the next 20 years for capital investment in plants, water
distribution systems, and wastewater collection systems.
All this results in systems that inherently are becoming
more inefficient; it is estimated that 20% of treated
drinking water is lost from pipe leakage in many urban
drinking water systems. [2]

Other factors affecting the industry today:
♦ Utilities are facing increasing competition and
  privatization due to tax law changes in the late 1990s.
  The switch from public utility operation to private
  contract operators has slowed from previous years pace,
  but is still increasing.
♦ Anti-terrorism security projects have been given top
  priority, and require additional funding not considered
  before 9-11.

Environmental Impact on Energy Use

As major stewards of our nation's watersheds, lakes, rivers
and bays, water/wastewater utilities' first priority is to
maintain or improve our nations precious resources and
deliver clean drinking water to an ever-increasing
population. That responsibility is becoming more expensive
in light of new regulations coupled with security concerns.
Major developments are as follows:

♦ As part of the Clean Water Act, the EPA is proposing
  reduced nitrogen concentrations from wastewater
  treatment plants, which could increase the use of
  electricity for aeration.
♦ Water utilities are addressing new sources of pathogens
  in water with increasing application of ultraviolet
  disinfection technology, replacing or supplementing the
  use of chlorine.[3] This could increase electricity costs for
  treatment of water and wastewater.
♦ Wastewater utilities are considering replacing the
  production of Class A instead of Class B Biosolids, due
  to public acceptance issues with Class B. Movement to
  Class A will increase usage of natural gas and
  electricity.

WATER/WASTEWATER UTILITIES ENERGY STRATEGIES

A 2001 American Water Works Association Research
Foundation (AWWARF) study survey among 22 U.S. and
Canadian water/wastewater utilities verified that while there
is a strong need to manage energy costs, sophisticated

energy management programs are only beginning to take root. One reason is that unique features exist for each utility that makes it difficult to compare energy performance. These include differences in system design, age and condition of infrastructure, water storage, extent of gravity service, environmental permit requirements, and electric rate structures. In spite of these constraints, individual utilities are making important strides in improving energy efficiency and investing in future technology. These include:

- **Energy Efficient Equipment - Aeration**
  Over 50 % of the energy in waste water treatment plants is used by the aeration system, consisting of blowers and diffusers, which generate and inject air (source of oxygen) into raw influent reactor tanks to remove nitrogen and ammonia. State-of-the-art variable flow compressors and motors coupled with fine bubble diffusers with increased oxygen-to-air transfer efficiency can reduce aeration energy consumption by 50%.

City of San Jose's Water Pollution Control Plant (167 mgd) replaced existing air diffusers with high efficient fine bubble diffusers in 2001, is projected to save $500,000/yr.

Arlington County (VA) 30 mgd wastewater treatment plant is completing the installation of fine bubble diffusers as part of their conversion to a biological nitrogen removal process. [4]

Los Angeles County Sanitation District's Joint Water Pollution Control Plant (JWPCP), wastewater treatment facility (350 mgd) switched from coarse bubble diffusers to fine bubble diffusers in 2001, saving approximately $1 million a year in electricity costs, and significantly reducing demand. [5]

- **Cogeneration Using Anaerobic Digester Gas**
  More than 90% of the wastewater treatment plants in the United States generate anaerobic (without air or oxygen) as a by-product of their operation. There are over 500 municipal wastewater treatment facilities in the U.S. with anaerobic digesters capable of providing methane to fuel power plants of 250 kilowatts or larger. Digesters generate a significant source of gas fuel that can be used to power gas turbine generators or fuel cells to supply a major source of plant power/process heat for the plant.

East Bay Municipal Utility District (EBMUD) has been operating since 1985 an on-site cogeneration plant has three 2.4 MW engine generators, which burn waste methane produced by the facility's digesters. The station generates about half of the

facility's energy needs, saving approximately $1.7 million/yr. [6]

San Diego's Point Loma Wastewater Treatment Plant (190 mgd) uses methane gas fuels two generators that can produce 4.5 megawatts. The plant has become energy self-sufficient. In fact, the plant saved the City more than $3 million in energy costs to run the facility and was able to sell an additional $1.4 million in excess power to the electric grid. [7]

Yonkers (New York) Westchester County Wastewater Treatment Plant (90 mgd) began operation in 1998 a fuel cell power plant using gas produced during anaerobic digestion of sewage. Operated by the New York Power Authority with funding from EPA the system has generated more than one million kilowatt-hours of electricity. [8]

City of Portland Columbia wastewater plant (82 mgd) fuel cells converts anaerobic digester gas (60% methane) into 175 kW of electric power, which is fed into the local power grid. Portland expects to save over $60,000 a year in energy costs. [9]

- **Real-Time and Block Power Electric Supply Purchasing**.
  Advances in computer/controls technology coupled with electricity deregulation now allow users the opportunity to purchase power in ways similar to electric wholesalers. Sophisticated SCADA controls systems allows treatment plant operators to adjust the operations of specific equipment to accommodate low (off peak) or high (on-peak) hourly pricing, resulting in major cost savings.

Columbus, GA Wastewater Treatment Plant has opted to a real-time pricing rate offered by its electric supplier. Power costs for each hour of the day are made available via the Internet. Costs for the day are locked in at 4 p.m. of the previous day. The utility reschedules its next day equipment operation depending on the forecasted pricing, only if the projected hourly cost is greater than the average cost. Since a majority of the runtime hours is priced at low, off-peak rates, the utility has significantly lowered its energy costs.

Las Vegas Valley Water District (LVVWD) purchases electricity in a fixed annual block of a MW demand level. During daily or seasonal peak times, LVVWD shuts down the majority of its pumps and draws from the storage system whenever possible, or runs backup generators. Water quality levels are continuously monitored. Energy not used by LVVWD during the on-peak time is marketed to other utilities at on-peak price. Since beginning this practice in 2000, LVVWD has saved approximately 50% of electric energy costs.

♦ **Distributed Power Generation**.

The Edison Electric Institute reported in June 2001 that electric utilities have invested 50 percent less in their infrastructure in the past decade than in the previous decade - with growth remaining the same. The uncertainty of electric utility restructuring combined with terrorist concerns and the pressure for enhanced environmental performance increases the potential for service disruptions. Water/wastewater utilities are re-thinking their roles as not only suppliers of clean water, but also *reliable* suppliers of clean water. Current industry standards allow either backup generators or "dual feed" connection between water customers and water plants. Distributed power applications offer additional capabilities including peak shaving, and grid support, using technologies such as gas turbines, reciprocating engines, and fuel cells. [10]

The Cocoa Beach (Florida) Water Reclamation Facility (6-mgd) has installed a special stand-by generator at its wastewater treatment plant. In a period of peak power demand, FPL can activate the generator to provide electrical power to the facility and reduce the demand on the utility's strained power capacity. The Cocoa Beach plant realizes significant power savings through a lower cost per kilowatt-hour. By providing this level of reliability in a high demand situation, the city is able to continue its wastewater processing while helping FPL avoid area-wide brownouts.[11]

Jacksonville (Florida) 25 water treatment plants have backup power standards of performance raised to the current high level. Backup electric generators are installed at every plant to provide electric power during periods of electric grid power outages. The system is capable of maintaining water pressure during an extended power outage. [12]

The City of Detroit Water & Sewerage Department (DWSD) operates of 44- 2 MW generators to provide emergency power backup and peak-shaving at thirteen facilities including three water treatment plants, five water booster pumping stations, and five stormwater sanitary pumping stations.

Miramar (Florida) wastewater plant was constructed with an energy management system that compares demand trend peaks of energy intensive equipment to the power company's peak demand cycles, and sets optimum times for energy cost reduction. The plant's backup generator is operated during the highest peak demand cycle to alleviate the cost of operation. [13] Fresno, CA 80-mgd wastewater treatment plant; purchased a used combined cycle cogeneration plant from a site which had closed in 1998. The 9 MW power plant, designed to burn natural gas and diesel fuel oil, was modified to use a blend of low-Btu digester and natural gas supplying all of the plant's electrical power.

WSSC earned $105,000 in credits during the summer of 2001 through the Pennsylvania-Jersey-Maryland (PJM) transmission grid emergency load curtailment program. The load curtailment was achieved at a water treatment plant, 2 wastewater treatment plants and 2 water pumping stations over a course of 4 days.

♦ **Greater Attention to Life Cycle Cost Considerations for Capital Projects.**

New pumping stations are being designed and constructed with multiple pumps of smaller horsepower rather than one large pump, optimum pipe sizes, variable frequency drives, and double precision laser alignment of pumps to determine the optimum equipment configuration. Life cycle costing (incorporating partial as well as full load efficiency, power factor, etc.) is being used as a basis for bidding projects where the total life cycle cost, not only initial capital cost, is the basis for award. Studies have shown that 64% of the total life cycle cost (including the cost of construction) of a typical pumping station, installation is energy. In some cases, consulting engineers have been rewarded for cutting energy cost or total life-cycle cost.

Water Distribution Energy Optimization. Because every water utility has varying hydraulic gradients, piping conditions, pumping and storage configurations, there is no uniform computerized "system" that will optimize energy usage while meeting water and water quality constraints. However, specialized computer programs are being created to interface with existing SCADA platforms, that schedule optimizations include operating parameters such as quality, costs, and variances in demand. The interface also displays all aspects of the distribution system, forecasting for operators how a schedule will affect each part of the water/wastewater system (see Figure 1). Stations automatically increase pumping during off-peak hours to build up water in elevated storage towers (potential energy), and limits pump use during peak pricing times. A 1998 report published by the American Water Works Association Research Foundation (AWWRF) to quantify the extent to which SCADA systems suggests that altering the operating schedule of pumping stations can reduce costs as much as 20 percent annually.

Using pumping optimization in conjunction with its existing SCADA system, the City of Irving (Texas) has saved roughly 14 percent on its energy costs over a 5-year period.[14]

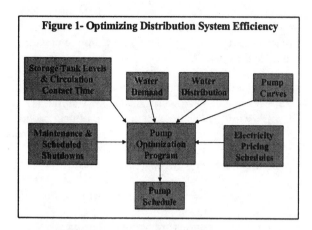

Figure 1- Optimizing Distribution System Efficiency

♦ **Energy Performance Contracting**

Bergen County Utility Authority (BCUA) wastewater treatment plant (60 to 109 mgd) engaged Onsite Sycom Energy Corp., an ESCO to replace base load electric motors with a natural gas engines to drive the aeration blowers. Using the plant's methane byproduct to fuel the gas engines and using the heat from the engines to heat the buildings enables the plant to save an estimated $942,300 per year. The switch to gas engines also was made so that natural gas can be used as a secondary fuel source when the methane waste gas supply does not meet the plants full fuel demand. In addition, the electric motors that were replaced by the gas engines remain as backup when one of the gas engines is down for service.

King County (Washington) South Wastewater Treatment Facility used FuelCell Energy to install and operate a 1MW fuel cell power plant through a cooperative grant to the County from the U.S. Environmental Protection Agency (EPA). The fuel cell plant is fed by anaerobic digester gas. [15]

City of Allentown Wastewater Treatment plant (40 mgd) contracted with PPL Spectrum to design and install a microturbine energy generation system using digester gas (65 % methane, 630 BTU/ft.³ heating value) producing more than 2 million kWh per year. A total of 12 - 30 kW generators were installed, producing 18% of the plant's electricity and all of the plant's thermal requirements. PPL Spectrum assumed all performance risks and guaranteed the savings, which were used to pay for the new installation. [16]

♦ **Energy from Biosolids**

A Sludge-To-Oil Reactor System (STORS), which dewaters untreated, digested, or waste activated sludge in a hydrothermal reactor that converts the material into high-energy "biofuel", has been successfully tested at a 5-mgd facility in California. Developed by Battelle Laboratories/EPA, the biofuel

can be produced as an oil with 90% of the heating value of diesel fuel, and used onsite to generate power. Nitrogen can also be extracted from the STORS derived wastewater and converted to ammonium sulfate, a commercial grade agricultural fertilizer. It is anticipated that the STORS process can significantly reduce the overall cost of sludge disposal, a major component of wastewater treatment.

WSSC ENERGY STRATEGY

The Washington Suburban Sanitary Commission (WSSC) is a publicly owned and operated water/wastewater utility, providing 280 mgd of potable water, collecting and treating 160 mgd of wastewater. WSSC serves approximately 1.6 million customers in Montgomery and Prince George's Counties in Maryland. In the late- 1990's, WSSC was the focus of a privatization study authorized by the State of Maryland. An independent competitive assessment that compared WSSC's then current organizational business practices with best utilities in the private sector resulted in a "competitive gap" in controllable costs of 20% between actual costs and "best in class". As a result, WSSC launched a "Competitive Action Program" to provide its customers with the best possible service at the least possible cost, without any reductions in quality, service and safety. Energy- one of the major items identified under achievable cost reductions- represented, after personnel costs, the largest cost component in the operating cost budget (approximately $12 million/yr.). A recommendation was made to formalize Energy Management to control related costs in the light of a newly de-regulated market. Since that time, WSSC has identified a strategy including ten major objectives:

1. **Reduce Annual Energy Cost by 20%.**
   Using FY 2000 as Baseline, improve energy efficiency by 20%, incorporating equipment upgrades (demand side), efficient new equipment (demand side), and electric supply procurement. Do so without any degradation of water quality or operational efficiency.

2. **Develop an Energy Usage and Cost Tracking System.**
   Since deregulation opened up the need to verify that a myriad of different electrical supply rates were applied correctly to hundreds of invoices per month, it was decided to develop a computerized system that automatically calculates (and verifies) billing, usage, and costs. In addition, it was decided that real-time metering information for electricity and gas was essential to identify usage patterns of major sites/equipment and to optimize procurement. The information will be available on WSSC's Intranet, will enable plant superintendents and plant operators involved with the day-to-day management of energy use and cost control.

3. Develop Performance Metrics to Demonstrate Efficiency Performance

The core of any management program, including energy is the measurement of progress. Although it is difficult for utilities to measure performance against one another, there are individual yardsticks available. Energy usage (kWh or BTU) per million gallons treated or pumped (sometimes referred to as wire-to-water ratio), energy cost per kWh, load factor (% of peak demand maintained) are all indications of how efficiently an organization is using and purchasing their energy supply. For wastewater plants, the Water Environment Federation (WEF) has published typical ranges of wire to water (WTW) ratios for a number of different processes. The range of WTW or averages can then be compared to a utility's performance to see where there is room for improvement. WSSC's WTW numbers for two of its wastewater plants shows one plant-Western Branch-above the average WEF WTW and the Piscataway Plant within average WEF WTW numbers (Figures 2 and 3). This lead to further investigation to identify inefficient equipment needed upgrading at Western Branch.[17]

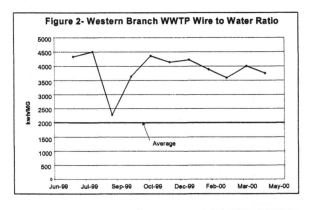

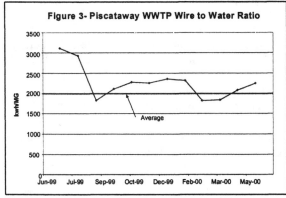

4. Conduct a comprehensive energy audit (with periodic updates).

Develop detailed load profiles, energy efficiency data about power use for all major sites, by specific processes, and whether there are opportunities to alter how and when power is needed, reduce peak demand, shift load to lower cost periods, etc. Identify inefficient systems/equipment for possible upgrading or replacement, in conjunction with expansion and operating plans.

5. Conduct a comprehensive energy audit (with periodic updates).

Develop detailed load profiles, energy efficiency data about power use for each site, by specific processes, and whether there are opportunities to alter how and when power is needed. Identify inefficient systems/equipment for possible upgrading or replacement, in conjunction with expansion and operating plans. Figures 4 and 5 show the energy efficiency (kWh/MGD) and energy cost efficiency (energy $ per MGD) of WSSC's water treatment plants during the last 5 years.

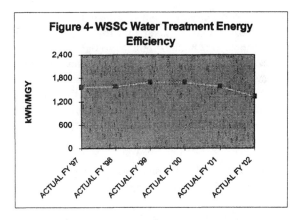

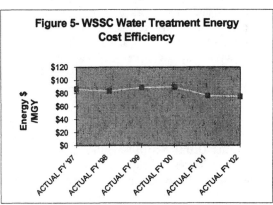

6. Develop an implementation strategy incorporating the following components

Demand: Improve efficiency of existing systems through upgrade, replacement, with more efficient equipment. Consider peak shaving to lower supply unit costs. Prepare for real-time pricing, if site has the capability to adjust load and instrumentation sophistication to take advantage of pricing fluctuations.
Supply: Knowing suppliers, procurement, risks, consumption and demand patterns and costs all

221

contribute to determining the right mix of gas & electric suppliers, billing options, and support decisions relating to on-site generation and alternative fuels usage.

Design and Construction of New Plants, Additions, Pumping Stations: Insure that the planning stage of all new or upgrade project incorporates life cycle costs (LCC), using Hydraulic Institute LCC Guidelines. LCC analysis should take into account entire pumping system (including pump, motor, piping, and operating controls) and interaction between the pump and the rest of the system and the calculation of the operating duty point(s). Also insure that thorough commissioning is included as part of construction process.[18]

7. **Implement Performance Incentives to Compensate Employees for Optimizing Energy Use.**

The most efficient equipment or plan to save energy can be easily undermined by the inability of operations personnel to "buy in" to the project. Plant personnel must take ownership of any new plan or design before it can be successful. If made an integral part of the decision process, plant operations are more apt to embrace new technologies and even help create new solutions. They should also share in the savings.

8. **Use Energy Performance Contracting wherever feasible to Expedite Improvements in Energy Efficiency.**

Instead of a separate array of planners, consultants, engineers, and contractors (all under separate contracts), one energy service company (ESCO) provides a turnkey service and guarantees the design, construction, and savings over a long-term period. Annual CM and PM is also included. As a result, fund, and construction, can be completed in 2-3 years.

9. **Procure Electricity Supply through Aggregation with other Utilities with Complimentary Load Profiles or Metering Capabilities.**

Water utilities have attractive load profiles and often can shift some of their energy intensive operations into not-peak periods. If their bills are aggregated with other municipal operations, they could end up subsidizing those with less attractive load profiles, including schools and office buildings, which consume all their power during peak periods. Use Internet bidding to reduce turnaround time for contract awards. In California, more than 380 utilities have banded together to form the Association of California Water Agencies to purchase power and, as a group, purchase roughly $710 million of electricity annually. The time it takes for board approval of a large contract may wipe out the savings potential of a temporarily favorable market.

10. **Participate in Industry Research and Benchmarking Studies, such as:**
   - American Water Works Research Foundation (AWWARF)- Best Practices to Energy Management. 22 member water/wastewater utilities (including WSSC) to develop Best Practices for Energy Management. The program was member funded and included case studies from water/wastewater organizations, "Best Practices" organizations outside the industry, and extensive benchmarking to illustrate how utilities were performing against each other.
   - Water Environment Research Federation (WERF)- Best Practices, innovative ideas, and effective wastewater plant operating procedures. Comparable data available on operations and maintenance costs to develop cost models through case studies from throughout the U.S.
   - Electric Power Research Institute (EPRI)- Under the Municipal Water and Wastewater program, EPRI supports research and development of new treatment processes which help utilities save on energy costs. Processes include aeration and ultraviolet (UV) disinfection systems.
   - Federal and State Development and Funding Organizations, such as the New York State Energy Research and Development Authority (NYSERDA)- Offers cost-sharing research and demonstration programs for New York's municipal water, wastewater, and solid waste facilities to adopt innovative technology that is more energy-efficient and economical, while preserving environmental standards.

CONCLUSION

As water/wastewater utilities cope with an ever-aging infrastructure, more complex environmental regulations, and added security responsibilities, new complexities brought about by deregulation in the electric industry will mandate different approaches in controlling energy costs and managing risk. This must be accomplished without sacrificing water quality and reliability of service. However, these increased responsibilities coupled with energy efficient technologies offer new opportunities for utilities to generate direct benefit to their ratepayers.

REFERENCES

[1] R. Neal Elliott, Ted Jones "Motor Systems Efficiency in Water and Wastewater Systems: A Call to Action", May 3, 2002.

[2] "Future Investment in Drinking Water and Wastewater Infrastructure", Congressional Budget Office, May 2002.

[3] "A Need for Disinfection Alternatives", Energy Delivery and Utilization Division, Municipal Water and Wastewater Treatment Target, Electric Power Research Institute, December 1999.

[4] Upgrade and Expansion of the Arlington County Water Pollution Control Plant, Arlington County Water Pollution Control Division Program Overview. Web Site.

[5] Karen E. Weber, "Sanitation District a Bright Spot in the Energy Picture", Civic 2001 Leadership, Sanitation Districts of Los Angeles County.

[6] "Success Story, East Bay Municipal Utility District, Special District 1, Wastewater Treatment", California Energy Commission, Process Energy, Energy-Water Connection, Waste Water Treatment Case Studies.

[7] Web Site-The City of San Diego, General Information, Point Loma Wastewater Treatment Plant.

[8] "Fuel Cells", Climate Change Technologies, Environmental Protection Agency State and Local Climate Change Program, January 2000.

[9] "Columbia Boulevard Fuel Cell", Oregon Office of Energy, June 7, 2002.

[10] "A New View on Energy Use", Distributed Power Power Systems, Office of Fossil Energy, U.S. Department of Energy, Electric Power R&D, Distributed Power.

[11] Cocoa Beach Water Reclamation Facility, City of Cocoa Beach Web Site.

[12] "JEA Water System Sustains No Serious Damage From Monday's Power Outage", JEA News, May 2, 2002.

[13] "Maximizing Membrane Water Treatment Plant Performance", Nadine Barnes and Marc Larson, *Florida Water Resources Journal*, January 1997.

[14] "Water Utilities Venture Into Energy Generation To Save Money", Energy Efficiency Forum, WaterWorld Magazine and PennWell Corporation, Aug. 30, 2000.

[15] "FuelCell Energy Signs with King County, Washington for Digester/Direct Fuel Cell Energy Project", *WaterWorld*, Jan. 25, 2001.

[16] John K. Steckel Jr., "City Uses Microturbines to Generate Electricity from Biogas", *WaterWorld,* January, 2001.

[17] Energy Conservation in Wastewater Treatment Facilities, Water Environment Federation, 1997.

[18] *"Pump Life Cycle Costs: A Guide to LCC Analysis for Pumping Systems"*, Office of Industrial Technologies, Energy Efficiency and Renewable Energy, U.S. Department of Energy, The Hydraulic Institute, December 2000.

Chapter 34

WORKING OVERSEAS ON ENERGY MANAGEMENT PROJECTS: CULTURAL AND FINANCIAL CONSIDERATIONS

Bruce K. Colburn, Ph.D., P.E., C.E.M.
EPS Capital Corp.
Villanova, PA

ABSTRACT

The author has had the privilege and pleasure of working in 20 different countries outside the US on energy management projects, working with owners, engineers, and financial people in developing energy performance contracts. Projects were predominantly industrial plants and larger medical facilities, and a few commercial/governmental complexes, of a size and operation which lent themselves to energy performance contracting because of the utility consumption magnitude. There are some major differences between methods, procedures, guidelines, ecological rules, and "rules of thumb" which make sense in North America and much of Western Europe in general, but do not in many other locales. Availability (or lack thereof) of financing, equipment selection, labor savings benefits, past operating practices, the historical procedures from which plant equipment was planned and originally built, and cultural and philosophical factors in a given country all contribute to the final equipment and system selection process for an energy performance contract.

The twenty foreign countries in which the author has provided services include Finland, Russia, South Korea, Czech Republic, Slovakia, Poland, Hungary, Portugal, Brazil, Chile, Peru, Canada, South Africa, Philippines, India, Thailand, Japan, China, Romania, and the Caribbean islands. These countries could be divided into Soviet Bloc countries, China, Japan, other Asian countries, West Europe, South America, South Africa, and then Canada (which is virtually transparent to US methods, procedures, pricing, practices and laws). The education levels of the plant personnel, makeup of staff, past investigative efforts by plant personnel into energy cost reduction opportunities, historical trends in utility costs, availability of fuels, past government regulations and restrictions on importing or taxing such technology, and the manner of operation of the facility all vary greatly with the historical background of the country as well as the market issues. Working through

these issues to secure an implementation contract, and seeing through the implementation and acceptance testing of the final systems given the local conditions, is explored.

INTRODUCTION

The author has had the privilege of working on engineering and energy performance contracts, working with operations and people in over 20 countries around the world. As a result of this experience, spanning 27 years, certain general points and trends can be ascertained which are shared in this paper. There are certain distinctive aspects of developing contracts, prosecuting the work, and certain logistical problems which are substantially different than working in Boston, San Francisco, or Peoria which can have a profound effect on the timely and cost-effective completion of retrofit and new construction projects.

In performing engineering, construction management, project commissioning, and post-construction operation, there are many major differences between methods, procedures, guidelines, ecological rules and desires, and even "rules of thumb" which all make sense in North America and Western Europe, but do not in many other locales. Availability of financing of a length of time, with low enough interest rates, with the ability to repatriate moneys out of country to pay back project loans, and historical procedures from which plant equipment was planned and originally constructed, and the cultural and philosophical factors in a given country can contribute to the final equipment and system selection process. The work discussed will be based on the efforts by the author working with energy performance contracts, and the Investment Grade Audits (IGA) required as a prelude to the final financing and construction implementation of these projects.

The twenty foreign countries in which the author has provided services include: Finland, South Korea, Czech Republic, Slovakia, Poland, Hungary, Portugal, Brazil, Russia, Chile, Peru, Canada, South Africa, Philippines,

India, Thailand, Japan, China, Romania, and the Caribbean. For purposes of similarity, these can be categorized as Eastern Europe, Scandinavia, Southeast Asia, North America, South America, South Africa, Japan, and the Caribbean. There is a wide range of utility costs in these regions, and these utility prices can have a profound effect on the level of opportunities from energy performance contracting, and the overall attitude of plant management on energy conservation in general.

Table I below provides a comparison of electricity rates around the world (in 1998), comparing them to a common

TABLE I. UTILITY PRICE COMPARISONS

Country	Fuel Price Comparison 1998 Reference Gasoline All Prices in US Cents Per Liter	Electricity- Industrial Low	High	% Import
South Africa	43	2	3.5	
USA	33	3.5	12	49
Canada	39	2.5	5	
Dominican Rep	40	9.4	11.3	93
Brazil	80		5.8	
Chile	49		5	
Peru	55		5.5	
Philippines	34	5	6	
Thailand	30		6	
Russia	28	2.2	4.4	
Japan	102	9.5	12	97
South Korea	93		5.6	
China	28		3.2	
Portugal	102		8.1	
Poland	54		3.7	
Czech Rep.	72	3.8	5	
Slovakia	61		4.1	
Hungary	72		5.5	
Romania	53		5	
Bulgaria	66		5.5	70
Finland	117		5	
Germany	96	6	8	
India	81	7	10	
Saudi Arabia	16			5
Untaxed Retail Pump Price	21	Theoretical Base		

commodity, automobile gasoline. Since gasoline is one of the fuels often imported, its local price is a rough

indicator of other imported fuels such as diesel and coal. As can be readily seen, Brazil, Japan, Portugal, Finland, Germany, and South Korea are nearly 3 times the cost of the US prices for gasoline. Electric rates for industrial plants are shown, with approximate lows and highs; in many countries, as in the US, electric rates vary widely over the country, as can be clearly seen in Russia.

Owners Beating on Contractors for Price Concessions - A common thread in many US and Eastern European plants seemed to be a tendency to bring a project down to the absolute lowest cost possible, even stripped further than was businesslike. The author's teams witnessed a number of instances where past construction work was poor, and the subcontractors made to feel like peons. Many items of work were half done, or incomplete. We saw similar results recently in the US in a steam plant, where recently completed renovation work on a boiler system had not been done well, and inspection revealed poor materials were used (only met minimums and barely that), and poor workmanship. In the end, almost all of the work had to be thrown out by the ESCO team on the boilers and steam lines, and had the work done correctly a second time, with proper materials, new controls, professionally supervised, with written guarantees of quality and performance from competent contractors who were financially stable. So quality work was negotiated, not bid, based on quality, and results. In the end, this aided in solving some serious operating problems, improved reliability and performance, unquestionably extended the life of older equipment which otherwise would have failed in a year, and set in place retrofits with a long life, instead of saving a few dollars and leaving lots of future problems for 1-2 years from now. Basically, the owner had been "taken to cleaners" due to an overzealous push for cheap first cost. In the energy performance contracting work performed by the author's groups, certainly cost is important, and hard bidding and negotiations take place also, but from the standpoint of high quality workmanship and long term system performance, with written guarantees on performance and longevity, as opposed to simply lowest first cost. The contractor's past response to service needs, past implementation schedule adherence, quality of work, amount of extras fought for in the past are all relevant to determining the "total" cost. These issues came up repeatedly in Eastern Europe also, and there was a constant re-education process of the plant managers and engineers as regards first class workmanship suitable for long-term investments, and low first cost work meeting an arbitrary budget without regard to "performance benefits". In no way was this reflective of ignorance on the part of management, but of expanding ones horizons to include quality, performance, cost/benefit, and associated parameters such as lower maintenance costs, less labor, and more reliable operation.

NORTH AMERICA

The two countries covered here are the US and Canada. The situation in North America is well documented. Straightforward financing of almost every type, for the long term, is available. Canada has rules almost identical to the US, even as it relates to financing, and tracking, if not always precisely following FASB accounting rules. Virtually every project the author's team participated with in Canada had the same rules and procedures as anywhere in the US, with the sole exception of Quebec Province, which has special laws requiring all contracts and reports to be in French first (although English could then be used incidentally). However, there is still a certain mindset on the part of some industry management, that suggests that they saw energy savings investments more as "costs" with limited regard for the "benefit" side, even though from an intellectual viewpoint there was no question they understood the concepts completely. It was as if their businesses had been so tortured to minimize expenditures, that any expenditure for any reason other than direct productivity was virtually treated as suspect, regardless of short and long term benefits. It just goes to show that shortsightedness was not limited to Eastern Europe. Mexico, on the other hand, is quite different, with currency that is highly variable with respect to the US or Canadian dollar, with a history of graft and corruption in both government and business, government control of many industries, debt repayment problems, and currency devaluations.

EASTERN EUROPE

Eastern Europe includes all areas formerly under communist influence. What has been identified as a base situation is that the vast majority of industrial plants were designed for 100% capacity, run flat out all the time, with few provisions for efficient operations at part load; from the perspective of forced, managed economy this might make sense, but in the current free market economy with widely fluctuating demands for goods, this has been very difficult on many smaller businesses privatized or attempting to become so, due to limited capital to correct the fundamental design deficiencies. What has been quite astounding, repeatedly, is that in the majority of facilities there was an extremely high level of trained technical personnel, but with each person having a very narrow focus. Whereas a comparable US or Canadian factory might have a few technical specialists for the factory, each of these plants would have something like 5 people for every one in the North American equipment plant. For example, in Russia, each specialist was extremely well versed in his sub-discipline, but was fairly vague as soon as you got out of his narrow specialty, often referring to other persons. They tended to be amazed at the wide range

of responsibilities and knowledge that our North American technical people had, and how a small group from North America could be authorized to do so much. The expertise these people shared as a group was great and quite useful, but for our team to get decisions made by them was very time consuming, often their side referring to "needing to confer", or "others" made the final decision. Most every decision was a joint decision, made after the plant people had many, many private consultation sessions. The author also noticed that by no means were these Eastern European groups ignorant, in fact they often used this "lack of authority" to their advantage in negotiations.

It is appropriate to separate Russia proper, other CIS countries (Ukraine, Bellorus, Kazakhstan, etc.), and the other nations (so-called "Eastern Europe" excluding the Soviet Union proper) who had been under Soviet domination since WWII. Russia, as could be expected, is the most difficult to work in and obtain financing for.

Many of the factories in Eastern Europe employed large numbers of "bodies" in production tasks, somewhat to exclusion of automation; this was by far most prevalent in Russia proper. One example in a mining and mill works in Russia was for a slurry pumping system for hydrocyclones. There were manual pressure gauges located up about 30 feet above the level of pumps, and it was important to control the pressure into the hydrocyclones to control quality of output. Full time people were assigned to monitor and manually adjust the pump discharge pressure (discharge valves right off pump), a most inefficient way to do so. They had people constantly running up and down stairs, or yelling in a very loud factory trying to do their best to maintain process parameters. We showed them as part of automation upgrade how to include this as part of a variable speed drive system, eliminate manpower, reduce energy wastage, and improve process parameter control. The plant management shared that during Soviet times part of the mandate was for full employment, so there was an impetus to use people over cost effective automation, even if their technical people knew better. This type situation was encountered many times, and overcoming the historical situation was not only based on economic factors, but on the need to gradually, not quickly, convert to automation and the necessary level of production personnel.

At one large factory in Russia which our team developed and were building a retrofit project, the factory, now privatized, had previously engaged a large US management consulting firm to study and recommend management and personnel solutions; the study determined that out of 10,000 employees, the factory needed only 3600 after reorganization and training. However, factory management was slow to follow the recommendations, because of the "people problem". In remote towns there was only one factory, no other businesses, and firing everyone who was not needed could have led to senior managers being murdered in the night; one director told the author that he could have been found dead in the snow, frozen, with a bullet through his brain, and the finding would have been "death from natural causes", since the employees and indeed the whole community were so desperate for jobs after the downfall of communism and the economic upheavals which occurred in some portions of the former Soviet empire. Therefore, businesslike decisions had to be tempered by a reality of social welfare, and the need for transition, but at a pace which was relatively slow for Westerners, so that the displaced persons had time to find other employment. Also, when the soviet empire collapsed, what was owned by whom was vague. In many places, the local factory "was" the town, so there had been no separate municipal police, fire, taxing authorities, mayor, or City Council. Now these are developing. In many locations, the local factory owned the housing and was responsible for the winter space heating, plus solving social problems (how do you find housing if you are getting a divorce and everything is owned by the factory, a la the "state" who is the sole landlord and controls all apartment assignments?). Top managers acted as "God"-in free Russia, most of those managers did NOT like that at all-but had to post public hours for people to come and attempt to help them solve personal problems.

An interesting issue that came up in Russia dealt with operating window air conditioners in factory offices in the middle of winter. The majority of Russian managers smoke, and heavily, and they have decided that running air conditioners helps the situation, at a time when the outdoor temperature is 0 F. Operation of these DX units was considered a "management" function, not related to energy conservation, and no amount of sharing how the outside air could be brought in without running the DX on recirculating air (while naturally the radiators are belching out excess heat) would suffice. Therefore, an unusual case of "re-cooling" the heat in winter.

An interesting observation appeared to be that the further the country was from Moscow, the less stringent communism was, and therefore the more towards normal business practices. The Czech Republic clearly was the first to pull out of the communist malaise, and interestingly was one of the furthest away in distance from Moscow. In the Czech Republic, since it had much more experience at freedom anyway, had private ownership of homes, farms, and such, and somewhat of a normal local government structure, whereas in Russia, it was much more centralized control.

All over Eastern Europe there was an attitude of protectionism where possible with locally made equipment, even if it was inferior in most respects to other equipment. Changes were noted since 1993, however, to the point that today in the Czech Republic for instance, high quality Western equipment competes with locally made equipment, and most likely the best cost/benefit decisions will prevail, regardless of the impact on local machine companies.

Interestingly, at first the Russians were very protective of Russian equipment, and tended to insist that only Russian equipment could be purchased; this was at a time about 5 years after the downfall of Communism. Our team had to interact with the local factory engineering and management team extensively to better understand what their thinking was. Typically, it had been ingrained in them to be "cheap", since there was never enough money under the Soviet system, whereas as energy performance contractors, the author's team have endeavored to be focused on value, not merely first cost (sometimes the most expensive item is the cheapest long term investment). In one area, we broke a deadlock on disagreement by asking them "if cost was not a criterion, would they buy magnetic ore separators from Russian supplier, or from Sweden" – they would buy from Sweden they said, because it lasted much longer, and was more rugged. After reviewing the financials with these experienced Russian engineers, even they agreed that if they had the freedom, they would buy a quality product, since it lasts so much longer that on a life cycle cost basis it paid for itself to buy the better, higher cost item. They had not had much ability to consider this in the past, given that unless they could justify to Moscow, they generally were forced to purchase in-country gear, regardless of quality or reliability (they were usually allowed, however, to buy foreign manufacturing equipment if they were willing to go through a great deal of documentation and defense of the approach, even though it caused problems with hard currency transfers during the Soviet era). It should be noted, however, that to some extent that philosophy prevails in the North American industrial sector, in that lowest first cost is an extremely strong motivator, and has been a point of conflict with the performance contracting community also, requiring "enlightenment" and persuasion.

Electric utility rates varied throughout Russia, as in the US. Industrial rates varied from about 2.2 cents/KWH to 4.4 cents, which is very low relative to US costs. However, when one considers a disconnect between what the "country" spent on the electric infrastructure, and the current utility rates which were more designed to capture certain costs and not recover all the true sunk capital, one understands better that some of the legacy of the old regime continued distortion in the electric markets. However, when one goes to add a new electric generating plant, or build new transmission capacity, there can be some shock when the true costs of this infrastructure are revealed, and political issues arise as to how the cost recovery can be implemented without some major dissatisfaction with business and residences when they learn of "rate shock", namely being exposed to the real cost of electric power generation, transmission and distribution.

Interestingly, power reliability tended to be high, perhaps because there was not necessarily a relationship between charged rates and real costs. What was apparent was that the low utility rates made it difficult to develop programs which paid for themselves from energy savings. One area, however, where electric rates were unusually high was in demand. In most of Eastern Europe, they had very high demand charges, and many different demand charges. In one area in Karelia in Northwest Russia, each large user had to "order" his demand for one month in the future, and there was a "reservation charge" for ordering this demand. Separate from this was the measured actual demand and charges. However, if the factory had a demand use higher than the previously ordered peak demand, then the entire bill had the demand charges increased 10 times, not just on the increment over the peak projected, but on all demand use. As a result, it was almost unheard of for a firm to exceed the projected demand, since it was far cheaper to shut portions of a factory down and send workers home paid, rather than face the penalties on electric demand surcharges. Interestingly, in such cases, plant management would claim that electric demand was a pure factory management control function, and had nothing to do with technical control, so they would not allow electric demand savings to be counted as a "benefit". Only the incremental KWH cost, which was often less than 2 cents US/KWH, could be counted toward savings. They would only allow demand credits if we saved a large amount on the demand usage, say more than 25% of their entire projected electric demand bill, and could prove it. It is a situation which had not been encountered anywhere in the world by our team previously. Naturally, as a result, some very reasonable electric savings measures were rejected.

Customs duties and border crossing issues were a concern for imported equipment. For countries like the Czech Republic and Poland, this was not a problem, since they had always had close ties with West Germany, and other European countries due to proximity. However, with Russia there was great concern. Our team members had all heard of problems with bribes, and Mafia connections with customs offices, and as a result, the EPS first project in Russia was specifically selected near the Finnish border, where the factory actually wanted to do the project, and understood the import rules well, since they had been dealing with the West since the factory first opened in the 1970's. As a result, the factory became our ally in avoiding customs problems, and with a contract which was open book, could assist in controlling costs through

insuring only the essential customs duties were charged, and avoiding issues of lawlessness and graft with local government employees. Our team heard of one case where some gas turbines were shipped into a northern port in Russia by a US firm, loaded on trucks, but by the time the trucks got to their destination (about 1000 km away), all the copper had been stripped off the generators, and the truck drivers seemed to know nothing about how this occurred; the next time that US firm shipped a series of recip generators, they hired soldiers of fortune, one for each generator unit, and they carried Uzis and sat on the equipment across the ocean, and on the trucks, and when confronted by some suspicious trucks, they all showed their Uzis and they looked threatening, and all the equipment was safely delivered to end user-a form of "insurance" (the guards were only paid on successful receipt of goods by owner, but of course they were well paid for their services). There is still some of this, but lawlessness is better controlled now even in remote Russian areas. In Poland, Czech Republic, Slovakia, and Hungary these things were unheard of, and fortunately not issues to be confronted today as a project developer.

Obtaining insurances in the Eastern Bloc was a problem after freedom came, even in countries such as Czech Republic which had a history of close ties to the West during the Soviet era. Since everything had been state controlled during the Soviet era, there had been no need for payment and performance bonds (the government self insured themselves, since everything was expropriated by the "state" anyway), building insurance, shipping insurance, etc. and so implementing projects post-communism meant generally working with small firms which were simply groups of individuals who had been part of state owned large operations. One had to use "gut" insight to identify those firms with no balance sheet, to ascertain who was worthwhile to work with, since no insurance protection was available. A good point is that theft of equipment is rare, something that still continues in an inner city construction project in a poor area in the heart of the US.

Work in the western part of Eastern Europe was quite normal, and the problems were just businesslike. Utility rates, although lower than in Western Europe, were beginning to increase, as part of a push to free market rates to rid the government of subsidies which distorted free market planning.

An interesting sideline was that all over Eastern Europe, the fresh water was clean, without worry of getting "Montezuma's Revenge" or something as debilitating. This is even more amazing when you consider that the waste treatment was very poor to non-existent, with rivers and lakes very polluted in the past due to direct dumping of human waste and industrial effluents, much as used to occur in North America and Western Europe.

Czech Republic and Slovakia – These countries, formerly the single Czechoslovakia, had the best set of commercial and business codes shortly after the overthrow of communism, and therefore were poised for Western investment the earliest. Clearly, the Czech Republic was the first to privatize the former state owned businesses in Eastern Europe, and the quickest to adapt; unfortunately, Slovakia was stigmatized with former communist leaders who were more focused on cronyism for awhile than with honesty and helping the citizens. However, because of the countrys' locations near Western Europe, and a long history of cooperation with West Germany even during the Cold War, these nations moved rapidly to privatize and encourage private investment. This has paid handsome dividends in particular for the Czechs, whose standard of living has increased dramatically over the last 12 years of freedom. At one point, in Prague the unemployment rate was about 0.8%, at a time when substantial numbers of foreign workers were streaming in to support the expanding economy there. One area which also set a pattern was that after the end of communism, the government vowed to move towards free market prices for utilities, and to make their currency convertible to the West and they did just that. The strong industrial tradition dates back to when Bohemia and Moravia were the economic engine of the Austro-Hungarian Empire.

An area where one normally considers energy cost effective payback to be a "slam dunk" is lighting retrofit, but in these two countries, that opportunity was gone because as soon as electric prices started increasing after freedom, people just turned the lights off except as absolutely necessary. During the day, lights were rarely on in offices, factories, schools, hospitals, and government centers. It is hard to have such measures pay when the baseline is near zero KWH consumption. To illustrate this point, the author was in Slovakia for a meeting at an industrial plant, and ushered into a large room, where the lights were off. Since it was relatively dingy in there, the papers which had been brought could not be read, so the author turned the lights on, which were fine; in walks the Plant Director and goes through formal introductions, looks around the room, leaves and comes back with some burly men who promptly moved all the furniture over to the window, turned off the lights, and left – unfortunately, the glare was so severe that it left the author with a headache, but it did result in reduced utility expenses!

Financing projects is much less of an issue now in the Czech Republic, due to the crown Czech becoming fully convertible for most business purposes since the latter 90's; as a result, Czech Republic is the first post-communist country to receive an investment-grade credit rating by international credit institutions. In Slovakia, financing projects is still somewhat of a problem.

Romania – One problem still experienced in 2002 is that the real cost of district heating is still not being passed through to the end users in Romania, by law/decree. Municipalities may have operators run the facility, but by law the municipality must take responsibility for providing heat regardless of the ability of people to pay for the heat (the poor often pay nothing for their heat), and as a result municipal governments in general see 20-40% of their budgets still taken up as heating subsidies. From an energy efficiency standpoint, this is serious, since end users have little incentive to conserve (seeing only low, subsidized utility rates), and the municipalities have a great incentive to improve energy efficiency because of the cost burdens, but because of the past communist governments and the subsidies, the municipal governments are poor, and obtaining financing is difficult. One special difficulty is that the law does not allow the district heating assets to be pledged for debt; only the taxing authority revenues in general can be employed.

The national government, and municipalities have been slow to respond, but are hampered by lack of economic growth and real increases in consumer spending, hence the political difficulty of merely passing the real fuel costs through, for fear of a backlash at the polls, or worse, rioting due to lack of heat, which is considered a basic right in this country.

Similarly the past political system due to a virtual dictatorship during the communist era led to inefficiencies in manufacturing, and a disconnect between factory systems and market demand. Utility rates are low, about 5 cents/KWH. Fuel prices are not necessarily seen by heat users, since they are subsidized. So even in the year 2002 district heating systems are still being run something akin to that under communism, even though it is clear that free market prices is the best way ultimately. It is a sad legacy of the days under communist rule, where free market and incentives were not allowed.

Hungary – This country was much like Czech Republic and Poland, in that industrial plants were stifled in innovation, and utility costs were not free market originally. Now fuel prices and electricity prices have been rising, reasonable investment is occurring, and the industrial plants are modernizing. Environmental rules continue to be stiffened, which is causing reinvestment in order to stay in business; as a result, the air and water quality is improving, and the "forced" improvements in the plants is aiding in the energy conservation area also. The language is not Slavic or Roman, having roots the same as the Finns, so the language is quite unique. It is one of the leaders of the Eastern European countries in eliminating the shackles of communism quickly. Except for the language barrier, contract negotiations are quite normal.

Poland - Poland follows much the same way as the Czech Republic, with a strong economic push for privatization and economic reform. It was a key part of the Austro Hungarian Empire in the 19th Century, and in the 1980's made headlines because of the Solidarity Movement which challenged communist control. It is a country deeply rooted in the Catholic religion, something even the Communists could not destroy, with strong Christian values. As a result, it has been one of the leading Eastern European countries to pull out of the Post-Soviet malaise, along with the Czech Republic and Hungary. Projects can be financed there, although there are problems, and the governments have been honest, and the utility prices increasing, although in a predictable manner. Plant managers and engineers, as elsewhere in Eastern Europe, are highly educated, but in the main the factories are still in major need of overhaul. Contracts and business negotiations are normal, and reasonable.

PORTUGAL

Portugal has a fairly robust economy recently, and has national legislation encouraging cogeneration, with rules similar to the PURPA laws of 1978, with similar requirements for need for utilizing process heat. In return, the cogenerator could sell back to the electric grid at published prices. In general, a reasonable concept.

However, in Portugal, the approach for ESCOs became one of requiring them to do all the work up front for free, with no signed agreements of any sort, and then finally someone (not necessarily the most cost effective proposal) would be selected. Unfortunately, in Portugal in particular, some distorted sense of reality led many large users to seek proposals from firms, based on the false premise that the Owners would receive huge cash benefits from on-site cogeneration projects, expectations which were completely unreasonable, and not borne out anywhere else in the world. As a result, there has been much talk and little action, but much cash and effort outlay by performance contractors. Portugal being one of the poorest countries in Western Europe, still allowed use of bunker fuel for generators, which then only added to air pollution. Because most of the fuels were imported with high taxes, fuel was expensive. During the late 90's natural gas lines were being developed as gas from France and North Africa was gradually brought in, displacing heavy fuel oil (bunker fuels) in many instances. Energy efficiency has been encouraged through membership in the EU, which has provided energy savings grants to encourage both energy efficiency and pollution reduction. Factory engineers were quite experienced, but the model was more like the US in

that the ranks were very thin, with each engineer technically capable in multiple areas. The majority of managers and engineers spoke English reasonably well.

JAPAN

For Asia, Japan stood out as somewhat unusual, so is singled out here. They have been very successful in developing a large heavy industrial base which supports itself through massive exports throughout the world. Once considered the junk capital of manufacturing, it is now perceived as one of the world's leaders in quality manufacturing. The companies have been successful despite the fact that approximately 97% of all energy is imported, and therefore utility costs are high. Industrial electrical rates on the order of 10-14 cents/KWH are the norm. Natural gas and and propane cost on the order of 10-12 dollars/MMBTU when US prices were about $3/MMBTU nat gas or less. Therefore, in order to be competitive, the Japanese have become very energy efficient, as the counter to high unit energy prices. Their labor costs have also become very expensive, equaling or exceeding US costs, and this has imposed burdens on them, which are partially balanced through high use of automation in factories. It just goes to show that high utility costs do not necessarily lead to stunted growth, as long as there is progressive management looking at cost and benefit, and not merely first cost.

However, what was surprising is that equipment prices were very high for Japanese products, and sky-high for imported goods. They place high import duties on foreign gear, or use arguments why such equipment could not be accepted into Japanese society. For example, 2 lamp T-8 electronic ballasts cost about $44 in Japan in 1999, versus about $12 in US for comparable products; more astounding, the companies we worked with did not wish to use foreign products even if they were better or cheaper. For example, solar film which we would pay about $1-$2/sq ft installed in the US, was being charged at about $6-$7/sq.ft in Japan, even for the same material (we had one specific material, for which they provided us cutsheets, which is manufactured in US and was the basis for the pricing-when the local Japanese suppier was asked why the pricing was so high, one got a circular story that made no sense, including our following up with the US supplier and its pricing in the US)

For project financing, interest rates are extremely low in Japan, about 3% (passbook interest for general consumers was often less than 1%). This was a positive point, naturally, but with the extremely high equipment prices and high labor costs, it was still difficult to develop a cost-effective energy performance program.

One also felt that at all times, the technical parties on the other side were extremely attentive, and carefully evaluating all that was said and shown. This US project developer, however, tended to feel that every bit of knowledge was being "sucked" out of us, and then we would be left high and dry, which is essentially what happened after limited success. The technical skills of the teams interacted with were superb, however, and their focus on business was near absolute. An interesting sideline was that after a long meeting at a company concerning financing, at about 9 PM we broke up and when walking out, noticed that the main work floor was full of people still, and inquiries indicated that about 90% were still there from day shift, because they "chose" to stay late.

SOUTHEAST ASIA

The countries covered are South Korea, Thailand, and India.

South Korea – a somewhat unique situation in this country is that all ESCO work is expected to be free until the final implementation agreement is signed; no one will commit to have an ESCO do study work and then have a contingent liability. They are brutal on profit margins. KEMCO, the national electric utility, somewhat controls electricity prices in the country, and has been a bit discouraging for other ESCOs. Despite these shortcomings, ESCO work has begun and had some success; individual relationships seem to be critical to success, with the contracts later being more of a formality; in the interim, however, any ESCO would likely be gnashing their teeth in fear of "the deal" collapsing before final signing approval. The industrial plants all had very capable technical personnel, but generally they viewed ESCOs as almost vendors, not as partnership arrangements.

India - India could be viewed as a sleeping giant that has awakened. It has a population equal to the combined sum of Europe, North America, and South America, with a large industrial base which continues to grow and expand. Profits are up, and there are the beginnings of an in-country push for air and water pollution reduction, even at the expense of jobs. Therefore, the industries are very concerned about total operating costs, because the environmental demands require ever more growing amounts of capital (read profits) to be deployed. The electricity situation varies widely, as in the US. In some of its states, there are severe power shortages, such as Karnataka, and in other areas such as Mumbai (Bombay) there is plenty of power. West Bengal used to have power shortages, but allowed IPPs to come in (previously controlled by the various state electricity boards only), and now prices there are down substantially and there is plenty

of reliable power in that state; it seems to show that free enterprise can work there.

All electric power for industrials is expensive, though because of a government plan to capture more of the costs from industrials to subsidize agriculture and low end residential users. In fact, the rate tariffs are the reverse of most of the world, in that the last KWH will be the most expensive, not the least expensive. This is great for energy cost savings, but bad from the plant management viewpoint. With utility rates averaging about 8 cents/KWH or more, there are usually reasonable energy cost savings opportunities.

One drawback is that many plants are owned by individuals or small family groups, who run them in a paternalistic manner, with decisions made by one or two people, sometimes on a whim, which makes it difficult to pin down management attitudes until late in the situation. The larger businesses, however, are run much like the US and Europe, with business concerns and needs similar. An interesting anecdote is that all public companies must provide details on energy usage in their annual reports, by law, and some provide detailed information on past investments, current plans, separating cogenerated power from purchased electricity for instance.

An observation was that most electrical equipment with motors were equipped with surge supressors to protect devices from repeated, unscheduled power interruptions. For example, virtually all window A/C units have this feature in homes and apartments for protection. The author was in Delhi on business when repeated power outages occurred over a three day period, which turned out to be a complicated situation with weather, lack of coal (caused by lack of payments by electric company, caused in turn by lack of payments by citizens and businesses) and continuing economic growth which was not being matched by new electrical capacity.

In offices, most computer and telecommunication circuits are special, isolated circuits and may have UPS's plus generators on that line, so as to insure reliable power for business purposes. If the power goes out on the grid, they can keep the main business matters running or at least perform orderly shutdowns, even though there were no lights, and it was very hot, since often the A/C was not backed up, even though many of the office buildings did not have operable windows; it was not unusual to arrive for a meeting and find that the power went out 3 hours before, but doors are propped open and people were expected to work with no lights, no air flow, and high outdoor temperatures (95F or so). However, in many other places, the facility had 100% diesel backup, with automatic switchover gear, so that about 60 seconds after power outage full standby power was in operation. All the better hotels had 100% diesel backup, and some were even driven on cogeneration equipment, with the grid as backup, due to the concerns on power reliability.

In business meetings, almost all discussions were in English. Virtually every factory dealt with had extremely competent technical personnel, most trained in India, Britain, or North America (due to English language being the primary Indian business language). The drinking water almost throughout the country is not suitable for Westerners, so one learned to carry bottled water almost everywhere each day for protection. The normal business in a factory is somewhat contrasted by the roadways with the poor. In some areas, people were so poor that they used pick axes to dig up the highway blacktop and burn as fuel for cooking; this was personally observed, in addition to the slums of Calcutta, which are as terrible as any description ever written. Because of the high electricity rates, businesses are focused more on cost control. Fuels are very expensive also, since much is imported. The coal used in-country is generally very poor quality, leading to high air pollution, which is now under attack by the government. In North America in industrial plants it is common to focus on thermal savings, whereas in India the focus tends to be more on electricity consumption reduction due to the very high electric rates.

Some impediments to energy retrofits are that (1) one must have governmental approval to import anything, based on its "foreign currency balance", and (2) customs duties on much non-Indian equipment is on the order of 35% of cost, clearly designed to encourage in-country products and services, even when no quality product equivalent existed. Therefore, even something as simple as standard T-8 lamps and ballasts were quite expensive, since at the time of work no in-country production was found; the only places with both a large need and the foreign currency reserves available tended to be large hotels. Also, it tended to be only in the hotels that lighting was run all the time and of a type and quantity similar to the US ; most of the offices and factories used lighting quite sparingly, again because of high utility costs, costs which, relative to the salaries of people, would be the purchasing power equivalent of about 60 US cents/KWH, a situation that clearly would also force North Americans to rethink the importance of lighting in daily work tasks. The very high customs duties generally forced one to find ways to use in-country resources, or to uncover joint ventures with Western organizations where the product was built in country, but strictly based on the Western design and technology tools; even then, the product was often inferior, but at least cost effective.

One trivial point that Westerners must get used to is that most of the automobile drivers on the highway seem to be somewhat crazy. In towns, taxis routinely travel about 6"

apart going 45 miles an hour in extremely high density traffic. The author probably lost 10 years of life due to fright. But again, it is just the way the Indians have learned to cope with overpopulation and yet "get the job done". India is clearly a place where business is thriving, high utility rates have been met with adaptive solutions, customs duties have not thwarted obtaining the key benefits of worldwide innovation, and poverty has not stifled innovation.

Thailand - In Thailand, many Western businesses have set up joint ventures, or separate in-country corporations; Kimberly Clark, ABB and many others are among those firms. Electric utility rates are medium priced, with average industrial KWH charges of 5-6 cents. Because so much energy is imported, the government is focusing more on energy efficiency. The first national ESCO program for industrials was funded in 2001. There are procedures for applying for customs reductions on selected energy efficiency equipment.. Pollution in Bangkok is so severe that people are dying from the air; an article in Fortune magazine referred to a scientific study done on dogs in Bangkok, and it was learned that about 70% of the dogs had the lungs of a human smoker who had been smoking heavily for 50 years. The government is beginning to crack down on pollution now, though. Auto traffic is terrible in the larger cities, and is a major source of energy wastage.

Because of the "Asian Flu", many firms have been reluctant to upgrade their facilities, due to the unknowns of future product sales, and in general the reduction in sales they have experienced over the last few years. However, there are always good firms interested in controlling their operating costs long term. Business negotiations are quite normal there.

Much of the electricity is via the PEA (Provincial Electric Authority), with EGAT (Energy Generating Authority of Thailand) the overall electricity supplier. The PEA power was quite reliable, but some of the MEAs (Municipal Electric Authorities) could demonstrate voltage sags and power dropouts which can be quite disruptive to many industrial processes, especially those such as spinning and weaving, which then requires resetting each machine, and in many locations sending out maintenance and production people to manually restart each device, and then reset, stabilize, restart and tune up, and then finally allow production to restart.

Philippines – The Philippines are actually over 7000 islands, spread North to South. As a result, electric power and fuel are a problem on many of the smaller islands (after Luzon and Mindanao, the largest ones), since not all have the same mineral and forest situations. As a result, Napacor, the national electric grid, has faced a daunting task over the decades, providing reliable power at a reasonable price. Because the country is so poor, many policies are based on forms of barter. For example, in processing sugar cane at mills, refineries routinely "charge" a portion of the output product as the "tolling fee"; in such cases, any operating cost reductions in practice accrue to the refinery owners, who tend to be wealthy private individuals. Electric rates are medium prices, but due to this situation with operating cost reductions, and the razor thin margins, unusual practices sometimes occur, which are difficult to bring value to from energy performance contracting. For example, at one sugar mill, the owner, believing he had found a "good deal" on a generator, purchased an old 2400 volt unit, which then after delivery the plant engineering people discovered in fact was 2400 volt diesel generator which then required special transformers and switching gear, used of course, and then a lot of work to get functioning, whereupon the unit threw a rod and was useless until rebuilt, which since the generator was on a remote island, required dismantling, and shipment by barge (on a space available basis to save money), and then many weeks to repair. All in all, an expensive "cheap" piece of (used) equipment. Although an extreme example, this is the backdrop to many factories as regards equipment upgrade. In addition, since many of the island industries hark back to the days of the Spanish Empire before the Spanish-American War of 1898, the plantations have workers, who by law now are almost guaranteed ownership of cane fields of 80 acres, are splintered so if one wanted to negotiate a "deal" to sweep the fields a second time after harvesting (for cane trash as fuel for cogeneration boilers), it is a major social effort, whereas many years ago one could get a half dozen planters in a room and make a deal in a few hours that would cover thousands of workers. Because the Philippine peso is so variable, it is difficult to obtain long-term financing in anything except Western currencies, which then exposes the borrower to currency devaluation and currency conversion risks. One has the other extreme, where in Makati City, a suburb of Manilla, it looks like Suburban Atlanta, with very expensive shops and restaurants. In general, doing business in this country is very difficult, although the larger factories had very capable technical people who were innovative in order to aid the factory in making money during this period of "Asian Flu" economically.

SOUTH AMERICA

Chile/Peru - Chile is a highly stable economy, with low inflation, deregulated electric markets, and stable financing situation. Electric rates vary from 4.5-6 cents/KWH all in. Since electricity is deregulated, one can negotiate rate programs under a free market. Chile looks like one is in the middle of Western Europe, and all the factories dealt with were staffed by highly professional managers with excellent technical staffs. It was much like the US in terms of business practices and business negotiations.

Next door neighbor Peru is not as industrialized, much poorer, but with similar electric rates as Chile. Financing projects is much more difficult in Peru. Most financing projects, even for house mortgages, were tied to the US dollar, so that effectively the local interest rates were irrelevant in determining loan interest rates, they instead tied to US dollar purchasing power. This is good for the finance companies, but potentially bad for the citizens if their local currency (Solas) substantially devalued with respect to the US dollar. The electric grid was unusually dependent on hydro-electric power. When a flood occurred in 1998, factories and towns were flooded and shut down for months, either due to direct flooding or lack of electricity for operation. Just as in the US, however, hydroelectric power is cheap when available; the problem is when no more hydro of consequence is available, the next fossil fuel plant built generates power at much higher costs, as has happened elsewhere in South America.

Brazil – Brazil is a dynamic economy, with about 160 million people and a substantial industrial base, with professional management and highly skilled plant technical personnel. Because of serious past problems with the currency, however, financing projects is difficult in country, and almost all loans are tied to Western currencies such as US dollar, Japanese Yen, or similar (Deutschmark, Euro). Electric power rates have been historically quite low, and as a result, plant designs and layouts are geared more for production. However, a national problem for years has been lack of peak power, and it is common throughout the country for the period from about 4PM – 7 PM weekdays to be "blackout", wherein if an industrial plant wants the power, they can have it, but the rates during that period are about 10 times normal, with both special demand and energy charges. As a result, most of the factories shut down production during that period. This is most wasteful. About 93% of the electricity in country is generated by hydro, and due to severe droughts for the last few years, there is a national push from the President down to reduce permanently electricity consumption. This has been difficult in the past, because with such low electric rates, energy retrofit measures for electricity had poor payouts, and there were few financial incentives available from government agencies to "buydown" energy efficiency measures.

One of the problems in Brazil is still the old tendency for "baksheesh", wherein some management and government personnel still expect extra compensation on the side; our team was fortunate not to personally encounter this. This would distort the free market selection of energy services based on pure free market benefits and performance; it has continued to distort opportunities for energy cost reduction in the country, and is part of an on-going, old problem for about 100 years. There is mounting evidence, however, that through education and reform, this old practice is slowly dying out, to the betterment of the country and its businesses.

SCANDINAVIA

Finland – Finland was the only country in Scandinavia where direct work was performed by the author. Other projects in Eastern Europe did require interaction with firms in other countries in Scandinavia, but no particular factories were involved, except Finland. Finland is a highly developed country, with very clean, energy efficient factories, with a very high standard of living. Having worked at a factory in Russia only 40 km from Finland, even the Russians in the town noted that the lowest level Finnish truck driver lived quite well, and the Russian learned that even truck driver had summer houses on lakes in Finland, so the Russians had first hand information that what they had heard surreptitiously from VOA and BBC about the economic strength in the West was true. Finnish electric rates run from 5-6 cents/KWH, which is higher than in Russia, but not that much higher. Environmental laws have forced substantial reworking of industrial processes, and as part of this effort, energy efficiency was included, since if you have to spend much money just to meet government environmental regulations, it is often not that much more expensive to add a high level of energy efficiency. Therefore, the environmental movement might be more the basis of the high energy efficiency achieved in Finland, although due to the high profit levels in general, on-going re-investment has occurred on a continuing basis.

In business matters, the Finns can be very tough in negotiations. But being Western in nature, they are focused on business in a way which is not that much different from the US. They are tenacious, however, as the Russians and the Germans learned in WWII when for a long time about 3 million Finns held off the Nazis and Soviets who invaded them. Unusual to many Americans is that there are two official languages in Finland, Finn and Swedish; the third, unofficial language, is English, which is spoken by the majority of college educated managers and engineers.

CHINA

The work experience was limited to Yunnan Province in Southern mainland China, dealing with biomass power generation from rubber trees. The Chinese Yuan, or Renminbi, is not directly convertible except through Hong Kong, and continues to devalue. One of the major impediments there is that individual business relationships have much more meaning than a signed legal contract; some parties feel almost insulted when one insists on signed contracts such as in North America and Europe.

Being that the government is communist, contracts and payments from the Chinese side can be ignored anyway, if a government official wishes. Government graft and corruption have been a problem in developing contractual relationships in many cases. The profit motive was not huge issue in this remote province. Solving social problems was important, such as providing jobs for people Following negotiating sessions, there was a need for the other side to always prepare formal "protocols" and make up documents, decorated with pretty ribbons, to prove that effort occurred, even if the substance of a series of meetings was to decide that another set of meetings would occur in the future; the meeting and process was proof to their bosses that good work was underway. From US business perspective, this is expensive, time consuming and wasteful. One also learns that very few Chinese will tell you they do not have the authority to negotiate or sign a contract, and in fact will go out of their way to convince you they do, but when the moment of reckoning occurs, things fall apart. But in fact, bosses with legal authority are very few.

There was a clear lack of understanding of business needs, risk, interlinked contracts for various parts of the work scope, and the reasons for this; it was as if their perspective was a need, and "fill the square" by shaking hands, and that was that. Their typical cost/KWH was low, but for the biomass project, it was discussed the need to receive about 8 cents/KWH, since fuel was not available all year, due to the Monsoon season. A large problem there was a lack of transmission capacity in the Southern region – it is difficult to build a power plant if there were no means to distribute the power to end users. There was strong resistance to change – resistant to ways to upgrade lines to promote investment. To them, it was have the new electric generator first, then build the new electric line later to service it, and we tried to get them to understand that the load capacity had to be there to encourage people to come and invest. To build a power plant, we needed to know we could sell the power and get it distributed. Some mental philosophical differences due to the communist thinking, and therefore a challenge for businessmen experienced at free market decision thinking.

One important point in China is that for power projects, the ultimate purchaser is almost always the local, state or national government, or national utility. If one has a contract with them, and the state is upset with the private power plant or its managers, for any reason, perceived or real, it is simply amazing how the moneys due do not come in a timely manner, but after "renegotiation" of the contract under terms favorable to the state or key individuals, the moneys due the private company start coming reliably again, albeit at a lower amount. In China, the contract is not as important as the long term relationships, and this naturally hurts the ability to obtain long term international financing under reasonable terms.

SOUTH AFRICA

The utility rates in South Africa were especially low, due to extensive use of low cost, poor quality coal, and the past labor practices which kept worker wages low. As a result, there were very low electric rates, but with very polluted air, which generally looked blue green and definitely had a smell of smoke near some of the urban areas (just as used to happen in the US in the 1950s). Lighting opportunities were limited, because, although from the outside most buildings looked normal to North Americans, inside most of the lighting was what would be considered cheap, poor quality, and clearly not part of interior design considerations. Similar findings occurred with the HVAC systems in new buildings; they existed, but in most cases seemed to be a hodge podge of pieces of equipment, with little regard for central heating and cooling. However, lest one think that the people were not creative, the very situation of very low electric rates had spawned entire cottage industries of electric heat pump storage systems, special design configurations for utilizing cheap electric power off peak (usually no demand charge at night), and storing heating and cooling generated at night, much as is done with thermal (cooling) storage in the US, but with both heating and cooling. Special sizing considerations then came into play to allow equipment to run during the day at low load levels, yet over a 24 hour period meet the overall comfort demands, whether in factories or offices, and yet keep the capital costs down, a typical trade off situation common with such configurations in North America. However, the innovative engineers there had taken such design considerations to the extreme, yet the results worked, and the costs were reasonable; just another example of where innovation and creativity in energy conservation can overcome very low utility rates. Some of the cooling projects at large, underground mines led to very challenging situations, since the cooling was not only part of a mine comfort issue, but a key part of life safety, since the cooling was required to allow for humans to work in very deep mines where temperatures otherwise could reach 150 F consistently, which is unworkable.

CARIBBEAN

The Caribbean is somewhat unique, with many of the locations being isolated island nations, which each need to provide sufficient electricity and fuels for tourism, business, industry, and general commerce. Therefore, because of their isolated locations throughout the Caribbean Sea, a vast area, each entity generally has to be complete, with its own backup and all reserve margins required with no help from any other island. Distances in many cases preclude undersea power cable connections.

Imported fuels are 80-100% of the total used. Except for islands such as Bahamas, Bermuda, Martinique, and the Netherland Antilles, fresh water is not up to US standards. Resort areas on most of these islands expect, but rarely achieve, US and Canadian standards for air, water and electricity reliability. Very high electric utility rates – typically 10 cents to 14 cents per KWH average, with industrial plant rates slightly lower. Some island nations have problems with government rules and regulations for foreign exchange repatriation to pay for debt service for investments, which creates impediments for long-term investment.

Construction often costs more than in the US because generally everything must be shipped in, including cranes, tools, materials, and related items, depending upon the particular island; one can not expect to go down to the nearest lumber yard, steel yard, or hardware store and have all of the supplies immediately available. In places like Puerto Rico that is not the case, but in places like Haiti and Aruba, one must plan all logistics, and bring most of the basic construction tools and equipment along with them.

Some locations, such as Dominican Republic, are a dichotomy; next door to Haiti on the same island, the Dominican Republic has a thriving economy attracting foreign investment while next door Haiti seems to get worse, and with no end in sight. In the Dominican Republic, for example, most of the key infrastructure utilities are in place, but more quality infrastructure utility systems are needed, and the crane (i.e. construction) seems to have become the "national bird" of the island, due to all of the new construction underway, and the government focus on growth.

Chapter 35

ACHIEVING ENERGY EFFICIENCY IN BUILDINGS THAT UTILIZE SUBSIDIZED ELECTRICAL ENERGY

Fatouh A. Al-Ragom, CEM
Kuwait Institute for Scientific Research – Kuwait

ABSTRACT

This paper explores the potential of improving energy efficiency in buildings that utilizes subsidized electrical energy. As an example, in Kuwait the government subsidizes 85% of the cost of electricity. In addition, the customer pays a fixed figure cost that is 2 fils/kWh (0.006 $/kWh). This has lead to escalation in the demand of electrical energy until it reached alarming levels at the early eighties. For this reason a code of practice for energy conservation was developed to set out limits for the electrical requirements of air-conditioning systems for buildings incorporating energy conservation measures. The code stipulates energy conservation measures and limits for different types of buildings. However, the code does not recommend measures to optimize energy consumption. In view of this, the work demonstrated in this paper aims at controlling the wastage in building energy consumption, particularly in office buildings and improving their energy efficiency. The procedures considered to achieve efficient energy utilization, focused on improving building operation strategies particularly the operation of the air-conditioning and lighting systems.

The methodology involved a walk-through energy audit followed by a standard energy audit. In addition, building historical energy consumption data were collected and analyzed to determine the waste in energy consumption and thus establish opportunities for energy savings. Several energy efficient operation strategies were recommended, out of which few were actually implemented and their actual energy savings were verified.

Since the improvement of the building energy efficiency involved modifications of operation strategies for the building systems, estimated savings are achieved at no cost. It was found that the savings are substantial from two different perspectives the financial and environmental one. Although, the energy audit was actually conducted to a single office building, the savings were reflected on 800 office buildings in order to determine the national benefits. The estimated national financial benefits were found to be 22 million KD (70 million $). Moreover, the predicted environmental benefit indicated a reduction in the power plants emissions by 749 million kg of CO_2.

This paper concluded that the foreseen benefits of improving buildings energy efficiency on the national level, outweighs those on the individual level. For that reason, it is suggested that the government should adapt a national energy efficient building operation campaign.

Keywords: Energy monitoring and analysis, Performance contracting, Energy Efficiency

INTRODUCTION

The availability of cheap electrical energy in Kuwait created an ignorant sense among the users in all building classifications with regards to their consumption. Whether the buildings are privately owned or owned by the government, the sense of awareness for energy conservation is almost negligible. Consequently, there has been a significant increase in the national annual electricity consumption. During the past decade the per capita annual electricity consumption increased by over 50% [3]. Future consumption trend will continue to escalate if energy conservation and efficient energy management polices are not enforced. Energy efficiency of buildings can be achieved through energy auditing by reducing energy consumption. For that reason, the upper management of the Kuwait Institute for Scientific Research (KISR) has wisely decided to audit the institute's main building. Although the building energy consumption was being monitored by the Facility Management and Service Department (FM&SD), only minimal efforts were taken to cut down the building's energy consumption and it was mainly concerned with the lighting system. For that reason KISR's upper management requested the Department of Building and Energy Technologies (BET) of KISR to conduct an energy audit for the building in order to minimize the building energy consumption with minimal cost.

BUILDING CHARACTERISTICS

The Kuwait Institute for scientific Research owns several buildings scattered throughout the country.

The management and the majority of the employees are situated in the main building. The building was built in 1986 and can be categorized as an office/research building. The building envelope is considered energy efficient as it incorporates insulation materials in the wall and roof sections as well as double-glazing system. The building utilizes electrical energy for the provision of the building energy requirements. The major electricity end users of the building are the air-conditioning system (A/C), the lighting system, and the office and lab equipment. For the past few years the building energy consumption was almost constant. The annual electricity bill for KISR's main building is approximately KD 25,000 ($80,645). Working out the consumption from the rate that is 2fils/kWhr ($0.006/kWhr), the bill indicates an annual energy consumption of 12,500 MWh.

The building comprises of private offices, partitioned offices, a library, an auditorium, a cafeteria, meeting rooms and labs. The building has a 23470 m^2 of living space area. A huge area of the building is dedicated for experimental labs. Almost 54% of the air-conditioned area is dedicated to the labs excluding the basement area. The building is a two-story building with a basement that includes emergency shelters, tunnels and enclosure of electrical cabling and connections. The architectural plans of the building are shown in Figures 1 and 2. The building incorporates a building automation system (BAS) that is utilized as an alarm-monitoring station [7]. Furthermore, It is used to monitor the air-conditioning system operation, mainly the inlet and outlet temperatures of the chillers and air-handling units (AHUs). The BAS is also used to monitor alarm status of fire distinguishing system.

To meet the building air-conditioning (A/C) requirements, the A/C system comprised of 10 air-cooled chillers, each of 373 kW rated capacity. Two are standby. The A/C system included 4 chilled water pumps to circulate the chilled water, one of which is a standby. The chilled water pumps require 75 kW each. The building is regularly utilizing three chilled water pumps all year round as well as a minimum of one chiller during the winter season to a maximum of six chillers at the peak of the summer season [8].

The building lighting system mainly consists of fluorescent lamps. Other types of lamps were utilized including incandescent, parlamps and spotlights. In addition special task lights were utilized such as the emergency lights [1].

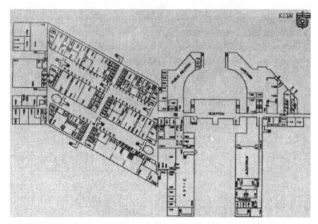

FIG. 1 MAIN BUILDING ARCHITECTURAL PLAN - GROUND FLOOR

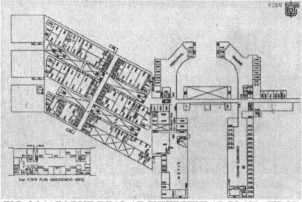

FIG. 2 MAIN BUILDING ARCHITECTURAL PLAN - FIRST FLOOR

METHODOLOGY

As a first step in energy auditing, a walk-through was conducted to determine easily spotted misuse of energy by end user, mainly A/C and lighting systems. A detailed survey was conducted later to investigate the possible operation and maintenance strategies (O&MS) by inspecting the A/C and lighting systems equipment and their operation strategies. Moreover, monthly power consumption data were collected from the FM&SD who regularly keep a manually logged record of the

monthly consumption. The historical data since 1998 were used in the analysis of the base load, that is the minimum constant amount of energy consumed in a building throughout the year.

The monthly consumption data collected by the FM&SD were from the meter readings. The readings were not taken exactly on the same date of each month. This made the meter reading inconsistent. Thus in order to compare the consumption of different years, the meter values were corrected to include the same number of days for a specific month. To correct for the meter reading inconsistency, a daily average power consumption data were calculated. Then, the monthly consumption was determined by exploiting the calculated daily average power consumption.

Weather parameters including the dry bulb temperature and the relative humidity were also gathered. The data were monthly averaged to represent the weather characteristics for the same period of the meter readings. This was done to correlate the seasonal energy consumption with the weather conditions.

BUILDING BASE LOAD

To estimate the building base load, the monthly power consumption of the two previous years (1998-1999) was plotted against the monthly averaged outside temperature as its shown in Fig. 3. The historical data provided an indication regarding the major building energy consumers. As it has been explained before, the base load is the minimum load consumed throughout the year. A horizontal line that coincides with the minimum consumption in Fig. 3 represents it. The base load analysis is very important for building management. Its importance resides in the fact that, once it is determined, it will provide building operation manger with a mean to check for any abnormalities in energy consumption.

Since the building is an office building, the major power consumers are the A/C system, the lighting system and lab/office equipment. During winter season one chiller is in operation as well as three chilled water pumps and the air handling units fans and motors. Thus the lighting system and office/lab equipment are utilizing the rest of the consumed power. The base consumption of the building is 800 MWh per month. This amount is being consumed regularly throughout the year. The base load of 800 MWh, actually represented not only the lighting system and office/lab equipment consumption but also the energy requirements for minimum air-conditioning required throughout the year.

Further analysis of the base load revealed more findings with regards to building energy consumption as shown in Fig.3. The area on the right side of the curve (i.e. the triangular area) represents the energy consumed by the air conditioning system in the summer season that is weather dependant [6]. Correlation between the outside weather temperature and the monthly power consumption required for the building air-conditioning was established.

It is clearly shown that the maximum monthly-consumed energy in the summer months reached a value of 1600 MWh on July 1999, this consumption is double the base load. Out of this maximum consumption, the A/C system consumed 1155 MWh this represents 72% of peak month total consumption.

Another important finding was the balance temperature (T_b). The balance temperature is defined as the minimum outdoor temperature at which cooling of the building is usually required. For KISR's main building, it was found

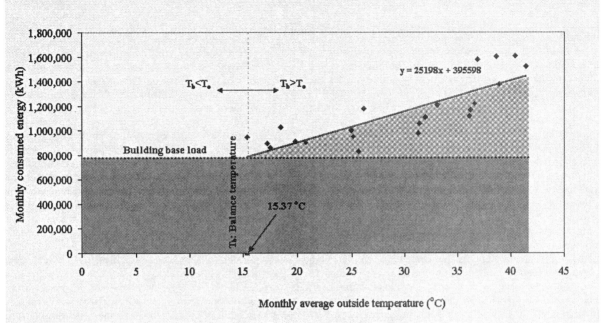

FIG.3 MAIN BUILDING BASE LOAD

that the cooling would start whenever the outside temperature exceeds 15°C. Since the building is using minimum cooling around the year with one chiller in operation, then whenever the outside temperature exceeded 15°C, the building utilized at least two chillers.

BUILDING ENERGY USE PROFILE

Since at least some energy consumption data are available for most existing buildings, a great deal of information can be obtained from an analysis of whatever data exist. The quantity and type of data available depend upon the type of metering that is installed in the building [6]. In KISR's main building, four substations were installed to provide the electrical requirements. The Ministry of Electricity and Water (MEW) has installed twelve energy consumption meters in the main building. The meters continuously display the building power consumption. The readings of the meters are collected manually every week and manually logged by FM&SD personnel to estimate the weekly and monthly power consumption. Some difficulties were

encountered when hourly consumption data was required for energy auditing analysis. The difficulties were mainly associated with allocation of service personnel for data collection. This lead to limit the analysis on whatever data that were available, namely the weekly and monthly consumption.

The building power consumption for consecutive two years from 1998 to 1999 as well as that of 2000 and 2001 is plotted in Fig. 4. The project duration was one full fiscal year commencing from March 2000 till February 2001. The consumption is recorded from the meters at different days of the month. This made the monthly data collected by FM&SD inconsistent. For that reason the consumption data were corrected as it was explained in the methodology section. The corrected data for years 1998 till 2001 that are shown in Fig. 4 describe the consumption pattern for the those four years.

The minimum consumption was just over 800 MWh for 1998 and 1999. The consumption of 1999 in general was more than that of 1998. This is linked greatly to the higher outside temperature (refer to Fig. 5). Although the outside

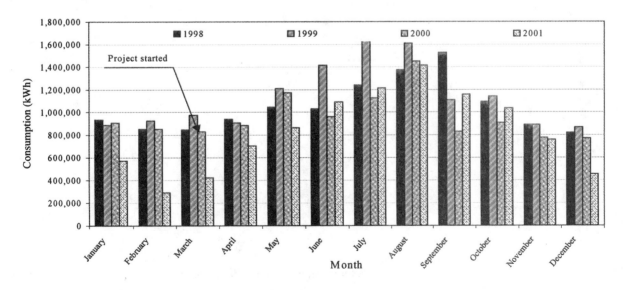

FIG. 4 CORRECTED KISR'S MAIN BUILDING POWER CONSUMPTION FOR 1998-2001

239

temperature in September 1998 was one degree higher than that of 1999, there is a large increase in the power consumption of 1998 as compared to that of 1999. This is attributed to a poor building operation strategy. The total energy consumed for the building were 12.587 and 13.563 MWh/yr for 1998 and 1999 in respectively. Year 1999 was selected to be the base year for the energy audit analysis thus energy savings will be worked accordingly.

In order to compare the building energy consumption with similar buildings that are considered to be energy efficient, the building energy density was estimated. The building electrical energy density, which is the annual consumed electricity per air-conditioned space area, was found to be 578 kWh/m². This value was found to be very high when compared to good practice benchmark density of 234 kWh/m² for prestigious air-conditioned office buildings specified by the Chartered Institution of Buildings Services Engineers (CIBSE) [7]. From the base load analysis and the energy use, it was decided to reduce the base load and the energy density as much as possible. The energy density provided by the CIBSE was not targeted; it was rather used to provide a guideline in achieving energy efficiency.

MODIFICATIONS OF BUILDING OPERATION STRATEGIES

The base load analysis and the historical annual energy consumption profiles indicated that building electricity consumption was enormous, and that inefficient operation strategies were utilized particularly for the air-conditioning system. Opportunities of efficient building operation were investigated. After that several operation strategies were recommended out of which some were adapted and implemented by the facility operators. The recommended operation strategies are listed in tables 1 and 2. The details of the recommended operation strategies of the lighting and air-conditioning systems are discussed separately in the following sections:

Lighting System

The building architectural design permits the utilization of daylight through skylights and large efficient glazing areas. In spite of that, the light system is utilized primarily to provide the required luminosity. The main reason behind this misuse of the lighting system is the design of the lighting control switches. Each switch controls multi fixtures of different task areas. For example, in the library, the reading desks area which is located near the windows have the lights on all the time as the switch for this area controls the lights of the reception area which is located further away from the glazed surface. Similar situations occurred at other areas within the building. In view of this, delamping strategy was investigated, and implemented in several areas of the building. The luminosity level was measured after implementing this strategy and it was found that it matches the recommended levels by Ministry of Electricity and Water (MEW) [1].

Another strategy was recommended which involved modifications to lighting utilization periods. After conducting night-time light luminosity measurements, it was found that the luminosity exceeded the recommended values. For example, the MEW standard recommends a value of 5 lux for corridors during night-time while the measured was 62 lux. In view of this it was recommended to switch on only 20% of the lights in the main entrance area to maintain the recommended lux level and achieve energy savings.

During the walk through audit, it was noticed that some employees were using side lamps to provide adequate light level in their offices. They've opted to switch off the fixed florescent lights and use the incandescent side lamps. Moreover, some employees that have access to daylight, did not utilize it, instead artificial lighting was used. All these inefficient practices were adapted to avoid the light reflection and glare on the computer monitor that was due to improper placement office furniture. For that reason a survey was prepared and distributed to the employees. The survey aimed at determining the utilization habits of the building employees and their requirements. The results of the survey indicated that out of 263 employees that are located in the building, 113 have access to natural daylight in their offices.

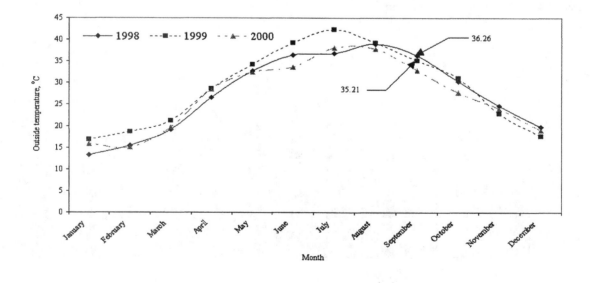

Fig. 5. Outside temperature profile 1998-2000

Out of the 113 employees, only 8 utilize natural light. In addition, 94 employees have side lamps in their offices. The estimated annual consumption of the side lamps assuming an average lamp rating of 60W and that they are used 5 days a week for 7.5 hours per day will be 11 MWh/year (refer to Table 1). To change the employees habits with regards to utilization of lighting system, the third strategy was recommended. This strategy suggested rearranging the office furniture in accordance with the light angle to prevent glare on computers monitors. This would motivate the employees to utilize day lighting and prevent them from using side lamps that will further reduce the consumption.

TABLE 1. RECOMMENDED OPERATION STRATEGIES FOR THE LIGHTING SYSTEM

Strategy	Notes	Savings MWh/year
1. Delamping	Cafeteria, corridors, workshops, labs and offices	81.7
2. Modifications to lighting utilization schedules (during non-working hours)	Working hours 23% turned off Non-working hours 50-70% turned off	55
3. Reorganization of office furniture	Eliminate the need to utilize side lamps and promote the use of daylight	11

Air-conditioning System

The building air-conditioning system was operating almost under a fixed strategy. Six chillers are utilized during the peak summer (i.e. July through August) and a minimum of one chiller is always in operation during wintertime, which is from November through January. Throughout the year all three chilled water pumps are in operation. The indoor temperature of the building is usually maintained at 18-22°C. The occupants mostly complain from the over cooled working environment. A detailed study for the chilled water distribution system and the air-conditioning system revealed that the air-conditioning system is oversized [8]. Moreover, it was found that the chilled water

could be circulated with only one pump olny. This oversizing was intentional as it was assumed that there would be future expansion of the building, which did not take place. Moreover, the operation of the A/C system had a huge opportunity for energy consumption savings. The two chilled water pumps were not needed for the year round operation. For that reason it was logical to recommend switching them off all year round. This strategy contributed greatly to the savings, as it is shown in the next section.

The daily operation of the A/C system was found to be fixed within the season. The A/C system was running continuously right through occupancy and non-occupancy periods even during weekends and holidays. In view of this different operation schedules are recommended for the A/C systems components. The supply air (SA) fans and return air (RA) fans that were continuously running, are going to have a certain operation schedules that are weather and occupancy dependant as shown in table 2. In addition, the corridors are usually very cold; their temperature was maintained at 18-19°C during occupancy period that dropped down to 11-12°C at night. To overcome this uncomfortable situation, the closure of the corridors supply air fans was recommended during non-occupancy period through out the year.

The operation strategies for the A/C system included an assertive operation strategy that is recommended for winter season. In this strategy, the closure of the chiller and the chilled water pump throughout the season as well as the closure of SA and RA fans for all AHUs during non-occupancy period is recommended. Basically only free cooling is utilized during the winter season, by supplying 100% fresh air to the building during working hours.

Equipment

Since the main facility building is categorized as an office/research building, the equipment are either office equipment such as computers, printers, fax machines and copiers or lab equipment that are usually used for specific experimental work and testing procedures. Other than those, are the equipment or appliances that are required for other building requirements such as those used in the cafeteria and the auditorium. The annual consumption in the lab area represents about 90% of the total equipment annual consumption.

The importance of the equipment energy consumption lies in their continuous use throughout the working hours and

TABLE 2. RECOMMENDED OPERATION STRATEGIES FOR THE AIR-CONDITIONING SYSTEM

Strategy	Implementation schedule	Savings MWh/year
1. Closure of third chilled water pump	Year round (168 h/week)	822.5
2. Closure of SA and RA fans of corridors AHUs during non-occupancy period	Year round (128 h/week)	404.2
3. Closure of second chilled water pump	Year round (168 h/week)	822.5
4. Closure of chiller and pump	Winter (9 weeks – 168h/Week)	347.8
5. Closure of SA fans of corridors AHUs during occupancy period	Winter (9 weeks – 168h/Week)	11.9
6. Closure of RA fans of all AHUs during non-occupancy period	Winter, RA (22 weeks-128 h/week)	344.1

Note: RA (return air), SA (supply air), AHUs (air handling units)

sometimes throughout the day, especially in poorly managed buildings. This equipment utilization pattern amplifies the energy consumption. Unlike the HVAC system energy consumption that is weather dependent, the equipment's energy consumption is user dependant. This makes the utilization pattern governed by factors that are difficult to control. Another important fact that emphasizes the importance of the equipment energy consumption is that it's considered as a major part of the building base load.

The office equipment are standard, they comprise personal computers, monitors, laser printers and scanners. The manager's offices include fax machines, photocopiers and electronic typewriters. The total energy consumption of KISR's main facility building is presented in Table 3.

There are 38 laboratories in the main building, which support KISR's applied research programs. The total area located by the laboratories is approximately 3,973 m^2, which is 17.0% of the air-conditioned area.

The equipment electrical consumption was either measured when possible, or determined utilizing the nameplate rating. As for the operation schedules, they were estimated based on interviewing the staff member in charge of the specific equipment in question. The estimated monthly energy consumption for laboratories equipment was found to be 215,781 kWh. Thus the total yearly energy consumption of KISR's main laboratories equipment was estimated to be 2,589.4 MWh [2]. The laboratories equipment electrical density was found to be 652 kWh/m^2.

ESTIMATED SAVINGS

Since, the aim for the energy audit is to reduce the energy consumption. For that purpose, the recommended operation strategies energy savings were determined. The savings are listed in tables 1 and 2. The savings achieved by implementing the recommended strategies for the lighting system would be 147.7MWh/year. Out of which, 81.7 MWh/year was estimated for delamping only. It is recommended that when a fluorescent lamp is removed, the ballast should be removed as well and used for maintenance when required.

Additional savings are estimated when energy efficient operation schedules are utilized while adhering to the recommended luminosity levels during nighttime. This strategy would save up to 55 MWh/year.

Since energy auditing aims also at increasing the building energy efficiency, recommended procedures should not affect the occupant's comfort. Actually, increasing comfort level whether thermal or visual is considered one of the targets for energy auditing. In view of this, the third recommended strategy aimed firstly at lowering the electrical consumption by diverting the occupants from using side lamps and encouraging them to use natural daylight. Keeping in mind that rearranging the office furniture was suggested to eliminate the glare on computer screens. Furthermore, this strategy would improve the working environment thus achieving additional benefit that is increased productivity.

In view of the A/C system, the savings that can be realized from adapting the recommended operation strategies for the A/C are substantial. The over design of the A/C system and the energy ignorant operation of the system by the building operators created a vast opportunity for energy savings. The total estimated savings that can be achieved by improving the operation of A/C system are 2753MWh/y this represents 20% of the annual consumed energy of the building base year.

The major savings were achieved by switching off the chilled water pumps. The achieved savings by the closure of the two pumps represented 60% of the total achieved savings by modifying operation strategies for the A/C system.

The modifications of the winter operation of the A/C system estimated savings are over 26% of the total saved by implementing the A/C system O&MS. In addition the estimated savings that can be achieved by adapting energy conscious operation strategy during non-occupancy period are 12%.

The achieved savings estimated for the implementation of the O&MS for the lighting system represent 1.1 % of the total building energy consumption. These savings when compared to those of the A/C system are considered trivial. But any savings that can be achieved; especially when they're free will be beneficial from environmental perspective if not from monitory one.

As for the equipment, the audit team was faced with the some resistance of laboratories equipment operators. They did not want to change any operational habits and they believed that their operation was energy conscious. Since the focus of this audit project was to reduce energy consumption with minimum disturbances, the operation of laboratories equipment were not looked into. Only the operation of office equipment, kitchen exhaust fans and vending machines was investigated. Few operation strategies were recommended including the closure of office equipment when not in use, as well as the kitchen exhaust fans and the vending machines.

The scanners were selected as it was found that from a questionnaire that was distributed among employees to investigate their operational habits with regards to office equipment, that they were left in operation even when not in use. Thus the closure of the scanners was recommended, this

TABLE 3. RECOMMENDED OPERATION STRATEGIES FOR SELECTED EQUIPMENT

Strategy	Recommended Period	Savings MWh/y
- Closure of office equipment - Scanners 19 unit 40 W utilized for 3hrs/Wday	When not in use (21h week days, 24h week end)	6
- Closure of exhaust fans	Non-working hours 15 hours (3 p.m. – 6 a.m.) 24 hrs on weekends	12.1
- Closure of vending machines	From Wed. 3p.m. till Sat. 6 a.m.	5

would save up to 6.0 MWh/yr for an average rating of 40W per scanner for a total of 19 scanners.

Another strategy that was recommended is the Closure of the exhaust fans in the main kitchen during non-working hours. This strategy recommends switching off the exhaust fans in the main kitchen during non-working hours; usually these fans are running 24 hours. It is advised to turn them off for 15 hours during working days and 24 hours in Thursday and Friday. Thus this strategy is recommended for a total of 6396 hours.

The closure of the vending machine located in the cafeteria is also suggested, when not in use that is during weekends and after working hours on Wednesday (i.e. from 3:00 p.m. to 12 a.m.).Only the vending machine in the cafeteria is targeted in this strategy, as employees working during non-working hours might use the others scattered in the building. When adapting these strategies, the estimated annual savings will be 12.1 MWh and 5 MWh for the closures of exhaust fans and the vending machine respectively.

The overall savings achieved by controlling the use of selected equipment were estimated to be 23.1 MWh/yr, an additional 0.17% savings of the annual consumption of the base year. This savings may be considered trivial, but the audit team believe that there is more opportunities with regards to reducing consumption of office and lab equipment that can be targeted separately in future studies. In addition, the savings achieved did not require any initial investment, other than the time required one professional the conducted the audit. The overall savings of the O&MS of the equipment will be 46KD/y ($149), and the salary of the professional is 32KD/d ($103/d). Thus the cost of achieving such strategies are covered within the first year assuming that the professional will spend one day to recommend such strategies.

The over all savings that can be achieved if all recommended O&MS were implemented will be 2923.8MWh/yr, which is equivalent to annual savings of 5848 KD ($18,863). The savings when compared to the annual energy consumption of the base year were found to be equivalent to 21% although it was proposed to achieve 15%.

From another perspective, the building base load was reduced from 800 MWh/month to 300 MWh/month in fiscal year 2000-2001. Thus building operators shall maintain a conservative figure of 450MWh/month as the recommended building base load for the time being. Thus 44% reduction in the base load can be easily achieved.

In view of the building energy density, 26% saving can be achieved as the energy density was reduced from 578 kWh/m^2 to 425 kWh/m^2.

VERIFICATION OF ESTIMATED SAVINGS

The savings that were estimated in the previous section were based on hand calculations utilizing the available data including nameplate power rating, load factor for the chillers and their coefficient of performance in addition to the measured ampere of the chilled water pumps and the air handling return and supply fans [10]. As for the lighting system, the data utilized were mainly from electrical drawings and walk through inspection. The total estimated savings as it has been shown in the previous section are 2923.8MWh/yr, which is equivalent to 5848 KD ($18,863). The estimated savings when compared to billing data that is 5875 KD ($18,950) per year equivalent to 2937 MWh/yr annual meter reading. Thus the savings were underestimated by 0.46%. Although not all recommended O&MS were actually implemented for the whole suggested period, among those that were not actually implemented are the closure of the scanners (6MWh/yr), reorganization of office furniture (11 MWh/yr).

ENERGY AUDITING NATIONAL BENEFITS

Though the energy audit discussed in this paper was actually conducted on one office building, the savings were reflected on 800 [4] similar buildings to estimate the national benefits, if similar practices were adapted throughout the country.

The savings were estimated based on the total cost of electricity, which is 0.015KD/kWh (0.05$/kWh) not the subsidized cost of 0.002KD/kWh (0.006$/kWh). In addition, two conservative assumptions were made, the first is the buildings annual energy consumption is 12000MWh/yr and the seconded is that the estimated savings that can be achieved are15% achieved by modifications of their O&MS. The predicted annual savings for 800 buildings are 22 million KD (71 million $).

From another perspective, the foreseen electricity savings will reduce the power plant emissions by 749 million kg of CO_2. The CO_2 emissions are estimated using a conversion factor of 0.52 kg CO_2/kWh for electricity production at 1997 figure [5].

CONCLUSIONS

Considerable savings can be achieved by simply modifying the operation strategies of the building systems.
At least 15% savings can be promised when adapting energy conscious operation strategies. In Kuwait, in spite of the fact that buildings are designed efficiently with respect to the building envelope, the building operation is habitually energy ignorant. This behavior is generally associated with the enforcement of energy conservation code by MEW [9] that controls the peak load requirements but not the consumption of the buildings. Another factor that is seriously contributing to the overuse of electricity is the government subsidy of electricity prices. The government covers over 85% of the total price.

The energy audit procedure followed in this study focused only on the operation of the building. Thus achieved savings are costless. The total savings achieved represented 21% of the total annually consumed energy. In view of the base load, implementation of the recommended O&MS will drop it by 44%. The modified building operation not only will reduce the energy consumption but it will also enhance the indoor environment thus the employees productivity is expected to improve.

This paper anticipated the national benefits that can be realized when all office buildings operation strategies are modified and turned into energy conscious O&MS. The realized monitory savings would be 22 million KD (71 million $). Moreover, emissions by the power plants will be reduced by 749 million kg of CO_2. The anticipated benefits of energy auditing on the national level, outweighs those on the individual level. In view of that, it is recommended that the government should adapt an energy efficient building operation campaign especially for the governmental buildings.

REFERENCES

[1] Al-Nakib, D. and Al-Ragom, F., *Energy Auditing of the Lighting system at KISR's Main Facility Building*. Kuwait Institute for Scientific Research. Report No. 6105. Kuwait. 2001.

[2] Al-Ragom F., G. P. Maheshwari, D. Al-Nakib, F. Al-Ghimlas, R. Al-Murad and A. Meerza, 2002. Energy Auditing of KISR's Main Building. Final report. Kuwait Institute for Scientific Research. Report No 6287.

[3] Al-Ragom, F. and G. P. Maheshwari, 2000. Energy Auditing of KISR's Main Building. Proposal. Kuwait Institute for Scientific Research. Report No 5782. 2000.

[4] Almudhaf, H. and F. Al-Ragom, 1999. Development of simplified fast facts demonstrating the impact of energy

conservation in Kuwaiti buildings. Kuwait Institute for Scientific Research. Report No. 5575. Kuwait. 1999.

[5] Energy Efficiency in Buildings, 1998. Chartered Institution of Building Services Engineers (CIBSE) guide. London, UK.

[6] Krarti, M., 2000. *Energy Audit of Building Systems: An Engineering Approach*. CRC Press LCC, New York, USA.

[7] Mirza, A. and F. Al-Ragom, 2001. Building Automation System of KISR's Main Facility Building. Kuwait Institute for Scientific Research. Report No. 6168. Kuwait.

[8] Maheshwari, G. P., H. Hussain, and R. Rajeeve, 2001. Development and Implementation of Energy Efficient Operation Schemes for air-conditioning system. Kuwait Institute for Scientific Research. Report No. 6213. Kuwait.

[9] Ministry of Electricity and Water (MEW), 1983. Code of Practice for Energy Conservation in Kuwaiti Buildings. Report No. MEW R-6, Kuwait.

[10] Pawlik Klaus-Dieter E., Lynne C. Capehart, and Barney L. Capehart, 2001. Strategic Planning for Energy and the Environment Vol. 21, No. 2.

AUTHOR'S BIO

Holding a M.Sc. degree in Mechanical Engineering (Thermo-Fluids) from Northeastern University, Boston, MA 1995. Involved in a number of projects related to the field of energy conservation in buildings and energy auditing. Specialization areas cover the following:

- Energy auditing
- Energy conservation in buildings
- Refrigeration and Air-Conditioning
- Heat exchangers design
- Utilization of heat recovery systems
- Passive cooling systems
- Alternative refrigerants

Working in the Kuwait Institute for scientific Research (KISR) since 1990. Now holding a research associate position at the Building and Energy Technologies Department. A member at the Association for Energy Engineers since 2000. KISR's representative at the Kuwaiti National Ozone committee since 1998.

Holding Certified Energy Manager (CEM) certification, obtained from the Association of Energy Engineers (AEE) - USA in December 2001.

Chapter 36

Demand Exchange Trading Floor (Dex)
A New Opportunity for End Users and Utilities Under a Regulated Environment

Rafael Herzberg, PE
herzberg@amcham.com.br
Managing Director
Interact Ltda., Energy Consulting
phone 55 (11) 5686 5577 fax 55 (11) 5521 2560
R. S. Benedito 1729   04735-004 São Paulo, Brazil

This paper will show how a demand exchange trading floor can optimize the distribution's company investments and at the same time open new possibilities for its customers to change their demands and accordingly minimize their monthly electricity costs, in a win-win situation.

1. The Dex principle

Commercial, industrial and institutional energy users have to contract a demand before their distribution companies. Accordingly each month the electricity bill includes a kW demand charge which can be understood as the cost associated with the infrastructure that was required to connect the user to the grid thus enabling kWh energy to be supplied.

Real life indicates that the contractual demand never matches the registered (physical) demand. It can be higher or lower but it is almost never equal. In our days everything changes and fast! Products change, machines that are used to fabricate these products change, production mix changes, the market changes - almost everything in a business environment changes and so quickly. How could demand be unchanged?

Dex is a trading platform where users can adjust their demands according to their needs in a win-win situation for all parties involved:

* The user that is selling kW will reduce the monthly demand charge as opposed to paying an idle demand ,

* The user that is buying kW will be able to expand production and

* The utility company will sell more kWh with the same overall kW demand or in other words will make more revenues with the same investment.

2. Simplicity

Dex as indicated above is a service to be offered by a distribution company (disco) to its customers. It means that the overall demand (from the disco prospective) is kept unchanged.

No need of additional metering. The current meters will do! Once the transaction is completed the only additional action required is the change (by the utility company) of the contractual demands of the parties (buyer and seller). The contract wording will be unchanged.

3. Example of a transaction

A: is willing to sell 1 000 kW
B: is willing to buy 1000 kW

If the transaction value is finalized at US$ 10 000 then this is the business outlook:

Disco transaction fee: 10% (US$ 1 000)
B will pay US$ 10 000
A will receive US$ 9 000

Given this business model, everybody is potentially interested in always optimizing the contractual demand because of very simple reasons:

(a) The customer A will pay the demand according to the actual needs, not in excess. This is a US$ 10 000/month saving!

(b) The customer B will get the needed extra demand, without paying penalties that would be incurred if the original demand was to be exceeded and

(c) The utility company is selling the same overall total demand (2 000 kW) but more energy because the B will use the demand while A was not using it. Let's assume for the sake of one example that the load factor for this additional demand is 70%. It means that B will consume 1 000 kW x 70% x 720 hours/month = 504 MWh/month. If the utility is charging energy at US$ 20/MWh then this additional energy sales will result in US$ 120 960/year.

4. Retaining customers in the long run

If this Dex tool is offered by a disco to its regulated customers then it can be anticipated that they will think twice before they change from this disco to another one when the market in that area "de regulates". This because the disco is offering an added value service which helps customers to optimize their demand and this represents a significant fraction of the overall electricity bill.

5. The more transactions the better for all parties

Optimizing the demand is an activity that would add to the bottom line of all corporate energy users. Since the disco is receiving a transaction fee it makes sense for all parties to adjust their demands as much as they need to.

6. A menu of options

The Dex could be tailor made to accommodate the needs and wants of each disco. The transaction could be formatted in a kW sale or a kW "rental" for a defined extension of time. Additionally a market driven price could be selected or a fixed price system.

7. The most important challenge

The Dex is in itself is a very simple service. A fairly low investment to develop the trading platform should be anticipated - potentially existing auction type internet based platforms could be used .

The real challenge is the sale of the concept before distribution companies.

8. We are eager, as consultants, to help distribution companies around the world, and their customers benefit from this concept

I my consulting experience I see so many times the same problem: the registered demand is not matching the contractual one. More often than not, the difference is meaningful. A 10% difference is not hard to find.

Let's assume that for each GW of de Distribution Company's demand, there is a 10% volume for this type of trading and that this volume is traded 3 times per year. These are very conservative numbers because of the rapid changes that take place in our business environment of these days!

The value of these transactions would reach around US$ 40 Million/year/GW. A medium sized disco with a 5 GW demand could anticipate an added US$ 200 Million revenue with Dex.

Rafael Herzberg, 48, is the managing director and partner for Interact Ltd. (www.interact-energia.com.br/english) a strategic energy consulting company, based in São Paulo, Brazil.

His experience is associated with corporate energy users (typically in the 3 MW to 50 MW range) including "to the fence projects" and "inside the fence energy savings".

Recent consulting works include ADM, Cargill, Degussa, Daikin, KSP, Rhodia, Nestlé and Shopping SP Market.

Rafael is the vice chairperson of the energy committee at the American Chamber of Commerce in São Paulo and a frequent speaker in energy related events.

Chapter 37

FITTING FLEXIBLE WIND SPEED MODELS: A New Approach

Jason .C. Chadee. and Chandrabhan Sharma
Department of Electrical & Computer Engineering
Faculty of Engineering
The University of the West Indies, St. Augustine
Trinidad West Indies
Email: jchadee@eng.uwi.tt

Abstract

Defining a wind speed probability density function (PDF) model is a compact method of providing a scientific judgement of a regime resource and profile. Actual wind speed distributions are highly heterogeneous and deformed in nature and, modelling this phenomena demands flexibility in the chosen models. The new approach firstly validates hourly mean wind speed (HMWS) observations for the properties of randomness, homogeneity, independence and stationarity. It is found that the traditional PDF modelling approach is statistically invalid. A hypothetical PDF modelling approach based on an hourly basis within any particular month is suggested and tested to be valid. Outliers are removed and three parameter flexible models derived from the Gamma family, i.e., Pearson type III (P3), Log-Pearson type 3 (LP3) and Generalised Gamma (GG3) are fitted for possible new application in the field of wind engineering. Model estimation is accomplished by the natural Method of Moments (MOM) and validation is achieved by the heuristic visual examination and mean power densities comparison. A three year 1988-1990 unpublished HWMS data set for February logged at the Crown Point meteorological station is used to illustrate the approach. The performance of the flexible models can be assessed by the accuracy of the mean power density estimate and a comparison with the standard models, two parameter Weibull (WE2), Hybrid Weibull (HWE2) and the single parameter Rayleigh (RAY). It was found that the use of the WE2 and RAY as standards in literature is questionable and new and improved theoretical models must be sought. Particular attention should be focussed on the development of three or more parameter models since they offer much greater flexibility and accuracy.

Terminology

WE2- Two- parameter Weibull model
WE3- Three-parameter Weibull model
WECS- Wind Energy Conversion System
GG3- Three-Parameter Gamma model
HWE2- Hybrid Weibull model
LP3- Three-parameter Log- Pearson model
MLM- Method of Maximum Likelihood
MOM- Method of Moments
PDF- Probability Density Function
P3- Three-parameter Pearson Type model
RAY- Single parameter Rayleigh model
HWMS- Hourly Mean Wind Speed

1.0   Introduction

One of the most important aspects of wind resource assessments is the simulation of an accurate description of the wind speed distribution via a wind speed frequency modelling (WSFM) approach. Failure to apply a theoretically valid WSFM will result in wrong estimates of the Wind Energy Conversion System (WECS) power output and, hence, creates economic consequences. The three basic steps involved in the current Wind Speed Frequency Modelling (WSFM) approach are:

a) The logging of HMWS and associated wind direction data sets at different WECS hub-heights (10m as the reference).

b) The empirical modelling of the collected sample using the WE2 (eqn. 1) or, in many instances, the RAY (eqn. 2) and HWE2 (eqn. 3).

$$f(u) = \frac{k}{c}\left(\frac{u}{c}\right)^{k-1} e^{-\left(\frac{u}{c}\right)^k} \quad k > 0, c > 0 \qquad (1)$$

Where k = shape parameter and c= scale parameter

$$f(u) = \frac{\pi u}{2\bar{u}^2} e^{-\frac{\pi}{4}\left(\frac{u}{\bar{u}}\right)^2} \qquad (2)$$

Where $\bar{u}$ = mean of the distribution.

$$f_h(u) = p(u=0)\delta(u) + [1 - p(u=0)]f(u) \qquad (3)$$

Where p(u=0) = probability of observing zero wind speed and δ(u) = dirac function

The MOM or Least Squares Method (LSM) is the parametric estimation technique.

c) The validation of WE2, HWE2 and RAY with observed wind distributions using one of the following variety of methods and statistical tests:

- Visual examination.

- Mean power density comparison.

- Comparison of wind moments.

- Chi-square (χ^2).

- Kolmogorov –Smirnov (K-S).

d) The use of this model to make statistical inferences about the underlying population in order to provide important pieces of scientific information for the successful WECS utility applications.

The assumptions of the WSFM are that the data is independent, identically distributed, homogeneous, stochastic, space and time independent. In addition, the winds are not affected by natural or manmade changes in the wind regime. In practice, the true PDF model of the data at a site or region is unknown. The assumption that data in a given regime arise from a single parent model may be questionable when data from large areas are analysed. Quite often, many assumptions made in WSFM may be invalid.

2.0   Literature Review

The first statistical studies in this field began 40 years ago (Sherlock 1951) and various models have since been proposed. In the 1950's and 1960's, the modelling of upper winds by the bivariate Gaussian distribution system received the most attention (Brooks et al 1950, Brooks and Carruthers 1953, Crutcher and Baer 1962). In the 1970's, univariate models were sought on the basis of convenience, simplicity and ease of use (Justus et al 1976). The univariate speed distribution derived from the bivariate normal proved to be an unwieldy summation of the products of Bessel functions (Smith 1971, 1976). Wentink (1974) investigated methods of fitting a Planck distribution (f =3) to Alaskan data. Widger (1977) calculated square-root normal distributions using monthly mean wind speed and fastest mile data that was inaccurate for the case of highly skewed distributions. Attention was also diverted to other wind applications where the WE2 was applied in the study of wind loads on buildings (Davenport 1963) and fitted to upper air data (Baynes and Davenport 1975). Also, the Rayleigh model was applied in extreme wind phenomena (Baynes 1974, Court 1974) and the two-parameter Log-Normal (LN2) model in air pollution studies (Luna and Church 1974). However, the Rayleigh and Planck models are parametrised solely by the mean wind speed, and this can be inadequate for fitting heterogeneous and deformed surface wind speed distributions. Most attention was then focussed on the two- parameter Weibull model, WE2, (e.g., Justus et al 1976). In addition, many studies specific to the WE2 examined various methods of parametric estimation (e.g., Justus et al 1978, Stevens and Smulders 1979) and use in wind power statistics (e.g., Hennessey 1977). In comparative studies, the WE2 emerged preferable to the Rayleigh (e.g., Corotis 1977, Hennessey 1978) and LN2 (Justus et al 1976). The hybrid Weibull model (HWE2), a slight modification to the WE2, was provided in response to the problems at low wind speeds and assertions that actual wind speed distributions are too deformed or heterogeneous for a 2-parameter model (Takle and Brown 1978). The HWE2 produced some improvement in fit at stations with a huge proportion of calms but does not offer much advantage than the WE2 (Tuller and Brett 1984). A 3-parameter Weibull model (WE3) was also utilised in some studies and was found to provide improved fitness and flexibility than the WE2 (Stewart and Essenwanger 1978, Tuller and Brett 1984). However, the third parameter introduces estimation difficulties and a positive value of the WE3 location parameter leads to the unrealistic condition of zero probability of wind speeds less than the parameter value. Bardsley (1980) suggested the Inverse Gaussian model as an alternative to the WE3. While the WE2 has been justified to an extent empirically, Tuller and Brett (1984) exposed the theoretical shortcomings of the WE2 in representing real world wind velocity patterns since four unlikely conditions must be satisfied. In essence, the WE2 is, theoretically, not a universal model or no single model could be expected to give good results at all stations since wind patterns are different due to the diversity of topographies. In addition, the WE2 and Rayleigh respectively are not reliable for evaluating WECS output (Baker et al 1990, Pallabazzer 1995). Nevertheless, these arguments were largely ignored as various authors utilised the WE2 (e.g., Halliday 1984, Poje and Cividini 1988, Mulugetta and Drake 1996, Habali et al 2000) and HWE2 (e.g., Exell 1985, Katsoulis and Metaxas 1992, Persaud et al 1999) as the defacto in assessing the wind resource of their respective countries. The Rayleigh and LN2 also received some more attention (e.g., Lalas et al 1983, Garcia et al 1998). In many of these cases, no statistical testing criteria were employed to justify significance in the diverse topographical terrain. Currently, the WE2 is the industry standard. For instance, the popular computer modelling package, WASP, incorporates it solely for wind atlas development (e.g., Pashrades and Christofides 1995, Douglas and Saluja 1996, EWEC 1999, Karlis et al 2001). Also, modern offshore windfarm analysts have also embraced the WE2 (Coelingh et al 1997, EWEC 1999).

3.0 Methodology

A statistically valid methodology is proposed to replace the current WSFM approach.

3.1 Statistical Criteria testing for HWMS

In the literature, there is no evidence or attempt to determine the statistical validity of the widely used HWMS data sets for PDF modelling. Failure to examine the data sets for the basic statistical properties of randomness, independence, homogeneity and stationarity represents a lack of statistical rigour and a fundamental flaw in the analysis of time series data. It must be emphasised that the need for this scientific rigour requires application of careful logic and the use of well-tested statistical methods. Non-parametric tests will be employed for the following properties (Chadee 2002):

- Sample Autocorrelation Function (ACF) for Independence and Randomness.

- The Runs Test for Randomness.

- The Wald-Wolfowitz (W-W) Test for Independence and Stationarity.

- Mann-Whitney (M-W) test for Homogeneity and Stationarity.

All the tests are programmed into EXCEL.

3.2 Model Selection and Definition

Since there is no theoretical justification for deciding which model is to be used, an empirical approach is taken by considering several candidate models for suitability. Wind speed is bounded by physical limitations as the empirical distribution $y = f(u)$:

a) Describing the data takes very different forms with possible marked asymmetry or skewness.

b) Possess a lower bound set at $u=0$ to $+\infty$.

c) Normally starts at y= 0, rises to a maximum and then asymptotically approaches y= 0 at an often different rate.

The PDF models must conform to these limitations. In general, a model that can take on many different values of skewness and kurtosis is more flexible, from the shape point of view, than one that has a single value of skewness and a single value of kurtosis. The more flexible is a model; the better is its descriptive ability, and a good predictive model stems from its relative insensitivity to sampling error. Ideally, a model that is good for both interpolation and extrapolation is desired. Consequently, more attention is placed on the three or more parameter models of the Gamma family in contrast to the standard single and two parameter models that are utilised due to convenient computational properties. The MOM is a natural and relatively easy parameter estimation method. The LSM is inefficient, biased and introduces a large error in the estimation procedure (Bowden et al 1983). The Maximum Likelihood Method (MLM) and Probability Weighted Moments (PWM) are considered the most efficient, unbiased and robust estimation methods since they provide the smallest sampling variance of the estimated parameters. However, they demand computational rigour.

3.2.1   Defined Models: The Gamma Family

The flexible models of the Gamma family are extracted from the new catalogue of defined models for wind speed distributions (Chadee and Sharma 2002). The relevant mathematics is given in this section and programmed in Excel.

Pearson Type (P3) model

Putnam (1948) and Sherlock (1951) first suggested this model. However, no extensive application has been performed in the field.

$$f(x) = \frac{1}{\alpha\Gamma(\beta)}\left(\frac{x-\gamma}{\alpha}\right)^{\beta-1}\exp-\left(\frac{x-\gamma}{\alpha}\right) \qquad \gamma < x < \infty \qquad [4]$$

$\alpha = scale\ parameter$
$\beta = shape\ parameter$
$\gamma = location\ parameter$

If
$$\alpha > 0 \Rightarrow \quad x \geq \gamma \quad (Form\ A)$$
$$\alpha < 0 \Rightarrow \quad x \leq \gamma \quad (Form\ B)$$

For negative values of α, the model becomes upper bounded and may not be suitable for analysing maximum events. Forms A and B represent positive and negative skewness respectively of P3.

First moment $\mu_1' = \dfrac{1}{\alpha\Gamma(\beta)} \displaystyle\int_\gamma^\infty x\left(\dfrac{x-\gamma}{\alpha}\right)^{\beta-1} \exp-\left(\dfrac{x-\gamma}{\alpha}\right) dx \quad$ [5]

Let $let\ y = \left(\dfrac{x-\gamma}{\alpha}\right) \quad$ [6]

Substitute eqn. [6] in eqn. [5]

$$\mu_1' = \frac{1}{\Gamma[\beta]} \int_0^\infty (\alpha y + \gamma) y^{\beta-1} \exp-y\,dy = \frac{1}{\Gamma[\beta]}\left[\int_0^\infty \alpha y^\beta \exp-y\,dy + \int_0^\infty y^{\beta-1} \exp- y\,dy\right]$$

$$= \frac{1}{\Gamma(\beta)}\left[\alpha\Gamma(\beta+1) + \gamma\Gamma(\beta)\right] == \alpha\beta + \gamma$$

Similarly, the second and third moments and the skewness coefficient are:

$$\mu_2 = \alpha^2\beta$$
$$\mu_3 = 2\alpha^3\beta \qquad\qquad [7]$$
$$\gamma_1 = \frac{u_3}{u_2^{3/2}} = \frac{2}{\sqrt{\beta}}$$

Replacing μ_1', μ_2 and Υ_1 by their sample estimates m_1', m_2 and C_s:

$$\hat{\beta} = \left(\frac{2}{C_s}\right)^2$$

$$\hat{\alpha} = \sqrt{\left(\frac{m_2}{\hat{\beta}}\right)} \qquad\qquad [8]$$

$$\hat{\gamma} = m_1' - \sqrt{m_2\hat{\beta}}$$

Log-Pearson (3) (LP3) model

If the variable log x is assumed to have a P3 distribution then the distribution of variable x is a LP3 model.

$$f(x) = \frac{1}{\alpha x\Gamma(\beta)}\left[\frac{\log x - \gamma}{\alpha}\right]^{\beta-1} \exp-\left\{\frac{\log x - \gamma}{\alpha}\right\} \qquad [9]$$

The PDF of the LP3 may take many different shapes (Bobee 1975b). For wind speed frequency modelling, values of $\beta > 1$ and $1/\alpha > 0$ are of interest. Negative coefficients of skew correspond to negative α values that are not acceptable since LP3 would then have an upper bound. Based on eqn. [9], moments of the model can be derived as:

$$\mu_r' = \frac{\exp(\gamma r)}{(1 - r\alpha^\beta)} \quad [10]$$

and higher order moments of order r do not exist if the value of α is greater than $\frac{1}{r}$ (Bobee 1975b). For the first, second and third moments, if natural logarithms of eqn. [10] are taken:

$$\log \mu_1' = \gamma - \beta \log(1 - \alpha) \quad [11]$$

$$\log \mu_2' = 2\gamma - \beta \log(1 - 2\alpha) \quad [12]$$

$$\log \mu_3' = 3\gamma - \beta \log(1 - 3\alpha) \quad [13]$$

Manipulating eqns. [11] to [13]:

$$\frac{\log \mu_3' - 3\log \mu_1'}{\log \mu_2' - 2\log \mu_1'} = \frac{\log\left[(1-\alpha)^3 \Big/ (1-3\alpha) \right]}{\log\left[(1-\alpha)^2 \Big/ (1-2\alpha) \right]} \quad [14]$$

The L.H.S of eqn. [4] can be calculated from the sample moments m_1', m_2', m_3' as:

$$B = \frac{\log m_3' - 3\log m_1'}{\log m_2' - 2\log m_1'} \quad [15]$$

Eqn. [14] is then solved by Newton's Method for α. Alternatively following Kite (1977), if we define:

$$A = \frac{1}{\alpha} - 3 \quad [16]$$

$$C = \frac{1}{(B-3)} \quad [17]$$

then for $3.5 < \beta < 6.0$

$$A = -0.23019 + 1.65262C + 0.20911C^2 - 0.04557C^3 \quad [18]$$

and for $3.0 < \beta \le 3.5$

$$A = -0.47157 + 1.99955C \quad [19]$$

α, β, γ are estimated by eqns. [11] to [12]

$$\hat{\alpha} = \frac{1}{(A+3)} \quad [20]$$

$$\hat{\beta} = \frac{\log m_3' - 2\log m_1'}{\left[\log(1-\alpha)^2 - \log(1-2\alpha)\right]} = \frac{\log\left[1 + C_v^2\right]}{\left[\log(1-\alpha)^2 - \log(1-2\alpha)\right]} \quad [21]$$

$$\hat{\gamma} = \log m_1' + \beta\log(1-\alpha) \quad\quad [22]$$

The Generalised Gamma (GG) model

Unlike the LP3, the GG model cannot have a finite upper bound. This property is desirable for a flexible model in modelling wind speed. The four parameter generalised gamma distribution (GG4), which is the most general form of GG, is (Stacy 1962):

$$f(x) = \frac{|s\alpha|\exp-\left[\alpha(x-\gamma)\right]^s}{\Gamma(\beta)}\left[\alpha(x-\gamma)\right]^{s\beta-1} \quad [23]$$

$\alpha = scale\ parameter$
$\beta = shape\ /\ power\ parameter$
$\gamma = location\ parameter$
$s = power\ parameter$

Domain of variation: $\alpha(x-\gamma) \geq 0$

α, s, m can be positive or negative whereas β should always be positive.

Stacy and Mihram (1965) studied a special case of the GG4 obtained by setting $\gamma = 0$, i.e., the 3-parameter GG3. A practical form of the GG3 can be utilised in the field by having $\alpha > 0$ and allowing s to be negative or positive; giving:

$$f(x) = \frac{\alpha|s|\exp-\left[(\alpha x)^s\right]}{\Gamma(\beta)}(\alpha x)^{s\beta-1} \quad [24]$$

The GG3 has as special cases some of the most widely used 2 and 1 parameter models in practice such as the Pearson type V (s= -1), 2 parameter Gamma (s=1), WE2 (β=1), 1 parameter exponential (β=s=1). The GG4, in addition to the special cases in the GG3 population, includes as special cases such models as the Pearson type 3 (s= -1), WE3 (β=1), 2 parameter exponential (β=s=1). The LN3 is also a limiting case of GG4. The GG3 or GG4 models can be made as a first fitting approach for a given sample and then, to reduce the number of parameters, to choose among the simpler models the one which fits the sample best. The forms of the GG3 are as follows:

1. $s\beta = 1$: the model has a non-zero finite value at x=0 given by $f(0) = \dfrac{\alpha|s|}{\Gamma(\beta)}$

2. $s < 0 \; or \; s\beta > 1$: the model is unimodal and starts at the origin f(0)= 0.

3. $0 < s\beta < 1$: the model is unimodal and starts at +∞; f(0)=+∞.

The GG3 $(x;s,\alpha,\beta)$ is obtained from the 1 parameter Gamma G1 $(y;\beta)$ by the transformation:

$$X = u(Y) = \frac{1}{\alpha} X^{\frac{1}{s}} \qquad [25]$$

The non-central moments of the random variable Y= u(X) are given by:

$$\mu_r'(y) = \int y^r f(y)dy = \int [u(x)]^r f(x)dx \qquad [26]$$

Applying eqn. [26] to eqn. [25]:

$$\mu_r'(GG3) = \int_0^\infty \left(\frac{1}{\alpha} x^{\frac{1}{s}}\right)^r f_{G1}(x;\beta)dx = \frac{1}{\alpha^r} \int_0^\infty x^{\frac{r}{s}} f_{G1}(x;\beta)dx$$

$$= \frac{1}{\alpha^r} \mu_{\frac{r}{s}}'(G1) \qquad [27]$$

$$\mu_r'(GG3) = \left\{ \begin{array}{l} \dfrac{1}{\alpha^r} \dfrac{\Gamma\left(\beta + \frac{r}{s}\right)}{\Gamma(\beta)} \Rightarrow \; \frac{r}{s} > -\beta \\ +\infty \quad otherwise \end{array} \right\} [28]$$

α, β, s are found using the same method as for the LP3, whereby, the first three moments in real space of X are utilised (Kuo 1984).

3.3 Model Validation

A number of statistical tests have been suggested in the validation literature for defining a theoretical model with data from the corresponding real-world system. However, the fitting is not simple since the output processes of almost all real-world systems are non-stationary and autocorrelated. Thus, classical tests based on independent and identically distributed (IID) observations are not directly applicable. Relatively little attention has been paid to robust validation methods in the wind speed frequency analysis literature. This may be due to the early acceptance of the WE2 and RAY as the universal models. The visual examination by frequency comparison is a heuristic procedure (Kelton and Law 1991) will be employed with a mean power densities estimate comparison. The theoretical PDF mean power density is well known as:

$$\bar{P}_{wt} = \frac{1}{2}\rho\int_0^\infty u^3 f(u)du \quad W/m^2 \qquad [29]$$

Where ρ= air density (kg/m^3) and $\int_0^\infty u^3 f(u)du$ is the expectation of the third moment

about the origin of the PDF, f(u). Table 1 references the defined models formulae.

Model	$\bar{P}_{wt}$ (W/m^2)	Reference
RAY	$\frac{1}{2}\rho\bar{u}^3(\frac{4}{\pi})^{3/2}\Gamma(5/2)$	Chadee 2002
WE2	$\frac{1}{2}\rho c^3\Gamma(1+3/k)$	Chadee 2000
HWE2	$\frac{1}{2}\rho[1-p(u=0)]c_h^3\Gamma(1+3/k_h)$	Chadee 2000
LP3	$\frac{1}{2}\rho\left[\frac{e^{3\gamma}}{(1-3\alpha)^\beta}\right]$	Chadee 2002
P3	$\frac{1}{2}\rho[\alpha^3(\beta+2)(\beta+1)\beta+3\alpha^2\gamma(\beta+1)\beta+3\alpha\gamma^2\beta+\gamma^3]$	Chadee 2002
GG3	$\frac{1}{2}\rho\left[\frac{1}{\alpha^3}\frac{\Gamma\left(\beta+\frac{3}{s}\right)}{\Gamma(\beta)}\right]$	Chadee 2002

Table 1   Mean Power Densities Formulae for Defined Models

4.0   Example Run

The statistical criterion testing is applied to the 1988 HWMS data set (10m) for Crown

Point. The critical test limits of the ACF's at the 5% and 1% significance level is $\pm.021$

and $\pm.028$ respectively. An ACF (k=100) is generated and the approximate standard error

of the autocorrelation is 0.0107. Autocorrelations larger than two standard errors in

magnitude are 'significantly nonzero'. Ninety five percent of the lags were significant and fell outside the ±.021 bounds. This indicates that the conditions of both randomness and stationarity are not satisfied at the 5% significance level. Figure 1 suggests the strong presence of a deterministic sinusoidal process (period   24 hours) superimposed on the random process. This illustrates the diurnal deterministic component.

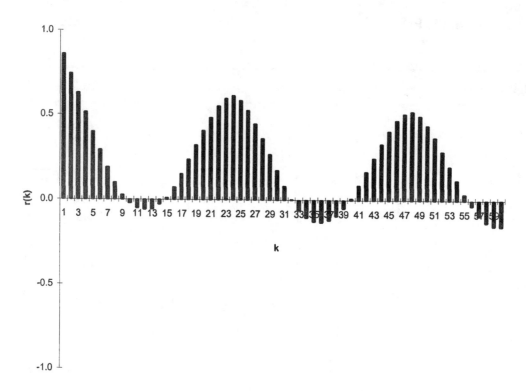

Figure 1 Crown Point 1988 Autocorrelation Plot

The lag plot suggests that a sinusoidal model might be appropriate and defies the use of PDF models. Table 2 shows the results of the runs test of randomness. The value of the test statistic |z| is 68.776; significantly greater than 1.96. The number of runs is 1145 as compared to the expected number of 4352.484 and the p-value is zero. Thus, the hypothesis of randomness is rejected at the 5% significance level. This indicates the presence of trends and supports the stronger notion of non-randomness in the HWMS. This is supported by the results of the W-W test of independence. The value of the test statistic |r| =80.32 >>> 1.96 and, thus, the hypothesis of independence at the 5%

significance level is rejected.

Number of observations	8705
Number above cutoff	4419
Number below cutoff	4286
Number of runs	1145
E(R)	4352.484
Stdev(R)	46.637
Z-value	-68.776
p-value (2-tailed)	0.000

Table 2   Test Statistics of the Runs Test of randomness

The analysis reveals the deficiencies of the 1988 HWMS data set since it does not exhibit

the statistical properties of randomness, independence and stationarity and is, thus, not

free from the deterministic component that is significant. Therefore, PDF modelling on

an annual basis is statistically invalid. A hypothetical approach is to model hourly within

a month (table 3), i.e., 24 PDF models/ month (Chadee 2002). The HWMS is divided into

12 one-month series on the basis that wind has a relatively homogeneous behaviour

within a month (Blanchard and Desrochers 1984). The hypothetical approach is tested for

validity with the February 1988-1990 HWMS for Crown Point. Chadee 2002 showed that

the hypothetical approach to PDF modelling with slight modification exposes the

stochastic component of the 1988 HWMS and removes any significant influence of the

deterministic component. This represents a substantial improvement to the statistically

invalid traditional annual basis approach and, thus, the validity of scientific conclusions

based on this new approach will not be suspect. The hypothetical approach is

recommended for use in the WSFM.

	1am	2am	....	12am	....	11pm	12pm
2/01/88							
2/02/88							
.							
.							
.							
2/28/88							
2/29/88							
	1am PDF model	2am PDF model		12am PDF model		11pm PDF model	12pm PDF model

Table 3   **A hypothetical PDF modelling approach (Chadee 2002)**

An empirical study is conducted with the RAY, WE2, HWE2, P3, LP3 and GG3 models. The 1am-4am models are defined and modifications similar to the HWE2 are made to the P3, LP3 and GG3 models to accommodate the zero wind speeds. Table 4 presents the MOM parameters for the models.

Model		Hour			
		1am	**2am**	**3am**	**4am**
RAY	$\bar{u}$	1.602	1.658	1.693	1.677
WE2	k	1.744	1.499	1.829	1.585
	c	1.799	1.875	1.905	1.869
HWE2	k_h	2.515	2.585	2.938	2.727
	c_h	2.072	2.340	2.214	2.323
LP3	α	-0.081	-0.097	0.089	-0.062
	β	29.255	20.192	19.071	42.282
	γ	2.893	2.599	2.299	3.270
P3	α	0.352	0.337	0.231	0.359
	β	4.993	6.621	10.045	5.223
	γ	0.081	-0.152	-0.345	0.191
GG3	α	4.394	1.757	1.503	8.567
	λ	6.626	4.434	4.270	8.894
	s	0.909	1.139	1.310	0.802

Table 4   **Model Parameters**

Figures 2, 3, 4 and 5 presents a histogram comparison of the defined models for visual examination.

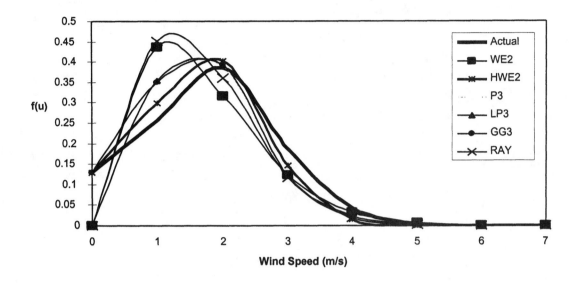

Figure 2   1am Models

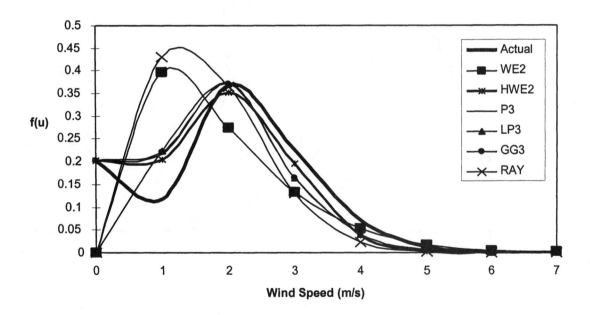

Figure 3   2am Models

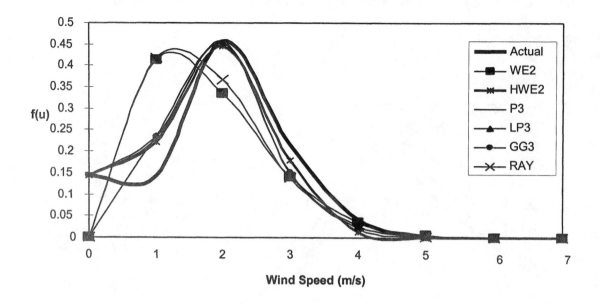

Figure 4   3am Models

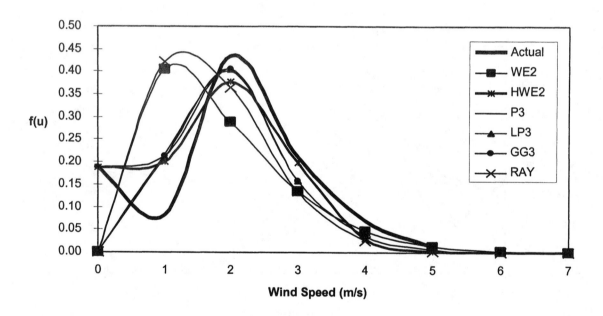

Figure 5   4am Models

Table 5 presents a mean power densities (W/m^2) comparison and an assessment of the models performance (%). Model performance is determined by:

$$\left(\frac{\bar{P}_{wt} - \bar{P}_{act}}{\bar{P}_{act}} \right) *100 \qquad \textbf{[30]}$$

where $\bar{P}_{wt}$ = Model mean power density estimate (W/m^2).

$\bar{P}_{act}$ = Actual mean power density (W/m^2).

Model	1am		2am		3am		4am	
	W/m^2	%	W/m^2	%	W/m^2	%	W/m^2	%
RAY	4.616	-9.710	5.109	-22.510	5.444	-2.280	5.296	-17.122
WE2	5.368	5.005	7.757	17.639	5.988	7.494	6.969	9.064
HWE2	4.998	-2.239	6.478	-1.753	5.513	-1.038	6.256	-2.099
LP3	5.110	-0.045	6.594	0.001	5.568	-0.051	6.390	-0.002
P3	5.150	0.742	6.637	0.656	5.605	0.614	6.429	0.604
GG3	5.152	0.772	6.637	0.654	5.604	0.593	6.429	0.607

Table 5   Mean Power Densities of Models

The visual examination clearly shows that the WE2 and RAY do not properly fit the actual wind speed distribution, especially for the lower wind speeds, whereas the Gamma and HWE2 models provides a good fit for all the modelling hours. The RAY performance is mediocre (-2.3 to -22.5%) and underestimates for all hours. The WE2 is slightly better (5 to 17.6%) and overestimates whereas the HWE2 performance is the best (-1 to -2.2%) of the standard models and underestimates. However, the Gamma models performed extremely well; LP3 (-.001 to -.051%), P3 (.604 to 742%), GG3 (.593 to .772%). Thus, the Gamma models do offer much greater flexibility and accuracy than the standard models.

5.0 Conclusions

The current WSFM was proven to be statistically invalid and a new WSFM approach is offered. An empirical study for illustration demonstrated that the flexible Gamma models were much superior to the standard WE2, RAY and HWE2 models. Thus, the WSFM area can be revitalised by focussing attention on the development of three or more parameter models. Consequently mathematical procedures are detailed. These may be computer modelled and then applied to other global wind data sets for more substantial empirical justification. A simple critique of the WE2 is that it is an extreme value model used for modelling hourly mean wind speed data (HMWS). However such models of extremes are for use in such applications as failure analysis, wind loading on buildings etc. The WE2 is critiqued further in Chadee 2002 with a larger HWMS data set. Using WE2 and RAY for the considerable effort of analysing wind regimes in many areas of the World for wind power development may be unjustified.

REFERENCES

Baker, R.W.; Walker, S.N. and Wade, J.E. (1983) *"Annual and Seasonal Variations in Mean Wind Speed and Wind Turbine Production"*, Solar Energy, Vol. 45, No. 5, 285-289.

Bardsley, W.E. (1980) *"Note on the Use of the Inverse Gaussian Distribution for Wind Energy Applications"*, Journal of Applied Meteorology, 19(9), 1126-1130.

Baynes, C.G. (1974) *"The Statistics of Strong Winds for Engineering Applications"*, University of Western Ontario Report, BLWT-4-1974.

Baynes, C.J. and Davenport, A.G. (1975) *"Some Statistical Models for Wind Climate Prediction"*, Preprints Fourth Conf. Probability and Statistics in the Atmospheric Sciences, Tallahassee, Fla., Amer. Meteor. Soc., 1-7.

Blanchard, M and Desrochers, G. (1984) *"Generation of Autocorrelated Wind Speeds for Wind Energy Conversion System Studies"*, Solar Energy, Vol. 33, No. 6, 571-579.

Bobee, B. (1975a) *"The Log-Pearson Type 3 Distribution and its Application in Hydrology"*, Water Resources Research, 11(5), 681-689.

Bowden, G.J.; Barker, P.R.; Shestopal, V.O. and Twidell, J.W. (1983) *"The Weibull Distribution Function and Wind Power Statistics"*, Wind Engineering, 7(2), pp. 85-98.

Brooks, C.E.; Durst, C.S.; Carruthers, D; Dewar, D. and Sawyer, J.S. (1950) *"Upper Wind Winds Over the World"*, Geophysical Memoirs, Great Britain Met Office, M.O. 499e, # 85, 1-50.

Brooks, C.E. and Carruthers, N. (1953) *"Handbook of Statistical Methods in Meteorology"*, Her Majesty's Stationary Office, London, England.

Chadee, J.C. (2000). *"Development of the Wind Potential of Trinidad and Tobago for Electricity Generation"*, Unpublished Report.

Chadee, J.C. (2002). *"A New Wind Speed Frequency Modelling (WSFM) Approach and its Applications"*, Unpublished M.Phil. Thesis.

Chadee, J.C. (2002). *"Wind Speed Distributions: A New Catalogue of Defined Models"*, Wind Engineering. Accepted for publishing.

Coelingh, J.P.; Van Wijk, A.J.M. and Holtslag, A.A.M. (1997) *"Comparing Wind Speeds on the North Coast and Offshore"*, Wind Engineering, Vol. 21, No. 5, 307-318.

Corotis, R; Sigl, H. and Cohen, M. (1977) *"Variance Analysis of Wind Characteristics for Energy Conversion"*, Journal of Applied Meteorology, 16(11), 1149-1157.

Court, A. (1974) *"Wind Shear Extremes."* Proceedings of the Initial Wind Energy Data Assessment Study, Asheville, North Carolina, July 29-31, M.J. Changery, Ed., published as a report NSF-RA-N-75-020, May 1975.

Crutcher, H.L. and Baer, L. (1962) *"Computations from Elliptical Wind Distribution Statistics"*, Journal of Applied Meteorology, 1, pp. 522-530.
Davenport, A.G. (1963) *"The Relationship of Wind Structure to Wind Loading"*, Proc. of the Conference on Wind Effects on Structures, National Physics Lab, London, England, pp. 19-82.

Douglas, N.G. and Saluja, G.S. (1996) *"Results and Verification of a Regional Wind Energy Resource Survey"*, Wind Engineering, Vol. 20, No. 1, 1-9.

EWEC (1999) *" Wind Energy for the Next Millennium"*, Proceedings of the EWEC Conference, Nice, France, James and James (Science Publishers) Ltd., London, UK.

Exell, R.H.B. (1985) *"The Wind Energy Potential of Thailand"*, Solar Energy, 35(1), 3-13.

Halliday, J.A. (1984) *"Analysis of Wind Speed Data Recorded at 14 Widely Dispersed U.K. Meteorological Stations"*, Wind Engineering, 8(1), 50-73.

Hennessey, J.P. (1977) *"Some Aspects of Wind Power Statistics"*, Journal of Applied Meteorology, 16(2), 119-128.

Hennessey, J.P. (1978) *"A Comparison of the Weibull and Rayleigh Distribution for Estimating Wind Power Potential"*, Wind Engineering, 2(3), 156-164.

Justus, C.G.; Hargraves, W.R.; Mikhail, A. and Graber, D. (1978) "Methods for Estimating Wind Speed Frequency Distributions", Journal of Applied Meteorology, 17(3), 350-353.

Justus, C.G.; Hargraves, W.R. and Yalcin, A. (1976) *"Nationwide Assessment of Potential Output from Wind Powered Generators"*, Journal of Applied Meteorology, 15(7), 673-678.

Katsoulis, B.D. and Metaxas, D.A. (1992) *"The Wind Energy Potential of Western Greece"*, Solar Energy, Vol. 49, No. 6, 463-476.

Kite, G.W. (1977) *"Frequency and Risk Analysis in Hydrology"*, Water Res. Publications. Fort Collins, CO.

Kuo, J.H. (1984) *"Evaluation of the Methods of Parameter Estimation for the Generalised Gamma Distribution"*, Master Thesis, Asian Institute of Technology, Bangkok, Thailand.

Luna, R.E. and Church, H.W. (1974) *"Estimation of Long Term Concentrations Using a "Universal" Wind Speed Distribution"*, Journal of Applied Meteorology, 13(8), 910-916.

Mulugetta, Y. and Drake, F. (1996) *"Assessment of Solar and Wind Energy Resources in Ethiopia II: Wind Energy"*, Solar Energy, Vol. 57, No. 4, 323-334.

Pashrades, S. and Christofides, C. (1995) *"Statistical Analysis of Wind Speed and Direction in Cyprus"*, Solar Energy, Vol. 55, No. 5, 405-414.

Persaud, S; Flynn, D. and Fox, B. (1999) *"Potential for Wind Generation on the Guyana Coastlands"*, Renewable Energy, 18, 175-189.

Poje, D. and Cividini, B. (1998) *"Assessment of Wind Energy Potential in Croatia"*, Solar Energy, Vol. 41, No. 6, 543-554.

Putnam, P.C. (1948) *"Power From the Wind"*, Van Nostrand, 224pp.

Pallabazzer, R. (1995) *"Evaluation of Wind-Generator Potentiality"*, Solar Energy, 55(1), 49-59.

Sherlock, R.H. (1951) *"Analysing Winds for frequency and Duration"*, Meteor. Monog., No. 4, Amer. Meteor. Soc., 72-79.

Smith, O.E. (1971) *"An Application of Distributions Derived from the Bivariate Normal Density Function"*, Proceedings of the International Symposium on Probability and Statistics in the Atmospheric Sciences, Honolulu, Hawaii, Amer. Meteor. Soc., 162-168.

Smith, O.E (1976) *"Vector Wind and Vector Shear Models, 0 to 27m Altitude for Cape*

Kennedy, Florida and Vandenberg AFB, California." NASA TM-X-73319.

Stacy, E.W. (1962) *"A Generalisation of the Gamma Distribution"*, Ann. Math. Stat., 33(3), 1187-1192.

Stacy, E.W. and Mihram, G.A. (1965) *"Parameter Estimation for a Generalised Gamma Distribution"*, Technometrics, 7(3), 349-358.

Stevens, M.J.M. and Smulders P.T. (1979) *"The Estimation of the Parameters of the Weibull Wind Speed Distribution for Wind Energy Utilization Purposes"*, Wind Engineering 3(2), 132-145.

Stewart, D.A. and Essenwanger, O.M. (1978) *"Frequency Distribution of Wind Speed Near the Surface"*, Journal of Applied Meteorology, 17(11), 1633-1642.

Takle, E.S. and Brown, J.M. (1978) "Note on the Use of Weibull Statistics to Characterize Wind Speed Data", Journal of Applied Meteorology, 17(4), 556-559.

Tuller, S.E. and Brett, A.C. (1984) *"The Characteristics of Wind Velocity that Favor the Fitting of a Weibull Distribution in Wind Speed Analysis"*, Journal of Climate and Applied Meteorology, 23(1), 124-134.

Wentink Jr., T. (1974) *"Wind Power Potential of Alaska: Part I"*, Geophysical Institute, University of Alaska, Fairbanks [NTIS, PN 238-507].

Widger, W.K. (1977) *"Estimations of Wind Speed Frequency Distributions Using Only the Monthly Average and Fastest Mile Data"*, Journal of Applied Meteorology, 16, pp. 244-247.

Chapter 38

PROSPECTIVE FORSCOM ENERGY INTENSITIES

Daryl R. Brown, CEM
James A. Dirks, CEM

Pacific Northwest National Laboratory

ABSTRACT

The U.S. Army's Forces Command (FORSCOM) has seen its energy intensity (MBtu/ksf[1] building floor space) drop from 118.8 in 1985 to 95.9 in 2000. Executive Order 13123 requires that energy intensity be reduced by 35% relative to 1985 by 2010. Thus, FORSCOM must further reduce its energy intensity to 77.2 by the end of this decade.

The objective of this study was to estimate the potential impact on FORSCOM's energy intensity in 2010 from key planned or prospective changes to installation energy-related infrastructure. This includes changes from the natural turnover of certain energy-related equipment, ongoing or currently planned programs, and retrofit with cost-effective energy efficiency measures.

The study results indicate that the combination of currently planned infrastructure changes coupled with cost-effective energy efficiency measures would allow FORSCOM to meet its energy goals. This paper describes these infrastructure changes, documents the analytical approach, and presents the results from the study.

INTRODUCTION

FORSCOM energy consumption per square foot of building floor space (hereinafter referred to as "energy intensity") has dropped from 118.8 MBtu/ksf in 1985 to 95.9 MBtu/ksf in 2000 or 19.3%. Executive Order energy goals require energy intensity to be reduced by 30% and 35% relative to the 1985 baseline for the years 2005 and 2010, respectively. This puts FORSCOM about 3%, or 4 MBtu/ksf, behind where it should have been in 2000 to be "on pace" for achieving the goals.

The objective of this study, conducted for FORSCOM by the Pacific Northwest National Laboratory (PNNL)[2], was to estimate the potential impact on FORSCOM's energy intensity in 2010 from key planned or prospective changes to the installation energy-related infrastructure. This includes changes from the natural turnover of certain energy-related equipment, ongoing or currently planned programs, and retrofit with cost-effective energy efficiency measures. The results of this assessment, providing an indication of the prospects for achieving FORSCOM's energy goals, should be used to guide the development of specific strategies for meeting those goals. The specific changes evaluated are briefly described below.

Replacement of Equipment on Failure

Existing building energy equipment (e.g., furnaces, heat pumps, chillers, etc.) is replaced with new equipment as it fails or wears out. This generally reduces energy consumption because new equipment tends to be more efficient.

Barracks Modernization

A significant fraction of the barracks stock is being improved in an Army-wide program impacting most FORSCOM installations. Many barracks have already been replaced or renovated, but the program will not be completed until the latter part of the current decade. In general, the new barracks are expected to use less energy than the existing units, although there may be exceptions to this rule.

Utilities Modernization

A significant fraction of FORSCOM energy consumption is associated with central plant energy conversion and thermal distribution losses. Many improvements have

---

[1] Per Army energy reporting practice, "MBtu" means million Btu.

[2] Operated for the U.S. Department of Energy by Battelle Memorial Institute under contract DE-AC06-76RL01830.

already been implemented or are in the process of being implemented as part of the Army-wide Utilities Modernization Program. While the Army-wide program is expiring, FORSCOM has initiated an Expanded Utilities Modernization Program for work to be completed from FY03-08. This represents a significant opportunity to improve the energy efficiency of these systems.

Housing Privatization

Housing privatization could affect future energy consumption per square foot in several potential ways. Privatization may result in housing being removed from the "goal inventory." With housing generally having lower energy intensity than other building types, this would increase FORSCOM's energy intensity for the residual goal inventory. If housing remains in the goal inventory, renovations and/or additions planned as a part of housing privatization will likely have a significant beneficial impact on energy intensity.

New Construction and Demolition

Improvements in energy-related equipment, stricter building codes, and larger buildings have generally resulted in the energy intensity of newer buildings being significantly less than older buildings. Continued new construction and demolition of older, less efficient buildings should help reduce the current energy intensity.

Cost-Effective Energy Efficiency Measures

Recent PNNL studies at Forts Hood and Stewart identified significant cost-effective energy efficiency opportunities with government funding and lesser, but still significant, opportunities with energy service company (ESCO) funding. With limited government funding available in the foreseeable future, the energy efficiency retrofit opportunity with ESCO funding is probably a more reasonable objective.

ANALYTICAL APPROACH

The general approach was to develop a model that represented the current energy infrastructure and energy use at each installation. The energy impacts resulting from the prospective changes outlined in the introduction were then estimated by making changes to appropriate assumptions in the model for one prospective change at a time. Building energy use was estimated with the Facility Energy Decision System (FEDS) model [1]. Non-building energy use, including central energy plants, thermal distribution, electrical distribution, exterior lighting, and water (waste, irrigation, and potable) pumping were modeled in a supplementary spreadsheet that incorporated FEDS model output.

FY00 building stock data were obtained for each FORSCOM installation from the HQEIS information system. These data were evaluated to develop 36 generic building proxies representing all FORSCOM square footage. The generic proxies were then tailored to match

the specific average building size and vintage characteristics within each of the building proxy categories at each installation. For some installations, the building inventory dictated using less than the full set of 36 proxies. Building energy use was then simulated using the specific proxies for each site with the FEDS model. Proxy characterizations were developed from multiple sources including 1) FEDS inferencing rules-of-thumb driven by building type, vintage, size, and location; 2) knowledge of building characteristics acquired from recent site visits to Forts Hood and Stewart; and 3) prior reports describing FORSCOM facilities.

Central energy conversion and distribution systems data were collected from the installations to help characterize loads and losses associated with these facilities. Data availability and quality varied significantly, so the specific approach taken to characterize the current situation varied significantly as well. Boiler fuel input and steam production data were available from some installations, so conversion efficiencies could be directly calculated. Steam production occurring during minimal demand periods (e.g., summer nights when space heating and service hot water heating demands are near zero) was used to estimate distribution system loss rates.

For some installations, central boiler data were not available, but the buildings served by central plants were known. This allowed FEDS to estimate the delivered steam or hot water load, with conversion losses assumed to be typical of other FORSCOM installations and thermal distribution losses based on estimates for other FORSCOM installations with adjustments for relative peak demand and length of the thermal distribution system.

Where no data were available, the buildings being served by central energy plants had to be assumed. Similar assumptions were developed for central chillers and their distribution systems. In general, less data describing chiller energy input and chilled water output were available than existed for boilers.

Prior studies of energy consumption at Forts Stewart and Hood yielded estimates of 0.60 and 0.70 kWh/building square foot per year for exterior lighting and water pumping combined. A value of 0.65 kWh/sf/year was assumed for the other nine installations. This is equivalent to about 2 MBtu/ksf/year. Electrical distribution losses were assumed to be 4% of purchased electricity.

Building and/or central energy system assumptions were adjusted within the uncertainty range for individual variables until modeled energy consumption and actual FY00 energy consumption were "reasonably close." The ratio of modeled to actual energy intensity ranged from 0.88 to 1.15 across the 11 installations, with a standard deviation of 0.08. Ratios of 1.0 and 0.99 were achieved for Forts Hood and Stewart, respectively, where more detailed site data were collected during recent visits. Although the absolute accuracy of the models was hurt because it was not possible to visit all sites, the models are believed to be reasonably accurate for estimating changes in energy consumption resulting from the prospective changes listed in the introduction.

Replacement of Equipment on Failure
Nothing lasts forever, including energy-related equipment. Through use and/or the passage of time, equipment wears out and eventually must be replaced. Some replacements are usually made with exactly the same equipment. For example, when T-12 lamps burn out, they are usually replaced with T-12 lamps with the same efficacy. Other replacements are usually made with the same type, but better performing equipment. For example, a new heat pump or chiller will likely operate with improved efficiency compared to the model being replaced. These types of equipment have shown evolutionary performance improvement over time as a result of manufacturer developments and more rigorous codes and standards.

Replacement of equipment on failure was assumed to affect the average vintage, hence performance, of all building-level space heating, space cooling, and service hot water equipment. The average vintage of such equipment was assumed to increase by 10 years. Improvements to unit efficiency were based on performance assumptions built into the FEDS model. Central plant heating and cooling equipment, although potentially improving over time as well, was not included in the calculation.

Barracks Modernization
The Army is in the middle of a decade-long program to modernize housing for single soldiers. Army-wide, the program affects approximately 160,000 spaces; within FORSCOM, 61,000 spaces are being modernized. 43,000 FORSCOM spaces will be modernized with funding authorized through FY01. The program is scheduled for conclusion (last year of new funding) in FY08.

In general, the degree of renovation is expected to be extensive. In most cases completely new barracks are being constructed. In other cases, the barracks are being torn down to their load-bearing support structures and are then rebuilt. For the purposes of evaluating the potential energy impact, the renovated barracks were assumed to be those that were generally older and larger. The renovated condition was assumed to be representative of new construction characteristics. Prospective energy savings were estimated with FEDS based on the presumed before and after characteristics of the renovated barracks.

Utilities Modernization
Energy conversion and distribution losses associated with centrally produced steam and hot water are estimated to be about 1.6 million MBtu per year across FORSCOM, or about 9% of total energy consumption. Data, where available, would indicate that boiler conversion efficiencies are generally good, in the 75% to 80% range. While some improvement may be possible in the conversion processes, much greater losses and potential room for improvement reside within the steam and hot water distribution systems.

Potential energy savings via utility modernization were estimated by assuming future loss rates of 0.30 MBtu/foot of piping per year[3], with adjustments where piping length data were judged to be unreliable. The total potential energy savings across FORSCOM was estimated to be 0.6 million MBtu per year. Fort Riley recently converted to building level boilers, so its distribution losses will be eliminated, as has already occurred at Fort Drum. Other Forts, such as Stewart, may also eliminate some of their current distribution piping in the next decade, which would increase the potential energy savings beyond that calculated. In addition, Fort Polk is currently considering replacement of its central heating and distribution system with distributed ground-source heat pumps, which would eliminate distribution losses and further improve space-heating efficiency compared to the existing boiler systems.

Lack of data made the estimation of current losses and potential improvements to central chilled water generation and distribution practically impossible. Improvements were only credited at Forts Riley and Stewart. Chilled water energy conversion and distribution losses will be reduced at Fort Riley as the current central absorption chillers are replaced with distributed vapor compression chillers. Chilled water distribution efficiency was assumed to climb from 77% to 90% at Stewart with the repair of insulation on chilled water and co-located hot water distribution piping.

Housing Privatization
Privatization is being used as a mechanism to address current inadequacies in the military's housing stock. According to the Army Family Housing Master Plan 2000, approximately 2/3 of the FY00 FORSCOM housing stock is inadequate and requires renovation. In addition, there is a housing shortage equivalent to about 15% of FORSCOM's FY00 housing stock.

Based on an assessment of inadequacies and shortages in the current stock, housing privatization is now planned for 8 of the 11 FORSCOM installations; privatization is less likely at Forts Drum, McPherson, and Riley, but still a possibility. Approximately 5300 new units are expected built via privatization, increasing the total housing stock to about 39,000 units. Note that the prospective impacts of government funded housing renovations and new construction are not included here, but were included with

---

[3] 0.30 MBtu/foot represents a modest improvement compared to current loss rates for the better performing FORSCOM distribution systems.

other planned new construction as described in a subsequent section.

Unlike barracks modernization, it was not as clear what degree of renovation would generally be required to repair the inadequacies found in the current housing stock. Renovation could mean anything from (for example) replacing carpet, which would not affect energy consumption, to completely replacing or rebuilding a structure, which would significantly affect energy consumption. Thus, it was not clear how to model the potential impact of housing renovation on energy consumption. Hence, the potential energy savings from housing renovation were ignored in this assessment.

The construction or conversion of approximately 6000 housing units will increase energy consumption and square footage. However, because housing generally consumes less energy per square foot than non-housing, a significant increase in the housing stock should result in lower energy intensities for the affected installations. In addition, new housing should generally be more energy efficient per square foot than the average existing unit. Energy consumption for the new housing was estimated by FEDS based on building characteristics typical of new housing for each installation.

True housing privatization could theoretically remove housing square footage and its energy consumption from the Army's management responsibility and energy intensity calculation. The potential impact of such a change was calculated by removing FY00 housing square footage and energy consumption from the energy intensity calculation. The prospects for such a change are discussed in the results.

New Construction

Lists of planned new construction for each Fort were developed by combining a FORSCOM-wide list of MCA (military construction, Army) projects with supplementary lists provided by each Fort, where available. The supplementary lists often included projects funded from sources other than MCA or were previously funded MCA projects that had not been completed by the end of FY00. The supplementary lists were screened to exclude items described as "long-range," "discretionary," or otherwise appearing to be more speculative than likely. Each building was categorized as either "new" (adding to total site square footage) or "replacement" (not adding to total site square footage).

The planned new construction data (building type, square footage, new or replacement) were used to modify the building proxies and/or the square footage represented by the proxies. Changes in energy consumption were then predicted via FEDS modeling of the adjusted proxies, with results multiplied by the square footage represented by each proxy.

Demolition

Lists of planned demolition for each Fort were created from FORSCOM-wide demolition lists developed for the FY01-03 Facility Reduction Plan (FRP). The FRP lists were supplemented with site-specific data, where provided and different. Although theoretically only covering planned demolition through FY01-03, funding constraints will probably delay completion of the planned demolition by several years. Therefore, the FY01-03 FRP demolition list should capture much of the demolition to be accomplished by FY10. Total FRP demolition across FORSCOM was 4 million square feet or about 2% of total building floor space.

The detailed FY01-03 FRP lists identified specific buildings scheduled for demolition. These buildings were removed from each site's inventory with subsequent changes to the average age and size (hence, other average building characteristics) for affected building proxies, as well as the square footage represented by the proxies. Changes in energy consumption were then predicted via FEDS modeling of the adjusted proxies and square footages.

RESULTS
Replacement of Equipment on Failure

The impacts of replacing equipment on failure are shown in Figure 1. Overall, this change in the energy infrastructure is expected to reduce the FORSCOM energy intensity by about 4 MBtu/ksf, which makes it one of the more important changes. Installation impacts are generally greater where the current energy intensity is high and little or no energy is provided from central energy plants. The evaluation of replacing equipment on failure was limited to equipment in buildings, i.e., similar potential impact within central energy plants was not evaluated.

Barracks Modernization

The impacts of barracks modernization are shown in Figure 2. Overall, the impact on FORSCOM's energy intensity is expected to be modest, resulting in a reduction of about 1 MBtu/ksf. Variation in site-specific impacts is generally explained by differences in the square footage of barracks being modernized and the fraction of total square footage this represents. The energy intensity reductions estimated for Forts Irwin and Lewis are lower than might be expected based on the square footage being constructed or renovated because the existing barracks were estimated to already have relatively low energy intensities.

Utilities Modernization

Utilities modernization impacts are shown in Figure 3. The overall potential impact for FORSCOM is estimated to be about 5 MBtu/ksf, which makes this one of the more important potential changes. As would be expected, installations with large thermal distribution systems in poor condition (e.g., Forts Campbell and Stewart) have the greatest opportunity for improvement. In contrast, there is little to gain at sites (e.g., Forts Drum, Irwin, and McPherson) with smaller systems (or none in the case of Fort Drum) in relatively good shape. The estimated reduction in energy intensity at Fort Riley is larger than might be expected from the size of its thermal distribution system because Riley is converting to distributed boilers, with central vapor compression chillers replacing the current central absorption chillers.

Housing Privatization

The estimated impacts brought by housing privatization are shown in Figure 4. As would be expected, the potential impact at individual installations varies considerably depending on the amount of new housing planned for construction. The overall impact for FORSCOM is significant, with energy intensity estimated to drop by about 3 MBtu/ksf from adding the new units.

The importance of housing to maintaining relatively low energy intensities is illustrated in Figure 5. If privatized housing were excluded from the energy intensity calculation, energy intensities would rise dramatically at the affected installations, with an overall increase of about 16 MBtu/ksf across FORSCOM. Variation in impact at the affected installations is attributable to differences in the fraction of building stock represented by housing and the energy intensities of housing and non-housing. Although privatized housing is expected to remain in the energy intensity calculation, FORSCOM would not meet its future energy efficiency goals if privatized housing were excluded and there were no adjustment to the 1985 baseline.

New Construction

The impact of new construction is shown in Figure 6. Overall, the impact on FORSCOM is relatively small, with an estimated energy intensity reduction of 1 MBtu/ksf. Variation among the installations is significant, reflecting variation in the planned new construction as a fraction of the current stock.

Demolition

Like new construction, the overall estimated energy intensity reduction for demolition is about 1 MBtu/ksf across FORSCOM. The impact of demolition on energy intensity is shown in Figure 7 for each installation as well as for FORSCOM. The prospective reduction in energy intensity is greatest at Fort Irwin, where 385 older housing units were assumed to be demolished in addition to the buildings on the formal FRP list. Unlike most installations, the energy intensity of housing and non-housing is essentially the same, so removal of inefficient housing improves the overall energy intensity. Note that demolition of relatively low energy intensity buildings at Fort McPherson is expected to increase its residual energy intensity, continuing an ongoing trend since 1985.

Retrofit

The potential impacts from implementing cost-effective retrofits are shown in Figures 8 and 9, for ESCO and government financing, respectively. Higher costs of capital and shorter cost recovery periods result in fewer cost-effective retrofits with ESCO financing, but with significantly less investment than for the government-funded scenario. In other words, ESCO financing eliminates the longer payback projects that would be economically possible with government funding. Of course, ESCO financing is generally more available in the current funding paradigm. The estimated reduction in energy intensity is about 14 MBtu/ksf with ESCO funding for FORSCOM overall, or about 2/3 of the estimated reduction with government funding. However, the estimated ESCO funding requirement to save 14 MBtu/ksf is $80 million, or significantly less than the $250 million estimated to save 21 MBtu/ksf with government funding. *Note that the estimated ESCO retrofit potential is approximately the same as the sum of all other impacts.*

Combined Impact

The combined impacts of all prospective changes for each installation and across FORSCOM are shown in Figure 10. These figures incorporate the potential impact of ESCO-funded rather than government-funded retrofits. The estimated reduction in energy intensity ranges from 11 to 44 MBtu/ksf for the individual installations and averages 28 MBtu/ksf for FORSCOM. *These figures were calculated by simply adding the impacts of the individual changes, so interactive effects, which will reduce the potential reduction in energy intensity, were not accounted for. For example, replacement of equipment on failure will hopefully not occur by 2010 in renovated barracks. Similarly, renovated barracks are unlikely candidates for cost-effective retrofits. Therefore, the potential reduction in energy intensity will likely be between 10% and 20% less.*

The impacts of individual changes across FORSCOM are shown in Figure 11. The combined impact of all changes across FORSCOM, with and without ESCO-funded or government-funded retrofits is shown in Figure 12. Included for comparison in Figure 12 are the actual FORSCOM energy intensities in FY85 and FY00 and the goal for FY10. The raw figures indicate that the combined effect of all changes, including full implementation of cost-effective ESCO-funded retrofits, would allow FORSCOM to beat its energy efficiency goal by 8 MBtu/ksf. If all cost-effective government-funded retrofits were implemented, FORSCOM's energy intensity drops by an additional 7 MBtu/ksf. Corrected for interactive effects, the potential reduction in energy intensity should put FORSCOM close to its FY10 goal.

Conclusions and Recommendations

- FORSCOM could potentially meet its FY10 energy efficiency goal with the combined savings of currently planned activities and ESCO-funded retrofits.

- The combined effect of currently planned activities (i.e., not including retrofits) could reduce FORSCOM's energy intensity by about 15 MBtu/ksf.

- Replacement of equipment on failure, utility modernization, and new housing constructed via privatization will reduce energy intensity the most of all currently planned activities.

- New construction, demolition, and barracks modernization will reduce energy intensity, but to a lesser extent than the three activities listed above.

- FORSCOM will not meet its FY10 energy efficiency goal if privatized housing is excluded from the building inventory with no adjustment to the 1985 baseline.

- Cost-effective ESCO-funded retrofits could potentially reduce energy intensity by about 14 MBtu/ksf; government funding, if available, would increase this figure by about 50%.

- Care should be taken in using the site-specific results from this study because most energy infrastructure characterizations were developed without the benefit of a site visit.

- The likelihood of compensating errors (rather than systematic errors skewing all results in one direction or the other) suggests greater accuracy for the FORSCOM results than for individual installation results.

Reference

1. Pacific Northwest National Laboratory. 1998. *Facility Energy Decision System, Release 4.0.* Richland, Washington.

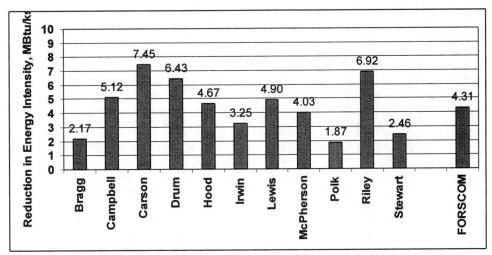

FIGURE 1. IMPACT OF REPLACING EQUIPMENT ON FAILURE

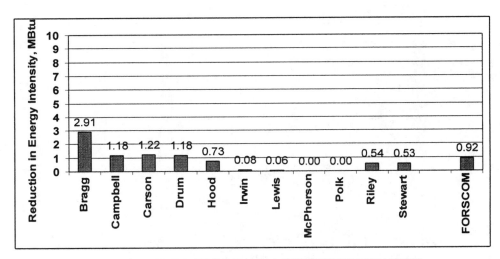

FIGURE 2. IMPACT OF BARRACKS MODERNIZATION

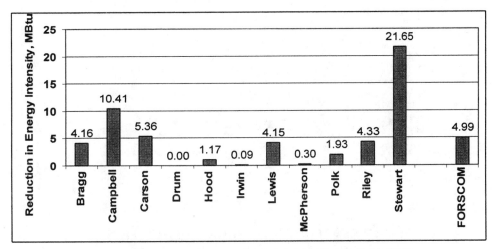

FIGURE 3. IMPACT OF UTILITIES MODERNIZATION

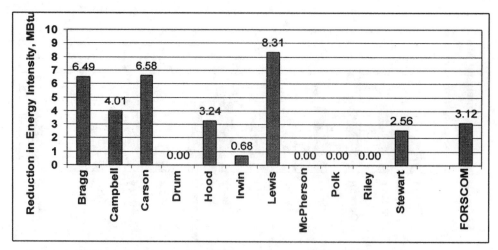

FIGURE 4. IMPACT OF NEW HOUSING WITH PRIVATIZATION

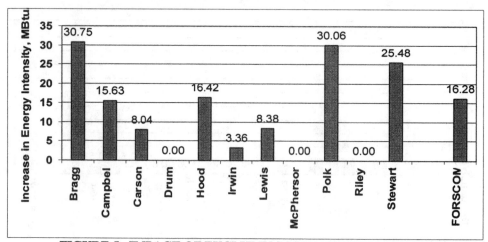

FIGURE 5. IMPACT OF EXCLUDING PRIVATIZED HOUSING

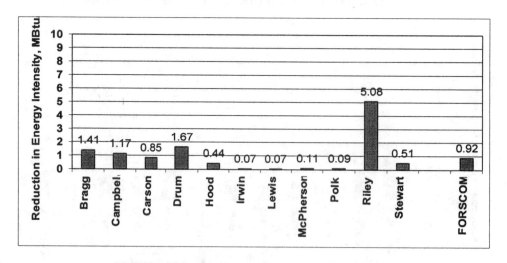

FIGURE 6. IMPACT OF NEW CONSTRUCTION

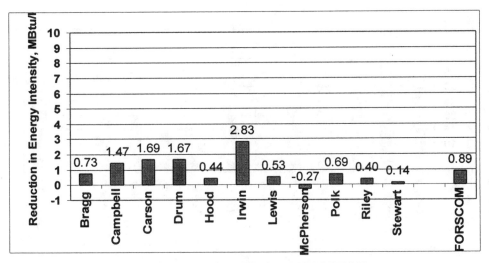

FIGURE 7. IMPACT OF DEMOLITION

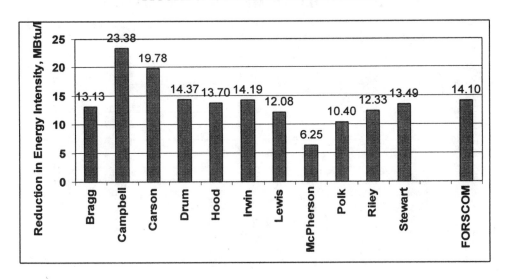

FIGURE 8. IMPACT OF COST-EFFECTIVE RETROFITS WITH ESCO FINANCING

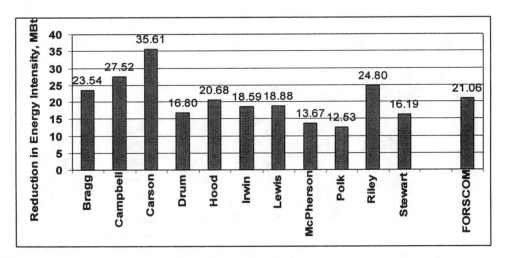

FIGURE 9. IMPACT OF COST-EFFECTIVE RETROFITS WITH GOVERNMENT FINANCING

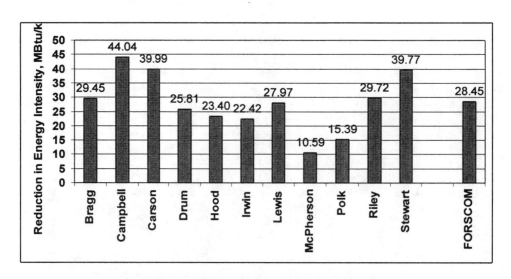

FIGURE 10. COMBINED IMPACT OF ALL CHANGES

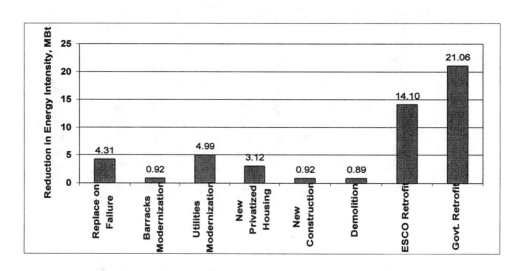

FIGURE 11. IMPACT OF CHANGES ACROSS FORSCOM

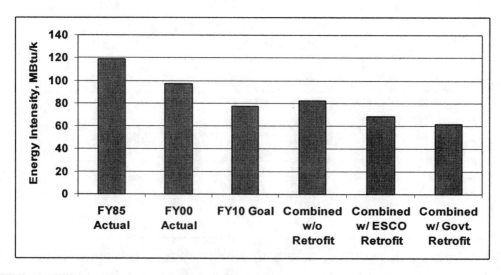

FIGURE 12. HISTORICAL AND PROSPECTIVE ENERGY INTENSITIES ACROSS FORSCOM

Section 2
GeoExchange

Chapter 39

GEOTHERMAL HEAT PUMPS – A CASE STUDY OF FEDERAL AGENCIES LEADING BY EXAMPLE

P. J. Hughes, Group Leader, Oak Ridge National Laboratory, Oak Ridge Tennessee, USA, and
J. A. Shonder, Research Engineer, Oak Ridge National Laboratory, Oak Ridge Tennessee, USA

ABSTRACT

The term geothermal heat pumps (also known as GHPs, ground-coupled heat pumps, and GeoExchange systems) refers to a family of systems that meet heating, cooling, and water heating needs while using 20 – 40% less energy than conventional space-conditioning systems. The GHP industry evolved from a few refinements in commercially available water-source heat pump and natural gas distribution pipe technology. Closed-loop ground heat exchangers made of high-density polyethylene, in combination with water-source heat pumps modified to operate over an extended range of entering water temperatures, enabled GHP systems to operate cost-effectively for both residential and commercial/institutional buildings in virtually any climate. Electric utilities in the United States, led initially by the rural electric cooperatives, embraced GHPs as a means to reduce utility peak loads, improve load factors, and gain market share. Policy makers took notice and estimated that widespread use of GHPs would enable the United States to save as much as 2.7 quads of energy, or over 3% of the nation's total. As part of the U.S. Department of Energy's overall GHP effort, several programs were launched to support mainstreaming the use of GHPs — including the Federal Energy Management Program's GHP technology-specific program. This paper introduces the technology and its history, describes the FEMP GHP program, reviews the success federal agencies have had in leading by example in the application of GHPs with FEMP's assistance, and discusses the lessons learned.

1. INTRODUCTION

The term geothermal heat pumps (also known as GHPs, ground-coupled heat pumps, and GeoExchange systems) refers to a family of systems that meet heating, cooling, and water heating needs while using 20 – 40% less energy than conventional space conditioning systems. GHP systems accomplish this by tapping heat sources and sinks that are near the buildings served — such as the ground, groundwater, surface water, wastewater streams, or potable water supplies (where allowed) — via water-source heat pumps (DOE FEMP 1999). These heat sources/sinks have moderate temperatures compared to outdoor air, the heat source/sink for conventional space-conditioning systems. GHPs are a renewable energy technology because the natural processes that sustain the sources/sinks at friendlier temperatures than outdoor air are always at work.

Water-source heat pumps (WSHPs) have been manufactured as a commercial product in the United States since the late 1950s (Hughes 1990). The original markets for WSHPs were primarily residential. The first market was in southern Florida, and these early systems used groundwater or canal water as the energy source/sink. Water was pumped from the source and discharged directly through the heat pump to the surface (canal, ditch, etc.).

In the early 1960s, systems for commercial and institutional applications using separate heat pumps for each zone, but connected to a common water loop, began to appear on the U.S.

West Coast. Referred to as the California heat pump system, the closed common loop was conditioned with an indirect closed-circuit water cooler for heat rejection and a boiler for heat addition to keep WSHP entering water temperatures within design limits. This concept quickly spread to the East Coast and elsewhere in North America. Today this system configuration is commonly referred to as the water-loop heat pump (WLHP) system (Pietsch 1988), and the market is primarily commercial office buildings but includes institutional buildings such as schools as well.

In the late 1970s and early 1980s the GHP industry began evolving from the older WSHP industry. With minor refinements WSHPs were made operable over an extended range of entering water temperatures. This enabled closed-loop ground heat exchangers to replace groundwater "pump and dump" as the geothermal source/sink in residential applications, and enabled ground heat exchangers to replace the boilers and towers in commercial and institutional applications.

The vast majority of GHPs in the United States are installed with the closed-loop system using continuous high-density polyethylene pipe buried in the earth, either in vertical or horizontal configuration. The closed-loop technology permits GHPs to be applied effectively almost anywhere, and this universal applicability was one of the keys to rapid growth in recent years.

The GHP industry started with very industrious entrepreneurs, including contractors and manufacturers, who built viable enterprises before any government or utility involvement. Since the early 1980s the utility industry has sponsored many modest but successful GHP programs in their service territories that clearly boosted the small industry in some localities. The U.S. Department of Energy (DOE), dating back to 1978, and utilities and their associations [the National Rural Electric Cooperative Association (NRECA) and the Electric Power Research Institute (EPRI)] sponsored modest R&D efforts in support of the fledgling GHP industry.

Some of the earliest and perhaps most widespread utility support of the GHP industry came from rural electric cooperatives (RECs) because of their unique circumstances. Most RECs are electric distribution companies that buy their power from statewide generation and transmission cooperatives (G&Ts) or investor-owned utilities (IOUs) on the wholesale market. The aggregate pattern of the electric loads they serve influences how economically RECs can procure wholesale power for resale to their customers. Lower peak demands and higher annual load factors are preferred. This pricing signal often encouraged RECs to seek ways to shave the peak loads — one of the main reasons the authors believe that hundreds of RECs helped the industry promote GHPs. A number shaved peak loads by 5 – 10 MW, others improved load factors by over 10%, and some even got directly into the GHP sales, installation, and service business.

Support of the GHP industry by IOUs came later, but their resources were orders of magnitude larger than RECs', so even a few successful IOU programs could have a noticeable impact. Since they could simply roll the cost of new power plants into the rate base, IOUs had less incentive to aggressively reduce peak loads. An informal review of utility programs, including both RECs and IOUs, found that the successful utilities often focused on a combination of commercial buildings, schools, and residential. One of the most successful GHP programs was developed by a utility that hired a vice president of marketing from a private-sector company. A benchmarking study found that utilities, which were regulated enterprises inexperienced in competitive business practices, often struggled as they ventured into the competitive market arena of GHPs and energy services (DOE 1997).

By the 1990s policy makers in Washington, D.C., noticed GHPs. DOE's Energy Information Administration (EIA), in a report supporting development of the National Energy Strategy, estimated GHP energy savings potential at 2.7 quadrillion Btu by 2030, up from less than 0.01 quad in 1990 (U.S. DOE 1990). A study by the U.S. Environmental Protection Agency (EPA) comparing the major HVAC options for residential applications determined that GHPs were the most energy efficient and environmentally benign option (EPA 1993). It became recognized that if — a *big* if — GHP technology were commonplace throughout the nation, the energy savings and emissions reductions would be significant. This set the stage for initiation of several major GHP programs, which are the topic of this paper.

In October 1993 the Clinton administration launched the Climate Change Action Plan as well as the voluntary Climate Challenge, a partnership between DOE and major electric utilities who pledged to reduce their greenhouse gas emissions. The Climate Challenge attracted over 50 utilities, whose chief executive officers sent letters to the Secretary of Energy stating their intent to either stabilize their greenhouse emissions at or below their 1990 levels or reduce their emissions to a different measurable performance level (DOE 1993). The Edison Electric Institute (EEI), supported by the NRECA and EPRI, selected GHPs as one of its five initiatives under the President's Climate Change Action Plan.

In 1994 DOE, EEI, NRECA, EPRI, the International Ground Source Heat Pump Association (IGSHPA), EPA, and several utilities initiated a collaborative effort for GHP market mobilization and technology demonstration called the National Earth Comfort Program (GHPC 1994). This program was supposed to build upon the GHP activities already underway led by industry, IGSHPA, DOE national laboratories, universities, EPRI, and NRECA. The Geothermal Heat Pump Consortium, Inc. (GHPC) was formed to implement the National Earth Comfort Program and original plans called for public/private spending of $100 million from 1994 to 2000 to do so. The initiative described below and intended to foster GHP applications in federal facilities was undertaken starting in late 1998.

2. DESCRIPTION OF FEMP'S GHP TECHNOLOGY-SPECIFIC PROGRAM

DOE's Federal Energy Management Program (FEMP) is one of the sectors within DOE's Office of Energy Efficiency and Renewable Energy (EERE). The primary mission of all the sectors within EERE except for FEMP is technology R&D. FEMP's mission is multi-faceted, but its most relevant aspect to this report is its effort to help U.S. federal agencies meet their mandates to reduce energy use in the 500,000 U.S. federal buildings (President Clinton 1999).

U.S. federal energy goals are expressed in terms of energy intensity (site usage in Btu per building area). The goals for 2005 and 2010 are 30 and 35% reductions in energy intensity, respectively, in comparison to 1985 energy consumption. To meet the 2010 goal federal facilities need to reduce their site energy consumption by an estimated 50 trillion Btu per year during the 2001–2010 period.

FEMP has many strategies for assisting agencies. These include design assistance to help agencies design and construct new buildings right the first time and guidelines making it easy for agencies to select equipment from among the most efficient available in each product category when making purchases. However, over 80% of the required annual savings of 50 trillion Btu is expected to come from retrofits of existing buildings. These projects include energy conservation measures (ECMs) such as lighting upgrades, insulation improvements, motor and drive upgrades, building control improvements, and HVAC equipment replacements. Because agencies rarely have all the appropriations they need to develop and fund energy-efficiency projects, FEMP supports agencies in the use of private-sector vehicles for project development and financing such as Energy Savings Performance Contracts (ESPCs) and Utility Energy Services Contracts (UESCs).

FEMP's agency customers are mandated to reduce building energy use, and they spend billions of dollars per year on new building construction, equipment purchases, major building renovations, energy, and energy-related operations and maintenance expenses. Therefore, it is not surprising that another FEMP mission is to help federal agencies lead by example in the use of advanced EERE technologies developed by DOE, industry, or partnerships between the two. FEMP is always looking for technologies that are commercially available, that are proven but underutilized, that save energy and money, have strong constituencies and momentum, and are wanted by, but not readily accessible to, agencies. GHPs met these criteria, so FEMP initiated a technology-specific program.

DOE's ongoing GHP programs sponsored by what was then called the Office of Power Technologies (EERE recently reorganized and OPT was carved into several pieces), including the National Earth Comfort Program and other initiatives, were essential contributing factors in preparing GHPs to meet FEMP's criteria. These programs created the initial interest in GHPs among agencies, and convinced FEMP that large public and private investments of other people's money would enable FEMP, with its very modest resources, to effectively help agencies gain access to the technology.

Perhaps most responsible for generating agency and FEMP interest in GHPs was a statistically valid evaluation study by Oak Ridge National Laboratory of a 4000-home GHP retrofit at Fort Polk, Louisiana. Under one of the first major federal energy savings performance contracts (ESPCs) in the United States completed in 1996 the energy services company (ESCO) installed GHPs, upgraded attic insulation, compact fluorescent lights, and low-flow shower heads. The results were significant: overall electricity consumption was reduced by 26 million kWh per year (33%) even though use of 260,000 therms per year of natural gas was also eliminated; the summer peak electric demand was reduced by 7.5 MW (43%); and the annual electric load factor increased from .52 to .62. (Hughes et al. 1998). In another study of about 50 schools in the Lincoln Nebraska school district, 4 of which had GHPs, it was determined that based on actual experience competitive first cost and energy and maintenance cost savings made GHPs the district's lowest life-cycle-cost HVAC option (Shonder et al. 2000).

Feedback from FEMP's agency customers indicated that DOE's GHP programs had stimulated their interest, but their efforts to move toward project development had proven challenging. The impediments to agencies were more related to shortcomings in the GHP delivery infrastructure than to problems with the technology. Shortcomings mentioned were lack of credible documentation of GHP benefits; no guides for surveying or auditing facilities and performing analyses to quickly determine whether GHPs were feasible; poor or no representations of GHP systems in the building energy analysis software programs used by agencies; no guides for construction or maintenance cost estimating of GHP systems; multiple ground heat exchanger design tools that gave conflicting recommendations and that required design inputs that were not readily available; lack of engineers willing to consider GHPs in their designs; and lack of quality (or any) GHP installation, commissioning, and service contractors in the area.

In short, federal sites were interested in GHP technology, were expecting to have all of the delivery infrastructure for GHPs that was available for mainstream ECMs, and were sometimes surprised to learn that it did not yet exist. Even more frustrating, in some cases where all of the technical barriers were overcome for particular GHP projects, the agencies lacked sufficient capital appropriations for implementation.

FEMP designed its GHP program to address these issues. The goal was to, within a few years, foster the transition of GHP technology from its status as a proven-but-underutilized technology into a mainstream ECM routinely considered for agency projects. There was no GHP unit or capacity shipment goal. Instead FEMP maintained its ongoing role as an unbiased, trusted federal advisor to its federal agency customers, available to help agencies apply GHP systems where they were economical and desired by the agency. There was no promotion of GHPs as part of FEMP's program. That was left to the providers of GHP systems and existing advocacy organizations such as the Geothermal Heat Pump Consortium (GHPC) and the International Ground Source Heat Pump Association (IGSHPA).

FEMP did not reinvent itself or even seek incremental appropriations to sponsor its emphasis on GHPs. Instead, it allocated a small portion of its existing funding to help agencies implement GHPs through its ongoing agency assistance programs. For example, existing building retrofit projects were the largest opportunity for GHPs, and the ESPC and UESC vehicles were emerging as the dominant means for implementing such projects. Some agencies have strong preferences for ESPCs or UESCs, so FEMP has ongoing outreach, education, and project facilitation programs to support both financing mechanisms. FEMP was able to cost-effectively support agency use of GHPs in ESPC and UESC projects by supplementing the existing FEMP ESPC and UESC teams with GHP technical experts.

FEMP geared its assistance to large commercial and institutional GHP projects. Observers noticing the military family housing emphasis may think otherwise, but when housing units are retrofitted by the hundreds or thousands, those projects share all the characteristics of large commercial and institutional projects. Why large projects? ESPCs and UESCs are best suited for multi-million-dollar projects because fixed transaction costs can be spread over a larger base and financing can be obtained at lower interest rates. Large projects enable bundling of GHPs with ECMs having shorter paybacks, increasing the number of feasible GHP projects under the ESPC and UESC vehicles where the project must be paid for by the cost savings generated by the retrofits. Small GHP projects require as much FEMP assistance as large ones, so large projects provide more leverage for FEMP's limited resources. Lastly, large GHP projects can bear the cost of attracting the necessary installation and service infrastructure to sites where none existed locally.

When FEMP's GHP program was being planned, only a small percentage of federal sites were served by electric utilities offering GHP projects through UESCs. And FEMP was not sure that the regional "all purpose" energy service companies (ESCOs) offering ESPC projects would emphasize GHPs either. Therefore, FEMP decided to include a special worldwide GHP Super ESPC procurement as a component of its GHP technology-specific program.

The GHP Super ESPC competitive procurement resulted in awards in 1999 of indefinite-delivery, indefinite-quantity contracts to five ESCOs who demonstrated expertise in the application of GHP systems through past performance and proposals for a specified project. This step ensured that every federal site worldwide would have access to several quality sources for development, financing, and implementation of GHP projects. Since every delivery order project implemented under these umbrella contracts must include GHPs, these ESCOs were also highly motivated to find agency sites where pay-from-savings GHP projects were feasible.

FEMP supported a few engineers at DOE's Oak Ridge National Laboratory (ORNL) to serve as its "GHP core team." The team's unique qualifications included involvement with GHP technology since the late 1970s, a technical leadership role in implementing FEMP's Super ESPC program, intimate knowledge of FEMP's UESC and design assistance programs, and knowledge of the cultures and design and construction practices at many different federal agencies. The GHP core team provided technical support to the DOE procurement officials who competitively awarded the GHP Super ESPC contracts. Then through FEMP's ongoing ESPC, UESC, and design assistance programs, the core team provided direct assistance to agency customers or the ESCOs/utilities and their subcontractors who were implementing GHP projects.

Since comparable resources are available for every other mainstream HVAC option, federal agencies and other building owners expect the GHP technical resources listed in Table 1 to be available for GHPs. The GHP core team's top priority is to provide direct assistance to federal

GHP projects. However, any remaining level of effort is applied toward using GHP project experience to advance the development of the tools listed in Table 1 that are as yet unfinished. The core team seeks partners and cost-sharing for all that it does. For example, core team members work within the technical community at ASHRAE — defining R&D work statements and serving on contractor selection and monitoring committees — because ASHRAE is currently the only sponsor of GHP R&D in the United States.

Table 1. GHP technical resources essential to achieving mainstream status by major project development stage – progress toward developing them.

Stage	Technical Resource	Progress
1. Credible evidence of benefits stage (evaluations)	a. Military Family Housing	(Hughes et al. 1998)
	b. Other Commercial/ Institutional	(Shonder et al. 2000)
2. Survey/audit stage	a. GHP Survey Guide— expandable for each GHP family member	To be completed in FY 2002
	b. GHP Survey Training—based on the GHP Survey Guide	
3. Feasibility/ decision-making stage	a. GHP Construction Cost Estimating Guide— expandable for each GHP family member	Enough vertical closed loop data is in the database to support statistically valid construction cost algorithm development, in progress. http://public.ornl.gov/BTC_MIC/logon.cfm
	b. GHP Maintenance Cost Estimating Guide— expandable for each GHP family member	Enough vertical closed loop data is in the database to support statistically valid maintenance cost algorithm development, in progress. (subset from ASHRAE 1998)
	c. Proven GHP Representations in (at least one, and hopefully all, commonly used) Building Energy Analysis Methods— expandable for each GHP family member.	Proven GHP representations now in research-grade software for use as a benchmark. Will begin testing commercial-grade software in FY 2002. Hope to find at least one commonly used method that is acceptable.
	d. GHP Feasibility Study Guide—expandable for each GHP family member	To be initiated in FY 2002
	e. GHP Feasibility Study Training—based on GHP Feasibility Study Guide	
4. Design stage	a. Proven In-Situ Tests for Soil/Rock Formation and Vertical Bore Backfill Thermal Property Determination	New method for analysis of in-situ test data developed and field tested (Shonder et al. 2000). ASHRAE Research Project 1118RP completed (Kavanaugh 2001)
	b. Proven Vertical Borehole Ground Heat Exchanger Design Tools	Technical papers documenting the comparison of available design methods and models calibrated to data, in ASHRAE Transactions (Shonder et al. 1999; Shonder et al. 2000). A report consolidating this information is in progress.
	c. Proven Borehole Completion Methods	ASHRAE Research Project 1016RP completed (Nutter 2001)
	d. Proven Standing Column Well Design Tools	ASHRAE Research Project 1119RP in progress (Spitler 2002)
	e. Proven Surface Water Loop Design Tools	ASHRAE work statement written but not yet approved for funding

	f. GHP Design Training	ASHRAE Short Course and ASHRAE Professional Development Seminar ongoing (ASHRAE 1997, ASHRAE 1995)
5. Implementation stage	a. GHP Guide Specifications— expandable for each GHP family member	GHP guide specifications have been developed for closed-loop and groundwater systems: http://www.eren.doe.gov/femp/ financing/espc/ghpspecs.html
	b. GHP Guide Covering GHP System Commissioning, Preventive Maintenance, and System Trouble-shooting— expandable for each GHP family member	(ASHRAE 2002)

To maximize GHP system acceptance, the various guides and training courses need to be developed, published, and offered to the public in accordance with the policies and procedures of the most recognized professional societies or associations in that mainstream field of endeavor. For example, designers of HVAC systems for large commercial and institutional projects generally turn to ASHRAE for their technical information needs; therefore the design items should be developed, published, and offered through ASHRAE. The Association of Energy Engineers (AEE), the National Ground Water Association (NGWA), and other groups may be the most appropriate mainstream organizations for some of the other items on the list. Of course IGSHPA continues to be the only industry association totally focused on GHP technology and applications.

The FEMP investment in GHP core team activities is summarized in Table 2. During the first year the team provided technical support to the DOE procurement officials who competitively awarded the GHP Super ESPC contracts. During subsequent years the core team's top priority has been to provide direct assistance to GHP projects. Remaining resources were applied toward using the GHP project experience to advance the development of the tools listed in Table 1.

Table 2. Federal Energy Management Program (FEMP) GHP Technology-Specific Program Funding

Fiscal year	DOE funding ($ millions)
1998	0.10
1999	0.25
2000	0.35
2001	0.35
All years	1.05

3. RESULTS OF FEMP'S GHP TECHNOLOGY-SPECIFIC PROGRAM

Government tracking of GHP industry shipment data provides an independent means of verifying the overall growth of the industry during the period 1994 to 1999. Data from DOE EIA based on a manufacturer's survey methodology are summarized in Table 3 (DOE 1999, DOE 2001). In the 1994 baseline year GHP capacity shipments were placed at 109,231 tons. Assuming shipments would have remained at the 1994 level without the major thrust of the public/private partnerships, 169,333 tons of above-baseline GHPs were shipped during the years 1995 – 1999. Therefore, it is theoretically possible that 150,000 of the 169,333 tons, or 89% of the above-baseline shipments, were influenced in some way by the National Earth Comfort Program as claimed by the GHPC.

EIA no longer tracks GHP shipments so industry growth after 1999 cannot be verified. The National Earth Comfort Program spent a total of approximately $60 million in years 1995 – 1999 and is believed to have influenced about 150,000 tons, which translates to an average of $400 per ton. However anecdotal evidence indicates that the overall GHP industry has continued to grow after 1999 and the continuing efforts of the GHPC and flywheel effect from earlier years deserve some of the credit.

Table 3. Annual GHP shipments according to EIA

Calendar year	Unit shipments (no.)	Capacity shipments (tons)
1994	28,094	109,231
1995	32,334	130,980
1996	31,385	112,970
1997	37,434	141,556
1998	38,266	141,446
1999	49,162	188,536

The federal boost to the GHP market began after 1999. Since FEMP launched its GHP emphasis program in late 1998, the annual federal investment in GHPs has grown from $6 million in FY 1999, to $33 million in FY 2000, to $76 million in FY 2001, as indicated in Figure 1 (Shonder 2002). FY 2001 investment includes about $49 million under ESPCs, $23 million under UESCs, and $4 million funded by appropriations. The trend is going strong, with another $70 million worth of federal GHP projects under development so far and potentially awardable in FY 2002. It is apparent from the investment trend shown in Figure 1 that essentially all of the increased activity results from the large financed "pay-from-savings" ESPC and UESC projects that FEMP is mostly involved with. FEMP examined the contract documents for the ESPCs and interviewed agencies with UESCs to determine that about 24,000 tons of GHPs were placed in these projects from FY 1999 through FY 2001.

As for progress on development of the GHP technical resources that federal agencies and other building owners expect for any mainstream HVAC option, FEMP has been a victim of its own success. There has been so much demand for direct GHP project assistance that progress on the tools has been slower than hoped. Nevertheless, significant progress has been made, as summarized in the right-hand column of Table 1.

As indicated in Table 2, FEMP has spent $1,050,000 on its GHP technology-specific program through FY 2001. With GHP capacity shipments of 24,000 tons, this corresponds to about $44 per ton. In addition FEMP and others have caused substantial progress to be made toward development of the GHP technical resources that both public- and private-sector building owners expect for any mainstream HVAC option.

However, in the view of FEMP and its agency customers, the primary motivation for embracing GHPs was to have another ECM useful for making progress toward their building energy use reduction goals. Based on the subset of GHP projects implemented under FEMP's Super ESPC program, agencies are saving, on average, 5000 site Btu annually for every dollar invested. For comparison, agencies save 7000 site Btu annually for every dollar invested under Super ESPC in general. Federal agencies will soon be moving on to "leading by example" with the next technology, and how well GHPs do will depend totally on their merits. To sustain federal market share the GHP industry will need to continue to improve its value by reducing costs, improving performance and reliability, and doing a better job of bundling GHPs into projects with other ECMs having shorter paybacks.

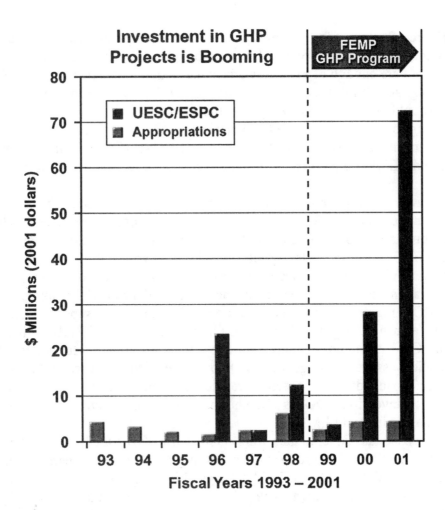

Figure 1. Federal investment in federal GHP projects for fiscal years 1993 – 2001. (UESC/ESPC numbers include the $19 million Fort Polk ESPC project in 1996 and the $9.4 million UESC project at Little Rock Air Force Base in 1998.)

4. DISCUSSION OF LESSONS LEARNED

Many actions and program components contributed to the success of the overall GHP program in recent years. GHP equipment and pipe manufacturers have reported very strong growth rates boosted partially by the rapidly growing federal sector demand influenced by the FEMP program. In the future federal agencies will most likely again lead by example in the use of advanced technology with assistance from FEMP. The following attempts to summarize the lessons learned from the GHP experience that may be useful in these future endeavors.

Look For Coattails. Federal agencies are always short of the funds they need to implement all of the building improvement projects they would like to do, and FEMP is a modestly funded program. In the case of GHP, it certainly did not hurt to have some $60 million of other people's money spent trying to expand the GHP industry. The chances of success for federal leadership by example are best when agencies focus on technologies with well-funded momentum, and FEMP customizes its assistance to match agency needs given the circumstances.

Public–Private Partnerships. Public-private partnership programs to advance the application of technologies have many benefits including shared cost and risk and broad-based buy-in. However there are enough of these nowadays that federal agencies and FEMP can afford to be selective. Big spending does not necessarily translate into applications momentum. Customer needs should be front and center — the customers are paying the ultimate bill. Technologies seeking to gain market share from entrenched products need to target small market niches where the barriers can be cost-effectively overcome first, and build from there. The best bets for agencies and FEMP are partnership programs that see the federal sector as an important market niche.

Build Programs Around Established Expertise and Organizations. Agencies and FEMP should beware of partnership programs inclined to re-invent the wheel. When DOE's Geothermal Division, as part of its overall GHP program, decided to explore opportunities to expand application of GHPs in the federal sector, it partnered with FEMP. FEMP already had a keen understanding of its federal agency customers, had respected ongoing programs that provided technical assistance and supported agencies' use of project financing, and had the infrastructure at DOE regional offices and national laboratories to support agency projects nationwide. FEMP also had as part of its team a few engineers at ORNL with a history of involvement with GHP technology since the late 1970s, intimate knowledge of FEMP's financing and technical assistance programs, and knowledge of the cultures and design and construction practices at many different federal agencies. By choosing established expertise and organizations over reinvention, DOE's Geothermal Division created a win-win-win for themselves, federal agencies and FEMP.

Meet Customer Needs. Federal sites were interested in GHP technology, were expecting to have all of the delivery infrastructure for GHPs that they had for mainstream ECMs, and were surprised to learn that it did not yet exist. FEMP designed its program to address the concerns of its agency customers. FEMP maintained its ongoing role as a trusted and unbiased federal advisor to its federal agency customers, available to help agencies apply GHP systems where they were economical and desired by the agency. Any new technology agencies take an interest in will pose challenges to application, and a customized series of actions will likely be required to address the impediments.

Large Projects Solve Many Problems. Large GHP projects can bear the cost of attracting the necessary installation and service infrastructure to sites where none existed locally. Federal agencies lack the funds they need for their projects and rely on partners to finance them via the ESPC and UESC vehicles. ESPCs and UESCs are best suited for multi-million-dollar projects because fixed transaction costs can be spread over a larger base and financing can be obtained at lower interest rates. Large projects also enable bundling of GHPs with ECMs having shorter paybacks, increasing the number of feasible GHP projects under the ESPC and UESC vehicles where "pay from savings" is required. Small GHP projects require as much FEMP assistance as large ones, so large projects provide more leverage for FEMP's limited resources. Nothing that was said in this paragraph is unique to GHPs.

Ensure Universal Access. When FEMP's GHP program was planned, only a small percentage of federal sites were served by electric utilities offering GHP projects through UESCs. And FEMP was not sure that the regional "all-purpose" ESCOs offering ESPC projects would emphasize GHPs either. Department of Defense and Department of State facilities around the world had no access to GHP systems. Therefore, FEMP decided to include a special worldwide GHP Super ESPC procurement as a component of its GHP technology-specific program. The ESCOs holding these contracts are motivated to find GHP project opportunities because all projects they do must include GHPs. There is plenty of evidence that utilities and regional ESCOs are now offering GHP projects to defend their markets. Federal agencies love options, and competition is good for the customer.

5. CONCLUSIONS

EERE technologies that are developed save energy and reduce pollutant emissions only if they achieve widespread adoption. Yet most governments focus virtually all of their resources on R&D. A much higher return on government investment to save energy and the environment could be derived from investing about 10% of the R&D funds on expanding adoption of EERE technologies that are commercially available, proven but underutilized, substantially reduce energy and emissions, are cost-effective, have a credible base and momentum, and are wanted by customers but to which access is not easy. It is clear from the GHP experience that even when EERE technologies meet these criteria, much research still needs to be done to help a fledgling technology grow. Applications research is needed to provide customers with all the guides and tools to make projects using the new technology no more difficult to develop and implement than conventional projects.

Market assessment and research is needed to target the market niches where the barriers to new technologies can be most cost-effectively overcome. It is clear from the GHP experience that federal agencies assisted by FEMP can be a powerful and cost-effective engine to lead by example in the application of new technologies.

ACKNOWLEDGMENTS

This work was funded by the U.S. Department of Energy, Office of Energy Efficiency and Renewable Energy, Federal Energy Management Program, and prepared by Oak Ridge National Laboratory, Oak Ridge, Tennessee 37831, which is managed by UT-Battelle, LLC, for the U.S. Department of Energy under contract no. DE-AC05-00OR22725. This paper represents the views of the authors and does not necessarily represent the views of DOE. The views and opinions of authors expressed herein do not necessarily state or reflect those of the United States Government or any agency thereof.

REFERENCES

Abnee 2002. Personal communication with Conn Abnee, Executive Director of the Geothermal Heat Pump Consortium, Inc.

ARI 1994. Statistical profile of the air-conditioning, refrigeration, and heating industry. Air-Conditioning and Refrigeration Institute, Arlington VA.

ASHRAE 1995. Commercial/institutional ground-source heat pump engineering manual. Caneta Research, Inc.

ASHRAE 1997. Ground-source heat pumps: design of geothermal systems for commercial and institutional buildings. Stephen P. Kavanaugh and Kevin Rafferty.

ASHRAE 1998. Operating experience with commercial ground source heat pump systems – final report of ASHRAE SP-863. Caneta Research, Inc.

ASHRAE 2002. Commissioning, preventative maintenance and troubleshooting guide for commercial GSHP systems – final report of ASHRAE SP-94. Caneta Research, Inc., Sachs and Sachs, Inc.

DOE 1990. Renewable Energy Excursion: Supporting Analysis for the National Energy Strategy. U. S. Department of Energy – Energy Information Administration. December.

DOE 1993. The Climate Change Action Plan. October.

DOE 1997. Geothermal heat pump benchmarking report. January.

DOE 1999. Renewable energy 1998: issues and trends – analysis of geothermal heat pump manufacturers survey data. U. S. Department of Energy – Energy Information Administration DOE/EIA-0628(98), p 59. March.

DOE 2001. Renewable energy annual 2000: with data for 1999 – 3. Survey of geothermal heat pump shipments. U. S. Department of Energy – Energy Information Administration DOE/EIA-0603(2000), p 27. March.

DOE Federal Energy Management Program (FEMP). 1999. FEMP Technology Focus – Geothermal Heat Pumps Deliver Big Savings for Federal Facilities, available at http://www.eren.doe.gov/femp/prodtech/pdfs/GHPTF.pdf

EPA 1993. Space Conditioning: the Next Frontier. U.S. Environmental Protection Agency. April.

GHPC 1994. National earth comfort program: summary edition. Geothermal Heat Pump Consortium, Inc.

GHPC 2001. Final report – national earth comfort program. DOE Contract DE-FC07-95ID13347. Geothermal Heat Pump Consortium, Inc.

Hughes P.J. 1990. Survey of water-source heat pump system configurations in current practice. ASHRAE Transactions, vol.96, Part 1, pp. 1021-1028.

Hughes P.J., Shonder J.A. 1998. The evaluation of a 4000-home geothermal heat pump retrofit at Fort Polk, Louisiana: final report. Oak Ridge National Laboratory, ORNL/CON-460. March.

Kavanaugh S. 2001. Investigation of methods for determining soil formation thermal properties from short-term field tests: final report, ASHRAE TRP-1118. University of Alabama.

Nutter D. 2001. Investigation of borehole completion methods to optimize the environmental benefits of GCHPs: final report, ASHRAE TRP-1016. University of Arkansas.

Pietsch J.A. 1988. Water-loop heat pump systems: assessment study. Electric Power Research Institute Final Report EM-5437.

Pratsch L.W. 2002. Personal communication with manager of DOE Solar Buildings Program, including Zero Energy Homes Program.

President Clinton 1999. Executive Order 13123: Greening the government through efficient energy management. Federal Register. June 3.

Shonder J.A., Baxter V.D., Hughes P.J., Thornton J.W. 1999. A new comparison of vertical ground heat exchanger design methods for residential applications. ASHRAE Transactions, Vol.105, Part 2, pp. 1179-1188.

Shonder J.A., Martin M.A., Hughes P.J., Thornton J.W. 2000. Geothermal heat pumps in K-12 schools: a case study of the Lincoln, Nebraska, schools. Oak Ridge National Laboratory ORNL/TM-2000/80. January.

Shonder J A., Beck J V. 2000. Field test of a new method for determining soil formation thermal conductivity and borehole resistance. ASHRAE Trans., Vol.106, Part 1, pp. 843-850.

Shonder J A., Baxter V D., Hughes P J., Thornton J W., 2000. A comparison of vertical ground heat exchanger design software for commercial applications. ASHRAE Trans., Vol.106, Part 1, pp. 831-842.

Shonder J.A. 2002. Personal communication from the leader of FEMP's GHP core team at Oak Ridge National Laboratory.

Spitler J. 2002. Standing column well model validation and design guide: final report, ASHRAE TRP-1119 (to be published). Oklahoma State University.

Chapter 40

Water+®
Geothermal Heating and Cooling from Municipal Water

Presented By:
Bruce Ritchey, President/CEO
WFI Industries Ltd. & WaterFurnace International, Inc.
9000 Conservation Drive
Fort Wayne, IN   46809
260-479-3224
bruce_ritchey@waterfurnace.com

Introduction:

Thank you for your interest in exploring the use of municipal water to heat and cool. The information in this presentation will give you an introduction to the concept and enough information to evaluate potential projects for this application.

The technology we are proposing is a patented and trademarked process called water+™. The technology was designed in the spirit of the United States Energy Act of 1992, which commands the Secretary of Energy to promote the use of Municipal Water as a source of heating and cooling (see Attachment A).

The system works by using the heat content of water from the water main to dramatically reduce the energy required to heat and cool. The water utility will be provided with a pumping station containing a heat exchanger that will transfer a small amount of heat to or from the water in the mains for use in a building. Water passing through the pump station is tested before and after leaving the heat exchanger to assure that the properties of the water remain within the parameters the utility desires. No water is destroyed or wasted.

The water passing through the pump station is altered in no way accept to raise or lower the temperature as it passes through. As the water returns to the water main, the earth surrounding the line and the large volume of water in the line absorbs the difference in temperature. Thus the water is a 100% renewable source of energy.

The water utility charges the building owner a fee for water used by the system. The profit for this service is normally not regulated, so it can be a great source of income for the utility while providing a very welcome advantage to the building owner.

The savings to the building owner are massive. The system operates at a 16 EER versus 9-11 EER for conventional heating and cooling. The system eliminates the need for roof penetrations, cooling towers, boilers, and expensive interior piping and expensive maintenance. The equipment is less costly and has an average life expectancy of 20 years versus 13 years for conventional outdoor units. (See Appendix B)

System Operation:

Water+ is a service offered only through the local water authority. Water purity and safety is their primary mission and they are the entity that will be held responsible. Therefore, the water in the system must be under the control of the water utility at all times.

The heart of the water+ system is the substation (Appendix C). The substation is owned and operated by the water utility. Like the water mains and fire hydrants, the substation is paid for by the developer or building owner and given to the city on a city right of way. The water utility will specify the contents of the substation in conjunction with the size of heat exchanger you select for the job.

Flo-pak, Inc. of Atlanta will build the substation as a module. The substation will be delivered to the job site in either an underground vault or an above ground building. The cost of the station will vary between $20k-45k. That amount replaces the need for a loop field, or in the case of a central system, you can eliminate the boiler, cooling tower and 2 of the 4 pipes.

Here's how it works: Water is drawn into the substation directly from the water main. An electronic sensor probe samples the incoming water and sends the data to a monitoring device that communicates to a Programmable Logic Control (PLC). The PLC can be programmed to sense whatever parameters the water utility chooses. Most would want to monitor Free Chlorine, pH, temperature and flow.

Once the water passes the sensor probe it enters the heat exchanger where it exchanges heat with the separate circuit serving the building. Flow through the heat exchanger is controlled to provide no more than a 5-degree F increase or decrease in temperature.

Water leaving the heat exchanger is again monitored to assure that it still meets the utility's standards. If the entering or leaving water is outside the parameters an alarm is sent either by radio signal or telephone line to the water utility. The water utility can then decide whether to dump the water to the drain or continue the flow through the pump, back into the main.

The water utility will also sample water at the facility on a regular schedule and send it to the state testing labs as they would with any ground source water source. From the utility point of view this pumping station is treated the same as a ground source water and point of entry to the potable water supply.

Design Considerations:
Most water utilities will not be aware of water+ and will need to be introduced to the concept. The best way to accomplish that is to have a building owner request it. When you are evaluating a potential geothermal installation that looks like it may be a good candidate for water+, have your customer request it. We have had no problem convincing customers of the benefits per the charts in Appendix B.

Once a specific building has been identified you can determine what it would take to apply water+ to the application. In general, we would like to see a location close to major water mains and a building that would not need more than 10% of the water produced from the water utility on a peak cooling or heating day.

Water will flow through the heat exchanger at 2 to 3 gallons per minute, per 12,000 BTUH at peak operating conditions. So, a 100-ton system could require up to 300 gallons of water per minute at peak. Over the course of a peak day it is conceivable that the peak condition could be maintained for 80% of the day. A 100-ton system could therefore require a flow of 345,600 gallons of water on the peak day. The water utility should be producing 10 times that amount in order to avoid temperature "creep" in the system.

Building and utility factors can effect temperature creep. The primary factor is load diversity. If the water is used to both heat and cool simultaneously the temperature increase and water required will be lowered. Many systems will use the water to heat hot water at the same time they are cooling the building. Cooling in some rooms will be required at the same time heating is required in others. The utility's schedule of "flushing" the mains will recycle the temperature of the whole main.

If the system requires more than 10% of the utility's output there are many steps that can be taken to solve the problem.

1. The utility can "flush the mains" at peak load times.
2. The water+ system can be supplemented with a small closed loop or well system.
3. The water+ system can be supplemented with a small boiler or cooling tower.
4. The water+ system could be supplemented with electric heat at off peak rates.

Designing the Building's HVAC system: The water supplied by water+ to the building's heat exchanger will vary with the temperatures of the water in the mains (usually 50-60 degrees F). The interior connections to the pumping station will be a simple in and out pipe to the heat exchanger with a variable speed pump to feed the watercourse heat pumps throughout the structure.

You will enjoy the benefit of saving all of the space normally taken by rooftops, chillers, boilers and cooling towers. The system can provide simultaneous heating in some areas and cooling in others with only 2 pipes rather than the usual 4-pipe system. Maintenance is greatly simplified dealing only with the pumping system and the self-contained watersource units that can be readily repaired or replaced without costly shutdowns.

Summary: Water+ provides all the benefits of a closed loop geothermal system without the initial cost of the loop. It requires no extraordinary design considerations on the part of either the HVAC designer or the water utility. Both parties are doing things they do every day. The system slashes the first cost of installation and can make geothermal the lowest cost as well as the most environmentally friendly way to heat and cool our buildings.

Appendix A

Energy Policy Act of 1992: Page 368

SEC. 3013. GEOTHERMAL HEAT PUMPS

The Secretary shall-

(1) encourage States, municipalities, counties, and townships to consider allowing the installation of geothermal heat pumps, and, where applicable, and consistent with public health and safety, to permit public and private water recipients to utilize the flow of water from, and back into, public and private water mains for the purpose of providing sufficient water supply for the operation of residential and commercial geothermal heat pumps; and

(2) not discourage any local authority which allows the use of geothermal heat pumps from-

> (A) inspecting , at any reasonable time, geothermal heat pump connections to the water system to ensure the exclusive use of the public or private water supply to the geothermal heat pump system; and

> (B) requiring that geothermal heat pump systems be designed and installed in a manner that eliminates any risk of contamination to the public water supply

Appendix B

180 Ton System

Water+ system at Fort Wayne
Geoexchange vs. 80AFUE/10 SEER Rooftops

Operating costs include heating, cooling and hot water.
Cost comparisons versus 10 SEER air conditioner, 80% gas furnace and gas hot water heater
Rates: 5.5 cents per kW for electric and 70 cents per therm for natural gas

<u>Air Conditioning Costs by Equipment Size:</u>	<u>Annual Costs</u>	<u>Start Up Costs</u>
Building operating hours 45%		
water+ line, substation and start up		$14,400
Energy savings per year	$ 69,098	
50% Demand charge reduction 111 kW x $120	<u>$ 13,348</u>	
Total energy savings and demand reduction	$ 82,436	
Total water+ charges per year	$ 14,400	
Net annual savings after water charges	**$ 68,036**	
Total Savings over 20 year Life of Equipment	**$1,080,454**	

water+ Installation with Heat Exchanger

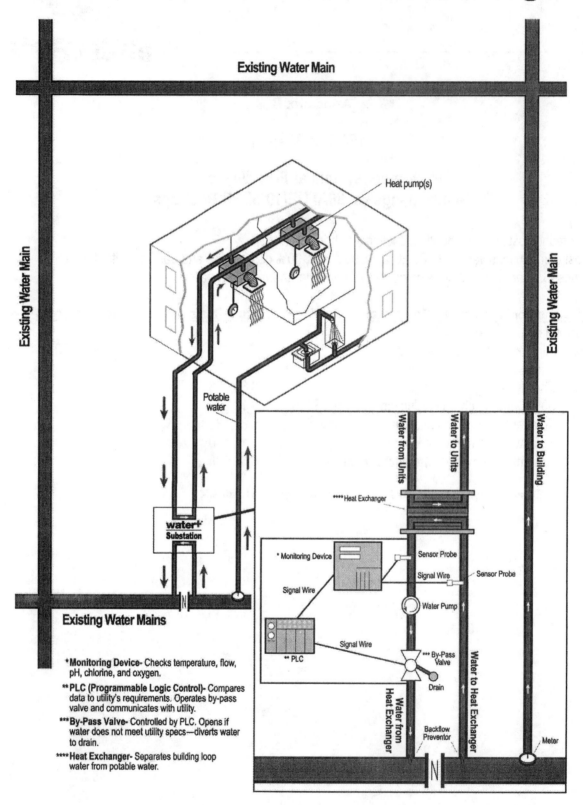

Existing Water Main

Existing Water Main

Existing Water Main

Existing Water Main

Heat pump(s)

Potable water

water+
Substation

Existing Water Mains

Water from Units

Water to Units

Water to Building

**** Heat Exchanger

* Monitoring Device

Sensor Probe

Signal Wire

Sensor Probe

Signal Wire

Water Pump

Signal Wire

** PLC

*** By-Pass Valve

Drain

Water from Heat Exchanger

Water to Heat Exchanger

Backflow Preventor

Meter

***Monitoring Device-** Checks temperature, flow, pH, chlorine, and oxygen.

****PLC (Programmable Logic Control)-** Compares data to utility's requirements. Operates by-pass valve and communicates with utility.

*****By-Pass Valve-** Controlled by PLC. Opens if water does not meet utility specs—diverts water to drain.

******Heat Exchanger-** Separates building loop water from potable water.

Section 3
Energy Service

Chapter 41

INVESTMENT GRADE ENERGY AUDIT

Ahmad R. Ganji, Ph.D., P.E.
BASE Energy, Inc.
San Francisco, CA 94103

Bruce Gilleland
Energy Management Division
California Department of General Services
Sacramento, CA 95814

25th World Energy Engineering Congress
Atlanta Georgia
October 9-11, 2002

ABSTRACT

The requirements of an investment grade energy audit for commercial, institutional and industrial facilities are reviewed. The results of review of investment grade audits for ten institutional facilities are briefly presented, and main deficiencies of the audits and their perceived causes are outlined. A checklist for the principal issues to look for in an investment grade audit is developed from the findings.

INTRODUCTION

Energy assessment/audit has become an accepted first step in identification and implementation of various energy efficiency opportunities in residential, commercial, institutional and industrial facilities. The objective of an energy audit is to identify economical energy/cost saving measures that do not adversely affect the quality of work/product and the environmental consequences of the equipment and processes. Energy audit is a needed step in implementation of any detailed and sizable energy efficiency project. Often there will be the need for engineering design before implementation/construction of the project.

The major impetus behind an energy audit is that the analysis of energy consumption and identification of potential conservation measures in facilities relate to various disciplines of engineering, that are often beyond the expertise of one person or small engineering firms. For example, on the less complex end of energy consumers, in the residential facilities, energy consumption depends on the structure, windows and doors, lighting, HVAC and refrigeration systems as well as cooking equipment. On the other end of the spectrum, in manufacturing facilities, the energy consumption is very process-dependent and greatly varies from facility to facility. Industrial facilities do not often lend themselves to standard prescriptive energy efficiency measures

customarily used in residential, commercial and institutional facilities.

There are two basic types of audits, walk-through audit and detailed audit, the latter considered investment grade audit. Investment grade audit is also called feasibility study by CEC (2000). An investment grade audit may be a comprehensive audit that is intended to identify all energy efficiency opportunities in a facility, or a more targeted audit which focuses on a specific piece of equipment or process, e.g. lighting, a boiler, a drying process, compressed air system.

Walk-through audits – Walk-through audits are usually done by utility representatives or equipment vendors. In an ideal case a person or a team knowledgeable in energy efficiency issues walks through the facility along with a facility personnel and identifies simple and standard energy efficiency measures such as lighting replacement, light and occupancy sensors, and high efficiency motors. The measures may be reported to the facility management with little substantiation and back-up information. Milan (2002) has prepared a guidebook for walk-through audits. Although the guide is for industrial facilities, it equally applies to commercial and institutional facilities.

Investment Grade Audits - According to CEC (2000), a detailed or investment grade audit (whether comprehensive or targeted) is a technical and economic analysis of potential energy saving projects in a facility that:

- Provides information on current energy-consuming equipment operations
- Identifies technically and economically feasible energy efficiency improvements for existing equipment, and
- Provides the customer with sufficient information to judge the technical and economic feasibility of the recommended projects.

Detailed or investment grade audits are the basis for further engineering analysis and design, and investment in energy efficiency improvements by facility owners or third parties. They can be also the basis for performance contract agreements. An accurate investment grade audit can result in identification of highly cost effective projects, and result in substantial cost/time savings in realization of the projects, while a low quality audit will result in unrealistic savings analysis, duplicate work in the engineering design process, and potential problems in performance contract agreements. More importantly, because some of these energy audits may become a basis for investment in, and establishment of distributed generation facilities in the present energy market, energy audit work may have significant economic repercussions.

It is the intent of this paper to review the requirements of detailed investment grade audit, including the audit of industrial facilities. A number of detailed audits for some institutional facilities in California are reviewed as cases, and their shortcomings are identified. The perceived causes of the shortcoming will be elaborated. Finally, a checklist for the basic contents of a detailed energy audit will be developed.

SOME ENERGY AUDIT CASES

BASE Energy, Inc. under contract with the State of California has had the opportunity to review some energy audit reports as owner representative for the State. The reports were prepared by energy service companies (ESCos), and in a few cases by energy engineering consultants. The audits and reviews have been performed since July 2001 after the peak of California energy crisis. The results from review of ten comprehensive audit reports are presented in the following table. The ten audits that are presented here were done by seven firms, some of them with national operations. The table has three columns, showing the facility that the audit report was prepared for, the recommended measures and the major issues that were raised by BASE staff after careful review of the audit reports.

It should be noted that despite shortcomings in some of these reports, many of the identified measures were deemed reasonable and were recommended for adoption. An eleventh report prepared by one of the firms was fairly complete and is not included in the table.

As noted in the third column "Issues Raised", there were significant deficiencies in most of these reports that stems from lack of adherence to the procedures outlined in CEC (2000). The important issue was lack of sufficient information in the reports for a design engineer to follow and complete the engineering of most of the projects. Additionally in most cases there was not sufficient information to repeat the analyses.

EXPECTATIONS FROM AN INVESTMENT GRADE AUDIT

CEC (2000) elaborates on the details of an investment grade audit. Although it may sometime be costly to follow the details of the process as outlined by CEC (2000), the final product of an investment grade audit (the audit report) needs to at least address the following issues:

- Clear operating hours per department (and equipment in the case of major energy users)
- Clear inventory of energy consuming equipment including their nominal ratings and capacities
- Energy rate/cost per unit of energy usage and for different types of energy (electricity, natural gas, etc.). In the case of electricity the customer may be paying for electrical demand too. In such a case, the demand cost and its basis should be clearly identified.
- Analysis of at least one year (as the base year) of energy consumption by type of energy/fuel
- Energy balance of the plant per type of fuel and preferably per meter based on rating, operating hour, utility factor and load factor of equipment. Utility factor is the ratio of the operating hours of a piece or group of equipment to the total operating hours of facility or department. Load factor is the ratio of the actual draw of equipment to the nominal rating of equipment, usually determined from measurement.
- Clear identification of major energy consuming processes and equipment in the whole facility
- Analysis of major energy efficiency measures identified in the audit process, which at least includes source of energy saving, amount and type of energy saved, cost savings, implementation cost and a pay-back analysis, as well as any major assumptions made in the analysis. In the case of computer simulation, a clear and succinct input/out put for computer programs needs to be included.
- Clear identification of the retrofit or control scheme/technology, and inclusion of cut sheets of the proposed equipment
- Clear identification of the measures that may have potential in similar facilities that do not exist or are not economical in the audited facility

It is expected that investment grade energy audits include realistic assumptions on the conservative side; be complete, self sufficient, and a clear guide to implementation, and serve as a roadmap to any future energy efficiency retrofit work in the facility. Assuming that an identified measure is chosen, and the detailed design is done, no more detailed energy consumption analysis should be needed to design and construct the measures.

SUMMARY OF ISSUES RELATED TO 10 REVIEWED COMPREHENSIVE ENERGY AUDIT REPORTS

Audit	Measures Recommended	Issues Raised

Office Building Southern California
 	
Firm A
	Retrofit part of the lighting system
	
	HVAC system upgrade
		Type of lamps and fixtures not identified, energy savings overestimated by about 40%
		HVAC system energy savings overestimated by about 50% (methodology problem)
		Various measures not identified:
		  VFD* for chilled water and condenser pumps
		  VFD for cooling tower fans
		  VFD for return fans
		  Proper control of supply fan VFD
		  Various control issues

Office Building Central Valley, CA Firm B	Installation of a New 400 Ton Variable Speed Chiller Upgrade Existing Partial Thermal Energy Storage System Install VSD* on Pumps and Fans Energy Management Hardware and Software Retrofit Lighting	No energy or demand balance presented Utility rate schedules were not identified DOE-2 simulation had been used but no input/output data were presented No equipment cut sheets presented, so performance data used in DOE-2 not clear It is not clear how cooling tower fans are controlled
Office Building San Francisco Bay Area, CA Firm A	Installation of VFDs on the Supply and return Fans. Installation of CO_2 Controls on the Return Air Fans. Installation of Damper Control.	Measured power of the motors is based on current measurement, lacks power factor measurement Fan curves have been used for VFD justification, not clear if flow and pressure were measured or assumed, fan curves are sensitive to both Numerical errors in power savings calculations resulted in overestimation of savings by 50% It is not clear why installation of CO_2 sensors are recommended and how it will result in any energy savings, maintenance cost savings, etc. Automating the on/off of the HVAC system not identified, while it is done manually now
Office Building Sacramento, CA Firm C	Lighting Retrofit Installation of a 100 kW photo voltaic Solar System	Rate schedules not identified Operating hours of equipment not identified Monthly utility data not included No equipment listing No energy balance has been done Inconsistent demand values has been used to size PVC system DOE-2 simulation done, but no conclusions were drawn
Prison Central Valley, CA Firm D	Lighting Retrofit Energy Management System Variable Air Volume HVAC Boiler Economizers and Fan VSDs Transformer Substation Cogeneration Replacement	Assumed plug load without justification No details of the HVAC system to be controlled by the EMS has been presented Measurement data for boiler not presented, but various measures recommended The basis for choosing the kW rating of the cogen is not clear FERC's criterion for cogen not clarified
Vocational Institution Central Valley, CA Firm D	Lighting Retrofit Thermal Energy Storage Programmable Timeclocks and Thermostats Boiler Economizer and Fan VSDs Dairy Chiller Heat Recovery New Water Booster Pump Cogeneration	Rate schedules not identified Boiler measurements not included Boilers optimization not taken into consideration Cogen calculations do not include actual plant data
Office Building Southern California Firm D	Lighting Retrofit EMS Controls Modifications VSD's for Pumps and Chillers Window Film Thermal Energy Storage	The schedule of operation of HVAC system and building temperature control (chillers included) are not clear. The specs for the HVAC system are not provided. The DOE-2 simulation has not been properly calibrated. There is a discrepancy of upto 50% in demand estimation

*Variable Speed Drive (VSD), the same as Variable Frequency Drive (VFD)

TABLE – CONTINUED

Audit	Measures Recommended	Issues Raised
Office Building Central Valley, CA Firm E	Lighting System Upgrade Power Conditioner (480V) Constant Volume to Variable Air Volume Energy System Management /Controls Cooling Tower Upgrades 120 kW Power Guard Photovoltaic System	Lighting energy savings significantly overestimated Cut sheets not included Energy and cost savings from Power Conditioner unsubstantiated Trace simulation input and output not included VFD is recommended for cooling tower fan, but motor size and info not provided No battery is recommended for the Photovoltaic cell, and it is not clear what will happen to produced energy when there is no need in the building
Office Building Central Valley, CA Firm F	Motors and Variable Speed Drives Air Handler Unit Upgrades Domestic Hot Water Heater Controls	Operating hours not clarified and inconsistent in the report No detailed equipment listing and energy balance presented Not clear how the savings in HVAC have been estimated, no analytical method presented
Office Building Central Valley, CA Firm G	Interior Lighting Retrofit High Energy Motor Replacement Retrofit Centrifugal Chiller with VSD	No energy balance presented Unrealistic cost savings of 43% has been presented for fluorescent lighting retrofit without delamping Effect of lighting retrofit on cooling not considered Overestimation of chiller operating hours by over 25% Overestimation of cost savings from high efficiency motors due to unrealistic unsubstantiated values in motor efficiencies

The following can serve as a checklist for preliminary screening of a detailed/investment grade energy audit:

_____ Are the energy rates based on historical (or projected) energy consumption and current (or projected) energy rates?

_____ Has energy usage (and demand in the case of large electricity users) been balanced for at least one full year of energy data, separately for different fuels and preferably per meter? The preferred forms of presentation is graphical (e.g. pie chart) or tabular.

_____ Are operating hours for different areas in the facility clearly identified and taken into consideration?

_____ Are major energy consumers clearly identified, and taken into consideration in the energy balance?

_____ Are the bases for implementation costs clearly identified?

_____ If a modeling software has been used, are the inputs and outputs clearly identified, so that another expert can repeat the work?

_____ For the proposed measures, is it clear why energy will be saved?

_____ Is it clear what form of retrofit is proposed and what are the advantages?

_____ Is it clear where the retrofit should take place?

_____ Have all potential energy efficiency measures been addressed?

MAJOR SHORTCOMINGS IN REVIEWED AUDIT REPORTS

The following have been the major issues with the audit reports we have reviewed:

- Lack of consistency in energy cost, demand cost, operating hours of various area of the facilities; often the basis for the considered demand cost is not clear
- Lack of energy balance, which often results in overestimation of the cost savings
- Lack of a clear description of the energy rate schedules, annual energy analysis, so that the customer is not really provided with a clear picture of how they are charged.
- Lack of equipment inventory and their ratings
- Lack of clear description and identification of retrofit scheme
- Overestimation of savings due to lack of consistency
- Lack of consideration of the latest retrofit technology
- Lack of pointing out the measures that may exist in similar facilities but do not exist in the surveyed facility

Overall, while the comprehensive detailed energy audit reports are supposed to provide a clear picture of the energy supply and consumption in the facility, and act as a roadmap for improvement of the energy utilization and cost reduction, they lacked some key components to serve the ultimate purpose.

PERCEIVED CAUSES

Some of the perceived causes of deficiencies in the audit reports seem to stem from:

- Lack of expertise of people who do the surveys, and more importantly those who prepare the report. Although taking inventory of equipment is fairly straightforward (filling out a site sheet), it often takes a clear understanding of complicated systems (e.g. a multiple-chiller system) to offer any meaningful energy efficiency improvements.

- Lack of basic knowledge of the fundamental engineering principles. Energy efficiency work is multidisciplinary, which necessitates a strong knowledge of fundamentals of mechanical and electrical engineering. It is always advisable to have a professional engineer oversee comprehensive energy audit projects.
- Lack of training in application of sophisticated simulation software such as DOE-2 and its various derivatives. Very sophisticated computer programs can produce incorrect results if they are not fed with the proper data (e.g. operating hours, load factors, etc.), and properly applied to the specific situation.
- Conflict of interest – Often the firm that conducts the survey and prepares the audit report, is the same or affiliated with the firm that will do the engineering design and implementation (such as full energy service companies). There may be cases that are not directly leading into a profitable project and get omitted, or some required steps and information are overlooked in the interest of "green lighting" a project. An example is when a firm is hired to do a comprehensive energy audit, but fails to take inventory of all equipment and evaluate them, in the interest of an attractive lighting retrofit project. Other examples are consideration of unrealistic operating hours, utility factors, load factors of the equipment. An oversized 50 hp fan motor may operate at 50% of its load, but it will not be known in the plant audit if its power draw is not measured!

MORE COMPLICATED ENERGY AUDIT CASES
Comprehensive energy audit of manufacturing facilities requires significantly higher expertise than commercial and institutional facilities. Energy consuming devices are highly varied and process/product-dependent, and many remote users may dictate the operation of major energy-consuming devices, e.g. boilers and compressors. In such cases understanding the process is as important as understanding the equipment. An auditor of commercial buildings will not necessarily have the expertise of auditing industrial facilities. While there are tens of energy saving opportunities in commercial facilities (refer to CEC 2000), there are hundreds of energy efficiency opportunities in industrial facilities. It is not uncommon to identify 10-30% energy efficiency opportunities with simple paybacks of zero to a few years in industrial facilities. Major guidelines for performing comprehensive energy audit of manufacturing facilities are the same as

those for commercial facilities. Some specific issues in audit of manufacturing facilities are:

- A much wider scope of measures and advanced technologies (inclusive of those for commercial facilities) can be identified in industrial facilities.
- While there are significant commonalties between industrial facilities with different processes, most facilities may have their unique energy efficiency measures that can be identified and analyzed based on fundamental engineering principles.
- Load measurements are required for major energy consuming devices. Some equipment may go through significant load variations.
- Energy usage in most industrial facilities are highly product and production dependent, and much less dependent on ambient conditions.
- Taking a detailed inventory (which includes the rating, usage pattern, loading) of energy consuming equipment is an essential component of a comprehensive energy audit of industrial facilities.

CONCLUDING REMARKS
CEC (2000), "Guide to Preparing Feasibility Studies of Energy Efficiency Projects" provides a comprehensive guide for reporting investment grade audits of various types of facilities. Although the guide has been mostly developed with institutional facilities in mind, its general recommended methods apply well to commercial, and for the most part to industrial facilities.

The results from review of investment grade audit of ten institutional facilities performed by seven ESCOs and engineering consulting firms show major deficiencies in their process and reporting, suggesting that closer adherence to the guidelines will significantly improve the works, and result in more realistic evaluation of the economics of the projects. Major deficiencies of the reviewed reports are outlined, and potential causes are briefly discussed. A checklist for initial evaluation of the investment grade audit reports is proposed.

At the end, in addition to the economics of the suggested measures, an investment grade energy audit should clearly define what the change/improvement is, and where it will take place, so that a designer would have specific knowledge for completing the design and specifications.

REFERENCES
1 - CEC (2000), "Guide to Preparing Feasibility Studies of Energy Efficiency Projects," Report P400-00-002, California Energy Commission.
2. – Milan, C. B. (2002), "A Guidebook for Preparing Walk-Through Energy Audits of Industrial Facilities,' Bonneville Power Administration, http://www.bpa.gov/Energy/N/reports/audit/index.shtml.

Chapter 42

A CONTRACTOR'S REAL WORLD PERFORMANCE CONTRACTING EXPERIENCES

Larry J. Fisher, President
ECT Services

ABSTRACT

Energy Services
WARNING—Parental Guidance Recommended—Sensitive material discussed which could be embarrassing, but truthful, some may even think humorous.

First, if you were expecting a technical paper, you're in the wrong room!

As I sit and wonder what to write on this very timely and hot, debated subject I reflect on my past experiences as a human being in the role of contractor. What does that mean?

Here I am delivering a paper in a room with of mix of people consisting of engineers (mechanical-electrical-energy), contractors, manufacturers, and end users. These are the same players in conventional contracting, and now I'm supposed to say something profound for the performance contracting.

This can be touchy to address all players at one time. How do you be truthful without offending at least one of the parties. After all does not the owner think their building is already perfect? Does not the engineer think all their ideas are a perfect fit for the owner? And does not the contractor(s) think they have a perfect plan to install the perfect energy cost reduction upgrade for the perfect owner? Oh, let's not forget about the manufacturer that when compared to other competition has the perfect answer to make the perfect upgrade fit.

Okay here we are—now what do I say? What can I say? Lie—that's it, lie!!!! No, Performance Contracting is still a very young field, and every player should know how the "installing contractor—me" sees the overall process of performance contracting.

First, there are two approaches to being awarded a portion of a PC. You can team up with a PC and have some input to the recommended ECO's, or just check the bid market for an opportunity to be low bidder. One has some advantages, the other has only disadvantages. (you figure it out!)

Let's discuss the low bidder PC market. First you have to make the biggest estimating mistake to be low bidder. Isn't that the way it works? The one that makes the biggest mistake is always the lowest bidder. As a PC, I would not want to be using the lowest bidder, as that bidder may want to take short cuts to make up for the bidding error. (Probably not cause all contractors are ethical, right?!) Should a PC get into bed with a low bid contractor, when the PC is going to guarantee savings for 15+ years to the perfect owner? This is a tough decision, (right). Think about it, the owner either requests an RFP or a PC presents the concept of PC to the owner. Either case, the owner (perfect, mind you) does not know any of the respondents of the RFP, nor do they know the PC direct sales approach. Does the owner ever really know them?

Now the PC has cut a deal (either thru the direct sales approach or the response to an RFP.) Now comes the detail engineering phase, lining up contractors (or bidders), and maybe clouding up the waters and inviting a few manufactures to throw in their two cents worth.

Here where we get to the title of the paper "A Contractor's Real World Performance Contracting Experiences" Now if it's a local project the contractor can simple go visit the site and see the conditions their selves. However, the arms of PC really stretch out to state, regional and national scales, so now you are dependent on the verbiage or narrative of a spec. What do you believe? Well, you would like to be low bidder, so listen to the "conditions" of the site, and how easy it is to get around in the building and how any piping to be removed or modified is like new and wiring is already in place, or all you have to do is a simple wiring connection. (There may be a hint of sarcasm in the air!)

Anyway, you succeed and are the low bidder! YES!!! Although you've never been to the site, you're sure the PC was right up front on stating conditions and you're raring to go. Contracts are signed, and finally a site visit is scheduled. This is to be followed by a pre-construction meeting with the owner. The project is only 2Ω hours from the office, an easy drive, plus all the way home you can plan the retrofits actual construction phases, piece of cake.

The day arrives, you even get to ride with the PC project manager, he has already seen the site once him self! The salesman is to meet us later in the pre-construction meeting with the perfect owner. I'm fired up!

This project is a large public high school. The building is only 12 years old, so nothing could be too tough. On arriving the envelope looks good, in fact, I can not believe the school is 12 years old. We check in the front office get visitors passes, and get an escort to the 12 year old mechanical room. So far so good! The outside mechanical room door opens and the lights flip on. Ugh! What happened to the 12 year old building? What was my scope of work? (By the way my contract consisted of the electrical, mechanical, and DDC web based controls). Okay let's get a little background of the mechanical system—Chiller, 2 boilers, 4 pipe system in the mechanical room, 4 zones that are two pipe systems with manual summer/winter changeover valves (4 for each zone).

I see no hot water reset valves, and the boilers are cast iron so there is no reset available here either.

I start going into shock, why is the insulation torn off in so many places? Is that thick rust I see on every flanged connection? Why is the existing insulation yellow stained everywhere? And why is it so cold in here? (November, mid-west state). To explain further, the domestic water heater and two boilers were gas fired, and there are four combustion air dampers that are supposed to operate (did you get the "supposed to" part?) in different sequences based on gas appliances burning. (okay, I said I was not going to get technical, well maybe a little). The maintenance escort (works for the perfect owner) says they haven't got around to closing them for the winter yet. I'm in trouble!

Next we visit a non working time clock that was to control separate zones in the building consisting of FCU's. There were supposed to be above ceiling control relays, all I have to do is wire in a couple control wires from the new BAS. You had to be there to see this. We found the panels, but what a mess they were, a total rewire was going to be required. Hm-m-m-m. Let's move on.

Next the gym has had a comfort problem for years. It seems the controls were installed, then abandoned, and other than turning on a "Mickey Mouse" switch, there was no control. Fortunately, the PC only promised the owner BAS occupied/unoccupied capability. May be an opportunity for service work.

Continuing our walk thru, we found mold growing on doors and walls in the lower level. The building design was like a walk out basement, with earth berm on two sides. IAQ was supposedly maintained by a 100% MUA unit This is not good. How can we save money by turning stuff off, when it appears dehumidification needs to be 24/7? Oh, just another challenge. I'm sure if the mold does not go away, it will be the controls fault and I'll never get paid. Man, I'm liking this performance contracting better every minute (sarcastic!).

Next we visit the chiller and it's current operation. Hey, this actually seems to be in pretty good shape, but there is not a low ambient controller installed. The interior parts of the building need to be cooled year around, so this is part of the upgrade, to allow for year around cooling to the interior zones. This will be accomplished by adding auto changeover valves in the mechanical room, and add hot water reset valves to the two interior zones so the introduction of hot water to a chiller can be avoided. Whew!

Time to go to the pre-construction meeting with the perfect owner. Driving to the meeting I'm reminded of the perfect engineering that has been done. We arrive and the perfect salesman is already there entertaining the perfect owner. We sit down and go thru introductions. The PM for the PC is a little baffled by what the salesperson sold as compared to what we saw. Me too!!

So we sit in the meeting and the sales person opens up the conservation by congratulating the owner for making the decision for participating in the PC world. As he continues on with the project scope of work and defining how the work is to be carried out, the PM is nodding his head in agreement. Wait a minute, is this the same person I just walked around the building with? Oh no, now they are asking me if I saw any problems. Now what do I do? If I tell the truth, the PC gets upset and they are holding the purse strings. If I agree everything is okay, the owner will eventually find out the issues at hand.

CONCLUSION

All kidding aside, performance contracting is one of the best opportunities to come along for the owners and contractors. Best advice. Get involved with a PC or two. Work on the design/build side of the contract—you spend more time up-front, but if you get the job, you spend a lot less time performing the work, plus you already know what is there.

If you have to go low bid, be careful, if you do not get an opportunity to visit the site and read the proposed scope of work in detail, don't bid it. The project in the above narrative is true. My power point presentation covers more ground, so contact me if you want a copy. The project made us money (it was supposed to was it not?) and we developed a direct relationship with the customer. This has resulted in several projects performed direct to the owner, plus future opportunities for additional work at some of their other buildings.

1501 S Preston
Louisville, KY. 40217
502-636-2402; Fax 502-636-0105; e-mail
lfisher@ectservice.com

Chapter 43

A Discussion of the Economic Aspects
of Implementing Energy Conservation Opportunities

By
Stephen A. Roosa CEM, CIAQP, MBA
Energy Management Alternatives, Inc.

ABSTRACT

The issue of urban energy consumption has an identifiable set of benefits and costs. Interestingly, energy usage is highly decentralized while energy generation and production tends to be relatively centralized. These issues have both a local and global impact. Concerns may include those associated with water and air pollution plus economic availability issues. Energy usage by the built environment has been increasing due to a large number of reasons. Increasing population and corresponding increase in the volume of conditioned space causes increasing energy use. The need for highly conditioned space has caused development of new standards for human comfort, especially in the workplace. The need to mitigate indoor air quality issues has risen to the forefront of the indoor environment debate.

More efficient use of energy in the built environment can have a significant impact in meeting certain urban goals. These goals include the ability to provide for urban expansion without constructing additional power generating facilities while improving environmental quality. Technologies are available to provide more efficient use of energy. Interestingly, energy efficiency technologies are often not employed.

There are also various means of justifying, financing and implementing energy reduction technologies. They include use of capital funds, maintenance (sometime referred to as overhead) funding, borrowing money, or allowing the projects to be funded and implemented by a third party. One type of third party approach is to use Performance Contracting.

The purpose of this paper is to explore issues concerning energy usage in the built environment and consider the use of Performance Contracting as a means of implementing energy conservation measures. It is possible to implement economically feasible energy conservation facility improvements without the incentives that performance contracting offers. However, performance contracting offers numerous advantages in the marketplace as a mechanism for implementing solutions. Project experiences in Kentucky will be cited as a case study to provide empirical evidence of the use of performance contracting.

INTRODUCTION

"In truth, of all great cities, London is the greatest....Even its antiquity is impressive; for London is more than two thousand years old....yet only seven hundred years ago, although already thirteen centuries old, it contained less than fifty thousand inhabitants; and five more centuries of growth were needed to raise its population to two hundred thousand. It had not reached a million, even, at the opening of this century; but now, in the amazing hive of human existence, included within the Metropolitan Police District of London, more than five and a half million men, women, and children, feast or starve, achieve or fail, amuse themselves or suffer, till, having played their several parts upon this murky stage, they are replaced by others. There are more people than in all the New England states combined, or than in the whole of Switzerland and more than twice as many as in Norway."

Stoddard, John L. 1898

Even Stoddard would have been surprised had he known that London's population would reach 8.5 million by 1950 before beginning a period of decline (Jones 1983). Rapid population growth on a world wide scale has placed an increasing burden on resources. The expansion of urban populations has long been recognized. Over half of the world's population lives in urban areas gaining over one billion in population in the last 30 years. Perhac noted that the use of energy in its many forms has impacted the urban experience. The availability of an inexpensive supply of energy, has often facilitated urban development and growth.

Taking a long term view, energy usage has increased significantly, from about 300 lbs. of equivalent annual usage of coal per person in 1860 to more than 4,000 lbs in 1984 (Perhac 1989).

There are numerous renewable and non-renewable energy sources available. Non-renewable sources include coal, oil, natural gas, nuclear and propane. Coal is used to generate heat and provide electricity. Oil is a fuel and lubricant source for automobiles and is widely used in the U.S. northeastern states as a domestic heat source. Natural and propane gas are widely used for water and space heating. These are a subset of energy sources commonly referred to as "fossil fuels." Nuclear power is a primary source of electrical generation.

The category of energy sources which are often referred to as "alternative fuels" or "renewable" energy sources include: 1) solar power used directly for space heating, with heat exchangers for water heating, or for direct electrical energy generation using photovoltaic cells; 2) wind power used for water pumping and direct conversion of electricity, 3) biomass fuels for heat production; 4) fuel cells for various uses; 5) hydropower for electrical generation; and 6) improved energy efficiency. It is clear that there are many options available to meet urban energy needs.

Energy usage is increasing worldwide. In the U.S. from 1970 to 1996, total energy consumption grew from 67.9 quadrillion BTUs to 93.9 quadrillion BTUs. Energy from renewable sources grew from 2.7 quadrillion BTUs, or 4% of the total, to 7.2 quadrillion BTUs, 7.7% of the total. In 1999 total U.S. energy usage was 96.6 quadrillion BTUs with transportation fuels totaling 25.9 quadrillion BTUs or 26.8% of the total. (U.S. Census Bureau 2000). To manage the growth in energy usage, energy companies have historically been involved in solving supply side issues associated with various energy related commodities while energy users and consumers have been concerned with the demand side of the equation. When supplies of energy exceed demand, prices tend to fall. When demand for energy (or a form of energy) increases relative to supplies, the price for energy tends to increase and substitutes may become viable. Fluctuating prices tend to confound efforts to mitigate increases in usage.

From a technological capability standpoint, we now have flexibility to select from multiple energy sources to satisfy a given requirement, allowing the most appropriate energy source to be used. In addition, we now have the technology to design and build new facilities which are extremely efficient. Are we doing that? Flemming and Goodman suggest that our nation is experiencing an energy crisis that we must learn to live with. Many of our

buildings waste energy needlessly and often incorporate few conservation or reclamation features (Meckler 1994).

Power production and use has urban regional impact. Where will the next power plant be constructed? Will the strip mine be allowed? Will the oil tank farm be allowed next to the river? How much longer will the nuclear power plant be allowed to operate? How large a commercial zone can be developed given the energy supply available? Is a new gas pipeline through the city really necessary? How can the coal plants be modified to be less polluting? Will we open more federal lands to drilling? The list seems endless.

Examples of the benefits of widely available, commercially usable energy are found everywhere. Energy is required to operate the means of transportation, cause appliances to function, create usable and comfortable interior environments, expedite communications, and operate all manner of equipment. The benefits also seem endless. Regardless, energy is a key infrastructure component of the world economy.

Each type of energy source has an identifiable set of costs. Many of the costs of the energy source are imbedded in the purchase price of the product. These include rights to the energy source, extraction, transportation, storage, losses and conversion. An example of acquisition rights might be an oil leasewhich offers the oil company the legal right to extract the oil. Extraction would include costs such as drilling or mining. Transportation costs are those which are incurred in delivering the unprocessed fuel to processing and the finished product to user or market. Storage applies whenever the fuel is awaiting use. Fuels are transformed or converted into usable energy (e.g. heat, electricity) and physical laws come into playwhich reduce the usable by-product. Most of the balance is waste, a portion of which can be recycled or reused.

In addition, there are other costs not imbedded in the product. The building owner must purchase a boiler, piping, and radiators in order convert the fuel source into heat. Infrastructure, such as interior electrical distribution systems must be installed. A sales or use tax may apply to the purchase.

There are hidden costs which may be extensive. As an example, imported energy (such as oil) has been long associated with national security concerns and implications of dependency on foreign oil suppliers. Consider the costs of providing defense related services to the friendly Arab oil exporting states (Roosa, 1988). Finally, there are negative externalities such as air and water pollution which occur from the use of fossil fuels.

Effects on a the U.S. national balance of trade can have a lasting economic impact. In 1972 the US trade balance was a negative $9.5 billion. By 1986, the trade balance had dropped to a negative $170 billion with the direct cost of imported oil accounting for roughly $37 billion of the total. (International Monetary Fund 1987). If this was an issue identified as early as the 1970s, what progress have we made? Very little it seems as the U.S. imports far more oil now than in 1986.

Urban growth increases demands for energy supplies. Growth usually means enlarging the urban service areas. One possible reason for the movement to the suburbs is that more land is needed because single story buildings are better suited to production processes. In addition, vast areas are needed for worker parking. Acres are graded and paved for parking rather than constructing more expensive multilevel parking structures. With improved highways, there is a shift from railroads to trucks as a means of transporting freight. New buildings, transportation systems, distribution systems are required to meet these demands.

As new facilities are constructed to meet urban requirements, energy usage must be considered in the planning process and this is usually performed by the utilities. What forces cause us to consume land as our cities grow? To create larger facilities, manufacturing tends to move to the urban perimeter where land is less costly. Roads are constructed. "Leapfrog" development requires costly extension of utility infrastructure. People then migrate to where employment is available. Shopping areas are constructed near where the people live. This cycle creates greater demands on energy.

It is interesting that despite improved design standards, many newer buildings use more energy than older ones. This is due to their design, location and the construction technologies employed. Causes for the increases include the changing standards for fresh air admission into occupied space. Increasing ventilation air means that greater energy costs are incurred in producing occupancy air (cooled or heated, humidified or dehumidified) from unconditioned air.

Consider the demands basic building design changes can have on urban energy usage. Assume that a production facility (needing 100,000 square feet of floor space) may be built in one of two types of buildings, each with a story equal to 10 ft high. Building X is ten stories high, 100 ft by 100 ft. Building Y is a single story building 500 ft X 200 ft. Assume that the roof and walls all conduct and absorb heating and cooling at the same rates and for the sake of argument ignore losses through the floor. Assume also that the internal loads and energy usage are the same regardless of model. The roof area of Building X is 100' X 100' =10,000 SF. For Building Y the roof is 500' X 200' or 100,000 SF. Building X has four walls each 100' x 100'

totaling 10,000 SF or 40,000 SF for all four. Building Y has two alls 500' x 10' and two walls 200' x 10' for a total of 14,000 SF. This data is summarized in the table bleow:

Table I – Summary of External Area

Area	Bldg. X (SF)	Bldg. Y (SF)
Roof	10,000	100,000
Wall	40,000	14,000
Total	50,000	114,000

The external surface to floor area ratio for Building X is 50,000 SF / 100,000 SF or .5. For Building Y external surface to floor area ratio is 114,000 SF / 100,000 SF or 1.14. All else being equal, the building envelope of the one story Building Y is likely to require roughly 2.28 times the energy as the ten story high Building X.

And what is happening inside those buildings? Inside we find more equipment and more computers. Consider the new high tech companies that are highly prized by cities competing to attract service industries.

Sioshansi notes that the demand for energy appears to be surging in the service and high tech sectors but has not fallen off appreciably in other sectors. High tech companies such as Cisco Systems, Oracle, Sun Microsystems, HP and Intel are major energy consumers of electricity. Oracle's complex in Silicon Valley uses an estimated 13 MW, Sun's campus over 26 MW (Sioshansi 2001).

Consider the urban growth of Las Vegas, Nevada, a city which by some measures, has the fastest growth rates in the U.S. Despite being born as a gambling mecca, the city spawned significant industrial and service sector growth. This growth has created the need to expand transportation systems, construct buildings, extend utilities and create additional urban infrastructure.

Figure 1: Lansat 7 Imaging of the Las Vegas Valley in 1972

Figure 1: Lansat 7 Imaging of the Las Vegas Valley in 1992

Enhanced Lansat 7 imaging of an approximately 50 by 50 mile (80 by 80 Km) area of the Las Vegas Valley shows the infrared urban footprint (urban heat island effect) of the city in 1972 to 1992 respectively. Heat generation (indicated in darker tones) is a clear

visual indicator of increased energy usage.[1] The increased infrared geographical impact is telling. Census data indicates that the area population increased from 273,000 to 863,000 from 1972 to 1992. The year 2000 Census lists the Las Vegas metropolitan are population at 1,376,000.[2]

Demand for energy tends to increase with new development. Gilling assesses the supply and demand pricing situation succinctly: Energy suppliers, focused on profits, will increasingly set prices to recover costs and eliminate subsidies while energy consumers, similarly attentive to the bottom line will seek to cut costs by reducing energy use (Gilling 1997).

SO.... WHAT IS THE PROBLEM?

Conversion of energy is the engine propelling our standard of living, the quality of our life style and the progress of our civilization. Access to energy is almost a birth right in the industrialized world. Access to space heating and hot water are considered necessities. Extended electrical power disruptions in our urban cities are often considered disasters. Simply adding buildings to the electrical grids can be fraught with uncertainty. Consider Jerry Adler's (1993) dilemma discussed in *High Rise* as he describes the difficulties that were encountered estimating energy use simply to get a skyscraper plugged into the grid on Manhattan Island:

> Gruter (an electrical engineer) added up all the electrical equipment in the building, including an estimate of all the lamps, typewriters, computers, copying machines, refrigerators, and coffee machines the tenants would plug into the walls. He wrote a kindly letter requesting Con Ed to provide service in this amount, approximately 15 million watts..... The utility was aware that this figure "total connected load" was a hypothetical number...
>
> The building's electric power consumption has a direct bearing on its air conditioning requirements, since virtually all the power ended up as heat. Modern office buildings are air conditioned year-round, even when they are simultaneously heated......*then*... He added a margin of extra

---

[1]Las Vegas Photographs: U.S. Geological Survey, 1997, Southwest U.S. change detection images from the EROS Data Center; Las Vegas, Nevada: Sioux Falls, South Dakota, USGS EROS Data Center. Images were obtained from the EROS Data at the following webstite: edcwww.cr.usgs.gov/Swworkshop.

[2] Other recent examples of rapid population growth in the US from 1990 to 2000 include: 1) Naples, Florida, 152,099 to 251,377; 2) Austin and San Marcos, Texas, 846,227 to 1,249,763; 3) Boise, Idaho, 295,851 to 432,345; and 4) Phoenix and Mesa, Arizona, 2,238,480 to 3,251,876 (U.S. Census Bureau).

capacity for high heat output tenants such as mainframe computers. Then he had to take into account the people.

Metabolism is the hidden adversary of the HVAC engineer. The average office worker, assumed to be essentially at rest, has a heat output of seventy watts.

Like so much else in New York, air conditioning technology has had to adapt to the ways of Tokyo and London, namely their .... insistence on working when it's past midnight in New York.[3]

The problems are best represented by a question. How best do we provide completely safe, totally dependable, easily transportable, seemingly inexhaustible, efficiently convertible, simply containable, environmentally sensible, preferably inexpensive, relatively convenient energy to our urban users without using too much land, hurting anyone, making too much noise, stopping traffic, having to buy lots of hardware, or creating/causing too many other associated problems?

There are negative externalities associated with the use of energy. How can they be mitigated while providing energy in the quantities needed to support continued growth? The problem is complex and solutions fall into a wide range of categories. The vision might be like Toffler's, who offered that ultimately, we see a civilization founded once more on self-sustaining, renewable rather than exhaustible sources of energy (Toffler 1980).

ENVIRONMENTAL IMPACT

Energy usage is a contributor to environmental pollution. With fossil fuels being the major source of energy, we would expect emissions of carbon to show a similar increase....they grew from 200 lb. per person per year in 1860 to more than 2000 lbs. in 1984 (Perhac 1989).

Environmental issues raise an additional set of concerns. Oil tankers can run aground on reefs and beaches (Prudoe Bay, Alaska). Coal sludge dikes can break and cause damage to rivers (Big Sandy River, Kentucky). Nuclear power plants have accidents (Three Mile Island, Chernobyl). Contamination of air and water due to sulfur and carbon dioxide emissions which has damaged the lakes in the northeastern United States. While there is significant debate over the environmental impact of increasing energy usage, there are known effects.

Man's activities produce a number of greenhouse gases in addition to natural water vapor. We have strong evidence that the atmospheric concentrations of these gases has been increasing, at least over the last few decades. If this continues, we will see a rise in average global temperature and a change in climatic patterns. The effects of such changes on society could be severe. The most prominent of the anthropogenic greenhouse gases is carbon dioxide, which enter the atmosphere when fossil fuels are burned....

- Ralph Perhac, Electric Power Research
Institute (1989)

Gillings states that the existence of adverse environmental externalities supports arguments for extending energy efficiency investments beyond levels justified on the basis of market considerations alone. Externalities at the local and regional urban level relate to emissions of particulates, nitrous oxides and sulfur dioxides. Carbon emissions are associated with non-renewable energy sources (Gillings 1997). Such externalities are rarely included in the price of the commodity. The accounting of projects which impact energy usage and costs may be complicated by attempts to deal with an assessment of environmental impacts.

SOCIOECONOMIC CONSIDERATIONS

Assuming reducing energy use is an appropriate thing to do, can we really modify human behavior? One of the management problems with energy usage has to do with the fact that production is often centralized while consumption is decentralized. It is difficult to convince an office worker to turn out the lights at the end of the day when she isn't personally responsible for the bill. How do you engender socially responsibility behavior? Stephen Viederman once said, "We have never learned, or we have forgotten, that the environment is the basis for all life. Rather than being an interest competing with other interests for attention, it is in reality the playing field on which all interests compete. We have consistently failed to recognize that the economic system is an open system in a closed and finite ecosystem."[4]

Naisbitt believes that a there is global consensus emerging that if we do not act now to protect natural resources, social responsibility could be a moot point. There is an emerging

---

[3] I enjoyed Adler's subtitle: High Rise...How 1,000 Men and Women Worked Around the Clock for Five Years and Lost $200 Million Building a Skyscraper.

---

[4] Stephen Viederman, past president of a philanthropic organization supporting environmental issues. Quote from "Sustainable Development: What It Is and How Do We Get There," presented at Stanford University (1991).

constituency that believes in approaching global environmental issues by managing resources at the local level (Naisbitt, 1994).

Some observers have been outspoken. Soleri (1971) in *Shetchbooks* suggest that "Time is running short. Environmental squalor, stretching over more than one generation, may overpower man's forbearance and sensitivity." He suggests that suburban sprawl is a land destroyer and a self defeating concept and that the earth is too small for a one story civilization (Soleri 1971). Al-Homound (2000) believes, "Usable resources are made available to mankind to be utilized for their benefit and well-being. Every individual bears the responsibility of not wasting or misusing usable resources. All moral codes are against such actions. Therefore, every individual should be educated and trained to become part of the management of resources for the benefit of generations to come." Having a moral belief that resource efficiency is beneficial certainly may have global social implications. Developing countries which are unable to obtain adequate energy resources due to the willingness of industrialized countries to pay a higher price for energy, may develop resentment due to a perceived lack of "equal access" to the commodity.

Recent events are causing a rethinking of the social impact of energy importation. Steffes flatly asserts that the U.S. , "We are overly dependent on foreign oil sources (58%), as are the other industrialized nations (Japan and Europe). There is a positive connection between foreign oil purchases and terrorism. It is common knowledge that some of the oil exporting nations expend oil revenues for arms and terrorism. So, in effect, the industrialized world is actually indirectly subsidizing terrorist activities with their oil purchases." Steffes also suggest that because our way of life is dependent on energy, particularly foreign oil, the U.S. will not be able to respond effectively to many terrorist threats.

The 1973 oil embargo contributed to a world wide recession. The 1979 Iranian revolution which provoked an increase in oil prices. These situations are often cited as examples of supply disruptions with political intent. So why hasn't there been had a major oil disruption since 1979? In a recent Louisville Courier-Journal article, Krugman asserts that " After the... 1970s, Western economies sharply increased their energy efficiency." He also suggests that a third oil "crises" is a distinct possibility as there is presently a world wide excess production capacity of only seven million bbl./day. Recently, Iraq decided to halt all oil exports for 30 days in protest of recent events in the Middle East. Thus oil prices are "once again hostage to Middle Eastern politics" (Krugman 2002).

According to the U.S. Census Bureau, in 1973, the U.S. imported an average 3,244,000 barrels (bbl.) of crude oil per day. By 1998, that figure had risen to an average of 8,706,000 bbl./day. Meanwhile domestic production declined from an average of 9,208,000 bbl./day to 5,925,000 bbl./day. Importation of oil from Organization of Petroleum Exporting States (OPEC) rose from 258 million barrels in 1973 to 746 million barrels in 1998. At the very least, efforts to implement energy efficiently may be a means of insurance against potential energy supply disruptions (U.S. Census Bureau, 2000).

THE COSTS OF DOING NOTHING

Do we do nothing and hope that technology will eventually solve all the problems? Once we pinned our dreams on atomic generation of electricity. Now we are concerned with nuclear safety and disposal of atomic wastes. Recently, fuel cells are have been widely hailed as a possible solution to our problems. Invented before the internal combustion engine in 1839, the fuel cell resembles both a battery and an engine. Extracting energy from a chemical reaction joins hydrogen (the universe's most abundant element) from the cell with oxygen from the air to produce water, they release electrical energy and do not "burn" fuel.

The first single standing residential application in the U.S. finally came in 1998 in Latham, New Jersey (Louisville Courier-Journal, 19 January 2002, p. C3). Many utilities are testing commercial fuel cell units. There are also fuel cell vehicles being developed. The current generated by fuel cells is direct current (DC) not alternating current (AC) which is the standard in North America. As a result, DC to AC converters must be employed to create usable power.

Fuel cells often require significantly larger space to house equipment than traditional generators. Interestingly, most fuel cells use fossil fuels and do release some greenhouse gasses. However, the emission amounts are only a fraction of traditional energy conversions. For example, the Pembina Institute for Appropriate Development showed that fuel cells can cut natural gas emissions by as much as 70%. Available for 175 years, fuel cells have not yet been widely deployed, in part due to their cost. However, if sustained increases in energy costs were to occur, fuel cells may become a more feasible alternative.

There are also empirical examples of the option to do nothing despite credible economic justification:

- I interviewed a manager of large hotel in downtown Louisville, Kentucky. He was provided with a set of energy conservation measures that in total would provide a 30-40% annual return. His reason for not implementing the project was that "hotels are bought and sold every couple of years." From his perspective, the

- improvements would not add adequate value to the sales price of the hotel to justify the expenditure despite the improvement to the company's net income.

- A mid-western industrial concern determined that an energy conservation project would provide an annual return of roughly 45%. This was inadequate to justify the project as it needed a 50% return to qualify the project. This was a "company policy" despite the fact that historically, the company's net profit margins were only 0-2%.

These examples may not be representative. However, the do demonstrate that despite substantial economic justification, energy efficiency is often not a primary concern.

The issues surrounding the use of energy suggest that to do nothing may not the wisest approach. Historical trends indicate that our cities will continue to grow. They will require multiple and dependable supplies of energy, both renewable and non- renewable, to ensure that growth is sustained.

Doing nothing effectively defaults to the continuation of current approaches. This tends to exacerbate the problems and sets into motion a series of events that not only supports the status quo but also causes new approaches and technologies to be stymied. Despite economic advantages, once infrastructure is in place, doing nothing often seems the most expedient alternative. It may also result in less immediate work for a decision maker and less perceived risk. One macroeconomic method of estimating the costs of doing is simply to multiply the costs of energy to an economy by a percentage lost to inefficiency and add a multiple for the costs of externalities. Such a sum would be staggering.

It is apparent that a range of solutions must be employed to solve the complex problems associated with increased energy usage due to urban growth. The approaches used must be both supply (production) and demand (consumer usage) orientated.

One interesting argument in support of doing nothing suggests that if measures such as energy conservation are implemented, demand for energy supplies will be reduced, thereby lowing their costs and causing the related commodities to be more competitive. This would result in less incentive to conserve.

MARKETS & MARKETING

Energy companies have in the past focused and specialized on providing an energy commodity, often from a single source. Electrical generating companies sold electrons, oil companies sold oil, coal companies sold coal and so on. What we are now witnessing in the marketplace is a redesign of utilities as they morph into energy service companies. Energy companies are marketing a wider range of products in deregulated markets through regulated subsidiaries. An example might be a utility selling window replacements to a university so that energy expenses will be reduced, then providing project financing, plus a financial guarantee of savings. Another example might be a mechanical equipment manufacturer selling lighting improvements to reduce loads on a new air conditioning system, allowing the downsizing of the mechanical equipment.

Bobker notes that in energy markets, long term consumer commitments will be sought from value added services. He states that the idea of selling energy services as opposed to a regulated commodity is part of an emergent sustainable development paradigm in which information systems and knowledge management will be key to energy services concepts and capabilities (Bobker 2001). He also observes that there is an emerging "technology cluster" which includes cleaner fuels, renewable sources of energy, process alterations, monitoring, product design, recycling, reuse and industrial ecology developments. He forecasts that end users will become a more active part of the energy sector rather than passive consumers (Bobker 2001). We may well see that markets may begin to fragment even further, as "ownership" of the customer becomes a key element in marketing services.

Is this concept really new or simply a reinvention of the times of Thomas Edison? He not only designed and constructed systems to generate electrical power, developed transmission systems but also invented consumer products and services which could be operated using electricity.

SUPPLY & DEMAND

The elementary economic theory is one of supply and demand. When inexpensive energy is available, it is often difficult to economically justify energy conservation. A recent survey of twenty-three Fortune 1,000 companies found that the mean energy usage per employee was 3,856 Mbtu. Energy costs as a percentage of revenues ranged from 0.5% to 15% with a mean values of 2.2% (Lind & Norland 2000).[5] Energy use is typically not a significant component

---

[5]Lind and Norland are to be applauded for this effort. The forwarded surveys to 410 companies and received a 5.6% response rate. The responding corporations were multi-plant, global

of product or production costs. If costs of a key energy input rise significantly in a short period of time, the unbudgeted costs are noted and alternatives may be considered. Finally, the costs of conservation technologies have difficulty competing with energy products since the initial costs can be significant.

Changes in future energy usage will be a function of changes in efficiency, population, conditioned space, vehicular usage and other factors. If demand increases without corresponding improvements in efficiency, prices have a greater likelihood of increasing. Prices will typically increase with reduced demand and simply increase prices to the point that demand subsides.

Is it reasonable to believe that energy usage can be reduced? There was a widely held belief in the 1950's and 1960's that increases in energy usage were necessary to drive improvements in the economy as a whole. This was commonly reffered to as the "Energy GNP" link. The belief was that the Gross National Product of a country could increase only if the energy usage increased as well.

Miller noted that the overall energy efficiency of the energy consumed in U.S. economy was 51%, indicating that 49% was being inefficiently lost as waste (Miller 1978). In addition, we might learn from the European experience. There is documented evidence that European cities have substantially lower per capita energy usage and lower carbon dioxide emissions when compared to North American cities (Beatly 2000).

There are historical events in certain markets which indicate that energy improvements can occur and that market segments can thrive with declining energy usage. U.S. industry uses about a third of the total energy consumed by our economy. Lind and Norland point out that between 1972 and 1983 (a peak price year), energy prices rose an average 520% (250% in real dollars). Between 1974 and 1985, industrial energy usage fell 44% relative to manufacturing output and 40% relative to the value of shipments (Lind & Norland 2000). This is a classic example of a lowering in market demand which responded to an increase in price.

Al-Homound asserts that as much as 5-15% in energy cost reductions can be achieved with little or no capital expenditure, 15-30% is commonplace and 30-50% can be obtained with capital investments (Al-Homound 2000). To what extent could this be applied? Among the first attempts to obtain to an order of magnitude image of the

---

operations, averaging 29 plants within the U.S. and 27 plants outside the U.S. (Lind & Norland 2000).

scale of the problem was by Victor Ottaviano who indicated that 25 billion SF of existing structures in the U.S. were obsolete when energy standards are applied (Ottaviano 1985).

THE ROLE OF GOVERNMENT

Is there a role for government? Gilling notes that by adopting policies that move energy prices to market levels, governments not only stimulate supply but also encourage efficiency and conservation in the delivery of energy supplies and in their consumption (Gilling 1997).

Are increased taxes one means of effective government intervention? Perhaps a tax on the amount of energy consumed would help reduce energy usage. Varno notes that an energy tax (he calls it a BTU, or The Energy Tax) would effectively cause higher priced power. Economic reasoning would suggest that the demand curve would adjust and that businesses with energy efficient equipment will be more competitive. Those with relatively inefficient manufacturing equipment or facilities will be more inclined to replace old equipment with energy efficient equivalents (Varno 2000).

Actually, the U.S. federal government has made efforts in this regard. Colvin noted that the Energy Policy Act of 1992 (EPACT) and other regulations open the door for Federal agencies to use utility programs to implement energy saving, environmentally friendly projects. EPACT and Executive Order 12902 together mandate a 30% reduction in consumption in all Federal buildings by the year 2005, using 1985 usage as the baseline (Colvin 1997). Both documents encourage the use of performance contracting. Recently, the U.S. Department of Energy has been developing public-private partnerships including its "Energy Star" trademark that provide standards and product identification for buildings and energy consuming devices.

JUSTIFICATION METHODOLOGIES

In the U.S., implementing such projects is not something you do simply because it seems to "makes sense" or it is viewed as the "right thing to do" or because it is "environmentally appropriate." Energy efficiency tends to fall into the category of purchases supported by some kind of economic analysis. Justifying energy reduction projects can be perplexing.

If the answer to the "Do Something" or "Do Nothing" question is to "Do Something" then it is inevitable that the next question is "Do What or Do Exactly What?" When answering the "Do Exactly What" question after being directed to "Do Something," the question becomes "Why are you Doing *that particularSomething*?" If part of the justification is economic, then it may be supported with an economic argument. Moving past the make vs. buy issue, the critical question becomes how does a project weigh in on economic merits. To make things even more complex, Flahery & Watters observed that energy economics are very site specific. The impact on savings calculations varies greatly with how a program is implemented as well the project's regulatory environment (Flahery & Watters 2000).

The basic data that is needed varies as a function of the economic analysis technique, the required detail and depth of the argument. To assess an energy efficiency project the minimum data needed includes unit energy costs, historical usage of all energy sources, project costs, project savings and life of equipment. Other costs and savings data may be needed to incorporate maintenance or other anticipated costs and savings not related to the direct energy impact.

There have been numerous approaches used to justify energy conservation projects based on the economic arguments for and against their implementation.[6] These include traditional justification and analysis approaches such as simple payback Period (SPP), Savings- to-Investment Ratios (SIRs), Net Present Value (NPV), and Internal Rate of Return (IRR).

The simple payback period (SPP) seems to be the most common technique. The SPP is simply equal to the anticipated annual cost divided by the anticipated annual project savings. If new environmental control system were installed in a building at a cost of $100,000 and the anticipated savings were $20,000 the SPP would equal 5 years.

Another approach, using a Savings to Investment (SIR) is calculated by dividing the present value of the benefits of a project by the present values of the costs of the project. If the SIR of a project is greater than one it is considered profitable. SIRs less than 1 are considered unprofitable. This technique is often used in the public sector by organizations such as the U.S. Army Corps of Engineers (Caphart et al 2002). This approach is also referred to as the Benefit to Costs Ratio (BCR).

The net present value (NPV) approach is performed by discounting the cash inflows over the life of the investment to determine whether they are equal or exceed the required investment. The basic discount rate used is often the cost of capital to the purchasing entity. Thus, inflows that arrive

in later years must provide a return that at least equals the cost of financing those returns (Block and Hurt 1984).

The Internal Rate of Return (IRR) calls for determining the yield on an investment, that is, calculating the interest rate that equates the cash outlays of an investment with the subsequent cash inflows (Block and Hurt 1984).

Finally, the economic cost of delay is worthy of consideration. Delaying a project often means that the status quo will be maintained and that current costs associated with lack of action will continue to occur. An empirical example is offered:

- An energy conservation project for a government entity in Southern Indiana was developed by the author costing $18,000 and saving between $28,000 and $44,000 per year in avoided energy costs. The project was finally implemented four years after it was developed. The government entity was unable to "budget" the money to implement the project since the "savings" accruing from the project would be credited to an account different from the debited cost center. This argument discounted the value of the fact that both accounts were budgeted from the same pool of taxpayer dollars. In this example, the non-discounted cost of delay for the four year period is estimated to range from $112,000 to $176,000.

PERFORMANCE CONTRACTING

Performance contracting is a method of implementing energy cost reduction technologies in which the facility owner (host) invests very little capital. It is viewed as a financially based partnership between the owner and the performance contractor. The relationship is symbiotic and can develop in one of many forms. In all cases, the facility owner capitalizes the reduction in predicted future utility and maintenance costs. Such reductions in costs can effectively become a form of collateral. This is due to the simple fact that utility costs are a manageable recurring business expense. To be managed they must be capable of being documented and be controllable.

One approach is to employ energy service companies (ESCOs). Gilling suggests that ESCOs have clear advantages over alternative delivery mechanisms for improving energy efficiency as it is their primary business focus and the contracting mechanism provides a clear

---

[6] There are in depth discussions in the literature with examples of how these are calculated and applied to energy conservation and management projects. Wayne Turner provides an excellent detailing (Turner 1997).

incentive. He suggests that the concentration of expertise within the ESCO permits the firm to become highly skilled in its core business, ultimately reducing transaction costs for all parties involved (Gilling 1997).

To implement the projects, performance contractors often employ a "design-build" approach rather than a "bid-specification" approach when implementing facility and equipment improvements. The "bid-specification" approach is seldom used in a performance contract since selection is most commonly due to low cost, with the project being awarded to the low bidder. Quality and extended product life are often sacrificed to achieve reduced proposal prices. In a "design-build" approach, higher product quality is required to meet performance guarantees during the economic life of the project. A performance contractor also provides a third party guarantee of cost reductions (Roosa 2001, June).

Hunt notes that unlike other ways of delivering energy services, a performance contract can be arranged in which the ESCO is responsible for all up front costs associated with the design, installation, operation and possibly maintenance of newly installed equipment in exchange for a share of the guaranteed energy savings realized over the life of the contract (Hunt 1997).

Turner indicates that ESCOs and other groups are providing energy assessments, energy and economic analysis, capital and monitoring systems to assist organizations in reducing their energy usage and their expenditures on energy services. By guaranteeing and sharing savings from improved energy efficiency and productivity, all parties may benefit. (Turner 1997).

CASE STUDY DISCUSSION

Performance contracts are in fact being used extensively in the U.S and elsewhere. There is recent empirical evidence that performance contracts are being used as a tool to implement energy conservation measures in Kentucky, a state whose electricity production is primarily coal based with a small hydropower generation component. As a result, electricity prices are among the lowest in the county. Despite the low cost of electrical energy in the state, there has been economic justification for performance contracting.

Initially, many of the larger energy reduction projects were utility based, shared energy savings projects. An allocation of the savings would pay for the project costs and financing of the project. An interesting example of this was a U.S. Postal Service project which involved two public utilities in Kentucky and achieved significant energy reductions.[7] A total of 60 buildings were involved. The project scope involved lighting and controls improvements (Roosa 2001).

---

[7] As energy engineer for the U.S. Postal Service project, I was pleased that it was selected in 1999 as the U.S.

A subset of the buildings were identified as being worthy of an analysis of environmental benefits. The analysis of this project indicated that the project had a positive environmental impact. The table below provides an estimation of its impact on air quality by summarizing the change in a few of the key emission components found in coal generated power. The table below (Roosa 2001) indicates that in all areas of the sample, energy savings yielded calculated declines in compounds of environmental concern.

Table II – Energy & Emission Component Reductions

P.O.	Bldg. SF	Change Btu/SF/Yr	CO2 Tons/Yr	So2 Lbs/Yr	NOX Lbs/Yr
#20	74,007	-2,250	-77	-1,147	-497
#29	425,000	-435	-624	-8,506	-3,805
#25	27,965	-4,911	-62	-982	-408
#30	29,730	-6,846	-92	-1,381	-597
#35	22,935	-3,895	-39	-595	-257
#37	22,700	-4,026	-41	-621	-289
Total	602,337	-22,363	-935	-13,232	-5,853

Similar performance contracting projects were also performed on medical campuses. Two of the largest to date were implemented at Norton Heath Care (formerly Alliant Medical Care in Louisville, Kentucky) and at the Bowling Green Medical Center. These projects involved were primarily lighting improvements.

In 1996, Kentucky Senate Bill 157 was passed enabling performance contracting. Prior to 1996, very few projects using this performance contracting were implemented in the state. As result, performance contracts have become a preferred method for providing energy services in Kentucky. In March 1997, John Stapleton, Director of the Kentucky State Energy Office, stated that his state could save as much as 25% of the $52 million that Kentucky State Government spends annually on energy for state facilities (Hanson & Weisman 1998). In 1998, House Bill 639 was passed broadening the availability of performance contracting to include state government facilities.

In Kentucky, elementary and secondary school facilities are operated by local school boards. Schools districts in

---

Department of Energy's Energy and Water Management Project of the Year.

Kentucky have a number of performance contracts completed or underway.[8]

Energy service companies involved in the K-12 schools market included companies such as Honeywell, Inc., ESG (formerly Energy Systems Group), Perfection Services, Trane, utility owned ESCOs and others. Lighting improvements were performed in most all of the projects. Other types of improvements included mechanical system improvements, control system upgrades, window replacements, building envelope modifications, ventilation changes, and water savings technologies.

A statistical analysis of the project data for the 39 K-12 projects performed through mid-2001 reveals that mean project size is $788,000 with a median of $672,000. The smallest project was awarded by Russellville Independent Schools ($137,000) and the largest was awarded by Marion County Schools ($2.2 million). The standard deviation was $555,300 and the average deviation was $448,000. An analysis of the data indicates that a typical project realized an annual savings of $70,000 to $100,000 per year.

The largest performance contract to date in Kentucky was recently issued by Jefferson County Schools (Louisville) in December of 2001 in the amount of $4.9 million. This project involves lighting upgrades in thirteen (13) buildings, window replacements in ten (10) buildings, and minor controls and mechanical improvements. This project is scheduled for completion in August 2002.[9]

Performance contracts were also implemented by Kentucky Colleges. Bellarmine College (Louisville), Georgetown College (Georgetown), and Center College (Danville), were among those who negotiated performance contracts. Western Kentucky University (Bowling Green) became in 2001 the first Kentucky State Government project.

It is clear by the experience in Kentucky that performance contracting has become an accepted method of implementing economically feasible energy conservation technologies. Recently, the Kentucky State Legislature passed 2002 Senate Bill 61 which further broadens and clarifies the availability of performance contracting to

State government entities, enhancing the prospects of additional similar projects in the future.

CONCLUSION

After exploring a few of the basic economic issues concerning energy conservation, there are conclusions that can be made. While there are numerous energy sources available, there are national economies such as the U.S. economy, which are strongly biased toward the use of non-renewable fuels rather than the use of alternative renewable energy sources. In addition, there is substantial evidence to suggest that additional improvements in the efficiency of how non-renewable fuels are consumed are possible.

Increases in energy usage are a function of many influences including population growth, urban expansion, changes in the built environment and other factors. It is clear that due to the centralized nature of energy production and the decentralized nature of usage, there are often few perceived incentives to support a decision to reduce usage despite the economic advantages which could be realized.

There are ethical and social concerns associated with dependency on foreign energy supplies. There are also negative externalities which apply with the use of certain types of energy which are worthy of consideration. Urban environmental pollution is a significant one.

While there are a number of methodologies available to assess the economic impact of energy conservation measures, projects are often not implemented due to a number of factors.

Energy companies and other companies have broadened their range of products to include services which result in lower demand for energy. These services not only reduce energy use but may also have resulting positive environmental impacts. Performance contracts have been used in recent years, to overcome some of the obstacles associated with traditional bid-specification acquisition approaches.

One feature of a performance contract is that it provides a third party guarantee of savings. The guarantee minimizes the facility owner's financial uncertainties that may be associated with the implementation of energy efficiency technologies.

In the last six years, performance contracts have become a widely used tool for implementing energy conservation measures in industrial, hospital and educational facilities in Kentucky. A statistical analysis of Kentucky K-12 projects indicated that the mean project size was under $800,000

---

[8] Actual project data used for the analysis which follows was provided the by the Kentucky Department of Education (KDOE), Division of Facilities Management in a public meeting in Richmond, Kentucky to the Kentucky State Board of Education in late 2001.

[9] The author was the lead energy engineer on this project while employed by a mid-west energy service company. This project was excluded from the analysis, as the data for the project was complete.

with an estimated average annual dollar savings of $70,000 to $100,000 per year. The breath and scope of these projects indicates that despite a highly competitive market, there is broad market acceptance of performance contracting in Kentucky.

REFERENCES

Adler, Jerry (1993). High Rise. New York: Happer Collins Publications, Inc. pages 143-144.

Al-Homound, Mohammad S. (2000). Total Productive Energy Management, Energy Engineering Journal. Vol. 98, No. 1, pages 21-38.

Edel Matthew & Rothenburg, Jerome (ed.) (1972). Readings in Urban Economics. New York: Macmillian Company.

Beatley, Timothy (2000). Green Urbanism: Learning from European Cities. Washington, D.C.: Island Press. p. 31.

Block, Stanley B. & Hirt, Gergory A. (1984). Foundations of Financial Management. Homewood IL: Richard D. Irwin, Inc. Pages 306-312.

Bobker, Michael F. (2001). Leveraging Knowledge: Transferring Energy Services To New Markets. Strategic Planning for Energy and the Environment. Vol. 20, No. 4, p. 62-77.

Capehart B.L., Capehart L.C. and Pawlik K. (2002). Part II: Energy Balancing - Making Financial Decisions. Strategic Planning for Energy and the Environment. Vol. 21, No. 3. Pages 58-80.

Colvin, Mary A. (1997). Alternative Financing Through Utility Programs for Federal Energy & Water Saving Projects. Energy and Environmental Visions for the Millennium, Proceedings of the 20th World Energy Engineering Congress. Pages 219-230.

Flahtery, Thomas J. and Watters, James L. (2000). Energy Savings Economics - Not Always What They Seem. Energy Engineering Journal, Vol. 98, No. 1, pages 47-60.

Gilling, Joseph W. (1997). The World Bank Role in an Evolving Energy Efficiency Market, Energy and Environmental Visions for the Millennium, Proceedings of the 20th World Energy Engineering Congress, pages 231-268.

Hunt, David M. (1997). Ways to Sell Alternative Financing to the Federal Government, Energy and Environmental Visions for the Millennium, Proceedings of the 20th World Energy Engineering Congress, pages 231-238.

International Monetary Fund (1987). International Financial Statistics, Yearbook 1987. Pages 698-699.

Krugman, Paul (April, 2002). The Third Oil Crises? Louisville Courier Journal. p. 8.

Lind, Laura and Norland, Douglas L. (2001). Corporate Energy Management: A Survey of Large Manufacturing Companies, Energy Engineering Journal. Vol. 98, No. 2, pages 53-72.

Meckler, Milton (ed.) (1994), Retrofitting Buildings for Energy Conservation, Lilburn GA: The Fairmont Press. p. 41.

Miller, James Grier (1978). Living Systems. New York: McGraw-Hill Book Company. p. 830.

Naisbitt, John (1994). Global Paradox. New York: Avon Books. Pages 206-208.

Ottaviano, Victor (1985). Energy Management. Melville NY: OTS Publications.

Perhac, Ralph M. (1989, September). A Critical Look at Global Climate and Greenhouse Gasses. Power Engineering. Pages 41-44.

Roosa, Stephen A. (2001). The Energy Engineer's Guide to Performance Contracting. Energy Markets and Environmental Protection in the New Millennium (Konferencia Dolgozatok). Sopron Hungary. Pages 315-319.

Roosa, Stephen A. (1988). The Economic Effects of Oil Imports: A Case for Energy Management. Strategic Planning and Energy Management. Vol. 8, No.1, pages 31-42.

Roosa, Stephen A. (2001). Measurement and Verification for the Real World. Intergrated Solutions for Energy and Facility Management. Pages 285-290.

Sioshansi, Fereidoon P. (2001). Will the New Economy Use More Energy or Less Energy? Strategic Planning and Energy Management. Vol. 21, No.1, pages 64-70.

Soleri, Paolo (1971). The Sketchbooks of Paolo Soleri. Cambridge Massachusetts: The M.I.T. Press.

Steffes, Dale W. (2002). United States Energy Dependency – and Terrorism, <u>Strategic Planning and Energy Management</u>. Vol. 21, No.3, pages 5-6.

Stoddard, John L. (1898). <u>John L. Stoddard's Lectures</u>. Boston: Balch Brothers Co.

Toffler, Alan (1980). <u>The Third Wave</u>. New York: Bantum Books. p. 351.

Turner,Wayne C. (1997). <u>Energy Management Handbook Third Edition</u>, Upper Saddle River NJ: The Fairmont Press, Inc.& Prentice Hall. Pages 1-67.

United States Census Bureau (2000). <u>Statistical Abstract of the United States</u>. p. 583.

Varno, E.J. (2001). Energy Conservation Projects - Putting It all Together, <u>Energy and Pollution Control Opportunities to the Year 2000</u>, Proceedings of the 16th World Energy Engineering Congress. Pages 247-253.

ABOUT THE AUTHOR

Stephen A. Roosa, CEM is the President of Energy Management Alternatives, Inc. with offices in Louisville and Lexington, Kentucky. During a recent five year period at a utility owned energy services company, he was the lead energy engineer on 26 completed energy service contracts.

Recent energy services projects include the first Kentucky State Government performance contract (Western Kentucky University, 2001), the largest K-12 school project in Kentucky (Jefferson County Schools 2001-2) and the largest lighting project in Kentucky (Alliant Health Care, 1998-9). Previous experience includes over 20 years experience in energy engineering and energy management with energy studies performed on over 3,500 buildings.

Mr. Roosa received a Bachelor of Architecture degree from the University of Kentucky and a Masters in Business Administration (MBA) from Webster University. He is presently completing a Ph.D. at the University of Louisville. He is an Association of Energy Engineers (AEE) Certified Indoor Air Quality Professional (1998) and an AEE Certified Energy Manager (1986).

Related professional awards include the Federal Energy and Water Management Project Award (1999); US Army Corps of Engineers National Energy Systems Technology Award, CENET (1991); US Department of Defense Energy Conservation Award (1989); AEE International Energy Manager of the Year (1987); US Joint Chiefs of Staff Citation for Energy Management (1983).

Mr. Roosa has served in the following organizational capacities: Director of the Louisville Resource Conservation Council (1990-1994); AEE Southeast Regional Vice President (1988-89); Tower Mutual Fund Group, Director (1986-87); AEE Bluegrass Chapter President (1986-7); Digital Information Systems of Kentucky, Chairman and Director, (1984-1988); Blackburn-Sanford Series Funds, Director, Portfolio Management (1983-86); Development World of Indiana, Inc., Vice President, Director (1980-81).

ACKNOWLEDGMENTS

The author wishes to thank the AEE for creating this forum and opportunity to present this approach to performance contracts and the opportunity to chair the WEEC 2002 session on performance contracting. Particular thanks to Al bert Thumann, Barbara Stroup and Patty Ardavin, for their help and support during my years as an AEE member. The author also extends thanks Dr. Peter Meyer, an economics professor at the University of Louisville, who provided encouragement and inspiration for this paper.

NOTE

The views expressed herein are solely those of the author and do not necessarily reflect the views of any other individual, organization, corporation or agency. Mention or reference to trade names, governmental agency or commercial enterprise does not constitute endorsement.

Your comments are invited. The author's email address is: stephenroosa@cs.com.

Chapter 44

Use of Measurement and Verification Systems for Continuous Commissioning

Martin A. Mozzo Jr., PE, CEM, CLEP
M and A Associates Inc.
PO Box 8693
Trenton, NJ 08650-0693

Introduction

This paper will discuss the use of Measurement and Verification (M&V) Systems as a tool for continuous commissioning. Commissioning is usually done with the start-up of building systems to insure that the system is operating as designed and producing the desired results including energy savings. Performance Contracting has been used extensively for energy savings projects, several times for HVAC systems. As part of the Performance Contract, an M&V System may be used to verified the energy savings of such projects. It is this author's belief, that with the proper application and expertise, such systems can be used as a continuous commissioning tool throughout the life of the project.

Performance Contracting

Performance Contracting has been used for the past several years as a tool to assist in financing and implementing energy projects. The structure of these contracts will vary on a case-by-case basis; however, the following generalization of them has been seen as most common. A contractor, ESCO, or an engineer identifies a potential project to an energy user, usually an industrial or commercial firm. This project could be the replacement of an old, inefficient chiller with a new, more efficient chiller. The premise of the project will be to reduce energy consumption, and thus costs. The project can be financed in several ways, complete payment upfront or possibly a shared savings. The project however, is based on the assumption that there will be energy savings involved. Proof of the energy savings may be required, usually by the entity doing the financial portion of the project. This may just be a stipulated savings, or an M&V System may be involved. This paper involves only the use of M&V Systems in the continuous commissioning process, stipulation, in my opinion, does not lend itself readily to this process.

Commissioning

The following statement is from ASHRAE's 1999 Application Handbook. "Commissioning is a quality assurance process of the installation of the systems in a building. It is a process for achieving, verifying, and documenting the performance of each system to meet the operational needs of the building within the capabilities of the documented design and specified equipment capabilities according to the owner's functional criteria. It is a process that ensures the quality of the installation." ASHRAE is also clear that commissioning applies to all systems of the building, not just HVAC systems.

It has been my experience, that excellent performance contracting projects, usually ones which are HVAC oriented, have a commissioning process which ensures the quality of the installation, and hopefully, will result in the desired outcome for the owner, that is energy savings and a comfortable environment. It also has been my experience that usually, commissioning is a one-time event at the completion of the project, once substantial completion has been obtained, the process is over.

There are several benefits to commissioning. Some of these are:

> The owner and contractor verify and agree that the system was installed properly and is functioning as designed.

> The system is providing a satisfactory environment to the building. If it is an HVAC system, the occupants are for the most part, comfortable. If it is an elevator system, the elevators work.

> If the project also has an energy savings component to it, then the savings levels that are anticipated should be achieved.

One of the other issues of commissioning is that the maintenance team for these building systems will have been provided with the proper training and tools to maintain the equipment over the life of the system or building.

If everything possible has been done properly through commissioning, the systems should continue to operate as planned. There becomes no need for re-commissioning or continued verification. Unfortunately, this is not a perfect world.

Re-commissioning

The re-commissioning process is similar to the commissioning process, that is, a team of experts will evaluate and test the system being re-commissioned to insure that it is functioning as designed and producing the quality results that were initially developed. Re-commissioning is required for the following reasons:

> Building use has changed, office building now a hotel for example.

> Occupancy has changed, either increased or decreased.

> New equipment has been installed, such as computers, which changes loads on the building.

> Maintenance of the system(s) has not achieved the high levels that were seen as required.

The benefits for re-commissioning are the same as for the commissioning basis,

330

improved environmental conditions, energy savings, proper operation of the equipment, to name a few.

Use of Measurement and Verification Systems as a Continuous Commissioning Tool

By virtue of cost, commissioning is a one-time, finite event. While it would be nice to have a continual commissioning process in place, the cost would be too high. If the project is a Performance Contract and if there is an M&V System in place, the system can be used as a tool for continuous commissioning to a degree. The M&V System is not designed to perform a commissioning function; it is only a measurement device. However, if key parameters are being measured on a continual basis, and if a qualified individual reviews it, then it can be used as a tool for continuous commissioning and identifying trends that indicate re-commissioning is required. It must be remembered that commissioning and re-commissioning is not a cheap event. Re-commissioning may be required in a year, two years, or maybe never. A tool, such as the M&V System, can help identify when re-commissioning is required. A couple of examples will help illustrate this point.

Example 1: Performance Contract using a variable frequency drive (VFD) on an air handler unit. The HVAC system is a variable air volume system (VAV) with VAV boxes located in the space. Space temperature controls the amount of air to each VAV box and a control mechanism is in place to vary the speed of the fan through the VFD to provide sufficient air to the entire system. In a Performance Contract, energy savings is calculated by subtracting actual electrical consumption (kWh) from baseline consumption. The M&V System will measure actual kWh during time intervals. If during the course of the project, maintenance is not performed properly and the VAV boxes now operate as a constant volume device, electrical consumption will rise and anticipated savings will not be achieved. If an individual is looking at the M&V System data, it should become obvious that the project is not performing as designed and actual, such as re-commissioning, may be required.

Example 2: A process improvement was installed as part of a Performance Contract. The improvement was better controls of an air distribution system used in the process through VFDs, reduction of excess air volumes, and control systems to monitor and correct air flows between zones. The M&V System measured the kW by time period before the retrofit and a baseline was established. After the retrofit, the M&V System measured that energy savings, as measured by kW in time intervals, decreased by 40%. Sometime after the installation and start-up of the project, it was noticed that energy savings decreased from 40% to 10%. Physical examination of the project showed that excess air had been allowed to be introduced into the system causing power requirements to increase. A re-commissioning effort was begun immediately to determine why this excess air was allowed, correct the actual problem, and restore the system to the design specifications. After this re-commissioning effort, the M&V System showed that the 40% energy reduction levels were once again being achieved, and the system was functioning as designed.

Needs

In order to use an M&V System as a continuous commissioning tool, the M&V System data must not only be reviewed continually, but the individual doing the review must be qualified to understand trends, ranges, and so forth in order to identify times when action must be done. One example where this was not done was on an HVAC chiller operation.

A new central chiller was installed to replace several remote chillers and DX units. The M&V System measured chilled water flow and delta-temperatures at each of the remote units. This measurement was required to calculate equivalent tons of air conditioning at these units. In this particular project, two disturbing observations were made of the M&V data. First, one process chiller, used year round, appeared to be maxed out at its nameplate rating for every time period. There was no variation in tonnage as should have been expected. What was discovered here was that the return water temperature sensor was broken and indicating a very high return water temperature. This resulted in a calculation where the chiller was producing its maximum capacity. Also, in the same system, there are DX units which are used for office cooling, primarily in the summer. Winter usage was expected to be zero; however, summer usage also was zero as well. What was discovered was that the flow meters measuring chilled water flow had failed yielding zero flows, even when there was flow, thus no savings. The end result of this review was the M&V System was re-commissioned, and now accurate data and savings are being achieved. A qualified individual who understood how the system was to work identified this need and implemented the re-commissioning.

Summary

Use of an M&V System can be a tool for identifying when re-commissioning activities are required. It is not a commissioning process, but rather an identification tool to point out problems that may exist. The use of an M&V System however, should be by a qualified individual who understands what the data states and how the system operates. In this fashion, the project can continue to operate satisfactorily and achieve the results that it was designed for.

Chapter 45

Using Advanced Metering to Measure and Verify Savings on Energy Projects

Randolph L. Haines, CEM, CLEP, CMVP, CPE
Energy Manager
Thomas Jefferson University
Philadelphia, PA

ABSTRACT

How do you know that after you spend a lot of money on an energy project that you will continue to save the amount you anticipated year after year? One way is to continuously monitor the consumption and demand with a near real-time metering program. Ideally, it would be nice to have a sub-meter on the one particular project you have installed, but it is not usually economic. By trending a group of devices, we can set alarms to alert if a value is exceeded.

BACKGROUND

Thomas Jefferson University and the Jefferson Health System make up the largest healthcare group in the Delaware Valley (Philadelphia) region. The Jefferson Health System is made up of four major healthcare groups: Thomas Jefferson University Hospital, Main Line Health System, Albert Einstein Healthcare Network, and Frankford Hospitals, as well as hundreds of small practices and other properties. We have more than 10 million square feet of clinical, research, teaching and housing property. JHS has an electrical peak demand of 60 megawatts, consuming more than 300,000,000-kilowatt hours per year. We spend about $45 million a year for all of our utilities. In April of 2002, we aggregated our load and purchased electricity for the entire health system. The new contract has a fixed price per kWh up to a cap, reducing our demand cost but increasing our use cost.

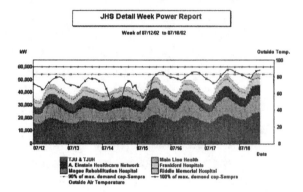

INSTALLED ENERGY SAVING PROJECTS

In January 2001, we hired an ESCO to finance and install Energy Saving projects and in the Summer and Fall of 2001, we installed the following projects: retrofitting of lighting from T-12 to T-8 lamps w/ electronic ballasts, installation of variable frequency drives on air handlers, adding building automation points to optimize start/stop, installation of fixed orifice steam traps, installation of removable steam insulation blankets and a near real time advanced metering system throughout the Jefferson Health System.

By bringing the metering in real time with the software trending, we can catch equipment running out of tolerance quickly. Other benefits include the use of monitoring, customized reporting, verification of utility bills, and remote site monitoring.

DESCRIPTION OF METERING SYSTEM

We decided to use a web-based client because of so many users at so many different locations (and to save money). At each meter location, the following equipment was installed: customer contacts for kWh and KQ (for power factor)—installed by the utility company; isolation contacts, data logger/recorder; terminal server and data jack. Cabling (CAT5ETR) was installed between each meter (including all subs) and the data logger. In our computer center we purchased and installed a data server, application server, and web server. We installed the software (Stark) on both the application server and my personal computer. We then set up the metering configuration and reports that are automatically sent out via e-mail.

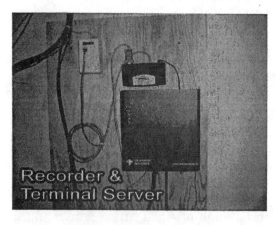

Every ten minutes, the application server, via the Ethernet, goes out to each data logger, collects the information, and stores it on the data server. All users can

access the information via their own PC using the web server.

Samples of reports:

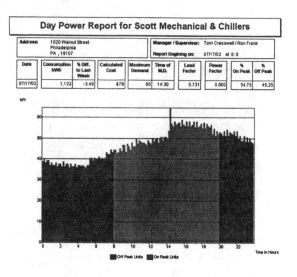

One Day Power Report of Scott Building Mechanical Equipment

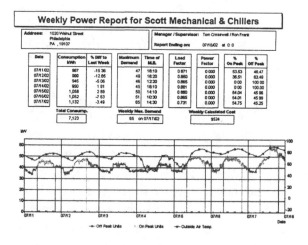

Weekly Power Report

The metering system calculates energy use every 10 minutes and compares the actual load to a setpoint and has the ability to e-mail a report if out of tolerance.

HOW DO WE MAINTAIN THE SAVINGS?

Now with the metering in place and the energy projects in place, how do we ensure we are getting our savings for the life of the project?

Installation of Variable Frequency drives on four supply and four return fans

One of our buildings on the campus is the Scott Building. Built in 1976, it is an 112,000 square feet Administration and Library Building which also contains our data center for the University and Hospital. The HVAC is a constant volume-dual duct system using a Siemens Building Automation control on the air handlers and chillers. The chillers in the building also feed two other adjacent buildings through underground piping. The chilled water temperature discharge setpoint temperature changes based on outdoor air temperature. The variable frequency drives (VFD) on the air handlers are changed based on occupancy times. The outside air intakes are controlled by calculating enthalpy both inside the building and outside air and the one with the lowest additional energy is used to heat or cool the building.

PROBLEMS

Some obstacles to easy measurement of the savings are: meters were installed after the project was installed and historical data was only manually read meters on a monthly basis (kWh only, no demand), only have one meter for the entire 480/277 volt system in the entire building, chillers feed three buildings and load varies greatly with outside air temperature and humidity.

All of the variables make this harder to verify savings, but by calculating the best fit correlation between outside air temperature and energy use when the VFD's are operating properly, we calculated an upper limit on both the demand (kW) and use (kWh) on a daily basis.

To test the system, we disabled the VFD's and ran them 100% and the alarms came in.

CONCLUSIONS

Although this has been a lot of work, the initial results are encouraging. With having a near real-time metering system, we have guaranteed that on a daily basis, we are truly saving the energy that was calculated during the development of the project.

Chapter 46

MARKET-BASED ENERGY PROCUREMENT

James S. Peters, Principal
JSP Associates

ABSTRACT

As retail energy markets emerge -- in fits and starts -- across the U.S. and the rest of North America, energy purchasers are becoming market participants, and market conditions are suddenly relevant to energy procurement. The dimensions of energy procurement that can be manipulated by end-users to optimize energy price performance are: 1) what is purchased, 2) how much is purchased, 3) how purchases are made, and 4) when supply contracts are initiated and purchases made. A market-based procurement strategy aligns purchasing processes with current and expected market conditions by relying on market signals for decision-making guidance.

INTRODUCTION

The notion of purchasing significant quantities of a commodity without being informed as to market conditions would, on the face of it, seem absurd. However, until recently retail energy purchasers faced markets intermediated by price controls and utility production cost-based pricing.

Consequently, energy purchasers required no market knowledge and had no need to view themselves as market participants. It should not be surprising that energy procurement strategies were designed accordingly.

Now, enabled by advances in information technology, retail energy markets are emerging – in fits and starts – throughout the world and especially in Europe and North America. Energy purchasers are becoming market participants and market conditions are suddenly relevant to energy procurement.

The principal rationale behind energy deregulation and the development of retail energy markets is that market-based exchange is more economically efficient than traditional utility monopoly arrangements. However, it is important to understand that realizing economic gains from deregulation requires action by end-users. Energy users must not only receive market-generated price signals. They must also act on those signals.

OPTIMIZING PURCHASING PERFORMANCE

The dimensions of energy procurement that can be manipulated by end-users to optimize price performance relate to fuel choice, volume, contract terms, and timing. The key issues are:

- what is purchased – i.e., fuel switching;
- how much is purchased – i.e., 2 years' volume, 1 year's volume, 1 month's volume, enough to fill storage, enough to meet minimum operating requirements, etc.;
- how purchases are made – i.e., in spot markets, under contract in a futures market with exchange for physicals (EFP), fixed price, capped price (maximum), indexed price, under contract with a staged commodity trigger, with interruptibility provisions, with fixed, minimum, and/or maximum volume requirements, with balancing and storage services, etc.;
- when supply contracts are initiated and purchases made – i.e., immediately, as late as possible, when a target price is reached, during off-peak periods, etc.

Choices that are controlled, or potentially controlled, on the demand-side frame end-users' market participation, and that participation begins as soon as an organization decides to conduct energy-using operations. Once an operating decision has been made, an organization is *short* the required energy until purchase is made. From that point on, an organization is *long* the energy until it is used. When an organization is *short*, it is financially at risk from higher prices. When it is *long*, it is at risk from lower prices.

As market conditions change, end-user response must also change if procurement is to be optimized. Market-based energy procurement strategies align purchasing and end-use with market conditions and, therefore, require that purchasers have a market view as well as an understanding of end-use requirements.

MARKET CONDITIONS and SIGNALS
Market-based prices are established by supply/demand balance. The market clearing prices signal suppliers to increase or decrease supply and consumers to increase or decrease demand.

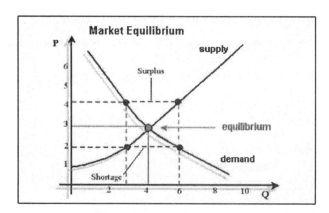

FIGURE 1: MARKET EQUILIBRIUM

Over time -- even from one moment to the next -- supply and demand curves shift and prices change.

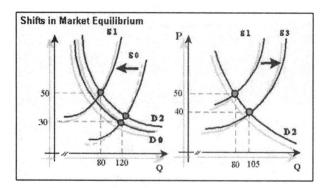

FIGURE 2: SHIFTS IN MARKET EQUILIBRIUM

Very high prices suggest that prices are unlikely to move much higher before beginning a return to mid-range (i.e., very high prices create strong economic incentives for demand reduction and increased supply).

Mid-range prices suggest that prices could move up or down with equal likelihood. (Periods of mid-range prices tend to be of longer duration than periods of high or low prices.)

Very low prices suggest that prices are unlikely to move much lower before beginning a return to mid-range (i.e., very low prices create strong economic incentives for increased demand and supply reduction).

Price volatility for energy commodities is quite high. For example, natural gas and heating oil prices are currently (July 2002) exhibiting implied volatility of about 60% and 40%, respectively. This means that the market anticipates natural gas and heating oil prices will move up or down by 60% and 40%, respectively, within one standard deviation of the average price expectation.

The *law of one price* suggests that differences in price from one location to another or from one marketer to another result from differences in non-commodity services such as transportation/transmission, balancing, storage, hedging, etc. and not from differences in the commodity portion of an energy's price.

The transparency of exchange-traded futures prices make these prices the best reference prices available. Figure 3, below, presents the forward price curve for natural gas constructed from successive months' NYMEX futures contract prices as of April 2002 with the implied volatility. This was the market's price expectation at that time.

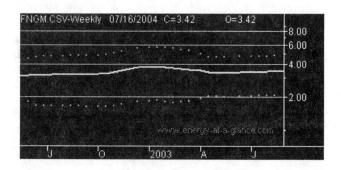

FIGURE 3: NG FORWARD PRICE CURVE

Figures 4, 5, and 6 present historical prices for 12-month futures strips (i.e., average price for the next 12 months) for natural gas, heating oil, and electricity (on-peak at Palo Verde, AZ; this and other NYMEX electricity futures contracts were discontinued in 2002), respectively traded on the NYMEX.

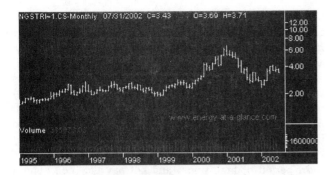

FIGURE 4: NATURAL GAS PRICES

During the period presented, the price of a 12-month natural gas futures strip ranged from under $2/MMBtu to over $7/MMBtu. Note the multi-month sideways price trend that lasted from 1996 through 1998 and the upward price trend beginning in early 2000. Also, note the trend reversal in early 2001, and the subsequent downward price trend through late 2001.

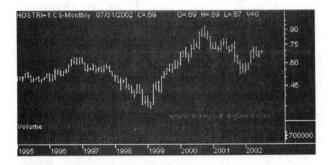

FIGURE 5: HEATING OIL PRICES

The price of a 12-month heating oil futures strip ranged from under $0.35/gallon to over $0.95/gallon. Note the multi-month sideways price trend in 1995 and 1996, and the downward price trend from mid-1997 to early 1999. Also, note the trend reversal and upward price trend beginning in early 1999 and ending in mid-2000.

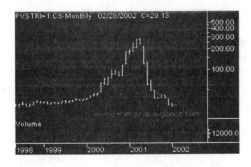

FIGURE 6: ELECTRICITY PRICES

During this period, the price of a 12-month electricity futures strip ranged from under $30/MWH to over $300/MWH. Note the multi-month sideways price trend from 1998 through 1999, the upward price trend that began in 2000 and reversed in 2001.

When prices are trending up, purchases should be made sooner rather than later. When prices are trending down, purchase should be later rather than sooner. When prices are trending sideways within a range, purchases should be made near the bottom of that range.

Figures 7 and 8 present historical cash (white), NYMEX nearest month's futures (yellow), 2nd month's futures, and 12-month futures strip prices for natural gas and crude oil, respectively, from April 2002 through July 2002. Note the fact that during most of this period the natural gas market was structurally *contango* (i.e., premium) – that is, prices for time periods further in the future were higher that prices for time periods closer to the present. Also, note that for most of this period the crude oil market was structurally *backwardized* (i.e., inverted) – that is, prices for time periods further in the future were lower that prices for time periods closer to the present.

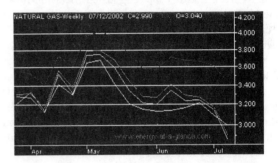

FIGURE 7: NATURAL GAS PRICE STRUCTURE

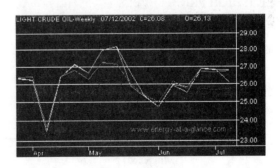

FIGURE 8: CRUDE OIL PRICE STRUCTURE

The *contango* (premium) price structure is considered normal. *Backwardized* (inverted) prices indicate short supplies. To the extent possible, purchasing should be avoided during *backwardized* periods.

MARKET-BASED PROCUREMENT STRATEGY

A market-based procurement strategy aligns purchasing processes with current and expected market conditions by relying on market signals for decision-making guidance. The decision-making context is an organization's short-term and long-term operating requirements. This point cannot be over emphasized. End-Users' strategies are not the strategies of traders or speculators. End-Users' market activities are determined by their operating requirements, and price performance cannot be optimized without reference to operating requirements and capabilities.

A simple topology of market-based decision-making is suggested in Tables 1 - 3, below. This topology is based on where a market is (i.e., price level, price trend, and market structure). The tables suggest appropriate decision-making with respect to contract length, price mechanism, and timing for contract initiation and purchasing. In general, contract terms appropriate to high cost markets are not appropriate to mid-range or low cost markets and vice versa. However, contacts written with staged commodity triggers provide customers with the ability to employ different price mechanisms, as desired, for the commodity portion. (In terms of the suggested decision-making outlined below, such contracts can be initiated at any time and can be long-term contracts. However, decisions related to employing the commodity trigger should follow the suggested decision-making.)

Table 1 suggests tactics for periods of high prices. Table 2 suggests tactics for periods of mid-range prices. Table 3 suggests tactics for periods of low prices. In all three situations the price trend of interest for contract initiation is the multi-month, intermediate-term trend. The price trend of interest for purchasing for prompt delivery is the short-term trend.

TABLE 1: HIGH PRICE LEVELS

Price Trend	Market Structure	Contract Approach	Contract Initiation	Purchase Timing
up	contango	short-term w/indexed prices	any time	sooner
up	Backward-ized	short-term w/indexed prices	any time	varies
down	contango	short-term w/indexed prices	any time	later
down	backward-ized	short-term w/indexed prices	any time	later
Side ways	contango	short-term w/indexed prices	any time	based on target price
Side ways	backward-ized	short-term w/indexed prices	any time	based on target price

Very high prices suggest (taking any underlying long-term trend into consideration) that prices are unlikely to move much higher before beginning a return to mid-range (i.e., as very high prices create strong incentives for demand reduction and increased supply). As a result, purchasers should neither lock-in prices (i.e., via fixed price contract) nor enter long-term contracts during periods of high prices. Price protection (e.g., price caps) can be considered in industries that are especially sensitive to high prices. However, most purchasers would be expected to weather a short period of high prices and not pay the (i.e., option) price of protection.

TABLE 2: MID-RANGE PRICE LEVELS

Price Trend	Market Structure	Contract Approach	Contract Initiation	Purchase Timing
up	contango	mid-term w/price caps	sooner	sooner
up	backward-ized	mid-term w/price caps	varies	varies
down	contango	mid-term w/price caps	later	later
down	backward-ized	mid-term w/price caps	later	later
Side ways	contango	mid-term w/price caps	based on target price	based on target price
Side ways	backward-ized	mid-term w/price caps	based on target price	based on target price

Mid-range prices suggest that prices could move up or down with equal likelihood. Periods of mid-range prices are of longer duration than periods of high or low prices. So, contracts can be of moderate duration. Fixed-price contracts would protect against higher prices but would also continue to lock-in mid-range prices if prices went down. So, price protection (e.g., price caps) is likely to be the best approach. The (i.e., option) price of protection is lower the further away the price cap is set from the current price. Purchasers could also accept a price floor (i.e., price minimum) which would offset some or all of the cost of a price cap. Taken together, cap and floor are referred to as a collar.

TABLE 3: LOW PRICE LEVELS

Price Trend	Market Structure	Contract Approach	Contract Initiation	Purchase Timing
up	contango	long-term w/fixed prices	sooner	sooner
up	backward-ized	long-term w/fixed prices	varies	varies
down	contango	long-term w/fixed prices	later	later
down	backward-ized	long-term w/fixed prices	later	later
Side ways	contango	long-term w/fixed prices	based on target price	based on target price
Side ways	backward-ized	long-term w/fixed prices	based on target price	based on target price

Very low prices suggest that prices are unlikely to move much lower before beginning a return to mid-range (i.e., as very low prices create strong incentives for increased demand and supply reduction). Consequently, purchasers should lock-in prices for as long as possible (e.g., via long-term, fixed-price contract).

CONCLUSION

Energy markets exhibit high levels of price volatility. However, this volatility can be viewed as an opportunity. Choices made and controlled or potentially controlled on the demand-side frame an energy purchaser's market participation. By employing a market-based procurement strategy, end-users' procurement decisions can be guided by market conditions (and expectations) and procurement and end-use can be aligned to optimize procurement price performance. A topology of energy procurement decision-making was suggested that outlines how procurement tactics should change in response to different sets of market conditions.

Chapter 47

UTILITY DEREGULATION
HOW TO MAKE IT WORK FOR YOU

John M. Studebaker
Studebaker Energy Consulting, LLC

UTILITY DEREGULATION BASICS

Basics of Deregulation

Deregulation of electricity is simply the purchase of the electricity commodity by a retail customer from a source other than their own serving utility. The process is very similar to retail customer purchase of natural gas; however, the effect on the electric utility is very different from that on the natural gas utility.

In the purchase of electricity from a utility, the commodity (electricity) being purchased is typically considered to be originated or generated by the electric utility. Even though electricity is generally considered generated by the utility that sends the monthly bill to the customer, no one really knows what actual electrons flow to the customer's meter point. All utilities that generate electricity actually flow that electricity into a power pool for ultimate distribution to the customer.

Currently there are 10 power pools that cover all of the contiguous United States and parts of Canada. No one can identify or track the actual flow of electrons from the point-of-generation to the point-of-use by a customer. Unless there is a specific physical single line that connects electricity generation with the customer of that electricity, (there are thousands of electricity generation units flowing electrons into the 10 power pools in the United States) it is impossible to identify the location where any particular electron was generated.

Electricity flows based upon the path of least resistance, not just where any particular utility wants it to go. There are no "good" or "bad" electrons; however, there are various levels of delivery classifications. Whether electricity commodity is purchased from the utility or through the deregulation process, the actual electrons being delivered to the customer will be the same quality and be distributed through the same transmission/distribution wires and meters that are used by the utility that serves the retail customer.

In the purchase of natural gas, in the majority of instances, the commodity (natural gas) does not originate within the utility's service territory but is simply purchased by the utility and resold to the retail customer.

Although these differences between electric and natural gas may seem to be of little importance to a retail electricity customer, they actually are critical to the utilities and their differing attitudes towards the customer's direct purchase of the commodities that they sell. Since most natural gas utilities purchase the commodity they sell from someone else, it does not disrupt their operation or profitability to any great extent whether their customers purchase utility natural gas or arrange for their own natural gas and simply utilize utility pipes, meters, and services. If the utility charges are based upon true cost of service principles, most natural gas utilities would probably prefer retail customers obtain their own natural gas since it could result in less supply problems for the utility.

An electric utility, however, takes a very different view of direct purchase of electricity by its retail customers since generally the serving electric utility, in theory at least, generates a quantity of electricity equal to what it sells to retail customers. When a retail electricity customer purchases electricity commodity from some source other than the serving utility, the lost electricity generation sales for the serving utility can result in loss of revenue. The lost generation volume may not be capable of being resold by the serving utility.

If this is true, as retail customers choose to purchase their electricity commodity from sources other than the serving utility, the utility will be required to increase electricity incremental rates to offset the reduced electricity commodity sales. As this happens, more and more retail customers might opt to obtain their electricity commodity from other sources than the serving utility. Ultimately, this could mean that as less and less electricity generation is sold to retail customers by the serving utilities, the incremental electricity cost could continue to rise. In time, the serving electric utility's incremental rates could become prohibitively expensive, resulting in financial losses for the utility involved.

Deregulation of electricity is inherently neither good nor bad, but a valid case can be made both for and against the process.

From a customer's viewpoint, due to the large variation in electric utility rates caused by a lack (in part) of true competition, deregulation of electricity would seem to be a welcomed option.

From an electric utility viewpoint, someone has to pay for its investment in materials and generation capacity; and, if customers can purchase their electricity anywhere on the power pool, the utility may have no way to recoup its costs. Both of these views have

some validity, but what will ultimately determine the reality of the process will be retail customers causing it to happen.

If retail electricity customers take a "wait and see" attitude, then deregulation will probably never be widely available since electric utilities, especially high generation cost utilities, are not going to push for a process that could ultimately force them into a smaller customer base.

Deregulation of electricity is not something that is technologically impossible to do since almost all electric utilities currently *wholesale* electricity purchase/sell between each other on a daily basis. The real problem electric utilities have with deregulation of electricity is that it will require them to obtain and keep their retail customer base through competition, not through regulatory commission mandated service territory boundaries.

It is always best to keep the lines of communication open between the retail customer and the electric utility, but it is especially important with the advent of deregulation.

Deregulation will affect each electric customer whether they ever utilize deregulated electricity themselves or not. Knowledge of what is going on in the deregulation of electricity is critical.

How Is Deregulation Evolving?

One of the real questions concerning deregulation of electricity is how will the deregulated electricity get from the point of generation to the point of use over various transmission grids? The stated problem is one of logistics—how to get the electricity from the point of generation to an individual specific retail customer that is perhaps located on a distribution grid different from the one on which the electricity is generated.

There are both obstacles to and advantages in deregulation of electricity. How quickly deregulation occurs will depend upon how involved retail customers become in the process. At this time, the process is evolving as follows:

1. Deregulation of electricity is, at least initially, occurring internally on each of the current 10 North American Electric Reliability Council Regions (NERC) (power pools) in the contiguous United States. (See Figure 1)

2. Retail customers that could benefit from deregulation of electricity may negotiate a discount with their serving utility to preclude their participating in the deregulation process.

Figure 1
NORTH AMERICAN RELIABILITY COUNCIL REGIONS & STATES SERVED

REGION NAME (POWER POOLS		GEOGRAPHIC AREA SERVED
ECAR	**East Central Area Reliability Coordination Agreement**	*Kentucky, Indiana, *Maryland, *Michigan, Ohio, *Pennsylvania, *Virginia, West Virginia
ERCOT	**Electric Reliability Council of Texas**	*Texas
FRCC	**Florida Reliability Coordinating Council**	Florida
MAAC	**Mid Atlantic Area Council**	*Maryland, *Michigan, New Jersey, *Pennsylvania
MAIN	**Mid American Interpool Network**	Illinois, *Missouri, Wisconsin
MAPP	**Mid Continent Area Power Pool**	Iowa, Minnesota, *Montana, Nebraska, North Dakota, South Dakota
NPCC	**Northeast Power Coordinating Council**	Connecticut, Maine, Massachusetts, New Hampshire, New York, Rhode Island, Vermont
SERC	**Southeastern Electric Reliability Council**	Alabama, Delaware, District of Columbia, Georgia, *Kentucky, *Missouri, North Carolina, South Carolina, *Virginia, Tennessee
SPP	**Southwest Power Pool**	Arkansas, Kansas, Louisiana, *Mississippi, *Missouri, *New Mexico, Oklahoma *Texas
WSCC	**Western Systems Coordinating Council**	Arizona, California, Colorado, Idaho, *Montana, *New Mexico, Nevada, Oregon, Utah, Washington, Wyoming *Partial

QUESTIONS ABOUT DEREGULATION

There are many misconceptions about what electricity deregulation means to retail customers. Based upon actual experience, following are some of the most frequently asked questions by potential deregulation customers concerning their fears or lack of understanding of the deregulation process.

1.   QUESTION: What about power quality?
      ANSWER: Power quality will remain the same.

The first thing that has to be determined is what is power quality. Power quality means different things to different people. Power quality can mean that if power is available it is good quality. To others, it can refer to variation in hertz (cycles), variation in voltage, harmonic levels, and electric line transmitted spikes, etc. The thing that has to be understood is that power quality will remain the same both before as well as after deregulation for both the utility and customer.

Quality of power is a function of the power pool in which the retail customer is located. It must be remembered that generally, retail customers are not directly connected to any single serving utility's generation sources. Retail customers are directly connected to their serving utility's distribution system, but the actual electrons that enter their serving utility's distribution system can be generated anywhere on the power pool of which they are a part. In fact, the origination point of the electrons may even be from a different power pool than the one, which directly serves the retail customer.

The truth is—deregulated electricity is the same electricity as what a retail customer is currently receiving from their serving utility. No one can track the actual path electrons take from the point-of-generation to a given electricity customer unless there is a direct, dedicated physical connection between the point-of-generation and the point-of-use, which is not the case between generators and customers today.

If a particular quality level is required by an individual customer, the best and most effective way of obtaining that quality level is to "condition" the electricity on the customer's side of the electricity delivery meter point.

Quality of power should not be a reason for not investigating electricity deregulation savings potentials.

2.   QUESTION: How can a company be assured that electricity will be there when needed?
      ANSWER: The required electricity will be available if you have opted for firm commodity, transmission, and distribution.

The real question is will you be able to afford the electricity you receive if your provider defaults (does not deliver) your electricity needs? Generally, there is no accurate way to track a specific customer's electrons from point-of-generation, transmission, and distribution to the customer's individual meter point on a real time basis.

The "truing up" of a specific customer's actual meter point usage on a monthly basis, with what the electricity provider actually delivered for that specific customer, is accomplished by comparing the serving utility receipt point quantities from the provider in the customer's behalf for the same period as the meter point reading period. At this point in time it is difficult, if not impossible, to compare actual specific customer serving utility receipts with usages on a real time basis.

In practice, the total deliveries by the retail customer's electricity provider and the usage quantity registered on the retail customer's use point meter are reconciled on a monthly basis. If there are discrepancies, especially deficits, the retail customer has to pay a penalty to the serving utility for system-supply electricity that was required to make up for the electricity provider's shortfall.

The question is not will electricity be available, but rather who will pay for any electricity-provider caused problems. In actuality, the retail customer is responsible to the serving utility for any electricity provider problems including, potential penalties for shortfalls, overages, balancing problems, etc. The way to minimize these potential cost problems is to structure the deregulated commodity provider contract in such a way as to shield or protect the retail customer from the serving utility cost penalties.

3.   QUESTION: How will a company know if they are getting the best deal?
ANSWER: It depends upon what you define as the "best deal."

If the best deal is absolutely the "cheapest" electricity commodity cost available, probably you will never be satisfied that what you are paying is the "cheapest" that could be had, since the "cheapest" cost changes every day or even more frequently. However, if your definition of "the best deal" is a reasonable cost with assured delivery from a provider that can supply all

of the assurances that you require, then that will be the "best deal" for your requirements.

Many times the "cheapest" initial cost does not translate to the best long-term value. Comfort with the (deregulated commodity) provider selected as well as a comprehensive contract that covers all of the variables that can occur, is the only way to assure reasonably cost and satisfactory assurance that the electricity commodity will be available when needed. Reasonable cost and satisfactory contract terms are a result of knowledge and negotiation with the potential provider. Luck/hope are not the means to accomplish either of these goals.

4.   QUESTION: Who maintains the customer's meters, and other electricity generation, transmission, and distribution infrastructure in electricity deregulation?
ANSWER: The same entities that currently do.

In deregulation, all areas of generation, transmission, and distribution of electricity continue to operate with the same federal/state oversight as prior to deregulation. Deregulation of electricity only allows a retail electricity customer the option of selecting electricity commodity suppliers, other than their serving utility. Federal/state regulatory oversight of maintenance, quality, and other electricity generation and delivery characteristics will remain the same in a regulated or deregulated environment.

Figure 2
STATUS OF ELECTRICITY DEREGULATION IN THE UNITED STATES

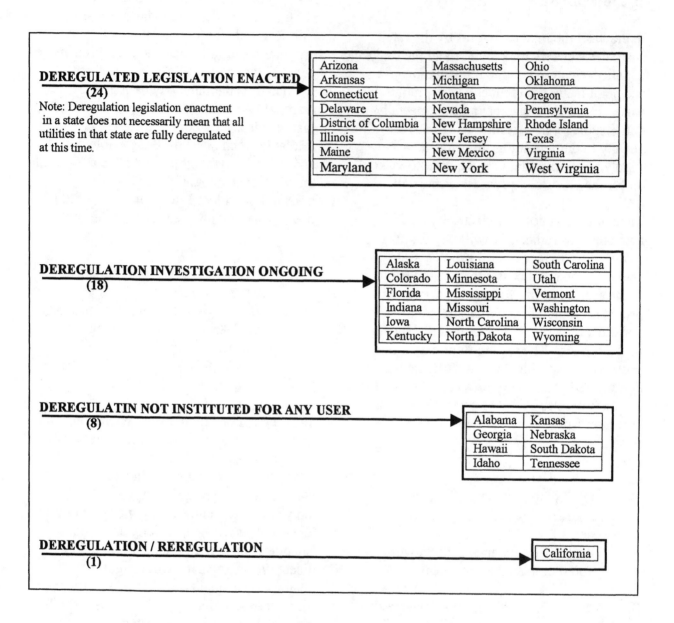

DEREGULATED LEGISLATION ENACTED
(24)
Note: Deregulation legislation enactment
in a state does not necessarily mean that all
utilities in that state are fully deregulated
at this time.

Arizona	Massachusetts	Ohio
Arkansas	Michigan	Oklahoma
Connecticut	Montana	Oregon
Delaware	Nevada	Pennsylvania
District of Columbia	New Hampshire	Rhode Island
Illinois	New Jersey	Texas
Maine	New Mexico	Virginia
Maryland	New York	West Virginia

DEREGULATION INVESTIGATION ONGOING
(18)

Alaska	Louisiana	South Carolina
Colorado	Minnesota	Utah
Florida	Mississippi	Vermont
Indiana	Missouri	Washington
Iowa	North Carolina	Wisconsin
Kentucky	North Dakota	Wyoming

DEREGULATIN NOT INSTITUTED FOR ANY USER
(8)

Alabama	Kansas
Georgia	Nebraska
Hawaii	South Dakota
Idaho	Tennessee

DEREGULATION / REREGULATION
(1)

California

THINGS TO DO PRIOR TO THE ACTUAL OCCURRING OF DEREGULATION

1. Know the current status of deregulation of electricity in the state that your facilities are located. (See Figure 2)

2. Utilize Internet web sites to keep up-to-date on electricity deregulation status. Following are two good sites that provide state-by-state deregulation information on a very timely basis. It is the best to utilize both web sites since they each provide deregulation information in a slightly different manner that seems to compliment rather than repeat each other.

www.serve.com/commonpurpose/dereg.html
www.EIA.DOE.gov/cneaf/electricity/chgstr

3. Know your current serving utilities' actions concerning deregulation. Contact your state utility regulatory agency concerning deregulation in general and your serving utility specifically.

4. Accumulate and itemize electric utility usage characteristics. The way to most quickly and accurately accumulate and document this type of information is to utilize a utility data form similar to the one shown in Figure 3—Utility Data Form.

Note: The following form (Utility Data Form) shown includes—electricity and cogeneration data. It is not necessary to utilize all sections of this form if not required but generally, it is easier to gather all of the utility data at the same time and retain what is not immediately needed for future use/reference.

Figure 3
UTILITY DATA FORM

Section 1—General Facility Data
1. Facility name_____
2. Facility address _____
3. Facility telephone/fax numbers_____
4. Facility contact person & telephone, fax, and email numbers _____
5. Facility function(s) _____
6. Facility size:
   a) Number of square feet _____
   b) Number of buildings   _____

Section 2—Electricity Data
7. Name of electric utility serving the facility_____
8. Name, telephone, fax, email numbers of electric utility service representative
   _____
9. Total number of electric meters _____
10. Is an energy management system utilized?_____
11. If an energy management system is utilized, is it used to load-shed/manage electrical usage patterns?_____
12. Does this facility have any off-tariff agreements or special contracts with the electric utility that may affect this project?_____
    (If *yes*, please attach a copy of the agreement/contract.)
13. Does this facility have any *current / pending / planned* energy services projects?_____
14. If the answer to #13 is *yes*, please include the following information:
    a) Describe the projects by status:
       (1) Current _____
       (2) Pending _____
       (3) Planned _____
    b) What are the project costs?
       (1) Current _____
       (2) Pending _____
       (3) Planned _____

Section 3—Cogeneration Data

15. Is backup or cogeneration equipment utilized at this facility?_____

16. If answer to #15 is *yes*, what is the equipment size? (kW capacity)_____

17. If answer to #15 is *yes*, can the equipment be utilized to peak shave/load-shed electricity, is it parallel wired? _____

18. If answer to #15 is *yes*, are the thermal characteristics of the process utilized, and if so, how? _____

19. What is thermal load, steam, hot water, etc. of this facility by hour, day, week, etc.?_____

Section 4—General Utility Data

20. Is this facility currently involved in any negotiations or discussions with the electric utility or other electricity provider not addressed in any other part of this questionnaire?_____

21. If answer to #20 is *yes*, please describe the discussions and include copies of proposals, agreements, etc. _____

THINGS TO DO WHEN DEREGULATION IS AVAILABLE

1. Obtain a copy of the electricity serving utility deregulated credits for the electricity commodity and costs for transportation to the serving utility receipt point.

This information can be obtained from the utility regulatory agency. This information will provide, generally in cents per kilowatt-watt (kWh) the amount of the retail rate that will be credited/deducted if the retail customer chooses to provide their own electricity commodity and transportation to the serving utility receipt point.

If the retail electricity customer can obtain the electricity commodity and transportation to the serving utility receipt point at a cost lower than the deregulated credit/deduction, they will save whatever the cost differential is, generally on a cost per kWh basis. The deregulated electricity flow chart process is shown in Figure 4.

Figure 4
DEREGULATED ELECTRICITY FLOW CHART

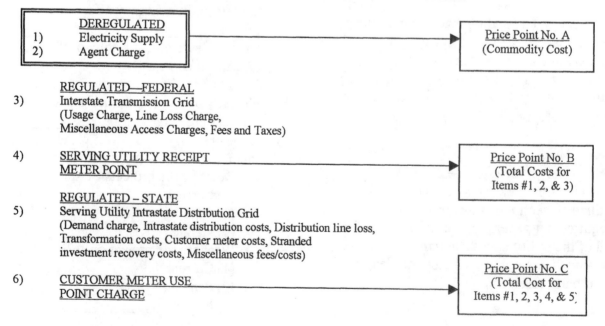

EXPLANATION OF FIGURE 4— DEREGULATED ELECTRICITY FLOW CHART

Deregulated Electricity Supply / Agent Charge—Price Point No.A

Costs included in this area include the actual commodity (electricity) and agent costs. These costs are calculated in MWh (megawatt hours—1,000,000 watt-hours). This unit of measure (MWh) is the standard utilized in all (10) power pools for all transactions between utility generators on a wholesale basis. One of the most readily accessible electricity price indices is the "D. J. Electricity Price Index" which is found daily in The Wall Street Journal in the "Money and Investment" Section. This electricity price data is generally located adjacent to the Futures Price sheets.

The electricity prices in this index represent actual weighted average prices for electricity traded at various delivery points in the 10 power pool regions. Prices are quoted in dollars per megawatt hour (MWh) and are—

- *Firm* delivery (*on-peak* and *off-peak)*
- *Interruptible* (non-firm) delivery (*on-peak* and *off-peak)*

Although not all delivery points on all 10 power pools are currently listed in this index, as electricity deregulation becomes more widely available more delivery points will be included.

Remember, if any index is utilized, it will only include the commodity (electricity) delivered to a common transmission power pool point. To the costs shown in an index will have to be added transmission costs to the wheeling customer's serving utility receipt point, plus serving utility distribution costs. The various types of electricity that can be purchased at a power pool delivery point are as follows:

1. *Firm*
This class of electricity generation service is expensive, but it is the only type of generation that is available 24 hours a day, 7 days a week with no interruption other than *force majeure* conditions. A customer that cannot be interrupted would utilize this class of service.

2. *Interruptible*
This class of electricity generation service is subject to curtailment based upon the stipulations contained in the contract between the generator and the customer. This class of service is generally less expensive since it can be curtailed, but it can be a very viable option for customers that can interrupt their electricity needs. Generally, interruptions will occur during periods of high electricity usage in the applicable power pool. In most areas of the country, high electricity usage periods occur in the summer months.

3. *On-Peak Generation Service*
This class of electricity generation generally can be either *firm* or *interruptible*. Generation in this class would occur during the highest usage of generation on the power pool. Normally, generation *on-peak* will continue for a period of—from 12 to 16 hours daily, Monday through Friday. Typically, Saturdays and Sundays and holidays are considered to be *off-peak* periods, 24 hours a day.

4. *Off-Peak Generation Service*
This class of electricity generation can be either *firm* or *interruptible*. *Off-peak* generation occupies all hours not considered to be *on-peak*. Electricity generation purchased during *off-peak* periods is less expensive than electricity generation

purchased *on-peak*. The least expensive electricity generation that can generally be purchased would be *off-peak* and *interruptible*.

Agent Charges

This charge represents the retail customers cost for the agent (marketer) utilized to acquire the electricity generation needed. Most customers utilize the services of a third party (agent) to initiate and follow-up on the deregulation process much as is generally done in customer transportation of natural gas. These third parties, whether brokers, marketers or producers, are technically know as agents since they act in the customer's behalf and can legally bind them to a contractual agreement. These entities will perform at least the following functions for the retail customer:

1.   Select an appropriate deregulated electricity supply source.

2.   Select an appropriate interstate transmission grid to move the customer's deregulated electricity from its origination point to the customer's serving utility meter/receipt point.

3.   Negotiate the least expensive deregulated electricity and transmission rates for the customer.

4.   Assist the deregulated customer in the contractual agreements that will be required. There are at least three distinctly different contracts required—

   A.   Between the deregulated electricity supplier and the deregulated customer;

   B.   Between the transmission grid utilized between the deregulated electricity supply and the serving utility meter/receipt point, and the deregulated customer; and

   C.   Between the customer's serving electric utility for the transmission and other services that they provide to the deregulated customer. These contracts in a flow chart form will look as follows:

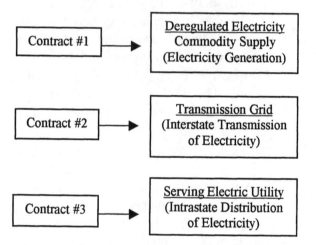

In addition to these (3) contracts, there will be a fourth contract between the customer and the agent utilized by the customer to facilitate the process.

Generally, the agent charge is a percentage of the actual electricity generation cost. Agent charges range in the area of ½% to 2% of the actual agent acquisition cost of the electricity generation required by the retail customer.

Interstate Transmission Charges

These changes represent the power pool's transmission cost to move the electricity generated, through the applicable power pool's transmission grid, to the retail customer's serving electric utility receipt or metering point. These costs represent rental or fees collected by the various power pool transmission line owners. These fees are subject to FERC approval and generally include "line loss" fees to account for electricity generation losses due to the resistance of flow of electrons through the transmission system. The loss factors are subject to FERC approval.

To minimize loss, electricity generation voltage levels in this portion of the transaction are generally between 100,000 volts to 385,000 volts. These high voltage levels are generally reduced to more usable levels on the serving utility's distribution system. Also, included in this portion of the transaction would be any miscellaneous regulatory fees and/or applicable taxes.

Electricity, Agent, Transmission Charges—Price Point No. B

This is the point at which the agent exits the deregulated electricity transaction. This is also the point at which the agent costs are accumulated and billed to the retail customer. The billing from the agent will include the following items:

1. *Electricity generation cost per MWh* (Item #1 on flow chart.)
2. *Agent charge* (Item #2 on flow chart.)
3. *Interstate transmission of electricity* (Item #3 on flow chart.)
4. *Total cost for items #1, 2, and 3* (expressed generally in cost per kWh)

Serving Utility Intrastate Distribution Charge—Price Point #C

This charge represents the serving utility cost to move the electricity received at price point #B (item #4 on flow chart) through their distribution system to the retail customer meter point. This portion of the wheeling transaction is under the jurisdiction of the appropriate state utility regulatory authority. Included in this portion of the transaction will be included miscellaneous costs as follows:

1. *Distribution line loss fees, if applicable* (See interstate transmission charges, item #3 for an explanation of line loss.)

2. *Transformation costs, if applicable*
   These costs are the result of the serving utility's need to reduce the electricity voltage level supplied from the transmission's power pool at serving utility receipt point. (Item#4 on the flow chart.) These costs may be included in the distribution charge or it may be listed separately.

3. *Customer use point meter costs, if applicable*
   These costs would compensate the serving utility for the meter, its usage and maintenance. This cost may be included with other items or it may be listed separately.

4. *Stranded investment recovery costs*
   These costs represent the utility's investment in generation infrastructure that may not be utilized by the retail customer when they utilize deregulated electricity through an agent. These costs are considered *stranded costs* since the serving utility, in theory at least, may have no other customer to utilize this infrastructure. These costs are approved on a utility-by-utility basis by the appropriate state utility regulatory agency. These types of costs will generally be different for each utility and may even vary for different customer classes served by the same utility based upon usage characteristic variations. Also, included in

this portion of the transaction would be and state regulatory agency fees and/or any applicable taxes. This price point includes all of the serving utility costs as follows:

1. *Intrastate distribution cost* (Item #5 on flow chart.)
2. *Distribution line losses, if applicable* (Item #5 on flow chart.)
3. *Transformation costs, if applicable* (Item #5 on flow chart.)
4. *Customer meter costs, if applicable* (Item #5 on flow chart.)
5. *Stranded investment recovery* (Item #5 on flow chart.)
6. *Any miscellaneous fees and/or costs, if applicable* (Item #5 on flow chart.)

All of these costs will be billed to the retail customer by the serving utility. This billing, together with the agent billing (item #4 on flow chart), will be the total electricity cost to the customer for the entire transaction (item #6 on flow chart).

Total Costs.

This total includes all costs from deregulated electricity supply point (item #1 on the flow chart) through the serving utility distribution costs (item #5 on the flow chart) and are as follows:

1. *Deregulated electricity supply cost* (Item #1 on the flow chart.)
2. *Agent charge* (Item #2 on the flow chart.)
3. *Interstate transmission grid costs* (Item #3 on the flow chart.)
4. *Serving utility distribution grid costs* (Item #5 on the flow chart.)

The total cost at this point would be compared to the total cost the retail customer had been paying to the serving utility prior to deregulation.

FINDING AGENTS TO ASSIST THE RETAIL CUSTOMER IN THE OBTAINING OF DEREGULATED ELECTRICITY

Generally, the best source for potential deregulated electricity suppliers (agents) is either the state regulatory agencies or the serving utility itself. Some states where electricity is deregulated require that interested suppliers be registered and have certain financial qualifications before they can serve as electricity supply agents in that state. In states where there is no registration required, the serving utility will have a listing of agents that would be qualified to serve that utility's deregulated retail customers.

SELECTING AN AGENT (Provider)

Questions to ask a potential deregulated electricity provider and points to consider prior to the signing of a contract.

1. Is title to the deregulated electricity for the entire term of the agreement?

2. How many electricity generation entry points to the interstate transmission grid are available?

3. Has non-delivery of deregulated electricity by this provider ever occurred? If so, why?

4. Always have a provider quote not only the deregulated electricity cost but also the total point-of-use cost. This point-of-use (commonly called "customer meter point") cost is what will be paid in total for the

deregulated electricity delivered. It includes—

- Electricity
- Agent fee
- Interstate transmission grid transportation and line loss
- Serving utility intrastate distribution grid transportation and line loss.

This is the customer use point meter cost and will be the one to use in determining savings.

5. Always obtain quotes and terms from more than one provider and compare them to see if one is more favorable than the other.

6. Do not be afraid to try to negotiate on agreement terms or electricity cost since most providers probably expect to have to negotiate on some items.

7. After doing the other six steps in this questioning exercise, do what is probably the most important step—find a provider you will feel comfortable working with and one that sincerely wants your business. If the right provider is selected, they will be able to provide much insight and assistance in all steps of this deregulated electricity process.

SUMMARY

Utility/energy costs and where they are headed are real questions that every commercial and industrial user has to face, resolve and control. Whether your company is large or small or somewhere in between, a strategy to survive is a 'must'.

Many companies are reacting to, rather than planning for, utility deregulation. Think about the information contained in this short presentation before concluding that "it may be good for someone, but not me." To utilize utility deregulation programs, information at the right time and in the right format is critical to success.

ABOUT THE SPEAKER

John M. Studebaker, President Studebaker Energy Consulting, LLC, brings a combination of technical expertise and knowledge developed over many years of industrial and consulting experience. He has assisted many organizations, including industrial and commercial companies, hospitals, multi-family property owners, municipal, state and federal agencies.

As an energy consultant and negotiator, he regularly utilizes his abilities to reduce utility costs. His knowledge of the energy industry, federal and state regulatory developments and the negotiation process, combined with his own experience, make him a uniquely qualified consultant.

He has a Ph.D. in Industrial Engineering and has taught utility fundamentals at 19 leading universities including— Clemson, Columbia, Cornell, Georgia State, and Harvard Universities, Universities of Alabama and Oklahoma.

He is a member of the American Institute of Plant Engineers, the National Society of Professional Engineers, The Association of Energy Engineers and the Doctorate Association of New York Educators. He is a certified Plant Engineer (CPE).

He is a lecturer for the following national associations—Institute for Supply Management, National Association of State Facilities Administrators, International Facility Management Association, and Financial Executives International.

PUBLICATIONS

He is the author of the following
utility/energy cost reduction books—

*Complete Utility/Energy Cost Reduction
Strategies Handbook* (2003)
Fairmont Press/Prentice Hall

ESCO Services Handbook
PennWell (2001)

Electricity Retail Wheeling Handbook,
Second Edition (2000)
Fairmont Press/Prentice Hall

Utility Negotiating Strategies for End-Users
PennWell (1998)

Slashing Utility Costs Handbook,
Second Edition (1998)
Fairmont Press/Prentice Hall

Electricity Purchasing Handbook
PennWell (1997)

Natural Gas Purchasing Handbook
Fairmont Press/Prentice Hall (1994)

Chapter 48

MEASUREMENT AND VERIFICATION OF A UTILITY'S ENERGY MANAGEMENT PROGRAM

Prof LJ Grobler, WLR den Heijer, AZD Dalgleish*

INTRODUCTION

Eskom, South Africa's main utility, is embarking on a major drive to implement energy management or demand side management (DSM) solutions into the industrial, commercial and residential sectors. Its target for the first year is to reduce the national peak demand by 180 MW.

The aim of the DSM program is also to establish the concept of performance contracting in South Africa and to use this vehicle together with financial incentives to stimulate implementation of DSM solutions. Since the concept of performance contracting is not well established in South Africa there is currently a resistance from financial institutions to fund this kind of projects. As financial assistance is crucial for the establishment of a performance contracting industry, the utility will initially provide the financial assistance.

It is therefore of utmost importance that a proper measurement and verification (M&V) program be developed to track and evaluate the performance of the implemented DSM projects.

PROBLEM STATEMENT

In order to M&V the effectiveness of a DSM program the energy use and behaviour of program partici-

pants needs to be compared with what their energy use and behaviour would have been in the absence of the DSM program.

The first element—the participant(s) energy use and behaviour pre- and post-DSM—can be readily monitored/measured.

The second element—what the participant(s) energy use and behaviour would have been—cannot be measured because it does not exist; it can only be inferred. Such inferences are based on analysis of energy use data and other variables collected from program participants and non-participants (control groups). For this section baselines need to be developed which determine what the participant(s) energy use and behaviour would have been without DSM.

M&V PROGRAM DEVELOPMENT

Since public money will be used by the utility to implement DSM it is crucial that an independent and credible M&V program be developed and put in place. For this reason a measurement and verification steering committee (MVSC) has been established. It consists of representatives from four of the main Universities in South Africa namely:

- Potchefstroom University for CHE
- University of Natal
- University of Cape Town
- University of Stellenbosch

Eskom requested the MVSC to act objectively as a third party authority to set guidelines, establish pro-

*Prof LJ Grobler is an Associate Professor, Willem den Heijer and AZD Dalgleish PhD students at the School for Mechanical and Materials Engineering at the Potchefstroom University for CHE, South Africa.

tocols, and to develop procedures and operational plans for M&V of DSM in South Africa.

The strategic intent of the MVSC is to be the body that internalizes M&V expertise in the national interest and is recognized as an independent arbitrator in SA on all M&V related issues.

The objectives of the MVSC are to:
- Develop the procedures and methodologies to M&V the DSM projects on a local as well as a national scale.
- Develop the necessary standardized frameworks for M&V plans, pre-implementation baseline reports, post-implementation reports and monthly and annual savings reports.
- Build sufficient capacity of tertiary institutions and industry to M&V the projects across the country.
- Set up a national M&V Centre to track and evaluate the performance of all the DSM projects on a local as well as a national scale.

A summary of the tasks associated with the M&V program development is given in Table 1.

POSITION OF M&V

There are a number of stakeholders in any DSM project, which includes the client, the Energy Service Company (Esco) and the financier or financial institution. The clients want to reduce their energy costs when they reduce their peak demand. The financial institutions want to protect their investments in DSM projects. The Esco wants to share in the energy cost savings when they implement DSM under risk.

The Esco or the client usually does the project identification and/or savings calculations as part of the preliminary and design phases of the DSM project. Once the DSM intervention has been implemented, these savings need to be quantified to determine the effectiveness of the DSM intervention. Since project payback or performance-based contracts rely on accurate and impartial savings information, the task of saving assessment and quantification need to be performed by a party outside the DSM project.

The principal questions that all DSM stakeholders want answered are: How much have been saved and are we still sustaining our savings? The dynamics in DSM projects make it difficult, and certainly not preferred, to assign any one of the stakeholders to de-liver an objective assessment of the savings. The quantification and assessment of the savings must remain impartial and the process transparent. The long-term success of many DSM projects is often hampered by the inability of project partners to agree on the quantity of savings that have been obtained. It is for this reason that another party needs to be included in the DSM process to determine and verify to savings.

M&V is the vehicle to provide all the DSM project stakeholders with an impartial quantification of the savings.

One of the first tasks that had to be performed by the MVSC was to identify and propose a structure of measurement and verification for Eskom's DSM activities. International measurement and verification protocols were utilized to develop an M&V system for South African DSM. These protocols were the International Performance Measurement and Verification Protocol (IPMVP)[1], as well as the M&V Guidelines for Federal Energy Management Projects (FEMP)[2]. Although these protocols were internationally used, they proved to be cumbersome and tended to neglect crucial stages of the M&V process, such as the development of the baselines. Baselines are covered in the protocols, but very little information is provided on the process of constructing the baseline. This resulted in the development of an additional M&V framework that was streamlined and focused for Eskom's DSM needs, without compromising on integrity or accuracy.

Why Should We Measure and Verify?
The importance of M&V for the success of DSM in South Africa is becoming more apparent. The whole process is designed to quantify and assess the savings that result from DSM projects in an impartial manner. If the DSM impacts are known, stakeholders can M&E the performance and progress of all the DSM activities, which will help to identify focus areas for DSM, as well as potential problems. M&V will enable Eskom to evaluate the verified savings against their DSM targets and help with proper implementation of DSM projects. M&V is therefore an essential part of any DSM activity.

M&V encourage investment in the DSM industry and reduce the risk for financial investors. M&V thus help to overcome barriers to DSM implementation. It will also become a crucial requirement when participating in international markets such as the clean develop-

No	Task	Objective (s)	Aspects Involved
		TABLE 1: SUMMARY OF TASKS	
1	Program planning and resource allocation.	Proper planning and costing of M&V projects.	• Prioritizing M&V program implementation. • Timeframes. • Resources. • Costs.
2	Development/ identification of KPI's.	Establish WHAT needs to be measured to meet Eskom's need(s).	• Develop detailed KPI's, these include technical, social and economic indicators. • Communicate KPI's to all relevant stakeholders. • Obtain stakeholder buy in/agreement.
3	Development of M&V procedures and protocols.	Establish HOW to measure—ensure consistency across all programs to allow subsequent "apples to apples" comparison.	• Develop detailed procedures and protocols on how each KPI indicator should be measured. • Develop questionnaires required to obtain information such as customer willingness, customer usage patterns, etc. • Investigate, test and recommend instrumentation required to obtain reliable and cost-effective measurements.
4	Develop IT infrastructure.	Ensure a reliable, accessible and consistent means of data capturing and storage.	• Development of SQL M&V database. • Development of user-friendly Internet based front end for data input.
5	Develop M&V training materials, programs and procedures.	Ensure consistency of data capturing methodology and accuracy. Build capacity to continually improve M&V	• Development of M&V training material (manuals, slides and videos). • Development of M&V training course format. • Development of outcomes based assessment procedures to ensure trainees are suitably qualified.
6	M&V training.	Obtain multiplier effect. Maximize the value of information.	• Train prospective M&V fieldworkers. • Fieldworkers should know how to collect M&V KPI data as well as how this data should be updated in the M&V database. • Fieldworkers should be able to diagnose and report problems to DSM critical performance in the field. • Examine/evaluate fieldworker competency.
7	Data collection.	Collect required KPI data.	• Launch M&V program. • Monitor data collection progress and costs. • Ensure database integrity is maintained.
8	Data processing.	Extract information required for M&V from captured data.	• Data mining. • Data censoring and validation • Development /refinement of M&V models. • Correlation of measured and inferred data. • Verification of accuracy.
9	M&V reporting.	Produce comprehensive M&V reports for each program undertaken.	• Establish a standard reporting format, which meets Eskom's needs. • Reporting of findings according to previously agreed reporting format. • Conclusions and recommendations based on findings. • Improve DSM planning data and assumptions
10	Continuous improvement process.	Continuously improve all aspects of M&V program implementation.	• Revise/enhance KPI's, procedures and protocols, training format and delivery, IT systems, data collection process data processing process and algorithms, reporting format, etc.

ment mechanism, which allow countries to benefit financially from emission reductions that result from DSM activities. The process of M&V provides credibility and broad-based acceptance to the energy market.

The process of M&V provides valuable feedback to stakeholders regarding the savings and how it is influenced. Efforts can thus be focused to optimize the impacts of DSM. The fact that the savings are measured and verified encourages better design and management of DSM projects. M&V not only give demand and cost savings, but can also provide energy consumption and emission impacts as well.

How Does One Measure and Verify?

A DSM project has three basic stages. These stages are the pre-implementation phase, the implementation phase and lastly the post-implementation phase. The timeline for each of these phases may vary according to the project complexity and a range of other factors. These stages can be seen in Figure 1.

A system has a characteristic energy usage before DSM intervention. After implementation the energy usage is reduced by a certain amount. In order to determine what the savings are, we need to establish what the energy usage after implementation would have been, had DSM intervention not taken place. This is achieved through the use of baselines that describe the energy usage based on certain known and/or measurable input variables or patterns. This enables calculation of the savings that were achieved by the DSM intervention by obtaining the difference

between the baseline and the actual energy usage. All baselines are based on certain assumptions and criteria. Adjustments are made to the baseline when any of these assumptions become invalid or criteria is no longer satisfied by the baseline.

Baselines are critical to the process and care need to be taken during the development of baselines. It is not enough just to look at what happened the previous year and use it as a baseline. It can happen that energy cost increase after implementation, and a baseline should be able to pick it up. Consider Figure 2. A DSM intervention is implemented, but soon afterwards the actual cost start to rise. Saving would thus occur only to a point X in time. This can result in disputes if baseline 1 is used (simple extrapolation of previous behaviour). An accurate baseline (baseline 2) shows that the energy cost would have risen as well in the absence of the DSM intervention and that savings are actually being achieved.

The fact that measurements are used during M&V to obtain the baseline, actual energy consumption and demand, makes the M&V process a negotiated process. The number of measurements is determined by the possibility of measurement and the cost to measure. If it were possible to measure everything, an almost perfect baseline and actual energy consumption would be available. However, the high cost to measure decrease the number of measurements and the overall accuracy of the baseline. All the involved stakeholders (the client, the Energy Service Company and the financier) must agree on the method of sav-

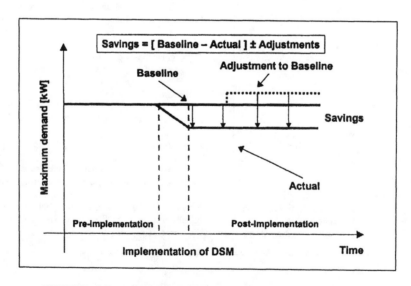

FIGURE 1: BASIC DSM PROJECT STAGES AND APPROACH
OF SAVING CALCULATION.

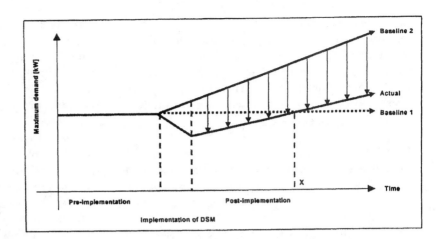

FIGURE 2: BASELINE
DEVELOPMENT ISSUES.

ings calculation. The level of detail of the M&V efforts should be in proportion to the size of the savings. Small savings will be measured and verified by a simple M&V process. The level of detail of the M&V process will increase as the size (quantity) of the savings increases.

DSM Project Stages

This section describes the different stages that are associated with the implementation of DSM projects[3]. The stakeholders in this process are the client, the financial institution and the Esco. The project stages are shown in Figure 3.

Project Identification

The Client or the Esco identifies the need, potential or opportunity for DSM and energy efficiency savings during this stage. On most occasions an Esco would be contracted to determine the potential impacts and savings.

Energy Audit/Assumptions

An energy audit is conducted to determine the type, quantity and rating of all relevant energy using systems. This information is used to determine the potential savings that can be achieved with DSM activities. The audit usually consists of a preliminary walk-through audit followed by a detailed audit. Assumptions are also stated regarding system information that isn't available. Factors that could influence the potential to generate savings through DSM are identified.

Recommendations for Implementation

A better estimate of the potential savings can be calculated once building and system information has been gathered. Upon evaluation of the various potential DSM activities, and a feasibility study, the DSM activities that show the greatest potential are recommended, based on their individual and combined feasibility.

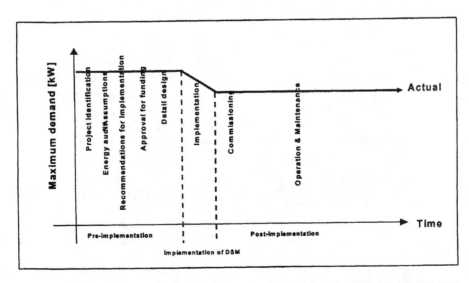

FIGURE 3: BASIC DSM PROJECT STAGES TRANSPOSED ON DSM IMPACTS.

Approval for Funding

Approval for project funding is granted once it has been established that the recommended DSM activities will deliver satisfactory results within an acceptable budget, timeframe and risk. M&V plays an important role during this phase since it will reduce the risk for the stakeholders.

Detail Design

A detail design is made of the recommended DSM activities once project funding has been approved.

Implementation

The DSM activities are then implemented based on the detail design. This phase may be characterized by fluctuations in energy usage.

Commissioning

Commissioning of the installed equipment is necessary to ensure that actual implementation has been done in the correct manner and the equipment and systems are performing to specified requirements.

Operation and Maintenance

The systems need to be maintained to ensure that the DSM activities deliver the optimum level of performance and continue to save energy and energy costs.

M&V Project Stages

The stakeholders in the M&V process are the M&V team, the client, the financial institution and the Esco. These stakeholders provide valuable information to the M&V process and need to give buy-in for M&V to continue through its various stages.

The M&V project has a total of five deliverables. They are:

- Pre-feasibility assessment;
- M&V plan;
- M&V baseline report;
- Post-implementation M&V report; and
- Monthly and annual saving reports.

Each of these reports and deliverables will be discussed in more detail in the sections that follow. Figure 4 shows the basic stages for each of the above M&V deliverables as they are transposed on the energy usage of the system that underwent DSM intervention.

Pre-feasibility Assessment

This stage of the M&V process is not compulsory and is purely an optional stage. The pre-feasibility assessment is basically an audit done by the M&V team together with the project management office DSM team. The purpose of this stage is basically to assess the feasibility of the proposed DSM activities.

Develop M&V Plan

The M&V plan describes the activities and procedures that will be followed to M&V the DSM activities. The plan should include a description of the project and give the assumptions and variables that could influence the savings potential of the DSM activities. The M&V activities are described together with the manner in which the baselines will be constructed and adjusted. All the information necessary for the M&V plan is obtained by means of energy audits. The M&V plan also contains a detailed analysis of the DSM proposal.

A metering plan must be included to state the equipment and schedule that will be used during metering. An overall schedule for the project must be provided as well as the costs to M&V. The M&V plan will be used to obtain buy-in for the manner in which M&V will be conducted. The M&V plan is the first key contributor to project buy-in. The M&V protocols, framework document and guideline documents are used to develop the M&V plan[4].

The M&V process and procedures need to be mutually acceptable to all the parties involved in the process (Esco, Client, M&V team), since it will form part of the tripartite contracts between the various parties. All parties need to review the M&V plan upon delivery and state any changes that should be made to the plan. The M&V plan must be revised until buy-in is obtained from all parties.

M&V Baseline Report

Pre-implementation measurements need to commence once buy-in has been obtained for the M&V plan. The pre-implementation measurements will be used in the construction of the baseline(s). These measurements need to be taken for an acceptable period prior to implementation to allow for sufficient data and project buy-in.

The M&V baseline report must contain the actual baseline that will be used during the saving calculations. All other information relevant to the baseline also needs to be included in this report. This includes:

- Variables used to characterize baseline;
- Data used to construct baseline;

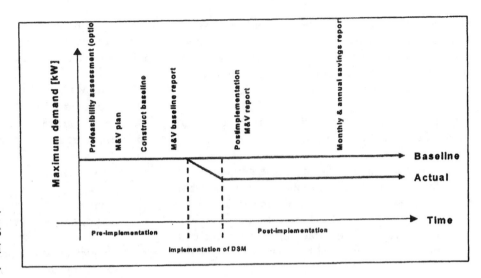

FIGURE 4: BASIC M&V PROJECT STAGES TRANSPOSED ON DSM IMPACTS.

- Construction procedures;
- Assumptions used during baseline construction; and
- Baseline adjustment procedures.

Upon delivery of the M&V baseline report, all parties need to review the report and state any changes that should be made. Once they all are satisfied and buy-in is obtained in the M&V baseline report, M&V can proceed. If this is not the case, the M&V baseline report must be refined and submitted again until buy-in is obtained. The final M&V baseline report is delivered only after all parties have met mutual agreement on all the issues involved with the development and use of the baselines.

Post-implementation M&V Report

The post-implementation audit goes hand-in-hand with the commissioning of the equipment and systems after implementation. This forms part of the M&V team's responsibility to verify that the implementation have indeed taken place to specification. This stage usually consists of a walkthrough audit. The post-implementation measurements are taken during this stage.

The data obtained from the post-implementation measurement phase are used to obtain the baseline energy usage. The actual energy usage, also obtained from the post-implementation measurement phase, is subtracted from the baseline to obtain the savings.

The post-implementation M&V report contains all the information relevant to the M&V project. The most important section of this report is the verified savings. This report need to be accompanied by all the

raw and processed data for archiving purposes to ensure project repeatability and calculation validation.

Monthly and Annual Savings Report

The monthly saving reports provide a summary of the savings that were achieved for each month. These reports are submitted on a monthly basis to all the DSM stakeholders.

An annual savings report is generated once a year. This report is generated from all the monthly data and serves as a summary report. Both the monthly and annual savings reports are required for the duration of the DSM project.

PROCEDURES AND METHODOLOGIES

The DSM projects vary between industrial, commercial and residential projects. Procedures and methodologies are therefore needed to M&V the impact of DSM of all these project types which includes the following and more:

- Industrial, commercial and residential lighting projects.
- Residential electrical hot water geyser load control of suburban areas.
- Industrial and commercial electrical hot water control.
- Industrial, commercial and residential energy efficiency projects.
- Industrial, commercial and residential load shifting projects.

The diversity of the projects provided the biggest

challenge to the MVSC in order to develop transparent procedures that can be used to M&V these projects. Secondly there was the issue around the cost of M&V. The utility set a guideline of M&V costs at maximum of 10% of the project life cycle cost.

The following factors were critical in the development of the M&V procedures:

- A decision was made to set the boundaries of the M&V as close as possible to the actual DSM intervention, but still within the 10% budget. The M&V process development for each type of project is therefore a trade-off between the cost of M&V and the level of detail needed for the M&V.

- The procedures and methodologies as described in the International Performance Measurement and Verification Protocol (IPMVP) were used as the starting basis for development of the M&V procedures.

- A crucial part of the M&V procedure development for the different project types were to find the most appropriate means of establishing the baselines. The baseline for each project was defined as the output of the model that describes what the energy consumption would have been without the DSM intervention.

- Since the aim of the DSM program is also to postpone the building of another power station, the M&V procedures should also be able to determine by how much each project contribute to a reduction in maximum demand when the utility is experiencing a maximum demand. The challenge was therefore to develop a credible and trustworthy M&V process for each project type within the 10% budget guideline that is also able to determine the impact on the utility's maximum demand.

- It was also decided that the boundary should be chosen such that DSM intervention will have an impact of more that 10% on the energy consumption within the chosen boundary.

M&V CENTRE

Overview
The purpose of the M&V-centre is to establish the infrastructure to M&V impacts of DSM on local, regional and national levels due to DSM implementation projects in South Africa. The impacts is mostly related to electricity, cost and emission savings.

What the M&V-Centre Is
The sole purpose of the M&V-centre is to show if DSM-targets are being met. It therefore must be able to assist users in quantifying savings and determining if the savings are sustainable. Typical results that can assist the user in that is the following:

- Savings (Electricity consumption, maximum demand, cost and emissions)

- Financial implications of project implementation (Net Present Value, Internal Rate of Return, Straight Payback)

All these must be given by the M&V-centre and are essential to determine if DSM is successful.

What the M&V-Centre is Not
The M&V-centre is not a METERING and verification centre. Metering (devices) is an important part of Measuring and Verification, however metering and measurement is not the same. Metering is performed when loggers or metering equipment are installed to meter the necessary parameters. Measurement includes all facets of the process used to determine the savings.

The M&V-centre is not a verification centre for control equipment. Data must be supplied in intervals that correspond with Eskom's tariffs intervals, i.e. 30-minute intervals. The only results the user will see is that the equipment are actually helping to meet the DSM target. The user will be responsible for data management software on his machines to verify that installed control equipment actually is working correctly.

Inputs for the M&V-Centre
The inputs to the centre must be kept a minimum but should be sufficient to calculate all the parameters required by the M&V-Centre. The following inputs are needed:

Project Information
Project information includes information about the project so that the project can later be classified under selected criteria. Typically one would like to see what the impacts of DSM are in a specific city, regionally or even on a national level. Information that needs to be

included under project information is the following:

- Project description,
- Address of the site,
- City of the project,
- Region,
- SIC-Code,
- EP-Code,
- Category,
- Contact persons,
  —Client,
  —M&V-Team,
  —Esco,
- Implementation cost,
- Project life,
- Company discount rate,
- Month for which the report should be generated,

Electricity Data

Electricity data include data about the baseline and the actual. Information that must be uploaded is the following:

- Electricity consumption (kWh),
- Maximum demand (kVA or kW depending on tariff used).

All the data are supplied in 30-minute intervals so that it corresponds with Eskom's tariff intervals.

Tariffs

All tariffs are not Eskom tariffs. Most buildings in cities are billed according to that city's municipality tariff structure. It might be that the intervals are the same as Eskom's but in most cases the costs will vary. It is therefore necessary that the user must be able to enter, edit or upload (in a form that corresponds to that of Eskom) the specific tariffs for the project.

Calculations Performed by the M&V-Centre

The inputs given are sufficient to perform the following calculations:

- Reduction in Maximum demand (kVA or kW depending on input),
- Reduction in Electricity consumption (kWh),
- Reduction in reactive power (kVAr),

- Reduction in electricity costs (R),
- Reduction in emissions emitted (CO_2, NO_x, SO_x, and particulate matter).

Outputs of the M&V-Centre

The M&V-Centre gives outputs on two time scales. They are a monthly basis and a yearly basis.

Outputs are the following:

- Reduction in maximum demand,
- Reduction in electricity consumption,
- Reduction in reactive power,
- Cost savings,
- Reduction in emissions emitted (CO_2, NO_x, SO_x, and particulate matter),
- Project internal rate of return (IRR),
- Project net present value (NPV),
- Project straight payback (SPB),

CONCLUSIONS

The development of a M&V program for a utility is quite a challenge, especially if you have to develop a cost-effective and credible M&V system that is able to determine the half-hourly impact of DSM on project, regional and national levels. However, in order to establish and maintain a successful DSM program, it is of critical importance that the M&V process and procedures be accepted and respected by all stakeholders.

BIBLIOGRAPHY

[1]U.S. Department of Energy, Office of energy efficiency and renewable energy. International Performance Measurement and Verification Protocol: Concepts and options for determining energy savings. October 2000.

[2]U.S. Department of Energy, Office of energy efficiency and renewable energy. M&V Guidelines: Measurement and Verification for Federal Energy Projects. Federal Energy Management Program. September 2000.

[3]Radloff, F.G.T. Monitoring and Verification Framework Document: Existing/Retrofit projects. September 2001. Report developed for Eskom under the Measurement and Verification Steering Committee.

Chapter 49

The Energy Engineer's Guide
To Performance Contracting Opportunities

By
Stephen A. Roosa CEM, CIAQP, MBA
Energy Management Alternatives, Inc.

ABSTRACT

Energy engineers and energy managers have in the last twenty years seen how performance contracting has become a viable method of implementing a wide range of energy, water and maintenance saving opportunities. Over this period, energy engineers have been key team members in developing and implementing performance contracts. By clearly defining their role and the services they offer, energy engineers can expand their service to include all phases of an energy services program. Is performance contracting an opportunity to create new business for energy engineering professionals? What set of services does the energy engineering professional provide? What are the deliverables required for engineering support of a performance contract? How do the requirements for engineering support of performance contracting projects vary from those required for projects implemented without performance contract? This paper responds to these questions and clarifies the role of the energy engineer participating in the performance contracting arena.

INTRODUCTION

Energy conservation projects are often justified on a financial basis as a result of the savings resulting from their implementation. Savings may accrue from reductions in energy cost, reduction in other utility costs,, avoided maintenance costs, etc. These can be categorized as quantifiable benefits.

Lower utility bills due to energy savings were just one of the benefits of the project. Other benefits may include the positive environmental effects achieved by the project. Lighting projects are often used as an example. Discarded florescent lamps may be recycled. Ballasts containing potentially hazardous materials can be properly disposed of. Non-hazardous ballasts can be recycled with materials reclaimed. Replacement lamps often have a significantly lower mercury content, which provides for easier disposal. The reduced electrical usage can provide reductions in carbon dioxide and sulfur dioxide emissions. Such benefits are typically categorized as non-quantifiable, since there is often not a direct or immediate dollar savings to the host facility.

In the past, little justification other than an engineer's calculations or a manufacturer's data sheets were used to justify the any identified cost savings. In order to more fully justify longer term capital improvements, the demand grew for longer term solutions which created the opportunity for a partnership between the energy services provider and the facility owner.

Performance contracts allow property holders the opportunity to finance facility improvements with quantified operating savings accruing from the improvements. As Hansen and Weisman noted, performance contracts as a simple concept, "a contract with payments based in performance."[1] Performance contracts employ a "design-build" approach rather that a "bid-specification" approach when implementing facility and equipment improvements.

A performance contractor also provides a guarantee of performance and costs reductions. If all or a portion of the guaranteed periodic savings is not provided, the performance contractor is obligated to pay any shortfall amount to the owner. The guarantee is distinctive in that it involves measurement and verification (M&V) of savings.

In addition to energy conservation projects, performance contracts are being employed to mitigate indoor air quality concerns and to implement projects that reduce water and sewer usage.

---

[1] Hansen, Shirley J. & Weisman, Jeannie C. (1998). *Performance Contracting: Expanding Horizons*. Lilburn GA: The Faimont Press, Inc. p. 5.

A performance contract may be appropriate for almost any facility. Likely candidates include schools, universities, health care facilities, central plant facilities, governmental buildings, office buildings and, military bases. The performance contract process will often be initiated from an owner request, an owner issuance of a Request for Qualifications (RFQ), or an owner issuance of a Request for Proposals (RFP).

Since energy engineering support for performance contracts is unique in many ways, energy engineers often employ a step-by-step process when providing engineering support for successful performance contracts. There are a number of variations. For the purposes of this paper, five project stages in the development of performance contracts are outlined. These stages are: 1) The initial Opportunity Assessment; 2) Preliminary Energy Services Program; 3) Development of the Detailed Energy Services Proposal; 4) Implementation of the Energy Services Program; and 5) Performance Assurance, Measurement and Verification (M&V) Services. For each stage, the deliverables typically required of the energy engineer will vary in extent and detail.

STAGE I:
THE OPPORTUNITY ASSESSMENT

The goal of this phase of the project is to determine if an opportunity exists to finance facility improvements with maintenance and operating cost avoidance. Information relative to utility usage, utility fuels used, the physical nature of the site(s), facility occupancy, building and equipment operating schedules, building plans and a listing of any specific needs are provided by the facility owner.

During this project stage the energy engineer interviews the potential customer to gather information critical to determining if a performance contract is an appropriate alternative for implementing improvements. As a result a qualification process is initiated. The engineer will evaluate whether or not energy saving (or other resource, e.g. water and sewer) opportunities exists and provides a descriptive list of potential energy conservation opportunities. Examples of these technologies include:

- Lighting system replacements, upgrades, or control improvements
- Mechanical, heating, ventilating and air conditioning improvements
- Installation of new or upgrades of existing energy management systems
- Architectural and building envelope improvements (e.g. insulation or window replacements)

- Water and sewer system conservation measures (WSCMs)
- Power conditioning or power factor correction
- Central cooling and/or heating plant construction or improvements
- Systems which provide metering or monitoring of critical utilities

If the preliminary assessment determines that opportunities to reduce recurring operating costs and the list of identified opportunities suit the needs of the owner, it may be determined that a qualified opportunity exists.

STAGE II:
PRELIMINARY ENERGY SERVICES PROGRAM

During Stage II, the energy engineer will further investigate the energy and/or water conservation measures, developing engineering documentation into a preliminary proposal. In support of this effort, the engineer visits site facilities, documents current conditions, evaluates energy conservation measures (ECMs), develops in-house project costs, identifies and quantifies cost avoidance, and compiles a preliminary financial model. A thorough evaluation of utility costs will be performed. This data will ultimately form the basis for a usage and cost baseline. Finally, a preliminary Measurement and Verification (M&V) Plan will be developed. M&V techniques are defined in various standards including the International Performance Measurement and Verification Protocol (IPMVP 2000). This protocol identifies measurement and verification techniques and procedures to follow when using each.

After a review of Stage II documentation, ECMs are selected for implementation. The parties involved may mutually agree to pursue a performance contract. A Letter of Intent (LOI) is often used for this purpose.

STAGE III:
DEVELOPMENT OF DETAILED PROPOSAL

During this stage the detailed engineering, final scope of work and selection of measures for implementation is completed. The energy engineer will obtains vendor and subcontractor quotes, provides an investment grade audit of selected measures, develop a project specifications, select equipment for installation, complete the project cost projection, develop a preliminary project schedule, prepare a financial model, and identify consultants and installers.

In the view of many facility owners, the bundle of energy conservation measures (ECMs) can become complex. ECMs may include mechanical system improvements, controls, lighting upgrades and building envelope modifications. The costs of measuring and monitoring the energy savings may become excessive. It is the responsibility of the energy engineer during this stage todevelop the most appropriate M&V plan which best satisfies the needs of the project and the owner's comfort with the projected guarantee amount.

An M&V Plan will be produced along with utility baselines. Developing an energy usage baseline for each of these projects involved the following: 1) defining a time period (typically 12-24 months) for the facility's historical baseline usage; 2) selecting a period for project implementation, during which energy usage is not evaluated; 3) defining a date for the beginning of the performance assessment period; and, 4) identifying future assessment periods for reporting purposes.

Any required pre-construction spot measurements of utility usage will be logged and verified. In addition, an investment grade audit of the proposed prioritized measures will be completed. A project financial model is often provided. At the conclusion of this stage, the performance contractor and building owner enter into a service contract.

STAGE IV:
PROJECT IMPLEMENTATION

At last the time arrives to implement the energy services project. Implementation refers to the actual site construction and installation of the equipment to be installed. A construction schedule with identified project milestones is negotiated.

All final changes to the engineering designs and specifications will be completed. Typically, performance contracts avoid the "bid-specification" procedure and contractors are engaged based on their qualification to implement the selected measures.

The energy services provider may choose to employ a project manager at this stage to provide oversight. The project scheduling and project site coordination activities will progress as construction and installation of equipment occurs. Prior to completion, the energy engineer may hold site inspections, perform additional monitoring, develop punch lists, verify equipment efficiencies and perform project commissioning.

STAGE V:
PERFORMANCE ASSURANCE AND M&V SERVICES

Upon physical completion of the project, the performance assurance service may continue for perhaps 2 to 25 years. Typically, the length of the performance assurance contract will last until financial amortization of the project I achieved. However, some owners do not wish to pay recurring fees for M&V services after they feel that the savings is being achieved. Some performance contracts allow the owner to opt out of the M&V contract after a period of three years.

The energy engineer can provide M&V services including periodic measurement and verification inspections and reports. M&V reports will compare utility usage and costs to the appropriate baseline. Installed metering and monitoring equipment may be employed to verify and validate utility usage. In addition, another engineering firm, a performance contractor or a consultant specializing in M&V services can provide M&V services.

As a result of recent improvements in monitoring and measurement technologies, it is possible for energy engineering professionals to log and record most every energy consumption aspect of the energy conservation measures they implement.[2] Examples include the use of a wide range of data loggers, infrared thermography, metering equipment, equipment to measure liquid and gaseous flows, heat transfer, air balancing, and temperatures.

Afterwards, periodic M&V inspection and analysis are performed and provided to reconcile the annual energy usage on a per building basis. The goals of the inspection were to: 1) ensure that installed equipment was performing as intended; and 2) to assess the energy impact. The analysis may be performed by the energy engineer with perhaps support from an M&V specialist.

If a project fails to achieve a cost savings guarantee, the performance contractor is financially responsible and may implement additional measures to ensure future savings.

---

[2] In addition to improvements in measuring equipment, accepted measurement and verification guides are also available. Examples include the North American Energy Measurement & Verification Protocol (NEMVP, 1996), the Measurement & Verification Guideline for Federal Energy Projects (1996) and the International Performance Measurement & Verification Protocol (IPMVP, 2000). Each provides details of M&V options and guidelines for verifying energy savings. The IPMVP is the current state of the art. It is available electronically at www.doe.gov/bridge.

Additional aspects of the final stage of the project include verification of warranty, provision of shop drawings and submittals, owners acceptance documents, etc.

CONCLUSION

A unique aspect of performance contracting is the third party guarantee of identified savings. At every stage of the development of a performance contract, there are opportunities for the energy engineer to exercise his or her skills. Energy engineers and energy managers can use performance contracting as one of their strategies to implement projects for their clients. Performance contracting is especially effective when supported by energy engineering professionals who follow a systematic approach to planning and providing engineering support. In addition to developing energy assessments, engineering analysis and project scope, measurement and verification of savings is one aspect of performance contracting which requires the skills of the energy engineer.

REFERENCES

AEE-ETE Conference, Energy Efficiency, Energy Markets and Environmental Protection in the New Millennium, Sopron, Hungary. (June 2001) *"The Energy Engineer's Guide to Performance Contracting,"* Stephen A. Roosa. This was the first published paper defining the five stages of a performance contract from the perspective of the energy engineer. Substantial sections of the article have been reproduced herein.

Hansen, Shirley and Weisman, Jeannie (1998). *Performance Contracting: Expanding Horizons.* Lilburn GA: The Faimont Press, Inc.

ABOUT THE AUTHOR

Stephen A. Roosa, CEM currently serves as the President of Energy Management Alternatives, Inc. with offices in Louisville and Lexington, Kentucky. During a recent five year period at a utility owned energy services company, he was the lead energy engineer on 26 completed energy service contracts.

Recent energy services projects include the first Kentucky State Government performance contract (Western Kentucky University, 2001), the largest K-12 school project in Kentucky (Jefferson County Schools 2001-2) and the largest lighting project in Kentucky (Alliant Health Care, 1998-9). Previous experience includes 20 years experience in energy engineering and energy management with energy studies performed on over 3,500 buildings.

Mr. Roosa received a Bachelor of Architecture degree from the University of Kentucky and a Masters in Business Administration (MBA) from Webster University. He is presently completing a Ph.D. at the University of Louisville. He is an Association of Energy Engineers (AEE) Certified Indoor Air Quality Professional (1998) and an AEE Certified Energy Manager (1986).

Related professional awards include the Federal Energy and Water Management Project Award (1999); US Army Corps of Engineers National Energy Systems Technology Award, CENET (1991); US DoD Energy Conservation Award (1989); AEE International Energy Manager of the Year (1987); US Joint Chiefs of Staff Citation for Energy Management (1983). Mr. Roosa has served in the following capacities: AEE Bluegrass Chapter President (1986-7),ASHRAE Kentucky Chapter Vice President (1992-93), and AEE Southeast Regional Vice President (1988-89).

ACKNOWLEDGMENTS

The author wishes to thank the AEE for creating this forum and opportunity to present this approach to performance contracts and the opportunity to chair the WEEC 2002 session on performance contracting. Particular thanks to Al bert Thumann, Barbara Stroup and Patty Ardavin, for their help and support during my years as an AEE member. I also wish to thank Shirley Hansen for the advice she has provided me on numerous occasions.

NOTE

The views expressed herein are solely those of the author and do not necessarily reflect the views of any other individual, organization, corporation or agency. Mention or reference to trade names, governmental agency or commercial enterprise does not constitute endorsement.

Your comments are invited. The author's email address is: stephenroosa@cs.com.

Chapter 50

THE EFFECT OF BUILDING GEOMETRY ON ENERGY USE

By Geoffrey J Gilg, EIT and Cisco L. Valentine, PE
Select Energy Services, Inc.

ABSTRACT

Energy service companies (ESCOs) use the Energy-Use Index (EUI) as a tool to evaluate a building's potential for reduction in energy use. Select Energy Services, Inc. (SESI) has found that consideration of building geometry is useful in evaluating a building's potential for energy use reduction. Building load and energy-use simulations using TRACE® and PowerDOE®, respectively, were conducted to gain insight into how building geometry impacts Heating, Ventilation, and Air-Conditioning (HVAC) sizing and energy use. The ratio of gross wall area to gross floor area, A_{wall}/A_{floor} has been found to be a useful factor to consider when making EUI comparisons. Simulations suggest that buildings with higher A_{wall}/A_{floor} ratios require higher central plant capacities and use more energy per unit area to satisfy the heating and cooling loads. Taking a building's geometry (A_{wall}/A_{floor}) into account while estimating savings potential may produce more accurate results.

INTRODUCTION

SESI has conducted a multitude of building evaluations in the course if its performance contracting and design work. SESI has many energy engineers with real-world HVAC design experience which often provides insight into peculiarities. One such peculiarity is "Why a building of the same square footage and use as another exhibits an EUI significantly different from another?" In an attempt to answer this question, SESI conducted a series of simulations which focused on building geometry and its contribution to heating and cooling loads and annual energy use.

The tools of choice are Trace® and PowerDOE®. TRACE® is a software package published by C.D.S. Software that is used to determine equipment loads. PowerDOE® is published by the Department of Energy and is used to simulate annual energy building energy use. Both software packages allow the easy and economical means by which to evaluate a building's HVAC capacity requirements and resulting energy use.

EUI

Even before setting foot on site, an ESCO can get a preliminary estimate of the potential for energy cost reduction. This can be done by analyzing the fuel and electric rates, looking for credits or rate restructuring, and by evaluating EUI. EUI is defined as the ratio of total annual energy used, in kBtus, divided by the square footage of the building.

$$EUI = \frac{kBtu}{ft^2}$$

EQUATION 1

The EUI is used as a barometer for estimating the potential for energy savings. However, it must be applied with discretion or an ESCO could pass on a great opportunity or overestimate the potential for energy cost savings.

How the EUI is Used

Once utility billing data, equipment data, and building square footage have been provided, an EUI evaluation can be conducted. The calculated EUI of the building is compared to an "ideal" EUI. The difference between the building EUI and the ideal is the potential for energy savings (see Figure 1). However, it is often cost prohibitive to attain the entire EUI differential, so ESCOs often prescribe a maximum, economically attainable, EUI improvement. Fifty percent is often used, but this depends on many factors.

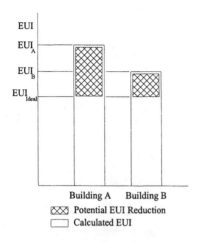

FIGURE 1

From the above methodology it is easy to see how comparing EUIs, based solely on square footage, can sometimes result in an inaccurate evaluation of the energy savings potential.

BUILDING GEOMETRY

Building geometry is an important factor to consider from a design standpoint. It influences heat loss, heat gains, infiltration, and solar gains which influence the heating and cooling load. Typically, the more wall (including windows) area available, the higher the heating and cooling loads. The first 10-15 feet from the exterior wall is considered the perimeter zone. The perimeter zone heating/cooling load is constantly changing because it is under the influence of the weather via the building envelope (walls, windows, and roof) as well as internal loads (occupants, lights, equipment, etc.). Inside this area is the interior zone which experiences much less heating/cooling load variation (only internal loads). Therefore, if evaluating two buildings of equal floor area, use, occupancy, etc., the building with the larger interior zone will typically require less heating and cooling capacity and use less energy annually.

Building geometry is also an important factor to consider from an energy-use standpoint. If two buildings of same square footage, use, schedule, controls, occupancy, and construction exhibit significantly different EUIs, differences in building geometries may explain why. The building with more wall area will likely have the higher EUI. Therefore, it is not uncommon to find that buildings with multiple floors or eccentric shapes using more energy than single-floor, rectangular buildings of the same square footage. For example, Figures 2 and Figure 3 illustrates two-story buildings each of 32,400 ft². Building A is a building layout found on many military installations and educational campuses.

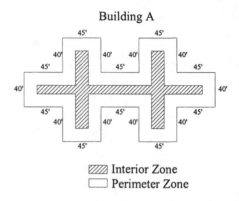

Building A

Interior Zone
Perimeter Zone

Gross Floor Area = 32,400 sq. ft.
Perimeter wall Length = 850 ft.
Gross Wall Area = 20,400 sq. ft.
Interior Zone Area = 8,700 sq. ft.

FIGURE 2

Building B is another building of the same square footage, but in the shape of a rectangle.

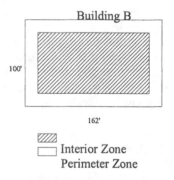

Building B

Interior Zone
Perimeter Zone

Gross Floor Area = 32,400 sq. ft.
Perimeter wall Length = 524 ft.
Gross Wall Area = 12,576 sq. ft.
Interior Zone Area = 18,480 sq. ft.

FIGURE 3

Given the same building load parameters, Trace® calculations indicate that Building A requires 15% additional cooling capacity and 25% more heating capacity than Building B. PowerDOE® energy use simulations indicate that Building A will use 15% more energy annually than Building B. This example shows that building geometry is indeed an important factor to consider when estimating the potential for energy use reduction based on EUI comparisons. With the realization that building geometry affects energy use, how can it be accounted for during an EUI comparison?

BUILDING MODELS

To evaluate the effect of geometry on energy use, several hypothetical models were defined, constructed, and analyzed using Trace® and PowerDOE®. The model definitions include such parameters as use (school, office, warehouse), geographical location, schedule, overall heat transfer coefficients (wall, roof, windows), and others. This methodology provides the ability to evaluate the effect of geometry in buildings with distinctly different uses and geometries. Models of the buildings were constructed in Trace® and PowerDOE® using the same building parameters. These programs allow parameters such as orientation, location, and geometry to be changed with a keystroke. A schedule of model assumptions is provided in Attachment A.

RESULTS

After conducting the building load and energy use simulations, a factor has emerged that often helps to explain why a building uses more or less energy per square foot than another. This factor takes into account differences in building geometry when evaluating energy use reduction potential. This Geometric Ratio (GR) is defined as the ratio of gross perimeter wall area (A_{WALL}) to gross floor area (A_{FLOOR}).

$$GR = \frac{\sum A_{Wall}}{\sum A_{Floor}} = \frac{A_{Wall}}{A_{Floor}}$$

EQUATION 2

Comparisons of Trace® load calculations indicate that buildings with higher wall to floor area ratios require larger heating and cooling plants. The effect of building geometry has been found to be more pronounced as outdoor air requirements decrease. For example, Trace® load calculations (heating only) for a warehouse indicate that with each percentage point increase in the GR, the peak heating requirement increases approximately one percent. Geometry, in this example, has such a significant effect because envelope load is a larger percentage of the total heating plant requirement. Thus the effect of geometry decreases, but it does not go away. Annual energy use predicted by PowerDOE®, on the other hand, is relatively flat for warehouse structures while showing significant geometric effects for school and office type occupancies. As the outdoor air requirements increase, the contribution of envelope loads to the total heating and cooling load decreases.

Simulations have also shown that it is important to consider the percentage window area per unit wall area. The amount of window in a wall has a significant impact in the overall heat loss/gain of that exposure. Buildings with higher window to wall area ratios typically require larger heating and cooling capacities and use more energy annually per unit floor area than buildings with lower window to wall area ratios.

Trace® and PowerDOE® simulations also indicate that orientation of a building is also an important factor to consider. If a building has a high (2 or higher) aspect (length / width) ratio and is oriented so that the long sides of the buildings are facing east-west, this building typically requires larger heating and cooling plant capacities and will consume more energy annually. Had this same building been oriented such that a long side was facing north-south, the heating and cooling plant capacity and energy use could have been reduced. Orientation of the long side of the building in a north-south direction also could have permitted more effective use of natural light to reduce lighting energy requirements which can further reduce the cooling load. Therefore, when considering the potential for energy reduction in this particular building, it is advisable to take building's orientation into account.

Differences in building energy use can also be explained by considering geometry as it relates to the original intended use of the building. On many military installations, especially those associated with airfields, there are numerous single level, high ceiling, marginally insulated buildings whose original intended use and design are not consistent with its present utilization. For example, storage buildings and aircraft hangers often converted to office space (without upgrading the walls, windows, or roof insulation). As such, they have undergone numerous HVAC retrofits through the years as the hangar/storage space is further converted to office space. Buildings of this type typically use more energy than buildings whose original intended use was that of an office.

The age of a building, in conjunction with geometry, also helps to explain differences in EUI. Older buildings have experienced much more wear and tear and typically have higher infiltration rates. HVAC equipment is typically at, near, or far past its useful life and requires frequent maintenance. In addition, older buildings typically are not insulated as well. Due to space restrictions, many older buildings have rooms or wings that have been added to the original building. This addition can significantly increase the perimeter wall area with only a small increase in square footage. Finally, older buildings do not benefit from recent quality control and construction standards. As a result, it is not uncommon for older buildings to exhibit higher EUIs than similar buildings of recent construction. PowerDOE® modeling has shown that building geometry, as indicated by the GR, has more influence on energy use in older buildings.

How the Geometric Ratio can be used

When evaluating the potential for energy use reduction, it may be to the ESCO's advantage to take into account the geometric ratio of the buildings under consideration. The GR represents the influence of building geometry on energy use and can be used to gauge the effectiveness of certain Energy Conservation Measures (ECMs). For example, ECMs associated with walls and windows such as window film, window replacements, and wall insulation upgrades may have a larger EUI impact in buildings with higher GRs. This is because wall and window conduction and solar gains are a higher percentage of the total HVAC load. Alternatively, ECMs such as air-side economizer, lighting retrofits, and roof insulation upgrades may have a larger EUI impact in building with lower GRs. This is because the percentage of contribution of outdoor air, lighting, and roof conduction to the total building load is typically higher for buildings with lower GRs.

CONCLUSIONS

At the conclusion of the calculations and simulations using Trace® and PowerDOE®, SESI believes that it has, at least in small part, contributed to a better understanding of building geometry and its impact on heating and cooling requirements and energy use. This understanding can be used to better estimate the effectiveness of certain ECMs which can help to avoid underestimation, as well as overestimation, of potential EUI improvement. This exercise has shown that there is value in considering building geometry while estimating the potential for energy use reduction.

REFERENCES

1. ASHRAE-Fundamentals, American Society of Heating, Refrigeration ,and Air-Conditioning Engineers, Inc., 2001.

2. Trane Air Conditioning Manual, The Trane Company, 1996

ATTACHMENT A

MODEL ASSUMPTIONS

Common Assumptions:

Location:	Washington DC
System type:	VAV w/ hot water reheat coils
Heating thermostat setpoint (°F):	68
Cooling thermostat setpoint (°F):	78
Floor to floor (ft) :	12
Plenum height (ft) :	3
Floor type :	Slab on grade (6" concrete & 12 " soil)
Roof type:	Flat - Built up
Infiltration rate (ft^3 per ft^2 wall):	0.15 ft^3 per ft^2 wall area
Sensible Load (Btu/hr per person)	250
Latent Load (Btu/hr per person)	200
U$_{wall}$ (Btu / (hr*ft^2):	0.1 Btu / (hr*ft^2)
U$_{window}$ (Btu / (hr*ft^2):	0.5 Btu / (hr*ft^2)
U$_{roof}$ (Btu / (hr*ft^2):	0.05 Btu / (hr*ft^2)
Schedule:	100% (weekdays, 8am to 5pm)
	20% (weekdays, 5pm to 8am)
	20% (weekends and holidays)
Ignore:	Gymnasium, library, locker rooms, restrooms, cafeteria, lounges, corridors spaces

Schools

Parameter	Model #1	Model #2	Model #3
Length x Width (ft)	200 x 80	100 x 80	73 x 73
Number of floors :	1	2	3
Orientation (long side)	15° south of due East	15° south of due East	15° south of due East
System type :	VAV w/ hot water reheat	VAV w/ hot water reheat	VAV w/ hot water reheat
Window percentage (of wall area) :	20	20	20
Occupancy (people / 1000 ft^2):	50 per 1000 ft^2	50 per 1000 ft^2	50 per 1000 ft^2
Ventilation (ft^3 / min / person):	15	15	15
Lighting Load (W / ft^2):	1.5	1.5	1.5
Equipment Load (W / ft^2) :	0.25	0.25	0.25

375

Offices

Parameter	Model #1	Model #2	Model #3
Length x Width (ft)	200 x 80	100 x 80	73 x 73
Number of floors :	1	2	3
Orientation (long side)	15° south of due East	15° south of due East	15° south of due East
System type :	VAV w/ hot water reheat	VAV w/ hot water reheat	VAV w/ hot water reheat
Window percentage (of wall area) :	20	20	20
Occupancy (people / 1000 ft^2):	7	7	7
Ventilation (ft^3 / min / person):	20	20	20
Lighting Load (W / ft^2):	1.5	1.5	1.5
Equipment Load (W / ft^2) :	0.5	0.5	0.5

Warehouse

Parameter	Model #1	Model #2	Model #3
Length x Width (ft)	200 x 80	100 x 80	73 x 73
Number of floors :	1	2	3
Orientation (long side)	15° south of due East	15° south of due East	15° south of due East
System type :	Gas unit heaters	Gas unit heaters	Gas unit heaters
Window percentage (of wall area) :	20	20	20
Occupancy (people / 1000 ft^2):	5	5	5
Ventilation (ft^3 / min / ft^2):	0.05	0.05	0.05
Lighting Load (W / ft^2):	1.5 W	1.5	1.5
Equipment Load (W / ft^2) :	0.25 W	0.25	0.25

Examples

Parameter	Model #1-Building A	Model #2-Building B	Model #2
Length x Width (ft)	See Figure 2	See Figure 3	100 x 80
Number of floors :	3	3	2
Orientation (long side)	15° south of due East	15° south of due East	75°
System type :	VAV w/ hot water reheat	VAV w/ hot water reheat	VAV w/ hot water reheat
Window percentage (of wall area) :	20	20	20
Occupancy (people / 1000 ft^2):	50	50	50
Ventilation (ft^3 / min / person):	20	20	20
Lighting Load (W / ft^2):	1.5	1.5	1.5
Equipment Load (W / ft^2) :	0.5	0.5	0.5

Annual Heating Profiles

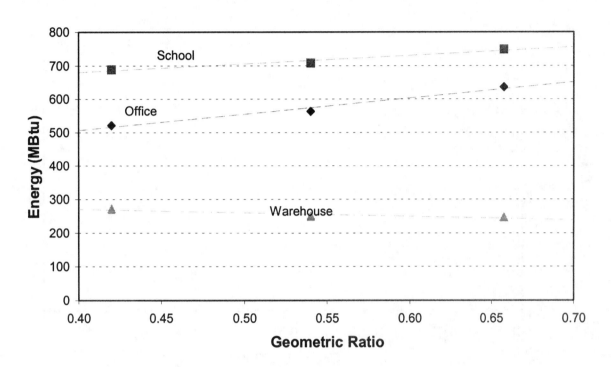

Annual Cooling Profiles

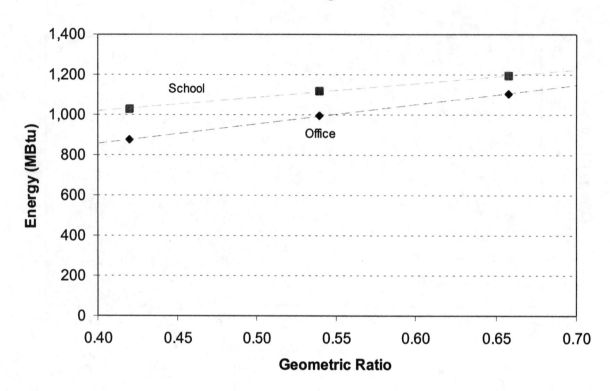

Chapter 51

PERFORMANCE CONTRACTING
–
TIPS TO GET WHAT YOU NEED, AND AVOID WHAT YOU DON'T

Andrew D. Holden, B.S., M.S., C.E.M.

Principal, Helios Resources, Ltd.

ABSTRACT

Performance contracting promises great things with little apparent risk to a host facility. Typically, there is no upfront expense involved to the facility, and payments usually start only when the project is complete and energy savings should already be accruing.

However, despite the typically intense attorney reviews and resulting reams of contractual legalese, there are significant risks inherent in this form of procurement. And the risks are on both sides of the table – both performance contractor and facility face hazards. While most of these risks could be mitigated through proper negotiation and preparation, most are not because they are not considered sufficiently early in the process, if at all.

For instance, what is the risk of spending too much, and of receiving too little, both in goods and savings, for your facility? How can you compare vastly different proposals from vendors of wildly different capabilities?

What is the risk to your facility if a project significantly under performs? Measurement and verification procedures are by necessity fuzzy and ill defined and yet part of the price premium you are paying is for M&V and the contractor's underwriting of this risk. If you are sure the savings are there, why pay for that underwriting?

If you and the performance contractor are not totally sure the savings are there, the contractor will try to structure the M&V procedures and guarantee in such a way so as to put the risk more on the facility. Why pay a premium for a project when the risk is back with you anyway?

Most qualification processes for a performance contract cause the contractor to provide a great deal of detail and work with no hope of compensation unless they are selected for contract. In this respect then there is tremendous jeopardy in performance contracting from the vendor's standpoint.

If you are a public sector entity then performance contracting may be your only logical alternative, despite the fact that it may not always be the most advantageous route to extracting the most energy savings for the least overall financial outlay. In this case, you need to be prepared with facts and strategy to extract as much from the performance contractor as you reasonably can.

However, in a facility where you have a choice between Performance Contracting, bid and spec or design/build then you should know the advantages and pitfalls of each and be able to make your decision on the right procurement vehicle from a position of knowledge. This paper will elaborate on typical performance contracting procedures and compare them to other contracting vehicles as appropriate.

STEPS IN THE PC PROCUREMENT PROCESS

A typical performance contract is let through a performance-based qualification process. After having been involved in performance contracts of varying sizes and complexities since 1987 this author has found that there are several vitally important steps in procuring a PC of any real size:

Internal Agreement

Even before writing any formal requests for responses from companies, it is vitally important that your physical plant, business and financial managers decide on what they hope to garner from a performance contract. Like a solid foundation under a building, this written understanding between senior management at your facility will serve as a solid base for evaluating performance contracting companies and their proposals. For the best performance contractors responding to your procurement documents this (confidential) understanding between the managers will better enable them to commit resources to making your project a success, and also to tailor their responses to your requirements.

The main decisions to be made internally are regarding capital improvements versus cash flow. Is it more important to get new equipment and virtually no cash flow, or to generate free cash? How will you treat capital avoidance, if a company replaces equipment at the end of its life will you allow them to take credit for that? How will you treat operating and maintenance savings? Can you envision outsourcing maintenance, or is that off the table? Are telecommunications savings and trash disposal savings allowable? Do you have minimum operating standards for parameters such as temperatures, humidity levels, lighting hours, minimum lighting levels, and a myriad other details.

Also at this stage is the question of energy metering of your buildings. Many campus environments have only a few meters serving dozens of buildings. A small capital investment up front now can pay dividends in subsequent stages as both you and the responding contractors will garner a better comprehension of your buildings.

A Reality Check

During this phase it can be useful to get a reality check from an outside consultant familiar with performance contracting to act as a mediator and a sounding board for ideas regarding what can be accomplished. Too many facilities have unrealistic expectations about just how much neglect can be undone with a single performance contract. So shoot high with your expectations, but understand the realities the contractor has in structuring a deal for your facility.

This reality check also helps avoid one of the most frustrating points for performance contracting companies – the facility that puts an RPF on the street, gets good responses (costing each of the companies anywhere from $10,000 to $100,000 to prepare), and then does nothing with them. This may occur anyway – after all priorities and people change, but this type of exercise should be minimized if for no other reason than companies that have been once bitten will be unlikely to take the chance on responding to your facility a second time.

The RFQ

Initiate a qualifications process through a "Request for Qualifications", or RFQ. By doing so, you will attract the widest possible variety and type of companies that can help you. It is much more cost-effective and lower risk for a company to respond to an RFQ than to a full-blown Request for Proposals (RFP) because there is little or no on-site field time required. Many more companies will want to respond and you will have a very nice set of documents from which you may select between three and five qualified companies to proceed to the next step.

But how do you qualify the respondents? Start by getting a selection committee together – it should consist of at least a facilities manager, high level financial and business managers, a technical advisor, and perhaps a purchasing agent. You will need to decide what is important to you. It is recommended that during the RFQ development phase you also develop a scoring sheet, to ensure that selection is fair and that your selection committee does not get blinded by one or two seemingly strong points that may obscure other, potentially more serious flaws.

You must decide whether it important to you that the company be local, national, or even international? Do you wish to exclude or actively solicit responses from the performance contracting divisions of manufacturers such as controls vendors and chiller manufacturers? Do you prefer independent companies, or do you have requirements for a company to have certain net assets and backing? Are the credentials of the staff more important than necessarily having a "brand name" company? Whatever you decide, a good reference list should be important, an overall attitude of partnership, and a local presence of some kind are usually helpful too.

Issue the RFP

Once your RFQ respondent's list has been pared down to a reasonable number of companies (three for a small to medium contract, up to five for a large one), an RFP can be issued to those pre-qualified companies to decide on your eventual contractor. Unfortunately, for many facilities, our step 4 is their step 1, as they blindly jump into an RFP, almost guaranteeing that a number of unqualified bidders will enter the fray and that the most qualified may opt0 to stay away from the RFP because of the large number of entrants.

Along the lines of paring the number of bidders, you will need to elect whether to put all your buildings into the RFP, or just a subset of them. This rather depends on how many buildings you have, and also what the political situation is like in your organization. For instance, many managers believe that if they select only a few buildings then the resulting sample project will not be of sufficient magnitude to attract backing and support from key decision-makers in their own organization. Against this, the respondents can do a much better job on four buildings than they can on twenty and if some believe the workload too onerous at this stage in the proceedings they may elect not to respond.

Part of the interest of a PC that distinguishes it from a bid/spec is the freedom that responding companies have to innovate. With suitably qualified companies, you will undoubtedly receive innovative and creative responses and in many cases they can really help solve some problems within your facilities while also saving operating costs. Often though, that creativity makes it impossible to truly compare responses, and many times companies can be too creative, proposing schemes that are too aggressive or that simply will not work.

It is therefore important to set guidelines within your RFP that state what the performance contractor can and cannot do. Setting forth lighting hours, for instance so that each company is on a somewhat level playing field, or restricting the shutdown of equipment to between certain hours. An alternate view of this is to have each RFP independently reviewed by technical experts who can evaluate the reasonability of each response. How each company handled such things as lighting hours can give a wonderful indication of how that company views your facility – and you. Some companies will install dataloggers for themselves so they can fully understand how the buildings operate. Others will bow to perceived competitive pressure and put in as many hours as they think you will stand for. Which company do you want to go forwards with?

Guarantees and Surety

Another element crucial to success in a performance contract is understanding each company's performance guarantee.

In fact the guarantee is what may have led you to consider PC in the first place rather than design/build or bid/spec, and indeed it may be a necessary part of your procurement process. But guarantees can be written in many different ways, and one way is to tell the customer that, since the contractor has no control over the way they operate their facility (and does not wish to control it), that operating hours are not part of the guarantee. Clearly then, you will want to make sure that operating hours are reasonable in any proposal that has this type of guarantee.

There are many other aspects of the guarantee that you will want to consult people who have experience in that arena, both legal and technical.

Another item that you need to consider is whether a bid bond or other surety will be required of the respondents. There is little downside, and a large upside to requiring bid bonds (but you need to make it clear during the RFQ process that you will be requiring them). Clearly, the downside is that some respondents will not respond at all if surety is required. No established company will object to surety though unless your requirements are unreasonable.

Performance requirements are another issue altogether, but an important consideration in the RFP process. In some cases, companies have taken advantage of the relatively haphazard comparison of various competitive proposals and deflated costs and inflated savings to ensure that their proposal looks the most economically attractive. They make the strategic decision that they will undoubtedly get a second chance at performing an IGA (Investment Grade Audit) prior to award of a contract, and at that time they will adjust costs and savings to where they ought to have been in the RFP response. To discourage that, many facilities have taken to adding provisions that require costs and savings in the IGA to be within a percentage of the numbers in the RFP response. This can certainly rein in those over-enthusiastic (or dishonest?) operators who seek to gain an advantage but it has limited affect because it is not until after the IGA is completed that the shortfalls are discovered. To eliminate that company and revert to another would mean losing anywhere from three months to a year in lost time - so many customers just have to bear it and continue with the original firm.

You should allow responding companies an appropriate length of time to assemble good quality proposals. Keep in mind that datalogging and metering take time, and so does engineering analysis, pricing and putting together a good financial package and proposal. A performance contract embraces so many different disciplines that it really does take time to assemble a good offering. Attempting to shortcut that is false economy.

Selection Process - Technical

Once you have sufficient responses to your RFP, selection of a performance contractor can begin. Because of the long term (usually 10 to 20 years) arrangement that most performance contracts require, personalities and egos definitely affect how well the project will go. For the best results, both parties should view a performance contract as a partnership. A vendor who is stubborn and cannot see a different point of view (and vice versa) is likely to make for very long and tedious negotiations, implementation and follow-up phases.

It is well worth scheduling oral interviews to see how the respondents interact with you, the customer. Orals allow respondents and customer to clarify parts of the proposals that were not necessarily clear, and you can get insight into the company and its personnel far better than through a written proposal.

The most unusual aspect of evaluating a performance contract, especially when compared to a bid and spec job, is that price is only one part of the selection equation, and depending on your requirements it may be a fairly small part. If you decided to run a qualifications process as we recommended earlier you may already have disqualified some low bidders, but again, with a contract term of anywhere from 7 to 25 years price is definitely secondary and more concern should be paid to technical ability and the overall package.

Each RFP response package will contain a very short qualifications section that you can quickly skip through, because you have already selected good companies for the RFP stage. More important will be the technical section, and included with the technical section should be specifics about who will staff your projects. Changes to this staffing should be with written notification only because you do not want to be teased with the prospect of getting the company's finest engineers and construction managers, only to be saddled with some lower grade personnel that you had not anticipated.

The technical portion will be difficult to evaluate, though the steps are easily delineated. For instance, you need to determine whether the respondents formatted their proposals as you outlined in your RFP document. If they did that shows a willingness to work with you. If they did not it suggests they think their way is the best way, never mind the consequences, and never mind what you require.

One by one, read the proposed energy conservation measures or opportunities (ECMs or ECOs) and see if you can determine what exactly the performance contractor intends to do, with what equipment and personnel, at what cost. Importantly ask where the savings will come from – and if you do not have sufficient technical knowledge to evaluate that then paying a technical consultant to do so may be a very good investment. If sufficient detail to perform this evaluation is not present then you need to look very hard at that contractor – if they are not forthcoming with information now, will it get any better as you travel this path together as contracting partners?

As you evaluate the technical sections, be aware of critical items that can affect the project. Such processes as Measurement and Verification (M&V), which is a subject that fills entire books, can markedly affect the project. The main question there is whether you (or your consultant) believe that the M&V strategies outlined are logical and defensible. Too much reliance on "utility bill" reconciliation and stipulated parameters could raise red flags because the contractor is transferring more risk to you, the customer. There are cases where stipulating savings values are appropriate, but it should be the exception rather than the rule.

Look at the savings detail provided – does the respondent intend to carry this analysis through the IGA stage, or will a different type of analysis be used once the contract is awarded? Whatever the answer, a reviewer with a logical mind should be able to clearly follow the calculations and the main assumptions and be able to assert that they are within reason and relevant. Hopelessly complex calculations such as those from many computer simulation applications seem to serve only as smokescreens, and we are left with the classic "garbage in, garbage out" phenomenon. No matter how good the software package, the initial assumptions need to be reasonable, and they should be listed for easy inspection.

A very valuable check into reasonability is to see how much savings a contractor predicts for each building analyzed. Hopefully, you were able to install metering on individual buildings as suggested earlier. From this you can relatively easily get a feel for what percentage of use the contractor predicts will be saved. If the percentage exceeds 20 to 25% then you need to start asking some serious questions – savings of over 50% are possible in the right circumstances, but anything over 20% begs for intense scrutiny.

Keep in mind that if you, the customer provided operating parameters to the companies, then those parameters could be at fault. For instance we have seen numerous instances of lighting hours being provided, only to discover when we use those hours that our anticipated saving exceed the entire facility's current electric bill! You have a responsibility for ensuring that you give the respondents adequate and factual information so they can do a good job for you.

In the savings calculations, look for excessive O&M (Operating and Maintenance) savings. Usually these are stipulated savings values, to which you are expected to agree and sign off on. Be extremely careful with O&M. In fact one suggestion is to request a financial model with no O&M included at all. This way you can evaluate the project without that distraction and you can always add it back if you find the assertions made to be reasonable. It is always reasonable to ask for backup support data, especially for O&M savings.

Selection Process - Financial
Once the technical sections are reviewed for accuracy and reasonability, your attention can be turned to the financial offering. There are so many different ways to present the financials that we can only cover some of the main points here. Senior financial management in your organization is sure to have very specific requirements about what type of financing, if any, they intend to use and how they wish to see the financial model presented. Clearly you will want to have communicated this to your vendors so that they can present the financials accounting for this choice. Most performance contractors are financing neutral – they generally have little desire in taking the additional interest rate and credit risk in-house along with the energy performance risk. However, most will assist in your decision regarding the best type and source of financing for your organization, and they generally have close ties to lenders familiar with the performance contracting business. You will want to ensure you understand whether there is any financial relationship between the contractor and the lender.

Make sure that any assumptions about such items as the construction period, the escrow payments and the overall interest rates are clearly delineated.

You also need to decide whether you wish to proceed on an agreed margins basis, or a closed book approach. Both have pros and cons. Many facilities like the initial promise of agreed margins, until they realize that they will share in any cost overruns, as well as any cost savings. With each, it is important to understand that performance contractors need to make money and so their margins can run anywhere from 20% to 40%. This can add a large amount to a project but you have to figure that each of the vendors was asked to produce proposals and only one will be selected, plus they are including the initial scoping and feasibility engineering, the design engineering, and the financial expertise and assistance. In a bid/spec job, these would all be separate fees from your engineering and financial services providers. However, you should be careful to find out how many hours each company has allocated for portions of your job, and at what hourly rates. Often the hourly rates are quite high when compared to engineering companies and you would like to know this for your negotiations.

Selection – Contractual

Part of the RFP response should be a sample contract that can be given to your legal experts for their review. Again, this legal advice may be from your regular counsel, but again outside legal advice can be obtained from people who are used to looking at performance contracts. Between them, your legal advisors will give you an impression of whether the playing field is level, or whether the contractor has a large number of potential outs that could leave you holding the bag months down the road. Areas to stress are the guarantees section, and the measurement and verification portions because these are really the backbone of the entire agreement. You also want to know what type of agreement you will be expected to sign, especially if the contractor is anticipating a shared savings plan, and the rights and responsibilities of each side.

Investment Grade Audits

Once all the reviews and interviews have taken place you will hopefully have selected a performance contractor that you trust, and who has given you a fair price for a project that you think is reasonable and workable. The contractor will then ask you to sign an agreement for them to perform an investment grade audit that has a back-out fee in it for you, if they meet their stated performance goals in the IGA and you do not proceed with the project you will owe them money.

That is reasonable of course, but you must make sure that the back-out fee is realistic otherwise you could find yourself married to this company just because you can not afford to back out of the deal. Not a pleasant position to be in.

When reviewing the IGA submissions, be careful to note any differences that may have occurred between the RFP response and the IGA. For instance, some companies will change their analysis technique completely, meaning that you will need to re-evaluate the proposal assumptions completely from scratch. In this scenario, it is reasonable to put much of the work on the contractor and allow them to assemble a chart of differences between the documents.

This IGA phase is crucial to the success of your project. For instance, it is at this juncture that you have the most leverage and can therefore obtain the best possible project for your facility. The contractor will generally listen to your desires at this point. Once the IGA is done, it will be very difficult for the contractor to change the proposal offering. So at the start of the IGA process is the time to get your wish list items considered and included.

Also understand that the performance contractor believes that they have some leverage over you at this point too. After all, presumably you selected them for good reason, so you would not really want to backtrack and go to the second choice. Further, by this time you will have spent some considerable negotiating time with the chosen company – going to the next company would mean throwing away most of that effort, and put the project behind schedule by several months too.

Implementation and Post-Implementation

Once the IGA is done and intensely reviewed for accuracy, and completeness the legal papers can be drawn up and implementation begin.

At this point, the performance contract begins to look much more like a regular construction project. You need to carefully manage the project to assure that everything promised in the IGA is done, including all commissioning, and training of personnel.

The major difference of course is that as time goes on, the performance contractor maintains a presence in your operations. How much of a presence depends on you, but there is a huge variety of performance contracting customers. Some of whom take no interest in the downstream monitoring, and others who are very active. Performance contractors tend to like customers who take no interest in the project once it is completed and the reference is assured. Even better is the customer who elects to stop paying any of the ongoing M&V reporting requirements because at that point the risk of performance transfers entirely to the facility. And for some customers that is exactly the correct thing to do – if everyone is sure the savings are there, then why pay to monitor them for ten or twenty more years? However, it often seems that it is the projects that are the least technically able, and the least sure of their savings stream that tend to buy out the contract, and that can be a huge mistake.

CONCLUSION

Compared to other procurement vehicles, performance contracting is quite complex. There are numerous pitfalls that even experienced facility personnel can fall victim to, despite their best efforts.

But PC is not without risk for the companies that sign deals each and every day either, as the reputable companies do have a performance risk for which they are responsible. Part of their job, however, is to attempt to transfer as much of that risk as possible to the customer. Before embarking upon a performance contract you must be prepared to ensure you leave the contractor with the majority of the risk that they are getting paid to take.

You can do that by:
- Understanding the process completely yourself – including the pressures the contractor is under
- Having all your senior management understand the realistic trade-offs that will arise throughout the process
- Having pre-agreed goals written that can simplify selection
- Pre-qualifying companies through a formal qualifications selection process

- Realize your limitations – use outside technical, financial and legal assistance where appropriate
- Ensure contractors provide sufficient detail in each of these three areas to adequately evaluate their proposals
- Measurement and Verification is very subjective, and also complex – the M&V plan must be logical and defensible
- Guarantees can range from excellent to horrendous, you need to understand each contractor's guarantee language very well
- Disproportionate stipulation of savings shifts risk from the contractor to the facility
- Be aware of excessive Operating & Maintenance savings – make sure they are real, and that you will truly realize those savings from your budget
- Separate the financial proposal from the technical to allow a true comparison of proposals
- Use your leverage during the Investment Grade Audit phase to your best advantage
- Carefully check that you are getting everything that was promised in the RFP response
- Manage construction like any other construction project, and make sure you are getting specified equipment as you normally would
- Follow up through post-implementation to make sure savings are there to your satisfaction
- Do not buy out the contract unless you are absolutely certain that the savings will persist for the contract term

ABOUT THE AUTHOR
ANDREW HOLDEN, CEM is principal of Helios Resources, Ltd., an energy and resource management company that consults to customers on both sides of the performance contracting table. Among other activities, Helios assists end use customers procure fair and safe performance contracts, and also assists performance contractors to tailor their offering to individual customer requirements.

Mr. Holden has over fifteen years of experience in the energy services and green buildings industry. Before leaving to start an independent energy services and resource consulting company, he was Director of Engineering for one of the largest independent "super-ESCOs". Here he took responsibility for the tactical deployment of at least 10 engineers who identify and qualify energy improvements. He ensured that only those opportunities that made the best business sense were targeted and evaluated. In addition, he determined the overall strategic direction for proposed energy improvements that were evaluated based on customer information, competitive threats and internal criteria. As an integral part of the business development team Mr. Holden was involved in financial modeling and decision-making.

Prior to entering senior management, Mr. Holden's responsibilities included the identification and qualification of energy improvements in lighting and HVAC systems, controls, and industrial processes. He also performed field audits of customer facilities, as well as overseeing data management for all lighting system projects.

Mr. Holden has expertise in the development of computerized energy use models for lighting, HVAC, chillers, air and water pumping systems, and other building systems. He is also proficient in accurate modeling of the effect of energy conservation measures on utility bills as well as the life cycles analysis of energy conservation measures. Many of the energy conservation measures installed have required the design, installation, and monitoring of complex measurement and verification systems which Mr. Holden has successfully undertaken.

Education
MS, Information Science, Pennsylvania State University, Malvern PA

BS, Applied Physics and Electronics, University of Lancaster, Lancaster, England

Certifications/Affiliations
Senior Member, Association of Energy Engineers (AEE)

C.E.M. Certified Energy Manager, Association of Energy Engineers

Member, Delaware Valley Association of Energy Engineers

US Green Building Council LEED Accredited Professional

EPA Green Lights Surveyor Ally

Contact
Mr. Holden may be contacted via email at info@heliosltd.com, or by telephone at 610-917-9111. You may also browse the Helios website at heliosltd.com and contact Mr. Holden from there.

Chapter 52

THE CITY OF CALGARY FIRE STATIONS
Replacing Technologies To Reduce Energy Use

Trina L. Larsen, P. Eng., Project Engineer
Keen Engineering Co. Ltd. / VESTAR

ABSTRACT

Since 2000, VESTAR, and the City of Calgary have worked together to improve the energy efficiency of the Fire Stations, throughout Calgary. The major work completed was lighting retrofits and replacements.

The majority of the fire stations were built in the 1970's and 1980's, and used T12 fluorescent lighting in the living quarters, with High Pressure Sodium lighting on the apparatus floors. As is standard for energy retrofit work, all of the T12 fluorescent lighting was retrofitted with new T8 fluorescent lamps with low power electronic ballasts. The keystone of the project, however, was removing the high pressure sodium lighting on many of the apparatus floors.

High pressure sodium lighting is often seen as one of the most efficient lighting technologies due to its high lumens per watt. Unfortunately, in most indoor applications, the colour of standard high pressure sodium is inappropriate for comfortable space usage. With the intermittent occupancy on the apparatus floors, and the fast lighting response time required, the existing high pressure sodium lighting prevented switching. VESTAR worked with the maintenance staff to determine the most effective solution for the apparatus floors that would both reduce energy costs and improve the working environment. The resulting solution was low-tech, easy to implement, and low maintenance.

This paper describes the full solution, outlining some of the challenges faced by the designers, and present actual energy saving data.

BACKGROUND

In the summer of 1999, The City of Calgary invited proposals for energy retrofits of 25 fire stations, and fire training facilities. VESTAR (formerly KeenRose) submitted the successful proposal.

The majority of Fire Stations were built in the late 1970's and early 1980's, corresponding to Calgary's boom times. Many of the facilities followed essentially identical plans, with minor changes. Space heating for the fire stations used force flow furnaces, and unit heaters. Lighting consisted of fluorescent fixtures T12 with metric (1160 mm) and imperial length (4') tubes, incandescents, and high pressure sodium high bays on many of the apparatus floors.

At the time of the proposal, the electrical rates in Alberta were amongst the lowest in North America. With the 24-hour operation of the facilities, the project was still able to fall well within the 9-year pay back window.

PROJECT DEVELOPMENT

From previous experience, the VESTAR team expected post retrofit building energy performance indicies (BEPIs) to range from 75 to 200 kWh/m^2/a. In analyzing the utility information, the fire stations had existing BEPIs ranging form 100 to 250 kWh/m^2/a. A preliminary target of 20% reduction in energy consumption was set.

Due to the low electrical rates the majority of the energy retrofit project was lighting retrofits, both in the main area and on the apparatus floors.

Within the main living quarters of the stations, the lighting retrofit consisted of a standard conversion where two lamp fixtures were reduced to one lamp operation and four lamp fixtures went to two lamp operation. In some instances, reflectors were used to maintain light levels within Illuminating Engineering Society (IES) standards.

Many of the apparatus floors were already lit with the most efficient light source – high pressure sodium with up to 150 lumens/watt (1). Combined with the 24-hour operation of the facilities, it was difficult to immediately see any solution to the lighting in these areas. However, the fire fighters were requesting a change, as they had a difficult time maintaining the vehicles under the yellow light. At many stations, the doors were left open during the day, even in the winter, to improve visibility, adding to the heating costs of the facility.

The VESTAR team monitored the facility operation and found the apparatus floors were not utilized continuously. In general, the lights were on for 24 hours a day, but the fire fighters used the floor for less than 12 hours each day. However, the lights could not be turned off due to restrike time, based on the requirement for the apparatus floor to be lit as soon as an alarm is sounded to allow the firefighter full mobility on the floors to quickly exit the building.

LIGHTING REDESIGN

Each hall was redesigned to use twenty 8' industrial fixtures, using 4, 4' T8 lamps. Two 4' sections in each hall were left as night lighting, while the remaining lights was to be controlled using occupancy sensors mounted to provide switching as soon as the fire fighters enter from any entrance, including poles. The sensors chosen were a combination of passive infra red and infra-red with microphone sensors to enable the lights to stay on when people are working on equipment. This low tech solution provided lower light levels (150 – 300 lux as compared to 250 – 400 lux) of higher quality light. In addition to the occupancy controls, the fire fighters requested switches to allow the lights to be turned off during the day when sufficient daylight exists to light the space.

CONSTRUCTION

During construction, the main challenge was placing and orienting the occupancy sensors. Dual tech sensors were chosen over infra-red because of the short lines of sight with fire trucks parked on the apparatus floor. However, fans and pump noise contributed to long hours of operation, and some of the far bays were still completely blocked by the trucks, though the distance was within the sensor range. Furthermore, the lights needed to come on immediately when the fire fighters came through a door or down a pole. With selective conversion to passive infra red sensors, and the installation of additional sensors, the project came together.

Feed back from the staff was immediate. They were quite pleased with the brightness of the space, and that they could now work on their equipment without guesswork. There were no problems with the reduced light levels, because the quality of the light had been improved so dramatically. Since the initial installation and commissioning, the sensors have become virtually transparent to the users.

POST CONSTRUCTION

The lighting work was completed in the summer of 2000. Figure 1 shows the maximum consumption savings on the

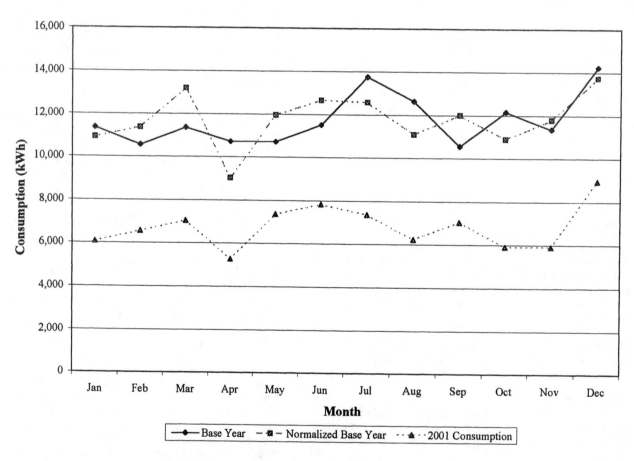

FIGURE 1 - CONSUMPTION SAVINGS FOR FIRE STATION #29

project, which occurred at Fire Station #29. The graph shows the actual base-year energy, the normalized base year, which provides seasonal adjustments based on the actual weather patterns of the year, and the actual energy consumption during 2001. As can be seen, the actual savings are averaging more than 40% for this facility.

Figure 2 shows the consumption savings for the entire project, including those facilities where only relamping and reballasting took place. In total, the electrical energy use over all the fire stations was reduced by 24%.

The savings have been better than predicted, both in energy units and in dollars. At the outset of the project, with electric utility rates of $0.031/kWh and $10.05/kVA, we projected a 5.5-year payback. Now, with rates at $0.089/kWh and minimal demand charges, the payback is projected to be 2.7 years, allowing the City of Calgary to expand the overall energy project to include an upgrade of the heating systems.

CONCLUSIONS

In energy projects, there is more to look at than objective numbers. Subjectivity plays a large role in the success or failure of a project, in order to effectively meet the needs of the staff. In this case, the objective numbers showed that the lighting in the apparatus floors was as efficient as possible, with more than enough light to meet IES standards. However, a subjective analysis showed great potential for energy savings, by using a less efficient light source, but lowering the actual light levels. The success of the project hinged on working with the client to find a solution that achieved the energy savings while improving their working conditions.

REFERENCES
(1) Rea, Mark S., IESNA Lighting Handbook, Ninth Edition 2000, Chapter 6.

BIO
Trina Larsen is a professional engineer with Keen Engineering, a partner of VESTAR. She has been working in energy management for seven years, primarily as a lighting designer, but also working on green engineering design and alternative energy projects. She has been involved in both international and North American projects, and has been a member of AEE since 1996.

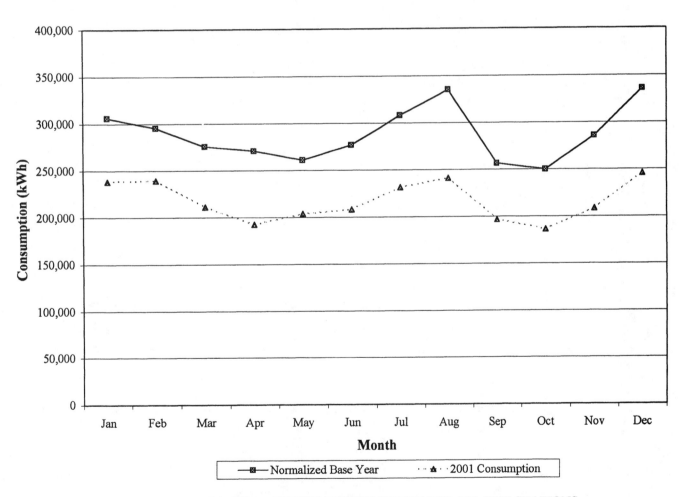

FIGURE 2 - CONSUMPTION SAVINGS FOR ALL FIRE STATIONS

Section 4
Combined Heat &
Power/Cogeneration

Chapter 53

Enabling Distributed Generation and Demand Response with Enterprise Energy Management Systems

by Rene Jonker and Patricia Dijak
Power Measurement Ltd., Victoria, BC
May 7, 2001

Introduction

An escalating demand for power has created two challenges for the energy industry: today, the problem is lack of generation; five years from now, it will be bottlenecks in the transmission and distribution infrastructure. Although demand response can solve the short-term problem, only distributed generation can solve both.

Demand response and distributed generation programs are becoming reality thanks to breakthroughs in enterprise energy management (EEM) and alternative generation technologies. These tools can deliver the quantity, quality and cost of power mandated by an expanding digital economy, growing environmental concerns and deregulation.

As greater numbers of power producers enter the picture and energy traders ask for more real-time information, the decentralized monitoring and control of energy and power quality is becoming a critical requirement. Information about every aspect of the power system is being shared at lightning-fast speeds and all players have to react just as quickly.

The Drive towards Distributed Generation

The digital economy, environment and deregulation are defining a new set of power supply requirements — requirements that can only be served through *distributed generation*, a system of small decentralized power plants situated close to end-users. Distributed generators can supply electricity to a single location, or pump power directly into regional or national electricity grids. The plants are owned or leased by utilities, energy service providers, independent power producers or end-users.

Distributed generation is becoming more feasible now that small-scale power plants are dropping in price and technologies for data communications and control are increasingly intelligent.

The Digital Economy

Digital economy enterprises — data centers, call centers, semiconductor fabrication plants, and other computer-controlled mission-critical businesses — are the fastest-growing segment of power consumers.[1] Unfortunately, the current infrastructure cannot meet their

---

[1] Stephens Inc.

escalating needs for quality or quantity of power.

These enterprises require nearly 100% "uptime" to guarantee the integrity of their products or services, but the power grid can deliver only 99.9% uptime or "three nines" of power, the equivalent of eight hours of outages per year. Improving reliability is difficult and expensive because long-distance transmission lines are routinely exposed to damage from animals, trees, lightning and other intrusions. These types of disruptions can be tolerated by lighting systems, industrial motors and air conditioners, the three waves of 20th century invention, but not the data and communication assets of the digital economy and, increasingly, the process control assets of the "old economy" as well.

Now expectations for reliability are around "six nines" (99.9999%) and as high as nine nines; however, even these indicators of "power on/power off" conditions are not sufficient to measure the level of power quality necessary for sensitive process equipment. Microprocessor-based devices are especially sensitive to voltage sags, swells, spikes or outages that can cause lost or corrupted data, equipment damage and process shutdowns. The only way to manage power quality is through an EEM system that can continuously monitor voltage and current waveforms and capture momentary disturbances for later analysis.

Decentralized power plants, which connect to end-users directly or through shorter transmission lines, are inherent sources of "higher nines" power. EEM systems monitor and control the operation of these plants, communicate real-time generation and consumption data, verify power quality, and trace the origins of power quality events.

These distributed generation facilities also provide a remedy for deficiencies in the power supply. Demand for power to support the Internet alone is skyrocketing. The Internet currently consumes 10% of the electricity in the

US, and this figure could rise to 50% in 10 years as usage increases. Both old economy and digital economy enterprises rely heavily on the Internet for supply-chain management systems that require access to information "24-seven." *Telecom hotels* and *server farms* host data and communication assets for corporate clients and their power densities are approaching 100 to 150 W per square foot, roughly double the most energy-intensive industrial facilities.[2]

Along with more reliance on the Internet comes rising energy bills. Large organizations already spend tens of millions of dollars per year on electricity, so a 10% increase in usage is a huge sum. Businesses can minimize costs by using an EEM system to monitor their load profiles and control the operation of small on-site generators during demand peaks.

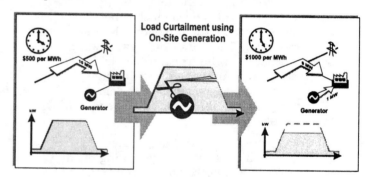

New Approaches under Deregulation

One effect of deregulation is that generation and transmission companies are reluctant to risk expenditures on large capital projects while their load growth is uncertain, competition continues to increase, and grid requirements are in flux. Load curtailment has always been an attractive alternative to the more costly options of purchasing power from neighboring producers or creating extra generation capacity, particularly large-scale generation facilities that take years to build and then sit idle most of the time.

Today, load curtailment programs and power plants with long development

---

[2] Stephens Inc.

timeframes are not enough to meet the growing demand for power. In the last ten years, California's electricity needs have risen 30%, but virtually no new power plants have been introduced. Demand in New York state has grown by 2700 MW in the last five years, but generating capacity has not kept up, increasing by only 1060 MW. In fact, New York has not brought a new plant online since 1996.[3]

Even if additional centralized power plants are constructed, they will operate as isolated islands of generation trapped inside inadequate intra- and inter-state transmission grids. Investment in the transmission and distribution infrastructure has actually declined over the last decade. Between 1988 and 1998, capital improvements to New York's transmission system fell from $307.7 million per year to $90 million per year.[4]

Hence the need for smaller-scale power plants located closer to end-users. In addition to being more affordable, smaller local plants avoid transmission system bottlenecks and suffer lower transmission losses. Usually 68% of the energy used to produce power in a centralized facility is lost by the time it reaches the consumer.[5]

Industrial and commercial energy customers also support the emergence of *microgrids,* power networks made up of dozens of linked generation units, each monitoring, switching, and communicating through advanced EEM technology. A microgrid bundles the generating capacity of individual units at each facility and forms a virtual utility that can be run by the consumer coalition or an existing utility.

Microgrid

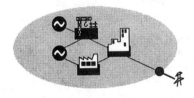

---

[3] New York Independent System Operator
[4] New York State Attorney General
[5] Stephens Inc.

Environmental Concerns

Developers of large-scale generation and transmission systems are finding it more expensive to negotiate rights-of-way and government approvals. Community groups have successfully blocked the construction of conventional power plants in their neighborhoods. Federal and state governments have determined allowable emission levels for various pollution sources and placed further restrictions on large generators. Even though some power plants could be retrofitted to meet these new standards, the costs to do so would be astronomical.

The permitting process for small-scale generators is much easier, if even required at all. Stationary pollution sources below a defined size do not need a permit to operate, and microgenerators fit into that category. Their emission levels are also quite low, with fuel cells and solar cells near zero.

While governments offer financial incentives to encourage the deployment of clean generation sources, aggressive environmental regulations are forcing other facilities to close. A large number of highly polluting coal-fired plants will be de-commissioned within the next few years, and the only way to replace that capacity quickly is through distributed generation.

As a result, small, clean, economical generating stations are now more attractive than big, expensive, polluting ones. Microgenerators such as fuel cells, solar cells, and microturbines have always been environmentally friendly, but now their decreasing cost is finally making their widespread deployment possible. Coupled with intelligent monitoring and control systems, these units can reduce the cost and environmental impact of electricity grids.

More advances are on the horizon with many companies cooperating on micropower research projects. In 1999 DaimlerChrysler and Ford joined a fuel cell partnership with Ballard, Arco, Shell, and Texaco, and later abandoned a coalition that opposed the Kyoto Protocol's limits on greenhouse gases.

Real-Time Management of the Power Grid

Energy is a unique commodity. It cannot be stored, so its generation, delivery and consumption must be managed in real-time, otherwise price and availability become unstable.

In the last few years, real-time monitoring, communications and control occurred mainly at the independent system operator (ISO) and regional transmission organization (RTO) level because of the need to control centralized generating facilities.

Now a power grid with decentralized generation must be supported with a spectrum of new energy management tools that help all players, from the ISO to the end-user, stabilize prices and maintain grid stability.

Stabilizing Demand and Price

The supply/demand imbalance in electricity hinders corporate operations and threatens competitiveness across the globe. New York and the Pacific Northwest have reported the lowest reserves in years, and California has resorted to rotating blackouts in addition to industrial/commercial load curtailment.

Prices on the spot markets have become extremely volatile with astronomical hourly spikes.

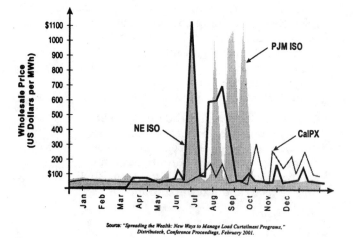

Source: "Spreading the Wealth: New Ways to Manage Load Curtailment Programs," Distributech, Conference Proceedings, February 2001.

During the summers of 1998 and 1999, electricity in some regions of the US sold at the margin for $1,000 to $6,000 per MWh, as much as 200 times higher than normal.

The main problem has been the inability of the demand side to participate in the market. Competitive markets usually encourage strong interactions between supply and demand forces, but this has not been the case for electricity markets. Until recently, energy consumers could not vary their demand in response to real-time prices, resulting in unnecessary price increases, load growth and threats to reliability. Considering the US energy market is worth $250 billion, a resolution to these inefficiencies would yield extraordinary savings for the entire economy.

Now EEM technology is providing end-users with the right information to make decisions and the real-time tools to act upon them. Instead of waiting for utilities to notify them of load curtailment sessions, end-users can decide to curtail loads based on spot market prices. Their actions, in turn, lower the spot price at peak periods, which benefits every business that needs to purchase that power. End-users are effectively participating in the wholesale electricity market because they can reduce overall demand and moderate price fluctuations.

ISOs and RTOs are introducing these capabilities through *demand response* programs where load curtailment credits are based on real-time pricing. Demand response programs are usually targeted at customers that can curtail loads of 100 kW to 5,000 kW or more. If smaller customers want to participate, they can aggregate curtailment with other customers through an energy service provider or load aggregator.

Demand response programs also save money on the supply side. According to Federal Energy Regulatory Commission (FERC) rules, every ISO must set up reserves to keep the grid operating during times of peak demand. These reserves can be in the form of spinning or supplemental reserves (online or idle generators), capacity contracts with other suppliers, or demand response or load curtailment programs.

By choosing a demand response program instead of a spinning reserve, a regional operator can save tens of millions of dollars. For example, ISO New England must maintain over 3,500 MW of generators that run at low levels just so they are available to produce additional power on short notice, and this is costing $30 million.[6] A demand response program reduces that need.

Stabilizing the Grid

Demand response is the interim answer to the supply/demand imbalance. It's also accelerating the development of a real-time technology infrastructure for the long-term solution: distributed generation. Distributed generation, in the form of standby generators, currently accounts for 10% of generation capacity in the US, and is expected to increase to over 30% of capacity in the next 10 years.[7]

One question concerning distributed generation is the stability of the power supply. Historically, utilities and ISOs have been responsible for grid stability, but as soon as hundreds of independent power producers start pumping power onto the grid, they need to bear part of the burden. That's where affordable, real-time EEM technologies come into play.

For all supply and demand side equipment to function properly, electrical voltages must be maintained within a reasonable range, usually within ±5% of nominal. Voltage control is becoming more complex as the energy industry is restructured and responsibilities are segregated across a number of different generation, transmission, marketing and regulatory entities.

Real-time EEM systems must be able to control voltages by automatically managing *reactive power*, the power wasted by any load that stores energy and transfers some of that energy back to the generator. Inductors and capacitors store energy. Nearly all power system components and end-user facilities — overhead lines, underground cables, transformers, motors, and fluorescent lights — are inductive or capacitive loads. That means some current carried by the transmission system transmits wasted energy (reactive power) and the rest transmits useful energy (real power).

Because transmission lines and transformers can only carry a limited amount of current, the reactive current increases congestion by lowering the capacity of the system to move useful energy. Power providers want to minimize reactive power flows because they reduce the ability of generators to supply real power.

Conveniently, the source of the problem also points to the solution: the currents in capacitors and inductors on the same transmission system move in opposite directions. Because current in a capacitor rises while current in an inductor drops, the two can be used to cancel reactive power flows. End-users often install capacitors to compensate for their inductive loads. Load serving entities (LSEs) install capacitor banks, synchronous condensers and generators at various points in the transmission and distribution system. All these devices can generate or absorb reactive power.

The requirements for reactive components on a transmission system are constantly changing with load levels, generation patterns, and contingencies like generator failures or line faults. A real-time EEM system must control these reactive loads in real-time to prevent them from affecting end-users.

Distributed generators also need EEM to respond to these changing conditions and supply some reactive power, or they would create voltage control problems for the grid. But induction generators such as windmills and solar cells only absorb reactive power; they don't supply it. Moreover, since their output fluctuates, their demand for reactive power fluctuates as well. So to control system voltages, they are isolated from the grid

---

[6] ISO New England, March 2001
[7] GilderGroup, Power Report, 1999

with solid-state electronic devices that simulate reactive power output. This scheme also allows a generator's frequency to be controlled independently from the power system frequency so that gas-fired turbines can operate at very high speeds and solar cells can generate direct current.

Frequency is another grid stability issue. Power must be maintained within a narrow window around 60 Hz. Frequency variations occur on a small scale when there is a slight supply/demand imbalance, and on a large scale when a generating unit suddenly fails. To ensure that frequency deviations are contained, distributed generators must react instantly by coming online within seconds or end-users may be surprised with interruptions.

Overall, an EEM system can stabilize the grid all the way down the power delivery chain by controlling voltage and frequency, managing congestion, coordinating protection and fault clearing, and automatically activating reserve capacity. Because operations have to happen in real-time, all EEM devices need direct connections to public communication networks such as the Internet, wireless and paging infrastructures.

Deploying Real-Time Technologies and Distributed Intelligence

The success of demand response and distributed generation depends on the technology behind real-time data gathering and communications. An EEM system has to alert thousands of sites to spot-market prices, confirm remote operations in seconds, and correlate all events with sub-second precision. It must immediately and accurately verify curtailment and generation activities to help operators maintain grid stability, and assign the appropriate credits or penalties.

To carry out all these activities, intelligent monitoring and control devices should be distributed at inter-ties, generators, and customer service entrances. Also, every command-and-tracking workstation from

the ISO to the end-user should be equipped with EEM software for system-wide or local situation analysis, load aggregation, remote control and reporting.

This combination of hardware and software can only answer the energy industry's needs if it meets four basic criteria:

- **High Accuracy:** It must meet nationally-recognized revenue-metering accuracy standards because regulatory bodies, LSEs and end-users need an audit trail to prove exact sequences of events and finalize transfers of money.

- **Reliability:** It must be an industrially hardened platform able to continue operating and store data in the event of power disturbances or communication interruptions. It must withstand a variety of conditions defined by ANSI or IEC for revenue meters.

- **Affordability:** It must be cost-effective to deploy and maintain, both in labor and equipment, or else the investment cannot be justified to owners, directors and other stakeholders. It should maximize the intelligence in each device, minimize the number of separate components, and allow easy data access through public Internet, wireless, satellite and paging networks.

- **Instant Communications:** Each device must automatically transmit raw or pre-analyzed data directly to public communication networks, and leverage the existing Internet infrastructure for easy scalability. The device should also issue control signals directly to other equipment, and support simultaneous data transfers to ISOs, LSEs and end-users so that all participants have the same information.

All four criteria call for the use of intelligent power meters with support for load profiling, power quality analysis, control, and multiple communication ports and protocols. A combination of PCs, RTUs, PLCs and external modems at each site may have similar technical capability, but multiple discrete devices are more expensive to set up and maintain. They require more wiring, power supplies, and replacement parts, and more maintenance time to pinpoint the source of glitches should they occur. Some components may also be more susceptible to failure during power quality disturbances.

Intelligent power meters can also work within firewall restrictions that are set up by Information Systems groups to restrict outside access to corporate networks. The meters can transmit e-mail messages or serve data directly to web pages, assuring both worldwide data access and corporate security.

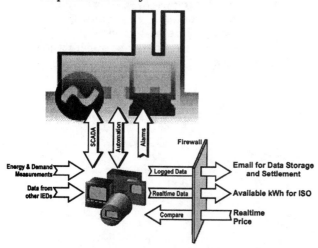

To optimize value and reliability on the software side, workstations should be located away from the "front lines" where only the industrially hardened meters need be. Also, people that just want information — not analysis or control capabilities — shouldn't have to install specialized EEM software. They can work with web browsers or e-mail to access data.

Other participants, mostly operators, need workstations with EEM software for enterprise-wide monitoring, dispatch, and reporting, along with a few high-performance servers to manage databases. These operators can exist anywhere in the power delivery chain —

at ISOs, LSEs or end-user facilities. Command-and-control software must also support multiple protocols and standards, such as MV-90 and ODBC (Open Database Connectivity), so that enterprise-wide data can be collected, analyzed and reported, and control actions determined.

To ensure proper functioning of the grid, every distributed generator should have an intelligent power meter for monitoring, control and communications. The meter must continually transmit current conditions at the generator's interconnect point to the ISO, distribution company or utility so they know when the generator is online, and can decide whether or not it should be. The meter should also receive control signals, and when a fault occurs, respond by quickly disconnecting the generator from the grid.

In a demand response program, an energy consumer's EEM system monitors the real-time market price of electricity through XML links to Internet wholesale exchanges. The EEM system correlates the data with building usage, manufacturing schedules or wastewater treatment functions. If the price of electricity climbs beyond the customer's threshold, and curtailment is the right alternative based on marginal costs of production, the EEM system sends a signal to the intelligent power meters to switch off equipment or start up on-site generators until the price drops again. Meters provide continuous real-time data to the ISO to show a drop in demand. The LSE's EEM software tracks the responses of all participants so that actual curtailment is verified and customers are paid appropriately by the power pool for their reduced consumption. EEM software generates reports that correlate billing data with curtailment operations and automatically adjusts customer bills with credits or penalties. The software and meters can automatically update a web page for each customer with real-time loads before, during, and after curtailment, and estimates of the credits earned. By tracking overall load reductions, the LSE can calculate real-time cost savings.

In a traditional load curtailment session, a utility's operations center (rather than the end-user) is constantly monitoring the availability and price of power, along with current and predicted demand. Depending on these key factors, as well as the time of day, the system operator may decide that the trend line isn't favorable and the utility cannot meet impending demand. If that happens, the operator activates the software to automatically notify thousands of customers by pager or e-mail, or dial out to the meters located at selected customer sites. A few minutes after first contact, customers must have reduced their loads by the agreed-upon amount, or pay premiums for the extra electricity used. Each meter captures energy readings to determine how much energy was drawn from the utility during the curtailment session. The meter also stores information continuously for billing and power quality monitoring purposes. After the session is over, EEM software uploads curtailment and billing data from the meters into an ODBC-compliant database.

Conclusions

We are on the verge of a new era in power generation and distribution. Breakthroughs in enterprise energy management technology and distributed generation are changing the way grids operate. Along with power generation, other functions are being decentralized: data gathering, analysis, control and communications.

The digital economy is one of the drivers behind distributed generation because of the need for a higher quality and quantity of power. In turn, the digital economy is solving its own problem by making communications more affordable and pushing intelligence to the microchip level.

All market players require EEM systems to monitor and control power usage, capacity reserves, costs and payments.

- **End-users** need to understand energy consumption patterns and power quality across their enterprises, and determine whether to participate in curtailment programs or distributed generation microgrids.

- **Energy service providers** want to aggregate loads for demand response programs, buy energy at wholesale levels, or offer distributed generation for premium power quality customers.

- **Application service providers** need to remotely maintain and control the generation assets of utilities, energy service providers and end-users.

- **Power producers and ISOs** have to address the supply/demand imbalance with demand response programs and, in the longer term, distributed generation.

The power grids of tomorrow will be more complex but more energy-efficient than the systems of today. With them will evolve EEM systems and service programs to benefit energy suppliers and consumers alike.

Chapter 54

NATURAL GAS PURCHASING STRATEGIES: MAKING SENSE OF IT ALL

Philip R. Walsh, P.Geol, M.B.A.
Managing Director, Energy Objective Ltd.

ABSTRACT

The increasingly competitive commodity markets for natural gas have seen greater volatility in pricing. In turn planners of distributed generation projects find themselves involved in making decisions on how they purchase their natural gas and at what price. Many capital project decisions of producers rely on a determination of future prices in evaluating the economic viability of those projects. Choosing the right strategy for determining the price of natural gas can mean the difference between a profitable capital expenditure and a losing one.

Prices for natural gas are a function of supply and demand. An analysis of the history of price, supply and demand forecasting shows a consistent trend for supply and demand that essentially mirrors the actual outcome. In the case of price the forecasts are less consistent and indicate that there is sufficient discrepancy between long term forecasted and actual values to warrant a bigger picture approach to choosing an appropriate strategy for price determination.

Increases in oil and natural gas prices in North America have been, over the past 30 years, strongly correlated to increases in economic growth. Establishment of a long-term equilibrium trend in economic growth identifies periods above and below this trend line. At those times where economic growth exceeds the long term equilibrium there is an increase in energy demand and a related increase in energy prices. Conversely, those periods of time when economic growth falls below the long-term equilibrium line coincides with energy price spikes and subsequent declines in energy prices related to lower economic growth.

Strategies for long-term price determination need to reflect the relative position of price to the long-term economic growth equilibrium.

INTRODUCTION

There is no question that the natural gas market over the last few years has become increasingly more volatile. This is due in part to the creation of a competitive marketplace and the influence of financial derivatives that allow for speculative profits or losses. In determining the economic viability of distributed generation projects a determination of price is a key component. Some guarantee of pricing can be determined by using the futures markets to hedge your commodity sales price. But is that the appropriate strategy? Perhaps the market is pricing natural gas at a discount to its real potential. Futures markets also are only beneficial in a shorter period of time (3 years or less) with market liquidity lacking in using the futures market to hedge longer term prices.

This paper will address the evolution of the natural gas supply, demand and pricing equilibrium. We will approach this analysis from what I believe is an interesting perspective. I have gone back in time to 1995 and pulled the forecast data for supply demand and pricing. We will review these forecasts relative to the actual history.

I will then address the current situation for supply, demand and pricing and where forecasters believe each of these components of the gas market is headed. Once we have seen the prognostication of others, I will provide our own internal conclusions regarding the short-term and long-term trend for these variables, the relative correlation of each and some recommended strategies that distributed generation planners today might make.

HISTORICAL FORECASTS

Demand Forecast versus Actual (1996 to 2000)

Back in 1995, the Natural Resources section of the Canadian government published in its annual review (1) a range of forecasts provided by prominent forecasting organizations such as the American Gas Association, Energy Information Administration, the Gas Research Institute and the Petroleum Industry Research Associates. Figure 1 shows the high, low and average demand forecast for the United States and Canada until the year 2000. The forecasts showed steady demand growth of about 2% per year. The actual demand exceeded the initial forecast but then slid downwards towards the lower end of the range and eventually settled at the upper end.

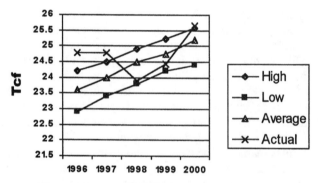

Figure 1. Demand Forecasts- US and Canada 1995

Supply Forecast versus Actual (1996 to 2000)

The supply forecasts shown in Figure 2 exhibited an assumption of steady growth with a delayed response to demand growth and then a steady increase averaging approximately 3% per year. The actual supply for that period fell within the range of forecasts initially but by 1998 it fell outside that range and only caught up with the lower end of the forecasts by 2000.

Price Forecast versus Actual (1996 to 2000)

The forecasts for natural gas prices at Henry Hub exhibited (Figure 3) steady growth consistent with the forecasted trends of supply and demand. Increasing gas prices resulted from increasing demand but were mitigated by the forecasted increase in supply growth.

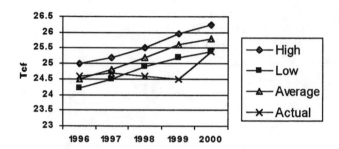

Figure 2. Supply Forecasts- US and Canada 1995

Interestingly, they all missed the boat when the actual price ended up higher throughout the forecast period. The unforecasted demand increase led to the higher prices that we see during the initial two years and in 2000 when the previous years had seen decreased supply. Why did the price forecasts underestimate the actual price by such a factor?

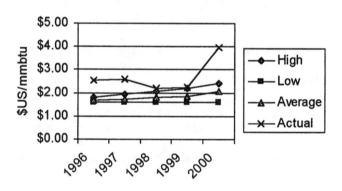

Figure 3. Forecasted Natural Gas Prices Henry Hub

Historical Natural Gas Price (1990 to 1995)

If we review the historical natural gas wellhead price on an average annual basis (See Figure 4) one can see that the general trend for pricing was downward. This established the starting point for price forecasting for the period 1996 to 2000. The starting price falls somewhere between $1.50 and $2.00 U.S. per mmbtu.

402

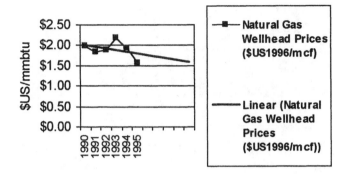

Figure 4. Natural Gas Prices 1990-1995

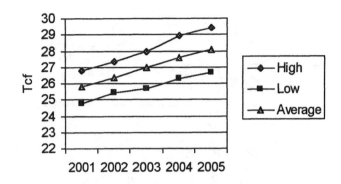

Figure 6. Future US and Canadian Demand

Future Price Forecast (2001 to 2005)

Now let's review the current pricing situation and forecast into the future (2). In Figure 5 we can see that the forecasters believe that the market price for gas in 2001 is too high relative to the supply/demand balance that they forecast. They predicted last year that prices would peak in 2001 and slide downwards until 2003 where they would re-establish themselves in a slightly increasing trend. The actual price for 2001 fell into the range forecasted and the market (NYMEX) is betting today that gas prices will stay within the forecasted range for 2002 but improve above the longer-term forecast.

Future Supply (2001-2005)

The forecasted supply picture (Figure 7) is also one of steady increases with a slight flattening out in 2005. The growth is estimated to be approximately 2% per year. This is down from the 1995 forecast for the following five years. It is interesting to note that the average of the 2001 forecasts for supply and demand were almost equal.

Past and Future Demand Forecasts (1996 to 2005)

When we merge the 1995 forecasts with the 2000 forecasts (Figure 8) we see that in the case of demand the

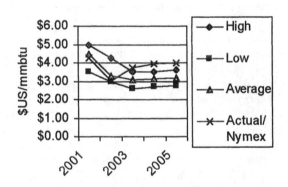

Figure 5. Price Forecast 2000 - Henry Hub

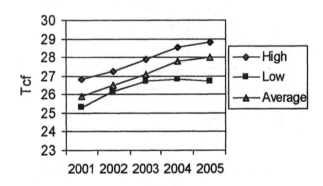

Figure 7. Future Forecasted Supply 2001

Future Demand (2001-2005)

In reviewing the forecasted supply demand balance we can see in Figure 6 that once again the forecasted demand is steadily growing, but at 2 % per year. This rate is consistent with the annual rate of growth forecasted in 1995.

merged results show a relative homogeneity between the forecasts with a greater range in predictions for demand over the next five years than what was evident back in 1995.

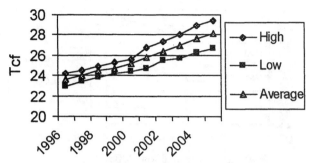

Figure 8. Forecasted US and Canadian Demand

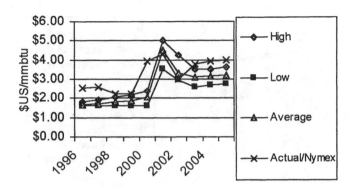

Figure 10. Price Forecast 2000 - Henry Hub

Past and Future Supply Forecasts (1996 to 2005)

The merged supply forecasts (Figure 9) also exhibit a divergence in the range of predictions but generally the forecasted trends are consistent on average.

Past and Future Price Forecasts (1996 to 2005)

Figure 10 summarizes best the discrepancy between the price forecasts and the supply and demand forecasts. There is a distinct break in pricing trend and an establishment of a new equilibrium for natural gas prices. This step up is due to the actual price response in 2000

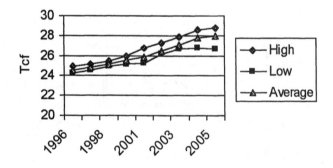

Figure 9. Forecasted US and Canadian Supply

and 2001. The question that needs to be raised is whether or not these new price forecasts are too positive relative to the long-term fundamentals i.e. demand and supply. As we saw in the previous figures there is no such "step up" in demand or "step down" in supply to correlate with the price forecast.

ESTABLISHING A LONG TERM EQUILIBRIUM

Our own evaluation of where prices are going is based on a longer-term view of the fundamentals. Of course short-term supply and demand issues such as cold weather, supply outages etc will affect short term pricing for natural gas. But in looking at the longer term we like the correlation between economic growth and demand. Falling out of the demand is the supply response. In turn the pricing variable adjusts based on the demand/supply imbalance. The demand variable is seen as more elastic than supply and so it reacts quicker than supply, which tends to be somewhat inelastic and slower in responding to changes in demand.

Figure 11 highlights the growth in the U.S. economy since 1960. I have established a trend line that exposes periods of greater than average growth and decline. When relating this period to the price of oil and natural gas we can see that the first price shock for oil in 1974 led to an economic decline. With stabilized oil prices the economy adjusted and began to grow again only to be hit with the 1980 price shock that resulted in an even greater decline in the economy. This economic decline lasted until oil pricing responded to lower demand and began dropping. A subtler decline in economic growth occurred in 1991 corresponding again with an increase in oil pricing. The latest economic growth period indicated on this chart is for the period 1996 to 2001 and it has been well in excess of the long-term equilibrium, with corresponding increases in oil prices resulting from increased demand. The size of the response of prices to economic growth has been mitigated somewhat by the decreasing amount of energy consumed per $GDP. Past pricing shocks have led to innovation and technology in energy efficiency that has helped reduce the demand for energy on a per capita basis.

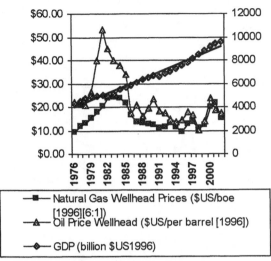

Figure 11. Prices vs. US Economic Growth (3)

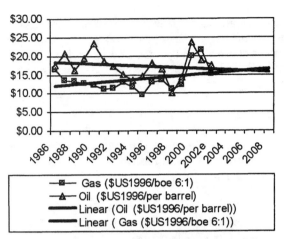

Figure 12. Relationship between Oil and Natural Gas Pricing

Now when we follow the price of natural gas we see that after wellhead deregulation in 1973 the price begins to move towards parity with oil on a price per thermal unit basis. Early issues of de-contracting, lack of pipeline interconnects between supply and market provided for divergence in pricing between the two. By the late 1990's the prices have converged as the energy marketplace has become more competitive as a result of deregulation policies and the participation of financial players in the market.

Relationship between Oil and Natural Gas Pricing

In Figure 12 we have narrowed the time frame down to the last 15 years. Note the convergence of oil and gas pricing. In fact, there continues to be a trend where natural gas prices follow the direction of oil prices. We have also established our own price equilibrium points for both oil and gas. Using this analysis combined with the current economic decline in economic growth it would appear that oil prices should continue downwards towards the $19 to $20 US dollar price level and probably below that for the short term. However, the impact of OPEC supply constraints may continue to keep prices in the $25 to $27 US dollar per barrel range which based on our analysis will continue to hamper economic growth and reduce the demand variable. It would appear that oil prices would need to stay below this range for 3 to 4 years to allow the US and world economy to be kick started from the benefit of lower energy prices.

For natural gas prices, they will tend to follow oil prices. We see a short-term price, barring any extreme weather conditions, having an equilibrium price between $2.85 and $3.00 US per mcf. Again, if we have a normal to milder than normal winter that price should be lower in the short term until we see an increase in economic growth.

When one is attempting to determine their strategy for pricing it is important to understand where one is relative to this equilibrium at the time they are making a pricing decision. For example, with the economic growth during the period 1996 to 1999 one could conclude that upward pressures on demand and the slow response of supply would lead to price increases. Accordingly a distributed generation planner would find their price below this equilibrium point and a longer term purchasing strategy would be appropriate. When the price eventually exceeded this equilibrium point a short-term (<1 year) purchase hedging strategy would be appropriate. A planner also needs to consider at what point one chooses to hedge their position.

Conclusions and Recommendations

In conclusion the following summarizes the key elements of determining a purchasing strategy. Economic growth creates demand. When demand begins deleting inventory (i.e. year over year storage balances) and because supply is more inelastic in responding, then the price will increase with demand. Eventually supply comes around as a result of the impetus provided by higher prices. When the economy corrects itself, demand decreases; supply is slow to respond and inventories build. Price decreases with lower demand and higher inventories. Eventually supply declines in response to lower prices. As seen in the historical data oil prices lead natural gas prices. In order to determine a successful strategy for long term pricing a distributed generation planner who is responsible for purchasing natural gas for their project must establish at what point the current price is relative to the long-term equilibrium between demand, supply and pricing.

References

1. Natural Resources Canada, Energy Resources Branch, Natural Gas Division, Market Review & Outlook 1995

2. Natural Resources Canada, Energy Resources Branch, Natural Gas Division, Market Review & Outlook 2000 to 2010

3. Oil & Gas Journal, Mid-Year Forecast, July 1, 2002, www.fintrend.com

Chapter 55

THE RAPIDLY APPROACHING MARKET FOR FUEL CELL POWER GENERATION

William H. Steigelmann, P.E., Technology Specialist
Aspen Systems Corporation

ABSTRACT

Fuel cell technology has been rapidly advancing during the past two years. The day when nearly every building will have its own source of power—via fuel cells—could be less than ten years away. This paper will summarize the technologies, their deployment and marketing approaches, and their expected technical and economic performance.

INTRODUCTION

As the title implies, this paper has a point of view. Many may feel that it expresses an overly optimistic viewpoint, and this may be true. But whether the timeframe is 10 years, 15 years, or longer, the main point of the paper is that this is the *Fuel Cell Century*, with regard to both electric power generation and transportation.

This assertion is made in the same way that a similar one could be made that the 20th Century was the Reciprocating-Engine Century for all forms of transportation that have wheels, whether these wheels run on roads, highways, rails, farmland, or even over the lawns that surround our homes. (Reciprocating engines are also an important prime mover in some elements of water-borne and air-borne transportation. For the first 50 years after airplanes were invented (in 1903), reciprocating engines had virtually 100% of the aircraft market, ultimately being mostly—but not entirely—supplanted by the jet engine.)

At the beginning of the 20th Century, steam engines were the dominant prime mover for railroads, had largely replaced sails for and water-borne transportation, and were beginning to find a role replacing horses on farms. The early automobiles and trucks were powered by a variety of prime movers, with steam and electricity being almost as popular as reciprocating engines. By the end of the century, the steam locomotive had disappeared (except for short tourist excursions on scenic routes in a few isolated locations.) Spark-ignition and Diesel engines are now powering virtually every locomotive, automobile, and truck that is manufactured anywhere in the world.

FUEL CELL POWER SYSTEMS

A fuel cell is an interesting electro-chemical device. It is basically a box in which hydrogen and oxygen react in a controlled way to produce water, heat, and the flow of electrons through an external circuit; rather than react quickly to produce an explosion. The fuel cell keeps the two reacting chemicals in separate sealed chambers; they can react only by means of the flow of electrical charges between the two chambers and through the external circuit. An explosion within the fuel cell is virtually impossible. One cell produces only a small voltage (less than 1.0 V), so to get usable power levels a large number of cells are stacked together, similar to the way 12-V and 48-V electrical batteries are constructed. The assemblage is logically named the *fuel-cell stack*.

Oxygen is readily available in the air, but a key question is, "where does the hydrogen come from?" One way is to use electricity to dissociate water into its constituent elements, but this is very energy-intensive. Another way is to reform the molecules of any hydrocarbon fuel (natural gas, propane, fuel oil, gasoline, methane generated in landfills, etc.), producing hydrogen and, unfortunately, also carbon dioxide. (This approach also requires energy input, and the conversion efficiency varies for different fuels.) As is discussed below, most types of fuel cells that are fueled by a hydrocarbon require an external reformer to generate the hydrogen gas that flows into the fuel-cell stack. One type features an internal reformer, where the needed hydrogen is produced within the stack itself.

Another issue—and one that is not as technically challenging as producing hydrogen—involves the electrical output. As noted above, the fuel cell produces a direct-current (dc) output. This is fine for most transportation applications, but for DG applications alternating current (ac) power is needed.

This means that the fuel-cell power system also must contain an inverter, which is an electronic "black box" that converts dc voltage to ac. Inverters are standard commercial devices that are also needed for DG units that produce electricity directly from sunlight (using solar photovoltaic panels) and from the wind (using wind-driven turbine-generators).

(For completeness, it should be mentioned that there is another market for fuel-cell technology that is not addressed here: the "micropower" market. Several companies are working to develop ultra-small battery substitutes for laptop and hand-held computers, cell phones, and other portable electronic devices. For these applications, a fuel cell powered by stored hydrogen and producing a dc voltage is expected to be feasible.)

The basic advantages of the fuel cell power system are that:

1) they operate at high efficiency;

2) they have low emissions of pollutants with a wide variety of fuels;

3) they produce useable heat as well as electricity, so they are suitable for cogeneration and CHP applications;

4) they produce little noise when operating;

5) they require very little operational attention and routine maintenance (typically are remotely operated); and

6) they can be fully factory assembled and thus entail quick and easy installation.

From a technical standpoint, engineers have known how to produce electricity from a fuel cell for more than a century. The first practical application was in the space program, producing auxiliary power aboard the Apollo vehicles and the Space Shuttles. One company has been producing a 200-kW stationary power unit for distributed-generation (DG) applications for the past 10 years, selling some 300 units. Another company has just recently begun marketing 250-kW units. An additional 20 or more companies are actively developing complete power units in the 0.5-kW to 1,000-kW range. Some companies are focused on the DG market, others on the transportation market, and some on both. Many are located in the U.S. and Canada, but there are also important activities underway in Japan, Germany, and other nations.

MARKET SYNERGIES

This paper is focused on distributed power-generation applications, but it recognizes that success there is closely linked to success in the transportation field, and *vice versa*. This is because many of the global efforts to develop a cost-effective fuel cell power source are directed toward vehicle applications, driven primarily by air-quality considerations. However, the same fuel-cell technology (i.e., stack design) that produces electricity to power a car or bus can produce the electricity needed to light a room, run a computer, drive a

fan, or cook a meal. In addition, there is the economy-of-scale factor: the more units of any product that are produced annually in a factor, the lower the per-unit cost. The automotive market typically involves production volumes that are measured in terms of hundreds of thousands of units per year. An automobile engine is a highly complex device that requires close-tolerance casting and machining of a variety of metal alloys. The are built to rigorous standards and involve stringent quality-control procedures. Yet the cost of the final product is approximately only $50/kW. Although today's price of fuel-cell power plants is nearly 100 times larger, production volumes are measured in terms of 50-100 units per year. As volume goes up, costs (and prices) will come down.

DESIGN OBJECTIVES

The problem being addressed by all the companies (even the two with commercial products now in the marketplace) is to identify fuel-cell power plant designs that:

1) operate reliably while in operation for periods that are measured in years;

2) operate efficiently using air and one or more commonly available fuels as input; and

3) are cost-competitive with electricity delivered via electric utility power lines, and with the motive power produced by the ubiquitous reciprocating engine (spark-ignition or Diesel).

A low-cost design may not have long life; a design that exhibits high efficiency may be too expensive. Companies in the field typically have been working for several years to develop optimum designs. The work involves design, build, and test, but while build and test efforts are underway, design refinements and improvements are being simultaneously developed. Every year, a new large-scale test program begins, with smaller component-level programs appearing along the way. All of this requires large capital resources and replenishments. Government contracts have helped, but most of the effort is privately funded.

One of the two fuel-cell systems now in the marketplace has demonstrated that it meets the first two criteria, but it is not even close to meeting the third. (The other commercially available system is probably in a similar position, but it is too new to have a demonstrated record of good reliability.) There is some market for high-priced units, such as for niche markets, sales to governmental agencies, and sales to organizations who want to show they are willing to pay extra for "green" technologies, but these markets are limited. The mass markets will require systems that are cost-competitive with electricity delivered via electric utility power lines, and with the motive power produced by reciprocating engines.

NICHE MARKETS

Manufacturers and distributors are focusing their initial efforts on a small number of niche markets where the current relatively high price levels pose less of a barrier to sales. One such market involves providing power at a communications relay station or tower located at a remote site. Two applications at these sites are: (1) backup power (in lieu of maintenance-intensive batteries), when utility power is normally used, and (2) primary power at sites where utility lines are not nearby and the alternative is the need to frequently deliver fuel to and perform maintenance on a continuously running engine-generator. Increasingly, electric utilities and utility customers are finding situations where it is less costly to install a DG system to serve a remote load than to upgrade or extend a utility power line. Another application is providing power to monitoring and control (e.g., reclosers and other switching equipment located at a utility substation. Here also, fuel cells are expected to be a viable alternative to batteries.

TYPES OF FUEL CELLS

The electrolyte defines the key properties, particularly operating temperature, of the fuel cell. For this reason, fuel cell technologies are named by their electrolyte. Five distinct types of fuel cells have been developed.

Alkaline: Using alkaline potassium hydroxide as the electrolyte, alkaline cells reach thermal efficiencies of up to 70%. Alkaline cells have been used on spacecraft for many years, but until recently have been too expensive for commercial use and are being phased out in favor of proton exchange membrane (PEM) technology for space applications. Only two manufacturers are working on the development of alkaline fuel cells for terrestrial applications.

Proton Exchange Membrane: This relatively low-temperature (~170°F) technology uses a moist polymer membrane as an electrolyte. Due to their high power potential, PEM fuel cells are the primary candidates for light-duty vehicles and for generating electricity for homes and other buildings, as well as for backup-power and "micropower" applications. The cell requires the supply of hydrogen, and therefore an external reformer is needed if tanks of hydrogen are not used as fuel. A catalyst at the anode strips off the electron from the hydrogen atoms. The resulting proton migrates through the moist membrane, and the electron flows through the external circuit. The constituents reunite at the cathode, where air is flowing. Two of the reconstituted hydrogen atoms link to an oxygen atom, forming water. The temperature of recovered heat is sufficient for domestic water heating and space heating uses.

Phosphoric Acid: The most commercially successful design to date, Phosphoric acid (PA) cells have been used to generate electricity in hospitals, nursing homes, hotels, schools, and other buildings. The cell operates at about 390°F, and therefore the recovered heat can serve moderate-temperature thermal needs in the building. As with the PEM fuel cell, the PA cell's catalysts are sensitive to fuel stream contaminants and the performance degrades slowly over time, necessitating periodic stack replacements.

Molten Carbonate: Because they operate at temperatures around 1,200 F, this type of fuel cell will probably be limited to large commercial, industrial, and utility use. Advantages of the higher operating temperature include more choices in catalyst, higher quality heat to recover for thermal needs, and the potential for fuel reforming within the stack. The cell reactions for molten carbonate systems (like the solid oxide fuel cells briefly discussed next) are different from those of the PEM and PA systems. The molten carbonate electrolyte transports negative carbonate ions from the cathode instead of positive protons from the anode so that the H_2O and CO_2 exhaust from the anode.

Solid Oxide: Like molten carbonate systems, solid oxide fuel cells operate at high temperatures (about 1,500-1,800°F) and are likely to be used for large stationary power plants. The high operating temperature eliminates the need for expensive catalysts, and allows for reforming of hydrocarbons within the stack. The high temperature heat is ideal for combined cycles, but also can cause high thermal stress on the equipment. The solid components allow flexibility in cell configurations.

FUEL CELL MANUFACTURERS

- Proton Exchange Membrane (PEM)
  Alstom Technology
  Analytic Energy Systems
  Avista Labs
  BCS Technology
  Ballard Power Systems
  DCH-Enable
  Fuju Electric
  General Motors
  H Power
  Hydrogenics
  IdaTech
  Matsushita Electric
  MTU Friedrichsha
  Nuvera Fuel Cells
  Plug Power (GE Fuel Cell Systems)
  Proton Energy Systems
  Proton Motor
  Teledyne
  Toyota
  UTC Fuel Cells

- Phosphoric Acid (PA)

  Toshiba International Fuel Cell Corporation

  UTC Fuel Cells (formerly ONSI)

- Molten Carbonate (MC)

  UTC Fuel Cells (formerly ONSI)

  FuelCell Energy (formerly Energy Research Corp.)

- Solid Oxide (SO)

  Acumentrics

  Ceramatec Advanced Ionic Technologies

  Ceramic Fuel Cells Ltd.

  Fuel Cell Technologies, Ltd.

  Global Thermoelectric, Inc.

  Hydrovolt

  Siemens Westinghouse Power Corporation

  ZTEK Corp.

FUEL OPTIONS

Transportation Applications

A key determinate of the future market for fuel cell power plants is the fuel required. A great deal of work is being done to develop small, economical reformers that convert gasoline to hydrogen, for use with automobile and truck applications. The thinking here is that it is best to use the existing vehicle refueling infrastructure: the nation's corner service stations with their gasoline tanks and pumps. Others are focusing on systems that can use methanol, which is also a liquid fuel that can be stored in tanks and pumped much the same way as gasoline is. The thinking is that it is a small step to add a methanol tank and pump at service stations. This was done with apparent ease when people started buying and using small portable kerosene heaters during the late 1970s, as a reaction to high energy prices and natural gas shortages that were then occurring. Research is also underway on ways to use hydrogen directly, either as a gas stored under high pressure or as a hydrate.

Stationary Power Applications

Those who plan to build and sell DG units for homes, commercial buildings, and other applications are focusing on systems that can be fueled with natural gas, propane, or fuel oil. The thinking is that natural gas is readily available in all but remote and rural locations, and the public is comfortable with using it. For rural applications, propane is the fuel of choice. Again, it is a commonly used and accepted fuel in those locations, and the distribution channels are already in place.

CONCLUDING REMARKS

One of the problems the developing fuel cell industry faces is that for more than five years its proponents have been saying an economical, commercialized product is only 3-5 years away—and they are still saying it. This time is it real? Only time will tell, but three reasons to be bullish are:

1. Considerable progress has been made during the past five years, and the rate of progress is accelerating.

2. A great deal of money is being spent to complete RD&D activities. Large companies with large financial and marketing capabilities are "in the game."

3. Some of the largest technical organizations in the world are involved, including the major global automobile manufactures, who know all there is to know about how to build complex devices that operate reliably, and to build them a cheaply as possible.

The potential market for fuel cell power plants is truly enormous, exceeding $100 billion. In fact, some proponents believe fuel cell power plants could largely replace large central-station plants by the year 2030. Before anyone can make such a prediction, however, a good deal of development work and testing to demonstrate that all design objectives are satisfied must take place. Also, the factories at which these power plants will be built in large numbers must themselves be built. Investments in mass-production tooling and in factories and will not happen until there is assurance that the product is ready and the mass market exists. On the other hand, such assurances could be available within a few years, and then things can move quickly. Look back at how quickly the automobile and the jet-engine use for aircraft became "mainstream technologies" after economic feasibility was demonstrated. Today, the infrastructure to support widespread fuel cell deployment already exists, which was not the case with those technologies.

Chapter 56

LESSONS LEARNED FROM
WORLD'S LARGEST FUEL CELL INSTALLATION:
CONNECTICUT JUVENILE TRAINING SCHOOL

James B. Redden, PE, President and Chief Operating Officer,
Select Energy Services, Inc.

ABSTRACT

This paper addresses the practical application of emerging distributed technology (fuel cells) in a real-life project constructed in Connecticut. Select Energy Services, Inc. (SES), formerly HEC Inc., has installed and is operating the world's largest commercial fuel cell installation. This 1.2-megawatt energy plant provides electricity, heating, and cooling for the state-of-the-art Connecticut Juvenile Training School (CJTS). The discussion chronicles the creative engineering and business solutions that overcame the obstacles faced by Connecticut State agencies in constructing this project, and how state government and private industry collaborated on this technically complex project.

INTRODUCTION

In 2000, the State of Connecticut undertook action to expand its juvenile detention facilities. At the time, the most appropriate site available for the facility was a large section of land located on the Connecticut State Hospital grounds. While the proposed construction site satisfied many of the project's criteria, it was also situated above an aquifer, subjecting any project to extensive environmental permitting and wetlands protection constraints. As part of the facility design, the State decided to supply heating, cooling, and electricity for the site from an "Energy Center," a central power plant located just outside the secured area, using buried pipes and cables to distribute the energy to each building on site. Once constructed, the Energy Center would provide all the heating, cooling, and electrical power needs for CJTS' 227,000 square feet of buildings on 35 acres, including residences, office buildings, and other campus facilities.

With this conceptual design in place, the project's construction and operation phases were offered for competitive bid to energy service companies. As part of its bid, SES offered a unique alternate. SES proposed to design, build, and maintain a freestanding Energy Center, delivering a guaranteed supply of "green power" through an innovative configuration of new technology—fuel cells—interconnected with the regional electric power grid and emergency generators for seamless system backup. Based on extensive life-cycle cost analysis and the environmental benefits related to using green power at the site, the fuel cell option was chosen. SES was selected to build the Energy Center and operate it for the next 30 years.

MAKING THE DEAL

In order to bring a project this unique to life, many parties had to contribute extensive time and effort in their areas of expertise. The State of Connecticut called on the Department of Public Works (DPW), the Department of Children and Family, the Department of Environmental Protection, the Department of the Treasurer, the Governor, and many others. The private sector called on energy services companies (ESCOs), engineers, lawyers, equipment manufacturers, and builders.

Two primary agreements were used to structure the deal: an engineering, procurement, and construction (EPC) contract, and an operations and maintenance (O&M) contract. The EPC contract addressed the

411

specifications, equipment capacities, schedules, terms, and other details relating to the Energy Center's engineering and construction. The O&M contract documented the duties, responsibilities, and requirements of the 30-year operating period.

The EPC contract was a fixed-price contract to construct the Energy Center. Equipment capacities and performance were specified and guaranteed by SES. For example, the fuel cells were required to meet a 1.2-megawatt electrical capacity test, the chillers had to produce 680 tons of cooling, and the boilers had to produce 9 million Btuh of hot water. Representing the State of Connecticut, the DPW maintained project oversight, approving all major equipment selections. The State's motto was "No change orders." SES met this challenge.

The O&M contract, which has a 20-year term with a 10-year renewal, covers staffing and operational responsibilities for the Energy Center. Chilled water, hot water, and electricity must be provided 24 hours per day, 7 days per week. Failure to provide these services would result in significant liquidated damages. To ensure that these services are reliably provided, the plant will be staffed with an operating crew to monitor the equipment and provide routine maintenance. The operator has full responsibility for repair or replacement of equipment.

The O&M contract also includes fuel purchasing for the plant. An innovative approach was devised whereby the State and SES meet annually to determine the gas purchase strategy to be used for the coming year. Based on input from the State's energy purchasing representative, annual or multi-year commodity purchases can be made. Increases and decreases in the unit cost of fuel are passed to the State.

FINANCING

The State chose to pay for the project over 30 years. SES financed the project through a combination of project financing and U.S. Department of Defense fuel-cell grants. The fuel-cell grants were obtained by SES in the amount of $200,000 per fuel cell and were used to buy down the price paid by the State. For the balance of the project cost, the State entered into a 30-year lease agreement with a limited liability company established by SES for the sole purpose of holding the lease for the energy center. Under the terms of the lease, the State makes fixed semi-annual payments and owns the plant at the end of the lease. SES raised

the money to build the energy center by selling tax-exempt certificates of participation (COPs) in the lease. Each certificate represents the right to a proportionate interest in the lease payments from the State. COPs may be traded and sold, and therefore are more marketable, typically carrying lower interest rates than a private placement of a project loan. In addition, Standard & Poors rated the COPS A+. Obtaining this rating required extensive discussions regarding fuel cell technology, the State's need for the facility (lease payments are subject to appropriations), and the structure of the transaction.

Attached to the lower tax-exempt interest rate were some strings. Connecticut's Department of the Treasurer spent considerable time on the transaction, prescribing terms of the transaction. In addition, under internal revenue rules, using tax-exempt financing for the energy center imposed limits on the operation and maintenance fees. SES worked within these requirements to preserve the economics of the transaction.

THE SCHEDULE

One of the project's biggest challenges was achieving construction schedule milestones. After SES was selected in June/July 2000, the first set of milestones focused on providing temporary electricity, chilled water, and hot water to the site. Since some school buildings had been under construction for several months, utilities were needed immediately to keep the construction schedule on track. SES project managers and electrical engineers designed and managed construction of a 13,200-volt temporary power line.

The line was energized within 2 weeks, preventing a possible slowdown of construction on the main facility. Chilled water was provided by August 1, a full 2 weeks ahead of schedule. Chilled water was required during construction to dehumidify the interior space to allow painting and other interior finish work to be completed on schedule. Later that year, in October, the temporary boilers were on site and started up to provide heat. There have been no outages or interruptions since these services started.

The next set of milestones involved installing and completing major components of the Energy Center. The building was constructed during the fall and winter of 2000; at the same time equipment vendors were filling orders for equipment with long lead times. Although the final Notice to Proceed was not issued until March 2001 due to contractual issues related to the financing, the Energy Center still retained a functional-use date of September 2001 with final completion by December 2001. The September date was met with power generated by all six fuel cells. Final completion is expected in December.

The State of Connecticut will confirm that SES exceeded expectations by meeting very aggressive deadlines during construction. Since the start of power production in July 2001, all services have remained on-line and available to meet the needs of the CJTS facility.

THE ENERGY CENTER

The Energy Center is a freestanding building located outside the high-security area of CJTS. It provides electricity, chilled water, and hot water to the entire campus through underground distribution. Physically, it is configured as follows:

Building and Site:
The building is approximately 4,000 square feet, housing all equipment and offices. Because it is outside of the secured area, the building has its own parking and admission area separate from CJTS. The fuel cells are located outside the main structure, as shown.

Electricity:
Providing reliable power is the most important mission of the Energy Center. To ensure reliability, the electric supply has three levels of redundancy: (1) the fuel cells, which are the primary power source; (2) backup power provided by the local utility; and (3) gas-fired emergency generators. Because there are six individual fuel cells, there is minimal chance of total equipment failure. If the fuel cells should malfunction, the local electric utility serves the facility with 13,200 volts from a relatively new line fed from a single substation and provided with state-of-the-art automatic reclosures. In the event of catastrophic failure, two 1,500 kW emergency generators are available to supply all the power needs of the facility for extended periods of time.

Chilled Water:
Chilled water is produced in the Energy Center and distributed to the facility. Over 1,000 tons of installed chilling capacity is available to serve a projected load of 680 tons. To maximize energy efficiency, an absorption chiller was installed to use waste heat from the fuel cells to capture "free cooling" when conditions permit. During the spring and fall, the absorption machine will provide most of the chilled water. During peak summer months, two centrifugal chillers will also produce chilled water. These chillers are equipped with variable-speed drives in order to track the load efficiently.

Hot Water:

In the course of normal operation, the fuel cells generate waste heat that can be used to heat the building during most periods. However, a fully redundant fire-tube boiler system was installed to ensure that heat is available under all circumstances. The building automated control system is designed to maximize waste heat use before drawing on the boilers.

Building Automated Control System:

A fully automated control system was installed to monitor and control the systems. This provides the system operator with information and scheduling inputs. Separate, integrated control systems operate the fuel cells and the rest of the mechanical systems.

FUEL CELL TECHNOLOGY TODAY

A fuel cell operates much like a battery: fuel cells produce power from chemical reactions rather than combustion, and thus do not produce air pollutants. However, unlike batteries, as long as a fuel is supplied to a fuel cell, it will continue to operate. Inside each fuel cell are 256 "cell stacks," which are stacked graphite plates containing phosphoric acid. Natural gas is processed through an external reformer, which converts it to hydrogen and carbon dioxide. By causing a chemical reaction between the hydrogen and the oxygen in the air, each fuel cell produces 200 kilowatts of electricity at 480 volts.

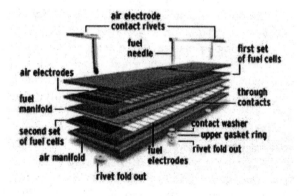

International Fuel Cells (IFC) is the largest company in the world devoted solely to fuel cells. IFC has manufactured more than 250 PC25 power plant systems (165 of which are the PC25C model installed at CJTS) that are installed in approximately 100 locations throughout the world. Installed PC25 commercial fuel cell power plant systems have accumulated more than 3 million hours of in-service operation.

LESSONS LEARNED

- Innovative approaches can bring unique projects to life
- Fuel cells are commercially available and can be used in suitable applications
- Long-term build/operate contracts can provide economic solutions to state needs
- Institutions need financially stable companies for these innovative projects
- Green power is still somewhat more expensive than commercially available alternatives
- The future is bright for the environment and for alternate power sources

REFERENCES

[1]Fuel cell illustration and details—Courtesy of International Fuel Cells

Author

James B. Redden, PE, is President of Select Energy Services, Inc. (SES), an unregulated subsidiary of Northeast Utilities Systems. Mr. Redden has over 25 years of progressive experience in energy services fields, including founding an energy services contracting firm in the late 1970s, providing project engineering on some of the world's largest buildings, providing project management on cogeneration projects, managing utility demand-side management programs, and profitably growing energy services businesses. His career has extensively involved project development and strategic planning. He has provided management and technical leadership on utility demand-side management programs, facility conservation programs, cogeneration systems, central plant improvements, fire safety upgrades, and diverse equipment retrofits at hundreds of facilities around the country. Active in professional societies, he has helped to promote energy efficiency as a career and an important part of today's energy mix. Mr. Redden earned his BS from Cornell University, College of Engineering.

James B. Redden, PE
President
Select Energy Services, Inc.
24 Prime Parkway
Natick, MA 01760
Phone: 508-653-0456
Fax: 508-653-0266
E-mail: jredden@hecenergy.com

Chapter 57

STEAM TURBINE VERSUS
PRESSURE REDUCING VALVE OPERATION

Greg Harrell, Ph.D., P.E.
Richard Jendrucko, Ph.D., P.E.
University of Tennessee

ABSTRACT

A question arising frequently in steam system design relates to the benefits and drawbacks associated with passing steam through a pressure reducing valve or a steam turbine to supply a low pressure steam demand. The most appropriate analysis of the economic benefits of operating the steam turbine utilizes an incremental systems approach.

A case study analysis based on a systems approach was used to demonstrate the role of incremental fuel and electricity costs, boiler and turbine efficiencies as well as steam flow and thermodynamic properties on the economic performance of the turbine-generator and pressure reducing valve options. An example analysis was performed for a boiler producing superheated steam at 600 psig and 800°F to supply a low pressure steam demand of 30,000 lbm/hr. Overall energy balances were computed for a turbine with an isentropic efficiency of 40%, a 90% efficient generator and an isenthalpic pressure-reducing valve as an alternative scheme. For a fuel unit cost of $3.00/$10^6$ Btu and an electricity unit cost of $0.035/kWh it is shown that 408 kW of electricity can be produced while supplying the steam demand. Use of the turbine-generator requires the total steam flow rate to increase to satisfy the process heating demand. The steam flow through the turbine would be 31,261 lbm/hr or about a 4% increase over the low pressure process base load. Assuming that the modest additional high-pressure steam demand can be met, a net purchased energy saving of $70,000/yr. could be realized. This analysis demonstrates that a substantial plant-purchased energy cost saving may be achieved for typical system operating conditions when a turbine-generator is used to produce low-pressure process steam rather than a pressure reducing valve.

BIOGRAPHIES

Greg Harrell

Dr. G. Harrell is a Senior Research Associate with the Energy, Environment and Resources Center at the University of Tennessee, Knoxville. He has worked as a design and utilities process engineer for BASF Corporation and he has served as the Director of Technical Assistance for the Energy Management Institute at Virginia Tech as well as an Assistant Mechanical Engineering Professor. Dr. Harrell has conducted many energy surveys for industrial clients worldwide. His current areas of specialization are industrial steam systems and compressed air systems.

Richard Jendrucko

Dr. Jendrucko is a Professor in the Department of Mechanical, Aerospace and Biomedical Engineering at the University of Tennessee, Knoxville. He has over twenty years experience in performing energy audits of industrial facilities under the University's Industrial Assessment Center Program. Dr. Jendrucko's professional publications include over 25 papers and presentations related to industrial energy conservation.

STEAM TURBINE VERSUS PRESSURE-REDUCING VALVE OPERATION

A question arising frequently in steam systems relates to the benefits and drawbacks associated with passing steam through a pressure reducing valve or a steam turbine to supply a low pressure steam demand. The most appropriate analysis of the economic benefits of operating the steam turbine utilizes an incremental systems approach. The information of primary importance to the analysis is:

- Incremental electric cost
- Incremental fuel cost
- Boiler efficiency
- Steam turbine efficiency (or the properties of steam entering and exiting the turbine)
- Steam flow rate (or process demand)

The term "incremental electric cost" relates to the rate structure or tariff applied to electrical purchases at a facility. In particular, the actual economic impact of any change in electrical consumption is the incremental cost. Many times the price of electricity is dependent on the amount of electricity consumed, the rate of electrical consumption as well as the time of use. Most electrical tariffs for industrial sites carry fixed charges, which do not change with respect to electrical consumption. A change in electrical demand will typically not incur the "average" electric cost for a facility but the "incremental" electric cost.

In order to compare the operation of a steam turbine to a pressure reducing valve an example is investigated. The example focuses on a boiler producing high pressure steam, which is operating in support of a site which demands low pressure steam and shaft power (or electricity). The investigation considers a facility capable of operating under two different scenarios. In the first operating scenario the system receives fuel to produce high pressure steam. The high pressure steam passes through a pressure reducing valve to supply the site's low pressure steam demand. Electricity is purchased to meet the site electrical power demand. In this scenario both fuel and electricity are purchased to support the activities of the site. In the second scenario fuel is also consumed to produce high pressure steam; this high pressure steam is passed through a steam turbine to produce shaft power. The turbine is connected to an electric power generator which supplies a portion of the site electrical demand. Low pressure steam is exhausted from the turbine and is utilized in site operations. In this scenario fuel is the only purchased utility for the site.

The example system consists of a boiler, a low pressure steam demand and a steam pressure reduction component (pressure reducing valve or turbine). The steam turbine drives an electric generator. Figure 1 is a simple schematic of the system.

The analysis procedure first determines the cost of fuel supplied to the facility when the pressure reducing valve is in operation. Electricity purchased during this operating mode is not considered until the amount of electricity produced through the turbine-generator set is determined in the second scenario. The second analysis scenario determines the cost of fuel supplied to the boiler when the turbine is operating and allows the electricity produced in the generator to reduce the total site electrical consumption.

One primary factor is held constant in the analysis; the thermal energy supplied to the low pressure steam demand. This is not to say the steam flow rate

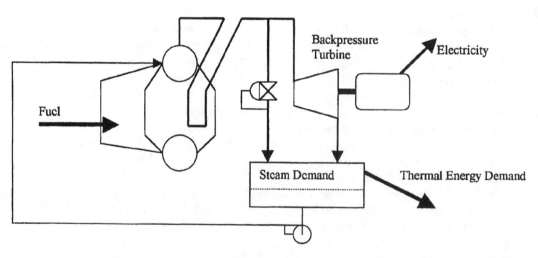

FIGURE 1

416

supplied to the steam demand is equal in both cases. In fact, the steam mass flow rate will change because the turbine converts some of the steam's thermal energy into shaft energy. Therefore, the steam exiting the turbine will have a reduced energy content when compared to the steam exiting the pressure reducing valve. As a result, when the turbine is operating the mass flow rate of steam must increase to supply the same thermal energy to the steam demand. This additional steam flow is provided by the boiler, which requires additional fuel.

EXAMPLE

In the example scenarios high pressure steam is produced in the boiler and is supplied to the pressure reducing valve or the steam turbine. Steam exhausted from these components is supplied to the low pressure user. For the example analysis the fuel unit price is $3.00/10^6 Btu and the electrical unit cost is $0.035/kWh. High pressure steam conditions for this example are 600 psig and 800°F at the boiler outlet. The turbine and pressure reducing valve export steam at 200 psig. Condensate is discharged from the steam user and is returned to the system at 0 psig and saturated liquid conditions. This is a simplified analysis; however, the main operational and economic factors are incorporated. In other words, this analysis accurately represents the economics associated with a typical steam system.

The example analysis provided here does not attempt to explain electric rate structures but merely utilizes a fixed electric cost for simplicity. This may not reflect the actual conditions at a given site. Similarly, fuel unit price is a fixed value in the example. Care should be exercised to accurately incorporate the appropriate fuel and electric costs for a given facility.

The example begins with the pressure reducing valve in operation and a low pressure steam demand of 30,000 lbm/hr. This steam flow corresponds to the steam flow exiting the boiler as well. The cost of fuel supplied to the boiler, K_{fuel}, is determined by Equation 1.

$$K_{fuel} = \kappa_{fuel} \frac{m_{steam}\left(h_{steam} \pm h_{feedwater}\right)}{\eta_{boiler}} T$$

EQUATION 1

Where, h_{steam} and $h_{feedwater}$ are the enthalpy values of steam exiting the boiler and feedwater entering the boiler, respectively. These properties can be found in thermodynamic property tables for the given fluid conditions. Boiler efficiency, η_{boiler}, is the first law of thermodynamics efficiency of the boiler; also known as the fuel to steam energy conversion efficiency of the boiler. For the example boiler, efficiency is taken as 85%. Fuel Cost, κ_{fuel}, and operating period, T, are incorporated in the calculation to allow the fuel consumption of the boiler to be represented as an operating cost. In this example the period of operation is taken as 90% of a year (7,884 hrs/yr). The steam mass flow rate from the boiler is represented as m_{steam}. The operating cost of this system is calculated below.

The amount of thermal energy, Q, supplied to the low pressure steam demand is determined by Equation 3. Equation 3 is a representation of the first law of thermodynamics applied to the steam demand.

$$K_{fuel} = \kappa_{fuel} \frac{m_{steam}\left(h_{steam} \pm h_{feedwater}\right)}{\eta_{boiler}} T$$

$$K_{fuel} = 3.00 \frac{\$}{10^6 Btu} \left(\frac{30,000\frac{lbm}{hr}\left(1,407.01\frac{Btu}{lbm} \pm 180.07\frac{Btu}{lbm}\right)}{0.85} \right) 7,884\frac{hrs}{yr}$$

$$K_{fuel} = 1,024,220\frac{\$}{yr}$$

EQUATION 2

$$Q = m_{\text{steam}}\left(h_{\text{PRV steam}} \pm h_{\text{condensate}}\right)$$

$$= 30{,}000\frac{\text{lbm}}{\text{hr}}\left(1{,}407.01\frac{\text{Btu}}{\text{lbm}} \pm 180.07\frac{\text{Btu}}{\text{lbm}}\right)$$

$$= 36{,}808{,}200\frac{\text{Btu}}{\text{hr}}$$

EQUATION 3

The energy (enthalpy flow) required by the steam demand is held constant for each analysis scenario. An important point to note is the fact that the steam exiting the pressure reducing valve has the same enthalpy content as the steam entering the valve. The pressure reducing valve is a classic throttling process when heat transfer to the surroundings is negligible, which is most often the case. Therefore, the valve is an isenthalpic (constant enthalpy) process. The isenthalpic process results in steam exiting the pressure reducing valve with a temperature of 7677. Recall the steam entering the valve had a temperature of 800°F.

The second scenario begins with the selection of a steam turbine or at least identification of the operating characteristics of the turbine. Steam turbine efficiency is an important parameter in the analysis of the economics of this type of system. Typically, steam turbine performance is defined by "isentropic efficiency." Isentropic efficiency is a comparison of the actual shaft power export of the turbine to that of an ideal, isentropic (or perfect) turbine. The equation for isentropic efficiency of a turbine is provided below.

Where h_{inlet} designates the enthalpy of the steam entering the turbine and h_{exit} designates the enthalpy of the steam exiting the turbine. The designation "actual" expresses the given turbine's operating conditions; in other words, the conditions of a real turbine operating in the steam system. The designation "isentropic" references perfect turbine operation. Equation 4 has been developed assuming kinetic and potential

energy changes are negligible and heat transfer is negligible for the turbine. These are good assumptions for typical steam turbines. Isentropic exit conditions are determined from thermodynamic property references. Isentropic exit conditions are assumed to occur at the same exhaust pressure as the actual turbine operation. The term "isentropic" denotes "constant entropy." Therefore, if the inlet conditions are known (inlet entropy), the isentropic exit entropy is known. Thermodynamic properties can be obtained for the isentropic exit conditions knowing the exit pressure and entropy values.

Isentropic work is the maximum theoretical work output of the turbine, which is the output of a perfect turbine. Isentropic efficiency is typically expressed (as most efficiencies are) as a percentage. Industrial steam turbine isentropic efficiencies range from less than 20% to over 80%, which is an exceptionally broad efficiency range. Isentropic efficiency has a significant effect on the economic evaluation of a steam turbine system. Therefore, actual turbine data or manufacturer's data should be utilized to improve the accuracy of the analysis.

The steam turbine utilized in the example analysis operates with an isentropic efficiency of 40%. This is typical for small industrial steam turbines. Equation 4 will be utilized to determine the exhaust conditions of the turbine.

Alternately, if the steam turbine exhaust conditions are known, then an evaluation of isentropic efficiency is not required. The measurements required to determine turbine exhaust conditions are steam temperature and pressure. These values are the only required measurements if the steam exiting the turbine is superheated. If the steam exiting the turbine is saturated the evaluation is more difficult requiring the use of a throttling calorimeter, which is a special measuring device for saturated steam. The example

$$\eta_{\text{isentropic}} = \frac{\text{Actual Work}}{\text{Isentropic Work}} = \frac{W_{\text{actual}}}{W_{\text{isentropic}}}$$

$$= \frac{m_{\text{steam}}\left(h_{\text{inlet}} \pm h_{\text{exit}}\right)_{\text{actual}}}{m_{\text{steam}}\left(h_{\text{inlet}} \pm h_{\text{exit}}\right)_{\text{isentropic}}} = \frac{\left(h_{\text{inlet}} \pm h_{\text{exit}}\right)_{\text{actual}}}{\left(h_{\text{inlet}} \pm h_{\text{exit}}\right)_{\text{isentropic}}}$$

EQUATION 4

$$\eta_{\text{isentropic}} = \frac{\left(h_{\text{inlet}} \pm h_{\text{exit}}\right)_{\text{actual}}}{\left(h_{\text{inlet}} \pm h_{\text{exit}}\right)_{\text{isentropic}}}$$

$$0.40 = \frac{1{,}407.01\frac{\text{Btu}}{\text{lbm}} \pm h_{\text{exit actual}}}{1{,}407.01\frac{\text{Btu}}{\text{lbm}} \pm 1{,}283.31\frac{\text{Btu}}{\text{lbm}}}$$

$$h_{\text{exit actual}} = 1{,}357.53\frac{\text{Btu}}{\text{lbm}}$$

EQUATION 5

turbine would be discharging 670°F superheated steam with a pressure of 200 psig.

Once the steam turbine exit enthalpy value is known it is used to determine the steam flow through the turbine required to satisfy the thermal demand of the system. A variation of Equation 3 is utilized in this evaluation.

$$Q = M_{steam} (h_{turbine\ exit\ steam} - h_{condensate})$$

$$36,808,200 \frac{Btu}{lbm} = m_{steam} \left(1,357.53\frac{Btu}{lbm} \pm 180.07\frac{Btu}{lbm}\right)$$

$$m_{steam} = 31,261\frac{Btu}{lbm}$$

EQUATION 6

This is the steam flow passing through the turbine; it is also the steam production of the boiler. Therefore, Equation 1 can be utilized to determine the operating cost of the boiler.

Fuel consumption increases when the turbine is operated. The increase in fuel consumption is seen by comparing Equation 7 and Equation 2. In other words, fuel consumption increases \$43,050/yr.

In order to determine the amount of electrical power produced from the steam turbine generator the first law of thermodynamics must be applied to the turbine. The shaft power exported from the turbine (W_{shaft}) is determined by the following equation.

$$W_{shaft} = m_{steam} (h_{inlet} - h_{exit})_{actual}$$

$$W_{shaft} = 31,261\frac{lbm}{hr}\left(1,407.01\frac{Btu}{lbm} \pm 1357.53\frac{Btu}{lbm}\right)$$

$$= 1,546,794\frac{Btu}{hr}\left(\frac{1\ kW}{3,413\ Btu}\right) = 453\ kW$$

EQUATION 8

Equation 8 is an expression of the shaft power exported from the steam turbine. If the shaft power is converted into electrical energy then generator efficiency must be incorporated. Electric generator efficiency is an expression of the ratio of electrical power export to shaft power input to the generator and will generally be greater than 80%. In this example the generator is assumed to operate with 90% efficiency.

$$W_{electricity} = W_{shaft} (\eta_{generator}) = 453\ kW\ (0.90) = 408\ kW$$

EQUATION 9

The electrical power export represents a savings to the site because the amount of electrical power generated reduces the amount of electricity required to be purchased. The generated electricity savings is calculated below.

$$K_{elec} = \kappa_{elec} W_{elec} T$$

$$K_{elec} = 0.035\frac{\$}{kWh}\left(408\ kW\right) 7,884\frac{hrs}{yr}$$

$$K_{elec} = 112,580\frac{\$}{yr}$$

EQUATION 10

$$K_{fuel} = \kappa_{fuel}\frac{m_{steam}\left(h_{steam} \pm h_{feedwater}\right)}{\eta_{boiler}} T$$

$$K_{fuel} = 3.00\frac{\$}{10^6 Btu}\left(\frac{31,261\frac{lbm}{hr}\left(1,407.01\frac{Btu}{lbm} \pm 180.07\frac{Btu}{lbm}\right)}{0.85}\right)7,884\frac{hrs}{yr}$$

$$K_{fuel} = 1,067,270\frac{\$}{yr}$$

EQUATION 7

Many times the electric power savings ($112,580/yr) is reported as the potential savings associated with operating the steam turbine because this is the avoided electrical purchase. However, recall the fact that fuel consumption increased to maintain the thermal energy supply to the site. This resulted in an increased fuel consumption of $43,050/yr. Therefore, the actual savings potential is $69,530/yr or approximately $70,000/yr.

Many systems incorporate desuperheaters to control the temperature of the low pressure steam exported from pressure reducing stations and steam turbines. An analysis of a system including a desuperheater is fundamentally the same as presented here; the difference is the obvious requirement to incorporate the operation of the desuperheater. Because the desuperheater controls steam temperature the steam flow supplied to the steam demand would be the same for both scenarios. The amount of desuperheater water will change based on turbine operation or pressure reducing valve operation.

In summary, the principal analysis parameters are the incremental cost of fuel and electricity, the efficiency of the boiler and the efficiency of the turbine (or steam properties). Steam flow will not be the same through the turbine and the pressure reducing valve. This has a significant effect on the analysis results.

Section 5
Renewal Energy Technology

Chapter 58

SOLAR ELECTRIC TECHNOLOGIES AND APPLICATIONS

Tara Willey
Steve Hester
The Solar Electric Power Association
Washington, DC

ABSTRACT

Solar electric power or photovoltaics (PV) utilize sunlight to produce electricity. PV cells are connected to create modules that, along with the balance of system, comprise a PV system. The electrical output of a PV system is determined by using design models, or measuring actual performance over a period of time. PV is a versatile, modular technology that can be adapted for almost any application, including residential and commercial applications, using a variety of business strategies. The costs of PV have decreased for large applications, however for smaller systems the costs remain unstable. Costs are only one of the barriers to commercialization, others include interconnection, an uneducated market, and technology reliability issues. SEPA's Solar Power Solutions program has been designed to address these and other barriers.

INTRODUCTION

In 1992 the Solar Electric Power Association (SEPA) was formed to bridge the gap between energy service providers and the PV industry. During the ten years of its existence SEPA has developed unique knowledge of PV based on the Association's relationship with both the energy service and PV industries. The six year long Technology Experience to Accelerate Markets in Utility Photovoltaics (TEAM-UP) program, and now, Solar Power Solutions (SPS) have provided an opportunity for SEPA to study a wide range of PV technologies and applications.

SOLAR ELECTRIC POWER OR PV BACKGROUND INFORMATION

Solar electric power or photovoltaic cells utilize solid-state technology to produce electric energy directly from the sun. Cells are wired together and laminated in a sealed package called a module, which can be mounted on a roof, packaged into roofing or other building products, or installed on the ground. The solar electric power is produced as direct current, or dc power. PV modules are usually measured in kW, and come with a nameplate rating in kW STC (Standard Test Conditions). An alternating current (AC) power rating in kW PTC (PVUSA Test Conditions) gives a closer estimate to the actual system output.

Since utility grid systems operate on alternating current, or ac power, grid-connected applications of photovoltaic modules require an inverter to convert the dc output to ac power. These inverters also provide intelligence to disconnect the PV module from the grid when the grid is de-energized. Solar electric systems designed to operate independently when the grid is "down" require energy storage, typically in the form of a battery, similar to a car battery.

Solar electric power systems, therefore, can have different requirements, can utilize different types of solar modules and, indeed, can be mounted in a variety of building and on-ground environments. Further, they can provide different and varying amounts of benefits to the consumer or building owner and local utility or other energy service company, depending upon the characteristics of the installation and the local electric service. Thus is born an environment whereby the development of useful, profitable business models is of interest to those whose mission is making solar electric service a mainstream energy choice.[1]

AVAILABLE TECHNOLOGIES

There are a number of different technologies available, each varying in cost and efficiency. A few examples of the available technologies are listed in Table 1.

TABLE 1. PHOTOVOLTAIC TECHNOLOGIES[2]

Single-crystal silicon with its high efficiency, is the technology of choice for telecommunications and other industrial applications, where "best performance" is a criterion.
Multi-crystalline or polycrystalline silicon is a prevalent technology for rooftop applications, where there are some space limitations - hence relevance of efficiency - but also price sensitivity. Similar technologies developed with new manufacturing processes include "ribbon" or "sheet" silicon.
Amorphous silicon (a-Si) is a thin film technology, and tends to have lower efficiency than crystalline silicone but also tends to have a lower cost per peak watt. It has been the technology of choice for small demand consumer products, such as watches and calculators, and for applications requiring performance under low-light conditions or partial shading.
Thin-film technologies such as cadmium telluride (CdTe), and copper indium diselenide (CIS) are valid for many of the same applications as amorphous silicon. Some environmental concerns exist about the materials used in their manufacture.
Concentrator PV may use a number of technologies; a small area of cells receives sunlight under high concentration. Concentrator PV is most effective where sunlight is intense, direct, and rarely interrupted, and so is well suited to geographic areas such as the Desert Southwest.
Multi-junction cells include emerging technologies such as gallium arsenide and gallium indium phosphide. These cells show high conversion efficiency either under concentration or normal sunlight, and are a promising technology for the future.

---

[1] *TEAM-UP - Business Models Report* pg. vi
[2] *Solar Power Solutions: A Business Case for Capturing Total Value* pg. 9

Dye-sensitized solar cells include a number of emerging technologies such as the TiO2- based Gratzel cells and new developments such as self-assembling organic PV layers.

PV SYSTEM COMPONENTS

The PV modules are only one component of the entire system. The other components are the inverter, mounting system, and wiring, etc.

The inverter converts the direct current produced by the PV modules to alternating current to either power the home/ building it is associated with or is directly fed into the utility grid. The inverter is generally acknowledged to be the weak point in the PV system, and is the most frequent cause for failures and malfunctions. The inverter industry has been making progress to correct that, and inverters are becoming increasingly more reliable.

Most PV systems are ground mounted or roof mounted, and both have advantages and disadvantages associated with them. Ground mounted PV systems can take up considerable amounts of space, and there is a potential for vandalism or theft and the system can pose a safety hazard. Ground mounted systems can be stationary, one axis tracking, or two axis tracking systems. Tracking systems have a greater power output, but generally have a higher initial cost and may require additional maintenance.

Roof mounted systems take advantage of unused roof space, however, there is a risk of compromising the roof's integrity by installing PV systems that penetrate the roof. This may invalidate the roof's warranty and may cause leaking. Structure and foundation costs can be minimized with roof mounted PV systems. The roofing structure's orientation, roof shape and shading may cause the PV system to perform below the expected rating.

PV SYSTEM RATINGS

In the final analysis, what customers most want to know is the level of energy production they can expect, which, in turn, depends not only on the system characteristics but also on the weather at the specific site, a variable which can be enormously inconsistent.

To determine actual AC ratings the system output must be measured under real operating conditions (which vary with time). There are some design models that will also give accurate estimates of the system's output. That data is used to calculate a rating for each system. Data acquisition systems can be used to provide measured data points for AC output, plane of array irradiance, ambient temperature, and wind speed. These data points can be used to estimate the rating, using a mathematical regression with the following equation:

$$X = A*Irr + B*Irr^2 + C*Irr*T_{amb} + D*Irr*WS^3$$

where: X = system output power, kWac;
Irr = irradiance, W/m^2;
T_{amb} = ambient air temperature, degrees C;
WS = wind speed, m/s.

PV APPLICATIONS

One advantage PV has over many renewable energy technologies is its versatility; the systems are modular and can be adapted to almost any shape or size, and can be sited close or at the intended electrical load. There are several applications for PV, including residential, commercial, and utility scale. The various technologies can be used to develop the ideal PV system for a specific application. Each application has advantages and disadvantages, which will be discussed in the "Barriers to Solar Electric Power" section.

Residential PV systems are usually roof-mounted and less than 5kW. These systems, due to their smaller size, generally have a higher cost/watt than larger systems because the balance of system (BOS) costs are somewhat independent of size. Reliability and maintenance are also challenges that face residential systems. The smaller inverters used for residential systems are often the most unreliable portion of the system, and without a some form of monitoring it is difficult to determine if their system is operating correctly.

Large commercial and utility-scale PV systems are usually more cost effective than residential systems. Systems over 70kW have shown a decrease in costs since 1996[4]. Commercial systems and utility-scale systems tend to be larger than residential systems, however their size varies considerably. Data acquisition systems are important for large systems because

a loss of power equates to a loss of money; generally accounted for as savings on an electric bill.

Recently there has been a movement toward utilizing building integrated photovoltaics (BIPV). BIPV can be incorporated into the design of a new building or added on to an existing building. When a building is designed with the PV system in mind PV system performance can be optimized.

PV MARKETS AND BUSINESS MODELS

Through working with its members and with the TEAM-UP and SPS programs SEPA has identified a number of sustainable, replicable business models that can be used to move PV into mainstream energy markets. SEPA has identified the following widely used business strategies:

TABLE 2. BUSINESS STRATEGIES[5]

The Community-Based Model involves a public-private partnership between community groups, local businesses, local utilities, local government, and others. Community involvement and support can help to resolve problems and address barriers to implementation by strengthening the local infrastructure.
Green Pricing programs create special energy products or mixes for which customers pay a premium on their electric bills to support "green" electricity. Green pricing can refer to wind, biomass, and other generation resources.
Schools and Public Buildings that utilize photovoltaics help to increase the visibility of solar and raise community awareness of solar. Schools and, to a lesser degree, public buildings with PV systems provide an excellent educational opportunity for students and the community to learn about energy, the environment, and related issues. In addition to the educational benefits, schools usually have flat roofs ideal for PV systems, and their peak demand coincides with the peak output of PV systems.
Dealership Networks consist of multiple strategic alliances with distributors who market and sell similar products. Distributors are local or national businesses that earn their revenues and profit from the product sales and

---

[3] *TEAM-UP - Performance Data Report*
[4] *TEAM-UP - Large Scale Cost Report*

[5] *TEAM-UP - Business Models Report*

the labor sold for installation and maintenance. This model is expanding to include homebuilders and developers who are partnering with the PV industry and energy service providers to build new homes with PV systems incorporated into the design.

Utility Partnerships use the strengths of the local utility to promote PV. Utilities can augment the technical knowledge of the venture by bringing additional resources and customer credibility. By pooling their resources, all partners benefit. Utilities are judged by some to be the key to taking PV into the mainstream with the lowest marketing and financing costs.

PV SYSTEM COSTS
From 1995 through 2000 SEPA collected detailed cost data on the 1100 systems installed as part of the TEAM-UP program. This data showed that large-scale systems (systems over 70kW) had the lowest costs on a dollar per watt basis, and that costs for these systems decreased steadily over time. Costs for residential systems remained relatively stable.

Large Systems
Cost data were collected from 23 PV systems with a generating capacity of 70kW to over 400kW. System costs ranged from a low of US$5.31/W to a high of US$11.82/W. Large PV systems differ in many ways, which posed some difficulty when comparing system costs. For example, single-axis tracking systems require tracker mechanisms and installation, while roof-mounted systems may require cranes and expensive roof modifications. The availability of state tax credits or incentives, site-specific installation and interconnection requirements, and varying labor costs may all have significant effects on total project cost.

As shown in Figure 1, system costs decreased from 1996 to 2000, with the exception of the year 1999. The increase in 1999 was most likely caused by an increased demand for PV systems. Several systems completed in 1998 and 2000 were installed by experienced project leaders, partially explaining the steep decline in costs in 1998 and 2000.

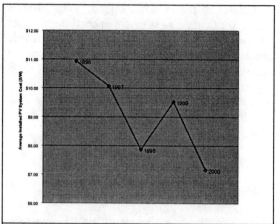

FIGURE 1: AVERAGE INSTALLED COST FOR LARGE SCALE SYSTEMS VS. INSTALLATION YEAR

Several factors contributed to decreasing cost trends. Module costs declined by year, with the exception of 1999; project leaders learned to reduce costs as they gained experience; long term contracts ensured stable prices; and installation experience lead to system ratings at or near the expected level. However, module cost data indicates that they were the largest factor in the overall cost reductions from 1996 to 2000.

Residential Systems
Over 600 residential PV systems were installed as part of the TEAM-UP program from 1995 to 2000. The data collected from these systems shows that the installed cost of small PV systems continues to be unpredictable.

Early in the TEAM-UP program the residential systems installed were large, customized systems. By the later years of the program (1999 and 2000) the majority of the systems installed were 1.5kW or less, and many were standardized packages. Many of these later year systems were AC modules with ratings of 500 watts or less. As standardized systems are developed costs will stabilize, and installation will become easier.

Figure 2 illustrates the cost per watt for residential systems when organized by size. As is expected, system costs are notably higher per kilowatt for systems less than 1.5 kilowatts (AC) in size. The total installed cost for systems larger than 1.5 kilowatts are relatively stable. Smaller systems must incorporate installation and overhead expenses, increasing the cost per watt. Also, many of the smaller systems are AC modules that have a relatively higher cost due to being a relatively new technology.[6]

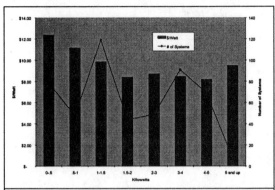

FIGURE 2: RESIDENTIAL SYSTEM COSTS AND NUMBER OF INSTALLATIONS BY KW

BARRIERS

Despite the advances that the PV industry has made over the years, a number of barriers still exist. The primary obstacle to market penetration is the high initial cost of the systems. Currently there are various federal, state, and local programs available to help bring down the cost of solar. The key to market penetration is increased demand, which is needed to enable manufacturers to expand factories and implement new manufacturing processes. This will lead to economies of production, and reduced costs.

The technology has made significant improvements in efficiency and reliability, however these issues remain an obstacle for the industry. As some manufacturers move to standardized systems, many of the problems are being resolved. However, inverters remain the weak element of the system, and the systems still require frequent maintenance. One problem that consumers encounter is that it is difficult for the average person to determine if their PV system is operating properly. This results in a loss of potential electricity generation. The alternative to this is to install a monitoring system, however for small PV systems this can be very expensive.

When compared with traditional electricity production, solar is prohibitively expensive. However, the true value of solar is difficult to define, and is dependent on perspective. Many consumers lack basic knowledge about solar and even if they have that information, they may not know where or how to procure a solar electric system. Educating the consumer on both the values and the industry are critical to market penetration.

Many areas are developing a strong local infrastructure to support the needs of the PV industry. This development is critical to providing installation and maintenance support to large- and small- scale consumers. There has been significant progress strengthening the local infrastructure in some areas, but the majority of the US lacks the local support for the PV industry that is necessary to advance commercialization.

Energy service providers can be both the key and a barrier to the advancement of solar technology. While ESPs often have available capital to finance large projects, they may lack basic PV technology knowledge. The interconnection of solar to the electricity grid is often technically and financially difficult. ESPs are in a position to make interconnection very easy or prohibitively difficult and expensive. Several ESPs have mechanisms in place for easy interconnection, however the majority does not. Net metering compensates the owner of a PV system for the excess electricity that the system produces and feeds back into the utility grid. This is another issue that faces the PV industry and directly involves ESPs. A number of states and ESPs have developed net-metering policies, but these are not uniform.[7]

SOLAR POWER SOLUTIONS

The Solar Electric Power Association, with funding from the U.S. Department of Energy has developed Solar Power Solution (SPS), a program designed to address the barriers to commercialization and market penetration. SPS has two components, a report entitled *Solar Power Solutions: A Business Case for Capturing Total Value*, and funding awards for two "showcase projects". The report, available on SEPA's website www.SolarElectricPower.org, analyzes the past, present, and future of the solar industry; identifies the barriers to commercialization; and offers recommendations on how to overcome those barriers. The showcase projects were selected because their programs are innovative examples of ways to accelerate the solar market. More information

---

[6] *TEAM-UP Residential Cost Report*

[7] *Solar Power Solutions: A Business Case for Capturing Total Value*

on SPS and the showcase projects is also available on SEPA's website.

CONCLUSIONS

Photovoltaic technologies are advancing, and fill a unique niche in the energy market. Because PV can be adapted for any need or size, whether residential or commercial, it has an important advantage over other renewable technologies. Through TEAM-UP and SPS several market strategies have been identified that have lead successful business ventures. Costs have been stabilizing, and for some applications costs are decreasing. ESPs and the PV industry have progressed toward making PV a more mainstream technology. ESPs are working with a variety of stakeholders to develop interconnection and net metering policies, and the PV industry has made improvements in efficiency and reliability. While there are still a number of barriers to commercialization, PV is rapidly advancing toward that goal.

REFERENCES

[1] *TEAM-UP - Business Models Report* - Solar Electric Power Association, 2001

[2] *Solar Power Solutions: A Business Case for Capturing Total Value* - Solar Electric Power Association, 2002

[3] *TEAM-UP - Performance Data Report* - Solar Electric Power Association, 2001

[4] *TEAM-UP - Large Scale Cost Report* - Solar Electric Power Association, 2001

[6] *TEAM-UP Residential Cost Report* - Solar Electric Power Association, 2001

Chapter 59

SOLAR HEATING FOR EMERGENCY DIESEL GENERATORS

John P. Archibald
American Solar, Inc.
8703 Chippendale Court
Annandale, VA 22003-3807

Abstract

Emergency diesel generators use large amounts of electric resistance heat to keep the engines warm and ready to start, all year. The annual electric use for mid sized generators (150KW - 1,000 KW) in outdoor enclosures can be 10,000 to 30,000 kwhr in mild climates with 4,000 heating degree days (65 F base). With over 600,000 emergency diesel generators installed in the US, standby electric heating consumes an estimated 6 billion kilowatt hours and $360 million per year.

The electricity is consumed to heat the jacket water of the engine by means of an electric resistance cartridge heater. The heaters deliver 130 degree F water to the engine. An alternative to electric heating of the jacket water, is to solar heat the air in the enclosure up to 110 F. This reduces the heat loss from the engine and therefore reduces the electricity consumption of the electric resistance heater.

The paper describes the opportunity to solar heat emergency generators. The design and construction of three systems for the US Geological Survey in Reston, VA is described.

Introduction

Emergency diesel generators (EDGs) are designed to provide electric power for buildings and processes when normal utility service is interrupted. The generators provide power for operation of critical equipment, building systems important to life and safety of the occupants, and high value services such as telecommunications and utility pumping stations. Many generators are installed outdoors in metal enclosures. The enclosures are typically no more than ventilated rain shelters which cover the engine, generator, and controls

To start the generator, the diesel engines rely on the compression of air in the cylinders. The compression generates enough heat to cause combustion of the injected fuel. If the engine is cold, combustion may not occur or it may occur unevenly across all cylinders. Failed starting or rough starting causes stress on engines and wear on internal components. After starting, most engines warmed up before the electric load is applied. In many cases, the engines may be loaded as quickly as they reach operating speed. Loading the engine before it reaches

its normal operating temperature adds stress to the bearing components.

Most diesel generators are fitted with electric heaters, to ensure that the engines will start in cold operating conditions,. Typically, these heaters are electric resistance cartridge heaters. The heaters are connected to the cooling water (jacket water) circuit that surrounds the cylinders of the engine. For large engines, (>1,500 KW) the cooling/heating fluid may be pumped through the engine. For smaller and most mid sized engines, the heater is usually set up in a convection loop. Heating of the jacket water in the cartridge heater causes it to rise up in the fluid loop and flow up through the engine. Within the engine, this warm water flows through the cylinder jackets where it cools slightly. It then sinks back to a pipe connected near the bottom of the engine, and back to the cartridge heater.

The heaters are typically set to maintain 130 degree F water temperature exiting the heater. Water returning from the engine is about 10 degrees cooler than the water leaving the heater. The onset of boiling can often be heard within the cartridge, when the heaters operate. This is typical in cartridges that are undersized for the heating loads experiences.

There appears to be no standard practice followed in sizing and arranging the heaters. Several different settings and arrangements can be observed. A water temperature of 170F leaving the heater was noted at one EDG on a military base. Several cartridge heaters have been observed to be oriented with the long axis horizontal instead of vertical. This severely reduces the convective flow forces in the cartridge. Often heaters are inoperative through neglect or failure of the system.

The heaters are generally sized at about 1 KW of heater capacity for each 100 KW of engine capacity. The energy use varies as ambient temperatures change. Heaters may only operate at rated capacity during the coldest winter conditions. However, the electricity use during warm summer conditions or in heated mechanical rooms, can still be quite high.

Even with properly installed heaters, the engine is not evenly heated. Typically, the engine "block" will show varying temperatures, increasing from bottom to top, with the bottom of the engine near floor temperatures and the top at 80 to 90 F. Similarly, the engine temperature decreases rapidly with increasing horizontal distance from the supply and return lines of the heater. The mass of fluids in the radiator and lube oil sump are often not heated. During a start cycle, these fluids must be heated along with other engine components before the engine reaches operating temperatures that are adequate to impose the electric load of the generator on the engine.

An additional benefit of the heaters is that they reduce condensation and corrosion on and inside the engine. The daily temperature swings experienced in outdoor enclosures would result in condensation on the cold metal parts when humid morning air is above the dew point temperature of the slower warming engine. By maintaining the engine at slightly above the ambient temperature, the heaters help to minimize this condensation.

Finally, there is no consistent construction to the enclosures housing the generators. The most typical construction appears to be the fully ventilated enclosure. This type of enclosure is built of sheet metal panels with open louvers on the sides and one end and a radiator exhaust grill on the opposite end. Air enters through the open louvers for combustion and engine cooling during engine operation. When the generator is shut down, in a standby mode, the air in the enclosure moves freely out of the enclosure as wind or thermal currents occur.

A second type of enclosure is the well insulated enclosure. These enclosures usually have perforated metal sheathing covering sound dampening fiberglass insulation in the walls. Motorized or spring actuated shutters cover air exhaust and intake louvers. The engine heating helps maintain the air temperature inside the enclosure higher than the outside air temperature. These enclosures are noticeably warmer and drier than fully ventilated enclosures.

ALTERNATIVE HEATING METHODS
There are many ways to reduce the need for electric resistance heating. Some methods involve the displacement of utility supplied electricity with another form of energy. These methods include: use of heat pumps for water heating, solar water heating, improved enclosure insulation, and solar electricity to supply the resistance heaters. One obvious approach would be to substitute one form of energy for electricity at the point of energy use in the heater. However, these individual alternatives generally solve only one of the several problems with the current heating system. These solutions may also add other problems in terms of complexity, cost, and administrative issues.

When the airflow requirements force the installation of shutters and controls and secure attachment of batts and blankets in tight enclosures, insulation becomes expensive. Air to water heat pumps for jacket water heating can reduce loads during warm days and nights, but they revert to electric resistance heating when temperatures drop below about 38 degrees. Solar electricity from photovoltaics can power the existing heaters, but is not likely to be cost effective for another decade when compared to these grid connected applications. Solar water heating is technically feasible. However, the high supply and return temperatures reduce the efficiency of the solar water heating systems compared to their more typical use in residential water pre-heating systems. Evacuated tube solar collector systems can provide the high temperatures with high efficiency. However, they are not generally capable of disconnecting from the load under full sun conditions when the generator is running. In addition, all these systems that only heat the jacket water, do not solve the problem of continuing heat loss to the enclosed space. Furthermore, problems such as high systems temperatures and pressures, the administrative issues such as manufacturer approved connections and controls for the generators (heat pumps, PV systems), and compatible fluids (solar water heating) raise difficult challenges for most of the obvious alternatives.

A less obvious approach to reduce the heat loss from the electrically heated engine is to use solar air heating within the enclosure. In this approach, the solar air heating system does not recognize the electric heater as the problem. Instead it addresses the problem of the loss of heat from the engine. Instead of substituting solar heat in the water for electric heat, the solar air heating systems substitutes a thermal blanket of air around the engine. This warm solar heated air eliminates the conduction and radiation of heat from the engine. The approach used, floods the enclosure with air that is solar heated up to 110 F. The solar heated air envelopes the engine and generator. It also heats the interior of the enclosure structure and operating fluids with warm air. In this warmer environment, the generator will give up less heat to the surrounding air by reduced conduction and radiation to the surrounding enclosure surfaces. Even though the electric jacket water heater continues to deliver 130F heat to the engine, the engine loses far less of this heat. The jacket water returning to the heater is at a higher temperature and requires less energy for reheating by the electric heater.

There is a much wider range of benefits with this approach. There are also fewer drawbacks than with the alternative heating systems listed above. The advantages are listed below:

1.   The primary heating system remains the reliable existing jacket water heating system. It is capable of handling 100% of the heating load and raising jacket water temperature from the ambient temperature to 130F.

2.   No new fluids or materials are brought in contact with the engine by the introduction of the solar air heating system. Therefore, issues of fluid compatibility between the solar air heating systems and the jacket water systems, are not a problem, as might occur if a solar water heating system substituted for the jacket water heating. Such compatibility issues could involve metallic components, liquids, freeze and boiling protection for the collector, and the engine operating pressures and flow rates.

3.   Engine manufacturer warranties are not an issue, since there is no direct connection between the engine and the solar air heating system. Only the maximum air temperature within the enclosure may be an issue, but is easy to maintain a temperature below the upper ambient operating temperature of the engine.

4.   The solar heated air evenly heats all the exterior surfaces of the engine, generator, controls, and the enclosure structure. This is one advantage of completely filling the enclosure with solar heated air. This provides a lower 'delta T' between the surroundings and the engine

surfaces than would otherwise be available if just the jacket water were heated but the surroundings were at ambient air temperatures. This lower delta T on all surfaces, reduces the radiation and conduction losses along "all" the heat transfer paths on the engine. These heat transfer paths include the metal engine body itself where it is connected to the heated portions of the jacket water systems.

5. Heating of the enclosure puts warm air in the vicinity of the engine air intake. During the start cycle of the engine, this warm air will be ingested into the cylinder, and should help to ensure high compression cycle temperatures, quick combustion, and a rapid start. The volume of warm solar heated air available in an enclosure during the start cycle is sufficient for about 15 to 30 seconds of operation.

6. Heating of all the air in the enclosure provides a greater heated thermal mass than is currently the case for the electric jacket water heaters. The solar heated air in contact with all the surfaces of the generators and enclosures heats the entire mass of steel, copper, liquids, concrete and aluminum of the engine, the generator, the support structure, the auxiliary equipment, and the enclosure. When subjected to 100+ F heating during the day, the mass of the equipment, as much as 5 tons for the weight of a 350 KW diesel generator alone, and the structure, act as a thermal mass that maintains elevated temperatures in the enclosure after solar heating stops.

7. Heating of the oil in the sump will maintain the lubricating oil in a less viscous state. This results in more rapid lubrication of the bearing surfaces during startup. When insignificant lubrication exists on the bearing surfaces, during the initial revolutions of the engine, high wear on an engine takes place. Reducing the viscosity of the oil by heating will accelerate the flow of oil through the lubrication circuit compared to colder more viscous oil.

SOLAR AIR HEATING GENERATORS AT THE US GEOLOGICAL SURVEY HEADQUARTERS

There are 4 emergency generators installed in outdoor enclosures at the US Geological Survey Headquarters in Reston, VA. Two generators are located next to each other. The other two are located at opposite ends of the campus.

One Cummins natural gas fired generator is enclosed in a well insulated enclosure. The walls of the enclosure are weather tight aluminum panels. They are insulated with 1.5 inch thick fiberglass contained behind perforated aluminum sound dampening panels. The air supply and exhaust openings provide a relatively dead airspace between the interior of the enclosure and the exterior.

The temperature in the enclosure varied between 71 and 56 degrees F, as the outside ambient temperatures varied from 62 to 23F, during two October days, with no solar heating. The enclosure temperature, generally varied within 7 degrees of the daily high temperature.

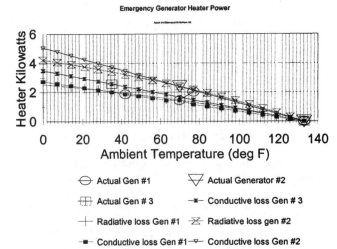

Figure 1 Heater power vs temperature

Other generators on the site are in fully ventilated enclosures. These enclosures have no insulation and open louvers with large screens that merely protect the generators from rain or flying debris such as leaves or paper. One can see through the enclosure to the other side. The temperature within these enclosures is generally within a few degrees of the ambient outside air temperature. Conductive or convective heat transfer from the engines is accelerated by movement of the air within the enclosures from the slightest wind and thermal currents from the warm engine

Three solar thermal tile air heating systems were designed to reduce the electricity use of the jacket water heaters on these four engine. Two have been installed and a third is under construction.

DESIGN CRITERIA FOR SOLAR AIR HEATING SYSTEMS FOR EMERGENCY GENERATORS

The following design criteria were used in developing the solar air heating system designs:

- Avoid interference with the primary function of the diesel generators, which is to provide reliable emergency power in the event of a power outage
- Reduce electric energy used in heating the diesel generators in standby mode
- Repay the initial cost with reduced life cycle cost of energy
- Improve the enclosures in order to improve the operations and maintenance environment of the diesel generators
- Minimize life cycle maintenance of the solar heating system by using standard industrial control technology and minimizing moving parts
- Design the components and structure for long operating life
- Provide aesthetically pleasing enclosed support structures using standard prefabricated industrial building materials

ESTIMATING THE ENERGY BENEFITS

Measurements of the electric energy use of the heaters were taken between July and December. The results are shown in Figure 1 plotted against the air temperature in the enclosure at the time of the test. The heaters for the 750 KW generator in the well insulated enclosure drew a total of 1.4 KW in air temperatures of ~70 F. A second reading showed 1.9 KW at 45 F air temperature. Each of the 800 KW generators drew 2.4 KW in 70 degree ambient air in fully ventilated enclosures.

These readings, allow the calculation of heater energy curves for temperatures encompassing the full annual range of daily air temperatures. Assuming zero energy use by the heaters at 130 F air temperature we therefore, plot two points (e.g.70F, 2.4KW and 130F, 0KW) These points lie on curves of heater energy use (engine energy loss) at any temperature. By making the simplifying assumption that all energy loss from the engine is conductive loss from the metal to the air, then the energy loss is proportional to the difference in temperature between the engine and the air. A proportionality constant can be determined from the data point at the 70 F air temperature, that applies across the entire temperature range. The lines in Fig. 1, labeled "Conductive loss", use such a calculation. The lines in Fig. 1 labeled "Radiative loss" use an approach which assumes that 100% of the heat loss from the engine is radiative. This energy loss is calculated based on the proportionality of the difference

Heater KWHR use per month
Based on average monthly temp

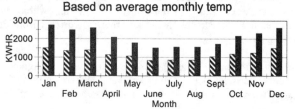

| NNN 750 KW generator insulated enclosure |
| ■ 800 KW generator, open enclosure |

Figure 2 Heater energy use per month

of engine temperature (130F) raised to the 4th power minus the air temperature raised to the 4th power. Both lines are in good agreement over the temperatures that represent average high and low daily temperature throughout the year in Washington, DC (26 to 89F).

A simple estimate of the value of the air heating approach can be made using the curves in Fig. 1. Based on the average annual temperature in Washington, DC of 57 degrees, and assuming that the enclosure could be maintained at 110 degrees throughout the year (ignoring nighttime cooling), we can determine the difference in energy use for the difference between the enclosure and average air temperatures. The curve for the 800 KW generators in fully ventilated enclosures shows a potential reduction in heater demand from 2.9 KW to 0.8 KW, a 72 % reduction. Obviously, nighttime cooling will reduce this potential. However, heating of the large thermal mass of the generator will lessen the night time cooling effect, particularly in

the well insulated enclosures. A 50% reduction is expected for a properly sized system.

Given the average monthly temperatures for the Washington DC area and, the curves of Fig. 1 for heater energy use at different temperatures, the average monthly electrical use of the generators can be determined. Expected electrical use per month of the two different generator

Figure 3 40' x 6' Solar thermal tile system

types is shown in Figure 2. Annual electrical energy use for the 750 KW generator in the tight enclosure is 13,962 KWHR (48 million BTU). Each of the 800 KW generators in the fully ventilated enclosures are expected to use 25,147 KWHR (86 million BTU) throughout the year. To put this in perspective with a more familiar solar application, typical electric energy use for hot water heating in a single family home is 3,017 KW per year. Therefore, emergency generators represent a much higher load and a higher value sale to a single customer (~5 to 8 time larger in this case of 750-800 KW generators), than do sales to meet average residential solar water heating loads.

The USGS purchases electricity at an average cost of $.046/kwhr. To satisfy the demand to heat each generator with electric resistance heating, costs $642 per year for the 750 KW generator and $1157 for each of the two 800 KW generators. A fourth generator on the site is a 250 KW generator in a fully ventilated enclosure. The heater energy use of that generator is also shown in Figure 1 (Actual Gen. 3) It is equivalent to the other fully ventilated generators but with lower heat loss due to the smaller size of the engine and heater.

Design and Construction
Based on the potential heat delivery from the solar air heating systems and the current heat loss of the generators, two of the systems were sized at 250 square feet. One system heats the 750 KW generator in the insulated enclosure. The enclosure is 11' x 23' x 10' high. The solar tile system is sized at a nominal 40' x 6', Figure 3. This system is 160 feet from the generator enclosure. No dedicated thermal storage is provided, however, the mass of the

Figure 4 30' x 8' collector

generator and enclosure themselves are providing some thermal storage. The system delivers solar heated air when the sun shines and shuts off when collector temperatures drop below the enclosure temperatures.

The second system heats the 250 KW generator in the smaller, fully ventilated enclosure. This enclosure is 4.5' x 10' x 5' high. The solar tile field is nominally 30' x 8'. See Fig. 4. The shorter length and taller height were used to meet the tighter area available between the nearby building and the roadway. See Fig. 5. Since the solar thermal tile systems can accommodate any variation in width or height, designing different sizes to meet the space constraints is no more complicated than sizing any surface for coverage with slate or tile roofing materials. This system is 35 feet from the generator enclosure.

In both of these systems, air is moved by a small, 240 watt, 10" tubeaxial fan within the solar tile support structure, through a 6" insulated duct to the enclosures. The duct is buried underground in a plastic liner. For the 40'x 6' system, a 120 foot portion of the duct is run above grade but below a ground cover. This routing was selected to prevent trenching damage to tree roots along the edge of a wooded area.

Both systems use switches to disconnect the system fan when the generator is running. While this is not entirely necessary, it

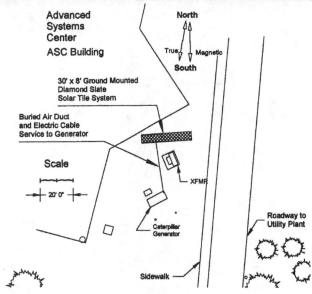

Figure 5 Site Plan 30' x 8' solar tile system

433

is considered good practice to prevent the introduction of excess heat around the operating generator. In fact, the radiator fan on the engine, and the engine combustion air requirements move about 15 times more ambient air though the enclosure when the engine is operating,, than the solar fan delivers for standby heating. Both solar tile systems ensure that delivered air temperatures do not exceed 110F. Certain diesel fuels can degrade above this temperature, and engines are not generally rated for higher temperatures. Additional automatic controls are designed to shut off the fan if temperatures within the space exceed 130 F. However, heat loss from the enclosure to the outside air will likely prevent such high temperatures from ever being reached.

The 40'x6' and 30'x8' solar heating systems use a diamond slate solar thermal tile as the principal collector component. See Fig. 6 and References 1, 2, and 3. This mid temperature (110-190 F) solar air heating system can deliver heated air at temperatures that meet the needs of the generators during typical winter conditions. The tile system uses 12" x 12" glazing tiles installed over corrugated metal absorbers to form a continuous weather tight collector surface. The tiles are fastened through the absorbers in a manner similar to the installation of slate roofing, using the French slate method. Air is drawn from the enclosed space beneath the system through airflow channels formed by the corrugated absorbers and the tiles. As the air moves across the tile field, beneath the glazing tiles, the air is heated to about 70 degrees above ambient temperatures at an air flow rate of 1 cfm per square foot of tile surface. Air temperatures can be adjusted up to about 100 degrees F above ambient by varying the air flow rate.

The tiles are supported on a structure of self framing walls and corrugated steel roof deck. The systems are tilted to 45 degrees and face due south. The walls and the roof line of each system enclose 170 square feet of space from the weather. Although no use is intended for these spaces at the USGS, they are relatively unobstructed and could be used as covered storage space in other installations. Increasing the height of the self framing walls is possible up to about 12' clear height.

The two 800 KW generators are being enclosed in a new solar heated building currently under construction using these self framing walls. The new 45' x

Figure 6 12" x 12" Diamond slate solar thermal tiles

14' x 19' high building (See Fig. 7) will incorporate 450 square feet of 9"x18" Classic Slate solar thermal tiles (Fig. 8) as the weather tight roof of the building. The exterior color of the wall panels will be a dark brown. These walls incorporate a 3" deep cavity in the self framing panels. Air heated by the south facing wall will be contained within the cavity and drawn up to the roof air inlet as preheated air for the solar thermal tile system. This will increase the total solar heating surface to 990 square feet.

INITIAL OPERATIONS
The 40'x6' ground mounted system began automatic operation on October 13, 2001. The 30'x8' system began automatic operation on December 7, 2001. A brief summary of the data collected on initial operations is as follows:

On October 24, 2001:
Airflow of about 200 CFM in the 40'x6' system resulted in a typical temperature rise at the fan of 60-75 degrees above ambient temperatures. Ambient temperatures reached 85 degrees. System temperatures at 2PM were as follows: collector fan temperature 145 F, delivered air temperature into the enclosure was 122 F. (Note: The thermally activated outside air damper had not yet been installed to limit delivered air temperature to 110F.)

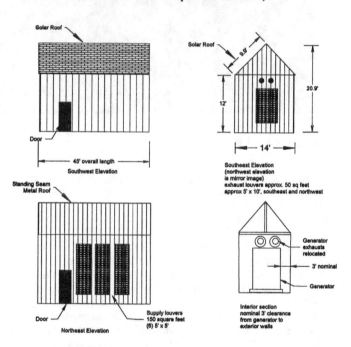

Figure 7 Solar heated generator building

Figure 8 9" x 18" Classic Slate Solar Thermal Tiles on Generator Building

On November 9, 2001

~9:45 AM   Differential controller signals that the collector is warmer than the generator enclosure and activates the solar fan.

2:00 PM;   Sky conditions -Sunny, Outside air temp 55F, air temp at solar fan, 120F, delivered air temperature to enclosure 108 F.   NIST solar monitoring station, 17 miles away, registers 134 BTU/sq ft pyranometer reading at 1:55 PM.

3:20 PM;   Sky conditions -Sunny with high thin clouds, Outside air temp 56F, delivered air temperature to enclosure 98 F. NIST pyran. reading 67 BTU/sq ft.

4:16 PM;   Differential controller senses that collector temperatures have dropped below enclosure temperature and shuts off the fan. Note: The sun angles for this date indicate the collector was shaded by the nearby building, for about 30 minutes prior to the shut down.

Initial operations have consistently shown a 10 - 12 degree F temperature drop through the 160 foot duct with a 55-70 degree F temperature difference between solar heated air at the fan and ambient mid-day air.

CONCLUSIONS

The opportunity to solar heat emergency generators represents a large potential market for appropriate solar heating technologies. The high (130 F) temperatures required indicate that a mid temperature collector system is best suited for this application.

Solar heat can be provided at much lower life cycle cost than the electric resistance heat currently used for most emergency generators.

Direct substitution of solar hot water or solar electricity to replace the electric resistance jacket water heating system appears technically feasible but mechanically and administratively complex and expensive.

Solar air heating of the enclosures can significantly reduce the heating by the electric resistance jacket water heater by reducing the engine heat loss.

Solar air heating also provides other benefits in terms of reduced complexity, increased heating of all components and liquids within the enclosure, provision of heated air available to the engine during startup, and no warranty issues with the generator manufacturer, improved air quality within the space, and improved working conditions where new solar buildings cover the generators.

The solar thermal tile air heating systems are currently delivering mid temperature air to emergency generators.

The solar thermal tile system has been demonstrated to provide a weather tight "solar roof" over the enclosed ground mounted systems.

References

1.   Archibald, J.P., 1999, Building Integrated Solar Thermal Roofing, Solar 99 Conference Proceedings of the ASES Annual Conference

2.   Archibald, J.P., 2001, Measuring Tree Shading and Collector Response on Large Solar Thermal Roofs and Walls, Forum 2001Proceedings of the ASES Annual Conference

3.   Archibald, J.P., 2001, A New Desiccant Evaporative Cooling Cycle for Solar Air Conditioning and Hot Water Heating, Forum 2001Proceedings of the ASES Annual Conference

Acknowledgment

The author would like to acknowledge the support of the US Geological Survey during the construction and initial operation of the solar thermal tile systems.

Chapter 60

POLICIES AND INCENTIVES FOR BIOMASS POWER TO BECOME A REAL PLAYER IN THE COMPETITIVE ELECTRICITY MARKET

Katherine H. Hamilton, CEM
Co-Director, American Bioenergy Association

ABSTRACT

Biomass has produced energy for hundreds of years, but only in the last twenty years has the production of electricity become viable. While biomass is plentiful and the benefits many, the industry has not grown at the rate of other, traditional generating sources. We will examine policy barriers renewable energy development has faced and pose solutions that in a new competitive market could level the playing field with traditional generation. This paper reviews the Federal policies in existence today, analyzes what several states have done, and discusses legislation that may be signed into law this fall.

INTRODUCTION

Biomass power is the generation of electric power from biomass resources—usually urban residues, crop and forest residues and crops grown specifically for energy production. Biomass power reduces emissions, including greenhouse gases, compared with fossil fuel based electricity. Increased use of biomass for energy would reduce greenhouse gas emissions, lessen dependence on foreign oil, improve U.S. balance of trade, boost the rural economy, and support a major new American industry.

BIOMASS POWER MARKET TODAY

The existing biomass power sector, nearly 1000 plants, is mainly comprised of direct combustion plants, with about two-thirds of those providing power (and heat) for on-site uses only. Plant size av-erages 20 megawatts with a biomass-to-electricity conversion efficiency of about 20%. Grid-connected electrical capacity has increased from less than 2000 megawatts in 1978 to over 7500 megawatts in 2000. More than 75% of this power is generated for their own industrial processes by the forest products industry. In addition, about 3,300 megawatts of municipal solid waste and landfill gas generating capacity exists. The cost of generation with biomass ranges from 6 to 12 cents per kilowatt-hour, depending on the feedstock (residues or energy crops); with the development of highly efficient gasification units, the price could be driven down to 5 cents per kilowatt-hour.[1]

BIOMASS POTENTIAL

The U.S. has the land and agricultural infrastructure available to produce enormous quantities of biomass in a sustainable way —enough, for example, to replace half of the Nation's gasoline usage or all of the Nation's nuclear power without a major impact on food prices. Shifting part of the $50 billion now spent for oil imports and other petroleum products to rural America would have a profoundly positive effect on the economy, in terms of jobs created (for production, harvesting, and use) and industrial growth (facilities for conversion into fuels and power). The Energy Information Administration projects that the largest source of non-hydroelectric renewable energy generation will be from biomass. Electric generation from biomass power is projected to increase from 38 terawatt-hours in 2000 to 64 terawatt-hours in 2020, or 1% of the total electricity supply.[2]

BARRIERS TO DEVELOPMENT

If biomass has such tremendous potential, why aren't investors clamoring to develop biomass power plants? Many are, as a matter of fact. But many of these investors are backing companies who will develop overseas rather than in the United States. Europe, Japan, and many other governments have determined that their emissions problems and power needs are such that renewable energy provides solutions that conventional generation cannot. They have invested heavily in research and provide substantial incentives to developers of clean energy resources. While the U.S. conducts some of the best research in renewable energy, the government does not facilitate the movement of technology past the demonstration stage into the marketplace. Investors and financiers are also hesitant to back plants for which a price of energy cannot be guaranteed. At this time, a policy solution is needed to close the gap between traditional and renewable energy generation.

POSSIBLE POLICY SOLUTIONS

Why aren't consumers provided energy generated from biomass power just as they are from nuclear, coal, and natural gas? We need to remember that traditional generation industries, when they started up were and even today are given tremendous incentives and subsidies to provide low-cost, reliable power. Consumers should have access to affordable, reliable energy that is also clean and sustainable. Unfortunately, sustainability and low emissions are not given the same value as bottom line cost. Economics will be the way to level the playing field; policies will need to be put into place that reward energy generators for using renewable energy sources. A production tax credit could be paid to generators (as it is with wind power today) per kilowatt-hour generated with biomass. Another policy would be to set a standard or requirement for generation, allowing that a certain percentage of generation comes from renewable energy resources, including biomass. Finally, continued research and development funding to find more efficient and cost-effective means of generating with renewable energy resources will be necessary to develop new and better technologies.

Current Federal Biomass Policy

Currently, a production tax credit of 1.7 cents per kilowatt-hour is given to producers of electricity who used "closed loop" (dedicated energy crops such as switchgrass) biomass and generation with poultry litter. Since no one has made energy crops economically viable solely for electricity generation, and since a poultry litter plant has not started operation in this country, this credit has cost the taxpayer not one penny. In other words, no one can use it. The definition of biomass should include "open loop", meaning non-hazardous cellulosic residues from urban, forest, and agriculture waste streams.

State Initiatives

Several states have passed legislation that gives incentives for renewable energy and energy efficiency. In Maryland, a production tax credit for biomass and other renewable energy is in place. In Texas and in eleven other states, a renewable portfolio standard ensures that some portion of the electric generation in the state will come from renewable energy resources. All of these state incentive programs have met with overwhelmingly positive public support. Most are already oversubscribed; customers are simply waiting for more renewable energy plants to come on line. While it may take a couple of years for generators to begin using renewable energy sources, these incentives made it viable for developers to begin construction.

Federal Legislation Under Consideration

Congress has been working to pass serious energy legislation for two years. While each house has passed a bill, differences in the two versions will need to be reconciled in a conference committee. As with most other provisions, the biomass measures differ somewhat in the two bills. The Senate contains the most inclusive production tax credit, allowing for open and closed loop biomass as well as co-firing with coal. The House includes only open loop biomass. The Senate also has a renewable portfolio standard that would require 10% of generation come form renewable energy sources by 2010. The House has no such renewable requirement. Both the House and Senate bills contain funding authorizations for important programs such as renewable resource assessment and biomass research and development. This funding, however, does not become "real" until appropriators put it into their spending bills.

CONCLUSION

Thus, while biomass power has the potential to continue to be the leader in renewable energy generation, only with policy incentives on a federal level will the industry truly take off and become a "real" player in the electricity market. Several large petroleum companies are investing in renewable energy and we can only hope that those corporations can help drive the market and enable legislators to realize that biomass is not a "fringe" technology but should be mainstream. One day consumers should be able to purchase all of their power from what would normally be considered a waste steam going to a landfill—and not go broke doing it.

REFERENCES

[1]National Renewable Energy Laboratory, 2002 Fact Sheet
[2]Energy Information Administration, Report#:DOE/EIA-0383(2002) December 21, 2001

Chapter 61

USING FACILITY INTELLIGENCE TO MANAGE ENERGY COSTS AT MULTIPLE SITES

Gerry D. Crooks, Founder and Chief Strategic Officer
Avista Advantage

ABSTRACT

On its face, processing utility or telecommunications invoices seems a relatively straightforward exercise. But the steps involved and the potential for error open the door to decreased operating expenses — particularly for companies with multiple sites — through the services of a facility intelligence provider like Avista Advantage. Both anecdotal evidence gathered from Avista Advantage customers and industry research confirm the savings can be substantial.

In 2000, the Institute of Management & Administration conducted its most recent *Managing Accounts Payable (MAP)* benchmarking survey[1] of more than 900 payables professionals. Survey participants were asked to indicate the average individual cost to process a vendor payment, taking department salaries into account, but excluding corporate overhead, rent, etc. The average figure totaled $10.15, up from $9.59 two and a half years earlier, with the median figure ringing in at $6.15.

In a January 2001 report[2], the Gartner Group, a leading business technology research firm based in Stamford, Connecticut, projected the business process outsourcing (BPO) market (excluding manufacturing services) in the United States would expand from $59.4 billion in 1999 to $174.8 billion in 2004. That rate of increase demonstrates a clear trend among American businesses to send back-office functions to subcontractor specialists, a trend further substantiated by the growth in the value of bills managed by Avista Advantage (see Figure 1).

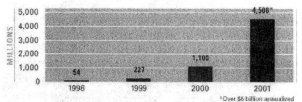

FIGURE 1[3]

The results of these two studies coupled with the recent volatility of the nation's energy market, well known to even the casual consumer of business and political news, build a convincing case for Avista Advantage's business model. This presentation will address the convergence of the demand identified by the Gartner Group, the hard business costs calculated by the *MAP* survey, the value represented by Avista Advantage's energy and facility expertise, and the potential that expertise holds to reduce a number of costs — including vendor payment processing expenses as well as those related to various utility services and facility operations — for organizations operating more than 100 sites.

SCOPE OF SERVICES

Through Facility IQ, a proprietary Internet-based customer interface, Avista Advantage provides access to aggregated facility expense data and simplified payment of expense invoices. Avista Advantage's clients — some 200 companies with 100,000 sites in the United States, Canada, and Puerto Rico — in turn use that information to track trends, identify relatively expensive or inefficient facilities, develop cost management strategies, and budget more precisely.

Avista Advantage's services currently cover two primary areas, utility and telecommunications expenses; three ancillary offerings deal with waste expenses, energy recon, and opening and closing accounts. The company's goal is to find minimum net savings equal to one percent of total bill volume annually for each customer organization. For the month of July 2001, for instance, aggregate client savings amounted to more than $4.3 million, or 1.1 percent of total bill value.

Technology

Avista Advantage holds five patents for its proprietary technology platform. These patents cover computerized resource accounting methods and systems, computerized utility management methods and systems, multi-user utility management methods and systems, energy-consumption based tracking methods and systems, computerized bill consolidation, billing and payment authorization with remote access to billing information, and electronic bill presenting methods. Together, these patents make up the company's two critical business systems: Facility IQ, a bill management and consulting solution, and AviTrack℠, a database that captures, analyzes, and provides reports on data collected from utilities. The software platform runs numerous tolerance checks to ensure the accuracy of all bills and helps time bill payment to avoid late fees while maximizing the client's treasury. Its open architecture eases information sharing with clients' internal accounting and reporting systems.

Process

Once an organization contracts with Avista Advantage, all relevant client bills are delivered to one of two Avista Advantage processing centers for initial scanning and data entry into the Facility IQ system. The company manages, on average, 2.7 bills per site each month and it interfaces with nearly 13,000 different providers.

Verification routines identify variances outside of predetermined tolerances and the system generates a billing exception report. A client's account team reviews the report and resolves issues with service providers, delivering considerable financial benefit — as the case studies featured later in this presentation will attest.

Once paid, all bill data is immediately made available to customers through the Facility IQ Internet portal which also supports a number of reporting and analytical tools for site-to-site comparison, site-to-benchmark comparison, energy use or costs per square foot calculations, and more. The data — which includes information regarding energy load profiles, usage patterns, cost metrics, and service providers — belongs to the customer and is accessible at any time. It's protected by 128-bit encryption, an alternate secure socket layer (SSL), and a redundant firewall system.

Service Categories

Facility IQ comprises two stand-alone components, utility and telecommunications services.

Through its original offering, utility services, Avista Advantage manages bills from gas, electric, water, and sewage providers. Facility IQ utility services may also include Energy Recon, wherein staff members analyze deregulated commodity opportunities and their appropriateness for each subscribing client, evaluate provider bids, and present the client with those bids deemed most advantageous along with an explanation of the differences among them. Customers also have the option of engaging Avista Advantage for open and close services. In that event, the Avista Advantage team sets up utility accounts in a client's name, negotiates deposits, identifies possible discounts, determines the appropriate rate schedule, verifies accurate initial billing information, closes accounts, and monitors resulting credits or refunds. The close service is also available to telecommunications customers.

Avista Advantage's telecommunications services component, the second principal offering, handles all local exchange carrier (LEC) bills, tests them for such anomalies as overlapping periods and previous balance reconciliation, and provides the option of resolving billing exceptions or producing a report for clients who prefer to address these issues themselves.

Customers who contract for Facility IQ waste services receive similar oversight of their waste and recycling providers.

THE VALUE OF AVISTA ADVANTAGE'S EXPERTISE

As a subsidiary of an investor-owned utility in business for more than 110 years, Avista Advantage possesses inherent and deep understanding of the utility industry and its processes. The value of that knowledge can be illustrated by a brief look at one client organization. The coffee chain Starbucks operates more than 3,600 locations nationwide, adding a new store every eight hours. Those facilities represent 900 utility service providers, 1,000 different bill formats, 500 separate rate schedules, and 50 unique regulatory environments. Given that level of complexity, Starbucks — like Avista Advantage's other customers — deems it strategically advantageous to turn the management of its utility services over to an organization that specializes in facility intelligence.

CASE STUDIES

HealthSouth

HealthSouth Corporation is the nation's largest healthcare services provider, with more than 2,000 outpatient rehabilitation, outpatient surgery, and diagnostic imaging facilities across the U.S. and abroad. They provide integrated health services for as many as 100,000 patients every day.

As part of a cost-cutting initiative, HealthSouth chose to outsource the management of its utility services in 1999. Specifically, management sought a vendor to: process and pay utility bills while aggregating usage data in an easily accessible format; provide detailed financial analysis of bills by facility, metro area, or region; audit all bills to identify incorrect rates, water leaks, and other savings opportunities at its facilities; and aggregate demand across all facilities for optimal purchases in deregulating energy markets. Initially, that task was divided among three service providers; by November 2001, Avista Advantage was serving all 1,500 HealthSouth facilities in the U.S.

Through the use of Avista Advantage's Facility IQ services, HealthSouth processed 7.5 percent fewer invoices in 2001 and saved 1.27 percent of its annual utility costs. Such savings are net to the client; Avista Advantage retains no portion.

Over a 12-month period, Facility IQ audited and paid more than 20,000 utility bills for HealthSouth facilities, finding direct savings exceeding $140,000 and opportunities for additional annual savings of $280,000. The following illustrate the real and potential savings uncovered by Avista Advantage's staff:

- Facility IQ analysts identified 34 sites across the country where gas, electricity, and water/sewage usage was significantly above average. By bringing these facilities down to average use,

HealthSouth could achieve estimated annual savings of $280,933.

- A gas meter misreading at an Oklahoma facility produced an inaccurate bill that, once revised at the behest of Facility IQ staff, saved the site $62,576.

- A second gas meter misreading, this one in Missouri, resulted in an overcharge of $9,638. Facility IQ staff members caught the error and had the bill adjusted.

- Facility IQ analysts found 12 sites in five Midwest and Southeast states with incorrect utility rates and facilitated a change to the appropriate rates, saving approximately $19,105 annually.

Circle K

With 2,100 stores in 18 states, Circle K is the largest chain of company-controlled convenience stores in the country. In order to capture accurate data on energy usage and costs, Circle K contracted with Avista Advantage in September 2000. Today, data from each store's utility bill is entered into an online database, giving Circle K's finance and energy personnel Web access to bill images as well as reports on invoice status, energy costs, and usage trends from specific sites or across the enterprise. Avista Advantage audits each bill against previous month and previous year data to detect billing errors, incorrect rates, and other avoidable costs. Over a 12-month period, Avista Advantage audited and paid more than 55,000 Circle K utility bills, realizing $429,000 in savings through measures such as these:

- Facility IQ analysts tracked down seven Western stores on the wrong electric rates. They advised Circle K to change the rates, resulting in annual savings of $22,700, more than $10,000 of which came from a single store.

- When a Southwestern utility over-billed and double-billed multiple accounts an amount totaling $63,146, Facility IQ staff found the errors and arranged for a corrected bill including a small credit.

- The Facility IQ system caught duplicate bills sent to five different stores from just one utility in the month of January 2001 alone. Staff members worked with the utility to save those five stores $17,856.

- The utility for a Southwestern store read its electric usage as 884 kWh rather than the actual 49 kWh. Avista Advantage personnel discovered the mistake, and requested a correction, reducing the bill by $7,725.

- A broken car wash hose at a store in the Southeast caused water usage to soar from 71 kgal to 267 kgal in a single month. Facility IQ staff alerted Circle K and estimated savings will total $1,678.

Comerica Bank

Detroit-based Comerica maintains banking subsidiaries in Michigan, California, and Texas, with operations in several other states. It serves its customers through more than 300 regional, branch, and supermarket offices and more than 600 ATMs. The property management firm Trammell Crow provides energy management for those facilities. After initially outsourcing utility bill management to another vendor, Trammell Crow sought a new partner to continue the savings derived from outsourcing bill processing, identify savings opportunities at existing sites, accurately open and close utility accounts and recover refunds, offer immediate Web access to bill data, supply managers with usage data for making energy purchasing decisions, and provide detailed financial analysis of energy bills by site, metro area, or region.

In the first six months of Avista Advantage's contract with Trammell Crow, Facility IQ audited and paid nearly 5,000 utility bills. Over that same period, staff members delivered a number of additional benefits reducing Comerica's facility costs by $32,000:

- A Michigan facility experienced water leaks in its sprinkler system and cooling tower that showed up in water bills audited by the Facility IQ system. Fixing the leaks immediately saved about $6,795.
- Facility IQ staff recovered refunds from utilities for three previously closed sites in California and Michigan totaling $6,559.
- Electric bills for two Michigan facilities showed unexpected increases from inaccurate meter readings. Revised bills from the utilities saved Comerica $3,973.
- Two facilities in Texas showed dramatic jumps in water usage during the summer of 2001. Fixing the leaks Facility IQ uncovered should yield about $2,750 in savings.
- Another leak, this one at a Michigan facility, showed up in an unusually high bill. Facility IQ staff advised the client, producing an estimated savings of $2,254.

EFFICIENT USE OF RESOURCES

The opportunities for operational efficiency revealed through facility intelligence clearly affect the bottom line. But most organizations do not possess the financial and human resources required to manage facility costs proactively. Indeed, those resources generate more ROI if used to perform core business functions. Therein lies the rationale for services like those of Avista Advantage. When the average cost to process an invoice exceeds $10 and outsourcing that function yields net savings of one percent of total bill volume, the appropriate course speaks for itself. Moreover, the identification of faulty or inoperative equipment expedited by closely monitoring invoice trends further promotes the best use of existing resources.

Critical to that effort is the establishment of benchmarks. Since one cannot manage what one cannot measure, Avista Advantage helps customers determine baselines against which to gauge trends. In the case of Facility IQ utility services, for instance, staff members obtain 12 months' worth of historical data to integrate into client account files, immediately creating a month-to-month comparison tool.

Providing facility managers with the ability to measure — one location against another, one location against itself, one location against the entire enterprise — may prove as valuable as the direct cost savings facility intelligence delivers. Armed with detailed knowledge about energy usage, customers can make well-informed decisions about capital expenditures, retrofits, budgeting, energy purchases, and more. And there is significant potential to affect more than the 5,200 megawatts (MW) Avista Advantage's clients consume today. Beyond the company's existing client base lie 5.8 million discrete sites among U.S. multi-site retail and Fortune 1000 companies[4]. Facility-related expenses continue to make up a material portion of those organizations' operating costs and many of them process bills from multiple service providers for hundreds or thousands of sites. The trend detected by the Gartner Group indicates that a host of these businesses will recognize the efficiencies inherent in outsourcing that function.

REFERENCES

1 "MAP Benchmarking Survey 2000," Institute of Management & Administration, 2000.

[2] Rebecca Scholl, "100%: The Rise of BPO in 2000," Market Analysis January 8, 2001, rpt. by The Gartner Group.

[3] "Growth in Value of Bills Managed," Avista Advantage management, 2002.

[4] United States, Department of Commerce, Census Bureau, Economic Census 1997 (Washington: U.S. Department of Commerce, 1997).*

*Public sector sites per Avista Advantage management estimates.

Chapter 62

Evaluating Building Performance Using Interval Meter Data

James M. Bolton, P.E, CEM
Honeywell Atrium

Dagfinn Bell, MS
Honeywell Atrium

Abstract:

Previously, energy managers had to make do with only monthly utility bill data to analyze building energy performance and to summarize historic trends in a buildings energy usage. However, as the cost of collecting interval data has continued to decline, an increasing number of facilities now have access to whole building interval meter data. The question must now be answered as to what can and should be done to make the best use of all this data. Using this whole building interval data along with ambient temperature and a few other pieces of building specific data, a detailed analysis of the buildings static performance as well as trends over time can be made. This paper examines some tools, techniques and limitations in mining this new data stream for maximum value.

Introduction

As energy mangers, we must understand how our buildings are using energy. Historically, utility bill information has been the primary source to quantify energy consumption. Over time, we might accumulate sufficient information to construct a basic model of energy usage. A good summary of electrical utility information might look as in Table 1.

Table 1

Billed Month	Billing Period Start	Billing Period End	No. of Days	Consumption (kwh)	Average Monthly Temperature (F)
Jan-01	4-Jan-01	3-Feb-01	30	103,025	44.5
Feb-01	4-Feb-01	5-Mar-01	29	85,974	48.2
Mar-01	6-Mar-01	6-Apr-01	31	103,319	57.8
Apr-01	7-Apr-01	6-May-01	29	91,222	57.9
May-01	7-May-01	8-Jun-01	32	133,928	75.5
Jun-01	9-Jun-01	8-Jul-01	29	138,474	77.4
Jul-01	9-Jul-01	8-Aug-01	30	149,082	78.4
Aug-01	9-Aug-01	7-Sep-01	29	152,597	77.9
Sep-01	8-Sep-01	8-Oct-01	30	141,523	73.4
Oct-01	9-Oct-01	7-Nov-01	29	126,608	65.2
Nov-01	8-Nov-01	9-Dec-01	31	103,498	54.2
Dec-01	10-Dec-01	8-Jan-02	29	108,412	46.0
Jan-02	9-Jan-02	10-Feb-02	32	102,101	44.1
Feb-02	11-Feb-02	12-Mar-02	29	91,732	50.6
Mar-02	13-Mar-02	11-Apr-02	29	102,388	54.6
Apr-02	12-Apr-02	12-May-02	30	111,074	61.5
May-02	13-May-02	14-Jun-02	32	133,725	68.8
Jun-02	15-Jun-02	15-Jul-02	30	128,048	76.4

From the data in Table 1, we could produce a chart showing the consumption by month, as the one shown in Figure 1.

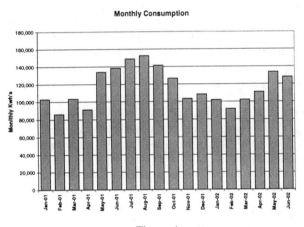

Figure 1

We should immediately recognize several shortcomings with this chart. First, the utility company usually does not make things easy for us. As illustrated in Table 1, billing periods typically do not start and end exactly at the beginning and end of each month. It can be difficult to determine in which month to assign the cost and consumption if the billed start and end dates occur in the middle of the month as they frequently do. Second, the number of days billed for each month varies. It's usually around 30 days but can range between 29 and 32 days. The difference in billed consumption between a 32-day billing cycle and a 29-day billing cycle could be 10% or more. Nevertheless, accounting cycles do begin and end at fixed dates. To put the data in terms that fit accounting periods, it is necessary to force fit our data into monthly bins. We can remove the differences caused by the varying number of days by normalizing the monthly consumption into an average daily consumption. Our chart would then look as shown in Figure 2.

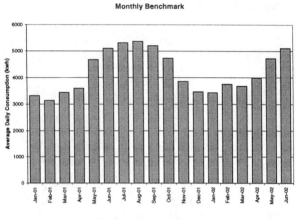

Figure 2

We could take this one step further to account for the fact that the data shown for the month of January really incorporates part of February. However, it would not do to tell Finance that they would have to wait until the February utility bill arrives in March before you can tell them what January's energy cost was!

With the data provided, we could also match consumption data with weather data to produce a scatter chart of average daily consumption versus average daily temperature as shown in Figure 3.

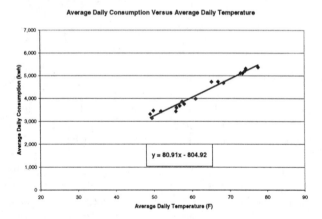

Figure 3

Applying a simple linear regression technique, we can plot a best-fit line through the data and develop an equation that describes the monthly consumption as a function of average daily temperature. Using this model, we can now project the monthly consumption based on the average monthly temperature. A practical use might be to develop a weather risk adjusted energy budget or to explain variances in our current utilities budget using this model.

If this were all the data we had available, then this is probably the best we can do. In reality, our analysis is

poor for several reasons. First, because of the duration required for data collection, it is likely that we have an inaccurate model. Buildings are seldom static, especially over the time frame required for data collection. Second, and more importantly, can we have any confidence in a model with such a limited set of data? Would it be abnormal if our next month's consumption total were 10% higher than other similar temperature points? What does the average daily consumption or the average monthly temperature represent? A major problem here is one of granularity. We know nothing of the daily ranges of the consumption and temperature or the frequency of those numbers. For example, to get to an average monthly temperature of 50 degrees, we could have two completely different sets of data as shown in Table 2.

Table 2

Date	Store A Average Daily Temperature	Store B Average Daily Temperature
1-Mar-01	45	26
2-Mar-01	46	27
3-Mar-01	47	28
4-Mar-01	48	29
5-Mar-01	49	30
6-Mar-01	50	50
7-Mar-01	51	70
8-Mar-01	52	71
9-Mar-01	53	72
10-Mar-01	54	73
11-Mar-01	55	74
Average	**50**	**50**

Both sets of data produce an average temperature of 50 degrees but the daily temperature ranges are quite different, and likely so is the energy required for heating and cooling. The same holds true for the average daily consumption. Without additional granularity, we cannot confidently predict what might happen in the next time period.

In order to compare buildings, we want to know for certain what the base load is. But with this analysis, it's hard to define. Our regression line in Figure 3 appears to provide a reasonable fit; but what happens at the extremes. Given the averaging necessary to produce this chart, we cannot tell if the average consumption would continue to decline with lower average daily temperatures or has the load bottomed out at 50 degrees. Similarly, at the upper end of our chart, have we really reached the upper end of the consumption? We might suspect that there is an average monthly temperature below which comfort cooling is not required. However, during that month, were there temperatures above which cooling was required? Thus, we might be tempted to assume that our model looks as shown in Figure 4.

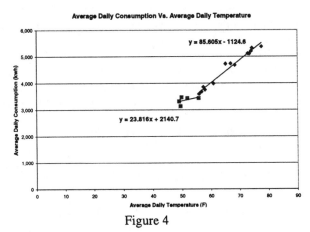

Figure 4

In this way, we might end up with several prediction equations, none of which has very much validity given the limited data set. With such limited data and the dynamic nature of buildings, there is little certainty which is correct and even less chance of detecting a trend. As we get new data points, we would probably only be able to plug them in and adjust our model as necessary.

Basic Benchmarking

Assume we have many similar buildings that we wish to compare. We could benchmark our buildings against one another using the utility bill data from each building, as shown in Figure 5. This chart tells us which buildings are consuming the most energy, but not when and why. We have not accounted for any of the differences that could drive energy consumption such as building size, weather differences, or building types.

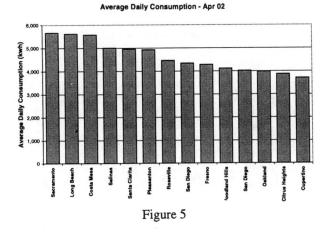

Figure 5

Normalizing the data by dividing by the building area allows comparison of buildings with size differences. A chart of the monthly benchmarks might then appear as in Figure 6.

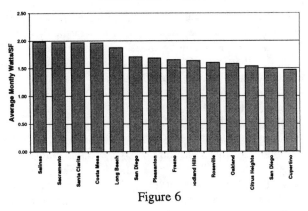

Figure 6

In the past, this level of analysis had to suffice. However, a better way to collect, summarize and analyze energy data is available.

Better Data, Better Decisions with Interval Meter Data

Most other areas in corporate resource management and marketing management have been using business information systems (BIS) for a long time to improve their decision making. Inventory control systems provide Materials Managers data for just-in-time inventory control. Transportation managers control their fleet with GPS tracking systems. FedEx can tell you where any given package is at a moments notice. With point of sales information systems, restaurant chains can track the popularity of each entree and adjust menus seasonally or daily. The latest experiment in the grocery store industry is to equip the grocery carts with micro transmitters and then monitor how much time shoppers are spending in each isle at each time of the day. All in an effort to aid marketing and sales, and thereby improve the bottom line, often by the smallest of margins.

The cornerstone of all these systems is data, enormous amounts of data, organized and mined in a timely and systematic manor. Imagine if the energy manager had access to equivalent interval meter data. They could track energy consumption in greater detail. Not only would you be able to say how much energy was used, but to a certain extent when and how the energy was used. Proper use of this data would improve decision-making and provide an unprecedented look at how a building uses energy over time.

The question is then, how do we acquire interval meter data? We could read our electric meter daily and collect the average daily temperature for each of our buildings. However this would be too time consuming, so for most energy managers, the next logical level of data collection beyond utility bill data will be automatic interval meter data collection. The cost of data collection has been reduced and installation simplified to such a point that it is affordable to almost every company, particularly so if real time data is not required. In addition to metering the consumption data, one should match it with the drivers of the variances. Key among those drivers for most typical buildings that provide comfort cooling and heating is ambient temperature and humidity data.

Defining Interval Meter Data

We should step back briefly now and define what we mean by "interval meter data". Starting with the utility bill data, we could say that consumption and demand information contained in the bill is one consumption reading every 30 days, or one interval per 30 days. Daily readings of utility meter consumption would be one interval reading per day. With automated recording, we could sample the consumption at nearly infinite granularity. Hourly readings would result in 24 points per day and 15-minute intervals would result in 96 consumption points per day. Further refinement is of course possible. Smart current transducers available today can record 26 electrical variables including voltage, current, power factor and load factor. At 15-minute intervals, that's nearly 2500 data points per day!

Analysis with interval data shorter than 15 minutes has shown some usefulness. However, for our purposes 15 minute or hourly data provides a manageable data set that suffices for most decision support requirements.

Some benchmarking is done by normalizing our raw data by building static data. By this, we mean deterministically fixed variables such as building size, building type, hours of occupancy, heating fuel(s), cooling fuel(s), etc. We might divide the consumption by the building area to compare buildings based on intensity as watts per square foot. However, we have found that provide building static data is frequently inaccurate, never being intended for this purpose. Before drawing any conclusions based on these inputs, we must make certain that the data is correct. Building size seems to be a particular challenge to measure consistently and record accurately. Before using building size to normalize building consumption, understand the source of the data. For most of our uses, it is not particularly important for the measurement to be accurate but it can be essential for it to be consistent between buildings.

Improved Benchmarking

With these precautionary notes in mind, let us proceed to improve upon our benchmarks using interval meter data. At a minimum, we would like to know the building size, location, and hours of occupancy in addition to having 15-minute consumption data, hourly temperature and humidity data.

Having access to this data immediately solves several problems in developing the energy model. First, when we chart the consumption for the month, we know that's what it is. We no longer have to finagle the utility bill to fit the budgeting periods. We "know" how much energy we used this month. In addition, we "know" how much we used long before the utility bill arrived. Our charts would still look like they did in Figures 1 & 2; the difference is that they would now be accurate. Now that we have interval meter data, we could take the analysis to the next level of detail. We could examine how our building is using energy on different weeks or days or different periods of the day. We could benchmark our facilities by any hour of the day or by unoccupied and unoccupied periods. Our benchmarks might look as shown in Figures 7, 8 and 9.

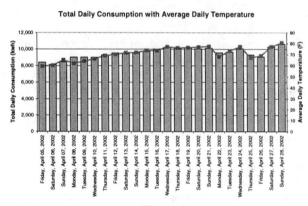

Figure 7

It would appear from the Figure 7 that the differences in consumption correlate with changes in temperature. Examining the occupied benchmarks in Figure 8 should prompt us to investigate what is causing the differences between the best and worst stores.

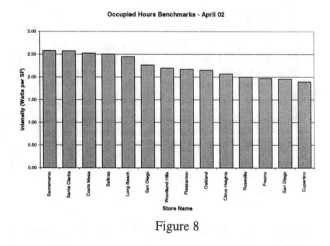

Figure 8

Moreover, the unoccupied benchmarks as shown in Figure 9 can be just as useful. For most facilities, one of the easiest places to begin making operational changes is during unoccupied hours. If there are major differences in the way that each store operates when closed, there may be a ready-made opportunity to lower the consumption without affecting daily operations.

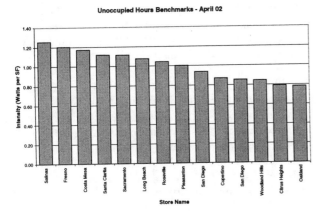

Figure 9

Within a relatively brief period, we could begin to construct the model for how the building uses energy at various temperatures. With only three months of data, we can begin to see how the building reacts to changes in temperature. The data plotted in Figure 10 is for one building over three months from February through April.

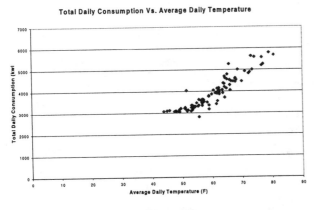

Figure 10

Compared to our earlier chart using 16 months of monthly consumption, we can now determine that the base load does in fact level out at average daily temperatures below 52 degree F. We can confidently conclude that our base load is right around 3,100 kWh per day. Note that this does not necessarily mean a non-air conditioning base load. We very well may have portions of the building that require air conditioning year round. However, this load would represent the minimum daily consumption at any lower temperature. We should also note that there does not appear to be any electrical heating occurring as would be evidenced by an upswing in the consumption at the lower

temperature range. In this case, the scatter chart would appear as a backwards check mark.

Adding the remaining daily data for the other months shows that our limited 3-month data set provided an excellent representation for the entire data set.

In Figure 11, we have compared our utility bill data model from Figure 3 with the interval data for the whole year. As expected, the data plotted from the monthly utility bill follows a similar pattern to the interval data. However, the utility data does miss the mark in several temperature ranges. Using the interval data set, we can now determine what happens at the ends of the ranges. We can see that the consumption continues to increase with increasing temperature and stops decreasing below a certain temperature.

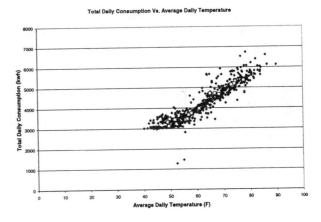

Figure 11

An interesting observation in Figure 11 is that the two outlier points below 2000 kWh total daily consumption correspond to Christmas and Thanksgiving; the two days that our building was closed.

Taking the analysis down to the next level of granularity, we could plot the hourly consumption versus the hourly temperature, as shown in Figure 12.

Figure 12 is created from only one month of data. Already, the pattern of consumption is quite clear. However, we have also introduced considerably more "scatter" in our scatter chart. In some cases, an analysis of this "scatter" provides some rather interesting information. For many facilities, an analysis of the variances can be thought of as a measure of control. How well in control are the dynamic systems such as the heating, air conditioning and refrigeration systems for this facility.

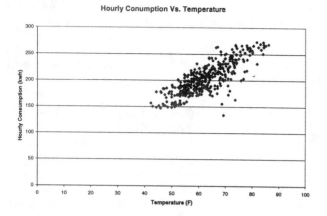

Figure 12

In one facility where an analysis of variances seemed particularly out of align, further examination revealed that this facility had a significant amount of simultaneous heating and cooling occurring. The controls systems were not functioning properly. As shown in Figure 13, after minor upgrades to the system, control is noticeably better along with an improvement in overall customer satisfaction. Additionally, the energy consumption at all temperature ranges was significantly reduced.

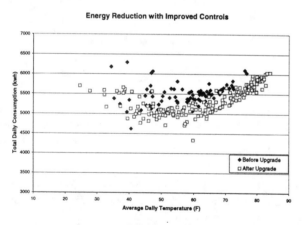

Figure 13

Even more interesting is that with interval meter data, energy managers can detect anomalies and trends. Within a short period after beginning interval metering, a model for the facility can be constructed as we have shown. It is not difficult to imagine that we would want to plot each day's or each hour's energy consumption on this model to see if the building is performing as expected, and to investigate further those occurrences when it is not. The challenge here is in picking a range of data for when the building is performing at its optimum. One of the key concepts behind the use of interval meter data is what one might call continuous commissioning; i.e. to achieve

optimum building performance and then to maintain that performance. Far too often, energy improvement initiatives are undertaken with expectations of great savings. Without keeping an eye on those investments, the effort often goes for naught. The rapid feedback and ease of analysis afforded by interval meter data allows the energy manager the opportunity to more easily keep an eye on those initiatives and to quickly detect when the building is performing outside of established ranges.

Notwithstanding, one trap to avoid when constructing our model is the tendency to allow our model to follow a drift in consumption. Within a few months after interval meter data becomes available, we can construct a good model of how the building is currently performing. For better or worse, our model is based not on how well the building could perform but on how well it is performing. Now say we spot a new unexpected upwards trend in the consumption. If we allow this new trend to creep into our model, then the new trend is averaged into the model.

For example, plotting the daily consumption versus the average daily temperature for a facility revealed a substantial change in the consumption pattern, particularly for average daily temperatures above 65 degrees F as shown in Figure 14.

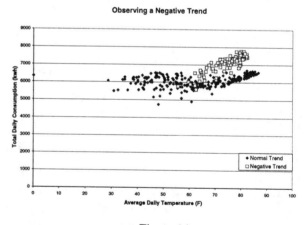

Figure 14

Had we allowed our model to simply keep building on the daily data, we could have easily overlooked this change. The chart would look quite normal otherwise as shown in Figure 15. It might later become impossible to tell that a costly change had occurred.

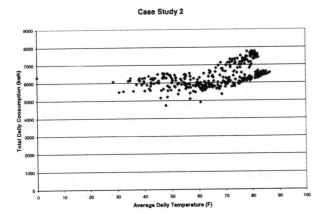

Figure 15

On the other hand, if we make improvements to the building that reduces energy consumption, we should establish a new model based on the new set of data. Once again, with interval meter data, this is done in a matter of weeks or months, not years.

More Benchmarking

As energy managers, we often go to great lengths to determine which of our buildings are doing the best and which are behaving poorly for several reasons. With limited resources, we want to make certain that we are putting our money where it will make the biggest difference. We also want to provide feedback to our designers and engineers as to how new facilities are performing relative to existing facilities.

Done properly, benchmarking provides us with confidence that we are focusing on the worst of our problems. Done poorly, benchmarking can mislead and misguide our conservation efforts and cause us to spend money addressing the wrong things. As a simple example, examine the benchmarks for 11 mid-west grocery stores as shown in Figure 16. Upon initial inspection, it would appear that some stores are performing far better than others are.

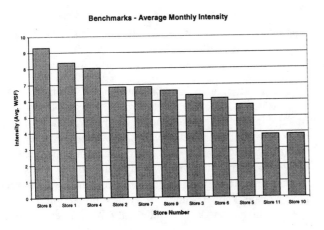

Figure 16

However, are we making reasonable comparisons? Are these facilities sufficiently similar whereby these benchmarks make sense? Upon closer inspection, we find that Store 10 and 11 are big box retail stores with a grocery section. The remainder are grocery stores of various designs, sizes and ages. The basic problem is that buildings are like fingerprints; no two are built or operated exactly alike. Even buildings that were constructed with the same template will in short order change.

That said, what could be done to make our benchmarks more meaningful. First, we must determine what we want to do with our benchmarking information. Once that is well understood, then we must make sure that our comparisons are relevant. In the case above, let's say we want to compare similar facilities by store type. It turns out for the 11 stores, we have three different types; two are big box retail with some grocery, five are older model stores and four are newer model stores. Rearranging the data, we can now compare the three different sets as shown in Figure 17.

Figure 17

But unless we know what drives the energy consumption in this type of store, we cannot be certain that our results are not misleading. For example, how do differences in sales volume affect the consumption? Is the weather the same at each of these sites for this month? Does that play a role in explaining some of the differences? Are all stores using the same fuels for heating and cooling? Are the hours of occupancy the same for each of these sites? All of these factors could potentially play a role in defining different consumption profiles. Therefore, before our next set of benchmarks, perhaps we should either begin to understand the key energy drivers for our facility or take them out of the equation altogether.

Given that benchmarks should be used as only one measure for evaluating performance, there are better ways of comparing geographically diverse buildings. With interval meter data, an assessment of building performance at various temperature bins is possible. For example, examining the scatter charts for a sample of buildings reveals that below 52 degrees, little if any comfort cooling is occurring.

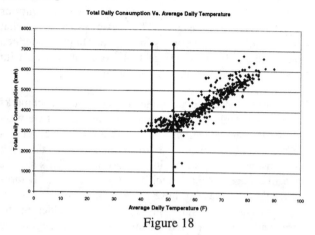

Figure 18

Taking a slice the data as shown in Figure 18 from each of the scatter charts provides us with a data set to compare at the same temperatures. Averaging the total daily consumptions for each building in temperatures between set ranges would allow comparison of buildings in nearly all geographic areas. The result is shown in Figure 19.

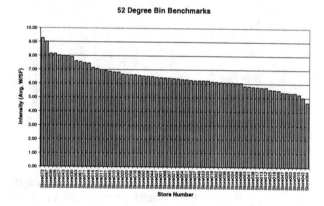

Figure 19

It is important to make sure that there are a sufficient number of data points to provide a representative sample for each site. If using hourly data, the data set should span more then a few days so that one unusual weather pattern does not skew the results.

The benchmarks in Figure 19 could be thought of as baseline benchmarks. We could also create similar benchmarks for other temperature bins that could provide insight for when comfort cooling is required. Benchmarking the same set of buildings at 72 degree or 82 degree bins might produce a different result as shown in Figure 20.

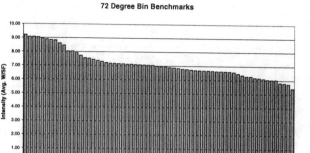

Figure 20

Notice that our best and worst performing stores shift around at different temperature bins. Placing the 10 worst performing stores in each temperature bin in a table would show how the rankings shift, as is done in Table 3.

Table 3

Store Number	Rank at Temperature Bin		
	52 Degrees	72 Degree	82 Degrees
Store061	10	1	1
Store057	5	5	2
Store067	2	4	3
Store039	3	6	4
Store071	nr	8	5
Store055	7	7	6
Store030	8	3	7
Store049	nr	10	8
Store072	1	2	9
Store023	nr	nr	10
Store026	4	nr	nr
Store043	6	nr	nr
Store063	9	9	nr

nr: not ranked in the bottom ten for this temperature bin.

Using interval meter data in this way, we have a much improved method to rank and to target improvements to the poorest performing stores.

Conclusion

Interval meter data analysis provides energy managers with an exciting opportunity to gain insights into the functioning of their buildings as never before on a continuous and cost effective basis. Used properly, the information available will assure that not only are our energy investments being applied in the correct areas, but that our investments will be maintained. Energy managers have always known where the energy dollars were being spent with current utility bill data. With interval meter data, energy managers can now begin to have answers as to when and why those dollars are being spent.

About the Authors

James Bolton holds a B.S.M.E. and an M.B.A. from the University of Maryland, College Park. He is a registered professional engineer and a Certified Energy Manager. As a Senior Engineer with Honeywell's Atrium project, he has helped to develop many of the analytical processes and techniques in use.

Prior to joining Honeywell Atrium, Mr. Bolton served for 13 years in various capacities at the University of Maryland Medical System in positions ranging from Energy Manager to Facilities Director.

Dagfinn Bell holds a BS ME from the Norwegian Institute of Technology and MS CE, Building Systems Program from University of Colorado, Boulder

Mr. Bell has been actively involved in research in whole building diagnostics, control, and energy performance modeling at the Joint Center for Energy Management in Boulder, Colorado. He has also organized, administered, and taught courses in Energy Management, Building Systems Simulation, and Environmental Design at The Norwegian University of Science and Technology in Trondheim, Norway. At Honeywell, he has been involved in developing analytical tools and techniques that are in daily use through Atrium.

Section 6
Environmental Technology

Chapter 63

INDOOR AIR & ENVIRONMENTAL QUALITY (IA&EQ) INVESTIGATION INTRODUCTION (INCLUDING TOXIC MOULD)

Dewayne R. Miller, REPA, CIAQP, CRMS
Walter H. Carter, REM, CIAQP, CRMS

ABSTRACT

This presentation will assist professionals in understanding Indoor Air and Environmental Quality (IA/EQ) and how these issues relate to them. The presentation introduces the history of IA/EQ from the beginning of recorded time through the present. This is accomplished by employing easily understandable thoughts and information that each professional will understand and will focus them on the total IA/EQ picture, as we know it today.

After IA/EQ recognition, this paper addresses governing Scientific Principles, Invasive Pathways, IA/EQ Issues along with Investigation and Resolutions. This paper will also discuss some of the variations in client's needs

The IA/EQ evaluation process presented will enlarge the scope of understanding for professionals and stretch the range of client and employee services strengthening environmental professionalism and improve client's quality of life.

INTRODUCTION

Outdoor air quality has improved in recent years whereas indoor air quality issues have not. In fact, some estimate IA/EQ to be as much as 70 times worse. Governmental IA/EQ inquiries have increased dramatically in recent years. WHY? Is this a "fad," a preconceived scare tactic to feed our already over active imagination of phobias, or is it really an issue that needs to be addressed?

Poor Indoor Air and Environmental Quality can affect:

> *Any Occupant*
> *in Any Structure*
> *in Any Economic Class*
> *at Any Time*

This paper is not meant to frighten the reader but to bring a balanced technical awareness to a "current hot topic." History and modern technology shed light into this deep and confusing subject.

BACKGROUND

Historically, there have been governmental restrictions in the United States regarding air quality. Chicago, Illinois, had restrictions on the generation of smoke from shipping, rails, and other emission sources as early as the 1850's. Closer to Atlanta and our home consider Ducktown, Tennessee. One of the first, if not "the" first, Federal lawsuit filed in the late 1890's dealt with improving air quality. The air was so bad in the Ducktown area; in order to see where you were going at 10:00 AM it was reported that one needed to use a lantern. They used an open pit burning method of treating the ore to remove the sulfur (content approximately 25%). Acid rain has played havoc with the vegetation and environment in this area. Improvement in the surrounding environment is slowly recovering with noted areas void of trees some 100 plus years after the fact.

Benjamin Franklin a noted 18th century statesman, scientist, inventor, and a signer of *The Declaration of*

Independence made the following statement:

> I considered fresh air an enemy and closed with extreme care every crack and crevice in the room I inhabited. Experience has convinced me of my error. I am certain that no air is so unwholesome as the air in a closed room that has been often breathed and not changed.

Approximately 1,400 BC techniques were written down that we follow in part today. The text is recorded in the Bible in Leviticus 14:33-47. A note for the non-Biblical scholar: The Hebrew word "tsaraath" means a number of items other than Leprosy. "tsaraath" covers a broad range of afflictions other than Leprosy and is analogous to any type of microbial agent such as mould and fungi. A shortened interpretive version of Leviticus 14:33-47 is as follows:

> If mildew reappears in the house after the stone has been torn out and the house is scraped and plastered the priest is to go examine it and, if the mildew has spread in the house, it is a destructive mildew. The house is unclean. It must be torn down—its stones, timbers, and all the plaster—and taken out of town to an unclean place.

> Anyone who goes in the house while it is closed up will be unclean till evening.

> Anyone who sleeps or eats in the house must wash his clothes.

Throughout history a shift has occurred from spending time outdoors (hunting, gathering and farming) to spending more time indoors within our structures (residences). Our structures are meant to provide us with warm (in the winter) or cool (summer) seasonally conditioned air, safety, and keep us dry and away from elements of weathering. Today people spend a greater percentage of their time indoors. In fact, people in the United States spend their time going from a conditioned residence to a conditioned vehicle to a conditioned work place to a conditioned vehicle to a conditioned store back to their conditioned residence. Some report that in the year 2002 in the United States we spend upwards from 70 to 90% of our time indoors. Being indoors in 2002 generally means being in an artificially conditioned environment. The question is: "Conditioned with WHAT?"

If this is true, that we spend more of our time indoors than at any other time in history, then what are the ramifications? It has been reported that there is a 20+% increase in asthma and related allergenic/allergic conditions over the last 20 years. Litigation in IA&EQ issues was almost non-existent in 1980 and now the judicial system is seeing a ground swell of these issues flow into their arena. The Ballard vs Farmers court case announced a verdict in the summer of 2001 awarding the Ballard's over 32 million dollars. The verdict was reached because of an IA&EQ issue. One of the services our firm provides is litigation support and we are currently involved with many cases in various stages of development. Through the media we are bombarded daily with reports of "sick" office buildings, schools, and single-family homes to large residential structures. Cartoons and comics address these same IA&EQ issues in their own particular way. Rex Morgan in the Sunday comic had an IA&EQ issue (mould) brought to light in its September 23, 2001 edition. Rex Morgan's comic was about Stachybotrys, a mold/mould/fungus.

A recent article quoted Dr. Harriet Burge, Ph.D., associate professor of environmental microbiology at Harvard University School of Public Health, in Cambridge, Massachusetts as saying "People should not live in moldy houses." This seems simple enough, but is it?

SCIENTIFIC PRINCIPLES

How do the various components related to IA&EQ get into my conditioned space? I believe the Second Law of Thermodynamics has some help for us to understand the methods of transportation (a simplified approach): Heat moves from Hot to Cold, Water moves from Wet to Dry, and Air moves from High to Low pressure. The Second Law of Thermodynamics has a variable helper called the Entropy; order verses disorder where disorder rules. To help us understand this complicated principle think of a house that is left in a state of neglect. Does it look better with age and neglect or does it look worse. Things will follow the path of least resistance. It takes work (energy) to make a house look good over time. There is upkeep, maintenance, and enhancement. If left to nature the house would be in a state of disrepair or disorder.

There are Threshold Limit Values (TLV)®[1] for a number of the more common chemical substances and physical agent and Biological Exposure Indices(BEI) ®. TLVs by definition refer to air concentrations of substances and represent conditions under which it is believed that nearly all workers may be repeatedly exposed day after day without adverse health effects (1998)[1] BEI's® are related to TLVs®. BEI® determinants are an index of an individual's "uptake" of a chemical or chemicals. Air monitoring to determine the TLV® indicates the potential "inhalation exposure" of an individual or group. There are Time Weighed Averages (TWA), Permissible Exposure Limits (PEL), and Excursion Limits (EL) for a number of similar chemical entities. These relate mainly to particulates and volatile organic compounds (VOC). There are acoustic, ergonomic, vibration, ionizing and non-ionizing radiation, thermal and cold stresses, etc. These are used to assist in determining the potential health concerns for individual or groups encountering the common chemical substances and physical agent.

One of the least known areas of IA&EQ is mould/mold/fungi. There are no TLVs® for most bioaerosols because sufficient information is not yet available. There are few, if any, standards established that relate to this class of IA&EQ bioaerosol issues. The ACGIH BIOAEROSOLS Assessment and Control book adopted the phrase "biological derived airborne contaminants" to describe bioaerosols (airborne particulates composed of, or derived from, living organisms) and VOCs released from living organisms. Bioaerosols include whole microorganisms as well as fragments, toxins, and particulate waste products from all varieties of living things (e.g., bacteria, fungi, plants, and animals). The ACGIH BIOAEROSOLS Assessment and Control book refers to their standard in the following definition. The publication states:

> Standards to prevent harmful exposures to air contaminants have five primary components: (a) the criteria or scientific basis for the standard, (b) a sampling method, (c) an analytical method, (d) a sampling method, and (e) a limit value. ACGIH has considered the possibility of recommending TLVs for bioaerosols and concluded that sufficient information is not yet available on these five components to which workers are exposed in non-manufacturing environments ACGIH (1998[a1]). TLVs exist for certain substances of biological origin, including cellulose; some wood, cotton, and grain dust; nicotine; pyrethrum; starch; subtilisins (proteolytic enzymes); sucrose; vegetable oil mist; and volatile components produced by living organisms (e.g., ammonia, carbon dioxide, ethanol, and hydrogen sulfide). However, there are no mandatory numerical limits against which investigators can

compare measurements of air or source concentrations for the majority of substances of biological origin that are associated with building-related exposures. Thus, in the U.S., sampling for biological derived air-borne contaminants is not conducted for the purpose of complying with any federal or state regulations other than for the agent for which existing TLVs have been adopted as standards.

Fungi are all around us all the time and almost everywhere. It went into space with the astronauts and clouded the pane of a space window. The mould clouded an otherwise clear sharp vision. The Fungi soul function is to break down cellulose to its simpler parts. If mould could do that then there is practically no reason why mould cannot be inside our place of work or residence.

Mould mainly needs food and moisture to survive. There generally is not a shortage of food so let's concentrate on moisture. Our favorite phrase to assist people to understand the current concern is: *It is all about Moisture. Follow the moisture trail. Repair the source and remove the mould.*

INDOOR AIR & ENVIRONMENTAL QUALITY

If we accept that IA&EQ issues are real, known in the past, and recognized in the present; then, how do they arrive into our residence, place of work or other structures we frequent. They get in through the doors, attics, crawlspaces, basements, holes in the structures such as windows, vents, etc. They come from indoor amplification sites and are transported to our space and breathing zone through any number of means. The *means* follow our preceding simplified version of the *Second Law of Thermodynamics*. We classify them as particulates, vapors or odors, and bioaerosols. These can be individual concerns or multi-factor issues encompassing all three classifications.

PARTICULATES

Many particulates are allergenic to certain individuals. Particulates are in the form of smoke, pollen, animal dander, dried saliva, cockroach, dirt, soot, dust, lead, asbestos, fecal matter, etc.

The ill effects of smoking are well documented in individuals. Along with the aforementioned there is the effect of Secondhand Smoke (SHS) or better known as Environmental Tobacco Smoke (ETS). ETS is defined as a mixture of the smoke given off by the burning end of a cigarette, pipe, or cigar and the smoke exhaled from the lungs of smokers. The health effects from ETS are: eye, nose, and throat irritation, headaches, etc. ETS is estimated to cause 3,000 lung cancer deaths in non-smokers each year. This is in question but what is not questioned is the serious respiratory health effects of ETS in children.

Pollen is one of the most annoying and common allergens causing suffering for over 30 million people. Plants produce these microscopic grains used for reproduction. These microscopic grains are generally between 20 to 120 microns in size (human hair diameter = 70-100 microns). Pollen was designed for efficient transportation and is extremely light. Pollen can remain airborne for many hours, even days at a time. Ragweed pollen has reportedly been found up to 400 miles from its original source and up to 2 miles high in the air.

Another common particulate is dust mite allergens. Dust mites digest human skin cells and are commonly located in bedding, upholstered furniture, and other textile materials. Then there are allergens from pets such as cats and dogs as well as unwanted indoor inhabitants such as cockroaches and other insects. Equipment frequently used in an office environment is a noted producer of particulate matter. Copy machine toners and microscopic paper bits are two types of irritants we have encountered during our investigations. Ordinary indoor dust can contain significant quantities of similar particulate allergens.

Deposits of black soot inside structures were first reported in 1994 in both single and attached housing. Occurrences of soot deposits were first noted in Florida. Soot was associated with installation of new central heating and air conditioning (HAC) systems and the moderate use of candles. Following is a list in order of the greatest occurrence of soot deposits: burning of candles, cigarette smoke, fireplace, natural gas, and oil lamps.

Other particulate issues would include lead, asbestos, etc.

Volatile Organic Compound (VOC), Gases, & Odorants

Volatile Organic Compound (VOC), Gases, and Odors are also common to indoor environments. They come in the form of odorants, gas irritants, Total Volatile Organic Compounds (TVOC), Aldehydes, Semi-Volatile Organic Compound (SVOC), Microbial Volatile Organic Compound (MVOC). VOCs can often lead to irritation for those exposed. Common irritation symptoms include headaches and eye and upper respiratory irritation. High levels can lead to additional and more severe symptoms such as dizziness and mental fatigue.

VOCs are organic or carbon-based compounds, which vaporize or turn into a gas at normal room temperature and in addition to causing odor and/or irritants some are neurotoxins. VOCs are easily emitted through the air during use (e.g., liquid solvent) or after the manufacture of a product (e.g., particle board, plastics, etc.). Because VOCs are easily evaporated, they can quickly pollute the air and are easily inhaled by people. The boiling points for VOCs are generally in the range of 50-160°C. Some common VOCs would be toluene, Xylene (meta and/or para), benzene used in cleaning; decamethyl (DM) pentasiloxane used in deodorants; and Limonene to give a lemon fresh smell. TVOC values are a collection or sum of all the VOCs.

Aldehydes are semi-volatile to volatile organic compounds that are known irritants in indoor air with a aldehyde functional group (HC=O). These are usually found in wood and paper products such as 2-Butenal, formaldehyde, etc. SVOCs have boiling points of 240-400°C, generally have a higher molecular weight than VOCs, and are less likely to be airborne indoors. Some common sources include pesticides and manufacturing processes like di-n-butyl phthalate are plasticizers in plastics, 4,4'-DDD, Chrysene, Pyrene, etc.

MVOCs are VOCs that are produced by microbial organisms such as fungi and bacteria. These compounds are produced during the metabolism and/or decay of the microbial organisms. Most have a musty or dirty odor like a bag of potting soil. Examples of MVOC are methylfuran, 2-hexanone or the smell of vomit and 8 carbon alcohols. The MVOC 1-octen-3-ol generally suggest old microbial growth.

A recent study found toluene, which usually is an indicator of human-made pollution, emanates from plants as well. VOCs in the atmosphere react with other chemicals to form smog. "Globally, plants emit about 90 percent of the VOC concentration in the air" says Alex Guenther of the National Center for Atmospheric Research in Bolder, Colorado. In urban areas, however, human-made sources predominate.

If one is interested in finding out more on odors, there is an American Society of Testing Materials (ASTM) standard number D6165 on comparison, detection, and identification of the odors of paints, inks, and related materials.

Nova Scotia has instituted fragrance restrictions. Dr. Roy Fox is the director of the Nova Scotia Environmental Health Center and a professor in the Departments of Medicine and Community Health and Epidemiology, Faculty of Medicine at Dalhousie University in Fall River, Nova Scotia. Dr. Fox stated that the use of fragrances and products containing fragrances is widespread in society. In many instances, these products contain synthetic VOCs that have replaced natural scents. Some public buildings, hospitals, colleges, libraries, and public transportation adopted "No Scent" policies. Dr. Fox has further stated these products may be neurotoxic or carcinogenic and they may "trigger asthma, precipitate migraines, and irritate, or exacerbate various symptoms." From personal experience, a relative of ours would drop to his knees fighting for breath if he was near someone wearing a certain cologne or perfume. He always carried a portable fan with him in case he encountered such a situation.

Radon is a gas and has been studied well. Radon will not be treated in-depth in this paper other than being recognized as a gas that is known to cause cancer. Radon is reported to be the second leading cause of lung cancer behind cigarettes.

Bioaerosols
Bioaerosols are defined in the American Conference of Governmental Industrial Hygienists (ACGIH) BIOAEROSOLS Assessment and Control book as:

> "Those airborne particles that are living or originate from living organisms. Bioaerosols include microorganisms (i.e., culturable, nonculturable, and dead microorganisms) and fragments, toxins, and particulate waste products from all varieties of living things. Bioaerosols are ubiquitous in nature and may be modified by human activities. All persons are repeatedly exposed, day after day, to a wide variety of such materials. Individual bioaerosols range in size

from submicroscopic particles (<0.01 micron) to particles greater than 100 microns in diameter."

Bioaerosols are biologically derived materials, which are natural to outdoor and indoor environments. Like most natural products, they can be considered as contaminates under certain conditions if located indoors at a "trigger" concentration.

Viruses are organisms and one example of a disease agent is the Influenza Virus which causes respiratory infection. The Spanish Influenza of 1918 is reported to have caused over 25 million deaths over a three year cycle covering the world three times. Bacteria can be an organism such as *Legionella Pneumophila* which caused the 1976 Inhalation Fever Outbreak in the Legionnaire Convention in Philadelphia, Pennsylvania. Bacteria spores, cell fragments (endotoxins) and cell products (allergens) also contain disease agents.

Fungi are organisms such as the disease agent Sporobolomyces allergens. Histoplasma capsulatum is a fungi spore found in bird droppings that causes a systemic infection. Alternaria allergens cause asthma and rhinitis. Aspergillus toxins (aflatoxin, ochratoxin, sterigmatocystin) cause liver cancer. Fungi cell fragments and cell products have allergens, glucans, toxins, and MVOCs which cause headaches and mucous membrane irritation. There are other common bioaerosols such as Protozoa, Algae, Vascular plants, Arthropods, Mammals, and Birds that cause numerous health effects.

Mould and its spores are mainly a result of damp environments. As stated earlier in the paper, mould mainly needs food and moisture to survive.

For improved Indoor Air and Environmental Quality minimize particulates, reduce or eliminate VOCs, and because there generally is not a shortage of food for mould, concentrate on moisture. Our motto is: *"It is all about Moisture. Follow the moisture trail. Repair the source and remove the mould."*

REFERENCE
[1]American Conference of Governmental Industrial Hygienists (ACGIH)

Chapter 64

UPDATES ON LEGISLATION AND INSURANCE ACTIVITY IN THE NATION FOR MOULD, ASBESTOS, & LEAD

Walter H. Carter, REM, CIAQP, CRMS
Dewayne R. Miller, REPA, CIAQP, CRMS

ABSTRACT

There currently is a lot of activity in the legislation and insurance arena—some good, some bad. There is a large outcry from the public. They want to be protected both physically and financially (insurance) from the Indoor Air and Environmental Quality (IA&EQ) issues. Lawsuits are the boundary makers and need to be included to yield an understanding to the whole picture as the IA&EQ issues are woven into today's society. This paper will address the trends in the regulations, legal, legislation and insurance perspectives as they relate to the current needs of our society for asbestos, lead, and mould (mold/fungi).

INTRODUCTION

The asbestos and lead regulations have been set now for a number of years with only minor refining activity. There is an up-and-coming asbestos issue brewing in Libby, Montana. The story is Libby (Montana) could be the single biggest public health concern in the United States, and it swirls around vermiculite (which is contaminated with asbestos fibers). The inside and outside air surrounding the World Trade Center (WTC) will also be addressed in the coming months and years and will be comprised of particles, lead, asbestos, etc. Mould issues are still being addressed as we speak. Our firm is involved with these areas and we are able to speak from first-hand knowledge about these issues.

ASBESTOS

There are restrictions and a partial ban on asbestos products manufactured in the US. There are estab-
lished standard practices and controls for asbestos, such as the visual inspection of asbestos abatement projects (American Society for Testing and Materials [ASTM] Designation E 1368-99). The U.S. Occupational Safety and Health Administration (OSHA) has a number of specific industrial standards in the Federal Register such as 29 CFR 1910.1001 (General Industrial Standards), 29 CFR 1915.1001 (Shipyard Employment Standards), 29 CFR 1926.1101 (Construction Industrial Standards), and Respiratory Protection Standards 29 CFR 1910.134. The Environmental Protection Agency (EPA) 40 CFR Part 61 and Part 763. There have standards such as those under the National Emission Standard for Hazardous Air Pollutants (NESHAP), U.S. EPA Asbestos Hazard Emergency Response Act (AHERA), and ASHARA Amendment. These are some of the federal requirements and individual states have their own.

Asbestos is classified as a toxic substance and is known to cause adverse health effects in humans and the environment. There is an abundant amount of federal and state regulatory directives dealing with asbestos as compared with lead and the mould issues. There are fees for training, certifications, and other established programs. Often OSHA and EPA directives were different and have been resolved over time for the most part.

Vermiculite is laced (contaminated) with Tremolite asbestos fibers. Loose-fill vermiculite was widely used as an insulation material in attic spaces. Aware of the potential health threat, the U.S. EPA contracted with Versar, Inc. of Springfield, Virginia, (Versar Report) in 1982 to assess the extent of human exposure to vermiculite. Vermiculite is mined as a mica-like material and resembles a closed book with pages of thin flakes bound tightly together. The ore is heated 1000(F, evaporating the water trapped between the flakes. The vermiculite expands or exfoliates forming the final, low-density free-flowing product. In 1982, 52 exfoliation plants were operating in 32 states. Asbestos fibers were found floating in the air 30 miles away from the vermiculite processing and packaging plants. The Versar Report estimated that 476,000 tons of loose-fill vermiculite insulation had been installed during the nine-year period ending in 1980, exposing 1.6 million installers and 4.2 inhabitants to asbestos fibers. This study failed to take into account the houses insulated before 1972 or after 1980. The exposure of remodelers or homeowners who disturbed vermiculite already in place was not assessed. The Libby deposit is unique among commercial U.S. vermiculite deposits in having an average amphibote asbestos content of 4 to 6 percent. Miners and millers were, at times, exposed to high levels of dust containing asbestos. Many workers developed health problems as a result of those exposures. Some residents of Libby who were exposed to high levels of asbestos also have been diagnosed with asbestos-related symptoms.

Officials are concerned about the asbestos content of the soils around Libby and are using a hyperspectral remote-sensing survey in Libby to assist mapping the distributions of the asbestiform amphiboles in soils. The Libby vermiculite mine closed in 1990, and shipments of vermiculite from the Libby mill site ended in 1992.

LEAD

Lead-based paints is a "New Comer" to the federal and state regulatory agencies. Today, lead is classified as a toxic substance and is known to cause adverse health effects in humans and the environment. In 1978 lead-based paint for residential uses was banned by the Consumer Products Safety Commission. However, lead-based paint for industrial uses, such as bridges and other steel structures, is still permitted.

In the residential housing sector, the U.S. Department of Housing and Urban Development (HUD) estimates that there are 57 million privately owned and occupied homes built before 1980 that contain lead-based paint. Of those homes, approximately 9.9 million are occupied by children younger than 7 years old. Children under the age 7 are at the greatest risk to lead-based paint hazards. It should be noted that,

if it is in good condition and when it is left intact, lead-based paint as well as asbestos by itself is not likely to present a hazard. Like asbestos, deteriorating lead-based paint presents a significant public health challenge. However, for lead-based paint in residential housing specifically children under the age of 7 years old present significant health challenges whereas for asbestos the main thrust is for worker safety in an industrial setting.

There are federal and state regulations, rules, and memorandums dealing with the lead issue. Most of the driving force has come from the EPA such as from the HUD part VIII. The Federal Register's Wednesday, March 6, 1996, has 24 CFR Part 35 and 40 CFR 745 which deals with lead; requirements for the disclosure of known lead-based paint and/or lead-based paint hazards in housing; final rule. Most of us know this under the Residential Lead-Based Paint Hazard Act (Title X). The residential community is under an obligation to disclose to perspective buyers, etc. if there is lead-based paint present in housing built prior to 1978.

Then Attorney General Janet Reno and Housing Secretary Andrew Cuomo announced in mid summer of 1999 multiple court actions of over $1 million dollars against landlords who violated federal law by failing to warn their tenants that their homes may contain lead-based paint hazards. During that same time period EPA cites seven private and parochial schools in Washington, DC, for violating regulations on the inspection and management of asbestos in schools.

MOULD/MOLD/FUNGI

Fungi are all around us all the time and almost everywhere. It went into space with the astronauts and clouded the pane of a space window. The mould clouded an otherwise clear sharp vision. The Fungi soul function is to break down cellulose (complex carbohydrate) to its simpler components. If mould could do that, then there is no practical reason why mould cannot be inside our place of work, residence, or anywhere else we visit.

Mould mainly needs food and moisture to survive. There generally is not a shortage of food so we will concentrate on moisture. Our favorite phrase to assist people to understand the current concern is: **"It is all about Moisture. Follow the moisture trail. Repair the source and remove the mould"**.

Mould is a "Real New Comer" as compared to Asbestos and Lead to the public awareness, legislation, litigation, insurance industry, and regulatory agencies. There is activity on the federal and state legislation levels with certain states taking an early lead regarding mould.

There has been litigation in the court system dealing with asbestos and lead. There are some Insurance precedents and, as always, is still evolving and has been for years. Court decisions have been made in the asbestos and lead arena. Mould, on the other hand, is currently under a state of flux in activity both in the legislation and court arenas. The insurance industry is trying to get a handle on and manage this new risk. The Insurance Industry is accustomed to working with risk in an established field but they are not familiar with an evolving field such as what is occurring in the mould arena. To confound this subject even more is the time eternal question of what comes first "the chicken or the egg?" Is it: Legislation, Regulation or Litigation? What is driving whom? And Why?

LEGAL ISSUES

Many lawsuits have been filed in recent years and awards given out by the court system. Some of the more notable examples are:

- $65 million suit filed in New York for bodily injury due to exposure to toxic mould.

- $60 million awarded for toxic mould infestation in Florida that included building repairs, defense expenditures, relocation expenses, and workers' compensation claims.

- $32 plus million homeowners' awarded in Texas for insurers' failure to properly handle a mould claim. This was mainly a "bad faith" claim and was the one that served as a "wake up call" to the Insurance Industry in the U.S. This will likely spread around the world.

- $18 million awarded in California for failure to properly handle a toxic mould claim.

- $6.7 million awarded in North Carolina for construction defects, which resulted in water intrusion and mould infestation.

The previous litigation issues mainly deal with improper handling of covered water damage losses, which resulted in mould amplification so extensive and severe as to present potentially serious health hazards. In many situations, they had suffered actual health problems. Not only were the building inhabitants involved but also potentially to anyone who unwittingly entered the structure. Mould growth has and can cause structural damage as well as damage to other building materials that are cellulosic based such as paper and wood products. There are many other forms of litigation in various stages of development but the above gives a flavor of what has come about and what is to be seen in the litigation arena.

Potential defendants in litigation includes anyone who is connected to the mould invasion usually brought about through an elevation in moisture through a variety of reasons. Defendants in litigation could include insurance companies, architects, developers, engineers, contractors, building managers, construction material manufacturers, distributors, suppliers, testers (such as ourselves), remediators, property owners, and others.

REGULATION

There are Threshold Limit Values (TLV)®[1] for a number of the more common chemical substances and physical agent and Biological Exposure Indices (BEI)®. TLVs by definition refer to air concentrations of substances and represent conditions under which it is believed that nearly all workers may be repeatedly exposed day after day without adverse health effects (1998)[1]. BEIs® are related to TLVs®. BEI® determinants are an index of an individual's "uptake" of a chemical or chemicals. Air monitoring to determine the TLV® indicates the potential "inhalation exposure" of an individual or group. There are Time Weighed Averages (TWA), Permissible Exposure Limits (PEL), and Excursion Limits (EL) for a number of similar chemical entities. These relate mainly to particulates and volatile organic compounds (VOC). There are factors including acoustic, ergonomic, vibration, ionizing and non-ionizing radiation, thermal and cold stresses, etc. These are used to assist in determining the potential health concerns for individual or groups encountering the common chemical substances and physical agent.

One of the least known areas of IA&EQ is mould/mould/fungi. There are no TLVs® for most bioaerosols because sufficient information is not yet available. There are few, if any, standards established that relate to this class of IA&EQ bioaerosol issues. The ACGIH BIOAEROSOLS Assessment and Control book adopted the phrase "biological derived airborne contaminants" to describe bioaerosols (airborne particulates composed of, or derived from, living organisms) and VOCs released from living organisms. Bioaerosols include whole microorganisms as well as fragments, toxins, and particulate waste products from all varieties of living things (e.g., bacteria, fungi, plants, and animals). The ACGIH BIOAEROSOLS Assessment and Control book refers to their standard in the following definition. The publication states:

> Standards to prevent harmful exposures to air contaminants have five primary components: (a) the criteria or scientific basis for the standard, (b) a sampling method, (c) an analytical method, (d) a sampling method, and (e) a limit value. ACGIH has considered the possibility of recommending TLVs for bioaerosols and concluded that sufficient information is not yet available on these five components to which workers are exposed in non-manufacturing environments ACGIH (1998[a1]). TLVs exist for certain substances of biological origin, including cellulose; some wood, cotton, and grain dust; nicotine; pyrethrum; starch; subtilisins (proteolytic enzymes); sucrose; vegetable oil mist; and volatile components produced by living organisms (e.g., ammonia, carbon dioxide, ethanol, and hydrogen sulfide). However, there are no mandatory numerical limits against which investigators can compare measurements of air or source concentrations for the majority of substances of biological origin that are associated with building-related exposures. Thus, in the U.S., sampling for biological derived air-borne contaminants is not conducted for the purpose of complying with any federal or state regulations other than for the agent for which existing TLVs have been adopted as standards.

There are only guidelines for remediation:
A. United States Environmental Protection Agency (EPA) *Mold Remediation in Schools and Commercial Buildings* issued in 2001.
B. American Conference of Governmental Industrial Hygienists (ACGIH) in Cincinnati Ohio *Bioaerosols Assessment and Control* issued in 1999.
C. New York City Department of Health (NYCDH) in New York City, New York, *Assessment and Remediation of Fungi in Indoor Environments*. Issued in 2000 by the New York City Department of Health, Bureau of Environmental & Occupational Disease Epidemiology.

LEGISLATION

In the 2001 session of the California Legislature Governor Davis signed two bills SB732 and AB284. SB732 is a multifaceted attempt to protect the public from adverse health effects relating to indoor moulds. SB732 requires the Department of Health Services (DHS) to consider the adoption of PELs for moulds for indoor environments. In the previous section it was noted there are no PELs for mould at this time. SB732 requires the DHS to give special consideration to immune-compromised individuals, pregnant women, infants, the elderly, and other "eggshell" groups in adopting PELs. SB732 requires DHS to develop standards to assess the health threat posed by the presence of mould. AB284 is based on the idea of promoting a more thorough understanding of the options for addressing mould contamination. The law requires DHS to undertake a study, under the direction of a review panel organized by DHS, on fungal contaminations in indoor environments. A Texas bill SB859 relates to establishing mandatory guidelines for indoor air quality in newly constructed or renovated public school buildings. U.S. Congress (107th) Representative John Conyers from Michigan introduce his "United States Toxic Mold Safety & Protection Act" this summer (2002). The major components of his bill would: (1) Calls on the EPA to issue guidelines that specifically spells out what levels of mould are acceptable, what levels are dangerous; (2) Establishes EPA guidelines to set standards and government oversight over what has become an unregulated industry of inspectors and clean-ups by requiring states to license and monitor mould inspectors and mould remediators (mould removers); (3) Calls on the Center For Disease Control (CDC) to authorize a long term study of the health effects of mould, and publish these findings in a report to Congress and the President; (4) Allows states to tap federal dollars to clean mould disasters; (5) Establish a federal toxic mould insurance program that would provide adequate compensation for families that do not have home owners insurance, or whose private home owners insurance does not sufficiently cover the cost of toxic mould removal, or any other cost incurred such as moving into a new home or an apartment; (6) Families or individuals whose health has been adversely impacted due to exposure to toxic mould, and has been diagnosed by a physician, would be eligible to receive Medicaid, if they are (a) uninsured or (b) underinsured at the time they suffered physical harm due to toxic mould poisoning; (7) Mandate federal guidelines that states must adhere to that require home owners and residential real estate developers to disclose mould problems upon the sale of their houses.

INSURANCE

It is all about covered losses for the insurance companies and re-insurers. Texas' most popular homeowners' insurance policy (HO-B) covers water damage if it was the result of an "accidental" discharge. Because "accidental" is both vague and broad in scope, most states add the word "sudden," as in "sudden and accidental". It is a qualifier that tends to limit claims to events such as burst pipes and ruptured washing machine hoses, and to exclude events such as dripping pipes and leaking roofs. Thus, in Texas, to the extent the policies cover more instances of water damage than the policies in other states, and courts have ruled that mould resulting from such water damage must be covered. The net effect is that Texas homeowners have obtained more substantial coverage for mould than homeowners in other states.

Insurance policies can be like 'reading the complete unabridged congressional record in a single sitting after working a 12-hour shift.' That withstanding The *Wall Street Journal* May 14, 2002, edition had a headline that read, "Harsh Policies Hit With Big Losses, Insurers Put Squeeze on Homeowners."

Texas appears to be the Mould Capital of the U.S. with Corpus Christi as the hub. The City of Corpus Christi is reported to have 5 times more claims than any other city in Texas. It is logical to infer that California is the Mould Celebrity Capital of the U.S. Several large Insurance companies (they are reported to have written about 70% of the homeowners policies) in Texas have restricted issuing coverage for mould. If mould coverage is available it is high or higher and heaven forbid the individual that can locate an insurer to obtain mould coverage if they have previously had a mould related claim on their residence.

Since 1997 an average premium for a Texas comprehensive home insurance policy that offered between $125,000 and $150,000 worth of coverage cost $985 annually, according to the National Association of Insurance Commissioners. By comparison, the national average in 1997 for a comprehensive insurance policy was $481, a difference of some $500. Despite higher premiums, insurers claim that they are experiencing significantly higher losses in Texas than in other states because of the excessive number and severity of mould-related claims. As a result, Texas Insurance Commissioner, Jose Montemayer, issued an order on November 28, 2001 that allowed insurers, beginning January 1, 2002, to limit coverage under the modified HO-B policies for some mould damage that resulted from a covered peril. The new ruling orders comprehensive coverage for removal of mould stemming from "a sudden and accidental discharge" of water, but eliminates payments for costly remediation procedures such as testing, treating, containing, or disposing of mould "beyond what is necessary to repair or replace properly what is physically damaged by water." The order also makes it mandatory for insurance companies to offer "buy-back" coverage. This means that companies must offer enhanced coverage for mould remediation costs in increments of 25 percent, 50 percent, and 100 percent of their policy limits that includes remediation procedures. Under this order, insurers may offer the new coverage as early as January 1, 2002, but must offer it by January 1, 2003. Homeowners who elect to purchase the additional coverage will be subjected to underwriting on an individual basis.

Texas as well as other states are trying to come to grips with this very important aspect of being able to provide insurance to its constituents.

REFERENCES

[1]American Conference of Governmental Industrial Hygienists (ACGIH)

Chapter 65

BUILDINGS FOR A LIVABLE FUTURE

Nick Stecky

ABSTRACT

Today, owners, occupants and communities are beginning to hold buildings to higher standards. And industry leaders are responding by creating physical assets that save energy and resources, and are more satisfying and productive, as well as environmentally accountable.

Building owners who want the greatest return on investment can take a path that is green both economically and environmentally. How are they doing it? Through integrated building solutions.

An integrated, or whole-building approach, actually means that up-front costs can be less than conventional construction, and that costs over the life of the building will be significantly lower. By building in an integrated way, owners can expect high performance buildings that offer:

- Increased efficiencies of systems and use of resources and energy;

- Quality indoor environments that are healthy, secure, pleasing and productive for occupants and operators;

- Optimal economic and environmental performance;

- Wise use of building sites, assets and materials;

- Landscaping, material use and recycling efforts inspired by the natural environment;

- Lessened human impact upon the natural environment.

MAKING IT ALL COME TOGETHER: THE USGBC

The U.S. Green Building Council (USGBC.Org), a balanced consensus coalition representing every sector of the building industry, spent five years developing, testing and refining the LEED Green Building Rating System. LEED stands for "Leadership in Energy & Environmental Design," and when adopted from the start of a project helps facilitate integration throughout the design, construction, and operation of buildings.

MISSION STATEMENT

The U.S. Green Building Council is the nation's foremost coalition of leaders from across the building industry working to promote buildings that are environmentally responsible, profitable, and healthy places to live and work.

The resources required for creating, operating, and replenishing our current level of infrastructure are enormous, yet the resources available for such activity are diminishing. To remain competitive and to continue to expand and produce profits in the future, the building industry must address the economic and environmental consequences of its actions. This need is driving the building industry to develop and market products that are more environmentally and economically viable.

The diffracted building industry needed a single entity to provide it with integration, leadership, and education. Since its formation in 1993, the US Green Building Council has fulfilled this need, becoming the center for debate and action on environmental issues facing the industry's multiple interests.

471

The Council has grown to more than 800 leading international organizations including: product manufacturers such as Johnson Controls Inc., United Technologies/Carrier, Herman Miller, and Armstrong World Industries; environmental leaders such as the Natural Resources Defense Council, the Rocky Mountain Institute, and the Audubon Society; building and design professionals such as the American Society of Interior Designers and the American Institute of Architects; retailers and building owners such as the Gap and Target Stores; as well as financial industry leaders such as the Bank of America.

The mission of this unprecedented coalition is to accelerate the adoption of green building practices, technologies, policies, and standards. The USGBC is a committee-based organization endeavoring to move the green building industry forward with market-based solutions. Another vital function of the Council is linking industry and government. The Council has formed effective relationships and priority programs with key federal agencies, including the U.S. DOE, EPA, NIST, and GSA.

The Council's membership is open and balanced. It is comprised of leading and visionary representation from all segments of the building industry including product manufacturers, environmental groups, building owners, building professionals, utilities, city government, research institutions, professional societies and universities. This type of representation provides a unique, integrated platform for carrying out important programs and activities.

COUNCIL OPERATIONS

Committee-Based:
The heart of this effective coalition is the committees in which members design strategies that are implemented by staff and expert consultants. These committees provide a forum for members to resolve differences, build alliances, and forge cooperative solutions that add value to the membership rather than adding costs.

Member-Driven:
Issues identified by members are targeted as the highest priority. An annual review of achievements is conducted that allows the USGBC to set policy, revise strategies and devise work plans based on members' needs.

Consensus-Focused:
The USGBC works together to promote green build-

ings and, in doing so, helps foster greater economic vitality and environmental health at lower cost. The various industry segments bridge ideological gaps to develop balanced policies that benefit the entire industry.

Council Member Benefits
The strength and credibility of the USGBC is derived from the diversity and balance of the membership. No other organization represents the entire green building industry.

Members have access to a clearinghouse of the best green building-related information possible on emerging trends, policies, and products. These include product databases, case studies, staff papers, directories, and other resources. Information is the key to the success of any business, especially one evolving so quickly.

Members gain networking opportunities with industry leaders and policy makers. From forums to advisory boards, from conferences to committee meetings, the Council provides myriad opportunities to expand one's network and forge working relationships with industry leaders, key policy makers, and strategic partners like AIA, ULI, BOMA, IFMA, and CSI.

Membership Categories
- Building Product Manufacturers
- Building Owners, Managers, Users, and Brokers
- Financial and Insurance Firms
- Professional Societies
- Design, Architectural, Engineering and Technical Firms
- Contractors and Builders
- Environmental Groups
- Utilities
- Universities and Technical Research Institutes
- State, Local, and Federal Governments
- Building Control Service Contractors and Manufacturers

LEED™ OVERVIEW

The LEED Green Building Rating System™ is a priority program of the US Green Building Council. It is a voluntary, consensus-based, market-driven building rating system based on existing proven technology. It evaluates environmental performance from an integrated or "whole building" perspective over a building's life cycle, providing a definitive standard for what constitutes a "green building."

LEED™ is based on accepted energy and environmental principles and strikes a balance between known effective practices and emerging concepts. Unlike other rating systems currently in existence, the development of LEED Green Building Rating System™ was instigated by the US Green Council Membership, representing all segments of the building industry, and has been open to public scrutiny.

LEED™ is a self-assessing system designed for rating new and existing commercial, institutional, and high-rise residential buildings. It is a feature-oriented system where credits are earned for satisfying each criteria. Different levels of green building certification are awarded based on the total credits earned. The system is designed to be comprehensive in scope, yet simple in operation.

LEED organizes the Essentials of Integrated Green Design into five categories:
- Sustainable Sites
- Materials & Resources
- Water Efficiency
- Energy & Atmosphere
- Indoor Environmental Quality

Details on the LEED system of Green Building measurement and information for LEED Certification of buildings and LEED Accreditation for professionals are available on the USGBC.Org website.

BENEFITS OF LEED

The Environment
At the onset, LEED was created to standardize the concept of building green to offer the building industry a universal program that provided concrete guidelines for the design and construction of sustainable buildings for a livable future. As such, it is firmly rooted in the conservation of our world's resources. Each credit point awarded through the rating system reduces our demand and footprint upon the natural environment.

The following are a few examples of how LEED is changing the way we think about design, construction and its environmental impact. Choosing to build on a brownfield site means taking the necessary steps to clean the area prior to laying foundation. Buying local building materials reduces transportation emissions. Using rainwater for irrigation ensures an ample supply of potable water for drinking. And using daylight for indoor illumination reduces overall energy consumption.

Economics
Conventional wisdom says that the construction of an environmentally friendly, energy efficient building brings with it a substantial price tag and extended timetables. This need not be the case. Breakthroughs in building materials, operating systems and integrated technologies have made building green not only a timely, cost effective alternative, but a preferred method of construction among the nation's leading professionals.

From the USGBC:
"Smart business people recognize that high performance green buildings produce more than just a cleaner, healthier environment. They also positively impact the bottom line. Benefits include: better use of building materials, significant operational savings and increased workplace productivity."

In many instances, green alternatives to conventional building methods are less expensive to purchase and install. An even larger number provide tremendous operational savings. The USGBC and LEED offer the building industry a fiscally sound platform on which to build their case for whole-building design and construction. Green Buildings can show a positive return on investment for owners and builders.

Building green also enhances asset value. According to organizations such as IFMA and BOMA, the asset value of a property rises at a rate of ten times the value of the operational savings. For example, if green building efficiency reduces operating costs by $1/sq ft per year, the asset value of that property rises by ten times that amount or $10. For a 300,000-sq-ft office complex that annual savings could be $300,000 and the asset value increase would be approximately $3,000,000. It pays to be efficient.

Social Implications
In addition to the environmental and economic benefits of building green, the are also significant social benefits. These include increased productivity, a healthy work environment, comfort and satisfaction to name a few. The good news about green buildings can then be leveraged with local and trade media through press releases, ceremonies or events. By calling attention to the building and its certification status, owners speak volumes about themselves. The USGBC writes:

"Like a strong prospectus, building green sends the right message about a company or organization: it's well run, responsible, and committed to the future."

This too has a direct effect on the bottom line.

Benefits to the Architectural and Engineering Design Community

All too often, market forces drive a building design team to focus on minimum first cost regardless of what the overall life cycle costs of this minimum first cost design may be. The end result is that all elements of society, from owner, to occupants and to the community end up with a building which is less than what it could have or should have been. It used too many resources in construction, its energy and operating costs are high and it does not provide the optimum indoor environment for employee productivity.

However, installation of the LEED Process of forming an integrated design team on Conceptual Design Day One promotes the formation of a creative solution to the particular building's needs being planned for. Within this creative roundtable of equals, the Team is able to maximize use of the Collective Wisdom of the members and develop a design concept that can be both green and economic. For example, increased use of natural light to displace some artificial light results in a reduced load on air-conditioning systems. These AC Systems can then be downsized, resulting in reduced equipment first costs and reduction in electricity use, both through the artificial lighting reduction and reduced cooling loads. Small savings multiply and reverberate throughout the design, ultimately having significant impacts on overall first costs and operating costs.

The most significant benefit to the A/E design community is that LEED promotes and rewards creative solutions. For those A/E firms seeking to provide more value to their clients, LEED is a way to achieve this. LEED can become a standard for design excel-

lence, and at once providing an A/E with a brand differentiator versus the competition.

SUMMARY

When building "Green," the sum is larger than the individual parts only when all components are integrated into a single unified system. Integration draws upon every aspect of the building to realize efficiencies, cost savings, and continuous returns on investment.

Building owners and managers benefit from state-of-the-art building automation systems that can integrate and control all of the various technologies involved in being green.

And for the A/E community, ability to do Green Design offers a significant differentiator that enables a firm to demonstrate its abilities and design excellence. Sustainable and green design are not yet "commodity" skills that all firms can lay claim to. As such, LEED and sustainable design offer an outstanding competitive edge in the marketplace for firms seeking a Leadership Position of Excellence.

About the Author:
Nick Stecky, Business Development Manager for Johnson Controls, is a LEED Accredited Professional and a Certified Energy Manager, CEM. Currently he is on the Steering Committee for the formation of the New Jersey Chapter of the USGBC and the Membership Chairman. He has over thirty years experience in the design, construction, operations and maintenance of facilities including corporate headquarters and USDOE nuclear laboratories. He has a BS in Engineering and a Masters in Systems Science. He is very active in ASHRAE activities, and was the President of the New Jersey Chapter. In addition, he is a regional Vice President of the Association of Energy Engineers. He has taught courses on LEED Green Buildings, ASHRAE Standards, Energy Deregulation and Cogeneration.

Chapter 66

SUSTAINABLE AND HIGH PERFORMANCE BUILDING DESIGN, CONSTRUCTION AND OPERATION: AN ENGINEER'S PERSPECTIVE

Rob Bolin, PE
Vice President, Sustainable Design
Syska Hennessy Group

WHAT IS SUSTAINABLE DESIGN?

The term sustainable has found its way in to the building industry vocabulary by way of agriculture. As applied to the agriculture industry, sustainable refers to a process that uses or harvests a resource without permanently damaging or depleting that resource. Within the last several years, national and international organizations have defined sustainability as "meeting the needs of the present without compromising the ability of future generations to meet their own needs." So as we apply this concept to the design of buildings, sustainable design is fundamentally best design practice utilizing appropriate modern technologies to optimize return on investment. This is nothing new. Building designers and constructors have been doing this for centuries!

There are many drivers moving the design and construction industry back in this direction. Regulatory drivers include federal executive orders, state energy codes such as California's Title 24 Energy Efficiency Standards, and local government initiatives, such as those cities now requiring projects achieve a LEED™ Green Building rating. Energy market drivers including utility industry restructuring, energy cost volatility, and energy reliability and security concerns. Technology drivers as related to emerging technologies such as on-site generation systems, and how economies of scale impact them. Finally, market transformation programs such as the EPA/DOE EnergyStar program and the US Green Building Council's LEED Green Building Rating System™.

SO WHAT OPPORTUNITIES DOES THIS PRESENT THE BUILDING INDUSTRY?

The integrated design process involving more stakeholders allows us to make better informed decisions earlier, resulting in fundamentally better buildings. We can more fully incorporate energy management strategies—both on the demand side (energy conservation) and the supply side (on-site and renewable generation). Better indoor and outdoor environments are created for building users with regard to indoor air, thermal comfort, acoustic comfort, lighting, visual comfort and ergonomics. Fundamentally better buildings should result in better tenants, owners should expect better rents, and design professionals should expect better fees.

Why is this so important? According to the Department of Energy, commercial and residential buildings in the United States account for 1/3 of our nation's energy consumption, 2/3 of electricity consumption, 50% of the SO_x emissions, 25% of the NO_x emissions, 35% of the carbon dioxide emissions, and more than $200 billion per year in energy costs. The World Watch Institute estimates the construction industry accounts for 40% of processed materials (stone, gravel, steel, etc.), 55% of virgin wood consumption, and 25% of the landfill content. Industry estimates that 90% of a building's life cycle costs are in personnel, and we spend over 90% of our time indoors, in often unhealthy buildings (the World Health Organization estimates 30% of our buildings are unhealthy). That's why this is so important!

ECOLOGY, ECONOMY, AND EQUITY

Sustainability begins by addressing the "triple bottom line," ecology, economy, equity. Regarding environmental concerns, resource efficiency is significant, whether that be the efficient use of land, materials of construction, water or energy. In addition, prevention of the pollution associated with the use of natural resources for building development, the hazardous materials that are all too often used to build buildings (e.g. PVC, mercury, lead, VOCs, ozone depleting substances), and the waste that can be mitigated (e.g. solid waste, air emissions, waste water and storm water runoff).

More and more enlightened building owners are giving due consideration to life cycle costs, not just capital costs. All building projects have hard construction costs, soft construction costs, operating costs, taxes, renovation costs, etc. Life cycle costs also look at operating income, and resale/salvage values as part of the life cycle of a building. For sustainable and high performance buildings, there are also hidden economics that are real but often hard to qualify—flexibility and adaptability, waste mitigation, risk, public relations, and the holy grail of life cycle costs, occupant productivity.

Real case study information is now emerging, and indicates that sustainable and high performance buildings have measurable results indicating that occupant productivity increases (often dramatically). At the community scale, sustainable and high performance building planning must consider the impact on economic development. Adaptive reuse of existing buildings and development of brownfields is almost always more environmentally beneficial than new construction on a greenfield site, and have added benefit of access to mass transit and pedestrian access. Urban infill and "smart-growth" strategies and policies abound.

THE PROCESS OF SUSTAINABLE DESIGN

A deliberate process should be taken for a sustainable and high performance building. Through the integrated design process, and using energy simulation and life cycle costing tools, the design team focuses on minimizing the loads in the building (demand-side strategies). Energy use can be minimized by appropriate building orientation, high performance building envelopes, reduced internal loads (EnergyStar-rated equipment), and optimized

ventilation strategies. Low-flow fixtures and drought-tolerant landscaping minimizes water demand. And an appropriately-sized building eliminates unnecessary building materials and results in less material use.

Once the building has been made as efficient as possible, the designers need to investigate where passive systems can be incorporated. Use of daylighting and lighting controls is extremely effective when well integrated in to the building design. Natural ventilation should be used when and where possible, as a means of not only reducing the reliance on mechanical refrigeration, but also to provide building users the opportunity to have some control over their local environment (e.g. via operable windows). Passive solar heating and cooling techniques such as earth sheltering, ground-water coupling and night-sky radiant cooling can also help to reduce the reliance on air conditioning.

The active systems required to operate the building, complement the passive systems incorporated. The design team needs to optimize these systems to ensure energy efficient and appropriate operation. They should already be smaller since the building itself is fundamentally more energy efficient than conventional. Consideration of system zoning and diversity will result in appropriately sized systems operating efficiently. Mechanical ductwork and piping can be slightly oversized to reduce pressure drops and minimize energy consumption. Underfloor air distribution, displacement ventilation, and systems that de-couple ventilation from heating and cooling are fundamentally more energy efficient systems than conventional overhead all-air systems. Direct Digital Controls (DDC) are now standard for buildings, and, coupled with appropriate control strategies that integrate the passive and active systems, will result in the smooth operation of a healthy indoor environment.

Emerging technologies in environmentally benign alternatives for on-site energy generation now abound. With a fundamentally more energy efficient building incorporating passive systems and optimized active systems, smaller on-site generating equipment is required to power the building. In the energy realm, photovoltaics, wind turbines, fuel cells, microturbines and solar thermal arrays are all now viable technologies incorporated in to building projects. Economies of scale are beginning to drive the capital expense down to the point where life cycle paybacks are often less than 5 or 10 years. And many states and federal agencies are offering incentives and buy-down programs to further promote on-site energy generation. Many projects are also much more aggressive with regard to rainwater harvesting systems, grey water systems and on-site sewage treatment through "living machines."

Materials that go in to the construction of a building and the waste from the construction and operation of the building and its systems need to be carefully considered. Avoiding installation of toxic materials such as PVC, mercury, lead, volatile organic compounds and ozone depleting materials means these materials will not ultimately end up in landfills or the atmosphere. Many states now have public and/or private entities that recycle construction and operational waste for profit. And design teams should always look for opportunities to capture, treat and reuse waste heat, waste water and storm water.

Finally, there are advanced design tools that can be utilized to more carefully analyze sustainable and high performance buildings. These include physical modeling tools for daylighting and wind tunnel testing, and analytical modeling tools such as DOE2 energy simulation software, life cycle cost analysis software, and computational fluid dynamics for complex flows in and around complicated spaces such as atria. Lastly, comprehensive sustainable design assessment tools such as the US Green Building Council's LEED (Leadership in Energy and Environmental Design) Green Building Rating System have transformed the market and made it easier for building owners and designers to define a level of performance for buildings to achieve.

WHAT ABOUT THE ECONOMICS?

The picture is not complete without further discussion of that other "green," costs. Sustainable and high performance buildings have potential additional hard costs of better quality materials and systems, and possibly expensive new or emerging technologies. Potential additional soft costs include commissioning costs and higher design fees. But there are some potential savings as well. A more efficient building will be fundamentally smaller and use less material, and the systems will also be of smaller capacity. Soft cost savings include reduced disposal and hauling fees, reduced change orders, potentially expedited permitting, and tax credits. It is hard to say definitively whether an owner should expect to pay less or more for a sustainable and high performance building. It is very much project and strategy specific, and case studies are across the board. A sustainable and high performance building can cost anywhere from 5% less to 10% more than a conventional building using "standard practice."

SO WHY DESIGN SUSTAINABLE AND HIGH PERFORMANCE BUILDINGS?

Hopefully, the previous discussion has answered this question. With today's dwindling natural resources, be they land, materials, energy or water, consideration of the environmental consequences of our decisions in planning, designing, constructing and operating buildings is now critical. The status quo will simply not do. Winston Churchill had it right when he said:

"We shape our buildings, and afterwards our buildings shape us."

Chapter 67

THE HIGH PERFORMANCE SCHOOL, SUSTAINABLE, OBTAINABLE AND COST-EFFECTIVE

Jason Kliwinski, RA, LEED 2.0 Accredited Professional
Project Manager, The Prisco Group

Since the beginning of the 12 billion dollar school construction initiative in New Jersey, one universal need has been put fourth – *how can we get the best buildings for the money.* While all the parties involved – the taxpayers, the NJEDA, NJDOE, NJDEP and NJ School Business Officials have multitudes of requirements and needs – this is the one question that is repeated by all. The EDA and DEP recognize the impact of life cycle costs and know that these buildings need to last. School Administrators realize that both budgets and schedules are tight. Users – the school's staff and parents recognize the impact that the building environment can have on them; they are tired of their children feeling sluggish and sick, and being distracted by loud HVAC, poor lighting, and inappropriate acoustics.

An answer that addresses all these concerns can be found in "High Performance Design," also known as "Sustainable" or "Green" design. The components of a High Performance designed School are community integration, low construction costs, simple building maintenance, healthy relationship to the natural environment, healthy indoor environment, and low operating costs. The following will hopefully help make clear the value of incorporating high performance design principles as defined by the LEED (Leadership in Energy & Environmental Design) Green Building Rating System, the only nationally accepted system developed by the US Green Building Council, in any project from program and professional consultant selection through construction and operation of a building by asking and answering some very basic questions.

WHAT IS HIGH PERFORMANCE DESIGN?

The terms – Sustainable, Green, and High Performance, as the EDA likes to call it, are used quite interchangeably these days. They all essentially mean the same thing. A building that saves significant resources in construction, operation, and maintenance, provides a healthier indoor environment to live or work in, and is recyclable at the end of its useful life is a well-designed, high performance building.

The basic principles that embody this are as follows:

1. **Holistic Design**: the design team must look at a building and its systems and how they interact to minimize waste and maximize efficiency. This ensures the most cost effective design and lowest operating and maintenance costs.

2. **Site Preservation**: the design team must study the site to ensure natural features are protected. Site amenities, such as natural day lighting, views, and features, are incorporated in the building through proper orientation, and damaged sites are restored to the extent possible or required. *Proper building orientation alone can reduce energy demands by 50% and eliminate glare problems.* This results in lower operating costs.

3. **Water Conservation**: reduction in water usage through efficient fixtures can reduce water usage by over 30% and save thousands of dollars a year in operating costs. Additional measures such as a rainwater catchment system, waterless urinals, or gray water recycling can reduce water usage by 80 to 90% in a school within a project budget.

4. **Energy Conservation**: off-the-shelf technology exists to reduce HVAC and lighting energy demands by 50-90% yearly over conventional design without an increased first cost and dramatic maintenance and operating cost reductions.

5. **Indoor Environmental Quality:** On average Americans spend 90% of their time indoors. Ventilation effectiveness, control of contaminants, proper illumination, and proper acoustic design all result in fewer employee sick days, 26% better performance by students and staff, and no liability to the owner for sick-building related lawsuits.

6. **Materials & Resources Conservation:** Specifying materials with significant amounts of recycled content, manufactured from renewable materials, obtained from local sources, made from non-toxic materials, and themselves recyclable, minimizes the building impact on our natural resources, reduces disposal fees during construction and renovation, and creates a healthy, more durable indoor environment.

7. **Commissioning:** Commissioning is a third party process that ensures the environmental goals and conservation standards designed by the project team are met both in the design documents, construction, and testing of a building and its systems. Basic systems commissioning on HVAC and lighting is now required by the State of NJ as of the adoption of ASHRAE 90.1-1999.

8. **Education & Community Involvement:** The building is a teaching tool for math and science principles that are basic to the technologies utilized in high performance schools. Schools which are accessible to the community, representative of the community in form and flexibility, and which instill a sense of pride are buildings, which will be well-maintained, well-received, and well-utilized for generations. *We must design our schools for our grandchildren's grandchildren not just for tomorrow's generation.*

WHAT ARE THE BENEFITS OF HIGH PERFORMANCE DESIGN THAT MAKE IT A "NO-BRAINER"?

In listing the benefits, one has to also consider the Life Cycle Cost perspective of a building. First cost alone should not be a deciding factor. In fact, when you look at the first cost of a building compared to the operation cost of a building, as demonstrated in the 40 year life cycle analysis below by Johnson Controls, it becomes apparent that decisions made in the area with the smallest financial impact, Construction, result in the most significant consequences in the area with the largest financial impact, Operation. All of the decisions are made during the area that is even too small to show on the pie chart, in Design. This accounts for only 6 to 8% of the 11% initial Construction Cost. *In short, all of the decisions that effect the entire Life Cycle Cost of a building are made up front – in the smallest cost percentage of the building. That is why it is so critical to think about sustainability or high performance design up front.*

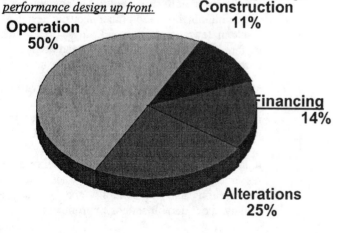

Operation 50%

Construction 11%

Financing 14%

Alterations 25%

For many of the reasons listed in the previous question, a high performance design should be a "no brainer" because:

1. **First Cost** is the same or less typically because it is making better use of resources, materials, and processes. This is contrary to the misconception that High Performance Design costs more. It does not! (*Typically 11% of building life cycle cost*)

2. **Operating Costs** are reduced by 50 to 90% because systems are more efficient and integrated. (*Typically 50% of building life cycle cost, including maintenance*)

3. **Maintenance costs** are sharply reduced because materials are more durable, systems are better designed and stress on individual components is reduced resulting in fewer failures & less expensive repairs.

4. **Performance** of staff and students/users has been documented to be increased by 20 to 26% with better indoor air quality from lighting & ventilation.

5. **Flexibility:** A sustainable building is flexible and easily adaptable to changing uses and users, reducing renovation costs by half. (*This is typically 25% of a building life cycle cost*)

6. **Financing:** Significant State rebates in New jersey through the Smart Start Program, & Clean Energy Program exists to reimburse Owners for part of the initial costs of many high performance technologies including sensors, efficient lighting & HVAC equipment, renewable energy systems like Photovoltaics & geothermal. In addition, other states like New York offer tax incentives and government grant with significant funding through private grants also more easily accessible with such a design. (*In a project under design in my office we are expecting to recoup $70,000 per school for the Howell School District's three new school projects by taking advantage of these programs that are funded through rate payer charges*)

HOW CAN YOU ACHIEVE A HIGH PERFORMANCE, SUSTAINABLE DESIGN ON TIME & BUDGET?

- **USE THE LEED GREEN BUILDING RATING SYSTEM AS THE BASIS OF ESTABLISHING YOUR ENVIRONMENTAL GOALS.**

The US Green Building Council has made this easy. The LEED Green Building Rating System provides a comprehensive basis for evaluating and designing buildings that meet and exceed basic code standards of design to deliver the benefits listed above. Codes are only a minimum to protect the public. The rating system is divided into five categories that include Sustainable Sites, Water Efficiency, Energy & Atmosphere, Indoor Air Quality, and Materials & Resources. A total of 69 credits are achievable for a maximum rating of Platinum. You do not have to be an expert to understand many of the common sense principles and applications LEED takes into account, nor do you have to know how to apply them, you just have to ask the right questions of your consultants.

- **REQUIRE YOUR CONSULTANTS TO USE THE LEED GREEN BUILDING RATING SYSTEM AS THEIR BASIS OF DESIGN FROM THE BEGINNING.**

As a father of two young children, citizen paying taxes in a school district, and environmentally conscious designer, it is particularly important to me that as we embark on this 12 billion dollar school construction initiative or any other major construction initiative, that school districts, building owners, the State, design professionals, parents, and staff make decisions based on **long term benefits** and not the first cost only. The first decision to make is in hiring a qualified design professional. Owners typically don't know how to ask their consultants to achieve a high performance design. Simply requiring your design consultant to be LEED Accredited or at least familiar and setting a goal to achieve at least a certified rating of 26-32 credits (there are higher ratings of Silver, Gold, and Platinum) will ensure that you are getting the best building for the money and lowering your operating and maintenance costs dramatically. Trying to overlay high performance design principles on a project after-the-fact or using a consultant who is unfamiliar with what it takes to design a high performance project from the beginning will result in higher design fees, higher first cost, and poorly designed and performing building. It is critical that the design team that is selected be chosen on the basis of being able to provide a high performance / sustainable / green design on-time and on-budget.

CASE STUDIES:
The Prisco Group has 4 of the State's 20 LEED Accredited design professionals on staff because the Owner, Scott Prisco who is LEED Accredited himself, firmly believes that this is the way every project should be designed for all of the reasons discussed above. To do anything less is a disservice to our client, their user, and the community at large. We recently completed the design of three new schools for the Howell School District (two

70,000 s.f. elementary schools, and one 110,000 s.f. middle school) to be LEED Gold certified – 39 Credits- on a tight budget of $137/s.f. for the elementary schools and $141/s.f. on the Middle School.

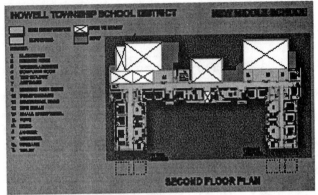

Middle School Second Floor Plan

These schools will use less energy than other schools in the district that are not air conditioned and do not provide 100% outside air while providing 100% outside air, full air conditioning throughout, use building materials made largely from renewable resources or with recycled content that are themselves recyclable, use rainwater to flush toilets instead of drinking water, offset power demands with two 50kW Photovoltaic systems, and reduce operating and maintenance costs as a result.

Bids recently received for Howell confirm what I have previously stated in this article- it does not cost more to build sustainably. The elementary school bids were $131.00/s.f. and the middle school bid was a shocking $111/s.f.. We are well over 3 million dollars under budget. These numbers include "bricks & mortar", built in furniture, and technology. They do not include site development or loose furniture.

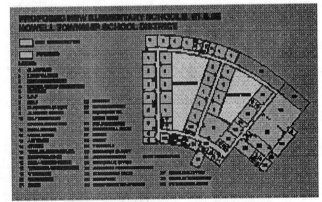

Elementary School Typical Plan

High performance design features included in the Howell Schools are as follows:

Holistic Design

- Overall building system efficiency improved by designing building as a whole and looking at effects of better building envelope design, energy efficient lighting & controls, water conservation and HVAC delivery systems & efficiencies in conjunction with one another. A balance between system components was achieved to produce the highest levels of efficiency overall. All of the stakeholders were part of the decision making process to ensure consensus a design.

Sustainable Site Development

- High reflectance roof coating reduces heat islands & the summer cooling load by up to 30%.
- Site lighting is specifically designed to "stay on site" and not contribute to light pollution.

Energy Efficiency

- Fact: Buildings consume 65% of all electricity in the US and produce 30% of all greenhouse gas emissions.
- High efficiency HVAC levels estimated to be 60% better then ASHRAE 90.1-1999 code requirements were achieved by using Lentz Engineering's innovative Regenerative Dual Duct System that uses as natural processes such as thermal storage, two stages of evaporative cooling, and heat recovery before having to apply energy to temper the air. HVAC equipment was able to be downsized to ¼ the typical size. For example, two 40 ton chillers fully air condition 70,000 sq. ft. with 40% redundancy built in and 20 % expansion capability. That amounts to almost 1,500 sq.ft./ton of AC
- Fluorescent indirect lighting that uses 1/3 the energy of standard direct lighting fluorescent fixtures was designed throughout the building.

Middle School Entry Courtyard Rendering

- Heat recovery from people, equipment, and fixtures virtually eliminates the need for winter heating and reduced the hot water boiler size to two slightly oversized residential units.
- R-27 walls, R-30 roof, and windows with a solar heat gain co-efficient of .3 dramatically reduce the heating & cooling requirements by almost 30%.
- Wherever possible, natural day lighting offsets the requirement for artificial lighting and photo sensors turn lights & HVAC equipment off or on as needed.

Water Conservation

- Fact: Buildings consume 12% of all potable water in the US.
- Low flush fixtures were specified as standard but in addition to that a rain water catchment system was designed that provided 100% of the school's toilet flushing water needs. This accounted for 80% of the school's overall water usage which we estimated would save $15,000/yr at current water rates and over 500,000 gal/yr of water.

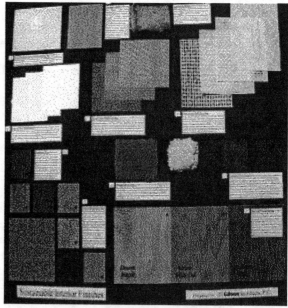

Sustainable Materials Finish Board

Materials & Resource Conservation

- Fact: Buildings consume 40% of all raw materials *globally* & building construction waste accounts for over 30% of all landfill material or 136 million tons annually.
- A Construction waste management policy requiring recycling of a minimum 75% of all construction debri materials was required.

- The majority of building products have a minimum of 20% post consumer or 40% post industrial content such as the concrete, steel, CMU, interior wainscotting, ceiling tile, toilet partitions, wall board, and carpeting.
- Many products are made from rapidly renewable resources or sustainably managed sources such as FCS certified hard wood gym flooring and formaldehyde free wheat board cabinetry.

Middle School Perspective Rendering

Indoor Air Quality
- Fact: Humans spend 90% of their lives inside buildings.
- 100% Outside air provided by our efficient HVAC system ensures constant flushing of the building
- 3 levels of filtration produce almost "clean room" quality indoor air. The filters used are bag filters that can be removed and cleaned and reinstalled easily.
- Interior finishes such as carpet, paint, wood, stains, and furniture fabric have been specified with low or zero VOC content, and no formaldehyde to eliminate off-gasing of toxins in the building.
- All of this in combination with reduce or remove the risk of "Sick Building Syndrome" that continues to plague many building today.

Howell Elementary School Entry Rendering

The one critical thing I have not mentioned yet, and that I need to, is the "Golden Rule" of sustainability. That rule is simple. Don't build anything new if you do not have to. It is better to reuse, renovate, and add on to existing buildings than to tear them down or build new buildings out in the middle of green fields with all of the infrastructure required to support them. The amount of embodied energy in buildings is tremendous. To throw that away doubles or triples them environmental impact of buildings. In this sense, historic preservation and adaptive reuse are among the most sustainable ways to meet the needs of todays generation without compromising the needs of future generations to meet their needs. For the last eight years, I worked on strictly urban adaptive reuse, addition, restoration, and preservation projects because the idea of sustainability or high performance design had not taken route yet beyond the 70'2 idea of energy conservation. One such project was the renovation and historic restoration of Thomas Edison State College Historic Townhouses in Trenton adjacent to the New Jersey State House. As a project manager with DF Gibson Architects, I worked as a key team member in the adaptive reuse and preservation of five early 19th century row houses as administrative offices for the college, a 30,000 s.f. distance learning center addition on the rear of the Townhouses, and interconnection to their adjacent five story building for full ADA compliance.

Thomas Edison State College State Street Elevation

The primary goal was not sustainability at the time. But, by reusing existing urban buildings, specifying non-toxic interior finishes, using a very energy efficient enthropy cooled gas fired HVAC system, natural day lighting, and creating large community spaces that were easily accessible, DF Gibson Architects was able to incorporate the basic principles of sustainable design on time, within the budget, and to the great satisfaction and pleasure of the Owner and end users. This facility has won two awards since opening in June of 2000, including the NJ Downtown Redevelopment Grand Prize and the American School & University Award for Design Excellence. The embodied energy saved by not demolishing the original townhouses coupled with the historic fabric preserved made this a truly sustainable project. Good planning enabled the reuse of the rear wall of the original townhouses (see photo below) as on half of the great hall. Natural lighting through clerestory windows and skylights lessened the need for artificial lighting.

Thomas Edison State College "Great Hall"

CONCLUSION:

There are a number of firms throughout the country and particularly concentrated in the Tri-State area with qualified LEED accredited professionals and/or an established history of successful high performance, cost effective sustainable projects. By establishing goals early

and working within the confines of your project's budget, it is very tangible for qualified firms to provide a high performance building on time and on budget that will delight users and administration for decades to come by creating healthy, efficient, beautiful buildings that are interactive with and respectful of their natural environment. The idea that building sustainably costs more is a myth propagated by those that do not understand or know how to do it. Looking at a project holistically, educating yourself to understand that there are better options out there that are readily available, off-the-shelf technologies, involving your community, and incorporating the principles of high performance design as clearly delineated by the LEED Green Building Rating System are the key elements to success in creating a healthy, cost effective, and productive building. It requires integration, forethought, and planning from schematic design through construction. Trying to overlay high performance design principles after-the-fact will result in higher project design , operating, and maintenance costs. As I have often said, "All of the mistakes are made in the planning," so plan well.

For more information on LEED and the USGBC visit www.usgbc.org or check out your local USGBC Chapter. In New Jersey go to www.usgbcnj.org for all of the local events and listings.

"The rule of no realm is mine. But all living things that now stand in peril, these are my concern. And I shall not wholly fail in my task if anything which may bear fruit and flower survives this night. For, I too am a steward, did you not know?" J.R.R. Tolkien

Chapter 68

THE ENERGY MANAGER'S ROLE IN SUSTAINABLE DESIGN

Kristyn L. Clayton, CEM, Senior Engineer
ARES Corporation

ABSTRACT

Problem

It is clear that the architectural and engineering views of what "sustainable design" means are not quite in line with each other. Furthermore, energy management during the entire building process is hit-or-miss at best, resulting in reactionary energy management. It is the intent of this paper to provide a precise definition of the term "sustainable" and to recommend ways that the energy manager can assist in all phases of the building process in achieving a truly sustainable design.

Method

Personal experience indicates that there are several ways that sustainable design practices can incorporate energy management and thereby reduce the life-cycle costs of a building. The first hurdle, however, is to define the concept in a manner that is acceptable to both disciplines. In order to reach a similar understanding from which architects and engineers can communicate, it is necessary to look at the current work and sustainable design programs that are in place. This paper focuses on creating a definition of "sustainable" for simplicity's sake by a discussion of the following topics:

- Provide an overview of the LEED^{TM} rating program,
- Discuss the current focus on sustainable design,
- Present a project example of a certified sustainable design by the LEED^{TM} rating program.
- Present areas where energy management should be incorporated into the building process.

Results

After a mutual definition of sustainable design is achieved, the task at hand for the energy professional then becomes to understand how to incorporate energy management into every phase of the building process and future operational planning of the facility. The primary ways to accomplish this are:

1) *Passively:* Assure that the project meets the applicable energy codes and standards
2) *Actively:* Design systems that minimize the fossil fuel energy use and maximize alternative fuel use.
3) *Comprehensively:* Project the potential costs of operation of the facility comparing different system concepts for the acquisition of energy to demonstrate how much the actual cost of traditional systems vs. energy managed systems will be for the owner.

Conclusion

By defining sustainability early in the process, design and construction professionals can understand each other and work cooperatively to provide clients with the best in "sustainable design". Energy management can then be incorporated into all critical steps of the building process passively, actively, or comprehensively depending on the project requirements.

INTRODUCTION

The term "Energy Management" presently refers to the control of the use of energy within an existing facility. Typically, it is reactionary in nature and sometimes it is too little too late for certain types of projects. This can be seen in Figure 1 where the certified energy manager (CEM) is shown as operating in the last one-third of the building's lifeline. There are many other ways that energy engineers can manage the use of energy throughout a facility's lifetime and it is imperative to think about these areas or the concept of energy management as understood today might become obsolete.

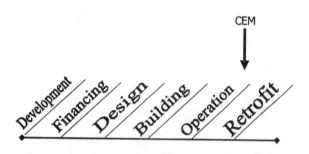

FIGURE 1 REACTIONARY ENERGY MANAGEMENT

Examples of the reactionary nature of energy management are:

- A system has become inefficient in an industrial process and is starting to cost down time and lack of productivity for a plant. A consulting engineer enters the picture and makes not only process upgrade recommendations but also offers up more energy efficient ways of accomplishing the same productivity at a lesser unit cost,
- Energy Services Contracting Organizations (ESCO) which retrofit the systems in an existing facility to upgrade the equipment to more efficient standards,
- Delay of occupancy permits for non-compliant clients caught during final inspection, and
- Retrofit installation of new generating equipment to prevent down times due to power shortages.

It is time to become proactive in the involvement with the life of a facility that actually begins during development. Soon in our society energy will become a prime driver in all aspects of design, construction and operation of facilities as the resources we have reveal their increasing scarcity. It will no longer be acceptable for engineers to quantify energy management as a process by which a building is controlled. Energy Management will have to include specific sustainable practices which are now gaining great momentum in the architectural field and with clients as well.

The building industry has a key opportunity to make a significant contribution through the implementation of the sustainable design approach.

DEFINITIONS

Engineers, architects and laymen often ask what "sustainable design" is when referring to building engineering. People in the building design professions aren't even clear about it themselves sometimes, at least between the various disciplines. So, for starters, it is important to define the word *sustainable* so that all parties who are using it in a particular context are clear on the meaning. The overall philosophy surrounding "sustainable" building is certainly a point that can be readily agreed upon. One definition to consider might be: "To design, build and consume materials in a manner that minimizes the depletion of the natural resources and optimizes the efficiency of consumption." Therefore sustainability encompasses not only design intent and construction practices, but also the use of the earth's resources before during and after construction. The term resources includes a very broad spectrum of resources starting with obvious ones such as water, coal, oil and natural gas, all the way to oxygen, vegetation and more esoterically, natural aesthetics. Figure 2 is a graphical representation of a triad that illustrates the concept well.

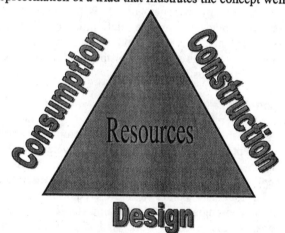

FIGURE 2. SUSTAINABILITY TRIAD

The chronologically last section of the triad of sustainability, or the consumption of natural resources, is simply the use of a substance without replacement. It begins during construction and continues throughout the entire building's lifetime. Most people have a reasonable understanding of the concept of consumption of natural resources.

The second leg of the triad is the construction of buildings by optimizing efficiency in material usage and site practices. There are a host of requirements for construction professionals to follow in order to satisfy a sustainable philosophy that will sometimes take a project by surprise if not considered early in the design phase. As an example, the particular focus on a certified sustainable project that will be used in this paper for discussion purposes was Indoor Air Quality. The project was a private middle school in Seattle, WA. This focus defined the term "sustainable" for the project and provided boundaries for other aspects of sustainability. Another area of focus in the same project was the accounting of all recyclable material during demolition and construction. The construction team had to actually count the number of tons of debris that left the site. This amount was then compared to the number of tons of recycled materials from the existing structure and from the site demolition as well. This project will be discussed further to illustrate the unique and custom nature of the definition of sustainable.

The final leg, or earliest activity of the scheduling of building sustainability, is design. This can be accomplished haphazardly with good Architecutral and Engineering (A/E) practices or it can be dictated in a consistent manner as it is in the U. S. Green Building Council's (USGBC) LEED™ rating system. LEED™ stands for Leadership in Energy and Environmental Design. The standards as set forth in the USGBC's program are briefly discussed in the following section.

THE LEED™ RATING SYSTEM

There is a power point overview from the USGBC website that is free to all and much more detailed than this paper can cover, however, the major points will be reviewed here. This discussion will help to illustrate where energy management can play a role in sustainable design.

The LEED™ Green Building Rating System is a voluntary, consensus-based, market-driven building rating system based on existing proven technology that evaluates environmental performance from a "whole building" perspective over a building's life cycle. The word voluntary is debatable because presently there are certain jurisdictions that now require a specific LEED™ rating for municipal structures.

There are five major categories for compliance in the LEED™ program. They are: 1) Sustainable site planning, 2) Safeguarding water (i.e. the protection of naturally occurring sources) and water use efficiency, 3) Energy use efficiency and renewable energy sources, 4) Conservation of materials and resources, and 5) Indoor environmental quality. There are precise areas of consideration for each of these categories that require research, discovery, documentation and verification to satisfy the USGBC's criteria. These areas are: Environmental benefits, Economic benefits, Health and safety benefits, and Community benefits. Each of these areas is analyzed in a

numeric rating system and then totaled to obtain the final rating or level of certification.

Chances are, there are a couple of areas that are good candidates for obtaining rating points for a specific project, and the rest are somewhat more difficult to make comply. The good candidate areas will define the definition of sustainable for a particular project. The example project of the private middle school had some very unusual governing criteria that mandated the highest level of Indoor Environmental Quality possible. Figure 3 shows the compliance matrix for the project. The dots represent the areas where points were obtained for sustainable design features. The blank areas were, for whatever reasons, not good candidates for achieving sustainable points through the LEED™ rating system.

	Environmental	Economic	Health & Safety	Community
Site	●			●
Water	●	●		●
Energy	●			
Conservation of Materials	●	●		
IAQ	●		●	

FIGURE 3 LEED™ COMPLIANCE MATRIX

The bottom line on the sustainable design process for this facility was that it was not very efficient in the energy conservation realm, but had a superior rating for the indoor air quality. Additional points were obtained by using innovative construction techniques such as the use of collecting and naturally filtering the site water run-off. Thus for people who think that sustainable means minimizing energy usage above all else, this example proves that just the opposite philosophy can still render a building certifiably sustainable. Indeed, energy efficiency is only one of the five categories in which compliance must be clearly shown to obtain certification points.

At the writing of this paper, there is only one building nationally that has reached the highest rating offered by the USGBC. Some interesting characteristics of this facility are: 1) it was designed on piers to minimize site disturbance, 2) all wood comes from forests managed according to the standards set forth by the Forest Stewardship Council, 3) cisterns are used to capture and use rainwater, and surprisingly 4) the use of composting toilets.

Building professionals will fall sadly behind if they do not jump on the band-wagon of sustainable design and become certified in the process. The federal government has worked the words "sustainable design" into most of their solicitations for A/E services as well. If this trend continues, the energy manager who is only versed in reactionary practices, i.e. the auditing and retrofitting of not-so-efficient facilities, may become obsolete in the next couple of generations.

WHERE DO ENERGY MANAGERS FIT?

As is evident from the overview of the five major categories in the LEED™ rating system, engineering is a crucial aspect of all of the categories. But what about energy engineering? After a mutual definition of sustainable design is achieved, the energy professional can begin to incorporate energy management into the design and future operational planning of the facility from the beginning of a project. The primary ways to accomplish this are:

1) *Passively:* Assure that the project meets the applicable energy codes and standards. As energy managers it is essential to be familiar with the codes that govern a particular design and to be able to see the effect that these codes can have on design and operation of a facility. The better the newer systems become at conserving energy, the lesser the need for audits and retrofits in the future (i.e. the dinosaur principle for reactionary energy management).

2) *Actively:* Creatively assist the design team in integrating all aspects of sustainability into the design to achieve a target building efficiency. Too often the architects and engineers don't communicate until the project is committed to a certain design approach. Then the mechanical and electrical design teams have to "just make it work" the best that they can. Working as facilitators in this process, energy managers can guide the process toward a totally integrated building that dovetails all of the sustainable features into one holistic building system. Site selection based on types of energy available and the potential for distributed generation and hydrogen infrastructure are just a couple of items that can be considered in the site selection area of sustainable design.

3) *Comprehensively:* Project the potential costs of operation of the facility comparing different system concepts for the acquisition of energy. This will demonstrate how much the actual cost of traditional systems vs. energy-managed systems will be for the owner. Another comprehensive effort would be to sell the idea of real time energy monitoring in manufacturing and industrial facilities to the owner, then model the results of such a system to show life-cycle potential. State-of-the-art technology allows for this to be done nicely from a remote location via the internet. This of course should be done in conjunction with design and would need to be priced early in the process to gain owner acceptance. Too often systems such as these are the first to go in budget reduction measures.

By employing an energy management professional from the start of a project the typical reactionary energy management in the last stages of a building's lifetime can be avoided. Sustainable design is a proactive concept that supports total energy management of a project.

CONCLUSION

As energy cost and availability becomes paramount in the profit calculations of industry and business, energy management will be a driving force in the development and design of large facilities. The two design disciplines of engineering and architecture can provide the global community with the best in "sustainable design" by incorporating energy management into all critical steps of the building design process. The Energy Manager's role can thus be expanded from a reactionary one into a comprehensive, proactive one in the building industry.

BIBLIOGRAPHY
www.USGBC.org

AUTHOR'S BIO
Ms. Clayton is a Senior Engineer with ARES Corporation, an engineering and management firm, specializing in Risk Management, Hi-tech Engineering Solutions and Project Management Software. Her experience incorporates engineering and architectural design, construction management, energy code compliance, and energy management design. She can be reached at: kclayton@arescorporation.com
ARES Corporation
1100 Jadwin Ave, Suite 400
Richland, WA 99352
509-946-8946

Chapter 69

BENEFIT-COST ANALYSES OF SUSTAINABLE BUILDING FEATURES

Benson Kwong, Senior Engineer
Project Management Services Inc.

ABSTRACT
Benefit-cost analyses (BCA) can be used to help select sustainable design features for a project and to complement the Leadership in Energy and Environmental Design (LEED) Green Building Rating System (1). LEED is a proxy rating system that assigns points to various sustainable building features; BCA measures economic and environmental costs and benefits on a monetary scale. BCA could help a project achieve the highest sustainability it can afford while also leading to a better appropriation of resources and providing direct justification for each sustainable design feature. To apply BCA to sustainable building features, it is necessary to develop a more accurate estimate of additional costs associated with variable sustainable design features. The most difficult task is to quantify the benefits of sustainable features, including initial savings, energy savings, maintenance savings, deferred replacement cost, productivity gain, improved quality of life, environmental benefits, and prestige factor. Cost and benefits to building owners, users, and society in general all need to be considered. Non-economic cost and benefits should also be incorporated in the analyses.

INTRODUCTION
This paper discusses how benefit-cost analyses (BCA) can be used to help select sustainable design features for a project. The first section compares BCA, as a measuring tool, to LEED. Subsequent sections provide more details on methodologies for estimating cost, and on the various types of benefits, including:

- Direct cost savings
- Indirect gains
- Reduced environmental externalities.

BENEFIT-COST ANALYSIS VS. LEED

What is sustainability?
The World Commission on Environment and Development states that, "Sustainable development meets the needs of the present without compromising the ability of future generations to meet their own needs" (2). There are two parts to this definition. The first, to meet "the needs of the present," can be readily evaluated using common economic tools such as BCA and life cycle cost analysis. The second part, "without compromising the ability of future generations to meet their own needs," poses new challenges since traditional economics deals with time frames no longer than one generation. New scientific models to relate today's activities to long term environmental effects and the economic valuation of these effects are being developed.

Effectiveness of rating systems
Our challenge is to measure how successful each design feature would be in achieving sustainability. The first problem is that "sustainability" is not very quantifiable. It is impossible to measure something objectively if there is no measuring scale available. Both LEED and BCA are attempts to invent measuring scales for sustainable building features.

The accuracy of a measurement depends on the correlation between the measured parameter and the target parameter. An example in physics may be helpful. Temperature may be measured with a mercury thermometer. However, we are actually measuring the volume of the mercury as a result of the thermal expansion. Fortunately, the thermal expansion of mercury changes linearly with temperature, so the correlation is excellent. Astronomers calculate the temperature of distant stars by measuring the wavelength of their emitting light. These measurements are indirect but accurate because the physical laws that correlate wavelength to temperature are well-known. These are indirect measures since a physical property other than the one in question is being measured. If I am deprived of thermometers and other instruments to measure temperature, I can devise a "proxy" method to measure the outside temperature by observing what people are wearing outside. However, there are no exact physical laws that dictate what people would wear in any given temperature. This method would be useful to a certain degree, but not be very accurate. The key to an effective rating system is to develop accurate scientific and economic models that reflect sustainability.

How LEED works

The LEED Green Building Rating System is a voluntary system that "evaluates environmental performance from a whole building perspective over a building's life cycle, providing a definitive standard for what constitutes a 'green building'" (1). LEED requirements are organized into the following categories:

- Sustainable Sites
- Water Efficiency
- Energy and Atmosphere
- Materials and Resources
- Indoor Environmental Quality
- Innovation and Design Process

To earn LEED certification, the applicant project must satisfy all of the prerequisites and attain LEED credits to achieve a minimum number of points. In LEED version 2.0, there are a total of 7 prerequisites and 34 credits for a total of 69 available points. Depending on the number of points a project achieves, the certification level could be Certified, Silver, Gold, or Platinum (the highest).

The LEED Rating System is a very useful tool in promoting sustainability. It puts together a comprehensive menu of sustainability-related issues and provides incentives for owners and designers to achieve sustainability goals. However, the LEED Rating System is like a menu without prices, which makes people who dine on a budget somewhat uneasy when it's time to order.

The LEED Rating System is a "proxy" measure that relies on subjective judgment to correlate with the concept of "sustainability." For example, there is no objective justification that could explain why "Light Pollution Reduction," using "Green Power," and using "Certified Wood" all have the equivalent effect (1 point) on sustainability.

What is benefit-cost analysis?

Benefit-cost analysis compares the cost and the benefit of a given measure, to evaluate if the benefit outweighs the cost. Cost can include the present cost of initial construction, plus the future cost of maintenance and operation. On the benefit side, both initial and future benefits need to be accounted for. Future benefits would include energy and material conservation, pollution reduction, occupant productivity, health, and satisfaction. All costs and benefits need to be converted to present value basis for comparison.

The minimum criterion for accepting a design element should be a situation in which benefit outweighs cost:

$$BENEFIT > COST$$

Alternately, a benefit-to-cost ratio (BCR) could be used, with a minimum ratio of acceptance:

$$\frac{NET\ FUTURE\ BENEFIT}{INVESTMENT\ COST} > X, where\ X > 1$$

(For a more detailed treatment of BCR, see the ASTM Standard on this subject [3].)

BCA can lead to better appropriation of resources and provide direct justification for each sustainable design feature. Economics is about the appropriation of resources. Human, natural, land, and capital resources are all limited. By considering sustainability, we are mindful of depletable resources such as fuel and mineral, and of environmental resources that need to be stabilized. Economic decisions are the choices we make to appropriate resources. Often the choices are difficult because all the options are good. It is hard enough to balance everyone's present needs. But we also have to balance the needs of the present with the ability of future generations to meet their own needs. By prioritizing projects based on BCR, we hope to optimize the benefits, both present and future, while applying our limited resources to the appropriate ventures.

Another usefulness of BCA is that it provides justification for each design feature based on its own merit. Granted, BCA may not be able to justify some sustainable design features now on the menu. But that shows that sustainable design should be project specific, and each project should have its own winning combination of sustainable design features.

Traditionally, BCA is used to evaluate the life cycle cost of a project, which is typically 20 to 40 years. BCA can readily handle the present and not-too-distant future, but not the "future generations" that sustainability needs to deal with. Cost for future generations can be evaluated by assigning cost for pollution and material depletion.

Although some of these issues are controversial, BCA can provide a forum for constructive discussion by identifying the reasonable range of cost and benefits.

How BCA can complement LEED
The LEED Rating System can use BCA as a testing tool to update future versions. The LEED Rating System provides incentives to select sustainable design measures with the most points at the lowest cost. BCA, on the other hand, optimizes benefits. The LEED Rating System is a constantly evolving document that is currently under a 3-year revision cycle. It has the advantage of being easily understood and applied. Benefit-cost analysis is a flexible analytical tool that can become more useful as more data are available from past projects and better methodologies for evaluating cost and benefits emerge from the fields of environmental economics. BCA can be a useful tool to provide feedback for future updates of the LEED Rating System.

COST ESTIMATE
Benefit-cost analyses for sustainable design features are most valuable at the conceptual design stage, when major design decisions are made. However, at this stage cost estimates often have to be made with little or no design information. There is a need for more accurate cost estimates based on historical data or typical design details.

Some sustainable design features have a negligible cost impact. For example, "Water Efficient Landscaping" typically involves the selection of more indigenous plants that require little or no irrigation. The cost of the plants depends on the species selected and many other factors, and is not a direct result of the decision for water efficient landscaping.

Other sustainable design features can be readily estimated using traditional cost estimating methodologies. These are usually cases in which the sustainable design features can be well-defined in the conceptual phase and a market of products is well-established. For example, low-emitting materials such as carpet and paints are well-defined, with multiple suppliers that can provide cost information. Cost comparisons with non-compliant material can be readily developed.

The need for more accurate cost estimates arises because there are many unique sustainable design features that are not well-defined at the conceptual stage, but that could make a significant cost impact. These include:

- Optimizing energy performance
- Additional commissioning
- Recycled content
- Daylight and views
- Construction waste management

- Construction IAQ management plan

There are other sustainable design features that are not typically part of the construction cost. For example, "Site Selection," has to do with real estate acquisition.

A conceptual costing guide would be helpful for most decision makers as they select sustainable design features. Such a guide would provide the common ranges of unit cost expected for various sustainable design features. However, a cost professional familiar with these features would need to be on hand to address site and project specific issues and to provide customized cost information for the selection of design features.

BENEFIT ESTIMATE
The most difficult task would be to quantify the benefits of sustainable features, including initial savings, energy savings, maintenance savings, deferred replacement cost, productivity gain, improved quality of life, environmental benefits, and prestige factor.

There are three main categories of benefits: direct cost savings, indirect gains, and reduced externalities. Direct cost savings are economic savings that are directly gained by the building owner through reduced initial construction cost, reduced energy consumption, lower maintenance requirements, and deferred replacement. This is the realm of traditional life-cycle costing (4). Indirect gains are benefits to the users of the building; an improved building environment enables people to be healthier, work better, and feel better about themselves. Both individuals and organizations gain indirectly from a more sustainable environment. Although many studies have been conducted to quantify some of these indirect benefits, the results are fragmented and not widely applied to benefit-cost analyses. There are some on-going attempts to organize and quantify these indirect benefits. The last category of benefits is reduced environmental externalities. Environmental externalities are negative impacts on the environment resulting from constructing and operating the facility, for which the facility does not have to pay. Developments in environmental economics have helped to identify the true cost of these externalities and to create mechanisms to charge for the degradation of the environment. However, many of the analyses are inexact and controversial. These costs seldom enter into the benefit-costs calculation of a project because the project does not have to pay the costs and usually is not aware of them. Some government projects do try to account for externalities, but more work is needed in this area to improve accuracy and promote the acceptance of analyzing the cost of externalities.

DIRECT COST SAVINGS
The following is a review of the conventional cost savings calculations in a benefit-cost analysis. Some of these

savings are directly related to sustainable design, such as utility savings and deferred replacement; others are indirect benefits of sustainable design.

Initial savings
Initial cost savings are achieved by either reducing project scope or attaining the desired function by an alternate means. An example of reducing potential project scope is the use of "Alternative Transportation," which would reduce the parking capacity required on site. An example of an alternate solution is to recycle existing asphalt paving on site for the new parking lot, thereby reducing the cost for new asphalt.

Utility savings
The reduction of natural resources required to operate a facility results in direct cost savings in energy and water bills. By optimizing energy performance, a facility can reduce operational costs for years to come. Although many energy conservation design features can be calculated using simple formulas, the complexity of the interactions between building geometry, occupancy, weather, and system control in a building often require building energy simulation to accurately predict energy usage. Simulation software such as DOE-2 is well-suited for this purpose.

Likewise, water conservation measures result in savings in the water bill, which may also include sewage charges.

Maintenance savings
Life cycle savings can also be achieved by lower maintenance. For example, xeriscape or dry landscaping not only conserves water but may also reduce garden maintenance requirements by reducing labor for trimming, mowing, and chemical treatment. Reducing site disturbance and conserving existing natural areas also reduces the need for maintenance.

Deferred replacement cost
One strategy to conserve future resources is to defer future replacement costs by installing more durable material today. A longer life component may cost more initially, but may have a lower life cycle cost, especially if a building is intended to last longer than the typical design life of 25 to 30 years. For example, brick veneer costs more than stucco. But with periodic cleaning and repointing every 25 years or so, a brick exterior wall could easily last a century. Stucco, on the other hand, needs more frequent refinishing and is not expected to last much more than 25 years. For a 25 year life project, stucco may have the lower life cycle cost, but if a building life of 100 years is considered, brick would probably have an advantage. LEED addresses the reuse of existing buildings. However, the future feasibility of reusing a

building now being designed depends on the construction material selected.

INDIRECT GAIN
Indirect gains of sustainability design are benefits to the occupants that are not typically reflected in the project benefit-cost analysis. Most of these are related to improvement in indoor environmental quality (IEQ). Sustainability design addresses indoor air quality, thermal comfort, environmental control, and daylighting. These are less quantifiable, and yet could be more significant than the direct benefits. In recent years, much work has been done to quantify these benefits. I am aware of three major efforts to collect, integrate and apply this research:

- ASHRAE initiated the Indoor Health and Productivity (IHP) Project to communicate the research results of relationships of IEQ to the health, comfort, and productivity of occupants (5).
- "Building Investment Decision Support," (BIDS) a benefit-cost analysis framework based on a body of published research, is being developed at the School of Architecture at Carnegie Mellon University (6).
- The Federal Energy Management Program is developing a business case for sustainable facilities (7).

Productivity gain
An improved working environment leads to better productivity. This is both intuitive and validated by empirical studies time and again. People perform better, faster, and with lower absenteeism when a better working environment is provided. For example, a study by the Heschong Mahone Group has documented faster learning progress and higher test scores for students in classrooms with daylight than for students in rooms with artificial lighting (8). Another study by the same group links daylighting to 40% increased sales in a retail chain (9). William Fisk estimated that the potential direct productivity gain for improving IEQ in office work is between 0.5% to 5% (10). Consider a typical office building with 416 sf per worker (11) and an average labor cost of $40,000 per year; the annual potential productivity gain range would be between $0.50 to $5 per square foot of building. This would roughly translate to a present value of $8 to $80 per square foot. Even at the low range, this represents a significant benefit when compared to the initial building cost.

Health care cost reduction
Indoor air quality improvement can reduce acute respiratory illness (ARI), allergies and asthma, and sick building syndrome. According to William Fisk (10), direct health-care costs and indirect productivity costs (value of lost work) for these illnesses are estimated at $70 billion for ARI, $15 billion for allergies and asthma, and $60

billion for sick building syndrome. The total annual health related cost, divided by the total office floor space of 12 billion square feet (11), is about $12 per square foot of building.

Improved quality of life

The benefit of a better indoor environment is not only to the employer who gains higher productivity or to the entity paying for health care, whether that be the employer, the HMO, or the employees themselves. The occupants would be healthier and feel better about themselves. One method to quantify the benefit of improved quality of life would be to survey and interview samples of employees to determine how they value an improved indoor environment. The ideal target for these surveys would be groups of building occupants who recently experienced a change in indoor environment due either to renovation or system breakdown. The key is to determine a shadow price on the environmental change. A question could be phrased such as: "All other things being equal, how large a pay raise (after tax) would it take for you to work in a building with the old _____ system?" However, a method based on a hypothetical decision can be distorted, as people react differently under real and speculative situations.

Prestige factor

Labels such as the EPA Energy Star or LEED certification also provide a prestige factor that carries value in itself. EPA considers the Energy Star as a brand applied to different markets from dishwashers to windows to entire buildings. As a marketing strategy, branding carries a price premium because the brand implies a certain quality guarantee. A building that carries a silver or gold LEED certification may be able to charge higher rent simply because of the LEED label. An employer in a LEED certified building may be able to attract many quality employees without having to pay a premium on salary. Again, marketing surveys would be needed to determine the value of LEED prestige.

REDUCED ENVIRONMENTAL EXTERNALITIES

Concept of environmental externalities

Environmental externalities are economic impacts which are not included in the market price of goods and services being produced. For example, a coal fueled power plant generates electricity and emits pollutants into the air. Society at large, not the power plant, generally has to bear the cost of the pollution, including the cost associated with reduction in visibility, increases in probabilities of certain illnesses, and green house effects that may have long term global climate impacts. Since the cost of these externalities is not borne by the power plant, it is not reflected in the price of electricity. Figure 1 shows a typical demand curve, which displays the prices that the consumers are willing to pay, reflecting the benefits

perceived by the consumers. The optimum price should be the cost including externalities, corresponding to a consumption level of Q2. But without accounting for externality cost, the consumption is higher at Q1. The quantities between Q1 and Q2 are those where total cost exceeds benefits. The market fails to achieve optimal economic value.

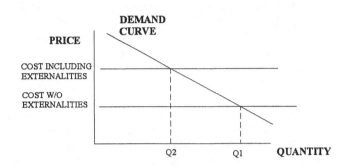

Fig. 1 – Demand curve considering externalities

Regulating environmental externalities

In order to remedy the market inefficiency caused by environmental externalities, government interference is needed. Regulation deals with externalities in three general ways: mandates, penalties, and quota trading.

1. Mandates – Governments can mandate a solution such as outlawing certain activities, setting a limit on others, or requiring a particular technology. An example of this would be the banning of the CFC gases that are present in older chiller units. These gases contribute to the depletion of the ozone layer, which leads to higher risk of skin cancer. Other examples are the requirement for a nitrogen oxide (NOx) emission limit (e.g., 5 parts per million) and for the use of the Best Available Control Technology that some air quality jurisdictions place on new power generation equipment.

2. Penalties – Another strategy to regulate environmental externalities is to set a penalty, in terms of a surcharge or tax. Ideally the penalty would be calculated to reflect the cost of the externalities and the revenue generated would be used to remedy the impacts of the externalities. However, political considerations often govern. An example of a penalty would be a tipping fee for a landfill. Typically, the fee would be much higher than the cost of operating the landfill. The fee should attempt to reflect the true cost to society for generating the waste material. The hotly debated carbon tax is another example of a penalty that attempts to reflect the cost of global warming in CO_2 emission.

3. Quota trading – A more market-oriented strategy for regulating environmental externalities is quota trading. A regulatory body would set a goal for reducing environmental externalities and assign each generator a quota. The quota creates an artificial shortage and a market for permit trading. This strategy is effective in allowing market forces to find the most economical way to reduce externalities. The industry, as a whole, will select the most economical combination of retiring old plants, retrofitting emission reduction technologies, and building new plants. Trading has been successful in reducing air pollutants such NOx and sulphur dioxides (SO2). However, although this strategy is useful in reducing pollution, it does not fully price the cost of pollution to society.

Estimating the cost of environmental externalities

Estimating the cost of environmental externalities often involves complex modeling based on scientific principles as well as empirical observations. One approach to costing environmental externalities is the "damage function" approach. This sums up the environmental damages associated with the polluting activities. Burtraw and Toman (12) described a typical model used for evaluating the cost of externalities for power plant emission. The overall model is made up of four modules:

1. Emission – This module calculates the amount of pollution emitted by the target plant (e.g., kg/yr of particulates). There is often more than one pollutant and each needs to be separately accounted for. The amount of emission depends on the abatement measures installed and their removal efficiencies as well as the capacity and output from the unit. Emission from the entire fuel cycle, not just at the power plant, should be accounted for. This would include fuel extraction, processing, and transportation.

2. Dispersion – This is the atmospheric dispersion module that calculates increases in ambient concentrations (e.g., g/m3 of particulates) for the affected regions as a result of emission from the target plant. This model accounts for space, time, meteorology, and air chemistry.

3. Impact – This module links the consequence (e.g., a change in the probability of a person developing asthma) to the increase in ambient concentrations. This module is based on epidemiology research.

4. Cost – The cost module puts a dollar value on the health impact, which would include the cost of health care, loss of productivity, and degradation in the quality of life.

The results of the studies examined by Krupnick and Burtraw (13) show an environmental externalities cost range for the coal fuel cycle of from $0.001 to $0.019 per

kWh. Externalities cost varies with site characteristics, fuel use, and the endpoints considered. The studies that were examined were for new power plants, which tend to be cleaner than existing plants. The impact of the greenhouse gas effect has not been considered in these studies.

When the above analysis is applied to all the generating resources of an electric company, we can calculate a cost per kWh for the electricity purchased from that company. This number can be directly applied to evaluate the benefits of "Green Power." It can also be used to evaluate the environmental benefit of power conservation.

Challenges in costing environmental externalities

Accurate pricing of environmental externalities can help us to make - and to communicate about - difficult decisions when allocating limited resources. In designing a sustainable building with a limited budget, we must choose which sustainable features to use. How much do we improve employee health with better indoor air quality? Or should some resources be diverted to increase energy efficiency in order to reduce outdoor air pollution? These and other important sustainability goals must be weighed and balanced through accurate pricing of cost and benefits. Although at present, pricing for many of these environmental externalities is uncertain, the science for evaluating consequences is emerging and the methodologies for pricing them are improving.

The following are environmental externalities that are still controversial or difficult to price:

- Light pollution
- Diminishing bio-diversity
- Global warming - greenhouse gas
- Fuel depletion
- Material depletion

In as much as LEED attempts to put into practice good sustainable design and go beyond what is required by law, we must attempt to quantify the benefits. Although there is little agreement in the scientific and political communities on these issues, BCA can serve as a common tool to communicate, clarify, and focus the issues.

CONCLUSION

The difficulty in understanding and quantifying the costs and benefits of sustainable design is perhaps the reason why a proxy rating system such as LEED is needed in the first place. LEED is simple to use, and encompasses diverse areas in sustainability. Benefit-cost analysis complements LEED by focusing on economic measurement and project specific parameters. BCA may provide the algorithm to improve future versions of the LEED rating system.

Further work needed to adapt BCA to sustainable design features includes:

- Development of a conceptual costing guide.
- Quantification of productivity, health, and quality of life benefits from indoor air quality improvements.
- Costing of environmental externalities originating from power generation.
- Monitoring of other issues involving environmental externalities.

REFERENCES

1. U.S. Green Building Council, LEED Reference Package Version 2.0, June 2001.

2. Bruntland, G. (ed.), Our Common Future: The World Commission on Environment and Development, Oxford University Press, 1987.

3. American Society for Testing and Materials (ASTM), "Standard Practice for Measuring Benefit-to-Cost and Savings-to-Investment Ratios for Buildings and Building Systems," E964-93(1998)e1.

4. American Society for Testing and Materials (ASTM), "Standard Practice for Measuring Life-Cycle Costs of Buildings and Building Systems," E917-99, 1999.

5. Kumar, Satish & William J. Fisk, "The Role of Emerging Energy-Efficient Technology in Promoting Workplace Productivity and Health: Final Report," February 2002.

6. Loftness, Vivian, et al, "Building Investment Decision Support (BIDS)," ABSIC Project #00-2 Final Report, 2000-2001.

7. Shearer, Beth, "Developing a Business Case for Sustainable Federal Facilities," presented at the Energy 2002 conference, Palm Spring, CA, June 2002. http://www.energy2002.ee.doe.gov/Presentations/susbldg/S8-Shearer.pdf

8. Heschong Mahone Group, "Daylighting in Schools: An Investigation into the Relationship Between Daylighting and Human Performance," August, 1999.

9. Heschong Mahone Group, "Skylighting and Retail Sales: An Investigation into the Relationship Between Daylighting and Human Performance," August, 1999.

10. Fisk, William J., "How IEQ Affects Health, Productivity," ASHRAE Journal, May 2002.

11. National Energy Information Center, "Commercial Buildings Energy Consumption Survey (CBECS)," 1999.

12. Burtraw, Dallas & Michael Toman, "The Benefits of Reduced Air Pollutants in the U.S. from Greenhouse Gas Mitigation Policies," November 1997, Resources for the Future, Discussion Paper 98-01-REV.

13. Krupnick, Alan J. & Dallas Burtraw, "The Social Costs of Electricity: Do the Numbers Add Up?" August 1996, Resources for the Future, Discussion paper 96-30.

AUTHOR'S BIOGRAPHY

Benson Kwong, P.E., CEM, CVS, CCE, is a senior engineer at Project Management Services Inc. in Rockville, Maryland. He holds masters degrees in mechanical and electrical engineering, as well as an M.B.A. He is a LEED 2.0 accredited professional. His work includes life cycle cost analysis, energy code compliance analysis, and DOE-2 energy simulation. He also facilitates and participates in value engineering studies, many of which focus on energy conservation and sustainable building design. Benson Kwong can be contacted at bkwong@pmsimail.com

FAST AND INNOVATIVE DELIVERY OF HIGH PERFORMANCE BUILDING: DESIGN-BUILD DELIVERS WITH LESS OWNER LIABILITY

P. Thomas Gard, PE, Esq., PMP
President
Dominion Project Management, Inc.

Abstract

This paper provides the argument that sustainability and high performance design and construction are best delivered through the design-build contracting method.

Sustainability is predicated on innovative design and a life cycle approach to project planning. High performance design and construction requires a systemic approach to design and construction. The design-build method of infrastructure delivery capitalizes on the synergy between the designer and builder, rather than exacerbating the traditional antagonism between designers and builders common with the design-bid-build method. Taken together, sustainability, high performance and design-build concepts are all founded on the principle of performance specifications.

In further argument for design-build, the owner is no longer at risk for the "implied warranty" for design accuracy and receiving only "substantial" compliance in its delivered facility. The owner is vulnerable to both with design-bid-build.

Thus, in the new sustainable and high performance environment, design-build is the contracting and project delivery method of choice.

Introduction

The design-build (D-B) delivery of buildings makes it less expensive and more certain that owners will get high performance and sustainability from their new buildings and renovation projects. With design-build, owner liability is significantly lower, construction change orders diminish, and claims are minor. In design-build, design and construction are fast-tracked and schedules are shorted by as much as one third compared to the traditional methods of construction delivery.

Design-bid-build (D-B-B), the traditional method of design and construction, does not work as well as design-build in the new sustainable environment. Design-bid-build segments and incrementalizes design and construction so that it is sequential rather than systemic in execution. When low initial cost is desired, and little innovation in design is acceptable, design-bid-build is an appropriate choice. But, design-bid-build is an antagonistic practice where the designer and builder are legally and practically pitted against each other. So, where the owner does not fully trust the builder, design-bid-build is a good tool to use the designer to police the project. However, none of these scenarios describe sustainable design and high performance building goals.

When high performance (in effect, energy efficiency) is coupled with sustainable design criteria, it is imperative that design-build always is considered, if not required, by owners. Design-bid-build does not provide our clients with the optimal mix of design, construction, cost and high performance demanded by owners in the 21st century, sustainable environment. In this paper, the reader will learn why design-build is often the better procurement choice and how it works in the sustainable, high performance environment.

To be effective, design-build requires a mastery of performance specifications rather than the commonly used design specifications. Thus, sustainable design and energy efficiency must be specified through a performance specification, rather than a detailed design specification. In this paper, sources for energy and sustainable criteria and standards will be provided that can be readily adapted to performance specifications. A performance specification-writing tool will be suggested that eases the task of writing performance specifications.

Then, standard form design-build contracts will be compared. And finally, presenting design-build in conjunction with sustainable design to your clients will conclude this paper.

The History of Design-Build and Design-Bid-Build

Design-build is not a new method of project delivery. Its roots go back to antiquity. The pyramids were built though design-build. Saint Paul's Cathedral in London was built through design-build. But, it fell into disuse in the United States about the time of the Civil War and gave way to the "new" design-bid-build process through the latter years of the 20th century. Now, in the 21st century, design-build is on the rise as the "new" delivery method of choice for many owners.

The primary difference between design-build and design-bid-build for an owner is that design-build places responsibility for infrastructure delivery into the hands of one party. That is the way construction was done when the building arts were simpler and a "master builder" managed the process. When design-bid-build arose, design and construction was bifurcated and done under separate contracts by parties that now have dramatically different legal liabilities and antagonistic interests. How did this come about?

The first of two driving forces in the move to design-bid-build was the perceived need for specialization in the design and construction industry. In the beginning of this country's history, construction was completed by master builders just as it had been done in Europe for centuries. But, by the end of the Civil War, it was a common practice for owners to hire separate disciplines for design (engineers and architects) and construction (contractors) as complexity of building increased.

These disciplines then organized professional associations to police and protect their standards. Two of the leading societies today were founded for this purpose. In 1852, the American Society of Civil Engineers (ASCE) began and in 1857, the American Institute of Architects (AIA) was chartered. Schools were endowed to educate entrants into the separate professions. The first engineering school in the United States was founded in 1802, which is the United States Military Academy. In 1868, the Massachusetts Institute of Technology (MIT) started its architecture school.

By the early 1900s, the Industrial Revolution provided new building technology, which prompted specialization in skills and accelerated separate educations in building arts and sciences. These technology advances spurred the split among the engineering professions and encouraged specialization among designers and builders. Notable advances that encouraged the specialization in the design and construction industry include the development of inexpensive steel by Andrew Carnegie, effective transmission of alternating current electricity by George Westinghouse, practical elevators by Elijah Otis, dependable cooling by Willis Carrier, and effective plumbing by the Kohler family from Wisconsin.

The second major force driving the use of design-bid-build was the graft and corruption that flourished during the Civil War and never seemed too far away all the way up to present time. Cheating in building construction was perceived to be easy when one party, the "master builder", controlled the entire process. So, splitting the process and making one party the "watchdog" over the other party seemed to be the right answer. Splitting procurement into two separate actions resulted in design-bid-build. A design contract based on technical merit, and a construction contract based on the lowest bid, was the anti-corruption remedy provided by design-bid-build.

In the design-bid-build system, the "watchdog" is the designer and the contractor is regarded as the "bad guy." Thus, the antagonism that is considered normal today in many projects was born over 150 years ago. Now, this antagonism, which is so destructive to construction budgets and supportive of legal budgets, is ingrained in our way of doing business. Most government entities and virtually all professional societies have codified this split of "watchdog" and "bad guy" in contracts, laws and procurement regulations. This codified process is known as "design-bid-build" and is based on design specifications and lump sum payment terms.

Shortcomings of Design-Bid-Build

By the 1970s, it was clear that design-bid-build was not the panacea that it appeared to be. The first issues were practical ones.

- There was minimal dialogue between the designer and builder during the design phase leading to confusion, conflicts and cost overruns during construction.
- As the antagonism increased between designers and builders, the owners were looking for responsible parties to shoulder unexpected costs and unreasonable delays. Finger pointing ensued as the designers and builders blamed each other. That finger pointing rose to become a vast body of construction law and cases.
- In response to the evolving law, inefficient designs evolved as designers protected themselves against legal liability through defensive specifications and plans, which resulted in higher costs, delays, and disputes.
- And, in response to the evolving law and the inefficient designs, builders claimed increased design errors drove their costs up and delayed their progress resulting in even more lawsuits.

But the greatest shortcoming of design-bid-build for the owner was the incredible liability placed on owners for accuracy of design. Under the implied warranty ruling from the *Spearin Doctrine* (United States Supreme Court, 1918), accuracy of design is the owner's responsibility, not the engineer's or architect's.

Under design-bid-build, the designer is only responsible for performing in a *non-negligent* manner as measured by the slippery "standard of care" criteria. And, builders only have to "substantially comply" with plans and specifications and have defenses to total compliance such as "economic waste" and "designer's errors".

Thus, under design-bid-build, the party who is least qualified to perform design and construction has the greatest legal and financial liability for the outcome. That party is the owner.

Finally, Design-Build Returned

By the early 1990s, it was apparent that a different method of project delivery was needed to place legal, financial and performance liability in the hands of the design construction professionals. Schedules were too long. Costs were uncertain. Owners were caught in the middle with designers and builders blaming each other. Design-build was the remedy that fulfilled all of these requirements.

In the 1990's, the use of design-build was resurrected as owners came to appreciate the benefits of choosing a single entity for design and construction. Design-build holds both of the parties, in the design-build entity, jointly and severally responsible for the facility delivery. This joint and several liability concept means that the designer and builder are responsible for their individual contribution to the project; and simultaneously, are each legally and financially responsible for the entire project. Thus under design-build, the designer and builder are genuine partners and must cooperate. Design-build became the answer owners were seeking.

The Design-Build Process

Under design-build, the owner specifies the performance characteristics and criteria of the building during procurement (the proposal stage). Several competing design-builders propose to meet those criteria with their unique designs that capitalize on the synergy and innovativeness of their design-build team. When the design-build contract is signed, the design-builder becomes responsible for the measurable standards (e.g., performance specifications) it agreed. The design-builder then writes the design plans and specifications that it will use to meet the performance specifications. The owner is off the hook for the implied warranty for accuracy of design.

Because the designer is, in effect, giving the design to itself (the design-builder) and is now agreeing to performance rather than specific details, design liability is square on the shoulders of the design-build team. Similarly, the builder is no longer in a position to say the design is wrong, compliance is impossible, or more costly, or more time consuming. The design-build team is now totally responsible for meeting the owner's performance goals and the owner is responsible for paying. Design-build is the answer owners were seeking.

Adoption of design-build was rapid throughout the federal government during the 1990s. Congress authorized all Federal contracting officers to use design-build by the turn of the century. States and local governments were close behind. Design-build is now approved for public agency procurement in over three-quarters of the 55 jurisdictions of the United States. Today, most large private owners recognize the value of design-build, and use it widely.

Sustainability and Design-Build

Design-build, sustainability and high performance project delivery come together through performance specifications.

- The design-build process is premised on performance specifications. Design-build assures that a facility is built that performs per performance specifications as opposed to design-bid-build that delivers projects that comply with design specifications.
- Similarly, sustainability demands a systemic approach to construction requiring that the owner, designer and builder to cooperate in a life cycle of performance.
- High performance is guaranteed when specifications for energy efficiency are specific, numerical and time-oriented.

Thus, the three concepts of design-build, sustainability and high performance are based on performance specifications.

Performance specifications are measurable (i.e., numerical) requirements for what a building must do, rather than what its components are or what it must look like. When using performance specifications in a sustainable environment, the owner's in-house designer describes maximum energy use, allowable environment impact, re-cycling parameters, and all other infrastructure and operations requirements of the building. These performance specifications are advertised in a Request for Proposal for design-build services. Design-build and performance specifications place responsibility for the detailed specifications and construction responsibilities on the party most able to perform – the design-builder.

But, Why Not Use Design Specifications? Does Not the Owner Lose Control Over the Project with Performance Specifications?

In contrast to design-build's approach to facility delivery with integrated services, design-bid-build was established to deliver separated and incremental design and construction so that the owner's designer could exercise project control. Design specifications are the key to a successful design-bid-build project because they deliberately limit innovation by any party other than the owner's designer and place tight controls on construction. Design specifications are the basis for containing and controlling design and construction during the design-bid-build process.

Using design specifications, the designer specifies the exact appearance of the facility, its components, its assembly and the standards for testing. Then, the builder must build the facility in substantial compliance with the plans and design specifications.

But, there are no guarantees that the owner will get what it wanted with design specifications. The concept of *negligence* in design-bid-build and detailed design specifications allows the designer to step away from the final responsibility – does the building perform? Obviously, with a builder in the process, the designer will complain that any non-performance is due to builder errors.

With design-bid-build and detailed design specifications, the builder only has to *substantially comply* with the design specifications and give the owner what was intended. The concept of "economic waste" will prevent the owner from getting what it really wanted as long as it's "close enough" and the cost to come to strict compliance is too high. Thus, the owner gets "close" to what it procured through design-bid-build (as subjectively interpreted by a jury in the final analysis), rather than performance that can be measured.

Further, design specifications are often used because they allow the owner to choose a builder based only on lowest costs. In theory, detailed design specifications allow all contractors to compete on exactly the same deliverable during the bid phase. Thus, it is commonly thought, with more detail in specifications and less variance in the parameters, costs can be precisely compared and controlled. Sadly, these assumptions have not proved to be true in practice.

First, design specifications have major shortcomings with regard to modern construction practices, especially in high performance and sustainability. There is little, if any, innovation allowed. It follows that as details in design increase, innovation is defeated. Innovation is a keystone to high performance and sustainable design.

Second, with detailed specifications and the design-bid-build delivery method, the owner is required to guarantee the accuracy of the design to the builder (the *Spearin Doctrine)*. While not widely understood, this is the law of the land. It is disappointing that the owner gets a lesser design guarantee from the designer, who only has *not-to-be* negligent.

Third, the builder must build the facility exactly as designed or face the potential for breach of contract. Ironically, this situation plays into the unscrupulous builder's hands. What design can be perfect the first time? This is a fallacy. Thus, as the inevitable changes and inevitable errors are found during construction, the builder obtains numerous changes orders and profits when the design omissions and errors are found and corrected. The owner has no choice but to pay.

Finally, when this process is complete, the owner only gets what the completed design specifications require. Typically, design specifications state what components must be in the building and how the building must look. While manufacturer warranties are granted for individual pieces of equipment, there is no assurance that building will deliver what the owner intended -- performance. That was never specified.

So, two major themes arise with design specifications and design-bid-build. Design specifications and design-bid-build promise to control costs, but at the expense of innovation, extra time and change orders. Design specifications and design-bid-build place the greatest liability on the party least able to perform – the owner.

To avoid these issues that are inherent in design-bid-build and design specifications, it becomes clear that design-build and performance specifications are the better option for the owner in a sustainable, high performance environment.

Performances Specifications Set The Parameters For The Sustainable, High Performance Project

With performance standards, the owner instructs the design-builder as to what the building *must do* as opposed to what it is *made of* or should *look like*. Design control is not lost as is commonly thought by the naysayers. The owner can tell the design-builder what it does not want the building to look like or what it does not want in the building.

Because the design-builder agrees to meet performance specifications, it additionally assumes the liability for final design and performance characteristics of the building. Thus, liability for design accuracy shifts from the owner to the design-builder through the use of performance specifications.

Using Performance Specifications

Using performance specifications is not easy, initially. The greatest impediment to using performance specifications is that designers have not been trained to write them.

First, virtually all engineers and architects were trained how to write and use detailed, design specifications. Second, manufacturers make design specifications readily available to the designer. That is because there is either a direct, or indirect, requirement to use their product that is imbedded in that specification. And last, the traditional and well-known method of design-bid-build depends on familiar design specifications.

Thus, to become sustainable design practitioners, engineers and architects must overcome many years of traditional practice and learn the new art of specifying performance.

Sources of Performance Specifications Criteria and Development Software

Many performance standards and criteria have been established to measure success for sustainability and high performance. These standards and criteria are the basis for the design-build performance specifications that engineers and architects must use.

Five such high performance and sustainable criteria systems are now widely used to develop the performance specifications.

The first such system is the Leadership in Energy and Environmental Design (LEED) program, which was developed by the United States Green Building Council (USGBC). It defines performance ratings from Bronze to Platinum, based on meeting sustainability and high performance design and construction criteria. Guidance for performance specifications is provided in five major design and construction areas.

The Green Building Challenge is an international effort to develop a sustainable building assessment tool that will be available soon.

The Army SPIRIT Program is similar to the LEED program, but expands on LEED's performance criteria with military specific standards for additional features unique to military installations.

The "Sustainable Facility Guide", prepared by John Barrie Associates Architects, Inc. and the United States Air Force Air Combat Command, is based on the Construction Specifications Institute (CSI) 16 Division format for specifications. It is quite "user friendly" for the new sustainable designer.

There are local systems that are useful for a sustainable design effort that are based on local economies and climates. The Austin, Texas "Green Builder" rating system is one of the better known.

And finally, the CSI now provides a software program through their on–line bookstore that leads designers and building professionals through the performance-specifying task with ease and thoroughness. The program, also available in trial version, is titled "Perspective®."

Standard Form Contracts

To obtain design-build services and reach agreement on sustainable performance specifications, a contract must be formed between the owner and design-builder. For owners and design-builders, contracts are often a challenge because they are written in a language that non-lawyers do not understand and appears to be threatening. In our American culture, we tend to fear contracts because there is the ever-present potential of litigation.

In response to this lack of understanding and threat of litigation, engineers and architects tend to choose standard form contracts that are sponsored by their respective professional associations. While these contracts can be easier to understand and have been favorably tested in court, they also favor the constituents of the society that wrote them. And for design-build contracts, the standard forms promulgated by the established societies are "cut and pasted" from other types of contracts with gaps and oversights. Thus, there is need to use these contracts with caution and understanding. Following is a critique of each of the commonly available standard forms.

AIA Standard Design-Build Contract Forms

With the AIA design-build contract forms, please be aware of the following.

Among the shortcomings, the AIA forms;

- Lack a set of comprehensive general conditions, that is, the A201 form.
- Split compensation into two amounts.
- Split the design-build tasks into phases.
- Heighten risk in litigation because the venue and choice of law clauses are unclear.
- Cut off the Phase One (designer) agreements from Phase Two (builder) through a poorly positioned integration clause.
- Must be used as a family of documents to include the AIA A191, A491 and B901 forms.
- Provide for payout at the end of Phase One allowing the architect to be paid and the builder to be left empty- handed.

NSPE Standard Design-Build Contract Forms

The National Society of Professional Engineers is a key organization in the Engineers Joint Contract Documents Committee (EJCDC) that developed the engineer's version of a design-build contract. The EJCDC contract also has shortcomings.

Among those shortcomings, it;

- Lacks a set of comprehensive general conditions.
- Assumes compensation to be lump sum rather than incentive based.
- Omits a non-assignment clause.
- Lacks a "no integration" clause cutting off previous agreements.

Among its better features, the EJCDC contract;

- Assumes the builder is prime.
- Uses only NSPE 2802, thus providing a single document for contracting.
- Does not assume a two-phase process.

Association of General Contractors Standard Design-build Contract Forms

The Associated General Contractors (AGC) set of design-build forms needs the most caution of all.

Among the cautions;

- One must use AGC 400, 410, 415, 420,430, 450, and 450.1 documents, which are not well coordinated.
- These documents are rigid about the builder leading the team as the prime, and the designer as a subcontractor.
- These documents are rigid that the builder controls the process.
- These forms lack a set of comprehensive general conditions.
- There is confusion among the documents on Guaranteed Maximum Price, lump sum and negotiation of price based on design changes.
- There is confusion among the documents in the role of the designers.
- There is confusion among the documents in the contract general conditions.

Design Build Institute of American Standard Design-Build Contract Forms

The Design Build Institute of America (DBIA), founded in 1994 promotes, sets standards for, and supports the design-build industry. Its forms are considered to be the optimal ones for design-build and sustainability. DBIA forms tend to be the most widely accepted among contract professionals because they best balance the risks and needs among the parties in the design-build process.

Among their attributes;

- DBIA forms have addressed the shortcomings of the other families of forms.
- Just like AIA, EJCDC and AGC forms, the DBIA documents come with explanatory notes and guides for the non-lawyer.
- DBIA documents allow the most flexibility in design-build team formation, compensation methods, and project performance.
- DBIA provides a wide assortment of forms covering virtually all types of design-build agreements except for international design-build.

Selling Sustainability and Design Build

Owner-clients need to see the bottom line advantage of sustainability and design-build for engineers and architects to win business. The moral imperatives of sustainment and shift in legal liability with design-build are appealing, but not compelling. It still comes down to dollars and cents in the final analysis. So, how is sustainment and design-build presented to the client to win business? Here is a six-step process.

First, learn the details of sustainable design and the process of design-build. Even experienced engineers and architects must have professional, hard-hitting and effective training in these subjects to beat the competition.

Second, when in front of the client, be prepared to answer the fundamental question every client poses. What is this going to cost me? The normal client measures design and construction costs in traditional paradigms. A client will be looking for either "best value", if a forward thinker, or "lowest cost", if a conservative thinker. Instead of these traditional methods of costing, show the client that life cycle costs overwhelmingly favor sustainability and high performance design. Then, show that design-build saves procurement costs and financial carrying costs. It is accepted that design-build normally saves at least 6% of the facility procurement costs required by design-bid-build for corresponding projects.

Third, be prepared to show your client that design-build saves a valuable commodity in addition to money - time. Authoritative studies have shown that design-build saves 33% of the time required by design-bid-build for corresponding projects.

Fourth, in addition to the money and time issues, clients are normally civic-minded and socially responsible. Show them the data regarding the moral imperatives for sustainability. Most clients do not know where to obtain sustainable information because it is not part of their core business. It is the designer's opportunity to assist them to meet their legal, environment and social obligations to society by educating them as to their sustainable responsibilities.

Fifth, most clients do not know of the significant legal liability that flows from design-bid-build construction. Most do not know that changes and claim submittals drop to almost 10% of that in traditional construction, when design-build is used. And, few know that design-build claim awards are a fraction of those experienced in design-bid-build.

And finally, to be most credible, the designer-builder needs to know the specific sources of sustainable and design-build tools, so that these can be cited and produced for the client.

Upon mastering these six steps, the design-builder will readily get the client's "yes" to a sustainable, high performance proposal.

Summarizing Sustainability, High Performance, and Design-Build

In summary, sustainability, high performance buildings, and the design-build method are a natural fit. This combination of moral imperatives, intelligent use of energy, and forward thinking design and construction is the combination necessary for responsible and economical building in the 21st century.

To be effective in this new market place, today's designers and builders must have these tools:

- Know the requirements for sustainability when presenting to government clients.
- Know the USGBC benefits of sustainability when presenting to private clients.
- Know the liability shift, change control and claims advantages of design-build.
- Know the sources of sustainability performance specifications, sustainable products and design-build contract forms

that suit the client.

As these tools are added to the practitioner's skill set, these paradigm shifts must be learned and become part of the practitioner's ethics and integrity.

- Sustainability is the moral and economic choice for building as our national and global resources diminish.
- High performance in terms of energy efficiency, re-use of resources and life cycle costing is the cornerstone of sustainability.
- Design-build provides the only fully innovative and cost-effective process for delivering sustainability where the designer, builder and owner are a genuine team.

Designers and builders are the catalysts that make sustainment and high performance happen. Therefore, designers and builders must learn more about these concepts and how to execute them for success in the 21st century.

The bottom line is bold and crisp. Sustainability, high performance and design-build are a triple win for the owner, designer, and builder, alike.

Author Biography

P. Thomas (Tom) Gard, PE, Esq. PMP, is a registered professional engineer with experience in energy engineering, an experienced litigator in construction and design, and a project manager with over thirty years experience in government and private industry. He holds engineering degrees from Michigan State University and Purdue University, a Masters in Business Administration from Northern Michigan University, and a Juris Doctor from The Catholic University of America. He founded Dominion Project Management, Inc. in 1997 to provide training in project management and construction law; consulting in design-build, sustainable design and energy efficiency projects; and, quality assurance and quality for high performance and sustainable design projects. He resides in Northern Virginia with his family and beloved classic sports car.

For more information, contact Tom Gard at Tom@Dominion-Project.com; or write to:
Dominion Project Management, Inc
26 H Plaza Street
Leesburg, VA 20176
(703) 443-2600

Section 7
Facilities Security

Chapter 71

Abstract

Security for utility and energy systems is of great importance to America and to the Department of Defense. Terrorism in today's world has made our vulnerability evident. We must deal with several areas of concern, while at the same time, addressing the security of our utilities and energy. Our utility infrastructure is subject to insufficient funding and resources to maintain adequate operating conditions. Market conditions have caused rising and unstable utility rates. In addition, we can no longer be dependent on traditional energy sources or methods of transmission.

To protect against our utilities and energy systems becoming potential targets or sources of weakness for the Department of Defense, we have undertaken an aggressive, integrated utilities and energy program. This paper describes the policies and procedures instituted to address these issues.

REDUCING THE VULNERABILITIES OF DEPARTMENT OF DEFENSE UTILITIES AND ENERGY USE

Dr. Get W. Moy, P.E.

Good afternoon. It's my pleasure to be here at the 25th World Energy Engineering Congress. Addressing this Congress on Reducing the Vulnerabilities of Defense Utilities and Energy Use is a topic that is critical to the Department of Defense and one that I deal with every day.

The Defense Department spends more than $2 billion annually buying electricity, gas and water, and hundreds of millions to operate and maintain systems to deliver energy. We do not normally generate power, but we do own, operate and maintain utility systems, including substations.....the pipes and wires, to deliver gas, electricity, water, etc. These systems are worth about $50 billion dollars.

The Department of Defense has developed an integrated program that optimizes utility system management by conserving energy and water, taking advantage of restructured energy commodity markets and privatizing our utilities infrastructure. Utilities are the backbone for operation of any installation, base, or city, for that matter. Think of the inability to use flight simulators or information management systems...of operating a hospital... without reliable electricity. Think of how unpleasant the quality of life and workplace environment would be without dependable water systems. Indeed, utility systems provide necessary support to the operational forces and quality of life on installations worldwide. At the same time, strong energy conservation and efficiency programs help the Department save real dollars and mitigate the effects of rising/spiking energy costs through demand reductions.

On September 11 our lives in America, and at the Department of Defense changed.....and they will never be the same. Security for utilities and energy has became an issue that is a foremost concern for all of us, and this means that we must look at our day-to-day operations....our policies, differently. In Vice President Cheney's letter to the president, delivering the Report of the National Energy Policy Development Group, he declares, " To achieve a 21st century quality of life – enhanced by reliable energy and a clean environment – we must modernize conservation, modernize our infrastructure, increase our energy supplies, including renewables, accelerate the protection and improvement of our environment, and increase our energy security." One of the greatest challenges facing America is the need to improve our aging energy infrastructure. The "energy infrastructure has failed to keep pace with the changing requirements of our energy systems.....The energy infrastructure is vulnerable to physical and cyber disruption that could threaten its integrity and safety. Disruptions could come from natural events, like geo magnetic storms and earthquakes, or could come from accidents, equipment failures, or deliberate sabotage.....any disruption can have extensive consequences." The Department of Defense utilities and energy programs are aligned, and we aggressively pursue the security of our utilities and energy systems.

Energy is a key ingredient of national security. An adequate, reliable supply of energy is essential to the performance of military missions. The Department of Defense is the single largest consumer of energy in the nation, and consumes about three-quarters of the energy used by the Federal Government. Threats against our country make the security of our utilities and energy critical.

507

For the issue at hand, Energy Security against Terrorism, let's look at the following three points of vulnerability:

- Aging utility infrastructure, with insufficient funding and resources to maintain our systems in adequate operating condition.
- Rising/unstable utility rates.
- Dependence on traditional energy sources.

To avoid having any of these areas become potential targets or sources of weakness for the Department of Defense, we've undertaken an aggressive integrated utilities and energy program. In each area, we've taken a deliberate approach to reduce our vulnerability. Our Services have applied heightened security at our installations worldwide, and the security procedures at those locations extend to the utilities and energy systems. We must avoid the potential for risks, detect threats before they materialize, and plan for rapid recovery in the event of the failure of our utility and energy systems.

Historically, military installations have been unable to upgrade and maintain utility systems fully, due to inadequate funding and competing installation management priorities. Normal appropriations have not been sufficient to properly maintain our utility infrastructure. This has made the systems vulnerable to unscheduled outages and failures. We cannot risk outages or failures when it could affect the defense of our country.

The Department cannot afford to own, operate and maintain its aging utility infrastructure and make the necessary capital investments to keep pace with future requirements, when others can provide these services more cost-effectively. This means that, with the help of the private sector's ability to leverage our appropriate dollars, we can convey these large capital assets to qualified owners and pay for the utility services with appropriated dollars. The Department of Defense has chosen utilities privatization as the preferred method of modernizing the utility infrastructure. Utilities privatization will allow military installations to benefit from private-sector financing, efficiencies, and innovations to obtain improved utility systems. The "end of the day" results are reliable, dependable, safe, and economical utility systems. The goal of our utility privatization program is to convey the major electric, natural gas, water treatment and waste water treatment utility systems at military installations to the private sector/municipalities.

With nearly 1,600 utility systems eligible for privatization, we have a lot of work ahead of us, but realize the long-term pay-off is a better way of doing business, using the private sector's talent and technology to improve our utility infrastructure. Today we have 30 privatization contracts for service in place, which includes electrical services at Fort McCoy, Wisconsin, and Fort Pickett, Virginia; natural gas services at Fort Sill, Oklahoma, Bowling Air Force Base, Fort Detrick, Maryland, and Naval Air Station, Tennessee; potable water at Fort Lee, Virginia; and water and waste water services at Aberdeen Proving Ground, Maryland. These examples are just the beginning of a very large program.

We are executing our privatization efforts in a deliberate way – incorporating economic analysis, and research with respect to the companys making proposals – so that we ensure they are in the best interest of the government. Utilities privatization is my personal number one priority since taking office as the Director of Utilities and Energy Use for DoD, but I want to be sure we obtain safe, technologically current, and environmentally sound utility systems, at a relatively lower cost than with continued government ownership. Since the office of Utilities and Energy Use was stood up last fall, we have begun regular meetings with the Services to share information about best practices, what works, and what doesn't work. We have extended the deadline for the Services to privatize from September 2003 to 2005. This does not mean we are slowing down, but we are moving forward as rapidly as possible to privatize, and to do it right.

On May 3, 2001, the President directed all Federal agencies to take appropriate actions to conserve energy use at facilities. Furthermore, conserving energy at DoD saves money that can be invested in readiness, facilities sustainment, and quality of life. Energy conservation and demand reduction projects make business sense. This dynamic becomes even more important when you consider that military installations spent nearly $2.8 billion in fiscal year 2001 to buy energy commodities. We continue to make progress in achieving the 2010 energy reduction goal for buildings of 35 percent per square foot, and have already reduced consumption by over 23 percent since 1985.

Much of the Department's performance to date has been based on efforts with the "low hanging fruit". We are not only paying attention to our consumption, but WHEN we consume. By consuming energy at non-peak times whenever practical, we reduce DoD energy costs, and make energy more accessible for the community. The Energy Conservation Improvement Program, known as ECIP, Energy Savings Performance Contracts, or ESPCs, Utility Energy Services Contracts, or UESCs and other investment programs, along with partnering with industry, are critical for us to reduce our demand for energy and, consequently, our vulnerability.

Additionally, the cold hard fact is that our supply of oil is finite and we control only a small portion of it. The power shortages we've experienced in California and elsewhere in recent years, as well as recent terrorist actions on our homeland have brought this fact to the forefront. We saw natural gas prices go up sharply and significantly raise electricity prices in some markets where gas was used more for power generation, and supply was strained to keep up with demand. Our water supply and quality are also becoming critical issues. We must ensure the quality, security, and availability of water and wastewater treatment facilities for our installations. We will look to the use of renewable energy sources, new practices, and technologies to increase our flexibility, combined with using the principles of sustainable development to reduce the resource consumption used in our new construction, and operation and maintenance.

We are challenged to be better.....smarter consumers. Technological advances in renewable power, fuel cells, distributive power, combined heat and power, biomass, and other renewable energy sources promise to provide improvement and efficiencies never before thought possible. Operations and maintenance costs are a major part of the Department of Defense operating budget. Energy conservation can reduce the life cycle O&M substantially. Increasing efficiency and reducing energy demand saves money that is better spent on Department of Defense readiness and quality of life, and helps to improve the environment.

Sustainable design....using design to incorporate energy efficiency and environmental protection into our installations, will ensure a healthful world for future generations, while reducing our costs. The Department of Defense is making a conscious effort to minimize non-renewable energy consumption, use environmentally preferable products, protect and conserve water resources and optimize operations and maintenance practices. Energy efficiency, building cost and energy access are essential aspects of the production of a sustainable design. Over the life cycle of a facility, energy savings are a huge part of the cost of ownership. New, more efficient heating, ventilation, energy generation systems and other technologies are constantly being developed, and these help the designer achieve energy efficiency objectives. These represent an improvement in our installation buildings and the quality of life for our military and DoD employees. The Services are actively pursuing sustainable design as a preferred method, and in some cases receiving national attention and recognition for their facilities, including the US Green Building Council's Leadership in Energy and Environmental Design (LEED) award.

Our National Energy Policy directs that the programs I have talked about.....energy conservation, renewable energy, and energy safety be a part of the program for all Federal agencies. President Bush has said "America must have an energy policy that plans for the future, but meets the needs of today." The Department of Defense stands ready to implement the National Energy Policy. The National Energy Policy has directed that agencies work together to achieve the highest possible security for energy in this country. The Department of Defense is working with the Department of Energy to develop a combined Joint Threat Policy that will be the basis for a protection strategy to be used at all DoD and DoE nuclear facilities. We will continue to work with others in the government, and with private industry, to ensure that we provide the security necessary for our energy and utility systems.

In conclusion, to combat terrorism, and ensure security for our energy and utility systems, it's important to look at the anti-terrorism/force protection measures needed, and equally important is how to reduce our weaknesses and vulnerability.....how to provide for the needs of our military, and at the same time ensure their "Quality of Life". We have undertaken a multi-faceted approach to achieve total utilities and energy security.

Chapter 72

ENERGY SECURITY & SMALL-SCALE GENERATION:
SOME THINGS NEVER CHANGE

Lewis Milford
Clean Energy Group

Distributed, renewable energy sources are vital to America's security. Now, after failing for decades to fully recognize their importance, it's important for the U.S. to start addressing the vulnerability of our centralized power systems and the possibilities that new technologies represent.

Historically, central energy systems have been targeted very effectively during times of war, most notably in Germany during World War II. While the German economy suffered heavily due to attacks on power plants, the decentralized nature of the Japanese power system made it a more difficult target. In the U.S., such risks are known but have not been adequately addressed by our current policies relating to the structure of our power grid. Our power companies are guarded, but many points of vulnerability to terrorist attack still remain in the form of structures like power lines, which are difficult to adequately defend. Emergency management of the U.S. energy system has its roots in military "civil defense" planning, where the primary governmental function is to maintain social order. With such roots, emergency management practices have largely focused on post-disaster planning, instead of focusing on elements like preparation for and prevention of attacks, which might be addressed through the development of a decentralized power system.

Emergency management agencies are aware of the risks posed by centralized power systems, but have largely failed to address them. A report commissioned by the Federal Emergency Management Agency concluded in 1980 that "Current US energy systems are highly vulnerable," but was not acted upon, despite the advice of some government agencies and outside advocates. Even after a 1990 Congressional investigation into the possibility of threats to central power systems, American perceptions of the likelihood of terrorist attacks were so low that no action was taken to change our vulnerability. Prior to 9/11, only a few states incorporated energy protection into disaster planning; California, for example, developed emergency plans to protect public health during electric disruptions, as a result of blackouts in early 2001. The facilities to which these plans recognized critical risks included water systems, medical facilities, schools, detention centers and day care centers. One other area of risk is disaster management services themselves; in Boston, for instance, electricity is needed to dispatch police, fire, and other emergency personnel.

After September 11, many experts dealing with the problem of energy system vulnerability have returned to solutions first advocated decades earlier. Former top government security chiefs endorsed clean energy options in a letter to Congress, explaining that "disbursed, renewable and domestic supplies of fuels and electricity" are the means to prevent threats to our safety posed by insecure power systems. After 9/11, many public commentators also recognize distributed renewable energy as a means of increasing our national security; an article in the Christian Science Monitor concludes "The events of Sept. 11 sealed the national security argument for a massive national investment in renewable energy."

If the U.S. is to meet the challenge posed by the vulnerability of our energy systems, many factors and technologies will have to be examined and considered. Fuel Cells and PV are potential aids in seeking security, but other useful technologies include microturbines, diesels, and UPS systems. Which technologies are most practical will depend upon competitive factors such as public funding and support, reliability, environmental constraints and benefits, operating and capital costs, and availability.

In 1997, President Clinton's Commission on Critical Infrastructure Protection raised several important points, writing that the entire nation's infrastructure would profoundly suffer from "prolonged disruption in the flow of energy." The commission reported that, "Our fundamental conclusion is this: Waiting for disaster is a dangerous strategy. Now is the time to act to protect our future." With these words in mind, states need to take steps now to protect our energy systems. Some of these are planning steps, such as identifying critical public facilities, and evaluating potential energy risks and losses. States should keep these factors in mind in considering distributed generation options to protect critical loads, working with other states on joint deployment, and incorporating energy security fully into emergency planning. These steps are important to the future of our nation's economic security and to the safety of American citizens.

50 State Street
Montpelier, VT 05602
(802) 223-2554
Fax: (802) 223-4967
Email: LMilford@cleanegroup.org

512

Chapter 73

HIGHLY RELIABLE ELECTRIC POWER SYSTEM DESIGN WITH PROBABILISTIC RISK ASSESSMENT

Stephen A. Fairfax, President
MTechnology, Inc. (1)

Abstract

Probabilistic Risk Assessment (PRA) has been applied successfully to military, aerospace, and civilian nuclear power for decades. PRA enables a formal, quantitative study of success and failure in complex systems, and can provide valuable guidance when contemplating new designs, upgrades to existing systems, or analysis of failures. This paper discusses the application of PRA techniques to a variety of power system studies including design, upgrade, and maintenance. The ability of PRA to produce quantitative guidance for responses to random, infrequent events is immediately applicable to evaluation of security measures. Several case studies illustrate the benefits and limits of these techniques.

What is PRA?

Probabilistic Risk Assessment: a formal, quantitative study of success and failure in complex systems, has been developed over 5 decades for applications in military, aerospace, civilian nuclear power. The techniques result in improved understanding of system responses to off-normal events, routine operations, maintenance, and changes. The results provide quantitative guidance for understanding component contributions to failure, evaluation of potential improvements, and the effects of maintenance and normal operation policies on system reliability.

The techniques used include but are not limited to hazard analysis, fault tree analysis, event analysis, estimation of failure distributions from sparse data, Bayesian updating of estimates, and failure modes and effects analysis. This paper will discuss the application of hazard, fault tree, and event analysis to a variety of power system applications.

Design Analysis

MTechnology, Inc. (MTech) was retained to evaluate the long-term availability of a highly redundant power system for the First National Bank of Omaha (2). The power system supports major credit card processing applications where the cost of outages is extremely high. Our analysis showed that the proposed system, which utilized redundant on-site fuel cells as the primary energy source, with redundant flywheel batteries, multiple Uninterruptible Power Supplies (UPS), redundant standby diesel engine/generators, and multiple gas and electric utility connections, would have a long-term unavailability against independent equipment failure of less than 1×10^{-6}. The results also highlighted a vulnerability to a particular component failure that was not obvious but easily mitigated. Operating policies and common-cause failures were evaluated as well.

Upgrade Analysis

We have evaluated proposed upgrades to existing corporate data centers for several clients . The analysis compared the expected improvement in long-term system availability offered by on-site generation versus additional utility feeders. Redundant utility feeders energized by separate substations are often employed in corporate data centers and other high-value applications, but our reviews have shown that the relatively high costs are not justified. Utilities charge large fees for these custom services as they consume feeder capacity, complicate operations and maintenance, and require substantial capital investments. The probability of high voltage transmission system failures and other dependencies between utility substations substantially reduce the protection offered by "independent" feeder circuits. A comparable investment in standby or baseload on-site generation assets has proven to be more cost-effective, even after including generous allowances of operations, maintenance, testing, and repair of the new customer equipment.

Hazard Identification:
Keystone of reliable, safe systems

Many failures in otherwise reliable systems are caused by unidentified hazards. Some designs that successfully mitigated the risks of certain hazards have been so successful that future owners and operators were unaware of the existence of the hazard, and so did not respect operating limitations or system isolation requirements during upgrades to critical facilities. The perverse result is that the most elegant and successful mitigation efforts can be disabled because of their success, if proper documentation is absent.

A hazard analysis report documents all hazards considered, assumptions about what hazards are credible and which were deemed too unlikely to require mitigation, and lists any mitigation measures. The effort required to produce such a report is substantial, but provides a valuable resource for future operations and upgrades. The report should be as complete as possible; investigators of future failures will assume that any hazards not explicitly considered were ignored.

Hazards that are discovered after the initial report require a revision of the analysis, not only to document the existence of a previously unknown hazard, but to evaluate the proposed mitigation measures against the existing safeguards and design assumptions. It is quite easy to violate a basic design assumption, or compromise an existing mitigation, during the process of improving the protection against a newly discovered threat.

Designers seldom anticipate abuses or improper operation of their systems. A hazard analysis is best conducted by a third party who is familiar with the equipment and application but not directly responsible for the design or operations. A number of checklists and brainstorming techniques are available to assist in the identification of hazards. Historical data from previous installations, hopefully with their own hazard analyses, is invaluable in this process.

Application of PRA to Security

The techniques developed to evaluate the reliability of complex, interconnected systems against random equipment failure are applicable to the analysis of security systems. Both reliability and security must protect against diffuse threats that can compromise equipment or targets at random times. The primary distinction is that equipment failures are generally treated as random while serious security breaches are usually the result of hostile intent. In both fields, layers of protection, passive mitigation rather than active responses, and careful ordering of the relative contribution of each component to system success or failure can be used to achieve the highest degree of protection for a given amount of effort and funds. The formal evaluation of events and consequences provides not only quantitative guidance for system design and operation, but provide a way to settle the otherwise intractable differences that arise due to individual experience and expertise.

Limits to PRA in theory and practice

The construction of a fault tree or event tree or other quantitative reliability/security model requires data on the frequency and distribution of failures for all system components. Availability analysis requires additional data on the time to repair failed equipment. These data are sparse and difficult to obtain. Manufacturers generally do not conduct robust investigations of equipment performance and failures. Data from warranty claims is useful but skewed towards early failures (when the warranty is still in effect) and rarely contains sufficient detail to ascertain definitive cause of failure or time to repair.

Some designers, frustrated by the lack of high-quality failure and repair data, eschew PRA techniques altogether. We have found that, particularly in high reliability applications where there is substantial equipment redundancy, the final results are not particularly sensitive to the failure rate of any single component. Indeed, such a sensitivity generally indicates a design defect. Further, the true value of the analysis lies in the formal, written evaluation of the system as a whole, and in the production of ranked estimates of the contribution of each component to the success or failure of the system. The lack of data may limit the accuracy of the estimates, but does not absolve the designer of the obligation to deliver a reliable, robust system.

Common cause failures, wherein multiple, seemingly independent components are affected or failed by a single event, are a serious limit. Common cause failures include human error, extreme weather, improper maintenance or repair techniques, and design or manufacturing defects. Experience at large corporate data centers suggests that over half of all "downtime" can be attributed to human error. (3)

Some common cause hazards can be mitigated if they are properly identified. Human error can be reduced by careful design and automation, adherence to well-written procedures for normal tasks, the use of a 2 or more person challenge/response approach similar to that used by aircraft pilots and controllers, and both initial and recurring training.

The effects of common cause failures grow more pronounced as system reliability improves. Our analysis of the First National Bank of Omaha facility showed that a hypothetical common cause failure occurring once per century would increase the estimated system unavailability against independent failures (less than 10-6) by a factor of 200 or more. If the system were less reliable, with unavailability of 10-4, the increase due the once per century event was essentially negligible.

Few enterprises have defensible estimates of the potential damages from power outages. Those that do often confine their analysis to marginal revenue loss, but our experience is that these are generally not the most significant damages. Lost or disgruntled customers, the possibility of lawsuits or regulatory action, financial market response, increased insurance premiums or loss of coverage, and other adverse affects can be orders of magnitude more costly than the loss of operating revenue.

This lack of understanding of the potential least and worst consequences of power system failure makes it difficult or impossible to economically justify the considerable expense of installing or improving premium power equipment and systems. Worse still, executives who do not appreciate the distribution of possible consequences, and the limits of risk assessment and mitigation, may mistakenly believe that they have completely removed the risk of power failure just because of the size of their investment in power equipment. PRA techniques offer a number of tools not only to assess the risks, but to present the results of the analysis to management and other non-technical reviewers in a manner that is understandable and defensible.

Failure, repair, and availability

The definition of failure and success has emerged as the most crucial part of our analysis in virtually all cases. We advocate a definition of failure that recognizes the effects on the end user of the system, rather than one based on the power supply. Modern computer-based equipment will generally fail if voltage is zero for more than 8 milliseconds. All too often, customers are mislead by utility statistics that show the availability of electric power in excess of 99.9%. The unwary will multiply the system unavailability, 0.1%, by the number of hours in a year and deduce that they will experience 8.7 hours without power each year. Not only does this not recognize the random nature of power failures, but it disregards the vastly different definition of failure used by utilities. Utilities must interrupt power to clear faults on their system. A circuit breaker that opens to clear a fault, then automatically re-closes a few seconds later, is counted as a success, but the user with sensitive equipment will experience a failure. Utility statistics generally don't include outages whose duration is less than one minute, the effects storms or other adverse weather, or planned outages for maintenance. Operators of critical facilities consistently report that it requires 12-24 hours to restore a corporate data center to normal operations following a system-wide power outage. This time to repair has profound affects on the availability of the system. Estimates of downtime based on multiplying system unavailability by the number of hours in a year are meaningless if the result is less than the time to repair.

A more useful approach is to use the repair time to estimate what mean time to failure is required in order to produce a given availability, then calculate the reliability over a period of interest. This approach leads one to characterize a "five nines" (99.999% availability) power system for a data center with a 16-hour mean time to repair as having a 10% chance of at least one outage in 20-year mission. "Six nines" availability yields 1% chance of outage in same lifetime. The oft-repeated contention that "five nines equals five minutes downtime per year" is revealed to be not only meaningless (as there is no such thing as a five-minute failure in a corporate data center) but completely misleading for purposes of evaluating the risk of failure.

Summary

The techniques of probabilistic risk assessment have been extensively developed for use in a variety of critical applications. The extension of these techniques to analysis of critical power facilities is straightforward and very useful. PRA offers the ability to justify investments in premium power equipment on the same quantitative basis used for most other business investment decisions. Careful consideration of the consequences of equipment or system failure can provide important insights to management and users regarding how much protection is realistic and affordable. The formal, quantitative evaluation of design and operating choices brings a degree of rigor to a field that has too often been dominated by decisions based on long experience, but not careful analysis.

References

(1) MTechnology, Inc., 2 Central Street, Saxonville, MA 01701. http://www.mtechnology.net

(2) *Long-term Availability of the SurePower System Installation at the First National Technology Center* D. Bruce Montgomery, Stephen A Fairfax, Prof. Michael Golay, Dept of Nuclear Engineering, MIT Frank Felder, Dept. of Nuclear Engineering, MIT http://www.hi-availability.com/ab_wh_papers.html#report

(3) Ken Brill, Uptime Institute, private communication

Chapter 74

MASSACHUSETTS AND ENERGY SECURITY:
WHAT ONE STATE IS DOING TO ENHANCE SECURITY THROUGH DISTRIBUTED GENERATION"

Raphael Herz
Director, Premium Power
Renewable Energy Trust
Massachusetts Technology Collaborative

ABSTRACT

The events of September 11, 2001, have indelibly marked requirements for a focus on energy generation and use strategies to protect public interests and manage emergency events. Security experts have concluded that current electrical systems could be vulnerable to conventional military, nuclear, and terror attacks. Disbursed, renewable and domestic supplies of fuels and electricity can be used to reduce these risks.[i]

As part of a larger state strategy to prepare for and respond to harmful events, Massachusetts is undertaking activities to reduce risk of harm to critical public facilities by considering distributed generation. The state's clean energy fund has begun an initiative to consider fuel cells and solar technologies as part of emergency planning and response. The early lessons from that effort indicate a strong willingness and need for distributed generation but a lack of resources to implement it. These lessons and plans for future activities are shared in this report.

INTRODUCTION

In early March, a powerful winter storm slams the Northeast, covering in ice and then crumpling into tangled modern art the electric transmission towers. The transmission lines for Boston, Springfield, and Worcester are frozen in the snow. The state's schools and major industries are shut down, as the workforce cannot navigate highways and roads, which are littered with fallen trees and branches. The state's emergency response agencies kick into action, and the governor and her administration plan their damage survey route. Masquerading as a state militia guardsman and bearing arms and bombs under heavy winter gear, an angry anti-government militant heads to the regional emergency response bunker. Unnoticed by all outside the facility in the turmoil of responding to the storm's aftermath, the militant sets off gateway metal detectors and is restrained by emergency officials before harm or loss of life. Local citizens, unaware of the narrowly averted loss of their governor, make their way to schools and other emergency shelters powered by photovoltaics and fuel cells that provide hot meals and warm shelter for homeless families and volunteers working to clear the roads for emergency crews.

Although the scenario above is fictional, it is not difficult to imagine in today's post-9/11 world, complicated by global climate change and national security issues. No longer is the question one of whether or not, but rather of how to build resiliency into our nation's energy supply, given a bleak economic climate in which state and local budgets are besieged with significant cutbacks. Distributed generation (DG) of renewable energy sources is often cited as a way to diversify the nation's energy supply and disburse the generation to smaller sites of supply. Combined with other energy efficiency practices, the use of DG can contribute to a more resilient power system capable of surviving the stresses of overload, deliberate attacks, and volatile regional and/or international market forces.[ii]

As part of a larger state strategy to prepare for and respond to harmful events, Massachusetts is undertaking activities to reduce risk of harm to critical public facilities by considering distributed generation. The state's Renewable Energy Trust, a fund receiving a system-benefit charge from electric bills, with a mission to foster renewable energy market sustainability and to spur growth in Massachusetts's renewable energy sector, has begun activities to consider photovoltaics and fuel cells as part of a strategy to evaluate market opportunities for DG technologies and to enhance the security of citizens of Massachusetts and beyond.

This report provides a background to the Renewable Energy Trust activities and its parent organization, the entities in the Commonwealth considering DG as part of their strategy to ensure public health and safety, and briefly set outs relevant definitions. The report then details a plan for evaluation and deployment of DG technologies.

BACKGROUND
The Massachusetts Technology Collaborative (MTC) is an independent economic development organization established to promote sustainable economic growth by supporting regional technology-based clusters and by serving as a public policy laboratory for technology-related initiatives. MTC administers the Renewable Energy Trust, which was created by the state legislature to help the Commonwealth shift toward greater reliance on renewable energy resources to meet its needs and to spur development of the renewables sector as an important source of economic growth in Massachusetts.

MTC seeks to be a catalyzing element for innovation by providing research and analysis to better understand economic forces and facilitating collaboration with public, private and academic leaders and decision-makers. It is in this vein that MTC, with its nimble ability to respond to and bring together varied stakeholders, sought to understand and test those activities that may reduce risk of harm to critical public facilities — especially DG.

Seeking to fulfill its renewable energy mission, and at the same time addressing a Commonwealth need,

MTC began discussions on security and disaster-related activities with the following state agencies:

The Massachusetts Emergency Management Agency (MEMA) coordinates federal, state, voluntary, and private resources during disasters and emergencies. MEMA develops state emergency readiness plans, trains response personnel, disseminates information, and helps communities recover from disasters. The agency operates the state emergency operations center and is developing a new state strategic plan to address terrorism-related vulnerabilities. MEMA has assisted all 351 cities and towns in developing local Comprehensive Emergency Management plans that identify all critical local facilities (including police, fire, medical, emergency shelters, etc.) and indicate whether those facilities currently have backup generation.

The Massachusetts Department of Capital Asset Management (DCAM) is the state building agency, assisting other state agencies with public-building design, construction, and real estate. Its scope of services includes planning, design, construction, repair and improvements, asset management, contractor certification, leasing, and acquisition. Properties under its charge include hospitals, courthouses, prisons, and police stations. The energy team at DCAM provides the initiative with an understanding of the current level of backup capability at critical state facilities, and insight into the state's pipeline of pending projects for security-related on-site generation opportunities.

The Massachusetts Port Authority (Massport) is an independent public authority that administers much of the state's transportation infrastructure. Massport operates three major airports, the region's largest seaport facilities and important surface arteries. Together, these facilities support more than 20,000 jobs and generate more than $8 billion in economic activity every year. Massport gains flexibility from its status as a self-supporting, independent public authority that receives no state tax dollars.

At a local level, police, fire, and medical facilities and personnel have responsibility for most emergency response, and local facilities serve as emergency shelters. In the larger metro-Boston area, the Boston

Emergency Management Agency (BEMA) has responsibility for emergency management response. BEMA operates three centers that dispatch police, fire and emergency management (911) calls for the city. The three centers can serve as backup for each other in emergencies. While public safety departments handle problems on a smaller scale, BEMA responds to large or long-term disasters. BEMA functions as MEMA's local liaison, as well as a liaison to the federal government.

To provide clarity in a post-9/11 world to organizations considering new tactics that may include DG technologies, we visualize an improved energy security standard defined using terms of disaster planning: mitigation, preparedness, response, and recovery. Mitigation is defined as "policies and actions taken before an event which are intended to reduce damage when an event does occur," and can be seen in the example of making buildings more resistant to earthquakes or fire. Preparedness involves implementing mitigation tactics and increasing a society's ability to respond to disaster. For example, such tactics may include development of emergency plans or training professionals and volunteers for improved disaster response. Response is simply seen as those actions, such as warning or evacuation, taken immediately when a disaster strikes, and recovery is defined as longer term efforts to rebuild both infrastructure and social fabric. [iii]

INITIATIVE TO IMPROVE ENERGY SECURITY
Initial Investigation Results
In response to the events of September 11, MTC began a rapid assessment of opportunities to assist the Commonwealth to enhance the public health and the security of critical public facilities by supporting the use of renewable generation (fuel cells and solar power) to provide high reliability power generation. Parameters confined the investigation within the MTC's legislative mandate, the organizational mission of developing new market opportunities, and the guiding principle of providing maximum benefits to Commonwealth ratepayers. The investigation results are as follows:

State, federal, and local officials with responsibility for security and disaster response have identified a pressing need for enhanced power protection, driven primarily by three factors:

- An increased likelihood of a power failure due to of newly recognized risks of terrorist attacks, including potential attacks on the electric grid or central generating stations. This risk adds to the previously recognized risks of power failure due to weather, grid failure, and other causes.
- Increased consequences of power failure due to increasing dependence on computers and other electric-powered devices to perform critical functions.
- Increased recognition that reliability is of paramount importance and that existing back-up power systems (diesels or batteries) may not be as reliable as had been assumed.

The state, federal, and local officials expressed significant interest in pressing forward with an exploration of the use of renewable generating technologies, including fuel cells and photovoltaics, in a variety of applications, including:

- Primary emergency management facilities, such as police dispatch centers and central emergency management operations centers. These facilities typically have some back-up generation today, but insufficient redundancy.
- Secondary emergency management facilities, such as emergency shelters and regional emergency management operations centers. These facilities typically have little or no back-up generation today.
- Private businesses that perform critical functions during an emergency, e.g., fuel pumping stations (which rely on electricity to run pumps). These facilities typically have no backup generation today. Such facilities could potentially be served by portable generation owned by the state emergency management agency, which would deploy these tools at individual communities during response and recovery periods.

Despite their recognition of the need for enhanced reliability, the public officials have little or no budget available for preliminary technical design or capital expenses for onsite generation and no staff resources for analyzing such projects. The problem is particularly acute at the state and local level, given the Commonwealth's overall budget shortfall.

The officials expressed interest in a partnership arrangement for analysis that could help them build internal support for DG, but they indicated that they require substantial financial support in order to move forward. In addition, officials recognized that buy-in would be required at all levels of responsibility, from agency heads to facilities managers and community emergency planners, and across all jurisdictions (local, state, regional, and federal).

INITIATIVE PLANNING
Following the assessment of these opportunities for security-enhancing DG, MTC crafted a flexible plan for a funded initiative assisting state and other government agencies to install more secure power technologies.

Study Grants at Selected Public Facilities
MTC will work in concert with a advisory group of interested agency personnel with charge for capital projects and/or facilities management to determine a comprehensive list of facilities of critical nature to public health and safety. MTC will then offer non-competitive grants to these state and local agencies to analyze the economic and technical feasibility of installations at about 10 public facilities, such as the state Emergency Operations Center, emergency management regional offices, remote telecommunications sites, and state laboratories.

Grants are to be used to assess the feasibility of installing on-site generation in security-related applications at specific facilities. Given the expected small value of the grants and constraints on staff at applying agencies, the solicitation application process will be simple and straightforward. The solicitation process will accommodate both applications to assess a single facility, and applications to assess multiple facilities that are under the control of a single agency, such as DCAM.

MTC staff will conduct outreach to identify target facilities and to encourage them to apply for funding. Funding will be available to any eligible facility that submits an application on a first-come, first-served basis for projects that meet the eligibility criteria.

Successful grantees will plan to participate in a preliminary feasibility study at each site to determine the threshold feasibility. A standard questionnaire or survey tool will be completed for each site to determine particular site characteristics and applicability for a variety of renewable energy products. For those sites for which the application of a renewable energy technology will clearly advance the agency's ability to avert or respond to disaster, an approximate project cost will be determined.

Solicitations for Grants for Design and Installation
At a later date, a second solicitation will be issued for grants for detailed design work and installation of on-site generation in security-related applications. Since the dollar value of these grants will be much greater, the application process will be more rigorous.

Although there will be a single solicitation, funding will typically be released in two stages: first for design work and second, if criteria are met, for installation.

Additional analysis is needed to determine the level and nature of the installation funding. It may be that information that would be helpful in making this determination would be gathered through the feasibility studies — therefore the design and installation solicitation should be finalized and issued after those studies are conducted.

Outcomes of the program, outside of enhanced security and disaster-response capabilities, will include data on distributed generation applications, so MTC will prepare case studies on of projects undertaken. Based on a rigorous methodology, the case studies will describe project major elements, present technical performance data, document costs and benefits, and highlight critical lessons that can be applied to similar projects in the future. Case studies will be widely disseminated as part of ongoing market development efforts.

Close accounting of the costs and benefits of any individual project activities, as well as of the cumulative impact of the activities funded by this initiative, is to be conducted to measure effectiveness and help to continually refine the program. Monitoring of program costs and benefits will include both those items that are immediately quantifiable (e.g., incremental costs and energy savings, quantifiable environmental improvements), as well as those that will require reporting on subjective measures, including social indices (e.g., project and program information dissemination, visibility).

Anticipated reporting activities will include regular, planned progress reports which will discuss project activities, rationale for investments and interventions, problems, barriers, partnerships and other leverage, and future activities. Reporting will not end with funded installations but will continue into the projects' operational life. This process might include monthly or quarterly energy production reporting, as well as semiannual or annual reports of project operations as a regular part of ongoing project monitoring.

OUTCOMES & CONCLUSIONS

As the electric marketplace continues to evolve, the argument for DG will so continue to be made on economics. It is fundamentally clear that purchasers for electricity need to evaluate associated benefits, and costs, associated with any purchase of power. In the end, the Commonwealth will realize the greatest benefits through projects demonstrating value beyond simply cost per unit energy generated. These benefits will need to be incorporated into value propositions for DG.

By building collaborative relationships with the public agencies and quasi-public authorities of the Commonwealth, and through prompt development of a funded initiative to explore the value of various renewable technologies, MTC has begun a pilot program to establish the use of distributed generation as part of a strategy to protect lives and properties and to respond to disasters with a diverse set of energy generation tools. This pilot program will test applications for renewable DG and give further insight into its viability.

The presentation of these results will include reporting on the lessons learned and the development plan for broadening the base of agencies participating in the initial program design. As the initiative gains headway through renewable energy generation installation, the development of a high-quality, broadly accepted framework of standards for the use of DG would provide government and end-users a

better means of responding to disasters, natural and man-made. With the industry and stakeholders working together, this framework will ultimately lead to the adoption of DG technologies in a cost-effective manner. Meetings with the potential partnering organization are, at the time of this writing, on-going. While no firm commitments have yet been made, these organizations continue to express strong interest in implementing DG projects at their facilities or sites.

REFERENCES

i Former head of CIA, Woolsey, former National Security Advisor to President Reagan, MacFarland, former Chairman of the Joint Chiefs of Staff, Moorer, September 19, 2001.
ii Lovins, Amory and Hunter, "Brittle Power: Energy Strategy for National Security", 1984.
iii Tierney, "Disaster Preparedness and Response", University of Delaware Disaster Research Center, 1993.

Raphael Herz leads programmatic efforts within Massachusetts Technology Collaborative to serve Massachusetts consumers and businesses needs efficiently, effectively, and economically, through shaping public policies, and private and public initiatives in the area of fuel cells and distributed generation systems. One such initiative currently under Raphael's purview seeks to improve the Commonwealth's security by harnessing benefits from distributed renewable resources. Raphael has been with the organization for several years, with heavy involvement in the Trust's $54 million Waste-to-Energy grant program. He is a graduate of the South Carolina Honors College, at the University of South Carolina, and earned a masters degree from Duke University in Environmental Management.

Raphael Herz
Director, Premium Power
Renewable Energy Trust
Massachusetts Technology Collaborative
75 North Drive, Westborough, MA 01581
tel (508) 870-0312, ext. 1-205
fax (508) 898-9226
eml herz@masstech.org   web www.masstech.org

Chapter 75

RENEWABLE and DISTRIBUTED ENERGY AS A SECURITY TACTIC

By Scott Sklar, President
The Stella Group, Ltd.
Washington, DC, July 2002
EE World Engineering Conference, October 2002

INTRODUCTION

Security implementation can be viewed from many perspectives. But whatever the issue and implementation approach, the supply and access to energy is a critical component.

This paper explores the options using distributed energy, primarily from renewable energy.

The three security areas covered are:

- low-power sensors, cameras, motion detectors and chemical sniffers—detection

- hardening infrastructure and buildings such as back-up power, sensors, uninterruptible power, and power quality—prevention

- scanners, electric fences, communications and emergency preparedness—offensive and defensive preparations and actions

In the ultra-high-security arena, advanced batteries, solar, small wind, and even on a more limited basis, fuel cells are utilized today. But in industrialized country settings, most is still interconnected with the electric grid or through the use of diesel generators.

DETECTION

From perimeter defense to remote sensing—all sorts of devices are utilized. These devices, in general, are small power to run cameras (traditional to night vision), heat and motion detectors, chemical and bio-logical sensors, and audio taps. As these devices have become solid state, digital, and miniaturized—use of batteries and transformers to grid interface is very common.

Obviously, batteries have limitations for long duration uses. So use of photovoltaics primarily have immense options in adding to the life batteries through trickle charging near or far from the units. Even mini-wind turbines and hand-held fuel cells have begun to enter the picture.

The real issue faces the sophistication of terrorists in deterring these devices. Using explosions or "arcs" that emit high electromagnetic pulses can essentially overpower many of these devices. But more easily, is pulsing through grid interconnects of electricity which more naturally burns out sophisticated equipment. The more that is detached from the grid and can be made "longer life" will be far more agile and resistant.

Newer systems can also be hardened from electromagnetic pulsing as part of the package if forethought is given.

The higher and harder to reach any sensing and detection equipment is placed, the harder t disable. PV, mini-wind, and micro-fuel cells all have great capacity to be co-located with these devices and hardened themselves appropriately.

Traditionally wired systems are easy to disable, and greater care needs to be given to the more sophisticated and better trained individual.

The military and intelligence agencies have had vast expertise with advanced distributed power technologies which have a solid record of performance.

PREVENTION

Systems that provide rust prevention (cathodic protection), pipeline protection (density sensors), spill and agent pre-detection (chemical and biological sensors), and crime and penetration sensing (heat and motion detectors, cameras and night vision)—as stated earlier—are generally run off of grid-intertied systems, conventional battery banks, and diesel engines.

These larger systems used in prevention of damage to pipelines, electric grid, area and perimeter security, building and facility defense—are even easier to disable than small detection systems.

Diesel engines, aside from their unreliability, generally must have their fuel tanks outside. Aside from fuel disruptions and general breakdowns, any individual with low training skills can damage diesel tanks. Not only can they disable diesel generators, but they can induce the flammable fuel to combust outside the tanks—and all this can be done from afar. Natural disasters have also shown diesel to be an absurd back-up strategy for emergency preparedness since they are susceptible to flooding by water and their fuel floats on water.

Larger systems that are grid intertied can have wires cut or transformers disable (which can be dome from afar). Battery banks are reliable for short power outages but not long ones. On-site PV along with small wind systems and even small fuel cells can lengthen battery life for long periods, and in some cases, indefinitely.

Clearly, it is time to invest in renewable-based back-up systems for police, fire, regional homeland security communications, and infrastructure hardening devices—in all its aspects.

Blending energy sources and having redundancy in sensing, communicating and powering should be the basic principle used by federal, state and local government—and private sector—approaches to security.

EMERGENCY PREPAREDNESS—DEFENSIVE/OFFENSIVE

"Drop and Plop" power for the military and traditional emergency preparedness is based upon the reliance of diesel generators. In the military, more than half the support structure relates to fuel delivery. Over-reliance on diesel will cause the cost and back-up logistical to become astronomical as we face homeland security challenges as well as trends to harsher weather patterns relating to global climate change.

Primarily PV and lately fuel cells are used by the military in "theater of war" activities. NASA employs these technologies in very harsh environments. Other technologies including solar absorption cooling, heat engines, micro wind turbines, micro hydropower, and modular biomass systems are all on the verge of becoming more easily available. Aggregated purchasing and training, will lower costs, increase availability, and enhance user confidence.

Systems that provide aggressive protection such as electric fences, eye scanners, and molecular sensors must be used in a more aggressive fashion to protect critical infrastructure. These systems can only be inviolate if power systems can be co-located and have low-maintenance and minimal fuel requirements.

Noise of traditional diesel systems actually create a lure for individuals wishing to cause disruptions. Power lines dropping from transformers are listed in most handbooks as to "what to look for" if anyone wants to disable security systems.

For those relying on diesel after natural disasters, always comment on the harsh environment of being housed near big diesels with their noise and fumes. A more sophisticated approach is needed in even traditional emergency response planning, and now a range of technologies are commercially available.

Lower weight photovoltaics, mobile fuel cells on hydrogen and methanol, micro-wind turbines that an be snapped on existing light and telephone poles, and micro-hydro systems that can be dropped on pontoons—are all now in the market place for very small niche applications.

CONCLUSION

The world is not a safe place but more technologies are available now than in any time in the past to provide reliable power for an increasingly digital age.

Market signals that allow US industry to evolve, hybridize, and harden technologies to meet security needs are critical.

Smarter training of procurement officials and security planners are critical to know what new technologies are available.

Military users of these new technologies must be allowed to be available for security planners and local governments, so they understand the options, limitation and benefits of these new technologies.

Greater technical support for potential users by experts within the security, distributed energy, smart controls, and wireless communications sectors must be encourages and funded.

Reliance on old technologies is a luxury that can no longer be supported. These traditional technologies—standard battery banks, diesel engines, and grid-intertied systems—are too easy to disable, are unreliable, and do not have long term "staying" power necessary for the emergencies we all may realistically face.

FOR FURTHER INFORMATION CONTACT:

Scott Sklar, President
The Stella Group, Ltd.
(733 15th Street, N.W., Suite 700, Washington, DC 20005)
Phone: 202-347-2214   fax—2215,   E-mail: solarsklar@aol.com
Message beeper: 7591858@skytel.com or 1-800-759-1858
Website: www.thestellagroupltd.com

Section 8
Plant & Facilities Management

Chapter 76

ENERGY MANAGEMENT OF WAKE COUNTY: A GROWING DEMAND

Phil Mobley, Energy Management Technician
Wake County Public School System, Raleigh NC

ABSTRACT

As one of the largest and fastest growing Public School Systems in the Nation, Wake County Public School System (reference as WCPSS) is continuously challenged to maintain energy cost, respond immediately to mechanical problems, and maintain comfortable temperatures within the school system. The Energy Management department of WCPSS is one of the first contacts for problems and complaints from the schools when proper temperatures cannot be maintained at a school.

Due to the number of schools, population, and physical size of the county (including 13 cities) the task of monitoring and maintaining temperatures, and diagnosing of problems for correction requires that an Energy Management System be installed and maintained for every facility.

INTRODUCTION

As with any growing business or in our case growing school system, someone who is not involved in the every day workings may wonder why or how the money to install an Energy Management System can be justified. One of the requests that school personnel make is to have Energy Management controls remove and give them a thermostat. The statement is normally made if the person is upset about the temperature in the area.

The justification of our system is recognized every day as a problem call is received. A basic need of our School System is to have enough personnel on hand to repair and maintain all of our Heating Ventilation and Air Conditioning (HVAC) equipment.

Because of staffing of HVAC and other critical departments, which will always be an issue, our concerns to be able to maintain and understand our "Real" temperature problems led us into the Energy Management System that we have today. Being able to monitor the room temperatures in the schools by using a Building Automation System (BAS) ensures that proper control can be maintained.

GROWTH VS. DEMAND

WCPSS:

- **All Schools and Facilities** = 15,000,000 sq. ft.
- **Trailers used at Schools** = 700 (Dec of 2002)
- **Number of School/Sites** = 126
- **Number of Students** = 97,583
- **Growth of Students** = >3,000 (avg / 4 yr)
- **Growth of Students for 2002/2003** = 4,200

Some of the main issues that were determined years ago in order to control budget requirements for WCPSS were that guidelines would be established. These guidelines were accepted and adopted as requirements by the Board of Education.

With the support of the Board of Education and School Administrations we are able to use the BAS and Energy Management to hold down energy cost, reduce equipment maintenance, and control space temperatures.

I stated that we have the support of the Board of Education before stating that the term Demand has many definitions. The definition the Association of Energy Engineers would use is; the amount of Energy required for usage at a given time. The definition that comes to mind when a classroom "demands" cooler temperatures, is to lower the temperature in the space until the teacher or school is happy.

COMFORTABLE TEMPERATURES VS. WASTED ENERGY

Since we have the support of the Board it helps Energy Management and the School Administration to explain the need for maintaning certain temperatures. Once a temperature problem has been investigated and determined there is no mechanical problem, then the task is up to Energy Management to resolve.

If a mechanical problem is determined we are able to use the BAS to reset the equipment in question and monitor it on restart. Resetting equipment and monitoring it allows us the abliablity to a report a true problem to the HVAC with more details and understanding than they would receive if the school called in the problem with out Energy Management checking it first.

Not all of our room temperatures are control by the BAS system. Some classes have systems that allow them to use a manual thermostat to select a temperature. In order to have some control, we have fixed the range in which the temperature can be selected.

The BAS uses the outside air temperature at each school to determine if heating or cooling is available. By controlling this the system does not over heat classrooms therefore reduces the need for cooling. The Energy Management Department determines these control heating and cooling numbers by monitoring the weather reports and forecasts.

Energy Management's purpose and goal in WCPSS is to maintain comfortable temperature levels in every school with out greatly increasing energy costs.

BAS AND ENERGY MANAGEMENT

Our Energy Management System is made up of BAS's and Load Shedding Receivers (mounted on trailers). We use the BAS to control and monitor HVAC systems, pumps, variable speed drives, chillers, hot water heaters, and lights.

For majority of the systems we use the same BAS Company. This allows us to stock fewer and the same replacement parts for the BAS.

We repair, upgrade, and maintain our BAS and all other devices, as well as and mechanical parts for the control portion of equipment in the WCPSS. Because we program, troubleshoot, and repair our BAS and all our other HVAC controls we gain the knowledge to keep our system operating and know when we need to upgrade through building renovations and new building construction.

USAGE AND SCHEDULING OF SCHOOLS

The HVAC system and lights in the schools are scheduled through the BAS to operate at the same hours as the normal school day. If any zone / area is required after normal school day hours, the school may turn that area on by pressing an over ride button which will operate the HVAC and lights for four hours.

Other users of the schools are both school and private before and after day camps. These camps use the large areas of the school such as gyms and cafeterias. The camps pay a fee to use the school's facility. Churches and Community Colleges (Night Schools) are common users of the schools.

Because the control of these groups in the school is very important, the Community School Department handles all of the paper work / fees and we in Energy Management schedule the requested areas. We make recommendations to the users to reduce the number of HVAC systems that are turned on helping reduce the energy usage.

TRAINING OF SCHOOL PERSONNEL AND REPORTING OF PROBLEMS

With the help of the Energy Savers Department (Ref. Proceedings of WEEC 2001, chapter 28), we give training sessions to school staff. Normally the classes are made up of custodians, office staff, assistant principals, and principals.

Training is given so that the school will have a better understanding of why we control the temperatures and how this is done. Once the staff is made knowledgeable and understands what they can do to help others at the school, the situation becomes a partnership.

Case:
Each school has been given a digital thermostat to use at the time a complaint is received in the office of the school that the classroom is either hot or cool. The properly trained person at the school takes the thermostat into the classroom and takes and reading at the location of the Energy Management sensor.

If the temperature in the classroom is between 71 and 75 degrees Fahrenheit then no problem is to be called in. This is the comfort range that we try to maintain.

If a reading is taken that is different than 71 to 75 degrees, then the person may call into an emergency line for WCPSS maintenance. Energy Management will then look up the area in question and determine if the problem is programming or equipment failure of the BAS or if it is a mechanical problem.

PROVING THE NEED FOR ENERGY MANAGEMENT AND A BAS

When looking at a school system as large as WCPSS and wondering if it makes sense from a financial and staffing standpoint, it doesn't take very long to understand the value that is added every day. Each school has a BAS that controls some or all of the HVAC system and lighting.

If the systems did not exist at the school then each call to maintenance would require a person to investigate every complaint locally on site. The manpower and training necessary for each person to be able to do this for 126 schools, as well as the lost driving time would be astronomical.

By looking at our growth in comparison to the amount spent on energy for the past years; we are able to determine the value that the Energy Management System provides for WCPSS.

The following Table 1 proves that with Energy Management and BAS in WCPSS has allowed us to maintain our operating costs for energy.

CONCLUSION

As requirements for air quality and HVAC systems increase, WCPSS uses the training and knowledge of the Energy Management Department to meet these requirements. The use of a BAS system enables us to achieve temperature comfort levels for the schools as required by Board of Education policy.

While meeting these requirements and goals we are able to contain the energy costs that WCPSS pays yearly by proper controls and understanding of the Energy Management System.

ABOUT THE AUTHOR

Phil Mobley is currently an Energy Management Technician in the Wake County Public School System based out of Raleigh, North Carolina. His background of professional experience includes HVAC, electrical, and electronics. Phil holds a degree of AAS in Electronic Engineering Technology. He can be reached via email pmobley@wcpss.net.

Table 1.

	1996-1997	1997-1998	1998-1999	1999-2000	2000-2001
Total Utility Cost	$9,767,722	10,236,354	10,607,686	10,853,978	12,999,559
Total Square Feet	10,827,692	11,547,507	12,518,685	13,240,650	14,204,567
Total Students	84,920	89,434	91,911	95,018	97,583
Cost per Student	$115.03	$114.45	$115.41	$114.23	$133.21
Cost per Square Foot	$0.91	$0.89	$0.85	$0.82	$0.91
Heating Degree Days	3335	3362	2962	3180	3716
Cooling Degree Days	1299	1677	1663	1837	1754

Chapter 77

From Tick Tock
to the Superhighway
to Save Energy Dollars

Allen R. Shrum
HVAC Foreman
Johnston County Schools

INTRODUCTION

When I first got stuck with Energy Management Systems I did not have any use for them. I thought it was just a big waste of money. I had the same feeling a lot of people had, which was "if you really want to mess something up, put it on a computer". I had enough problems with my HVAC system without adding more. Today that view has changed totally and I would not accept a system without one. Will the system work without Energy Management System. Yes. BUT your work will increase. Also in a number of ways your productivity will go down. Digital control automation will save you major energy dollars in several ways as well as saving wasted personal energy.

We first got into Digital Control Automation through a renovation project at four of our schools. They were basically fancy time clocks due to the type of equipment used in the renovation project (package DX window and wall-mounted equipment). We used it to schedule start/stop operations using a page like the one in Figure 1.

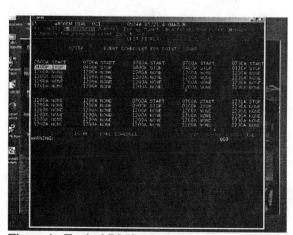

Figure 1. Typical DMS schedule page.

We were able to call up the site, reschedule equipment, and check a few temps with the page looking like Figure 2, and that was about it.

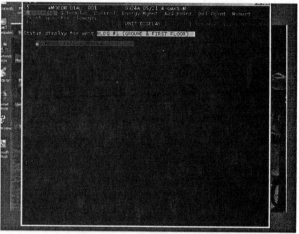

Figure 2. Typical point of early systems.

NEW SYSTEM

Then we built two new schools with DDC where the system included more points of information. It was then I was able to start seeing some points of benefits from the system other than just a fancy time clock. When I also started seeing some energy savings due to the schedule, I went to my boss and requested money to install a DDC system at Smithfield-Selma High School, a school that had extremely high utility costs. It basically had time clocks (Figure 3) that were controlled by the school personnel, a fact that caused the HVAC to run 24/7.

Figure 3. Typical clock panel at a school.

Why? People!!!! People took the pins off clocks and let them run 24/7. After months of discussion, the administration finally granted the money with the stipulation that the system pay for itself in two years or don't ask for more money for these systems. After thirteen months the system had a proven savings to cover the cost of the system plus additional moneys.

I also found that DDC controls could cut down on unnecessary service calls due to people not letting time clocks start the systems as they should.

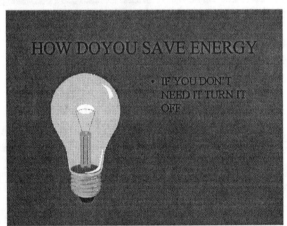

Figure 4. Basic creed of school system.

Figure 4 was the maxim by which we all lived- turn it off if not in use. That works fine for lights, but not for HVAC systems. School personnel thought they could save more money by waiting until they thought the system needed to come on. This caused occupants to be uncomfortable, who would then call the superintendent and board members saying the A/C was broken and asking why it could not be fixed. Then I would be called into my boss's office and questioned on why we could not fix the A/C at John Doe school (Figure 5).

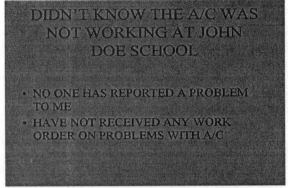

Figure 5. Reasons for inefficient A/C at non-automated schools.

I would have to explain that I was not aware of the problem there and that I would have it checked ASAP. Then I would have to send a tech out to find out what was wrong with the system. He would spend about 30 minutes to an hour travel time, another one to two hours checking the system out, only to find that the problem was simply someone not allowing the system to function as it was designed.

In essence, we were spending more money using time clocks. For example: forty miles X $ .35 per mile = $14.00 X 52 weeks = $928.00 in vehicle cost. $12.00 per hour (Labor) X 2 = $24.00 X 52 weeks = $1248.00 + $928.00 = $2,176.00. We would answer three or more calls each week like which would mean our service department was spending $6528 on unnecessary service calls.

Through automation, the internet, and with the systems we now have in place, those service calls are now gone. In addition to the energy savings afforded by the systems, we also save on service calls. Most of the time, I am able to see where we have a problem before the school personnel even know they have a problem. This is due to the front-end page that lists all of the schools with automated systems. Figure 6 shows those schools with the red highlighting where a system has trouble and an alarm has been sent to our front-end computer. This alarm is printed out and gives controllers, units, boiler, chiller, or system trouble.

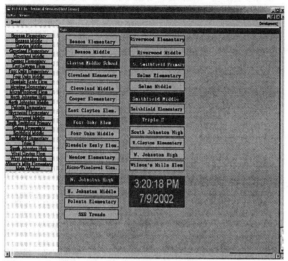

Figure 6. Monitoring front-end page.

Through further analysis and diagnosis of the system I then can give my technicians exact information including room location, unit number, and the nature of the problem (valve, belt, motor, etc.). Through 2-way immediate communication, the technicians can respond to HVAC troubles before the occupants know they have a problem. If they are performing PM service and an emergency call comes in, I can immediately pull them off one job and send them to another. I can also look at the system and tell what the problem is and make sure the technician has the necessary parts they need to fix the problem when they get there. Figure 7 and 8 are examples of the kind of information I can see for all HVAC units at a school.

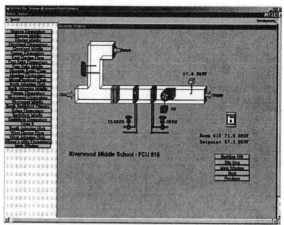

Figure 7. Typical fan coil unit.

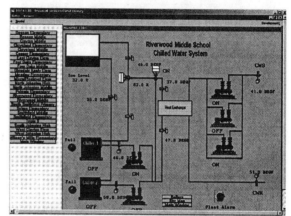

Figure 8. Typical chiller plant with ice storage.

As you can see, with this type of information we are able to eliminate many trips which saves energy and also reduces down time which makes the customer happier. It allows the technician to spend more time performing preventive maintenance on equipment which cuts down the problem calls even more.

ADDITIONAL AUTOMATION
Because of our automation system, we are further able to connect with an additional system that allows us to track and trend all types of information throughout our HVAC systems. It gives us an on-going log to better understand our systems, to see if we are operating at peak efficiency, and if not what we can do to improve efficiency. Figure 9 shows the kw reading at Polenta Elementary School for a day during our peak operating hours. We can use this to help lower our peak demand charges at this site.

Figure 9. KW trend at Polenta Elementary

We can look at a variety of points in combination to compare operational properties. In Figure 10, we look at ice supply, KW load, and outside air temperature.

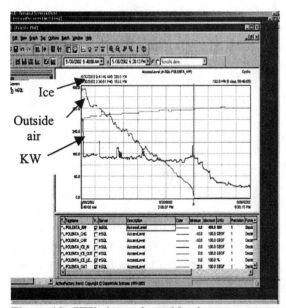

Figure 10. KW, ice and outside air temperature

The red line represents the ice level, the black line represents the KW load, and the purple line represents the outside temperature.

This graph shows that at 9:40 AM we have 100% ice that steadily decreases until 4:45 PM. The KW load was 286 kw at 9:40 AM, but drops to below 150 kw when ice usage begins at 9:45 AM. That represents a drop of 130 kw during peak or a reduction of $650 in demand charge based on $5.00 per kw demand. With this trending system, we can trend by the minute, hour, day, week, or month, or whatever interval of time needed to diagnose the operation of the system. We can also trend different sites for comparison to fine-tune each system.

CONCLUSION

As you can see from the previous figures and discussion, automatic controls in our schools has saved major energy dollars in a variety of ways. The addition of ice storage capability is saving huge energy dollars. These strategies have saved dollars, increased customer comfort, improved the HVAC Department's image in the eyes of the customer, quickened response time, and made our jobs easier. Complaints are almost non-existent and praise from all levels is much more frequent.

Chapter 78

POWER QUALITY SOLUTIONS TO
MITIGATE THE IMPACT OF
VOLTAGE SAGS IN MANUFACTURING FACILITIES

Trevor L. Grant, Vice President, Technical Sales and Applications
Dr. Deepak M. Divan, President and CEO; Fellow, IEEE

Soft Switching Technologies Corporation
8155 Forsythia Street, Middleton, WI 53562 – www.softswitch.com
tgrant@softswitch.com; ddivan@softswitch.com

ABSTRACT

The dominant power quality problems in industrial manufacturing applications are short duration voltage sags and momentary interruptions. For 'normal' grid customers, the EPRI Distribution Power Quality study clearly demonstrated that the vast majority of power line disturbances are of short duration. For customers connected to 'premium' grids, realized with dual independent distribution feeds with high speed make before break ATS systems, connection to transmission grids, or use of highly meshed grids, short duration voltage sags represent essentially 100% of the power disturbances they experience. Power quality solutions, which protect against all short duration power line disturbances, provide protection against virtually 100% of all the events experienced by those customers who have the highest cost of downtime, the 'premium' grid customers.

With the increasing demands for minimizing downtime in manufacturing operations, facilities managers have been challenged to identify cost effective solutions to address power quality related problems. This paper will provide an overview of the power protection issues faced by industrial facilities, based on a review of utility PQ problems, typical plant power distribution systems, and sensitivity of various equipment and processes. Select applications experience of power electronics based PQ solutions such as the Dynamic Sag Corrector® (DySC® – pronounced 'disk') in critical manufacturing operations will be presented. The selection criteria will be highlighted to demonstrate how the solution configuration, rating and placement within a facility impacts its economic viability. The pros and cons of 'facility wide' versus 'point of use protection will be discussed. Finally, the issues related to ROI for manufacturing processes will be discussed.

INTRODUCTION

The impact of power quality and power reliability problems on productivity and downtime in US industry range in the many tens of billions of dollars annually. Estimates from independent EPRI and DOE studies put this cost as high as $150 billion, yet, according to the results of the EPRI Distribution Power Quality (DPQ) study conducted several years ago, only 3 % of events experienced by distribution grid industrial customers were outages. The vast majority of the offending 'events' were found to be short duration disturbances, primarily voltage sags and momentary loss of power. This result has refocused many power equipment suppliers and end users in their efforts to address these problems, since the normally 'reliable' distribution-level utility service does not provide the high 'quality' of power delivery needed by many industrial and commercial electricity users. This distinction between power reliability (the absence of utility voltage) and power quality (the corruption of the 'ideal' utility voltage) problems is therefore becoming better understood as manufacturers attempt to identify solutions to their power quality problems.

Most manufacturers have only recently begun to develop an appreciation of the view of the quality of power entering their plants in the same way that they view other raw materials. Recent rolling black-outs in California (a power reliability/availability problem), have certainly heightened the awareness of the impact of power problems on operations, yet, with the exception of the semiconductor industry, there is not a broad organized approach to addressing the impact of power quality on industrial productivity. This is due in part to a lack of understanding of the nature of PQ events created on the utility grid (or internal to a plant) and of the sensitivities of manufacturing equipment and processes to the most common PQ events. In addition, effective solutions have only recently become available, thus the view 'there is nothing that can be done cost effectively' has prevailed.

Semiconductor industry initiatives through the SEMI organization (Semiconductor Equipment and Manufacturers International) have led to the development of the SEMI F47 standard, that is being specified in the procurement of 'tools' (very expensive high tech equipment) used in the manufacture of IC chips. This standard is more stringent than the old CBEMA Curve (Computer Business Equipment Manufacturers Association, now the Information Technology Industry Council, now the ITIC Curve) that provides a ride through specification for IT equipment design, but which is not stringent enough to be effective for industrial equipment. Semiconductor manufacturers (e.g. TI, IBM, Intel, etc.), pushed very hard for this standard since their cost of downtime due to power events is very high, and is well documented. This standard is having a positive impact, and there are efforts being made to 'move' this standard into the industrial arena.

SoftSwitching Technologies has been in the forefront in the development of cost effective solutions to power quality problems, beginning with the introduction of the Dynamic Sag Corrector (DySC, pronounced 'disc') in late '98, and recently with the introduction of the I-Grid™ web enabled power-monitoring system based on the I-Sense™ ultra low cost monitor. DySC systems have been successfully applied in a broad range of critical manufacturing applications, including semiconductor tools and chip fab plants, as well as automotive, fibre optics, plastics, paper, steel, and other manufacturing applications. Some of this applications experience is shared in this article.

This paper will further review the most common power quality characteristics of the electric supply to plants and equipment, the sensitivity of equipment and processes to these events, and the solutions that are currently available. Applications experience of SoftSwitching's power electronics based DySC solution will be provided, including selection criteria. In addition, the decision drivers, including the pros and cons of facility wide vs point of use deployment, as well as ROI, will also be discussed.

VOLTAGE SAGS AND THE IMPACT OF ELECTRIC DISTRIBUTION

Voltage sags are generally created on the electric system when faults occur due to lightning; accidental shorting of the phases by trees, animals, birds, human error such as digging underground lines or automobiles hitting electric poles, and failure of electrical equipment. Sags also can occur when large motor loads are started, or due to operation of certain types of electrical equipment such as welders, arc furnaces, smelters, etc.. In the case of a fault, the utility would detect the resulting over-current, and

perform a feeder breaker re-closure operation that disconnects the down-stream loads from the system, in its attempt to clear the fault and therefore maintain the reliability (availability) of the electric supply to the majority of its customers.

This scenario can be highlighted in Figure 1 that shows an elementary distribution system. The fault created on the feeder L1 is 'fed' from the entire grid, the utility operates the feeder breaker supplying L1, thus the downstream customers (e.g. A, in the circle shown) experience a voltage sag and a subsequent momentary interruption when the feeder breaker is open. Customers such as on feeder B, would experience a voltage sag until the fault is cleared. The magnitude and depth of the sag and momentary interruption outage depends on the nature of the fault, where on the grid the re-closure operation occurs, and how the utility operates its protective equipment.

Re-closure breakers on the transmission system (typically over 100 kV) operate faster compared to breakers on the lower voltage distribution system (3 to 10 cycle range vs 10 to 30+ cycles at the distribution level). In addition, the time when the re-closing breaker is left in the off state varies widely from utility to utility, and even within the same utility's service territory. The fastest first re-closure operation at the distribution level is in the 10 cycle range. Generally, if the fault is not cleared in the first attempt, the off interval is increased during each subsequent attempt. It should be noted that the voltage does not collapse immediately upon opening of the breaker due to voltage hold-up by the back emf (or generator action) of connected rotating loads.

From the scenario described earlier, it can be seen that the potential for voltage sags is much greater than for momentary interruptions, since the entire section of the grid that feeds the fault experiences a sag, whereas, only the customers downstream of the re-closing breaker experiences a momentary interruption. Many more customers (each with the potential for internally generated faults) are connected to the distribution system vs the transmission grid. Thus, with more distribution lines and substation exposure to the elements such as lightning, trees, squirrels, etc., many more sags occur at the distribution level compared to the transmission grid. At the transmission level, the very fast re-closure operations coupled with large loads with significant rotating motor content, result in very few momentary interruptions. This is less true at the distribution level where the re-closure operations are longer.

The distribution level electrical supply can therefore be categorized as a 'normal grid' compared to a 'premium' transmission grid. A premium grid at distribution level voltages can also be realized by a highly interconnected meshed distribution network like exists in New York City, or with dual independent distribution feeds with high speed make before break Automatic Transfer Switch (ATS) systems. The net effect is fewer, short duration voltage sag events on the premium grid, vs more sags and some long duration events on the normal grid. This is summarized in Table 1, which shows a typical distribution of events on both grids, and the type of customers that are generally fed by each service. Undoubtedly, critical manufacturing operations that use large amounts of power such as in the semiconductor, fibre-optic, automotive sectors, almost always command premium utility service, with its superior characteristics. It must be noted however, that the typical events that occur on the transmission grid, are sufficient to shut down critical manufacturing processes. Thus, while the utility reliability level characterized by the "9's" reliability concept suggests acceptable high 9's premium power, if each event results in a (conservative) downtime of 1 hour, the effective "9's" reliability level is essentially the same as for distribution level service.

The results of the EPRI Distribution Power Quality (DPQ) study, which is the only comprehensive distribution power monitoring study to date, provides clear validation that the majority of events are short duration voltage sags down to 50 % remaining voltage. The summary data from the DPQ study is presented in the Magnitude – Duration plot in Figure 2. This format is a common way of displaying voltage sag events, and enables the protective coverage zone of mitigation devices to be overlaid, thereby highlighting which historical events would not be covered. The SEMI F47 and the ITIC equipment susceptibility curves are also presented in this format.

The three phase nature of events (i.e. whether the event is a single line to ground, line to line or symmetrical sag) is not highlighted in this format. It may be helpful to know what the three phase nature of the event at the equipment being considered for protection since a single line to ground sag will be transformed to two phases through distribution transformers within a plant (due to delta : wye transformations). In addition, some mitigation equipment can correct for deep line to line sags, without using energy storage.

The issue of availability of PQ monitoring data that shows historical sag events has been problematic, since without this information, it is difficult to correlate a PQ event with process and equipment shutdown, thereby making it difficult justify some solutions. SoftSwitching's experience suggests the high valued manufacturers, particularly the semiconductor fabs, have their own monitoring and in many cases, several years of event data. The broader manufacturing sector generally has no historical data, but know from experience that when the lights flicker – their process or machine is down. While all the major utilities have some level of monitoring, this is done primarily at the transmission level, and to a much lesser extent at the distribution level. As a result, in most cases this data is not available. This is due in large part to the high cost of traditional monitoring equipment, and the need to become proficient at using what is sometimes complex applications software.

SoftSwitching has struggled with this lack of data, and is addressing this using a web enabled PQ monitoring system called the I-Grid that is based on an ultra low cost I-Sense monitor. Once the I-Sense monitor is installed, the user requires only a telephone line connection to the monitor, which dials out via the web when an event occurs, and transfers the key information of sag depth, duration, a time stamp and waveforms to the I-Grid server. In addition, a near real time e-mail notification of the event information is sent to designated recipients, who can log on to the I-Grid web site using any web browser to view detailed data from that monitor. This system offers a plant or facilities manager an affordable mechanism to monitor multiple facilities and/or sections within a facility, thereby providing the on-going historical event data upon which a sag mitigation solution can be based.

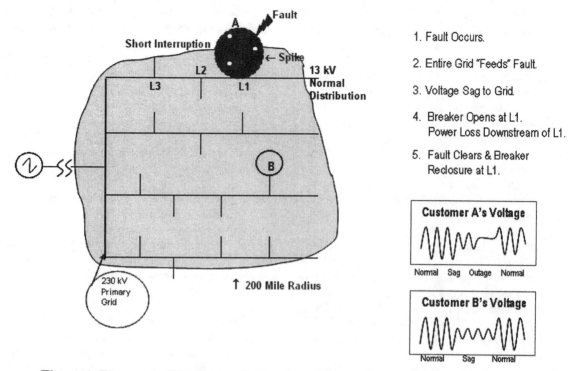

Figure 1. Elementary Distribution System Highlighting how Voltage Sags are Created.

NORMALGRID					PREMIUM GRID			
Normal Utility Events	Utility Reliability Level	Process Uptime 1 Hr Downtime per Event	Typical Applications		Premium Utility Events	Utility Reliability Level	Process Uptime 1 Hr Downtime per Event	Typical Applications

92% Events Protected with a DySC
2 events/yr, 2 hours total downtime/yr,
99.9% Process Uptime : **3-nines**

100% Events Protected with a DySC
100% Process Uptime : **9-nines**

9's = (time in a year – time in a year when voltage is out of spec.) x 100 / (time in a year) : Rounded to the least significant 9 >> No. of 9's

Table 1: *Availability vs. Process Uptime in Normal & Premium Grids.*

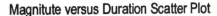

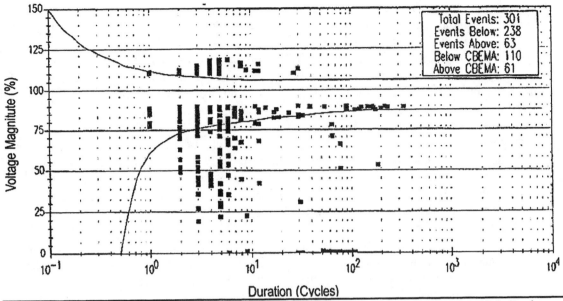

Figure 2. Magnitude – Duration Scatter Plot of summary data from the EPRI DPQ Study

EQUIPMENT/PROCESS SUCCEPTIBILITY

Today's industrial manufacturers increasingly utilize a broad range of sensitive electrical and automation equipment to control their operations and processes. These include variable speed ac and dc drives, servo drives, PLC's, contactors, starters, relays, instrumentation, sensors, industrial computers, and power supplies, to name a few. These devices have various levels of susceptibility based on their specified voltage tolerances. Thus, since these devices are configured to control various elements in a machine or process, the sensitivity of the process will be determined by the most sensitive device in the configuration. For example, many control panels use small inexpensive 'Ice Cube' 120 Vac relays. Some of these relays are known to drop out when the input voltage decreases below 90 % of nominal voltage. Therefore, if such a relay is used in a motor starter control circuit, that motor will drop out when such a sag occurs.

Continuous processes are most challenging to address. Examples include plastics extrusion, wire drawing, food processing, fibre-optic manufacturing, printing, textile manufacture, and bottling, to name a few. The difficulty is compounded because their control systems are highly integrated, thus, even though there may be a few critical components that are sensitive, the integrated nature of the controller makes it difficult to isolate the sensitive elements, thus the whole process may need to be protected. In addition, process control manufacturers may void warranties when the equipment end user inserts external components into 'their' system. Interestingly, while primary focus is to maintain a process or machine operating through a sag, one may easily overlook HID lighting systems which are very sensitive to sags, and can represent a safety hazard or limite productivity when sags occur.

With the advent of the SEMI F47 Standard, semiconductor tool vendors are pushing the requirements 'down the food chain' to the component suppliers. As a result, more robust contactors, relays, etc. are being developed that ride through events that traditional components would not.

SAG MITIGATION SOLUTIONS

There are currently a modest range of solutions available for mitigating voltage sags at the component, equipment, or plant entrance level. Devices are available in single phase, at low distribution voltages of 208/240/480/600 Vac, and at medium voltages for higher power plant entrance applications. Some devices use energy storage technologies such as capacitors, batteries, or flywheels to provide energy to ride through the sag event in the same as when there is an outage, essentially acting as a UPS. More recently, power electronics based devices have emerged that do not require energy storage, yet can provide very effective correction of the vast majority of sags and momentary interruptions. These devices use a series voltage injection principle, utilizing either transformer coupling or novel power electronics circuitry to achieve the voltage injection function. The traditional Constant Voltage Transformers (CVT's) which was designed to provide voltage regulation, has been applied to correct for sags, however, it requires over-sizing to correct sags and to operate without significant voltage distortion in the presence of load harmonic currents. In addition, CVT's are heavy, bulky and inefficient.

Additional component level solutions have recently been introduced such as coil hold up devices that can be added to contactor coils to provide additional hold-up time, thereby enabling them to ride through sags. The challenge with using these devices is the need to understand the detailed operation of the control system so that all of the sensitive components are identified and protected and to ensure that the addition of the hold-up device does not affect any control system timing. Ride-through of ac drives can

be achieved by adding storage energy to the dc bus capacitors to enable sag ride through. Care needs to be taken in applying these devices to ensure other sensitive system components are identified and protected. It should be noted that phase controlled dc drives have no dc bus, thus cannot benefit from dc bus hold-up systems, and require input side devices to enable ride through of sags.

In should be noted that battery based solutions are viewed with increasing disfavor in the industrial arena as can be seen by the SEMI F47 Standard, and with the advent of flywheel UPS's. Looking forward, there will be a strong move towards battery-less solutions for industrial applications. Table 2 provides a summary of various solutions available, with highlights of their ratings, and comments on their operation/application.

Device	Voltage Rating	No. of Phases	kVA Ratings	Comments
Coil Hold-up device	CV	1	<100 VA	• Applied to contactors, relays, and magnetic devices with low pf. • Surrounding controls and system remain unprotected.
CVT	CV, LV	1	<10 kVA	• Needs to be oversized to be effective with sags, inrush, & load current harmonics • Large, heavy and inefficient • 480 V:120 V versions avail.
Capacitor based UPS	CV	1	<5 kVA	• Responds to sags like an outage. • Sag correction interval limited by stored energy • Square wave output
Battery based UPS (Industrial)	CV	1	100 VA to 10 kVA	• Battery life is an issue in industrial environments. • Requires regular maintenance
Battery based UPS (Industrial)	LV, MV	3	500 kVA to 2 MVA	• Treats sags like they are outages • Many industrial facilities are moving away from battery based solutions (SEMI F47 recommends using battery-less solutions)
Flywheel UPS	LV, MV	3	300 kVA to > 5 MVA	• Lower efficiency, higher cost. • Primarily targeted for 15 second ride through to bring on back-up generators • Requires mechanical maintenance
DC Bus Hold-up Device for VFD's	LV	N/A (dc)	To 250 HP	• Applied to dedicated AC drive • Requires invasive integration into drive system • Surrounding controls and systems remain unprotected
Power electronics based series injection ride through device (e.g. the DySC)	CV, LV	1,3	250 VA to 3 MVA	• Offers flexibility to be applied at lowest cost point in process • Provides ride through of momentary interruptions • Requires no energy storage, but can be added for longer ride-through • Efficient and compact • Suitable for OEM equipment
Transformer based series injection ride through device (e.g. the DVR)	LV, MV	3	2 to 10 MVA	• Sag depth capability affects design and cost • Cannot ride through momentary interruptions without high cost • MV versions limited to plant entrance applications • Poor efficiency since transformer windings always carries current

CV = control voltages, 120 – 240 V; LV = low voltages, 208 – 480 V; MV = medium voltages, 2300 – 6900 V.

Table 2. *Basic Summary of Sag Mitigation Solutions*

SOLUTION SELECTION & DEPLOYMENT ISSUES

Plant operators, maintenance personnel, and production managers know from experience of the relationship between power line events and down time. The adage of 'the lights flicker and the process is down' is all too familiar to those who have to clean up scrap, restart processes, and explain why the process or plant went down and shipments are late. If the correlation between events and shut-down is strong, a power monitoring program may have been started to develop enough data to understand the nature of the power events so that cost effective solutions can be explored. Some manufacturers turn to their local utility for event data, sometimes with limited success. Increasingly, manufacturers look to power quality consultants to install power monitors and perform a site audit wherein the electrical distribution system, personnel experiences, equipment and processes are reviewed to identify obvious candidates for improvement. Sometimes, sag testing is performed on specific equipment to determine their susceptibility, and finally, recommendations to deploy various mitigation solutions are offered for consideration.

In general, deploying a sag correction device closest to the equipment that is susceptible, represents the lowest cost option. Conversely, a solution on the utility side of the meter can be the most expensive solution. The exception to this may be when there is a high percentage of sensitive loads within the plant, e.g. when there are multiple extrusion lines that are the primary loads in a plant. The overall cost of a large device coupled with the lower cost to install a single device, may be lower than for multiple smaller rated devices. In most applications, the optimum solution is somewhat between these scenarios, where a solution on a small line could be demonstrated, thereby providing validation and comfort that the solution does work, and the impetus to engage in a broad deployment. After the solution is installed, it is very desirable to validate the 'saves' to show improvements in operations compared to before installation. SoftSwitching's I-Grid provides a very cost effective mechanism to achieve this, wherein I-Sense™ monitors are permanently installed at the input and output of sag correction units

Table 3 provides an overview of the decision drivers that need to be taken into consideration when addressing voltage sag problems. In addition, comments on each of the issues are presented where applicable, to provide an awareness of how each of these issues may be approached.

Item No.	Decision Driver	Comments
1.	ROI	• Power quality is ultimately a financial problem. • A business case justification needs to be done. • Cost of ownership (not just equipment cost) should be considered. • Cost of downtime can be most difficult info to get.
2.	Availability of event data	• Your Utility may have historical event data. • The I-Grid power monitoring system will be of great value.
3.	Cost of down-time	• Need to consider all components, including scrap, stranded labor, time to get product quality and/or process parameters in spec., opportunity costs such as losing a contract due to late deliveries. • Equipment failure can result from repeated exposure to sags.
4.	Cost of ownership	• Some solutions are inefficient, with ongoing energy costs. • Consider extra air conditioning infrastructure required. • Maintenance costs add to this.
5.	Sensitivity of plant loads	• Need to understand which equipment is sensitive. • Wiring may make it difficult to separate non-sensitive loads.
6.	Installation costs	• Consider rewiring costs necessary to separate sensitive loads. • Consider process down time & logistics of installation.
7.	Evaluate on a small scale if possible	• In multiple line applications, evaluation on one line validates solution (especially when unprotected lines go down).
8.	Engineering effort to define and optimize solution	• Engineering effort may be required to integrate the solution, including drawing revisions, etc. • Don't spend $20,000 to find out the solution costs $4,000.

Table 3. *Decision Drivers for Identifying and Implementing Voltage Sag Mitigation*

While in general deploying a solution closest to the point of use is a more economical approach, it is important to understand the issues related to deploying point of use vs facility-wide protection. Some of these issues and consideration thereto are highlighted in Table 4.

Item No.	Point of Use Solutions	Facility Wide Solutions
1.	Available in 1 & 3 phase at 120V to 600 V	Typically are at medium voltage, 3 phase. Some LV solutions available
2.	Ratings range from 250 VA to 3 MVA	Ratings in the 1 to 10 MW range
3.	Protects only the critical loads	May protect significant non-sensitive loads
4.	Can be deployed in stages (evaluate on one process line)	All or nothing solution
5.	Engineering effort can be minimal	Typically requires major engineering effort
6.	Protects against internally generated PQ events (i.e. within the plant)	Does not protect against internally generated PQ events
7.	Failure of protection affects only connected load	Failure of protection affects entire plant
8.	Solution cost limited (rating of solution closely matches rating of sensitive load to be protected)	Overall cost of solution can be high (all loads may not sensitive)
9.	Deployment can be quick (short lead time)	Long delivery time
10.	Wiring of solutions to individual loads can be problematic. Sometimes it is not possible to separate sensitive loads.	Does not require re-wiring of loads
11.	Installation costs can be marginally higher, depends on number of units and required re-wiring	Installation costs can be lower. Generally, no re-wiring is required

Table 4. *Comparison of issues related to Point of Use Solutions vs. Facility Wide Solutions*

CASE STUDIES

The real world applications and experiences of actual companies are more illuminating than arguments based on statistics. Here are details from some actual installations.

I. Engines, Inc., a manufacturer/processor of large axles and rotors for railway and other applications located in West Virginia, was experiencing 10-15 sag events annually. This resulted in as much as 24 hours of downtime, scrapping of large expensive rotors, and delayed shipments. In cooperation with AEP and EPRI, SoftSwitching installed a 300 kVA PRODySC® unit to cover several CNC machines in the main production/processing line, as well as the offices. According the Engines, Inc. President Carl Grover, "The DySC has virtually eliminated the necessity for reworking damaged materials due to voltage sags." Unlike before the PRODySC was installed, the office personnel did not have to re-boot computers and restore data due to voltage sag events.

II. A major fiber-optic cable manufacturer was experiencing 6-10 voltage sags per year. As a premium grid customer, this company had over seven years of power monitoring data, which showed no power interruptions, only voltage sags. One cable finishing process line could realize losses reaching $150,000 - $500,000 per event. Due the integrated nature of the sheathing line control system that includes several dc drives, the only option was to install a single unit per line. Over a dozen PRODySC systems with a cumulative rating of over 3,500 kVA are now protecting a portion of the cable finishing area in this plant. In the first three months of operation two definite, documented 'saves' were recorded. The DySC investment was paid for with the first save.

III. A manufacturer of large-die plastic extrusion products, in cooperation with EPRI-PEAC, their local utility company, and SoftSwitching Technologies, installed a 300kVA PRODySC unit solution to protect several extrusion lines. Figure 3 shows how the PRODySC unit corrected a deep voltage sag to keep the process running. In this application, the economics favored using a single unit for up to 5 production lines, compared to utilizing a smaller unit for each of the extruder lines.

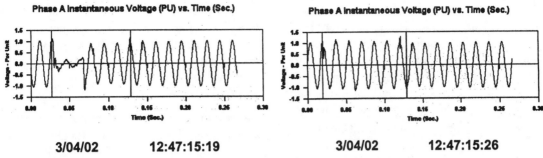

Figure 3. *Typical Event Showing Both Incoming Line Voltage & Corrected Output*

IV. A major automotive manufacturer required protection for the distribution bus that supplied one of their body shops, which includes robotic welding, PLC based material handling and ancillary industrial controls. The body shop was a critical production cell because a shutdown of the robots during a body welding operation may cause the whole body to be scrapped. The size of the bus is 1600 A but the actual load at present is less than 1200 A. The customer found it most cost effective and convenient to cover the whole bus but only to the current level that was presently being used. A modular 1200 A PRODySC system was installed, with expansion capability to increase the current capability to 1600 A at a later

date. Provisions were also included for future installation of capacitive energy storage, if warranted by PQ events identified through further monitoring data. The installation has also been equipped with I-Sense™ monitors, one for input voltage and one for output. The system has been operating since May of 2001 and several sag events have been recorded. One such event is depicted in Figure 4, and is based on reports derived from I-Sense monitors via the I-Grid system. The customer reports that for almost all events, the other equipment in the plant shut has down on 'power loss' while the bus protected by the PRODySC kept the body shop up and running.

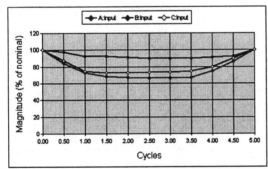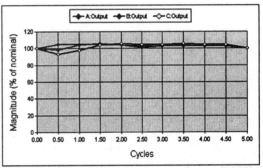

Figure 4. *Auto. Plant Data: Input voltage sag and PRODySC corrected output voltage (RMS)*

V. A major semiconductor manufacturer required sag correction for their photolithography tools. Voltage sags caused shutdowns resulting in scrap material and lost production capacity. This installation was ideal for distributing PRODySCs at the input of each tool. This was due to the huge logistical effort that would be required to gain access to the distribution transformer that powered several tools, since this would require shutting down all the tools that the distribution transformer powered. In the semiconductor fab business, access to tools for other than production is extremely difficult. Over ten 42 kVA PRODySCs were installed ahead of respective

tools. The DySC units fit nicely into the facility as their small size allowed them to be arranged in accordance with the space limitations of the fab's sub-fab area. This customer has reported several sag events since August of 2001, again resulting in continued operation of the semiconductor tools while other less critical unprotected equipment were shut down.

CONCLUSIONS
The availability of sag correction devices now on the market offers the real potential for broad deployment

x

to minimizing the negative effects of voltage sags and momentary interruptions on industrial productivity. Several of the more recently introduced devices have been validated and gained significant acceptance by both industrial users and Utilities, in a broad range of applications. While a number of applications have demonstrated an attractive ROI across a broad spectrum of industries, there is a significant need for PQ historical event data to help to identify the appropriate solution, and to support the business case justification for the capital expenditure. SoftSwitching's I-Grid web enabled monitoring system will be very beneficial to this end. In addition, there is a great need to educate end users about the availability and performance of mitigation devices, and how these devices can play an important role in significantly reducing the costs associated with voltage sags. It is hoped that this article has provided a sufficient overview of all the relevant issues to enable end users to ask and address the critical questions related to the application of sag mitigation devices.

REFERENCES

Electric Power Research Institute. "An Assessment of Distribution System Power Quality." TR-106294s-V1-3 Research Projects 3098-01. Palo Alto, Calif., 1996.

Semiconductor Equipment and Materials International (SEMI). Standard SEMI F47-0999. "Provisional Specification for Semiconductor Processing Equipment Voltage Sag Immunity." Mountain View, Calif.

Powering the Digital Revolution: Electric Power Security, Quality, Reliability, and Availability in the Digital Age

Marek Samotyj
CEIDS Program Director
Electricity Innovation Institute, EPRI
Palo Alto, California USA

Don Von Dollen
CEIDS Application Manager
EPRI
Palo Alto, California USA

Bill Howe, PE
Director, Information Businesses
EPRI PEAC Corp.
Boulder, Colorado USA

Introduction

The digital revolution of the past few decades has increased demand for electric power with higher reliability and quality than is typically delivered via the conventional centralized power system. As modern economies move into the 21st century, this requirement for high *SQRA* (security, quality, reliability, and availability) of an electric power supply will increase as more manufacturing processes and service industries become dependent on digital devices. Even residential customers are becoming increasingly digital-based as more homes use microprocessor-controlled appliances, and digital entertainment systems. Furthermore, the increasing use of home-offices is blurring the distinction between commercial and residential power users. Overall, in the future, all power users whether they be commercial, industrial or residential are expected to demand more reliability from the electric power delivery system than ever before.

Electric Power for the Digital Age

There is a clear economic and national security imperative for utilities around the world to understand the role that highly secure and reliable electric power supply will play in modern society. Specific capabilities are needed for electric power delivery to meet the needs of the digital society including:

- Security: The digital society is extremely productive and capable, but also vulnerable. Electric power is a principal vulnerability, but one that can be hardened against attack.

- Availability and Reliability: The digital society is expected (and designed) to be continuously operational, without interruption or denial of service. Electric power must support this availability.

- Self-healing and Redundant: Digital communications use a network of high-capacity nodes to route data efficiency and expeditiously. Electric power systems need the same capability.

- Massive customization: The digital revolution has revealed an inexhaustible appetite for instant and user-specific customization of service and support. Electric power must develop this capability to support this revolution.

- Rapid reconfiguration: The digital world has demonstrated its ability to rapidly adjust to changing requirements. For example, the Internet evolved from a simple document exchange system just a few years ago, to the now familiar capabilities of email, on-line transactions, and data presentation are even now being augmented by video conferencing, voice-over-IP, civic systems such as web-based voting, etc. The electrical supply system must be able to emulate this rapid adaptive behavior to support the digital society.

The role of electric power has grown steadily in both scope and importance over the past century. Developments in key digital technologies such as microprocessors, electric lighting, motor drive systems, computers, and telecommunications have continuously reshaped American life, as well as the productivity of its commercial and industrial foundation. These technology advances have steadily extended the precision and efficiency attributes of electricity. As a result, electricity has gained a progressively larger share of total energy use, even as the energy intensity of the U.S. economy (energy per dollar of GDP) has declined. Electricity accounted for 25% of all energy used in 1970 and now accounts for nearly 40% of the total in the U.S. and in other countries with similar levels of economic development.

The electricity system has emerged at the century's end as the most critical infrastructure, in the sense that it enables all other infrastructures. In the coming decades, electricity's share of total energy is expected to continue to grow, as more efficient and intelligent processes are introduced into industry, business, homes, and transportation. Electricity-based innovation—ranging from plasmas to microprocessors—is essential for enabling sustained economic growth in the 21st century.

The electric power system is one of the largest and most complex machines of the technological age. Managing this system will become increasingly difficult as overall loading continues to grow with deregulation. The U.S. Energy Information Administration (EIA), for example, predicts a 15% increase in demand in the U.S. over the next decade. Moreover, a growing fraction of this electricity will serve the highly sensitive electronics of the digital economy, thus placing an additional premium on reliability and quality of service.

A host of opportunities and challenges face electric power supply in the digital age, ranging from fully-realized distributed generation, to self-healing transmission and distribution systems. The goals for these efforts are equally diverse, spanning infrastructure needs to environmental challenges. Figure 1 illustrates the strong relationship between technology innovations and the important social and market goals they influence.

Science and Technology Drivers	Strengthening the Power Delivery Infrastructure	Enabling Customer-Managed Service Networks	Boosting Economic Productivity and Prosperity	Resolving the Energy/Carbon Conflict	Managing the Global Sustainability Challenge
Distributed Generation	●	●	●	·	●
Power Electronics	●	●	●	·	●
Microprocessor-based Electrotechnology	·	●	●	●	●
Real-time Information Processing Technology	●	●	●	·	●
Advanced Materials	●	·	●	●	●
Biotechnology	·	·	●	●	●
Environmental Knowledge and Technology	●	·	●	●	●

Figure 1. Technologies Drivers and the Objectives they Influence

Quality, Reliability, and Availability

Conventional bulk supply systems, from a service interruption perspective, deliver power with reliability in the range of 99.0% up to 99.9999% (also referred to as "two nines" up to "six nines" respectively), and average reliability being about 3 to 4 nines, or 99.9% to 99.99%. Rural electric customers typically experience the least reliable power in the range of 2 or 3 nines. Urban customers served by networks typically have the highest reliability with 5 or 6 nines. However, these reliability levels do not consider short duration power quality disturbances. When potentially disruptive power quality disturbances such as voltage sags, voltage swells, switching surges, poor voltage regulation, harmonics and other factors are considered, the availability of what we can call "disruption free" power can be one or two orders of magnitude worse than a more standard interruption based availability index.

For high value critical-process manufacturing or information services, an availability of nine-nines (99.9999999) is often stated as being the desired reliability level to avoid losses due to production downtime or the inability to deliver key services. This level of reliability should consider not only service interruptions but also power quality conditions that may cause process disruptions. Examples of high value critical processes and services include internet server farms, data processing systems, financial services, telecommunications providers, microchip manufacturing plants, digitally-controlled manufacturing, etc. (see Figure 2).

Achieving "high-nines" reliability is not possible using the existing bulk supply system without considerable enhancement. Such ultra-high reliability is, in practice, achievable at lower cost by the application of extensive redundant onsite (customer-side) generation, static switches and uninterruptible power supply (UPS) equipment coupled with various enhancements to the bulk supply system. The degree to which solutions focus on bulk supply system enhancements versus customer-side equipment investments is different for each case and depends on many technical and economic factors. As more customers demand such high levels of reliability, it is becoming clear that the power industry needs to better define how to serve this load, and there may be more opportunities to enhance the bulk supply system to reduce the need for customer-side equipment required to achieve high reliability. Of course, these enhancements only make sense if the cost can be recovered by the added value of enhanced reliability.

System Type	Unavailability Minutes/Year	Availability (Percent)	Availability Class
Unmanaged	50,000	90	1
Managed	5,000	99	2
Well-Managed	500	99.9	3
Fault Tolerant	50	99.99	4
Highly Available	5	99.999	5
Very H.A.	0.5	99.9999	6
Ultra H.A.	0.05	99.99999	7

Figure 2 Levels of Availability

Targeting the Most Significant Problems

EPRI has helped hundreds of electric power end-users solve difficult power delivery problems. These investigations have revealed that the single most potent cause of end user power quality problems is voltage sags or swells. The second most vigorous contributor is harmonics, unwanted frequencies in a facility's voltage or current waveforms. The next heavy hitter is grounding and other wiring issues. Collectively, these three PQ phenomena account for over 85% of power quality investigations conducted by EPRI over the years. Sags in voltage supplied to digital systems are a growing concern, and one of the most common causes of problems (see Figure 3).

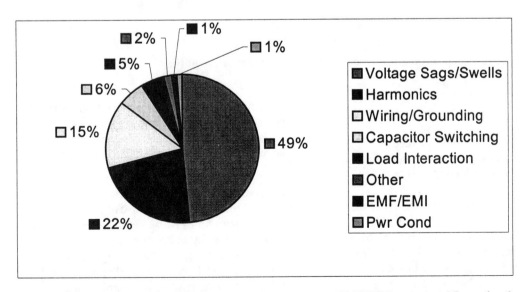

Figure 3. Breakdown of the PQ Phenomena found in over 500 EPRI-sponsored Investigations

549

One reason these sags are an increasing concern is that the amount of sensitive equipment modern businesses uses—including programmable controllers, adjustable-speed drives (ASDs), and computers—has increased dramatically. U.S. sales of microcomputers—those most likely to be employed in industrial settings—have nearly tripled since early 1993. Then, sales were just under 1.2 million units per quarter; in late 1998, sales were nearly 3.2 million units per quarter (see Figure 4).[1]

Providing end users with electric power that is free from voltage sags would seem to be the obvious responsibility of the local utility. Utility folks and electrical engineers have a saying: "The utility owns the voltage, and the end user owns the current"—meaning that the utility is responsible for generation, distribution, and regulation of the *voltage* at an end user's meter, but the end user's load is what characterizes the shape of the electrical *current*.

The challenge facing the utility side of this partnership is this: the voltage a utility "owns" is usually generated at power plants dozens (or hundreds) of miles from the loads the utility serves. Between the generation and the load are a wide array of systems and devices: transmission lines and interconnections with other utilities' grids, substations and distribution systems, switches, reclosers, step-down transformers, meters, and other equipment.

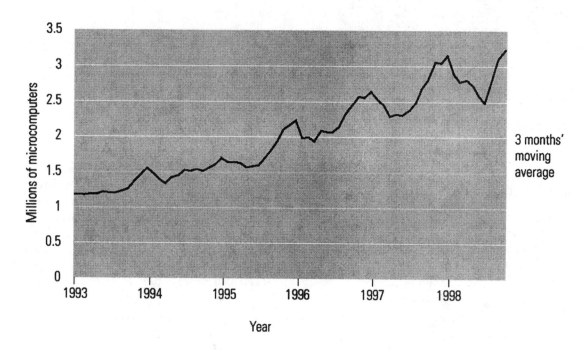

Figure 4. The Increasing Use of Microelectronics: Sales of Microcomputers in the U.S.

Security

The complexity of the electric power system, combined with its large geographic extent, makes it vulnerable to natural events, human error, and intentional attack. The industry has a great deal of experience in dealing with the first two of these, and recently has begun considering the urgency of protecting the physical assets of the power system against attack by terrorists or saboteurs. Perhaps even more difficult to protect against would be cyber attacks on the computers and software used to handle

the growing number of power transactions and the operation of the physical grid. Trends toward standardization of computer and software systems may inadvertently increase vulnerability to cyber attack.

Maintaining the security of electric power supplies to these systems will become increasingly important in years to come. An EPRI survey of electric utilities revealed real concerns about grid and communications security. Figure 5 ranks the perceived threats to utility control centers. The most likely threats were bypassing controls, integrity violations, and authorization violations, with four-in-ten rating each as either a 5 or 4 out of 5. Concern about the potential threats generally grew as the size of the utility (peak load) grew. In addition, utilities were asked to rank the types of intruder threats. Just under half of the respondents expressed concern over the threat of hackers and/or disgruntled employees. Other potential intruder threats were significantly likely to be rated as concerns.

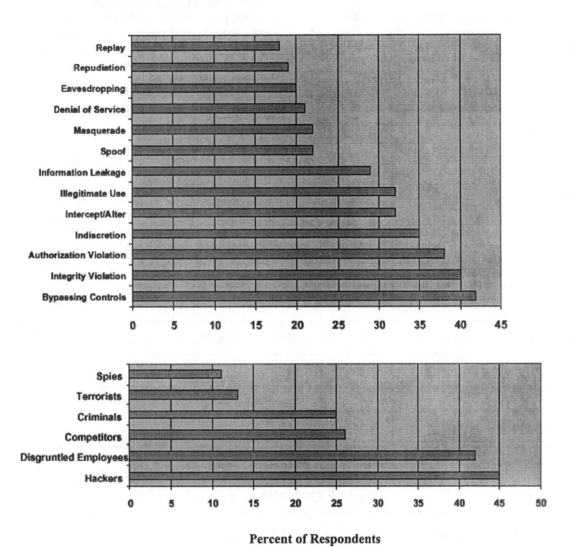

Percent of Respondents

Figure 5 Threats to Power Supply Control: Results of EPRI Survey of Electric Utilities

The Need for Highly-reliable Digital Power

The importance of reliable, high-quality electrical power continues to grow as society becomes ever more reliant on digital circuitry for everything from e-commerce to industrial process controllers to the onboard circuitry in toasters and televisions. With this shift to a digital society, business activities have become increasingly sensitive to disturbances in the power supply. Such disturbances not only include *power outages* (the complete absence of voltage, whether for a fraction of a second or several hours), but also *power quality phenomena* (all other deviations from perfect power, including voltage sags, surges, transients, and harmonics). Three sectors of the U.S. economy are particularly sensitive to power disturbances:

The digital economy (DE). This sector includes firms that rely heavily on data storage and retrieval, data processing, or research and development operations. Specific industries include telecommunications, data storage and retrieval services (including collocation facilities or Internet hotels), biotechnology, electronics manufacturing, and the financial industry.

Continuous process manufacturing (CPM). This sector includes manufacturing facilities that continuously feed raw materials, often at high temperatures, through an industrial process. Specific industries include paper; chemicals; petroleum; rubber and plastic; stone, clay, and glass; and primary metals.

Fabrication and essential services (F&ES). This sector includes all other manufacturing industries, plus utilities and transportation facilities such as railroads and mass transit, water and wastewater treatment, and gas utilities and pipelines.

The Costs of Non-Digital Power

There is little question that power quality and reliability issues are costly to world business. But what form do these losses take, and how sensitive are they to outage duration? IEEE Standard IEEE Standard 493-1997 (The Gold Book) provides practical guidance on the impact of power interruptions on U.S. businesses.[2] The standard demarcates business losses into four categories:

- Damaged plant equipment
- Spoiled or off-specification product
- Extra maintenance costs
- Cost for repair of failed component

If possible, the cost for each interruption of service should be expressed in dollars for a short interruption plus an amount of dollars per hour for the total outage time in order to utilize the reliability data and analysis presented (see Figure 6 through Figure 9).

All plants	$6.43/kW + $9.11/kWh
Plants > 1000 kW max demand	$3.57/kW + $3.20/kWh
Plants < 1000 kW max demand	$15.61 / kW + $27.57/kWh

Figure 6 Average cost of power interruptions for industrial plants[3]

| All commercial buildings[a] | $21.77/kWh not delivered |
| Office buildings only | $26.76/kWh not delivered |

Figure 7 Average cost of power interruptions for commercial buildings[4]

Power interruptions	Sample size	Cost/Peak kWh not delivered		
		Maximum	Minimum	Average
15 min duration	14	$67.10	$5.68	$26.85
1 h duration	16	$75.29	$5.68	$25.07
Duration > 1 h	10	$204.33	$0.48	$29.63

Figure 8 Cost of power interruptions as a function of duration for office buildings containing computers[5]

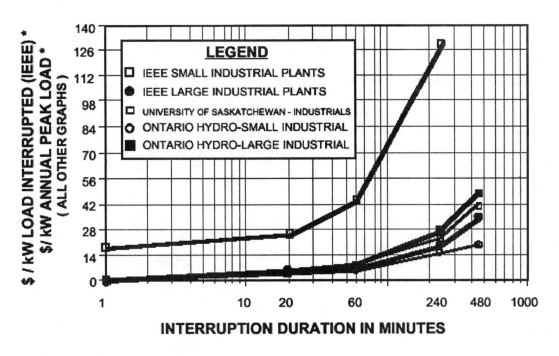

Figure 9 Cost of interruptions versus duration[6]

The size of an electric power end user's electric load is an important metric for understanding the market for reliability. Not only will different sized solutions be required to solve problems at large vs. small facilities, entirely *different* technologies may be appropriate. Shown in Figure 10 are the self-reported costs due to reliability problems of all U.S. electric power end users in the digital economy, continuous process manufacturing, and fabrication and essential services sectors. Costs are presented as a percentage of the facility's revenues. Making the assumption that facilities experiencing reliability costs in excess of 1 percent of their revenues are being injured by reliability costs, would lead us to conclude that approximately 12.7 percent of industrial end users are ripe for purchase of reliability enhancing measures.

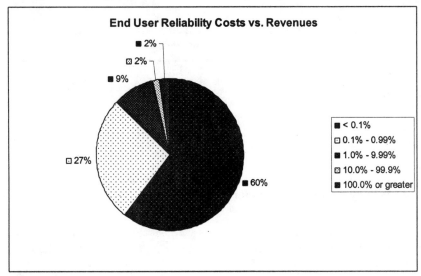

Figure 10 End User Reliability Costs vs. Revenue

Needed: A New Approach for Electric Power SQRA

There are several ways to define the "reliability" or the "quality" of electric supply. The approach described below is to extend the traditional utility measures of reliability and include short-duration power-quality events to come up with fairly straight-forward measures of the overall SQRA (security, quality, reliability, and availability) of an electric power supply system.

The first part of this optimization plan is to define quality levels. Defining quality levels helps characterize the quality of the supply, and conversely, helps define what level of quality we need from a power system (combination of the utility and local support equipment). Four levels of quality are specified:

> Quality Level 1 – moderate voltage sags, ITI (CBEMA) curve
>
> Quality Level 2 – severe voltage sags
>
> Quality Level 3 – momentary power interruptions
>
> Quality Level 4 – long-duration power interruptions

Quality levels provide more than just a way to characterize events. If the industry can standardize quality levels, much more is possible. Vendors can claim a certain testable quality for equipment. Users can specify that they want a device with a certain ridethrough. SEMI F47 has done this for semiconductor manufacturers, but much more is possible. Utilities can advertise (or guarantee) certain levels of quality that are more meaningful than SAIDI or SAIFI. Together, these effects lead to less downtime for end-use equipment.

The next part of the QRA analysis is quantifying existing reliability of components and systems; this report brings together such information including:

- Good reliability data—This report brings together a lot of hard-to-find data on utility-side and facility-side systems and equipment reliability.

- Characterizing and predicting utility quality—EPRI's Distribution Power Quality (DPQ) data is used to find out what factors really affect voltage sags and momentary interruptions. We can also predict quality (approximately) based on a small number of input parameters. Other sources of utility quality data are pulled together to provide a better picture of the quality of utility supplies (see summary, Figure 11).

	Utility Supply Quality Levels (typical number of events per year)			
	1 moderate voltage sags	2 severe voltage sags	3 momentary interruptions	4 long-duration interruptions
Rural distribution supply	28	13	7	3
Suburban distribution supply	19	8	3	1.3
Urban distribution supply	12	4	0.7	0.2
Urban network supply	12	4	0.02	0.02
Transmission supply	5	1.5	0.9	0.7

Figure 11 Default Utility Supply Characteristics for QRA Analysis

Finally, a QRA analysis approach ties these parts together. The approach is easy enough to implement in a spreadsheet. At the same time, it handles the complexities of redundant systems better than some complicated methods (especially with respect to common-mode failures). A complete QRA analysis to select optimal configurations includes several steps:

1. Find the mean time between failure (MTBF) of each configuration.

2. Estimate the annual equivalent configuration cost of each.

3. For each configuration, find the annual outage cost based on the MTBF.

4. Rank each scenario based on the total annual cost, which is the sum of the configuration costs and the outage costs.

New utility-side solutions are needed to address voltage sags and momentary interruptions. As part of the QRA development, some new configurations are presented. A "sag-resistant spot network" shown in Figure 12 is one of the configurations. This configuration is just in the conceptual stage, but we could implement it with existing technology.

Traditional Spot Network

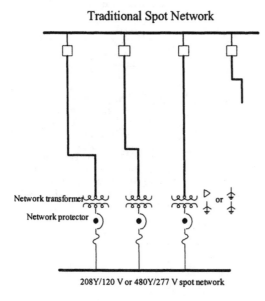

PQ-Enhanced Spot Network

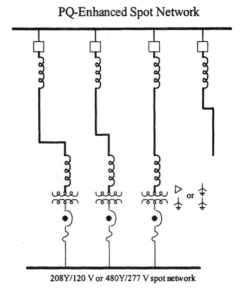

Figure 12 Comparison of a Traditional Spot Network to a Configuration With Added Reactors to Minimize the Voltage Sags Caused by Primary Feeder Faults

Optimizing Power System Design and Configuration: A Case-Study Approach Case studies are an effective means to best analyze and illustrate methods to provide optimized QRA configurations for digitally-driven processes. One case study focused on data centers, especially internet data centers, which have grown phenomenally in recent years.

In many ways, these facilities are considered great utility loads, as they have very high load densities and have a high load factor. Some of the highlights of internet data centers are:

*   Load densities of 25-50 W/ft^2 or more

*   Demand very high quality power

*   Most of the load is either critical computer or telecommunications load or air conditioning.

*   Data centers typically have redundant UPS systems and redundant generators

Figure 13 shows some of the utility-side and facility-side solutions that were investigated along with the cost of each. In each case study, care was taken to first analyze the potential losses incurred by the facility versus the generalized cost of potential solutions. Then, cost estimates for a wide variety of potential QRA solutions are estimated and ranked based on cost effectiveness.

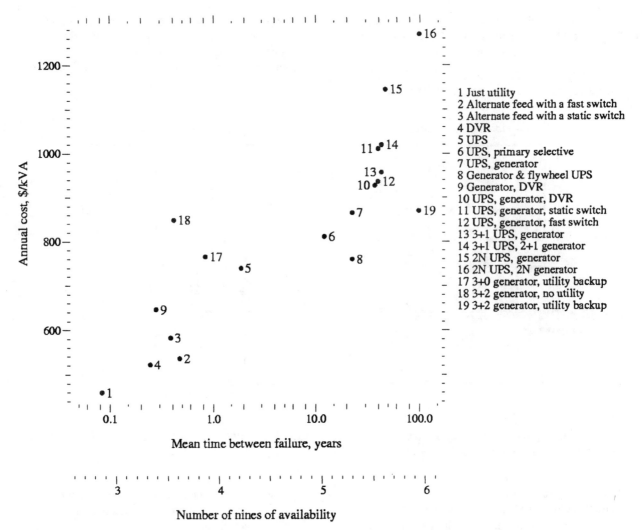

Figure 13 Cost vs. Performance of Several Utility-Side and Facility-Side SQRA-enhancing Equipment Configurations

Each of the case studies had widely differing results and optimal solutions. Some generalities were common in the case studies:

- One size doesn't fit all. The optimal solution depends on many factors: facility size, how convenient a second utility feed is, cost of facility interruptions, and the sensitivity and types of facility equipment.

- The outage cost plus the configuration cost does not represent what some facilities are willing to pay for performance. Some facilities are willing to pay much more for better performance (more redundancy, less chance of failure) than their actual outage costs.

- Load ride-through enhancements effectively increase performance in many situations for a relatively small cost.

- The utility-side options are most suitable for large commercial and industrial users.

- Distributed generation options look potentially viable for many high-performance needs (if the utility is present as a backup).

Conclusion

Significant investments in the bulk supply system and customer-side equipment will be needed to determine optimal solutions to digital end users' QRA requirements, but it is not clear at this stage what

556

balance of investment in the supply side versus the customer side is required to most cost effectively meet the needs of the growing digital power market. The ideal approach will be location dependent – based upon the characteristics of the existing power system and nature of the load at each specific site. Locations with more reliable utility supply systems (such as urban areas where networks could be used) will need to rely less on customer-side equipment to reach high levels of performance. Locations with poorer reliability (such as rural areas where radial distribution is used) will need to place more dependence, and, hence, investment in customer-side solutions such as distributed generation and UPS type equipment. In some cases, it may even be desirable to have an off-grid solution that is totally dependent on distributed generation and customer-side solutions. Some key factors that determine the optimal solution on the utility system side are the number of customers that demand high reliability, the amount they are willing to pay for it, the size of these loads and the spatial distribution of such loads within the service territory. These and other factors will determine the optimal balance of investment in bulk supply versus customer side solutions.

About the Authors

Marek Samotyj is Program Director of the Consortium for Electric Infrastructure to Support a Digital Society (CEIDS), an initiative established by EPRI and the Electricity Innovation Institute in 2001. Through a unique collaboration of public, private, and government stakeholders, CEIDS provides the science and technology to ensure an adequate supply of high-quality, reliable electricity to a digital economy and integrate energy users and markets. This mission is realized in the meeting of three critical CEIDS goals:

- Lead in anticipating and meeting tomorrow's electric energy needs
- Enhance value for all CEIDS partners
- Create and foster opportunities to enable a digital-quality power supply

Before joining CEIDS, Mr. Samotyj held the position of Business Line Manager responsible for EPRI Retail Sector's Technical and Business Services. He was also a PQ Product Line Team Leader. During 1984, Mr. Samotyj was a Consultant for Power Electronic Systems at EPRI

Mr. Samotyj received his B.S. and M.S. degrees in Electrical Engineering in Poland. He received an M.S. degree in Engineering-Economic Systems from Stanford University. From 1981 to 1982, he was a Fulbright Senior Scholar, and a Fellow of the Professional Journalism Program at Stanford University.

He is a member of the IEEE and a member of CIGRE, International Conference on Large High Voltage Electric Systems. He is a founder of the EPRI Power Quality newsletter, *Signature*. He is a recipient of the Year 2000 John Mungenast International Power Quality Award for his lifetime achievements funded by Power Quality Magazine and The Financial Times Energy's E-Source

Mr. Samotyj can be reached at tel: 650-855-2980 (USA), email: msamotyj@epri.com, web: www.ceids.com

Don Von Dollen is an Applications Manager for Consortium for Electric Infrastructure to Support a Digital Society (CEIDS), an initiative established by EPRI and the Electricity Innovation Institute in 2001.

Don joined EPRI in 1991 as Project Manager in Underground Transmission. He managed superconductivity research programs including wire and cable development, and research projects relating to transmission cable systems. He was also Target Manager for the same area, managing related research programs and laboratories. Don also managed the demonstration of a superconducting cable system at Detroit Edison.

Before joining EPRI, he was a Research Engineer with the Pacific Gas & Electric Company. Don holds a B.S. degree in Physics from California State University, Sacramento. He is member of CIGRÉ Study Committee 21; IEEE Power Engineering Society; and Material Research Society.

Mr. Von Dollen can be reached at tel: 650-855-2679 (USA), email: dvondoll@epri.com, web: www.ceids.com

Bill Howe is Director of Technology Information Businesses for EPRI PEAC Corp., a wholly-owned for-profit subsidiary of EPRI providing world-class resources in power quality, reliability, end-user site problem solving, product testing, and technology development.

Mr. Howe is responsible for all activities associated with defining and managing EPRI PEAC's businesses in the area of technology information. Key responsibilities include strategic planning, project management, information products, and multi-client studies covering a range of topics related to quality, reliability, and availability of energy delivery.

Before joining PEAC, Howe was Director of Power Integrity Businesses for Primen, a subsidiary of EPRI; and President of the PQ Group and Director of the Power Quality Series at E Source Inc. (now a part of Platts Energy), focused on the delivery of premium power quality and related services in the deregulated marketplace. Earlier, as Director of Corporate Energy Services at E Source, he launched that company's first product line targeted to the end-user market. Previously, Howe served in management and senior engineering positions within a number of Fortune 500 companies, and has experience in medium-voltage power quality product development, product testing, substation and distribution-system design and construction, motors and drive systems, and process automation. He is a registered Professional Engineer.

Mr. Howe can be reached at 303-417-1514 (USA), email: bhowe@epri-peac.com, web: www.epri-peac.com.

References

[1] "Microcomputer Unit Shipments in the United States, Total Industry Shipment Estimates, November 11, 1998," Information Technology Industry Council (ITIC), United States Microcomputer Statistics Committee,
1250 Eye Street NW, Suite 200, Washington, DC 20005, tel 202-737-8888, fax 202-638-4922, e-mail hsayadian@itic.org, web www.itic.org.
[2] "IEEE Standard 493-1997: IEEE Recommended Practice for the Design of Reliable Industrial and Commercial Power Systems (IEEE Gold Book)," (1997)
[3] IEEE Standard 493-1997, Table 2-5
[4] IEEE Standard 493-1997, Table 2-7
[5] IEEE Standard 493-1997, Table 2-8
[6] IEEE Standard 493-1997, Figure 2-6

Chapter 80

HOW ENTERPRISE ENERGY MANAGEMENT SYSTEMS HELP MAXIMIZE RELIABILITY

John Van Gorp, Marketing Manager
Power Measurement

Bill Westbrock, Business Development Manager
Power Measurement

ABSTRACT

The rapid adoption of information technology (IT) and increasing dependency on sophisticated production processes has dramatically increased the importance that organizations attach to highly reliable supplies of electrical energy. Enterprises such as large data and communications centers, Internet hosting facilities, online retailers, and manufacturers with sensitive processes find even brief interruptions to be disruptive and expensive.

These "digital economy" operations require near 100% uptime, and the aggregate load that these businesses represent is growing at a phenomenal rate. Even "old economy" enterprises are increasingly dependent on automation equipment and Internet-enabled solutions for manufacturing, procurement and 24-hour customer service call centers.

Unfortunately, there is a large disparity between the reliability that the power grid can provide and what these organizations require. Thus, nearly all organizations that require "high nines" power incorporate an array of specialized equipment to help ride through power interruptions. However, this specialized equipment often operates independently and not together as a cohesive power reliability system. An enterprise energy management ("EEM") system offers the distributed information and control capabilities that can help better integrate this specialized equipment, ensure their performance and, in turn, guarantee maximum uptime.

POWER RELIABILITY COMPONENTS

The power grid was developed to deliver "three nines" of clean, reliable power; that is, it provides a constant flow of energy 99.9% of the time. This translates to less than nine hours of downtime a year. This is sufficient for lighting systems and motor loads, but new digital assets and processes require very precise streams of electrons at highly regulated voltages, translating to power reliability as high as "six nines" (99.9999%, or less than 30 seconds of downtime a year) or higher [1].

Typical loads found within power-sensitive businesses can include banks of computer-based data servers, communications switches, or manufacturing processes run by automation equipment. To ensure these loads are kept fed with clean energy, these businesses normally deploy a variety of specialized power reliability equipment to make up the difference between what they need and what the power grid can supply (see Figure 1).

Transfer Switch
A transfer switch is responsible for connecting one or more power-sensitive loads to one of several possible power sources, ideally making the transition between sources as transparent as possible. A transfer switch may be used to switch from one utility feed to another, or from a utility feed to an on-site generator.

Generator
On-site generation is responsible for supplying power to critical loads when the utility supply is not available. In deregulated markets, a company's energy manager may also elect to turn on an on-site generator when it becomes more economical to run than the price of energy available from the power grid [2]. Diesel generators have traditionally been used to provide on-site generation, but new power sources such as microturbines and fuel cells are increasingly being used.

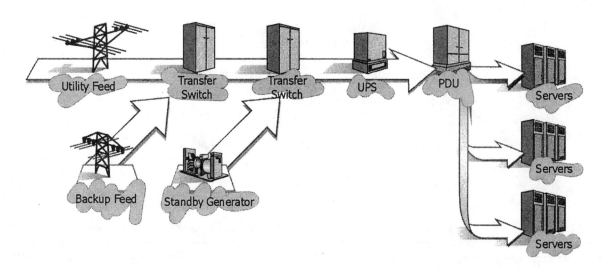

FIGURE 1: TYPICAL ASSETS IN A HIGH-RELIABILITY POWER SYSTEM

Uninterruptible Power Supply (UPS)

A UPS acts as the short-term *buffer* between the continuity and quality of energy supplied by the power grid and that required by critical loads. The UPS will draw from a temporary power source (such as batteries or a flywheel) as needed to maintain stability until on-site generation can be brought online to provide power.

Power Distribution Unit (PDU)

A PDU is the interface between the power reliability system and critical loads, normally accepting power from this system and distributing it to the loads on separate circuits. To increase reliability, the PDU may also include a static transfer switch (STS) that can transparently switch between a primary and backup power source.

Each of the components described above must interact seamlessly with the others to provide high-nines reliability. However, components often come from several different manufacturers and are not typically integrated tightly together.

A transfer switch, for example, may receive a signal indicating an outage on the main utility service and switch over to a feed from on-site generation without knowing the complete status of that on-site power source. A UPS may know that the primary utility service has failed and draw power from temporary power storage equipment (such as batteries or a flywheel) without knowing the status of on-site power generation.

This lack of comprehensive management over this collection of components has an impact on the highest level of reliability that can be achieved. Without an infrastructure for system management, failures can leave facility personnel in the dark as to exactly what happened. An outage lasting several hours can, depending on the customer affected, be very expensive. Personnel at SEH America (a semiconductor manufacturer) estimate that a plant shutdown for several hours would mean revenue and productivity losses of $1 million US [3].

How can long-term reliability be improved? What is needed is an information system that can monitor the electrical and physical characteristics of power reliability components and provide facility personnel with the tools they need to achieve the highest uptime possible.

EEM: A LAYER OF "ENERGY IT"

An enterprise energy management system is composed of intelligent devices, communication links and software that combine to form a layer of "energy IT" that rides on top of key power reliability system components and critical loads (Figure 2). The EEM system monitors the key electrical and physical characteristics of each power reliability component and critical circuit, within a single facility or across multiple facilities, and provides operations personnel with the information they need to extract the highest possible reliability from the system as a whole.

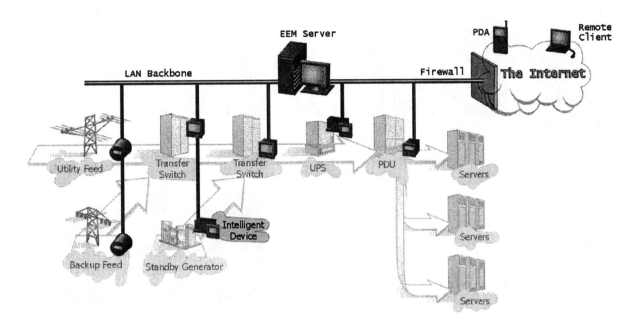

FIGURE 2: EEM SYSTEM "LAYER" ON TOP OF A POWER RELIABILITY SYSTEM

Intelligent Devices

Microprocessor-based devices within an EEM system are permanently installed at key power distribution points, or on critical equipment, turning electrical and other physical measurements into digital data (Figure 3). These devices are considered "intelligent" because they provide much more functionality than simple transducers. Often included are a variety of data manipulation features such as local data archival, power quality analysis, and alarming on critical conditions. Some devices also include manual and automated control capabilities over external equipment. Multi-port, multi-protocol communications allow each device to share its information with a variety of systems and users simultaneously.

Communication Links

A variety of communications technologies may be used to move data captured by intelligent devices back to head-end EEM software. Traditional methods include dial-up telephone lines and dedicated copper cabling, while newer systems make increasing use of existing corporate infrastructures and standard networks such as Ethernet LANs, public digital wireless and the Internet.

Software

The head-end EEM software retrieves data from the network of intelligent devices for further display and analysis, as well as permanent archival. From the important data gathered from each device "node" the EEM software

delivers the useful information in a form that operators require to properly manage their digital assets. The software can also aggregate and archive data in an industry-standard format, and provide access to real-time and logged information to multiple users simultaneously through customized graphical screens (Figure 4).

The EEM system also makes use of Internet and wireless technology to make critical reliability information and condition alerts more widely available (through web browsers, pagers, cell phones and PDAs).

MAXIMIZING UPTIME WITH EEM

With an enterprise energy management system in place, the important steps can be taken to ensure that a business achieves the level of "nines" of reliability they are targeting.

Benchmark Performance

The performance of the power reliability system as a whole as well as the performance of individual components can be benchmarked against design specifications and industry standards. For best results, the power reliability system should be monitored continuously, or what is termed "24/7", so that its performance can be reviewed over time and to ensure that no relevant data is missed. When configured to provide performance benchmarks, the EEM system can be used to help answer several questions:

561

FIGURE 3: TYPICAL EEM INTELLIGENT DEVICES

- When the electrical output of UPS equipment is compared to the electrical input, is this equipment performing to specifications in its ability to mitigate disturbances?

- When critical loads are subjected to electrical disturbances that are judged acceptable by industry standards (such as SEMI F47 and ITIC) do they "ride through" the disturbance and continue to operate as expected?

- Are increasing loads on facility electrical circuits stressing the capacity of certain power reliability system components?

Test Key System Functions
Critical system functions are tested whenever possible to ensure correct operation, and the EEM system can play an important role in the verification and documentation of these tests:

- Streamline system commissioning. During the construction of a data center the EEM system is used to verify and document the proper operation of the reliability equipment as it is commissioned. This helps provide consistency and decreases the overall cost and time necessary for the testing process.

- Perform start-up tests with on-site generation and document the results of the test. The EEM system can provide high-speed trending of relevant electrical and physical data (such as voltage and frequency stability, power output, and various generator pressures and temperatures).

- Monitor automatic transfer switch tests, such as transfers from the utility feed to on-site generation. Intelligent devices in the EEM system can capture the data required to assess the performance of transfer switches (including voltage and current waveforms as well as timestamps for switch operations).

- Verify UPS switching operation. It is important to test the ability of UPS equipment to switch between the

primary energy source (normally the utility) and a secondary energy source (often a bank of battery cells). An EEM system can be used to verify that the output of UPS equipment remains within specifications during switching tests and that the batteries are recharged correctly after a generator has switched in as the primary UPS source.

- Verify static transfer switch (STS) operation. In the event of a primary UPS failure the EEM system can verify that the static transfer switch inside a PDU successfully switched over to a backup power source.

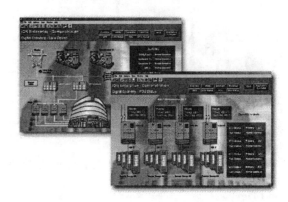

FIGURE 4: TYPICAL EEM SOFTWARE

Capture and Analyze System Failures
Power reliability systems are complex systems, and equipment or system failures can affect the supply of energy to critical loads. Intelligent devices in an EEM system can perform the same job as the "black box" flight recorders used on aircraft, providing the data needed to analyze failures and quickly identify what corrective actions are required. Consider the following scenarios:

- Backup systems fail to keep critical loads energized during a utility outage. Where in the normal sequence of events did the power reliability system fail? Is one piece of equipment responsible for the failure, or is a more complex interaction involved? The information provided by an EEM system can help in finding the answer.

- Several servers in a data center occasionally reboot for no apparent reason, and the electrical circuits feeding these servers are under suspicion. What did the electrical output of the UPS equipment look like at the time the servers rebooted? What about the quality of energy received from the utility? Disturbance data captured by an EEM system can help answer these questions.

CONCLUSION

The energy needs of the digital economy pose a great challenge: this sector is expected to consume a significant portion of the energy generated in the near future, and the quality of this energy must be exceptionally high. Yet the existing power grid infrastructure was never designed to support the reliability required by these new power-sensitive businesses.

Why do these organizations consider this greater reliability so valuable? Consider the following quote from Jeff Byron, former energy director for Oracle Corporation: "What's the self-sufficiency worth to us? Millions of dollars per hour. It is so important, you almost can't calculate the value to us and our customers... The digital economy depends on uninterrupted supplies of the highest quality electricity."[4]

Although it is common practice to increase uptime by deploying power reliability equipment, it is difficult to achieve the highest reliability possible when components are loosely integrated and the information required to manage a system of this complexity is missing.

The solution is an enterprise energy management system that acts as a "digital nervous system", pulling together all power reliability components into a single, coordinated system and providing the information required to maximize uptime. Given the cost that companies like Oracle assign to downtime, many digital economy firms will find the increased reliability made possible by an enterprise energy management system to be invaluable.

REFERENCES

[1] "The PowerChip Paradigm", Huber-Mills

[2] "Enabling Distributed Generation", Power Measurement

[3] "SEH America Ensures Power Quality", Power Measurement

[4] The Wall Street Journal, May 11, 2000

Chapter 81

BUILDING BUSINESS PARTNERSHIPS WITH YOUR ELECTRIC UTILITY:
A POWER QUALITY PERSPECTIVE

S. Kay Tuttle
Power Quality Specialist
Duke Power Company

ABSTRACT

This paper explores the role of the utility and the industrial or commercial facility engineer in developing a business partnership especially as it relates to the quality of electric power. The industrial or commercial facility engineer needs a thorough knowledge of the electrical power quality needs of equipment and processes critical to the business's financial success. Information relating to the operation of the electric utility system is essential to understanding what the utility can reasonably deliver and determining the best solution for bridging any gaps between process requirements and available power quality. The utility needs a thorough understanding of the equipment and processes of businesses they serve as well as a thorough knowledge of the power quality requirements of that equipment. Also, the utility should have available the best options for each process to resolve any gaps between the quality of power supplied and that required by the process. The utility has an obligation to its business partners to explain the operations of the utility system and to make available solutions to power quality problems or needs. Some utilities now offer to install power quality monitors, diagnose power quality problems, perform wiring and grounding assessments, and procure and install mitigation equipment within commercial and industrial facilities. When an opportunity arises for the facility engineer and the utility power quality engineer to work together to prevent or resolve a power quality issue, each should be prepared with the knowledge, information and resolve to do so.

INTRODUCTION

It is imperative for utilities and their customers to form a partnership in order for both to optimize their businesses. Electricity and productivity in industry are inherently linked. For a utility to remain profitable, it must have productive customers, and for a customer to be productive, he or she must have reliable, high quality power. Partnership implies trust. The utility must trust customers and disclose the reliability and quality of power on the electrical system, and the customers must trust the utility and inform the utility engineers regarding their processes. Working together both can meet their business objectives.

SHARING INFORMATION WITH CUSTOMERS ABOUT THE UTILITY SYSTEM

Before the utility can share information regarding typical system performance, the utility must first monitor and analyze the system. In an effort to characterize the utility distribution system, Duke Power and other electric utilities funded a study to determine what quality of service a distribution served customer might expect. This study called DPQ (Distribution Power Quality) was conducted by EPRI (Electric Power Research Institute) and focused on voltage sags, transients, and harmonics. The results for voltage sags are presented in Figure 1. This information is extremely valuable to customers when specifying new equipment or selecting the optimum power quality mitigation devices. For example, the data indicates that the great majority of voltage sags are 6 to 10 cycles in duration and from 60% to 90% remaining voltage. A customer can use this information when ordering new equipment by requesting equipment that can ride through these voltage sags. If the equipment manufacturer does not have the capability to test the ability of the new equipment to ride through voltage sags, the utility can do so. Or, if mitigation equipment is needed, this information is valuable when choosing which mitigation equipment to apply.

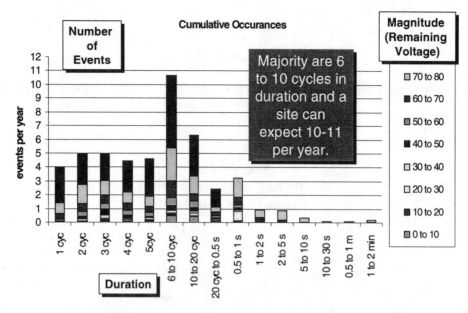

Figure 1
Voltage Sag Data from the Distribution Power Quality Study

UNDERSTANDING CUSTOMER PROCESSES

A utility gains valuable information by analyzing its system, but that is only part of the information needed to make businesses more productive. A detailed understanding of customer processes and what causes these processes to unexpectedly shutdown are also needed. Voltage sags are a common cause of process interruptions for many industrial customers. Voltage sags cause equipment and therefore entire processes to shut down, impacting productivity as well as product quality. In an effort to resolve many of the problems caused by voltage sags, utilities provided funding to EPRI to perform extensive testing of processes prone to shutdowns and to determine effective solutions. The information is in a web based tool called the Industrial Design Guide, IDG.

EPRI and the participating utilities prioritized industries for study each year. To date, plastics and polymers processing, metals fabrication, semiconductor fabrication, pharmaceuticals, printing and publishing, and healthcare and hospitals have been addressed. The plastics and polymers processing industry was the first completed. Processes within this industry were identified early and included pipe extrusion, plastic jacket extrusion, thermoforming, blown film – bubble, and injection molding. Each of these processes was tested in order to find the weak links within the process. One objective was to identify the most economical and effective power quality solutions and to do so required identifying what components within the process caused the process to shut down. A process diagram of blown film is shown in Figure 2. The equipment shown in dark gray are possible weak links and can be viewed in even more detail within the IDG.

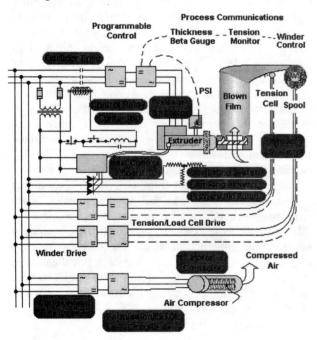

Figure 2
Diagram of Blown Film Process and Possible
Weak Links

A tool that enables component level testing was developed several years ago. This tool is connected to and powers the process being tested. The process is then subjected to controlled voltage sags of different magnitudes and durations originating at various points on the voltage sine-wave, while the response of process components is being monitored. The result is detailed information about the ride through capabilities of various components during voltage sags. A sample of the results from such a test is shown in Figure 3 This figure shows that for a sag to 87% nominal voltage for one cycle or longer, the photo eye, the most sensitive component in the process, will drop out causing the process to shut down. The next most sensitive component in this example is the double-pole, double-throw, DPDT, relay. A voltage sag to 75% of nominal voltage lasting two cycles or longer will cause this relay to dropout.

Once the process is characterized to the component level, solutions for each of the components can be identified as well as the cost effectiveness of each solution. With this information, the customer can make an informed business decision about the acceptable number of shutdowns per year and the cost he or she is willing to pay to achieve this level of ride-through.

Figure 4 shows contour lines generated from the DPQ Study. For example, a distribution served customer with equipment sensitive to voltage sags in the hghlighted area can reasonably expect between 10 and 15 process interruptions a year.

Figure 5 overlays the process component sensitivity found from sag testing with the distribution system characterization curves from the DPQ Study. By examining the contour lines that the equipment sensitivity plot is within, a customer can predict how often a particular component will result in process shutdowns each year. If the power supply were the weakest link in the process, a distribution served customer could expect between five and ten process interruptions a year. Unfortunately, the DPDT relay and the photo eye would cause far more disruptions.

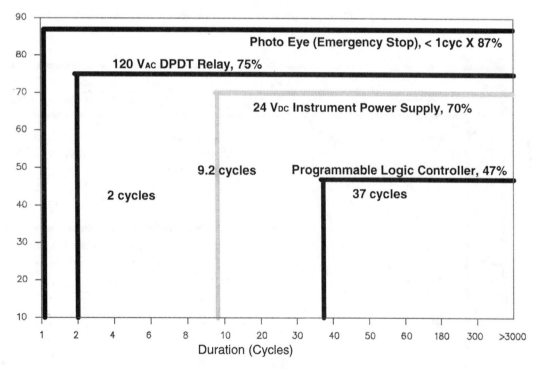

Figure 3
Process Component Sensitivity

567

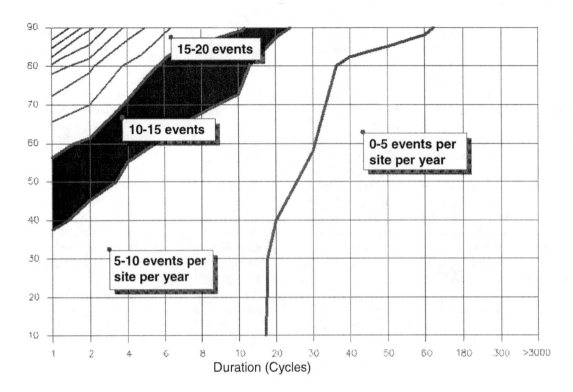

Figure 4
DPQ Study Distribution System Characterization Curves

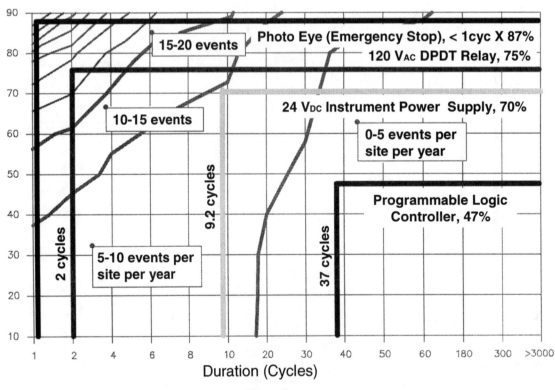

Figure 5
Compatibility

Power Quality solutions can be applied at the facility level to protect the entire facility, at the process level to protect a process, at the equipment to protect the piece of equipment, or at the component level for example to hold in a relay or contactor. In general, power quality solutions applied at the facility level are the most expensive while solutions applied at the component level are the least expensive. There are situations however when each is appropriate. For example, if the cost of a process interruption is minimal, then perhaps improving the power supplies would be all that could be economically justified. However, if the cost of a process interruption is substantial, then a process DVR, dynamic voltage restorer, or perhaps even a flywheel would be the right business decision. Armed with this information and the cost of each solution, the customer can select and justify the appropriate level of voltage sag ride-through.

manufacturer, and then at the recommendation of the manufacturer, contacts the utility. Unless there is an obvious problem with the equipment, the utility usually receives a call. This gives the utility the unique advantage of knowing what problems a particular business or industry is consistently experiencing. With this information, the utility can track and trend the data to determine what problems should be studied to find effective and economical solutions.

One tool used by utilities is the PQ Database. This database was developed by EPRI for utilities to use to store and sort power quality inquiry data. When a customer contacts a utility to request assistance with a power related problem, the description of the problem is entered into the database. As the information about the problem is gathered, it too goes into the database.

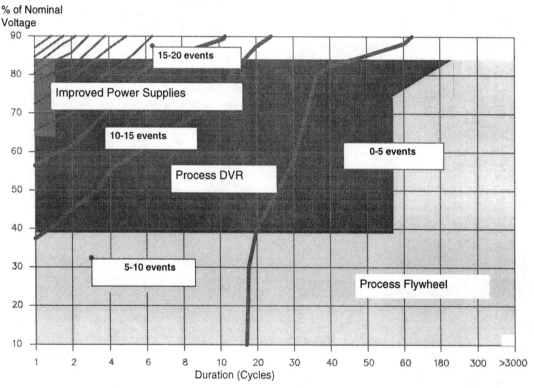

Figure 6
Selecting A Solution

TRACKING CUSTOMER REQUESTS
Each year customers contact their utility for help resolving reliability or power quality problems. If the customer and the utility already have a good working relationship, the utilities are usually the first contacted. Sometimes the customer first contacts the equipment

Monitoring data is often collected and saved, and the actual resolution to the inquiry is also stored. This data can then be sorted in a variety of ways. Samples from a few such sorts are shown. Tables 1-3 illustrate such data collected by Duke Power's PQ engineers from 1997 to 2000 [Ref].

569

Table 1 shows equipment affected by power quality events. Table 2 shows the responses of the equipment to the power quality events, and Table 3 shows the causes of the power quality events.

Affected Equipment	Count	Percent
Plant Equipment – in General	317	14.2
AC Drive	204	9.2
Process Controls	152	6.8
Motor	140	6.3
Other-Affected Equipment	97	4.4
PC	84	3.8
Breaker	73	3.3
LANS – Networks, Mainframes	62	2.8
UPS	61	2.7
Chiller, HVAC	61	2.7

Table 1
Affected Equipment from Duke Power PQ Database

Affected Equipment	Count	Percent
Equipment/Component Failure	501	27.5
Drop-out	334	18.3
Erratic Operation	232	12.7
General-Customer Request	207	11.3
Nuisance Tripping	154	8.4
Energy Usage Monitoring	65	3.6
Cycling – On and Off	52	2.9
Lights Dimming/Flickering	42	2.3
PQ Characterization	31	1.7
Fuse Expulsion	29	1.6

Table 2
Equipment Response

Affected Equipment	Count	Percent
Duke System; Fault, Operation	209	13.4
Customer Equipment Degradation	155	9.9
No PQ Problem	153	9.8
Other – Customer System Problems	148	9.5
Lightning Strike	115	7.3
Grounding/Bonding	94	6.0
Capacitor Switching	91	5.8
Equipment Specification	71	4.5
Problem Cause No Found	68	4.3
No Electrical Problem	61	3.9

Table 3
Problem Causes

Once the data is collected and sorted, it quickly becomes obvious which equipment is experiencing the most problems and what problems are most often encountered. Many utilities contribute to a collaborative effort, to research ways to better solve common power quality problems. Often solutions exist, and it is just a matter of identifying the most appropriate solution and where the solution would best be applied. Sometimes existing solutions are not appropriate and a new solution is developed, applied, and tested. This effort requires collaboration between utilities, a research and development team, customers, and equipment manufacturers.

DEMONSTRATION PROJECTS
When ideal solutions to existing power quality problems do not exist, new solutions that solve the identified problems can be designed, developed, and tested. One example is the low speed flywheel. This flywheel was specified by EPRI, developed by Active Power, and installed and tested at Shaw Industries, a customer served by Duke Power. This demonstration project required collaboration and cooperation of EPRI, Active Power, Shaw Industries, and Duke Power. The flywheel was applied to a process line that extrudes filaments to produce carpet backing. This facility was served by a distribution circuit and the process shut down frequently due to voltage sags and momentary interruptions.

The key to successful implementation of the flywheel as a power quality solution included:

- Characterizing the electrical system,
- Determining the sensitivity of the process components,
- Matching the solution to the process line power requirements as well as to the utility distribution system relaying schemes,
- Including specific and accurate language in specifying the solution,
- Meticulously diagramming the process,
- Properly installing the solution, and
- Monitoring the results.

Shaw Industries realized both productivity and efficiency gains from the operation of the flywheel.

UTILITY/CUSTOMER FORUMS
Some utilities have customer groups that meet regularly to discuss power quality and reliability issues, as well as utility standards and changes, and customer or industry challenges. This forum offers a unique opportunity for the utility and the customer to find ways to help each

other. Many power quality opportunities are discovered this way. Without this interaction, the utility could only guess what their customers needed and customers could only guess how and why utilities implemented policies and changes. One such group, the Power Quality Issues Forum, was established at Duke Power in 1992. This group meets quarterly and participates in activities that include: visiting the Clemson University Electrical Engineering Laboratory to see utility funded power quality research and development efforts; attending PQA, a yearly power quality conference hosted by EPRI; traveling to EPRI-PEAC to see equipment and product testing and research; sponsoring power quality training to stay current on industry initiatives; and visiting demonstration sites such as the installation of the flywheel at Shaw Industries.

WORKSHOPS

As information is gained from demonstration projects, Industrial Design Guide work, SagGen testing, equipment testing done by EPRI-PEAC, and research and development conducted by universities and funded by utilities, this information must be shared with utility customers. One effective way of doing so is by holding workshops, conferences, and seminars. Some specific examples include the Industrial Technology Information Exchange conference sponsored by Duke Power yearly for the past two years. This conference highlights new electric technology applications, power quality and reliability efforts, and innovative ways to reduce energy costs. Based on customer feedback from the first year, the conference was held twice in 2001 in both North and South Carolina and participation increased dramatically. Another successful way to share relevant power quality information is conducting workshops and seminars. Such workshops offered by utilities focus on wiring and grounding for enhanced equipment performance,

effectively applying surge suppression, improving process ride-through, selecting effective power quality solutions, improving drive performance, selecting appropriate monitoring equipment for the application, designing effective lightning protection systems, and solving problems with ungrounded electrical systems.

TRACKING COSTS OF PQ PROBLEMS

In order for a customer to make an informed business decision about power quality solutions, it is imperative to know the cost to the business when a power quality problem occurs. This cost should include scrap, unproductive labor, lost productivity, missed orders, risk, and recovery. A process for tracking these costs should be implemented if not already in place.

SPECIFYING NEW EQUIPMENT FOR RIDE-THROUGH

In order to minimize costly power quality solutions, ride-through specifications can be included when purchasing new equipment. Ideally, one would characterize the electrical environment to know exactly what specifications to include, but this is not always feasible. A generic ride-through curve can be included which would allow a process to ride-through most voltage sags. Figure 7 illustrates the ITIC, Information Technology Industry Council, Curve. This curve was developed to represent the sensitivity of most computer equipment. The region within the two curves represents conditions where computer equipment should operate without disruption or damage. A similar curve has also been developed for the semiconductor industry.

KEEPING ABREAST OF NEW PQ SOLUTIONS

Utility customers can keep abreast of new power quality solutions in a variety of ways. Power quality magazines have articles describing new solutions. Utilities offer

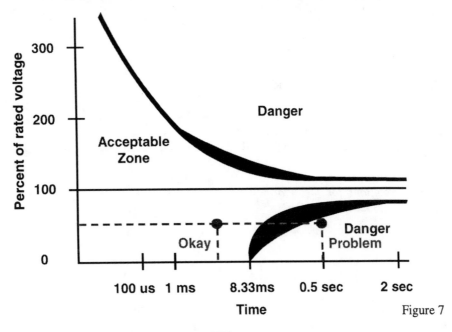

Figure 7

seminars and conferences outlining features of power quality solutions. Literature from equipment testing is available through EPRI utility members. With the tendency for business and industry to reduce personnel, it is not always practical to stay informed about power quality issues. In which case, one can contact utility power quality experts when power quality problems occur or when specifying new equipment.

EDUCATING UTILITY ON PROCESSES

In order for utilities to help when power quality problems do arise, it is imperative that the utility power quality engineers be familiar with the processes in question. This can only be accomplished if the utility customer experiencing the problem feels comfortable sharing process information with the utility. Much information regarding processes is confidential and proprietary and the utility must respect that confidentiality. It is much easier to expeditiously solve a power quality concern if the utility power quality engineer already has a good understanding of the process equipment. This requires resources and commitment from the utility management. Power quality expertise takes years to acquire and technology, equipment, and power quality solutions are constantly changing, requiring time and effort to remain informed.

CONCLUSION

By actively participating in a partnership, both the electric utility and utility customers can significantly improve their business results. This requires collecting and sharing information regarding utility system operation, studying and sharing process requirements—including sensitivity to electrical disturbances, and evaluating solutions to power quality problems.

Information can be effectively shared through customer forums, conferences, and workshops. A utility, customer partnership requires commitment from all involved, but the benefits are well worth the effort.

REFERENCES

1. *Industrial Design Guide*: Version 3.0, EPRI, Palo Alto, CA: 2001. 1005912

2. *Power Quality Applications Guide for Architects and Engineers*, EPRICSG, Palo Alto, CA: 1999. TR-113874

3. *Duke Power Energy Solutions for the Information Age Workshop*, May 23, 2002, Charlotte, NC

Chapter 82

ENERGY AND COST SAVINGS THROUGH EMS OPTIMIZATION

Mahesh Bala, Sr. Project Engineer, Select Energy Services, Inc.
Roy Michaelson, Energy Specialist, Howard County Public School System

ABSTRACT

An organization's energy management system (EMS) is not always effectively used to optimize energy use. This is often due to budget, labor, or time constraints. To demonstrate the energy and costs that could be saved through EMS optimization, two schools in Howard County, Maryland, were selected for a pilot study. The objective of the study was to demonstrate the savings from the EMS at a minimal cost to the County and to show the benefits of the EMS controlling as much of the equipment operation as possible. Clarksville Elementary School (CES) and River Hill High School (RHHS) were chosen after reviewing the energy use indices for all of the County schools. RHHS, a large modern high school, and CES, an older elementary school, provided a good contrast in terms of area and types of heating, ventilating and air conditioning (HVAC) equipment and controls. They represented a large fraction of the County schools.

Field observations and electricity-use patterns at the two schools revealed several energy conservation measures (ECMs). Typical ECMs included remote on/off capability of the chiller at CES; locking arrangement for thermostats to prevent unauthorized setpoint changes in classrooms; rescheduling "unoccupied" time for various rooms to more closely follow school's actual weekly use; and tightening weekday, weekend and holiday schedules of HVAC units to more closely follow the actual use. These ECMs were implemented in the two schools at a cost of about $4,500. The measurement and verification (M&V) plan consisted of monitoring and comparing the energy and cost savings from the monthly bills with historical data for a period of six to eight months. In order to affect a proper comparison with historical utility meter data, adjustments to weather and number of days in the billing cycle were made.

RHHS realized $1,700 of average monthly cost savings, while CES realized approximately $230. This case study clearly indicates the power and cost-saving potential of the EMS.

1. INTRODUCTION

The purpose of this project was to demonstrate energy and cost savings by optimizing the Metasys® energy management system (EMS) at Howard County Public School System (HCPSS). The project had two phases. In the first phase, a plan to achieve the project goal was formulated. In the second phase, the plan was implemented and its effectiveness in terms of energy and cost savings was measured and verified. Specifically, the project consisted of the following tasks:

1.1 Phase 1

1. From among the more than 50 HCPSS schools, two schools were chosen based on the following criteria:
   - Annual energy use
   - Types of controls
   - Completeness of the EMS installation
   - Investment required to carry out the energy conservation measures (ECMs)
2. From field surveys at the two schools, potential ECMs that could be implemented through the EMS were identified.
3. For the identified ECMs, the hardware, software or programming changes necessary to implement the ECMs were specified, and the associated cost estimates were obtained from the controls' vendor.
4. In order to minimize the cost, ECMs that required a minimum of investment were selected for implementation.
5. In order to identify and document the energy and cost savings, a M&V plan was developed.

1.2 Phase 2

Monthly energy and cost savings were measured and verified during the M&V period.

2. SCHOOL SELECTION PROCESS

Using the annual energy use data obtained from electric, gas, and fuel oil bills, and the average area of the schools, the site energy use indices (EUI) for various Howard County schools were compiled. The EUI, simply the energy used in a year per square foot of the school floor area (gross), was then used to rank schools. Table 1 provides the EUI (MBtu/ft²/year or 1000 Btu/ft²/year) for the various HCPSS schools for the years 1997-98 and 1998-99, including their ranking based on the EUI. The ranking simply lists the schools from the highest to the lowest EUI for the most recent year, 1998-99. The corresponding rank of the same school in year 1997-98 is also provided.

In the next step of the selection process, the types of HVAC equipment, their age and the types of controls in the schools were identified. Schools that required a capital improvement project to realize energy savings were excluded. For example, decreasing the energy use significantly in Oakland Mills Middle and High Schools would have entailed replacing the inefficient absorption chillers with modern, high-efficiency chillers.

We also wanted to select a relatively new school with modern direct digital control (DDC) and an older school with pneumatic local-loop control and DDC supervisory control. Such a selection covered a broader spectrum of the County schools.

Two schools, River Hill High School and Clarksville Elementary School, emerged as the top candidates from the selection process. RHHS is a relatively new school with modern DDC controls. Although its EUI was low among the various County schools, it had a higher EUI among the DDC schools. CES, an older elementary school, represented other County schools with pneumatic local loop controls and limited DDC supervisory control.

In summary, RHHS and CES were chosen for the pilot study because both schools have above average EUI in comparison to a group of schools that are similar to them in terms of age and controls technology. Also, because each school differs in terms of age, mechanical equipment, and controls, they are a fair representation of the Howard County schools.

Table 1 ENERGY USE OF HOWARD COUNTY SCHOOLS

School	1997-98		1998-99	
	Rank	EUI	Rank	EUI
Oakland Mills Middle School	3	111	1	139
Gateway School	6	102	2	128
Oakland Mills High School	2	115	3	117
Dunloggin Middle School	21	77	4	105
Phelps Luck Elementary School	5	105	5	103
Clarksville Middle School	1	119	6	99
Cedar Lane Special Education	8	95	8	99
Clarksville Elementary School	**20**	**77**	**9**	**97**
Patuxent Valley Middle School	16	81	10	96

Table 1 (CONTINUED)

School	1997-98		1998-99	
	Rank	EUI	Rank	EUI
Swansfield Elementary School	34	67	11	91
Bushy Park Elementary School	32	67	12	85
Worthington Elementary School	53	49	13	84
Clemens Crossing Elementary School	31	67	17	81
Thunder Hill Elementary School	18	78	18	80
Centennial Lane Elementary School	14	85	20	79
Burleigh Manor Middle School	11	91	21	77
Talbott Spring Elementary School	9	93	22	76
Patapsco Middle School	17	81	23	76
Bryant Woods Elementary School	27	70	24	75
Bollman Bridge Elementary School	12	86	25	73
Pointers Run Elementary School	36	65	26	72
Atholton Elementary School	58	37	27	72
Hammond High School	37	63	28	71
Centennial High School	23	71	29	69
Longfellow Elementary School	25	71	30	68
Hammond Middle School	39	61	31	68
Manor Woods Elementary School	35	66	32	67
Wilde Lake High School	30	67	33	67
Glenelg High School	42	59	34	67
Guilford Elementary School	29	68	35	65
Rockburn Elementary School	52	49	36	65
River Hill High School	**22**	**73**	**37**	**65**
Northfield Elementary School	28	70	38	63
Fulton Elementary School	63	19	39	63
Stevens Forest Elementary School	40	61	40	62
Wilde Lake Middle School	19	78	41	61
Atholton High School	50	51	42	60
Mayfield Woods Middle School	43	59	43	60
Waterloo Elementary School	33	67	44	60
West Friendship Elementary School	57	38	45	59
Mount View Middle School	26	70	46	59
Hollifield Station Elementary School	44	56	47	58
Running Brook Elementary School	38	62	48	57
Ilchester Elementary School	48	53	49	55
Long Reach High School	41	60	50	55
Elkridge Landing Middle School	47	53	51	53
Waverly Elementary School	51	49	52	53
Ellicott Mills Middle School	49	52	53	52
St. John's Lane Elementary School	46	55	54	52
Deep Run Elementary School	45	56	55	49
Howard High School	61	20	56	46
Howard High School	61	20	56	46
Dasher Green Elementary School	54	42	58	39

3. ECMs IDENTIFIED

Field observations of the two schools revealed several energy conservation measures. In general, the ECMs included shutting down equipment when not in use, scheduling the HVAC equipment to operate more closely with the occupancy, and scheduling the outdoor air so it is not conditioned unnecessarily during unoccupied hours.

Site surveys were conducted in RHHS and CES in September 2000 to identify potential energy conservation measures. In order to understand the schedules and how the schools were operated, the principals of the schools were also interviewed. As part of the field survey, the electricity use was measured for about a week at more than 15 locations throughout CES and RHHS. The measurements were made with electricity-use data loggers, which measure and store current flow data at regular intervals. These measurements allowed us to establish a pattern of electricity use at the two schools and to identify possible gaps in the EMS setpoints and schedules. We also obtained 30-minute interval electricity-use data for RHHS from July 1999 to June 2000. This data revealed the use pattern of HVAC equipment, lighting and other equipment in the school.

We observed the following from the data logger data, the 30-minute interval electricity-use data and the schedules provided by the schools' principals:

- The lights were on until 11 p.m. in both the schools so that janitorial services could be performed. We recommended that the lighting schedules be tightened through better scheduling and planning.
- In RHHS, a peak of 940 kW at 8 p.m. that occurred on 09/14/00 did not coincide with any scheduled activity at the school. We recommended that HCPSS investigate this occurrence.
- The relocatable classrooms at CES were active mid-afternoon on 09/24/00 (Sunday), and again at midnight on 09/27/00 (Wednesday). At the time of the survey we suspected that the electric heating coils became active at these times.

The preliminary list of ECMs for the two schools was developed from our site-survey observations, EMS setpoints and coincident school schedules, and the anomalies in the measured data.

3.1 Preliminary ECMs for CES

CES is a single-story brick-face building with a gross area of approximately 46,500 ft^2. A 150-ton air-cooled chiller and two hot-water boilers serve the cooling and heating needs of the school. Table 2 shows the multiple units that circulate the air, the zones they serve, and the original equipment schedules.

3.1.1 Tie in the air-cooled chiller into the EMS so as to provide on/off capability. The tie-in is to be provided without defeating the existing safeties, such as the safety interlock that ensures water flow in the evaporator, before starting the chiller. The ECM's intent is to allow better scheduling and control of the chiller operation through the EMS.

3.1.2 Tie in each of the two boilers into the EMS so as to provide on/off capability. Similar to the chiller, the tie-in is to be provided without defeating the existing safeties. The ECM's intent is to allow better scheduling of the boiler operation through the EMS. For example, both boilers are kept warm throughout the winter months. With this capability, one of the boilers can be turned off as needed, while the other boiler can serve the school. This will minimize boiler standby losses.

3.1.3 Prevent unauthorized setpoint changing on the pneumatic night setback thermostats by providing a locking arrangement. The pneumatic night setback thermostats in CES serve as a backup to the EMS. Typical night setback setpoint for the EMS is 55°F, while for the pneumatic backups it is 50°F. If the 50°F setpoint is changed to some value above the EMS setpoint of 55°F, then energy will be wasted at night. While this measure does not directly affect the EMS, it ensures that the control of night setback setpoint remains with the EMS.

3.1.4 Provide programmable thermostats in the relocatable classrooms. The electricity-use data from the loggers show nighttime electricity use, possibly from the electric heating coils in the relocatable classrooms. Through programmable thermostats the nighttime electricity use can be reduced.

3.1.5 Reschedule "unoccupied" time for various rooms. The time clock in the EMS shows the occupied time for the entire school to be from about 6:00 a.m. to 4:00 p.m. on Mondays and from 7:00 a.m. to 4:00 p.m. on other weekdays. The EMS schedule did not coincide with the schedule we obtained from the principal. We recommended that the schedules for different rooms be coordinated with the principal so that the room schedules could be tightened further without sacrificing comfort.

3.1.6 Provide capability to change the CHW output temperature. Chiller energy use can be reduced if the chilled water output temperature is maintained as high as possible without sacrificing comfort.

3.1.7 Fine tune schedules of ACUs 1 and 2. ACUs 1 and 2 serve the multipurpose room. The new schedules for the units had to be coordinated with the principal. In addition to developing tighter schedules, only one of the two units can be run during periods of light or moderate occupancy to provide comfort in the multipurpose room.

3.1.8 Provide outdoor air (OA) damper point to control its open/close in ACU 1 and 2. The units economize only during the heating mode. This ECM is recommended only if ECM 6 cannot be implemented.

Table 2 EXISTING EQUIPMENT SCHEDULES AT CES

Zone	Equipment	Rooms	Existing Schedule (Regular)
1	UV	12 and 13	Mon: 6:00 – 16:00 Tue – Fri: 7:00 – 16:00
2	UV	14 and 15	Mon: 6:00 – 16:00 Tue – Fri: 7:00 – 16:00

575

Table 2 (CONTINUED)

Zone	Equipment	Rooms	Existing Schedule (Regular)
3	H&V 1	Gym	Mon: 6:00 – 16:00 Tue – Fri: 7:00 – 16:00
4	UV & FCU	6	Mon: 6:00 – 16:00 Tue – Fri: 7:00 – 16:00
5	UV & FCU	Classes	Mon: 6:00 – 16:00 Tue – Fri: 7:00 – 16:00
6	UV & FCU	8, 9, & 10	Mon: 6:05 – 16:00 Tue – Fri: 7:05 – 16:00
7	UV & FCU	16 – 21	Mon: 6:05 – 16:00 Tue – Fri: 7:05 – 16:00
8	AHU 1	Media Center	Mon: 6:05 – 16:00 Tue – Fri: 7:05 – 16:00
9	UV	GI	Mon: 6:05 – 16:00 Tue – Fri: 7:05 – 16:00
10	UV	Audio/Visual	Mon: 6:05 – 16:00 Tue – Fri: 7:05 – 16:00
11	H & C 1	Office	Mon: 6:10 – 16:00 Tue – Fri: 7:10 – 16:00
12	UV	3, 4, and 5	Mon: 6:10 – 16:00 Tue – Fri: 7:10 – 16:00
13	ACU 1 & 2	Multipurpose	Mon – Fri: 6:10 – 18:00
14	UV	2	Mon: 6:10 – 16:00 Tue – Fri: 7:10 – 16:00
15	UV	Teachers' area	Mon: 6:10 – 16:00 Tue – Fri: 7:10 – 16:00
16	UV	Art Area	Mon: 6:10 – 16:00 Tue – Fri: 7:10 – 16:00
17	FCU	FCU Corridor	Mon: 6:10 – 16:00 Tue – Fri: 7:10 – 16:00

Key: UV = unit ventilators; FCU = fan-coil units; H&V = heating and ventilating unit; AHU = air-handling unit; H&C = heating and cooling unit; ACU = air-conditioning unit; GI = group instrument

3.2 PRELIMINARY ECMs FOR RHHS

RHHS is three-story building with a gross area of 234,000 ft². The school is served by two 200-ton Trane Centravac® water-cooled chillers and six hot-water boilers. Table 4 shows the multiple units that circulate the air, the zones they serve, and both original and modified equipment schedules.

3.2.1   Tighten schedule. Setup schedule (for switching on and switching off equipment) based on typical occupancy. The ECM applies to AHUs 1-12 and 14-20. Refer to Table 4 for AHU schedule details.

3.2.2   Control OA damper based on occupancy need. Setup separate schedule for OA damper. Requires EMS programming. The ECM applies to AHUs 1–5 and 12.

3.2.3   Provide zone or return-air (RA) temperature feedback to EMS. Needs temperature sensor installation, input to EMS and associated EMS programming. This ECM provides feedback about how the zones are responding to cooling or heating, and helps in fine-tuning the HVAC equipment schedule serving the zone. The ECM applies to AHUs 6–11, 14–17, and 20.

3.2.4   Tighten alternate Tuesday schedule for AHU 6 as needed. The existing schedule is from 6:35 a.m. to

10:00 p.m. Coordinate with the principal and modify schedule accordingly. The rescheduling can be done without further modification through the EMS.

3.2.5   Examine and reset holiday schedule for AHU 12 as required. The existing holiday schedule is from 5:30 a.m. to 8:00 p.m. Coordinate with the principal and modify schedule accordingly. The rescheduling can be done without further modification through the EMS.

3.2.6   Examine schedule for AHUs 14, 17, and 20. The AHUs are scheduled to start before the chillers on Mondays. Reschedule so that the chiller is started before the AHUs.

3.2.7   Examine and reset schedule as needed. The schedule on the EMS for AHU 19 calls fan shutdown at 2:00 p.m.; however, the fan was recorded in the EMS as running at 2:37 p.m. on 09/26/2000. This needs to be investigated and the schedule needs to be reset as needed.

4. COST ESTIMATES AND IMPLEMENTED ECMs

The cost estimates for the ECMs listed in this section were obtained from Johnson Controls, Inc (JCI). ECMs that required high investment were excluded from further consideration (refer to ECM Status column in Table 3). To further reduce the cost, HCPSS agreed to provide the material and the labor in-house; these costs are *not* included in the final cost shown in Table 3. The ECMs implemented at the two schools are shown in bold.

Table 3 COST ESTIMATES OF ECMs

ECM 3.1	JCI Cost Details, $				ECM	Note	Cost, $
	M	**L**	**P**	**Total**			
CES							
1	1,500	8,100	410	10,000	Incl.	(a)	**410**
2	450	2,150	410	3,000	Excl	(b)	-
3	0		0	0	Incl	-	-
4	0		0	0	Incl	-	-
5	0		0	0	Incl	-	-
6	300	1700	-	2,000	Excl	(c)	-
7	0	0	410	410	Incl	-	**410**
8	-	-	-	-	Excl	(d)	-
RHHS							
ECM 3.2	**M**	**L**	**P**	**Total**	ECM	Note	Cost, $
1	0	-	0	0	Incl	-	-
2	2,000	9,150	1,860	13,000	Excl	(b)	-
3	3,000	11900	1,130	16,000	Excl	(b)	-
4	0		0	0	Incl	-	-
5	0		0	0	Incl	-	-
6	0		0	0	Incl	-	-
7	0		0	0	Incl	-	-
TOTAL ESTIMATED COST							**820**

Key: M = Material, L = Labor, and P = Programming
(a) Programming done by JCI, material purchased by HCPSS, and labor done in-house. Total cost to the County was $4,500, including $820 for programming.
(b) ECMs excluded to minimize investment.
(c) Chiller did not have the capability to allow the EMS to do chilled-water temperature reset.
(d) Excluded because ECM 3.1.7 was included.

5. IMPLEMENTATION PLAN

The implementation of the pilot study consisted of the following steps:

- Installing the additional controls, including the required EMS programming
- The EMS operator meeting with the principals of RHHS and CES to develop new schedules for different rooms in the schools and further tightening the HVAC equipment schedules based on the new information. These modified schedules for both the schools were entered into the EMS.
- Implementing the M&V plan.

Our recommended M&V plan included HCPSS monitoring the energy and cost savings through the monthly bills for the two schools for a period of six to eight months. The simple plan provided a direct measure of the effect of the ECMs on energy and cost savings. In order to affect a proper comparison with historical data, adjustments to weather and number of days in the billing cycle were made. These adjustments were made using simple calculations in a spreadsheet.

The analysis of the M&V data included the following steps:

- *Compare post- and pre-M&V monthly period costs and energy use.* The M&V period started in March 2001 for RHHS and in April 2001 for CES. The M&V period for the project spans March through December 2001.
- *Adjustments made to the billing data.* Energy uses and the associated costs are dependent on numerous factors, including weather, the number of billing days in the month, the number of occupants, and building use changes. HCPSS also reported that for both schools, the number of occupants and the building use remained approximately the same in 2000 and 2001. Variations in weather and number of billing days were accounted for using hand calculations.

We also recommended that the M&V plan start in January 2001 and continue through July or August of that year. This ensured that winter, shoulder and summer months were included in the M&V plan.

We expected the implementation of the ECMs during the M&V period to be a dynamic process, in that the effects of one measure can affect other measures; thus, adjustments were made during the M&V phase depending on how the building system reacts to each measure. For example, reducing the building internal heat load can lead to increased space heating load during the winter months and decreased cooling load during the summer. The annual energy savings will be the difference between the saved energy (lighting as well as cooling) and the increased heating energy. Also, we did not want the M&V to adversely affect the day-to-day running of the school. Our plan was to incorporate the energy savings seamlessly into the schools' operations.

We realized that human supervision of the EMS was imperative for HCPSS to achieve energy and cost savings. The various EMS parameters, such as schedules, should be periodically verified to be consistent with the actual use at the two schools. We recommended that the principals notify the EMS operator of any required schedule modifications so that appropriate changes could be made to the EMS. We emphasized the interaction between the schools and the EMS operator and the supervision of the EMS to be essential to the success of this study.

5.1 Adjustments Made to the Billing Data

Billing days: The energy use was assumed to be directly proportional to the number of billing days. Since demand is rate of energy use and is typically determined by the energy used in fifteen minutes[1], no adjustment for the number of billing days was made to demand.

Weather: Both energy and demand were assumed to be directly proportional to the weather condition. For simplicity, the monthly outdoor-air average dry-bulb temperature was selected as the parameter that represented weather variations. To make the estimate more accurate, weather-independent loads (e.g., computers, lighting) were separated out from the weather-dependent (space heating, cooling and ventilation) loads. Since no electrical-load data were available for RHHS and CES, we estimated that for educational facilities[2] about 49% of the total load was weather-dependent, and the rest were weather-independent. The weather-dependent part was modeled as directly proportional to the temperature difference between the school inside temperature (setpoint) and the monthly outdoor-air average dry-bulb temperature.

5.2 Rationalizing the Savings

Energy savings were rationalized by comparing how much energy RHHS and CES used in 2001 in comparison to 2000 (adjusting for weather and billing days). If the savings reported in the M&V phase were "significantly" different, then we could conclude with reasonable certainty that the savings resulted from the EMS optimization.

In order to determine the natural variations[3] in electricity use so that statistically significant results could be delineated, three high schools, Wilde Lake, Oakland Mills, and Glenelg, were selected. According to HCPSS, no significant construction modifications had taken place in these schools in recent years, and the facility use and the number of occupants had remained relatively constant. Thus, significant factors that affect energy use were reduced to weather variations and number of billing days in the year. In an attempt to define the normal expected deviation of monthly electricity use for the three high schools from year to year, we corrected the bill for weather and the number of billing days.

---

[1] Demand charges are typically for the highest demand measured in two consecutive 15-minute periods.
[2] Refer to ASHRAE *HVAC Applications*, 1999, page 34.8, Table 2A.
[3] Due to limited data, similar analysis for elementary schools yielded inconclusive results. The results from the statistical analysis for high schools are applied to elementary schools.

After making the corrections, we found that the energy use varied by ±7% and the demand by ±4% in the three high schools. Thus, it is reasonable to expect that electricity-use variations beyond these values are brought about by EMS optimization.

During some months, the energy and demand listed in Table 5 and
Table 6 show a marked increase in 2001 compared to 2000. Whenever the variations are influenced by documented external factors, such as construction, or when the variations did not exceed the natural variations of ±7% for energy and ±4% for demand, the data are omitted from the summary. In other words, all data that are unaffected by the influence of any known external factors and exceed the natural expected variations are included in the summary below.

6. SUMMARY

Table 7 summarizes the results from Table 5 and
Table 6. We used the savings from the M&V period and estimated the annual savings for the two schools, assuming no influence of any external factor. Because M&V occurred in the summer months, when electricity use is high, we reduced the savings by 20% to account for the reduced electricity use in the winter months. The reduction was based on the average electricity use in the winter and summer months.

The total cost savings for both the schools attributable to EMS optimization during the M&V period amounted to $6,875. The projected annual cost savings are $17,500.

Some other benefits were realized when HCPSS maintained the EMS setpoints and equipment operation more closely during the M&V phase. For example, a controls malfunction in the RHHS auditorium unit was identified after detecting an increase in the electricity use. Similarly, a fault in the CES chiller schedule was discovered while investigating the increase in the electricity use.

Table 7 shows that the projected annual savings for RHHS are substantially higher than for CES not only because RHHS is larger than CES, but also because of the more sophisticated controls at RHHS. While the more sophisticated controls may initially cost more to install, they provide more flexibility to control equipment, thus lowering the operating cost during the life of the equipment.

The study results also show that for the purposes of fault identification and correction, and to exercise a better control over equipment operation and associated costs, having a full-time or at least a part-time operator to monitor the EMS schedules and equipment operation would be worthwhile. The energy and cost savings are from optimizing the EMS in just two schools. It is expected that the savings would be significant if similar measures are incorporated throughout the HCPSS.

Table 4. ORIGINAL AND MODIFIED SCHEDULES FOR RHHS

Eqpt.	Area Served	Original Schedule				SESI Recommendations			
		Weekdays (Monday - Friday)		Weekends & Holidays		Weekdays (Monday - Friday)		Weekends & Holidays	
		Fan	VAV	Fan	VAV	Fan	VAV	Fan	VAV
AHU 1	Main Gym	6:54-14:00	NA	Off	NA	6:54-14:00	NA	Off	NA
AHU 2	Gym Lobby	6:53-14:00	6:53-14:00	Off	Off	6:53-14:00	6:53-14:00	Off	Off
AHU 3	Auxiliary Gym	6:38-14:00	NA	Off	NA	6:38-14:00	NA	Off	NA
AHU 4	Backstage	6:37-14:00	6:37-14:00	Off	-	10:35-14:00	5:10-14:00	Off	Off
AHU 5	Auditorium	6:34-14:00	NA	6:00-13:00	NA	4:00-6:00	NA	Off	NA
AHU 6	Art Classrooms	Mon: 5:35-14:00 Tue-Fri: 6:35-14:00	Mon: 5:35-14:00 Tue - Fri: 6:35-14:00	Off	Off	7:30-14:00	6:16-14:00	Off	Off
AHU 7	Band & Choral	Mon: 5:30-14:30 Tue-Fri: 6:30-14:30	Mon: 5:30-14:30 Tue - Fri: 6:30-14:30	6:00-13:00	6:00-13:00	7:30-14:00	6:35-14:00	Off	Off
AHU 8	Lecture & Performance	Mon: 5:16-14:30 Tue-Fri: 6:16-14:30	Mon: 5:16-14:30 Tue - Fri: 6:16-14:30	6:00-13:00	6:00-13:00	7:30-14:00	6:55-14:00	Off	Off
AHU 9	9th Grade Classrooms	Mon: 5:20-14:30 Tue - Fri: 6:20-14:30	Mon: 5:20-14:30 Tue - Fri: 6:20-14:30	6:00-13:00	6:00-13:00	7:30-14:00	6:00-14:00	Off	Off
AHU 10	Media Productions	6:10-14:30	6:10-14:30	Off	Off	8:00-14:00	5:00-14:00	Off	Off
AHU 11	Admin Guidance & Health	5:30-16:00	5:30-16:00	Off	Off	5:30-16:00	5:30-16:00	Off	Off
AHU 12	Student Dining	6:46-14:30	NA	Off	NA	10:00-14:00	NA	Off	NA
AHU 13	Kitchen Hood Makeup Air	Linked to EF	NA	Off	NA	Linked to EF	NA	Off	NA
AHU 14	Center Classroom Wing	Mon: 4:54-14:30 Tue: 5:45-14:30 Wed-Fri: 5:54-14:30	Mon: 4:54-14:30 Tue: 5:45-14:30 Wed - Fri: 5:54-14:30	Off	Off	7:30-14:00	5:16-14:00	Off	Off
AHU 15	South Classroom Wing	Mon: 5:25-14:30 Tue-Fri: 6:25-14:30	Mon: 5:25-14:30 Tue - Fri: 6:25-14:30	Off	Off	7:30-14:00	5:35-14:00	Off	Off
AHU 16	Science Classrooms	Mon: 5:20-14:30 Tue: 6:20-14:00 Wed - Fri: 6:20-14:30	Mon: 5:20-14:30 Tue: 6:20-14:00 Wed - Fri: 6:20-14:30	Off	Off	7:30-14:00	5:46-14:00	Off	Off
AHU 17	Technology Classrooms	Mon: 4:58-14:30 Tue - Fri: 5:58-14:30	Mon: 4:58-14:30 Tue - Fri: 5:58-14:30	Off	Off	7:30-14:00	5:58-14:00	Off	Off
AHU 18	Wrestling & Weight Training	6:56-14:00	NA	Off	NA	6:56-14:30	NA	Off	NA
AHU 19	Locker & Shower Rooms	6:55-14:00	NA	Off	NA	6:55-14:30	NA	Off	NA
AHU 20	Reading Room	Mon: 5:14-14:30 Tue-Fri: 6:14-14:30	NA	Off	NA	6:14-14:00	NA	Off	NA
Chillers	-	5:35-16:00	NA	5:55-13:00	NA	5:35-16:00	NA	Off	NA
Boilers		Auto scheduler in place. Boiler operation through Johnson Metasys was not considered at HCPSS' request.							

NA = Not Applicable

Table 5. M&V SUMMARY FOR RHHS

Month	Use for 2000[a] Energy kWh	Use for 2000[a] Demand kW	Use for 2001[b] Energy kWh	Use for 2001[b] Demand kW	Savings or (Losses) Energy	Savings or (Losses) Demand	Remarks
March	220,400	908	188,200	599	15%	34%	Data included
April	163,600	813	208,200	990	(27%)	(22%)	Data excluded - Auditorium unit ran due to a controls malfunction
May	266,700	1,080	244,500	896	8%	17%	Data included
June	268,800	1,119	250,500	1,035	7%	8%	Both energy and demand data excluded due to statistical significance
July	238,200	918	230,700	916	3%	0%	Energy data excluded due to statistical insignificance. Demand (loss) included
August	310,500	1,077	296,500	1,185	5%	(10%)	
September	234,600	1,062	297,000	1,198	(27%)	(13%)	Two re-locatable classrooms added. All data excluded
October	215,700	1,059	256,700	991	(19%)	6%	
November	227,100	861	327,700	1,086	(44%)	(26%)	
December	203,100	690	260,900	985	(28%)	(43%)	

Table 6. M&V SUMMARY FOR CES

Month	Use for 2000[a] Energy kWh	Use for 2000[a] Demand kW	Use for 2001[b] Energy kWh	Use for 2001[b] Demand kW	Savings Energy	Savings Demand	Remarks
April	25,900	146	30,500	150	(18%)	(3%)	Demand data excluded due to statistical insignificance. Energy (loss) included
May	37,200	199	32,400	158	13%	20%	Data included
June	31,900	183	33,200	179	(4%)	2%	Both data excluded due to statistical insignificance
July	22,200	115	25,100	145	(13%)	(26%)	All data excluded due summer construction, for which the electrical power was taken from the school
August	26,900	167	37,300	210	(39%)	(26%)	
September	32,000	196	32,600	187	(2%)	5%	One re-locatable classroom added. All data excluded
October	29,700	185	31,050	163	(5%)	12%	
November	36,600	123	44,500	145	(22%)	(18%)	
December	39,400	135	50,700	171	(29%)	(27%)	

[a] actual metered data from the bills
[b] utility data adjusted for weather and number of billing days – reflects 'equivalent' year-2000 use
All of the data are shown for the sake of completeness, but not all data are considered directly attributable to EMS optimization. Data are excluded when external factors, such as construction or equipment malfunction affected the energy use, or when the results were not statistically significant. The included data are shown in **bold**.

Table 7. COST SAVINGS SUMMARY FOR THE M&V PERIOD

School	Period	Demand Savings		Energy Savings		Total Savings	Projected Annual Savings
		kW	$	kWh	$	$ in the M&V period	$/year[b]
RHHS	Mar–Dec 2001	469	4,522	72,725	1,881	6,403	15,300
CES[a]	Apr–Dec 2001	41	467	202	5	472	2,200

[a] Results may be inconclusive due to the limited M&V data.
[b] The reported savings occurred in summer months, when electricity use is rather high. The estimated annual savings were reduced by 20% (calculated from typical school use) to account for this fact.

M:\AESP\WEEC 2002\Energy and Cost Savings through EMS Optimaization.doc

STRIVING FOR COST-EFFECTIVE ENERGY INFORMATION SOLUTIONS: EMERGING WEB-BASED TECHNOLOGIES PROVIDE HOPE!

John M. Duff, CEM
VESTAR, a Cinergy Company

ABSTRACT

The Internet is providing a cost-effective method of providing energy users with valuable information that enables them to better control their energy usage. The days of solely relying on systems that are on-site to provide this information have passed. The ability of off-site energy managers to collect, process and disseminate this information using Internet based e-mail and web-pages accessible by the end-user's standard Internet browsers has become a much more attractive option.

While centrally monitored energy management is not new, it has been used primarily by high-end users with dedicated staff to perform the gathering and analysis functions. With low-cost Internet communications available, this service can now be provided to a much broader market. This market, consisting of K-12 school corporations, municipalities, medium sized commercial office buildings, and modest sized retail chains has been under-served by the energy management community, except in regions with high-cost energy rates. While energy retrofit activities have provided a significant amount of energy savings to much of this market, there is more savings to be had in the operational and system maintenance areas.

The only information that many of these underserved markets have is the monthly energy bills. They are generally used for billing only, though some energy cost savings can be achieved by analyzing them for mistakes or for rate change recommendations. When one tries to detect the cause of excess energy usage using monthly bills, inadequate results often happen because these bills are time-late and lack energy usage profile information needed to identify the cause of excess energy usage.

This paper provides information regarding the information systems necessary to manage a facility's

energy usage. It demonstrates the need for better, near real-time energy usage information for energy engineers and facility managers. In providing useful, timely energy usage information, the energy engineer and facility manager are better able to manage the energy usage in the facilities.

INTRODUCTION

Energy management has been around in one form or another for over four decades. This paper is written primarily for facility managers and the energy service industry to motivate the development of affordable energy management systems to provide near real-time energy usage information to the end user so that they can more effectively manage their energy usage.

Interviews with facility operators rarely uncover anyone who is provided routine information regarding energy usage, especially if the only source of information is monthly bills. Since these are time-late, their value for detecting and solving problems is quite low. If the month's usage has been deemed to be excessive, any of several reasons can be given. Was it the weather? Did we operate the facility differently last month? Was there construction going on? Without profile data, the source of a demand spike may go undetected for months or years, perhaps never being discovered. The excess usage may have occurred from a setpoint change or equipment problems.

It is difficult to create positive change unless there is accountability for under-performance. Facility operators and tenants make decisions every day that affect operations that impact energy usage. Maintenance personnel perform repairs and adjustments that often increase energy usage in excess of what is needed to correct a comfort problem. None of this is done maliciously, but is the result of a lack of knowledge of the impact of their actions and a lack of accountability that could be remedied by appropriate energy information feedback on the results of their actions.

Take, for example, a technician who receives a "hot call,"-- a space temperature that is too high, in the summer on a constant volume reheat system. To remedy this situation, the technician may reduce the chilled water delivery temperature, thus "solving" the problem. If the cause of the problem was a leaky reheat valve, not only is the space affected using excess heating and cooling energy, but the other space's reheats have to open up more to compensate for the lower chilled water temperature. All of this is on top of the chiller load increase to deliver the reduced chill water temperature. This phenomenon contributes to what is called 'energy creep', the slowly rising energy usage of systems that drift out of adjustment over time. If these actions can be detected and the proper personnel informed, better facility use practices can result in lower energy costs. A perfectly commissioned building may start with a low energy cost per square foot, but the actions of facility operators and tenants over the years, as well as undetected efficiency and setpoint changes can go unnoticed for years. If properly analyzed, even poor commissioning of buildings can be detected and remedied.

There are similarities between energy management and business management. To manage any endeavor requires expertise, motivation, and information. If one is managing a business, one must have knowledge of the business, a profit or other motive, and information on how the business is doing. The information might consist of sales, revenue, and profits. The information usually comes from an accounting department, who provides the information in a format that is useful to managers and executives running the business. Without this information, the business is operating in the dark.

Energy management requires the same principles. The expertise may come from a dedicated on-site energy manager, a corporate energy manager, handling many facilities, or an off-site energy manager. The motivation may be reducing operating costs to help the bottom line, reducing peak loads on over-loaded circuits, better customer relations by being a more responsible user of energy, or any of a number of benefits. The information required to accomplish the job might include the energy budget, the utility rate structure, the energy use profile - both historic and real time, and knowledge of the facility loads and their controllability. The quality of these three essential elements will determine the success of any energy management effort.

DATA OR INFORMATION?

There must be a clear understanding of the difference between data and information. While the data may hold the answers needed to solve a problem, until it is turned into information, it is often of little use. An example is the gathering of a year's worth of energy bills. Unless there is some standard to compare the information to, the only information that may be available is whether or not you are over or under budget. Normalizing the data using weather and operational data can provide year to year comparison information, but may not indicate whether or not less energy could be used to achieve the same outcome. If an expected energy usage could be constructed from a knowledge of the facility equipment and operations, plotting this against the actual usage profile provides valuable information and highlights possible deviations. These deviations can fall into three categories:

1. Random events that change energy usage
2. Detectable excess energy usage
3. Problems with the energy usage model

The need for more detailed energy profile information has resulted from the advent of competitive energy sources and real-time pricing. Many utility companies offer this service, sometimes in conjunction with beneficial rate options. It may come in the form of 15-minute electrical usage data that can be presented graphically. An experienced energy manager can determine quite a lot of information from this data, but the manager is the person who must review the data, make the determination what is and is not significant, and provide results or opinions on how to reduce the energy usage. The key here is that an experienced person needs to look for problems in the data. If this data were to be analyzed in a manner that alerts the manager to the problem areas, more time could be devoted to solving problems and less time to searching for them.

ENERGY MONITORING BACKGROUND

In the 1970's, energy shortages and available technology brought an increase in the usage of energy monitoring equipment. These primarily consisted of sub-metering plant equipment and runtime analysis to prevent excessive electric demand charges. Demand limiting technologies, consisting of startup controls and timing allows industrial plants to better control their energy usage. Nearly all of these efforts were performed on-site.

Beginning in the 1980's, computer based energy management systems became popular. The increased use of computer modems allowed the energy management function to be located off-site. Companies, such as Wal-Mart, made good use of this technology to monitor not only the base usage of their stores, but also the timing of the usage. A store manager who left his lights on after store closing hours would soon receive a call to explain the increased usage. Soon, all store managers became very sensitive to energy usage issues, and this resulted in a more competitive retail operations. This is an example of proper management generating accountability, thus motivating the operational changes that are desired.

The 1980's also saw the introduction of complex front-end building automation systems that were designed to operate in a stand-alone mode, capable of controlling the operation of more complex HVAC system, such as Direct Digital Control (DDC) systems. This added control allowed for better matching of system heating and cooling capacity to existing loads. These systems were able to record equipment usage, and in some cases recorded equipment energy usage. Few of these systems, however, were actually used to monitor the energy usage in a manner that allowed consumption to be managed. Demand thresholds were able to be set so that a dedicated system manager could be alerted to energy spikes, and could take corrective action. This is expensive in that someone had to monitor the system in order for it to be effective. Eventually, demand control strategies were able to be implemented that offered less hands-on control, but these were primarily used for the larger energy users. Little was done to monitor the routine usage, such as lighting, ventilation fans, and other controllable loads. The reasoning being that the loads were so small that the cost of monitoring them was not deemed to generate sufficient benefits.

As the Internet became more widely used, the economics of remote monitoring changed. Based on independent research, there appear to be two schools of thought on this. One school seeks to monitor smaller and smaller loads, so as to generate large amounts of detailed data that can be analyzed to detect excess energy usage. The other school of thought seeks to monitor key energy circuits and use system information and expected usage profiles to detect excess usage. This requires a detailed knowledge of the system, or a significant amount of usage history and the appropriate variables, such as weather, production numbers, and demographics in order to detect excess usage. The primary benefits of the second method are that the number of sensors is smaller, reducing installation costs, and that the data communications requirements were less expensive. The drawback was that, unless sufficient facility and operational information was available, such as energy audits and facility operational data, results could be less than adequate for the effort. Each method has its usefulness, depending on the type of facility that is to be monitored.

IN SEARCH OF WEB-BASED TECHNOLOGIES
The 21st century has seen an explosion in the number of Internet-based information systems. In researching the systems designed to provide energy information for the purpose of energy management, VESTAR found that either the existing systems were too costly, or did not provide the functionality needed to deliver adequate energy savings. The criterion was to find a system that would routinely provide benefits that were two to three times the cost for groups of facilities that average 50,000 to 100,000 square feet, such as K-12 school corporations. After several months of research, no existing systems were found that would adequately provide this service to our customer base in a cost effective manner. The target was to find a way of generating 5 to 10% energy savings with a cost of 2 to 3 % of their energy cost so that we could provide a reliable return on the customer's investment in the monitoring system. Many excellent systems with powerful graphics capabilities were available, but they were geared for large commercial and industrial markets.

GATHERING THE DATA
Several energy service providers are currently offering information delivery products with varying levels of analysis capabilities. Most services focus on month-end reporting of interval meter data only. Few others are able to acquire facility information such as temperature, operating status or alarms. The provider names have been omitted to prevent the release of potentially proprietary information.

As you can see from Table 1, most of the providers offer hourly interval meter data. The average cost for providing data-only service is $60 per meter. The big variable is the setup cost, which can run from $1,200 per meter to $3,000 per site. This cost includes installation of any special metering, connection to the data server, and data delivery to the customer. Many of these installations use dial-up phone lines to modems or other labor-intensive setups. New technologies are currently being developed to reduce these costs.

SHOW ME THE MONEY!
A number of papers have been written that indicate savings from proper energy management can be 5 to 10% from equipment control modifications and facility operational changes. Savings from proper demand control can be even higher.

Taking an average of $60 per meter monthly service fee, and amortizing the setup cost over three years, the average monthly cost is approximately $185. If we assume a 50,000 square foot building on one electric meter with annual energy costs of $1.50 per square foot, the annual energy cost is $75,000. Therefore the monthly cost is $6,250. In order to pay for the $185 per month monitoring costs, the system would need to generate 3% in energy savings. What is missing in this information, however, is the cost of the analysis and generation of recommendations needed to accomplish the savings. For this example, let's assume that monthly monitoring is adequate to generate sufficient savings. Assuming that an off-site energy manager can analyze 500 meters per month, and that his time costs $120,000, with benefits, software and systems costs, this adds $20 to the monthly cost. This increases the monthly cost to $205 increasing the required savings to just 3.3%, still below the 5 to 10% in savings potential. There are many cases when one electric meter serves well over 50,000 square feet, resulting in improved economics. If one used the above information on a 25,000 square foot building, the savings rate would have to be 6.6% to break even. See Figure 1 for more examples.

Since most of the meter data providers in Table 1 specify hourly interval meter data, they are evidently targeting customers that are interested in time-of-use information to take advantage of real-time pricing and load shedding. Most of these efforts are geared to hourly data, rather than 15-minute data. The benefit of 15-minute data is that it provides much better load profile information, and it corresponds to the demand charge time interval used by most utility companies. It is this interval that is of use to most energy managers, given the much greater cost of reduced intervals, such as 1-minute data. The electronic meters used by the majority of utility companies are setup to measure 15-minute data. Energy managers who analyze 15-minute data are interested in detecting improper or excessive system operation and to check the results of demand reduction efforts.

TABLE 1: INTERNET-BASED ENERGY MONITORING PRICING

Service Provider	Service Description	Pricing
Provider A	Dial -up hourly interval meter data (monthly) Dial -up hourly interval meter data (daily) Dial -up hourly interval meter data (hourly)	$20/meter/month $50/meter/month $150/meter/month
Provider B	Dial-up interval meter data	$1200 + $45/meter/month
Provider C	Dial-up interval meter data	$200/mo for up to 4 meters
Provider D	Installation Dial -up hourly interval meter data (monthly)	$1500/site up to 3 meter pts $100-150/mo up to 3 meter pts
Provider E	Installation Dial -up hourly interval meter data (monthly)	$1200/ meter pt $30-$80/mo (varies by pt type)
Provider F	Display hourly interval meter data (monthly)	$45/mo/meter pt (software only)
Provider G	Installation Dial or cellular hourly interval meter data (monthly) Forecasting Facility points	$3,000 per building, includes monitoring panel $75/meter/month $40-60/meter/mo $20-40/pt/mo
Provider H	Installation Dial -up hourly interval meter data (monthly)	$1800/site $75-150/meter/mo based on term
Provider I	Dial -up hourly interval meter data (daily)	$50/meter/month + service contract
Provider J	Dial -up hourly interval meter data (daily) Must put in new meters, 3yr term Access single meter at a time and download	$46/meter/mo meter data only +$30/meter/mo adds bill payment +15/meter/mo adds Power Quality
Provider K	Dial -up hourly interval meter data (daily) 1 yr min term	$75/meter set-up $125/meter/mo

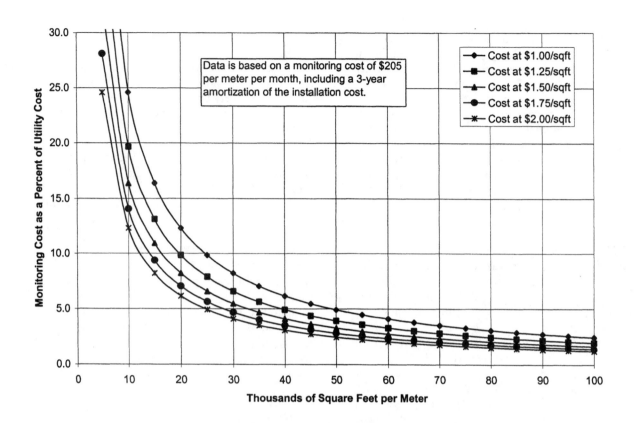

FIGURE 1: MONITORING COST AS A PERCENTAGE OF UTILITY COST

MOTIVATING THE MARKET

With such desirable benefits available, it would seem that this method of energy management would be quite widespread, but with less than 10% of the US market using some form of automatic meter reading [1], the initial setup costs can be quite a barrier to expanding the market into the medium and small sized customers. What is needed is a strong value proposition to justify the expense of installing the monitoring system.

Figure 1 shows the monitoring cost as a percentage of utility cost for five levels of energy usage from $1.00 per square foot to $2.00 per square foot and for meters that monitor up to 100,000 square feet. It is based on a monitoring cost of $205 per meter, including the amortization of the setup costs. By examining Figure 1, one can readily see that when the energy usage is greater than $1.00 per square foot and when the meter is monitoring at least 50,000 square feet, the monitoring cost is less than 5% of the utility cost. When the meter monitors only 25,000 square feet, the energy usage must exceed $2.00 per square foot for the monitoring cost to be less than 5% of the utility cost. One can see from Figure 1 why the larger facilities have been mostly served by the energy management industry.

UTILITY COMPANIES JOIN THE EFFORT

Many utility companies are utilizing new technologies to gather customer meter data, and provide other services. Deregulation has pushed many of these companies to reduce operating costs. Automatic meter reading technologies have proven to be beneficial in lowering the cost of obtaining meter data, and are widely used. Some utility companies are using the data for other uses, as well.

Cinergy Corp. (www.cinergy.com), an Ohio based gas and electric utility, is embarking on a new venture with Current Technologies, LLC by deploying a Current Technologies(TM) Powerline Communications (PLC) solution to 100 homes in the state of Ohio. The test will focus on utilization of distribution powerlines for broadband Internet access, automatic meter reading, outage detection and substation monitoring. [2] Bundling meter reading with other services should lower the cost of remotely available meter data. This endeavor will add to Cinergy's already mature portfolio of energy management services, such as Energy Merchant, that it provides to its customers.

Duquesne Light, Co. (www.duquesnelight.com), serving the Pittsburgh area, takes over 400,000 daily meter readings on a fixed network, nearly 46,000 readings using

587

telephone-based modules, and 80,000 monthly readings using mobile units for outlying areas. Duquesne's initial goal was to achieve improved meter reading and customer service, improve load forecasting, and outage management. [3]

As the number of utilities that implement automatic meter reading grows, the cost of implementing this technology in lower energy cost areas and smaller customers should decline. These efforts are further motivated by the utility's desire to manage load curtailment during peak hours.

TECHNOLOGIES ON THE HORIZON

Applications of new wireless technologies, such as Bluetooth, Shared Wireless Access Protocol (SWAP), and Wi-Fi [4] offer the hope that installation and communication costs of meter data gathering equipment will continue to drop. The low cost of many of these systems enable the installation of the necessary equipment with little cabling required. Inexpensive iButtons, small portable devices that utilize a 1-Wire® protocol for communications, offer many potential opportunities for use in energy management, including data logging and reporting, as well as event detection, such as when loads start and stop. [5]

CONCLUSIONS

The time to provide better energy management services to small to medium-sized energy users is here. Technologies are coming on line to reduce the cost of remotely available interval meter data. The use of Internet based information data gathering and information delivery systems is making the operational cost of these systems able to provide enough value to justify use in markets that have been largely underserved. History has shown that as new technologies become more widely used, the cost goes down.

What the market seems to be requesting is a low-cost method to turn this data into the information needed to accomplish effective energy management for small to mid-sized energy users. One of Cinergy Corp.'s non-regulated subsidiaries, VESTAR (www.vestar.net), is developing a web-based solution called CheckPoint and envisions that CheckPoint will become the energy management software application of choice for facility and energy managers. A key feature of CheckPoint is the use of an automated analysis process. This lowers the monitoring costs by automatically detecting the most common sources of excess energy usage, thereby reducing the requirement to have a person search for problems. This allows the service to be offered to K-12 schools and other small to mid-sized energy users.

Facility managers can team with energy managers via web-based systems, and can play a vital role in reducing the cost of energy management systems by providing quality facility system and operational information to the energy managers, thus allowing them to use interval meter data to diagnose and remedy excess energy usage. Perhaps with better tools, facility managers can play a more active role in energy management, adding their expertise to the energy management team.

REFERENCES
1. Energy Engineering, Vol. 99 No. 5, 2002, pg. 8
2. PR Newswire June 24, 2002, Financial News section
3. Transmission & Distribution World, February 2000
4. See **http://www.howstuffworks.com/wireless-network.htm** for more information
5. See **http://www.ibutton.com/ibuttons/index.html** for more information

Chapter 84

A New Approach to Maintaining Chiller Efficiency

Larry Seigel, President
Chillergy Systems LLC

Dan Durham, P.E., Principal Engineer
Medical College of Georgia

L.D. Kicak, HVAC Manager
Emory University

Abstract

At many facilities the chiller plants are the largest user of energy while being critical to the daily operation of the facility. The chillers themselves are subject to a wide variety of operating conditions that can reduce the operating efficiencies of the chillers and result in increased energy consumption. A centrifugal water chiller can lose as much as 30% efficiency and still appear to be operating satisfactorily. Common problems such as tube fouling, refrigerant leaks, water flow problems, non-condensables, oil contaminated refrigerant, etc. are difficult to identify and therefore do not get corrected until the chiller is obviously not performing. This session will present a unique new web based tool for monitoring chiller performance such that efficiency problems are identified quickly and energy cost impact is quantified in dollars making repair cost/ benefit analysis possible for the most common chiller efficiency problems. Case studies will be presented by Medical College of Georgia and Emory University.

Do you know how efficiently your chillers are running?

Driven by the CFC issue and the need to reduce energy costs many chiller plant owners have made substantial investments in upgrading their systems over the past decade. Dramatic improvements in chiller efficiencies, system design improvements, variable speed drives and upgraded controls systems have all led to the installation of chill water systems of far greater design efficiencies than we had in the past. These systems when properly installed and commissioned can provide an excellent return on investment through reduced energy costs.

From the day the chillers and system are commissioned and turned over to the owner the battle to maintain the chillers and systems at peak efficiency begins. The battle is very subtly waged, small incremental changes begin to occur; water flows can start to vary, control set points start to drift, water treatment systems can fail, cooling towers can develop fill or distribution problems, refrigerant leaks can develop, purge systems can lose efficiency, etc. Individually these problems may not amount to much and are difficult to identify on a daily basis but over time they can lead to significant efficiency losses and resultant increases in energy costs.

How do you monitor your chillers efficiency?

The most common method used today to track chiller operation and efficiency is the daily log sheet. An operator visits the chiller plant and records operating data usually on a clipboard left at the chiller. Interpreting log data in order to identify efficiency problems is a difficult process at best and generally is effective only when the problem or problems present result in the chiller not being capable of delivering the required water temperatures. In many cases a chiller can loose up to 30% efficiency and still appear to be operating properly! The explanation for this is that most chillers operate between 40% and 80% loaded thus the chiller delivers design temperature water at 70% load while using 100% kw. A common method for evaluating chiller efficiency is to ask the questions.

Is the chiller running?

Is the building cool?

If the answer is yes to both of these questions the assumption is made that the chillers are operating efficiently.

The cost of inefficiency

Using a university as an example, a 10,000 ton chiller plant could cost $1,000,000 to $1,500,000 per year in energy just for the chillers. An efficiency loss of 15% would result in wasted energy dollars of $150,000 to $225,000 per year.

The efficiency/reliability connection.

There is a very close connection between efficiency and reliability, that is the more efficiently you run your chillers the more reliably they will operate having less down time, fewer service calls, in other words a higher likelihood that they will perform when you need them the most.

A new approach to maintaining chiller efficiency.

In the summer of 2000 the Medical College of Georgia, Augusta, Georgia, participated in a *beta* test of a new Internet based program that allows chiller owners and operators to monitor chiller efficiency on a daily basis. The program called ChillerCheck provides a system for operators to log chillers using a PDA such as a Palm device. The Palm is then Hot-Synced to a website where the data is analyzed and problem identification is provided. Emory University, Atlanta, Georgia became the second beta test site in the spring of 2001. A review of the Medical College of Georgia and Emory University experience using the ChillerCheck program follows.

Medical College of Georgia

The Medical College of Georgia (MCG) is located in Augusta, Georgia. A total of 10 centrifugal chillers ranging from 333 to 2000 tons provide 11,500 tons of cooling.

Dan Durham, Principal Engineer, first met Larry Siegel during a presentation at the Medical College in early 2000. All of the MCG chiller log sheets were revised to show individual chiller design information for comparative purposes per Larry's recommendations.

Chiller problems were immediately identified once these log sheets were analyzed. Two of MCG's 450-ton chillers had a high condenser approach temperature which resulted in a 10% efficiency loss; a 1900-ton chiller had a high evaporator approach temperature which resulted in a 20% efficiency loss. These efficiency losses corresponded to estimated extra annual energy costs of $8,000 and $28,000 respectively based on chiller size, chiller efficiency, annual run-hours, average load, and cost of electricity.

The high condenser approach on the 450-ton chillers was due to calcium precipitating out of the condenser water onto the condenser tubes. The tubes were cleaned and the water treatment modified to prevent calcium deposition.

The high evaporator approach on the 2000-ton chiller was due to a variety of problems. The chiller was found to

have a blown division plate gasket, low refrigerant, and a sticking evaporator float valve. Repairs were made and the efficiency loss was eliminated.

Once the ChillerCheck Internet software was developed, the Medical College agreed to become a ChillerCheck beta test site. Operators originally completed chiller log sheets which were then entered into the ChillerCheck website manually. They now take chiller logs with a Palm PDA and download the information to the ChillerCheck website via a hot sync. Efficiency losses are immediately calculated on the Palm PDA with problem details and possible causes available on the website.

The use of ChillerCheck has produced several benefits for the Medical College. It has increased chiller problem awareness and quantified the cost due to efficiency losses. This has made it possible to address problems quickly and prioritize repairs based on cost. It has increased chiller reliability by catching problems early and has increased operator knowledge and morale. The end result is better service to the Medical College with lower utility bills.

Emory University

Emory University in Atlanta, Georgia, is located on a campus near downtown Atlanta. Cooling is provided by 39 water cooled centrifugal chillers totaling 24,694 tons in 29 separate locations. There are 3 large central cooling plants with the balance of the chillers located at remote sites.

L.D. Kicak. HVAC Manager at Emory became aware of the ChillerCheck program while attending a Chiller Operation Seminar at Medical College of Georgia in the spring of 2001. Recognizing the values the ChillerCheck program could bring to the HVAC Operations Dept at Emory Mr. Kicak volunteered to become a beta test site. Two 250 ton chillers located in a residence hall were selected at the initial test chillers. These chillers had recently been serviced and declared to be operating satisfactorily. The chiller instrumentation was checked for calibration and a lead operator from the Emory HVAC Dept was trained in the use of the PDA. Readings were taken and the data synced to the web site. The analysis of the data showed that one of the chillers had a high evaporator approach with the second chiller indicating excess non-condensables in the condenser.

On the first chiller the refrigerant charge was removed for reclaiming and the evaporator heads were removed to allow inspection of the tubes and division plate. When the inspection was complete the findings were:

- The chiller was over charged with refrigerant by 300 pounds (design charge was 500 pounds)
- There was 60 pounds of oil in the charge.

- The bottom third of the evaporator tubes were fouled with mud.
- The division plate gasket was partially blown out.

On the second chiller the findings were:
- A small air leak was found.
- The purge was inoperative.

Based on the results with the residence hall chillers eleven additional chillers were placed in the beta test program. An example of the findings on these additional test chillers was a 1200 ton chiller located in one of the central plants. The initial readings indicated a high evaporator approach along with a high condenser approach. This chiller uses a digital control panel for all operational readings. The digital readout was showing a leaving chill water temperature of 42 ° with a refrigerant temperature of 36 °. Investigation revealed that the actual leaving chill water temperature was 38°, four degrees colder than necessary to provide adequate cooling and resulting in an approximately 6.5% efficiency loss at full load conditions.

The overall results on the 13 beta test chillers showed an average efficiency loss of 19% with an estimated impact on energy cost of $169,704. At that point Emory decided to proceed with implementing the program on all 39 centrifugal chillers. A project was developed with the following goals:

- Reduce energy cost by operating chillers at higher efficiency levels (potential savings of $300k to $500k)
- Improve operational reliability of the chiller plant reducing downtime.
- Elevate skill level of chiller operators and technicians.

Program implementation

Using the ChillerCheck program as a focal point the maintenance department was reorganized into four maintenance zones with four operators assigned to each zone. A comprehensive operator/technician training program was implemented providing training on chiller fundamentals, log analysis and troubleshooting, and use of the PDA and ChillerCheck program.
Instrumentation was checked and upgraded where necessary. New digital readout thermometers are being used for all water temperatures and direct reading pressure differential gauges are being used to measure water flows. Handheld infrared thermometers are used for readings such as condensed liquid refrigerant temperatures. A set of log readings on a properly instrumented chiller now takes between 1 ½ to 2 minutes per chiller.

Results

Numerous efficiency and reliability problems have been identified through use of the ChillerCheck program for example:

- A 1000 ton chiller in one of the central plants started to experience excessive refrigerant loss due to a malfunctioning purge. The problem was identified quickly, the leaks were repaired and the purge replaced.
- A 1280 ton chiller in a central plant developed reduced condenser water flow due to a plugged strainer. The problem was identified immediately and corrected.
- A number of chillers experienced fouled condenser tubes due to microbiological fouling related to a chemical feed problem. The feed problem was fixed, the tubes brushed and chiller efficiency was restored.
- A number of excessive air leaks were identified through purge time analysis. The leaks were fixed and efficient operation was restored.

The Bottom Line

Implementation of the ChillerCheck program at Emory University has resulted in a number of benefits to the chiller plant operation:
- Significant energy savings have been realized as evidenced by the overall improvement in chiller operating efficiencies.
- Emory has gone to **a Demand Based Maintenance** program where specific maintenance tasks such as condenser tube brushing is no longer done on an annual scheduled basis but on an as needed basis.
- There has been a reduction in outsourced services due to an improvement in our in-house diagnostic capability.
- Shift from reactive maintenance to proactive maintenance.
- There has been a reduction in unscheduled chiller down time due to chillers operating at higher reliability levels.
- More effective monitoring of chiller operating parameters has resulted in identifying refrigerant leak issues early thus reducing refrigerant loss and maintaining compliance with EPA refrigerant leak requirements.

ChillerCheck.Com

Overview – ChillerCheck is an Internet based centrifugal chiller logging program that provides daily data collection using a PDA followed by data analysis and problem identification. The program also delivers long-term trend logging of all key operating parameters, maintenance record keeping, and logical sequences corrective action recommendations.

Problem Identification

ChillerCheck provides data analysis leading to the identification of the following problems:

- Fouled condenser or evaporator tubes.
- Loss of refrigerant charge.
- Cooling tower problems.
- Water flow problems.
- Non-condensable problems
- Incorrect condenser or chill water set point problems.

ChillerCheck Process

- Log chiller using PDA (Fig 1)

Fig. 1

- Sync data to Web site and review results

Fig. 2

- Review efficiency analysis and energy cost estimates. (Fig. 3)

Fig. 3

592

- Review trend logs (Fig. 4)

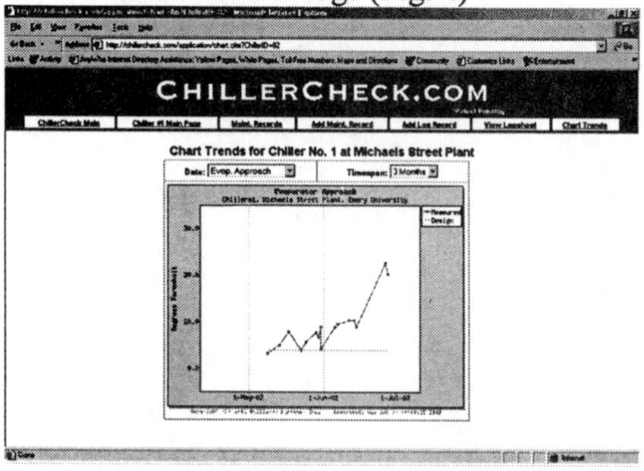

Fig. 4

- Simplified data collection
- Quantification of problems in $$$$
- Customized management access
- Online maintenance record keeping
- Unlimited geographical coverage
- Periodic comprehensive operator training programs

Conclusions – Detailed analysis of chiller log readings can result in more efficient chiller operation and reduced chiller down time.

ChillerCheck Features

- Daily chiller efficiency analysis

Chapter 85

Information Technology Basics for Energy Managers – How a Web-Based Energy Information System Works

Barney Capehart, University of Florida
Paul Allen, Reedy Creek Energy Services
Klaus Pawlik, Accenture
David Green, Green Management Services Inc.

ABSTRACT

Advances in new equipment, new processes and new technology are the driving forces in improvements in energy management, energy efficiency and energy cost control. Of all recent developments affecting energy management, the most powerful new technology to come into use in the last several years has been information technology –or IT. The combination of cheap, high-performance microcomputers together with the emergence of high-capacity communication lines, networks and the Internet has produced explosive growth in IT and its application throughout our economy. Energy information and control systems have been no exception. IT and Internet based systems are the wave of the future. Almost every piece of equipment and almost every activity will be connected and integrated into the overall facility operation in the next several years.

The Internet, with the World Wide Web – or Web - has become quickly and easily accessible to all facility employees. It has allowed the development of many new opportunities for energy and facility managers to quickly and effectively control and manage their operations. The capability and use of IT and the Internet in the form of Web based energy information and control systems continues to grow at a very rapid rate. New equipment and new suppliers appear almost daily and existing suppliers of older equipment are beginning to offer new Web based systems. Facility managers, maintenance managers and energy managers are all having to deal with this rapid deployment of Web based equipment and systems, and need to be prepared for current and future applications of Internet based technologies in their facilities. In some cases, facilities are developing their own information and control systems or at least subsystems and are trying to understand how to connect and interface new IT equipment to their older energy management or facility management systems.

The purpose of this paper is to help prepare energy managers to understand some of the basic concepts and principles of IT. We hope that they can successfully apply IT to their facility, and have the knowledge to supervise the IT work of a consultant or a vendor. Knowing what is going on and what is involved is important information for the energy manager if they are going to successfully purchase, install and operate these complex, Web-based energy information and control systems. Energy management is a very comprehensive area, and this paper is the first in a series whose purpose is to address the most significant concepts and principles that the typical energy or facility manager might need. The emphasis on this series is on computer networking, use of facility operation databases, and sharing data using the Web and the TCP/IP communications protocol. This first paper will introduce basic principles; structures and definitions needed for most facility IT applications. Future papers will cover general application principles and will discuss specific software and hardware requirements for typical energy information and control systems.

ENERGY INFORMATION SYSTEM (EIS)

The philosophy, "If you can measure it, you can manage it", is critical to a sustainable energy management program. Continuous feedback on utility performance is the backbone of an Energy Information System. A basic definition of an Energy Information System is:

Energy Information System (EIS): Equipment and computer programs that let Users measure, monitor and quantify energy usage of their facilities and help identify energy conservation opportunities.

There are two main parts to an EIS: (1) data collection and (2) web publishing. Figure 1 shows these two processes in a flow chart format

Everyone has witnessed the growth and development of the Internet – the largest computer communications network in the world. The Internet and the World Wide Web (Web), using the TCP/IP communications protocol, has made it much easier to access and distribute data. Using a web browser, one can access data around the world with a click of a mouse. An EIS should take full advantage of these new tools.

Intranet: An Intranet is a small, self-contained, private version of the Internet, using Internet software and Internet communications standards. Companies are increasingly using Intranets to give their employees and other approved people easy access to facility and corporate data.

TCP/IP: Transmission Control Protocol/Internet Protocol (TCP/IP) is a family of industry standard communications protocols that allow different networks to communicate. It is the most complete and accepted enterprise networking protocol available today, and it is the communications protocol of the Internet. An important feature of TCP/IP is that it allows dissimilar computer hardware and operating systems to communicate directly.

Web Browser: A web browser is a program used to display data transferred over an Intranet or the Internet. It lets users select, retrieve and interact with resources on the Web. The most commonly used web browsers are Internet Explorer and Netscape.

METERING EQUIPMENT

The first task in establishing an EIS is to determine the sources of the energy data. Utility meters monitored by an energy management system or a dedicated power-monitoring system are a good source.   These systems provide a good means to collect energy data. Metering equipment collects the raw utility data for electric, chilled water, hot water, natural gas and compressed air. Information from these meters is collected by either direct

analog connections, pre-processed pulse outputs or by digital, network-based protocols.

Direct Analog Connection: The utility meter produces a 4-20mA or 0-10V signal for the instantaneous usage continuously monitored by an energy management or process control system. The control system calculates the utility usage integrating the instantaneous values over time.

Pulse-Output: The utility meter outputs a pulse for a pre-defined amount of energy usage. A local data storage device accumulates the pulses.

Digital, Network-based Protocol: The utility meter calculates and totals the energy used within the meter. A dedicated local area network (LAN) links the energy meters together. A local data storage device polls these meters at predefined intervals to store the energy data until retrieved by the server.

DATA COLLECTION PROGRAM

Data gathered from all of the local data storage devices at a predefined interval (usually on a daily basis) is stored on a server in a relational database.

Relational Database: A relational database is a collection of tables, rows and columns used to store data, and is organized and accessed according to relationships between data. Examples of relational databases are FoxPro, SQL and Oracle.

There is a variety of methods used to retrieve this data:

Modem Connection: A modem connection uploads the data from the local data storage device to the energy data server. Typically, the upload takes place on a daily basis, but could be transferred more frequently, if needed.

LAN or WAN Network Connection: A Local Area Network (LAN) or a Wide Area Network (WAN) connection, established between computers, transfers energy data files to the energy data server.

FTP Network Connection: File Transfer Protocol (FTP) is an Internet protocol used for transferring files from one computer to another. It is used to move the energy data files from the local data storage devices to the energy data server.

Once the energy data has been transferred to the energy data server, an update program reads all of the various

596

data files and reformats them into a format that is used by the web publishing program

An essential feature of this process is to design the programs and tables so they will update quickly. Typically, utility meters can generate an enormous amount of data, so it is important to keep the table records manageable. Breaking the data up into yearly, monthly, weekly and daily files keeps the data manageable.

WEB PUBLISHING PROGRAM

To publish the energy data on an Intranet or the Internet, client/server programming is used. The energy data is stored on a central computer, the Server, and waits passively until a User makes a request for information using a web browser, the client. A web publishing program retrieves the information from a relational database, sends it to the web server, which then sends it to the client that requested the information.

Web Server: A web server is a program that runs on a network server (computer) to respond to HTTP requests. The most commonly used web servers are Internet Information Server and Apache.

HTTP: Hypertext Transfer Protocol (HTTP) is an application layer protocol used to transfer data across an Intranet or the Internet. It is the standard protocol for moving data across the Internet.

HTTP Request: An HTTP request is data sent from a web browser to a web server.

HTTP Response: An HTTP response is web browser content sent from a web server to a web browser in response to a specific HTTP request.

A CGI interface program coordinates the activity between the web-server and the web publishing program and allows for simultaneous multi-user access.

Common Gateway Interface (CGI): CGI is a method used to run conventional programs through a web browser.

The client/server process for an EIS uses the steps below (See Figure 1):

1. A User requests energy information by using their web browser (client) to send an HTTP request to the web server.

2. The web server on the network server activates the CGI interface program. The CGI program then starts up the web publishing program.
3. The web publishing program retrieves the information from the relational database, formats the data in HTML and returns it to the CGI interface program.
4. The CGI interface program sends the data as HTML browser content to the web server, which sends the content to the web browser requesting the information.

This entire process takes only seconds depending on the connection speed of the client's computer to the web.

HTML: Hypertext Markup Language (HTML) is the format of the file containing web browser content. Developers use HTML to create Web pages, and build graphical documents that contain images, formatted text, and links to other documents on the Web.

Browser Content: Browser content is data – text, numbers, images and links - displayed in a web browser. Content is the new name for information carried over a network. It may be words, numbers, pictures, sound, or any form of what we used to call information.

PROGRAMMING CHOICES FOR EIS WEB PUBLISHING

The following sections provide additional detail on programming choices used in the development of the web publishing programs. These are only a few of the many programs available. Both server-side and client-side programming environments are applicable.

Using Server-Side CGI programs to Create Content

Server-side programs are programs that run on the network server. CGI programming is the most fundamental way to access relational database information over the Internet or Intranet and display dynamic content. This is important to any EIS since the amount of data involved will undoubtedly require processing with a relational database of some kind.

Dynamic Content: CGI programs create dynamic content as a web page that is displayed in a web browser at the same time it is created.

Static Content: Developers create static content as a web page that is stored in a file and displayed later. The web browser retrieves the data and displays the static content.

Although CGI is a necessary piece of the puzzle in creating dynamic content it may just be a stepping-stone to some other program. Small CGI programs often times just launch secondary programs that run on the web server and return content to the browser. A secondary program could be nearly any custom program that has the ability to send data back to the web server. *FoxWeb* is a small CGI program that connects to a Visual FoxPro database application. The application then calls any number of custom designed queries and procedures to return results to the browser as HTML. More information about FoxWeb is available at http://www.foxweb.com.

PERL (Practical Extraction and Report Language) is an application used for CGI programming. One reason is that it is free. Another is that it is portable across operating systems. In other words, applications written in PERL will work on any operating system. It also has the ability to connect to many types of databases. A good source for information on PERL is at http://www.perl.com.

ColdFusion is a server-side application that uses a ColdFusion server. The server executes templates containing a mixture of HTML and ColdFusion instructions, and then returns the results to the browser as pure HTML.

Active Server Pages (ASP) are also a popular choice recently. The ASP program on the Windows web server will automatically interpret web pages ending with the extension ".asp". The web pages are a mixture of ASP instructions, Visual Basic code and HTML. ASP is not portable across operating systems. It only works with Microsoft web servers.

Java Servlets are Java programs that run on a web server and build web pages. *Java* is the latest of a long line of "higher level" programming languages such as FORTRAN, Pascal and C++. It is also portable across operating systems. Java Servlets written for one web server on one operating system will run on virtually any web server and operating system.

Java Server Pages (JSP) are similar to *Active Server Pages* except that the pages consist of *Java* code in place of Visual Basic code. This makes the code portable across operating systems. The web pages typically end with the extension ".jsp". This tells the web server to interpret the embedded *Java* code like any other *Java Servlet*. Information about *Java Servlets* and *Java Server Pages* is available at this Johns Hopkins University web site: http://www.apl.jhu.edu/~hall/java/.

Any organization wishing to develop an EIS should carefully consider which server-side applications to use. The decision should be a practical one rather than a popular one. All of the criteria below should be a part of the evaluation process:

- What operating system is predominantly available to the facility?
- What programming languages are the support personnel willing to work with?
- What applications are compatible with the existing database?
- How much of the budget is available to spend?

Using Client-Side Applications to Enhance Content

Client-side applications can create a deeper level of interactivity within web pages. Scripting languages such as *JavaScript* and *VBScript* are less complex versions of other languages like Java and Visual Basic, respectively. They reside within the HTML of a web page and provide a great deal of functionality that HTML itself cannot. Scripts such as these can validate input, control the cursor programmatically and much more.

Dynamic HTML (DHTML) is the result of scripting languages taking advantage of the extensions common to the latest browsers to make the pages change after they are loaded. A good example of this is a link that changes color when the User places the mouse cursor over it. Much more dramatic effects are possible using DHTML. However, the two most popular browsers Internet Explorer and Netscape interpret DHTML differently. Good information about DHTML is available at http://www.dynamicdrive.com/.

Cascading Style Sheets (CSS) are special HTML features that allow much more flexibility to format elements of a web page. The ability of CSS to describe the style of an element only once rather then every time you display the element provides a separation of content and presentation. This makes your web pages less complex, much smaller and therefore faster to load. Beware that CSS is only fully supported in the latest versions of browsers (4.0 and above).

Java Applets are small *Java* programs that are stored on a web server and are called for from the HTML in a web page. Statements in the HTML pass parameters to the applet affecting its functionality. Unlike *Java Servlets,* the browser downloads the applet and runs it using the browser operating system rather then the operating system of the web server. Free Java applets are widely available on the Internet. KavaChart applets are very useful for charting trends in data. KavaChart applets are available online at http://www.ve.com.

Extensible Markup Language (XML) XML is a meta-language and has a number of uses. A meta-language is a language used to explain another language. XML organizes data into a predefined format for the main purpose of sharing between or within computer systems. Furthermore, its uses include data organization and transfer, data presentation, data caching, and probably some that we have not invented yet. More information about XML is available at http://xml.com/.

Developers can use any or all of these to enhance the content of an EIS. Three important points to remember about using client-side applications to enhance your browser content are:

1. Many client-side applications require later versions of browsers to work correctly. Be sure all of your users are using the required browser versions.
2. Many client-side applications are available free. Search the Internet before spending resources developing your own custom client-side applications.
3. Client-side applications will make your web pages more complex. This adds to development and maintenance costs. Be sure to weigh the benefits of these enhancements against their costs.

Support for EIS Web Publishing

Support for an EIS is quite involved. It includes Help pages on the application itself to guide the user. There must be an email address and telephone number of someone for users to contact. Adequate system support personnel must be available to help with system or network problems. Developers should track and document updates to the application. Undoubtedly, at some point, the tools you use to develop your EIS will require support as well.

Help pages should be simple and to the point. Avoid long discussions about how the EIS is developed and why. Save that for the "About This System" section or something similar. Each menu item or function should have it's own Help page. That information should be accessible from the main menu or at anytime within the function itself. Contact information about where to get further help should be available on every page.

Email addresses and telephone numbers published for help should be those of the local data expert. Many problems arise due to missing data or misunderstanding of the data.

These issues should be resolved or discounted before sending the problem on to the programming or system support personnel.

IT system support may not be as responsive as we would like. These personnel have a tremendous job to do. It is important to maintain a good relationship with them since their expertise is critical to the success of the EIS. However, at times when they are not able to respond it helps to have as much control over the EIS system as possible. Perhaps locating the server or the data collection machine in a location that is more accessible can help. Many times simply re-running a data collection routine or making a minor change to the code is all that is needed to solve a problem.

The programming support personnel should track and document all changes to the code. A good version tracking system is necessary to preserve versions that may be useful later. Keeping a maintenance log will help to recall changes made to the EIS system as well as contact information for sources of outside help.

Outside support from vendors comes in various forms. There is "free", "free only by email", "paid by hour", "paid by the call" and many other variations. Due to the nature of the EIS data, these applications require a constant level of support. Not necessarily a great deal of support, but they seem to be in a constant state of evolution. There may be a new report for someone, new data available, anomalies in the data or new versions of tools to install. The value of outside support that is available for the tools used may be a deciding factor in choosing components of the EIS.

Choosing EIS Web Publishing Tools

We might define "tools", in this case, as utility applications that require more configuration effort than programming effort. There are some exceptions of course. In any case, tools fall into three categories:
1) open-source or free
2) purchased
3) developed.

Tools are needed to perform such functions as batch emailing, charting, scheduling application run times, and database to web connectivity. The relational database and web server are also tools.

Batch email applications can be of any category. There are good free ones and purchased ones. Some email servers have batch processing capability and some do not. Purchased batch email applications are relatively inexpensive. They have some variations in features such as whether or not they will send HTML or attachments. They are also easy to develop.

Charting tools are really too complex to warrant developing. There are some very good free and open-source charting tools that have all the features of purchased ones. If not, one could probably purchase extensions to the standard features of a free charting tool.

The EIS needs scheduling programs to launch data collection applications at predefined times. Some operating systems have scheduling programs built in. They may be difficult to configure though. A purchased version is probably the best choice since their cost is quite low.

There are some applications that do much of the database to web connectivity for you. These either require purchasing or, in the case of the free ones, a great deal of programming. The purchased ones are a good choice since much of the error reporting is part of the application. The purchased versions can be very expensive or relatively inexpensive. Each database has it's own connectivity options so much of this decision rests on which relational database is used.

The database used is likely a purchased one or may actually be open-source. There are open-source databases like MySQL competing with the best of the others. Commercial relational database systems range in cost from very inexpensive like MS Access to very expensive like Oracle.

Open-source web servers like Apache are available for some operating systems and are very widely used and reliable. Others are free with the operating system like MS IIS. Some are also commercially available for a few hundred dollars. The web server choice depends mostly on the operating system of the server itself.

The EIS tools will likely be a mix of open-source, purchased and developed applications. It is important to consider budget constraints, operating systems and support when deciding which and what type of tools to use. Always plan ahead of time for the compatibility of all the tools the EIS will use.

ENERGY INFORMATION SYSTEM EXAMPLE

In 1997, the Utility Reporting System (URS) was developed by Reedy Creek Improvement District (RCID) to provide a means to "publish" utility metering information and track the results of energy saving efforts at Walt Disney World using the Disney Intranet. The URS provides continuous feedback on utility performance and pinpoints energy waste for further investigation.

This section will "get under the hood" and describe the specific programming tools used to create the URS. The goal here is to relate some of the basic concepts presented earlier in the paper to a specific example of an Energy Information System.

Relational Database Table Structure

The URS uses a relational database program called Microsoft Visual FoxPro. The first step in the URS development was to organize the data table structures. Below are the basic tables:

Account definition table: Includes meter account level definitions and grouping variables used by the program.

Monthly data tables: Includes the monthly billing data from RCID Utility Billing System.

Daily data tables: Includes data recorded on an hourly basis from power monitoring systems and energy management systems.

Email data table: Includes names, email addresses and the utility reports sent.

Data Collection Programs

The next step in the development of the URS was to develop programs to pull the utility data into the data tables. Visual FoxPro reads the various data sources and organizes the data into common data tables. Shown below are the various data collection tasks in the URS:

Monthly Utility Data: An FTP transfer from the RCID billing system downloads this data in an ASCII comma delimited file on a monthly basis. The database administrator creates a new record in the account definition table each time a new billing account is available.

Power Monitoring Hourly Data: RCID's Supervisory Control and Data Acquisition (SCADA) power monitoring system records max, min and average hourly data for meters and outputs this data to an ASCII file each day. A Visual FoxPro program reads this data and reformats it into hourly data tables.

Energy Management System (EMS) Hourly Data: The EMS produces files that include trends of analog/digital points and consumable data from utility meters connected to the EMS. Data collection programs copy these files from the EMS servers to the URS Server after the EMS creates them each night. A Visual FoxPro program reads the data from these reports and reformats it into the hourly data tables.

Veris Industries Power Monitoring Data: Hourly data is recorded in local data collection devices called Eservers. On a nightly basis, a program supplied by Veris Industries automatically collects this data from each Eserver into an ASCII comma delimited file. A Visual FoxPro program pulls the data from these reports and into the hourly data tables.

Once the data collection programs collect all of the data from the various data sources, a Visual FoxPro program updates all of the URS data tables. Once completed, the program copies the standard data file tables to the URS Server data directory. The data is now ready for viewing on the web.

Email Utility Reports

To make the URS easy to use, it sends HTML-based reports via email on a daily basis (to report on hourly data collected) and a monthly basis (to report on monthly billing data). Email increases the likelihood that the User views the utility data. Instead of waiting for the User to visit the URS web site and figuring out how to generate the same report, the URS delivers the report via email.

By creating an HTML-based report, links to graphs can be embedded into the report to make it more visual (see figure 2). Users view the reports using their email program (Microsoft Outlook) and are able to produce graphs by simply clicking on links in the email. Sending mail on utility usage helps to increase employee participation in reducing their facility's energy consumption.

Web Publishing Program

The program language used to generate the web pages for the URS is Visual FoxPro. FoxWeb is the CGI program that interfaces Visual FoxPro with the web server. Different reports allow viewing and graphing both the monthly utilities billing information and the hourly utility data. Kavacharts Java applets, called from the Visual FoxPro programs, generate the graphs used in the URS.

The challenge of producing an effective EIS is to create reports that are both informative and easy to use. The URS makes extensive use of embedded links to sub-reports and graphs. Most reports in the URS show the data in tabular format with embedded links on numbers and data labels that the User can click on to either re-sort the data, produce detailed sub-reports or graphs showing the data various ways. This makes the use of the URS intuitively easy for the User.

CONCLUSION

Today's Energy Manager needs to be knowledgeable of the basic principles and concepts of IT, since this is a fast growing area of new systems and services. This first paper described the basics of how an Energy Information System is set up and how it works. Future papers on related energy management topics will help de-mystify the IT terms associated with them. A future paper will also address the general principles and concepts associated with an Energy Control System, since the foundation has been laid with this discussion of an Energy Information System.

ABOUT THE AUTHORS

Barney Capehart is a Professor Emeritus at the University of Florida College of Engineering, and is a member of the AEE Hall of Fame He regularly teaches five-day Energy Management Training Seminars for AEE. Barney is the lead author of *Guide to Energy Management* from Fairmont Press, and is a Fellow of IEEE, IIE and AAAS. Barney was the Director of the University of Florida Industrial Assessment Center for ten years, and was the recipient of the 1988 Palladium Medal from the American Association of Engineering Societies. (Capehart@ise.ufl.edu)

Paul Allen is the Chief Energy Management Engineer at Reedy Creek Energy Services (a division of the Walt Disney World Co.) and is responsible for the development and implementation of energy conservation projects throughout the Walt Disney World Resort. Paul is a graduate of the University of Miami (BS degrees in Physics and Civil Engineering) and the University of Florida (MS degrees in Civil Engineering and Industrial Engineering). Paul is also a registered Professional Engineer in the State of Florida. The Association of Energy Engineers (AEE) selected Paul as the 2001 Energy Manager of the Year. (paul.allen@disney.com)

David Green has combined experience in Intranet/Internet technology and database queries and has developed programming for Energy Information Systems. David has been the president of his own consulting company, Green Management Services, Inc., since 1994. He has a Bachelor of Science degree in Chemistry and a Master of Arts degree in Computer Science. David is also a Lieutenant Colonel in the Illinois Army National Guard and has 18 years of military service. David has successfully completed major projects for The ABB Group, Cummins Engine Company, ECI Telematics, the M.A.R.C of the Professionals and The Illinois Army National Guard. (dcgreen@dcgreen.com)

Klaus Pawlik is a consultant with Accenture working in the utilities industry. Klaus is the author of the *Solution Manual for Guide to Energy Management, Third Edition*. Klaus holds a Master of Business Administration and a Bachelor of Science in Industrial and Systems Engineering graduating with highest honors from the University of Florida. While at the University of Florida, Klaus worked in the Industrial Assessment Center leading teams of undergraduate and graduate students performing energy and waste minimization, and productivity improvement assessments for manufacturing facilities. Additionally, for two years, he assisted Dr. Barney Capehart with teaching Industrial Energy Management. Before attending the University of Florida, Klaus served six years in the United States Navy, where he worked as an electrical operator on nuclear power plants. For two of those years, he served as an instructor training personnel on the electrical operations for nuclear power plants. (klaus.e.pawlik@accenture.com)

Figure 1: Energy Information System Functional Layout

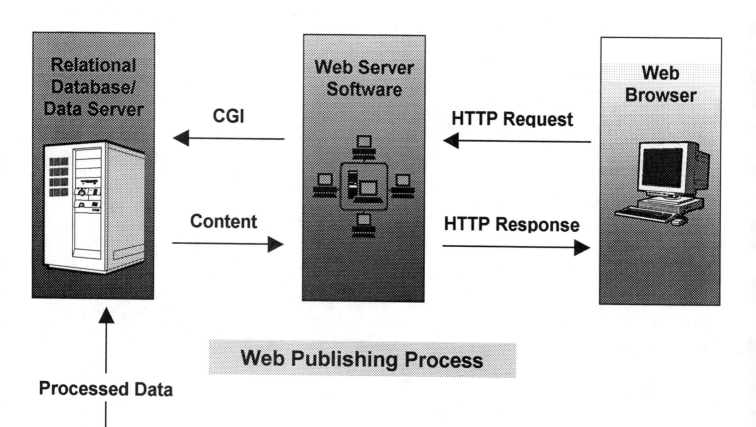

Web Publishing Process

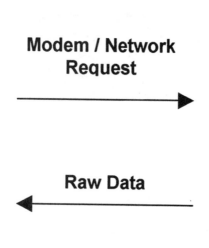

Data Collection Process

Figure 2: Utility Reporting System HTML-Based Report Example
Daily Chilled Water Report

Daily Utility Report
7/03/2002

HYPERLINK ACTION

Mid-6am	6am-Noon	Noon-6pm	6pm-Mid	DAILY

Re-generates Report – 6-Hour Averages

CHW-EPCOT - DELTAT	UNITS	DAILY Avg	7-DAY AVG	% DIFF
MAIN ENT GROUP SALES	DEGF	7.50	7.66	-2.2 %
NORWAY	DEGF	7.82	8.21	-4.7 %
WONDERS OF LIFE	DEGF	9.17	9.32	-1.5 %
PRODUCTION SERVICES	DEGF	9.23	9.17	0.6 %
MOROCCO	DEGF	9.24	9.61	-3.8 %
....	...	...	...	
DVC BEACH CLUB	DEGF	16.20	16.23	-0.2 %
CHINA RESTAURANT	DEGF	16.49	16.40	0.6 %
LAND SUPPORT	DEGF	18.14	17.92	1.2 %
MAIN ENT KENNEL	DEGF	18.85	18.54	1.7 %
SEAS SUPPORT	DEGF	21.91	19.65	11.5 %

Re-Sorts Based on Column Selected

Generates 24-Hour Profile Graph

Generates 30-Day Profile Graph

CHW-EPCOT - FLOW	UNITS	DAILY Avg	7-DAY AVG	% DIFF
MAIN ENT GROUP SALES	GPM	11	11	0.8 %
LAND SUPPORT	GPM	29	29	0.8 %
MAIN ENT EAST GATE	GPM	30	30	0.3 %
MAIN ENT KENNEL	GPM	35	35	-0.5 %
WORLD SHOWPLACE PAVILION	GPM	42	42	-0.2 %
SEAS SUPPORT	GPM	117	122	-3.8 %
....	....	...	...	...
WONDERS OF LIFE	GPM	621	588	5.6 %
TEST TRACK	GPM	722	715	0.9 %
LAND	GPM	990	980	1.1 %
INNOVENTIONS	GPM	1787	1739	2.8 %

ADDITIONAL INFORMATION

More information about Energy Information Systems as well as links to many of the tools discussed in this paper can be found at http://www.utilityreporting.com/.

BIBLIOGRAPHY

Allen, Paul J and David C. Green, *Managing Energy Data Using an Intranet - Walt Disney World's Approach, Proceedings of the* 2001 World Energy Engineering Congress Conference & Expo, Atlanta, Ga., October, 2001.

Bos, Bert, *Cascading Style Sheets* [article on-line] (2002, accessed 8 July 2002); available from http://www.w3.org/Style/CSS/ ; Internet.

Hall, Marty, *Java Programming Resources* [article on-line] (1999, accessed 8 July 2002); available from http://www.apl.jhu.edu/~hall/java/ ; Internet.

INT Media Group, Incorporated, *TCP/IP* [article on-line] (2002, accessed 6 June 2002); available from http://webopedia.internet.com/TERM/T/TCP_IP.html ; Internet.

Ireland, Blair, *Introduction to Perl - Become a Guru* [article on-line] (accessed 6 June 2002); available from http://www.thescripts.com/serversidescripting/perl/tutorials/introductiontoperl--becomeaguru/page0.html ; Internet.

Kington, Max, *ColdFusion - An Introduction* [article on-line] (accessed 6 June 2002); available from http://www.thescripts.com/serversidescripting/coldfusion/tutorials/coldfusion-anintroduction/ ; Internet.

Marshall, James, HTTP *Made Really Easy* [article on-line] (August 15, 1997, accessed 8 July 2002); available from http://jmarshall.com/easy/http/ ; Internet.

Murdock, Robert, *ASP Basics - What is ASP?* [article on-line] (accessed 6 June 2002); available from http://thescripts.com/serversidescripting/asp/tutorials/aspbasics/page0.html ; Internet.

NCSA Software Development Group, *CGI: Common Gateway Interface* [article on-line] (1999, accessed 6 June 2002); available from http://www.w3.org/CGI/ ; Internet.

Richmond, Alan, *Dynamic HTML* [article on-line] (2002, accessed 6 June 2002); available from http://wdvl.internet.com/Authoring/DHTML/ ; Internet.

SOFTWARE REFERENCES

Apache HTTP Server Project, Apache Software Foundation, http://www.apache.org/

ColdFusion MX, Macromedia, Inc., http://www.macromedia.com/software/coldfusion/

Eserver Energy Information Server, Veris Industries, Inc., Portland, Oregon, http://www.veris.com

FoxWeb, Eon Technologies, Alameda, California, http://www.foxweb.com

Java, Sun Microsystems, Inc., http://java.sun.com/

Kavacharts, Java Applet for graphing data, http://www.ve.com

MySQL, MySQL AB, http://www.mysql.com/

Perl, Perl Mongers - The Perl Advocacy People, http://www.perl.org/

Visual FoxPro, Microsoft Corporation, http://msdn.microsoft.com/vfoxpro/

Richmond, Alan, *Dynamic HTML* [article on-line] (2002, accessed 6 June 2002); available from http://wdvl.internet.com/Authoring/DHTML/ ; Internet.

606